# LEVIATHAN

Thomas Hobbes

*edited by A. P. Martinich*

broadview literary texts

**National Library of Canada Cataloguing in Publication Data**

Hobbes, Thomas, 1588-1679
Leviathan

(Broadview literary texts)
Includes bibliographical references and index.
ISBN 1-55111-331-7

1. Political science—Early works to 1800—State, The.
I. Martinich, A. P. (Aloysius P.), 1946- II. Title. III. Series.

JC153.H65 2002 320.1 C2002-900683-X
Broadview Press Ltd., is an independent, international publishing house, incorporated in 1985.

North America:
P.O. Box 1243, Peterborough, Ontario, Canada K9J 7H5
3576 California Road, Orchard Park, NY 14127
TEL: (705) 743-8990; FAX: (705) 743-8353;
E-MAIL: customerservice@broadviewpress.com

United Kingdom:
Thomas Lyster Ltd
Unit 3 & 4a, Ormskirk Industrial Park
Old Boundary Way, Burscough Road
Ormskirk, Lancashire L39 2YW
TEL: (01695) 575112; FAX: (01695) 570120; E-mail: books@tlyster.co.uk

Australia:
St. Clair Press, P.O. Box 287, Rozelle, NSW 2039
TEL: (02) 818-1942; FAX: (02) 418-1923

www.broadviewpress.com

Broadview Press gratefully acknowledges the financial support of the Book Publishing Industry Development Program, Ministry of Canadian Heritage, Government of Canada.

Broadview Press is grateful to Professor L.W. Conolly for advice on editorial matters for the Broadview Literary Texts series.

Text design and composition by George Kirkpatrick

PRINTED IN CANADA

*Contents*

## *Acknowledgments*

I want to thank the following people who graciously read and commented on parts of this edition: Jo Ann Carson, Leslie Martinich, Reid Pillifant, and especially Sharon Vaughan. Pat Fox of the Harry Ransom Research Center has been a joyful helper for several books. I dedicate my work in this volume to my students in TC 301.

## Introduction

Thomas Hobbes's *Leviathan* (1651) is generally regarded as the greatest work of political philosophy in English, even greater than John Locke's *Two Treatises of Government* (1690) and the contemporary classic, John Rawls's *A Theory of Justice* (1971). Although it was written 350 years ago, *Leviathan* remains an important treatise because of its compelling answers to some of the most basic questions of political theory. One of the most fundamental of these questions is 'Why do human beings need laws and government?' Hobbes's answer is that if there were no laws or government, then every action would be permissible and if every action were permissible, then each person would have the right to everything that another person had, including that person's life. In short, human life would be "solitary, poor, nasty, brutish, and short."

This answer may raise the question, 'Why do people come into conflict at all?' Even if everything would be permitted if there were no laws and government, why couldn't people stay out of each other's way? Hobbes's answer to this question is that every person wants to preserve his life. We know from our own experience that even people with painful, terminal illnesses try to stay alive as long as possible. A necessary condition for staying alive is having *desires* for those things that will preserve life or make life more comfortable. If people desired the wrong things or did not desire anything, they would die. But even the desires that are necessary for life produce conditions that threaten life. If there is one apple and two people who desire it because they are hungry, then the two people will have interests that conflict. And they will need laws and government to resolve them.

The actual human condition is even more serious than I have described it so far. In addition to conflict being unavoidable, each person would know that the potential for conflict with other people always existed. Each person, then, would have a motive for killing or otherwise neutralizing every other person before such a conflict actually arose. This itself is another source of conflict. Further, each person knows that every other person is thinking the same thing; and so the motivation for premptively killing other people is increased. There is still a third cause of conflict. Some people try to dominate others because they enjoy having control. Hobbes explains these causes of conflict in vivid terms.

Some readers are put off by Hobbes's dark view of human beings in 'the condition of mere nature', and they think that human beings are by nature better than he makes them out to be. Let's grant that these readers are right. Hobbes's philosophy would be objectionable if he provided no way out of the miserable condition that he describes, because his view would be unrealistic. However, he does explain how people can get out of the state of nature. So, he might be understood as beginning from a worst case scenario, and then showing that human beings do not have to remain in that condition. Through their own ingenuity they can create the conditions for a long and happy life. Hobbes's starting with the misery of the state of nature and ending with happiness in the civil state is analogous to the starting point of philosophers who begin with skepticism about human knowledge and end by showing that skepticism can be overcome.

I have said that Hobbes has a way to get people out of the state of nature but have not said how he does it. So, let's consider that issue. Hobbes holds that the lives of people are preserved and are made to flourish when government protects every citizen from every other citizen and from external enemies. How can a government be formed? Two intuitions about this seem to conflict. One intuition is that people have to give up some of their rights in exchange for protection. The other intuition is that the government is not merely the citizens' protector but also their representative. The government's actions are in some sense the citizens' actions. How can these two things be reconciled? Hobbes thinks that the act of giving up one's rights and the act of making the government one's representative are one and the same act. I think he is wrong about this, but that is beside the point. What is important here is that Hobbes gives detailed and often insightful answers to the basic questions of political theory; and I will soon return to them in this Introduction.

As great as *Leviathan* is as a work of political philosophy, it is much more than that. Its opening chapters adumbrate a worldview that is thoroughly materialist, mechanist, and reductionist.

Everything that exists is a body; all changes occur through the contact of one body against another; life is nothing but a certain kind of complex motion; human life is strictly analogous to the motion of machines; and qualitative experience of the world is reducible to motions in the brain and heart. In short, Hobbes challenged the most basic beliefs of his contemporaries.

The first words of the Introduction, "Nature ... [is] the Art whereby God hath made and governs the world," deconstruct the distinction between what is natural and what is artificial. Nature, the paradigm of what is natural, is artificial, because what is artificial is something made by a person and God made the world. The deconstruction continues with Hobbes's assertions that machines are alive, and human beings are machines.

Equally contentious is his position that man is not naturally a social or political animal, *pace* Aristotle. In their natural state, human beings are "solitary," as sketched above. The political or civil state is artificial, made by human beings themselves in a creative act. That is, humans create government just as God created the world. The government he calls 'Leviathan', after the monster described in the book of Job as "king over all the sons of pride." All humans are guilty of pride because they are disinclined to obey legitimate authority. Leviathan is also a "mortal god, to which we owe, under the immortal God, our peace and defense." Leviathan is a savior god because it does for humans what individually they cannot do themselves: it saves them from lives that otherwise would be wretched.

In the "Dedication," Hobbes indicates that he hopes to present a theory that steers a course between a government that allows subjects (citizens) too much liberty and one that allows too much authority. His theory fails not least because he argues for absolute sovereignty, the view that the government possesses all the political power—there is no division or separation of power—and the government can make laws about any aspect of life. In a word, absolute sovereignty does not give citizens enough freedom. Hobbes says that a subject (citizen) is free to do anything that the law does not forbid. That is, freedom is what is left over. Nonetheless, there are so many interesting arguments and observations in *Leviathan* that it is a great piece of political philosophy.

*Leviathan* was written in France mostly during 1650, the year after Charles I had been beheaded by the Rump Parliament. Anticipating bloodshed, Hobbes had fled England in November, 1640 for France, where he stayed during the English Civil War. (He returned to England early in 1652.) *Leviathan* was his third book of political philosophy. The first, *The Elements of Law, Natural and Politic*, was circulated in manuscript in May, 1640, just at the end of the Short Parliament, but not printed until 1651. The second, *De Cive*, was published in a limited edition in 1642, followed in 1647 by an expanded version, which was distributed widely on the Continent and made Hobbes's reputation as a political philosopher.

Like most great works of philosophy, *Leviathan* was often misunderstood by its first critics. For example, about the state of nature, Robert Filmer wrote,

> I cannot understand how this right of nature can be conceived without imagining a company of men at the very first to have been all created together without any dependence one of another, or as mushrooms (*fungorum more*) they all on [*sic*] a sudden were sprung out of the earth without any obligation to one another.... The scripture teacheth us otherwise, that all men came by succession, and generation from one man: we must not deny the truth of the history of creation. (*Observations on Mr. Hobbes's Leviathan: Or his Artificial Man: A Commonwealth*, section 3)

Filmer's mistake is to think of the state of nature as primarily historical and descriptive of the very earliest time in human history. In fact, Hobbes denies that the first humans, Adam and Eve, began in the state of nature. For him, the state of nature is primarily a concept, used in a thought experiment. He asks the reader to think about what it would be like *if* humans had no government at all. He would not have changed his view even if he had thought the condition never actually existed. However, he thinks that the state of nature does exist in three situations: among people too primitive to have a government, during civil wars, and between sovereign nations.

Since the state of nature is the condition in which there are no laws and only laws restrict behavior, there is no restriction on what people may by right take for themselves in the state of nature, including the life of another person. It is easy to see that the state of nature is a war of all against all and that human life in it is, to repeat, "solitary, poor, nasty, brutish and short." So it is important for humans to get out of it.

Hobbes claims that the escape is made possible by following the laws of nature, and he defines a law of nature as "a precept or general rule, found out by reason, by which a man is forbidden to do that which is destructive of his life, or taketh away the means of preserving the same, and to omit that by which he thinketh it may be best preserved." The individual laws are easily proved using the method of *reductio ad absurdum*. For example, in order to prove the first law, suppose that people do not seek peace. It follows from that proposition that people are not acting in a way that preserves their life. But this contradicts the definition of a law of nature. Therefore, the opposite of what was supposed is true, namely, "People are to seek peace."

Concerning the second law, suppose that people do not lay down their right to all things. It follows from that proposition that they are not seeking peace. But this contradicts the first law of nature. Therefore, the opposite of what was supposed is true, namely, "People are to lay down their right to all things."

Notice that the second law is ambiguous between (a) "every right should be laid down" and (b) "some rights should be laid down." People would be more likely to accept (b) as true, because it is a necessary condition for the existence of any government and does not justify an absolute sovereign. But Hobbes sometimes gives the impression that the second law means (a), precisely because he wants to justify absolute sovereignty. In either case, the sovereign is created according to Hobbes when people lay down their rights by transferring those rights to the sovereign, who is created in this very act of transfer. If the sovereign consists of one individual, then the government is a monarchy; if the sovereign consists of more than one but less than all, then the government is an aristocracy; and if the sovereign is composed of all, then the government is a democracy. He did not think there was any difference in meaning between 'monarchy' and 'tyranny', between 'aristocracy' and 'oligarchy', or 'democracy' and 'anarchy'. The difference is merely one of tone or connotation. 'Tyranny', 'oligarchy' and 'anarchy' are the words used when one does not like the government. Hobbes preferred monarchy over the other two forms of government, but acknowledged that the other two were fully legitimate.

About the earliest critics of *Leviathan*, a few points are worth making. First, most are respectful of Hobbes as a person and thinker. In the Preface to his *Observations Concerning the Original of Government, Upon Mr. Hobbes's Leviathan* (1652), Robert Filmer wrote:

> With no small content I read Mr. Hobbes's book *De Cive*, and his *Leviathan*, about the rights of sovereignty, which no man, that I know, hath so amply and judiciously handled: I consent with him about the rights of exercising government.

In his *The Prerogative of Popular Government* (1657), James Harrington wrote,

> It is true I have opposed the politics of Mr Hobbes .... Nevertheless in most other things I firmly believe that Mr Hobbes is, and will in future ages be accounted, the best writer at this day in the world; and for his treatises of human nature, and of liberty and necessity, they are the greatest of new lights, and those which I have followed and shall follow.

Edward Hyde, the earl of Clarendon, wrote that *Leviathan*

> receives great credit and authority from the known name of the author, a man of excellent parts, of great wit, some reading, and somewhat more thinking; one who has spent many years in foreign parts and observation, understands the learned as well as modern languages, has long had the reputation of a great philosopher and mathematician, and in his age has had conversation with very many worthy and extraordinary men ... In a word, Mr. Hobbes is one of the most

> ancient acquaintance [*sic*] I have in the world, and of whom I have always had a great esteem, as a man who besides his eminent parts of learning and knowledge, has been always looked upon as a man of probity, and a life free from scandal; and it may be there are few men now alive, who have been longer known to him than I have been in a fair and friendly conversation and sociableness … [Leviathan] contains in it good learning of all kinds, politely extracted, and very wittily and cunningly digested, in a very commendable method …

However, the praises are often tempered with negative judgments. Again Hyde:

> I have proposed to myself to make some animadversions upon such particulars, as may in my judgement produce much mischief in the world, in a book of great name … which has prevailed over too many, to swallow many new tenets as maxims without chewing. … if he [Hobbes] had been more indulgent in the more vigorous parts of his life, it might have had a greater influence upon the temper of his mind, whereas age seldom submits to those questions, inquiries, and contradictions, which the laws and liberty of conversation require: and it has been always a lamentation amongst Mr. Hobbes his friends, that he spent too much time in thinking, and too little in exercising those thoughts in the company of other men of the same or of as good faculties; for want whereof his natural constitution, with age, contracted such a morosity, that doubting and contradicting men were never grateful to.

And Filmer, after endorsing Hobbes's conclusions about government, says "but I cannot agree to his means of acquiring it [government]. It may seem strange I should praise his building, and yet mislike his foundations; but so it is."

The Appendices of this book contain representative criticisms from seven seventeenth-century thinkers. Some of the criticisms seem to me to be fair, but many are unfair, based either on a woeful or uncharitable misinterpretation or an unsound line of reasoning. But I leave it to each reader to decide whether this is true and if so, which is which.

The second point to be made about Hobbes's earliest critics is that they rarely read his words sympathetically or engaged him in debate. Their minds ran in the ruts of their time and they often simply denied rather than refuted his arguments. To a large extent, their criticisms are a record of the conventional wisdom of the time.

Third, many of his critics think that Hobbes regularly contradicted himself. Clarendon wrote,

> And to all that huddle of words in that whole paragraph, I shall say no more, but that it looks like the discourse of some men, which himself says … *may be numbered amongst the sorts of madness, namely when men speak such words, as put together, have in them no signification at all*, by their noncoherence and contradiction.

Here, the critics are on firmer ground, since Hobbes does seem to contradict himself. In some places, he says that the laws of nature are laws; and in other places, he says they are not. In some places, he says that the actions of the sovereign are the actions of his subjects; and in other places he says that they are not. I leave the adjudication of these matters to the reader.

### Suggested Further Reading


Bowle, John. *Hobbes and his Critics*. London: Jonathan Cape, 1951.

Hampton, Jean. *Hobbes and the Social Contract Tradition*. Cambridge: Cambridge UP, 1986.

Johnston, David. *The Rhetoric of Leviathan*. Princeton: Princeton UP, 1986.

Kavka, Gregory. *Hobbesian Moral and Political Theory*. Princeton: Princeton UP, 1986.

Lloyd, S.A. *Ideals as Interests in Hobbes's Leviathan*. Cambridge: Cambridge UP, 1992.

Martinich, A.P. *A Hobbes Dictionary*. Oxford: Blackwell, 1996.

—. *Hobbes: A Biography*. Cambridge: Cambridge UP, 1999.

—. "Interpretation and Hobbes's Political Philosophy." *Pacific Philosophical Quarterly* 82 (2001): 309-31.

—. *Thomas Hobbes*. London: Macmillan, 1997.

Mintz, Samuel. *The Hunting of Leviathan*. 1962. Bristol: Thoemmes, 1996.

Rogers, G.A.J. and Alan Ryan, eds. *Perspectives on Thomas Hobbes*. Oxford: Clarendon, 1988.

Skinner, Quentin. "The Context of Hobbes's Theory of Political Obligation." *Hobbes and Rousseau*, ed. Maurice Cranston. Garden City: Anchor, 1972. 109-42.

—. "John Milton and the Politics of Slavery." *Prose Studies* 23 (2000): 1-22.

—. *Reason and Rhetoric in the Philosophy of Hobbes*. Cambridge: Cambridge UP, 1996.

—. "Thomas Hobbes on the Proper Signification of Liberty." *Transactions of the Royal Society*. Fifth series 40 (1990): 121-51.

Sorell, Tom. *Hobbes*. London: Routledge & Kegan Paul, 1986.

—, ed. *The Cambridge Companion to Hobbes*. Cambridge: Cambridge UP, 1996.

Tuck, Richard. *Hobbes*. Oxford: Oxford UP, 1989.

# *Thomas Hobbes: A Brief Chronology*

| | |
|---|---|
| 1588 | April 5, Hobbes born in Malmesbury, Wiltshire, England; 'invasion' of the Spanish Armada |
| 1608 | graduates from Magdalen Hall, Oxford, and becomes tutor to William Cavendish, the future second earl of Devonshire |
| 1614-15 | tours Continent (France and Italy) with William Cavendish |
| 1619-23 | sometime secretary to Francis Bacon |
| 1622-24 | stockholder in Virginia Company, probably by the grace of William Cavendish |
| 1628 | William Cavendish dies |
| 1629 | publication of Hobbes's translation of Thucydides' *The Peloponnesian War* |
| 1629-30 | second tour of the Continent, with Gervase Clifton |
| 1634-36 | third tour of the Continent, with William Cavendish, the third earl of Devonshire; associates with Marin Mersenne, Pierre Gassendi, and others in Paris |
| 1636 | visits the aged and ill Galileo under house arrest; returns to England in October |
| 1640 | Spring, *Elements of Law, Natural and Politic* circulated in manuscript |
| 1640 | November, Hobbes flees to France |
| 1641 | contributes to *Objections* to Descartes's *Meditations* |
| 1642-49 | English Civil War |
| 1642 | *De Cive* published; 1647, second edition |
| 1646 | debates the issue of free will with John Bramhall in Paris; debate published in 1654-55 |
| 1648 | December, Pride's Purge of Presbyterians from Parliament |
| 1649 | January, execution of Charles I |
| 1649-60 | The Commonwealth |
| 1651 | about May, *Leviathan* published |
| 1652 | February, Hobbes returns to England; Robert Filmer, *Observations on Mr Hobbes's Leviathan* |
| 1654 | *Of Liberty and Necessity* published |

1655 *De Corpore* published

1656 English translation of *De Corpore* published; *The Questions Concerning Liberty, Necessity and Chance* published

1657 George Lawson, *An Examination of the Political Part of Mr Hobbes His Leviathan*

1658 *De Homine* published; John Bramhall, *The Catching of Leviathan, or the Great Whale*; death of Oliver Cromwell

1660 Restoration of the monarchy; Charles II succeeds to British throne

1661-65 Clarendon Code

1662 *Mr Hobbes Considered in his Loyalty, Religion, Reputation and Manners* [written by Hobbes] published

1663 William Lucy, *Observations, Censures, and Confutations of Notorious Errours in Mr. Hobbes His Leviathan*

1666 bill introduced into the House of Commons to prosecute Hobbes for atheism; no action taken

1667 Edward Hyde, the earl of Clarendon, dismissed by Charles II, flees to the Continent

1668 Latin version of *Leviathan* published

1670 Thomas Tenison, *The Creed of Mr. Hobbes Examined in a Feigned Conference between Him and a Student in Divinity*; Samuel Pufendorf, *Of the Law of Nature and Nations*

1673 translation of the *Odyssey* published

1675 Hobbes leaves London for the last time; last years spent at Chatsworth and Hardwick Hall, Derbyshire

1676 translation of the *Iliad* published; Edward Hyde, *A Brief View and Survey of the Dangerous and Pernicious Errors to Church and State in Mr Hobbes's Book, Entitled Leviathan*

1679 December 4, Hobbes dies, buried in parish church near Hardwick Hall; *Behemoth* published

1679-81 Exclusion Crisis: attempts to exclude James, brother of Charles II, from the succession

1680 *An Historical Narration Concerning Heresy, and the Punishment Thereof* published

1682 *An Answer to a Book Published by Dr Bramhall* published

1688 Glorious Revolution; James II flees England and William of Orange succeeds as king in 1689

# *A Note on the Text*

## This Edition

Since this is an edition for students, I have changed those things that I think unduly interfere with understanding and have retained some things that give the flavor of seventeenth-century grammar and typography, with one exception. The "Review and Conclusion" at the end of *Leviathan* is presented in this edition with its original spelling and punctuation in order to give the reader a sense of the original. For the rest of the book, I have modernized the spelling of most words (including changing 'then' to 'than' when appropriate). Greek words have been transliterated into the Roman alphabet. I have modernized punctuation, fully aware of the dangers of doing so. (In this matter, I follow the practice of the great scholar J. G. A. Pocock in his edition of James Harrington's political works.) In the original edition of *Leviathan*, italics were often used for proper names, emphasis, and to indicate a quotation. I have retained italics to indicate a quotation, sometimes retained them for emphasis, but rarely, if ever, use them for proper names. Hobbes's name was spelled in various ways, e.g. 'Hobbs'. I have kept the original form unless its form is an apparent typographical error.

I have been guided by the following rules of thumb. I have changed Hobbes's colons to semicolons or periods; his semicolons to commas; and dropped many of his commas, especially when they simply set off a prepositional phrase or a series of items that are marked by, say, 'or' ('beasts, or idiots, or children'). Sometimes I left Hobbes's punctuation unchanged because changing it would interfere with understanding, or because it is a memorable quotation, which the student should savor. When the word following a colon or semicolon in Hobbes's text is capitalized I have usually changed the punctuation mark to a period and have begun a new sentence. Typically, I have placed a semicolon in front of 'in effect', 'it followeth', 'yet' and 'though', when they logically divide the thought of the sentence in half. Students and other readers have told me that these changes have greatly aided their comprehension of the text.

Internal references to the Bible have often been moved to the more natural position at the end of a quotation. Some references have been expanded and some corrected silently.

Many scholars now refer to *Leviathan* by chapter and paragraph number; so I have inserted paragraph numbers into this edition, even though they do not appear in early editions. Since Hobbes's seventeenth-century critics referred to a 1651 edition of *Leviathan*, I have provided the original page numbers in brackets in the margin. (It is crucial to remember this when reading references to *Leviathan* in the appendices.) In the 1651 Head edition (and thus in my numbering) two pages are each numbered 247 and 248; and no pages are numbered 84, 194, 257-60, 332 and 388. The original page references also help one to find the same passage in other editions of *Leviathan*. Like the Bible for believers, no one interested in political philosophy should own just one edition of *Leviathan*.

Among the things that I might have changed but did not, are the verb-ending '-eth' and the full capitalization of words that Hobbes put in capitals, for example, 'HONOUR' and 'ENEMY'. But I have changed to lower case most nouns that were capitalized; for example, 'Commonwealth', 'Honour', and 'Nature' become 'commonwealth', 'honour', and 'nature'.

All items in brackets are my own additions to the text.

Words and phrases in brackets in the text either indicate the meaning of an unfamiliar word (e.g. 'propriety [property]') or fill out Hobbes's syntax a bit (e.g. 'for such [a man] know'). The context should make clear which is which.

Books of the Bible are set in Roman type.

When I refer to other parts of *Leviathan* in the footnotes, the instruction 'See also' means that other passages deal with the same topic. 'See' means that I am giving a reference that the text requires. 'Cf.' ['confer'] means that other passages give a different treatment of the same topic.

With a few exceptions, I have limited my cross-references in the footnotes to other passages in *Leviathan*.

I have prepared not a postmodern edition of *Leviathan* but a minimalist one.

## Some Tips on Understanding Hobbes's Grammar

Sometimes an independent clause or even a sentence begins with the word 'which', referring to something mentioned in the preceding clause, often something quite complex. For example,

> No man can know by discourse that this or that is, has been, or will be; *which* is to know absolutely,

means

> No man can know by discourse that this or that is, has been, or will be; *to know by discourse that this or that is, has been, or will be* is to know absolutely.

Sometimes 'which' occurs as if it were an adjectival pronoun. For example,

> All which causes … do manifestly appear in the examples following

means,

> All of these the causes [of religious changes, which were discussed in the preceding six paragraphs] do manifestly appear in the examples following.

Sometimes the word 'that' means 'in order that'. For example,

> to make known to others our wills, that we may have the mutual help of one another

means

> to make known to others our wills, in order that we may have mutual help.

Sometimes the word 'that' is used where we would use 'who'. For example, 'The man that [who] studies hard' or 'The Romans that [who] had conquered the greatest part of the then known world'.

Hobbes sometimes reverses what we consider the normal word order. For example, where he says, "in the body natural," we would say, "in the natural body."

Often he uses 'but' where we would use 'nothing but', e.g. 'multiplication is but adding together of things equal'.

## Editions of 1651

Three editions of *Leviathan* purport to be published by Andrew Crooke in 1651. These editions are referred to by the printer's ornament that appears on the title page: Head, Bear, and 25 Ornaments. The Head edition was the very first. It appeared in two large paper versions. The pages of one of these two contain a border formed by a red line. The Bear edition was probably printed in Holland at an unknown date. The 25 Ornaments edition was probably printed in London about 1680.

The Harry Ransom Humanities Research Center of the University of Texas at Austin contains seven copies of 1651 editions. Four copies come from the Ornaments edition, and three copies are from the Head edition, one of which is inscribed 'T Willughby'.

# *Abbreviations*

## Abbreviations Used for Hobbes's Books

| | |
|---|---|
| *Lev.* | *Leviathan* |
| *DC* | *De Cive* |
| *Q* | *The Questions Concerning Liberty, Necessity and Chance* |

## Abbreviations Used for Books of the Bible

| | |
|---|---|
| Acts | Acts of the Apostles |
| Deut. | Deuteronomy. |
| Apoc. | Book of the Apocalypse [= Revelation] |
| Chron. | Chronicles |
| Col. | Colossians |
| Cor. | Corinthians |
| Eccles. | Ecclesiastes |
| Ezek. | Ezekiel |
| Gal. | Galatians |
| Gen. | Genesis |
| Heb. | Hebrews |
| Is. | Isaiah |
| Jer. | Jeremiah |
| Josh. | Joshua |
| Matt. | Matthew |
| Mic. | Micah |
| Num. | Numbers |
| Prov. | Proverbs |
| Ps. | Psalms |
| Rom. | Romans |
| Sam. | Samuel |
| Thes. | Thessalonians |
| Tim. | Timothy |
| Zech. | Zechariah |

# LEVIATHAN

OR

THE MATTER, FORM, & POWER

OF A

COMMON-WEALTH

ECCLESIASTICAL

AND

CIVIL

BY THOMAS HOBBES OF MALMESBURY

Thomas Hobbes, *Leviathan* (1651) illustrated title page.
Harry Ransom Humanities Research Center,
The University of Texas at Austin.

# TO MY MOST HONOR'D FRIEND

## MR FRANCIS GODOLPHIN, OF GODOLPHIN[1]

Honor'd Sir,

1. Your most worthy brother, Mr. Sidney Godolphin, when he lived, was pleased to think my studies something, and otherwise to oblige me, as you know, with real testimonies of his good opinion, great in themselves, and the greater for the worthiness of his person. For there is not any virtue that disposeth a man, either to the service of God or to the service of his country, to civil society or private friendship, that did not manifestly appear in his conversation, not as acquired by necessity or affected upon occasion, but inherent, and shining in a generous constitution of his nature. Therefore, in honor and gratitude to him, and with devotion to yourself, I humbly dedicate unto you this my discourse of commonwealth.

2. I know not how the world will receive it, nor how it may reflect on those that shall seem to favor it. For in a way beset with those that contend, on one side for too great liberty, and on the other side for too much authority, 'tis hard to pass between the points of both unwounded. But yet, methinks, the endeavor to advance the civil power, should not be by the civil power condemned; nor private men, by reprehending it, declare they think that power too great. Besides, I speak not of the men, but (in the abstract) of the seat of power (like to those simple and unpartial creatures in the Roman Capitol, that with their noise defended those within it, not because they were they, but there), offending none, I think but those without, or such within (if there be any such) as favor to them.

3. That which perhaps may most offend are certain texts of

---

1 Sidney Godolphin (1610-43) was an MP in both the Short and Long Parliaments and died, as Hobbes says near the end of *Leviathan,* "by an undiscerned and undiscerning hand" ("A Review and Conclusion," 4). Hobbes may have met Godolphin when the latter was a member of the Tew Circle. In his will, Godolphin left Hobbes 200 pounds sterling, which was to be paid by his brother Francis. Hence the dedication.

Holy Scripture, alleged by me to other purpose than ordinarily they use to be by others. But I have done it with due submission, and also (in order to my subject) necessarily; for they are the outworks of the enemy, from when they impugn the civil power. If notwithstanding this, you find my labor generally decried, you may be pleased to excuse yourself, and say, I am a man that love my own opinions, and think all true I say, that I honored your brother, and honor you, and have presumed on that, to assume the title (without your knowledge) of being, as I am,

Sir,
Your most humble, and most obedient Servant,
Thomas Hobbes
Paris, April 15/25, 1651

# THE CONTENTS OF THE CHAPTERS

## Part IV: Of the Kingdom of Darkness

# THE INTRODUCTION [1]

1. Nature (the art whereby God hath made and governs the world) is by the art of man, as in many other things, so in this also imitated, that it can make an artificial animal.[1] For seeing life is but a motion of limbs, the beginning whereof is in some principal part within, why may we not say that all *automata* (engines that move themselves by springs and wheels as doth a watch) have an artificial life? For what is the *heart*, but a *spring*; and the *nerves*, but so many *strings*; and the *joints*, but so many *wheels*, giving motion to the whole body, such as was intended by the Artificer? *Art* goes yet further, imitating that rational and most excellent work of nature, *man*. For by art is created that great LEVIATHAN[2] called a COMMONWEALTH, or STATE[3] (in Latin, CIVITAS), which is but an artificial man, though of greater stature and strength than the natural, for whose protection and defense it was intended; and in which the sovereignty is an artificial *soul*, as giving life and motion to the whole body. The *magistrates* and other *officers* of judicature and execution [are] artificial *joints. Reward* and *punishment* (by which fastened to the seat of the sovereignty, every joint and member is moved to perform his duty) are the *nerves* that do the same in the body natural. The *wealth* and *riches* of all the particular members are the *strength. Salus populi* (the *people's safety*) [is] its *business. Counsellors*, by whom all things needful for it to know are suggested unto it, are the *memory. Equity* and laws [are] an artificial *reason* and *will. Concord* [is] *health. Sedition [is] sickness.* And *civil war* [is] *death.* Lastly, the *pacts* and *covenants* by which the parts of this

---

1 Hobbes is showing that normal beliefs do not pass scrutiny. Nature is actually artificial; machines are alive and humans are machines. Our beliefs must be reconsidered. Since Hobbes is the one to deconstruct these standard distinctions, he is in a good position to construct the correct view, or so he wants the reader to believe.

2 Cf. 17.13

3 Comparing the state to a living body was common in the seventeenth century: "The head cares for the body, so doeth the King for his people. As the discourse and direction flowes from the head, and the execution thereunto belongs to the rest of the members, everyone according to their office: so it is betwixt a wise King and his people" (James I, "The Trew Law of Free Monarchies," 1598); "As in natural things, the head being cut off, the rest cannot be called a body: no more can in politick things a multitude or commonality, without a head be incorporate" (*Examples for Kings: or Rules for Princes to Govern By*, 1642).

body politic were at first made, set together, and united, resemble that *fiat*,[1] or the *let us make man*, pronounced by God in the Creation.

[2] 2. To describe the nature of this artificial man, I will consider

First, the *matter* thereof, and the *artificer*; both which is *Man*.

Secondly, *how*, and by what *covenants* it is made; what are the rights and just *power* or *authority* of a *sovereign*; and what it is that *preserveth* and *dissolveth* it.

Thirdly, what is a *Christian Commonwealth*.

Lastly, what is the *Kingdom of Darkness*.

3. Concerning the first, there is a saying much usurped of late that *wisdom* is acquired, not by reading of *books*, but of men. Consequently whereunto, those persons, that for the most part can give no other proof of being wise, take great delight to show what they think they have read in men by uncharitable censures of one another behind their backs. But there is another saying, not of late understood, by which they might learn truly to read one another, if they would take the pains; and that is *nosce teipsum*, *read thyself*, which was not meant, as it is now used, to countenance either the barbarous state of men in power towards their inferiors or to encourage men of low degree to a saucy behavior towards their betters. But [it was meant] to teach us that for the similitude of the thoughts and passions of one man to the thoughts and passions of another, whosoever looketh into himself and considereth what he doth when he does *think*, *opine*, *reason*, *hope*, *fear*, etc., and upon what grounds, he shall thereby read and know what are the thoughts and passions of all other men upon the like occasions. I say the similitude of *passions*, which are the same in all men, *desire*, *fear*, *hope*, etc., not the similitude of the *objects* of the passions, which are the things *desired*, *feared*, *hoped*, etc.; for these the constitution individual and particular education do so vary, and they are so easy to be kept from our knowledge that the characters of man's heart, blotted and confounded as they are with dissembling, lying, counterfeiting, and erroneous doctrines are legible only to him that searcheth hearts. And though by men's actions we do discover

1 'Fiat' is Latin for 'Let there be'. 'Fiat lux' means 'Let there be light'. 'Fiat homo' means 'Let there be man'. These are some of God's words of creation in the Vulgate or Latin version of the Bible.

their design sometimes; yet to do it without comparing them with our own and distinguishing all circumstances by which the case may come to be altered is to decipher without a key and be for the most part deceived by too much trust or by too much diffidence, as he that reads is himself a good or evil man.

4. But let one man read another by his actions never so perfectly, it serves him only with his acquaintance, which are but few. He that is to govern a whole nation must read in himself, not this or that particular man, but mankind, which though it be hard to do, harder than to learn any language or science; yet when I shall have set down my own reading orderly and perspicuously, the pains left another will be only to consider if he also find not the same in himself. For this kind of doctrine admitteth no other demonstration.

# PART I [3]

# OF MAN

## CHAPTER I

## OF SENSE

1. Concerning the thoughts of man, I will consider them first singly and afterwards in train or dependence upon one another. Singly, they are every one a representation or appearance of some quality or other accident of a body without us, which is commonly called an *object.* Which object worketh on the eyes, ears, and other parts of man's body, and by diversity of working, produceth diversity of appearances.[1]

2. The original of them all is that which we call SENSE (for there is no conception in a man's mind which hath not at first, totally or by parts, been begotten upon the organs of sense). The rest are derived from that original.[2]

3. To know the natural cause of sense is not very necessary to the business now in hand; and I have elsewhere written of the same at large. Nevertheless, to fill each part of my present method, I will briefly deliver the same in this place.

4. The cause of sense is the external body or object which presseth the organ proper to each sense either immediately, as in the taste and touch, or mediately, as in seeing, hearing, and smelling; which pressure, by the mediation of nerves and other strings and membranes of the body, continued inwards to the brain and heart, causeth there a resistance or counter-pressure or endeavour of the heart to deliver itself, which endeavour, because outward, seemeth

---

1 Hobbes is conceding that there is qualitative experience of the world, as he also does in 1.1.

2 A standard philosophical view is that "nothing is in the intellect that was not first in the senses."

to be some matter without. And this seeming or fancy is that which men call *sense* and consisteth, as to the eye in a *light* or *colour figured*; to the ear in a *sound*; to the nostril in an *odour*; to the tongue and palate in a *savour*; and to the rest of the body in *heat*, *cold*, *hardness*, *softness*, and such other qualities as we discern by *feeling*. All which qualities called *sensible* are in the object that causeth them, but so many several motions of the matter, by which it presseth our organs diversely.[1] Neither in us that are pressed are they anything else but divers motions (for motion produceth nothing but motion).[2] But their appearance to us is fancy, the same waking [as] that dreaming. And as pressing, rubbing, or striking the eye makes us fancy a light, and pressing the ear produceth a din, so do the bodies also we see or hear produce the same by their strong, though unobserved action. For if those colours and sounds were in the bodies or objects that cause them, they could not be
[4] severed from them, as by glasses, and in echoes by reflection, we see they are where we know the thing we see is in one place, the appearance in another. And though at some certain distance the real and very object seem invested with the fancy it begets in us; yet still the object is one thing, the image or fancy is another. So that sense in all cases is nothing else but original fancy, caused (as I have said) by the pressure, that is, by the motion of external things upon our eyes, ears, and other organs, thereunto ordained.

5. But the philosophy schools, through all the universities of Christendom, grounded upon certain texts of Aristotle, teach another doctrine; and say for the cause of *vision*, that the thing seen sendeth forth on every side a *visible species*, (in English) a *visible show*, *apparition*, or *aspect*, or *a being seen*, the receiving whereof into the eye is *seeing*. And for the cause of *hearing*, that the thing heard sendeth forth an *audible species*, that is, an *audible aspect*, or *audible being seen*; which, entering at the ear, maketh *hearing*. Nay, for the cause of *understanding* also, they say the thing understood sendeth forth an *intelligible species*, that is, *an intelligible being seen*; which coming into the understanding, makes us understand. I say not

---

1 The qualitative properties that people naturally think of as in bodies are actually only motions of very small bodies.

2 Qualitative experiences in humans are also nothing but motions. Cf. 1.1. Thus, the Aristotelian view is false; see 1.5.

this, as disapproving the use of universities, but because I am to speak hereafter of their office in a commonwealth, I must let you see on all occasions by the way what things would be amended in them, amongst which the frequency of insignificant speech is one.

## CHAPTER II

## OF IMAGINATION

1. That when a thing lies still, unless somewhat else stir it, it will lie still for ever is a truth that no man doubts of. But that when a thing is in motion, it will eternally be in motion, unless somewhat else stay it, though the reason be the same (namely, that nothing can change itself), is not so easily assented to. For men measure, not only other men, but all other things, by themselves; and because they find themselves subject after motion to pain and lassitude think everything else grows weary of motion and seeks repose of its own accord, little considering whether it be not some other motion wherein that desire of rest they find in themselves consisteth. From hence it is that the schools say heavy bodies fall downwards out of an appetite to rest and to conserve their nature in that place which is most proper for them ascribing appetite, and knowledge of what is good for their conservation (which is more than man has) to things inanimate, absurdly.

2. When a body is once in motion, it moveth (unless something else hinder it) eternally; and whatsoever hindreth it cannot in an instant but in time and by degrees quite extinguish it. And as we see in the water, though the wind cease, the waves give not over rolling for a long time after, so also it happeneth in that motion [5]
which is made in the internal parts of a man, then, when he sees, dreams, etc. For after the object is removed or the eye shut, we still retain an image of the thing seen, though more obscure than when we see it. And this is it the Latins call *imagination*, from the image made in seeing; and [they] apply the same, though improperly, to all the other senses. But the Greeks call it *fancy*, which signifies *appearance,* and is as proper to one sense as to another.

*IMAGINATION*, therefore, is nothing but *decaying sense*[1] and is found in men and many other living creatures, as well sleeping as waking.

3. The decay of sense in men waking is not the decay of the motion made in sense, but an obscuring of it, in such manner as the light of the sun obscureth the light of the stars, which stars do no less exercise their virtue by which they are visible in the day than in the night. But because amongst many strokes which our eyes, ears, and other organs receive from external bodies, the predominant only is sensible; therefore the light of the sun being predominant, we are not affected with the action of the stars. And any object being removed from our eyes, though the impression it made in us remain; yet other objects more present succeeding and working on us, the imagination of the past is obscured and made weak, as the voice of a man is in the noise of the day. From whence it followeth that the longer the time is after the sight or sense of any object, the weaker is the imagination. For the continual change of man's body destroys in time the parts which in sense were moved, so that distance of time and of place hath one and the same effect in us. For as at a great distance of place that which we look at appears dim and without distinction of the smaller parts; and as voices grow weak and inarticulate, so also after great distance of time our imagination of the past is weak; and we lose (for example) of cities we have seen many particular streets, and of actions many particular circumstances. This *decaying sense*, when we would express the thing itself (I mean *fancy* itself), we call *imagination*, as I said before. But when we would express the decay and signify that the sense is fading, old, and past, it is called *memory*. So that imagination and memory are but one thing, which for divers considerations hath divers names.

Memory.

4. Much memory, or memory of many things, is called *experience*. Again, imagination being only of those things which have been formerly perceived by sense, either all at once or by parts at several times. The former (which is the imagining the whole object, as it was presented to the sense) is *simple* imagination, as

1 Hobbes's goal is to show that mental states and events, for example, imagination, are reducible to a few basic things, and ultimately matter in motion. Thus, imagination is really decaying sense, and a sensation is a motion in the brain. Memory is imagination, which is decaying sense, which is motion.

when one imagineth a man or horse, which he hath seen before. The other is *compounded,* when from the sight of a man at one time and of a horse at another, we conceive in our mind a centaur. So when a man compoundeth the image of his own person with the image of the actions of another man, as when a man imagines himself a Hercules or an Alexander (which happeneth often to them that are much taken with reading of romances), it is a compound imagination and properly but a fiction of the mind. There [6] be also other imaginations that rise in men (though waking) from the great impression made in sense. As from gazing upon the sun, the impression leaves an image of the sun before our eyes a long time after; and from being long and vehemently attent [attentive] upon geometrical figures, a man shall in the dark (though awake) have the images of lines and angles before his eyes, which kind of fancy hath no particular name, as being a thing that doth not commonly fall into men's discourse.

Dreams.

5. The imaginations of them that sleep are those we call *dreams.* And these also (as all other imaginations) have been before either totally or by parcels in the sense. And because in sense the brain and nerves, which are the necessary organs of sense, are so benumbed in sleep as not easily to be moved by the action of external objects, there can happen in sleep no imagination and therefore no dream, but what proceeds from the agitation of the inward parts of man's body; which inward parts, for the connexion they have with the brain and other organs, when they be distempered, do keep the same in motion; whereby the imaginations there formerly made, appear as if a man were waking, saving that the organs of sense being now benumbed, so as there is no new object which can master and obscure them with a more vigorous impression, a dream must needs be more clear in this silence of sense than are our waking thoughts. And hence it cometh to pass that it is a hard matter, and by many thought impossible, to distinguish exactly between sense and dreaming.[1] For my part, when I consider that in dreams I do not often nor constantly think of the

1 A partial response to Descartes. It is significant because Hobbes does not try to identify a criterion to distinguish dreaming from waking. Such a criterion would be useless, because one would need another criterion to judge whether one was correctly applying the first criterion, and so on.

same persons, places, objects, and actions that I do waking, nor remember so long a train of coherent thoughts dreaming as at other times, and because waking I often observe the absurdity of dreams, but never dream of the absurdities of my waking thoughts, I am well satisfied that, being awake, I know I dream not, though when I dream, I think myself awake.

6. And seeing dreams are caused by the distemper of some of the inward parts of the body, divers distempers must needs cause different dreams. And hence it is that lying cold breedeth dreams of fear and raiseth the thought and image of some fearful object, the motion from the brain to the inner parts, and from the inner parts to the brain being reciprocal, and that as anger causeth heat in some parts of the body when we are awake, so when we sleep the overheating of the same parts causeth anger and raiseth up in the brain the imagination of an enemy. In the same manner, as natural kindness when we are awake causeth desire and desire makes heat in certain other parts of the body, so also too much heat in those parts, while we sleep, raiseth in the brain an imagination of some kindness shown. In sum, our dreams are the reverse of our waking imaginations; the motion when we are awake beginning at one end, and when we dream, at another.

[7] Apparitions or Visions.

7. The most difficult discerning of a man's dream from his waking thoughts is, then, when by some accident we observe not that we have slept; which is easy to happen to a man full of fearful thoughts, and whose conscience is much troubled, and that sleepeth without the circumstances of going to bed or putting off his clothes, as one that noddeth in a chair. For he that taketh pains and industriously lays himself to sleep, in case any uncouth and exorbitant fancy come unto him, cannot easily think it other than a dream. We read of Marcus Brutus (one that had his life given him by Julius Caesar, and was also his favorite, and notwithstanding murdered him), how at Philippi, the night before he gave battle to Augustus Caesar, he saw a fearful apparition, which is commonly related by historians as a vision. But, considering the circumstances, one may easily judge to have been but a short dream. For sitting in his tent, pensive and troubled with the horror of his rash act, it was not hard for him, slumbering in the cold, to dream of that which most affrighted him; which fear, as by degrees it made

him wake, so also it must needs make the apparition by degrees to vanish. And having no assurance that he slept, he could have no cause to think it a dream, or anything but a vision. And this is no very rare accident; for even they that be perfectly awake, if they be timorous [timid] and superstitious, possessed with fearful tales and alone in the dark, are subject to the like fancies, and believe they see spirits and dead men's ghosts walking in churchyards; whereas it is either their fancy only or else the knavery of such persons as make use of such superstitious fear to pass disguised in the night to places they would not be known to haunt.

8. From this ignorance of how to distinguish dreams and other strong fancies from vision and sense did arise the greatest part of the religion of the Gentiles in time past that worshipped satyrs, fauns, nymphs, and the like; and nowadays the opinion that rude people have of fairies, ghosts, and goblins, and of the power of witches.[1] For, as for witches, I think not that their witchcraft is any real power, but yet that they are justly punished for the false belief they have that they can do such mischief, joined with their purpose to do it if they can, their trade being nearer to a new religion than to a craft or science. And for fairies and walking ghosts, the opinion of them has, I think, been on purpose either taught or not confuted to keep in credit the use of exorcism, of crosses, of holy water, and other such inventions of ghostly[2] men. Nevertheless, there is no doubt but God can make unnatural apparitions. But that he does it so often as men need to fear such things more than they fear the stay or change of the course of nature, which he also can stay and change, is no point of Christian faith. But evil men, under pretext that God can do anything, are so bold as to say anything when it serves their turn, though they think it untrue. It is the part of a wise man to believe them no further than right reason makes that which they say appear credible. If this superstitious fear of spirits were taken away and with it prognostics from dreams, false prophecies, and many other things depending thereon, by which crafty ambitious persons abuse the simple people, [8]
men would be much more fitted than they are for civil obedience.

---

1 Scholars dispute whether Hobbes wanted to restrict this problem to pagan religions or to extend it to Christianity also.

2 'Ghostly' may mean either spiritual or religious. In either case, Hobbes's use is sarcastic.

9. And this ought to be the work of the schools, but they rather nourish such doctrine. For (not knowing what imagination or the senses are) what they receive, they teach, some saying that imaginations rise of themselves and have no cause, others that they rise most commonly from the will and that good thoughts are blown (inspired) into a man by God, and evil thoughts by the Devil, or that good thoughts are poured (infused) into a man by God, and evil ones by the Devil. Some say the senses receive the species of things and deliver them to the common sense; and the common sense delivers them over to the fancy, and the fancy to the memory, and the memory to the judgement, like handing of things from one to another with many words making nothing understood.

Understanding. 10. The imagination that is raised in man (or any other creature endued with the faculty of imagining) by words or other voluntary signs is that we generally call *understanding*, and is common to man and beast. For a dog by custom will understand the call or the rating of his master, and so will many other beasts. That understanding which is peculiar to man is the understanding not only his will, but his conceptions and thoughts, by the sequel and contexture of the names of things into affirmations, negations, and other forms of speech. And of this kind of understanding I shall speak hereafter.

## CHAPTER III

## OF THE CONSEQUENCE OR TRAIN OF IMAGINATIONS

1. By *Consequence* or TRAIN of thoughts, I understand that succession of one thought to another, which is called (to distinguish it from discourse in words) *mental discourse*.

2. When a man thinketh on anything whatsoever, his next thought after is not altogether so casual as it seems to be. Not every thought to every thought succeeds indifferently. But as we have no imagination whereof we have not formerly had sense in whole or in parts, so we have no transition from one imagination to another whereof we never had the like before in our

senses.[1] The reason whereof is this. All fancies are motions within us, relics of those made in the sense. And those motions that immediately succeeded one another in the sense continue also together after sense; in so much as the former coming again to take place and be predominant, the latter followeth by coherence of the matter moved in such manner as water upon a plain table is drawn which way any one part of it is guided by the finger. But because in sense to one and the same thing perceived sometimes one thing, sometimes another, succeedeth, it comes to pass in time that in the imagining of anything, there is no certainty what we [9] shall imagine next. Only this is certain, it shall be something that succeeded the same before, at one time or another.

Train of thoughts unguided.

3. This train of thoughts or mental discourse is of two sorts. The first is *unguided, without design*, and inconstant; wherein there is no passionate thought to govern and direct those that follow to itself, as the end and scope of some desire or other passion; in which case the thoughts are said to wander and seem impertinent one to another, as in a dream. Such are commonly the thoughts of men that are not only without company, but also without care of anything, though even then their thoughts are as busy as at other times, but without harmony; as the sound which a lute out of tune would yield to any man, or in tune to one that could not play. And yet in this wild ranging of the mind, a man may oft-times perceive the way of it and the dependence of one thought upon another. For in a discourse of our present civil war, what could seem more impertinent than to ask, as one did, what was the value of a Roman penny? Yet the coherence to me was manifest enough. For the thought of the war introduced the thought of the delivering up the King to his enemies; the thought of that brought in the thought of the delivering up of Christ; and that again the thought of the 30 pence, which was the price of that treason; and thence easily followed that malicious question; and all this in a moment of time, for thought is quick.

Train of thoughts, regulated.

4. The second is more constant, as being regulated by some desire and design. For the impression made by such things as we desire or fear is strong and permanent, or (if it cease for a time) of

1 A scholastic maxim: Nothing is in the intellect that was not first in the senses.

quick return; so strong it is sometimes as to hinder and break our sleep. From desire ariseth the thought of some means we have seen produce the like of that which we aim at; and from the thought of that the thought of means to that mean; and so continually, till we come to some beginning within our own power. And because the end by the greatness of the impression comes often to mind, in case our thoughts begin to wander they are quickly again reduced into the way; which, observed by one of the seven wise men, made him give men this precept, which is now worn out: *respice finem*;[1] that is to say, in all your actions, look often upon what you would have, as the thing that directs all your thoughts in the way to attain it.

5. The train of regulated thoughts is of two kinds: one, when of an effect imagined we seek the causes or means that produce it; and this is common to man and beast. The other is, when imagining anything whatsoever, we seek all the possible effects that can by it be produced; that is to say, we imagine what we can do with it when we have it. Of which I have not at any time seen any sign, but in man only; for this is a curiosity hardly incident to the nature of any living creature that has no other passion but sensual, such as are hunger, thirst, lust, and anger. In sum, the discourse of the mind, when it is governed by design, is nothing but seeking, or the
[10] faculty of invention, which the Latins call *sagacitas*, and *solertia*, a hunting out of the causes of some effect, present or past, or of the effects of some present or past cause. Sometimes a man seeks what he hath lost; and from that place and time wherein he misses it his mind runs back, from place to place, and time to time, to find where and when he had it; that is to say, to find some certain and limited time and place in which to begin a method of seeking. Again, from thence, his thoughts run over the same places and times to find what action or other occasion might make him lose
Remembrance. it. This we call *remembrance* or calling to mind. The Latins call it *reminiscentia*, as it were a *re-conning* [re-examination] of our former actions.

6. Sometimes a man knows a place determinate, within the compass whereof he is to seek; and then his thoughts run over all

1 See Plato, *Protagoras* 343a-b. Reputedly, Chilon said, "Look to the end."

the parts thereof in the same manner as one would sweep a room to find a jewel, or as a spaniel ranges the field till he find a scent, or as a man should run over the alphabet to start a rhyme.

7. Sometimes a man desires to know the event of an action; and then he thinketh of some like action past, and the events thereof one after another, supposing like events will follow like actions. As he that foresees what will become of a criminal re-cons [recalls] what he has seen follow on the like crime before; having this order of thoughts, the crime, the officer, the prison, the judge, and the gallows. Which kind of thoughts is called *foresight*, and *prudence*, or *providence*, and sometimes *wisdom*; though such conjecture, through the difficulty of observing all circumstances, be very fallacious. But this is certain: by how much one man has more experience of things past than another; by so much also he is more prudent, and his expectations the seldomer fail him. The *present* only has a being in nature; things *past* have a being in the memory only; but things *to come* have no being at all, the *future* being but a fiction of the mind, applying the sequels of actions past to the actions that are present; which with most certainty is done by him that has most experience, but not with certainty enough. And though it be called prudence when the event answereth our expectation; yet in its own nature it is but presumption. For the foresight of things to come, which is providence, belongs only to him [God] by whose will they are to come. From him only, and supernaturally, proceeds prophecy. The best prophet naturally is the best guesser; and the best guesser, he that is most versed and studied in the matters he guesses at, for he hath most *signs* to guess by. Prudence.

8. A *sign* is the event antecedent of the consequent, and contrarily, the consequent of the antecedent, when the like consequences have been observed before; and the oftener they have been observed, the less uncertain is the sign. And therefore he that has most experience in any kind of business has most signs whereby to guess at the future time, and consequently is the most prudent. And [he is] so much more prudent than he that is new in that kind of business, as not to be equalled by any advantage of natural and extemporary wit, though perhaps many young men think the contrary. Signs.

9. Nevertheless, it is not prudence that distinguisheth man from

[11] beast. There be beasts that at a year old observe more and pursue that which is for their good more prudently than a child can do at ten.

Conjecture of the time past.

10. As prudence is a *presumption* of the *future*, contracted from the *experience* of time *past*, so there is a presumption of things past taken from other things (not future but) past also. For he that hath seen by what courses and degrees a flourishing state hath first come into civil war, and then to ruin, upon the sight of the ruins of any other state will guess the like war and the like courses have been there also. But this conjecture has the same uncertainty almost with the conjecture of the future, both being grounded only upon experience.

11. There is no other act of man's mind that I can remember naturally planted in him so as to need no other thing to the exercise of it but to be born a man and live with the use of his five senses. Those other faculties, of which I shall speak by and by and which seem proper to man only, are acquired and increased by study and industry, and of most men learned by instruction and discipline, and proceed all from the invention of words and speech.[1] For besides sense and thoughts and the train of thoughts, the mind of man has no other motion, though by the help of speech and method, the same faculties may be improved to such a height as to distinguish men from all other living creatures.

12. Whatsoever we imagine is *finite*. Therefore there is no idea or conception of anything we call *infinite*.[2] No man can have in his mind an image of infinite magnitude, nor conceive infinite swiftness, infinite time, or infinite force, or infinite power. When we say anything is infinite, we signify only that we are not able to conceive the ends and bounds of the thing named, having no conception of the thing, but of our own inability.[3] And therefore the name of God is used, not to make us conceive him (for he is incomprehensible, and his greatness and power are unconceivable), but that we may honour him. Also because whatsoever, as I said

---

1 Mistakes in universal propositions that express "general signification," that is, the meaning of the terms, are implicitly contradictory, for example, "All men are winged" and "Not all men are mortal." (See 4.13.)

2 See also 12.6, 31.28, 45.12, and 45.15.

3 Infinite magnitude or number is as hard to understand as infinite goodness.

before, we conceive has been perceived first by sense either all at once or by parts, a man can have no thought representing anything not subject to sense. No man therefore can conceive anything, but he must conceive it in some place and endued with some determinate magnitude; and which may be divided into parts; nor that anything is all in this place and all in another place at the same time; nor that two or more things can be in one and the same place at once. For none of these things ever have or can be incident to sense, but are absurd speeches, taken upon credit, without any signification at all, from deceived philosophers and deceived or deceiving Schoolmen.

## CHAPTER IV [12]

## OF SPEECH

Original [origin] of speech.

1. The invention of *printing*, though ingenious, compared with the invention of *letters*, is no great matter. But who was the first that found the use of letters is not known. He that first brought them into Greece, men say, was Cadmus, the son of Agenor, King of Phoenicia. A profitable invention for continuing the memory of time past and the conjunction of mankind dispersed into so many and distant regions of the earth; and withal [in addition] difficult, as proceeding from a watchful observation of the divers motions of the tongue, palate, lips, and other organs of speech, whereby to make as many differences of characters to remember them. But the most noble and profitable invention of all other was that of SPEECH, consisting of *names* or *appellations*, and their connexion, whereby men register their thoughts, recall them when they are past, and also declare them one to another for mutual utility and conversation, without which there had been amongst men neither commonwealth nor society nor contract nor peace no more than amongst lions, bears, and wolves. The first author of speech was God himself, that instructed Adam how to name such creatures as he presented to his sight, for the Scripture goeth no further in this matter. But this was sufficient to direct him to add more names, as the experience and use of the creatures should give him occasion,

and to join them in such manner by degrees as to make himself understood, and so by succession of time so much language might be gotten as he had found use for, though not so copious as an orator or philosopher has need of. For I do not find anything in the Scripture out of which, directly or by consequence, can be gathered that Adam was taught the names of all figures, numbers, measures, colours, sounds, fancies, relations; much less the names of words and speech, as *general*, *special*, *affirmative*, *negative*, *interrogative*, *optative*, *infinitive*, all which are useful; and least of all, of *entity*, *intentionality*, *quiddity*, and other insignificant words of the School.[1]

2. But all this language gotten and augmented by Adam and his posterity, was again lost at the Tower of Babel, when by the hand of God every man was stricken for his rebellion with an oblivion of his former language. And being hereby forced to disperse themselves into several parts of the world, it must needs be that the diversity of tongues that now is, proceeded by degrees from them in such manner as need (the mother of all inventions) taught them; and in tract of time grew everywhere more copious.

The use of speech.

3. The general use of speech is to transfer our mental discourse into verbal or the train of our thoughts into a train of words, and
[13] that for two commodities, whereof one is the registering of the consequences of our thoughts, which being apt to slip out of our memory and put us to a new labour, may again be recalled by such words as they were marked by. So that the first use of names is to serve for *marks* or *notes* of remembrance. Another is when many use the same words to signify (by their connexion and order) one to another, what they conceive or think of each matter and also what they desire, fear, or have any other passion for. And for this use they are called *signs*. Special uses of speech are these: first, to register what by cogitation we find to be the cause of anything,

1 Hobbes sometimes criticizes "the School" or "Schoolmen." He is referring to the tradition of medieval Christian philosophers that dominated Europe in the thirteenth and fourteenth centuries, and were influenced to a greater or lesser extent by Aristotle. St. Thomas Aquinas, John Duns Scotus, and William of Ockham are famous medieval scholastic philosophers. Although scholastic philosophy went into some decline during the fifteenth and sixteenth centuries, it was still influential in the seventeenth century. Francisco Suarez, for example, was a late-sixteenth-early-seventeenth-century scholastic philosopher, whom Hobbes sometimes singles out for criticism. Many of Hobbes's opponents, notably Bishop John Bramhall, were scholastic philosophers.

present or past, and what we find things present or past may produce or effect, which, in sum, is acquiring of arts. Secondly, to show to others that knowledge which we have attained, which is to counsel and teach one another. Thirdly, to make known to others our wills and purposes, that we may have the mutual help of one another. Fourthly, to please and delight ourselves and others, by playing with our words for pleasure or ornament, innocently.

Abuses of speech.

4. To these uses, there are also four correspondent abuses. First, when men register their thoughts wrong by the inconstancy of the signification of their words by which they register for their conceptions that which they never conceived, and so deceive themselves. Secondly, when they use words metaphorically, that is, in other sense than that they are ordained for and thereby deceive others. Thirdly, when by words they declare that to be their will, which is not. Fourthly, when they use them to grieve one another, for seeing nature hath armed living creatures, some with teeth, some with horns, and some with hands, to grieve an enemy, it is but an abuse of speech to grieve him with the tongue, unless it be one whom we are obliged to govern, and then it is not to grieve, but to correct and amend.

5. The manner how speech serveth to the remembrance of the consequence of causes and effects consisteth in the imposing of *names*, and the *connexion* of them.

Names proper and common.

6. Of names, some are *proper*, and singular to one only thing; as *Peter, John, this man, this tree.* And some are *common* to many things, as *man, horse, tree,* every of which, though but one name, is nevertheless the name of divers particular things, in respect of all which together, it is called a *universal*, there being nothing in the world universal but names, for the things named are every one of them individual and singular.[1]

Universal.

7. One universal name is imposed on many things for their similitude in some quality or other accident. And whereas a proper name bringeth to mind one thing only, universals recall any one of those many.

8. And of names universal, some are of more and some of less

1 A clear statement of Hobbes's nominalism.

extent, the larger comprehending the less large. And some again [are] of equal extent, comprehending each other reciprocally. As for example, the name *body* is of larger signification than the word *man*, and comprehendeth it; and the names *man* and *rational* are of equal extent, comprehending mutually one another. But here we
[14] must take notice that by a name is not always understood, as in grammar, one only word, but sometimes by circumlocution many words together. For all these words, *he that in his actions observeth the laws of his country*, make but one name, equivalent to this one word, *just*.

9. By this imposition of names, some of larger, some of stricter signification, we turn the reckoning of the consequences of things imagined in the mind into a reckoning of the consequences of appellations. For example, a man that hath no use of speech at all (such as is born and remains perfectly deaf and dumb), if he set before his eyes a triangle and by it two right angles (such as are the corners of a square figure), he may by meditation compare and find that the three angles of that triangle are equal to those two right angles that stand by it. But if another triangle be shown him different in shape from the former, he cannot know without a new labour whether the three angles of that also be equal to the same. But he that hath the use of words, when he observes that such equality was consequent, not to the length of the sides, nor to any other particular thing in his triangle, but only to this, that the sides were straight, and the angles three, and that that was all for which he named it a triangle, will boldly conclude universally that such equality of angles is in all triangles whatsoever and register his invention in these general terms: *Every triangle hath its three angles equal to two right angles*. And thus the consequence found in one particular comes to be registered and remembered as a universal rule and discharges our mental reckoning of time and place and delivers us from all labour of the mind, saving the first; and makes that which was found true *here*, and *now* to be true in *all times and places*.

10. But the use of words in registering our thoughts is in nothing so evident as in numbering. A natural fool that could never learn by heart the order of numeral words, as *one*, *two*, and *three*, may observe every stroke of the clock and nod to it or say *one*, *one*,

*one*, but can never know what hour it strikes. And it seems there was a time when those names of number were not in use; and men were fain to apply their fingers of one or both hands to those things they desired to keep account of; and that thence it proceeded that now our numeral words are but ten, in any nation, and in some but five, and then they begin again. And he that can tell ten, if he recite them out of order, will lose himself and not know when he has done. Much less will he be able to add and subtract and perform all other operations of arithmetic. So that without words there is no possibility of reckoning of numbers, much less of magnitudes, of swiftness, of force, and other things, the reckonings whereof are necessary to the being or well-being of mankind.

11. When two names are joined together into a consequence or affirmation, as thus, *A man is a living creature*, or thus, *If he be a man, he is a living creature*; if the latter name *living creature* signify all that the former name *man* signifieth, then the affirmation or consequence is *true*; otherwise *false*. For *true* and *false* are attributes of [15] speech, not of things. And where speech is not, there is neither *truth* nor *falsehood*. *Error* there may be, as when we expect that which shall not be or suspect what has not been; but in neither case can a man be charged with untruth.

Necessity of definitions.

12. Seeing then that *truth* consisteth in the right ordering of names in our affirmations, a man that seeketh precise truth had need to remember what every name he uses stands for and to place it accordingly; or else he will find himself entangled in words, as a bird in lime twigs; the more he struggles, the more belimed. And therefore in geometry (which is the only science that it hath pleased God hitherto to bestow on mankind), men begin at settling the significations of their words, which settling of significations they call *definitions*, and place them in the beginning of their reckoning.[1]

13. By this it appears how necessary it is for any man that aspires to true knowledge to examine the definitions of former authors and either to correct them, where they are negligently set down, or to make them himself. For the errors of definitions multiply themselves, according as the reckoning proceeds, and lead

1 These definitions may be stipulative and need not be descriptive of actual use.

men into absurdities, which at last they see, but cannot avoid, without reckoning anew from the beginning, in which lies the foundation of their errors. From whence it happens that they which trust to books do as they that cast up many little sums into a greater, without considering whether those little sums were rightly cast up or not; and at last finding the error visible and, not mistrusting their first grounds, know not which way to clear themselves, spend time in fluttering over their books, as birds that entering by the chimney and finding themselves enclosed in a chamber, flutter at the false light of a glass window for want of wit to consider which way they came in. So that in the right definition of names lies the first use of speech, which is the acquisition of science, and in wrong or no definitions lies the first abuse, from which proceed all false and senseless tenets, which make those men that take their instruction from the authority of books and not from their own meditation to be as much below the condition of ignorant men as men endued with true science are above it. For between true science and erroneous doctrines, ignorance is in the middle. Natural sense and imagination are not subject to absurdity. Nature itself cannot err; and as men abound in copiousness of language, so they become more wise or more mad than ordinary. Nor is it possible without letters for any man to become either excellently wise or (unless his memory be hurt by disease or ill constitution of organs) excellently foolish. For words are wise men's counters; they do but reckon by them; but they are the money of fools, that value them by the authority of an Aristotle, a Cicero or a Thomas or any other doctor whatsoever, if but a man.

Subject to names.

14. *Subject to names* is whatsoever can enter into or be considered in an account and be added one to another to make a sum or subtracted one from another and leave a remainder. The Latins
[16] called accounts of money *rationes*, and accounting *ratiocinatio*. And that which we in bills or books of account call *items*, they called *nomina*, that is, *name*. And thence it seems to proceed that they extended the word *ratio* to the faculty of reckoning in all other things. The Greeks have but one word, *logos*, for both *speech* and *reason*; not that they thought there was no speech without reason, but no reasoning without speech. And the act of reasoning they called *syllogism*; which signifieth summing up of the consequences

of one saying to another. And because the same things may enter into account for divers accidents, their names are (to show that diversity) diversely wrested and diversified. This diversity of names may be reduced to four general heads.

15. First, a thing may enter into account for *matter* or *body*, as *living, sensible, rational, hot, cold, moved, quiet,* with all which names the word *matter* or *body* is understood; all such being names of matter.

16. Secondly, it may enter into account or be considered for some accident or quality which we conceive to be in it, as for *being moved*, for *being so long*, for *being hot*, etc., and then of the name of the thing itself by a little change or wresting, we make a name for that accident which we consider; and for *living* put into the account *life,* for *moved, motion,* for *hot, heat,* for *long, length*, and the like. And all such names are the names of the accidents and properties by which one matter and body is distinguished from another. These are called *names abstract*, because severed, not from matter, but from the account of matter.

17. Thirdly, we bring into account the properties of our own bodies, whereby we make such distinction. As when anything is *seen* by us, we reckon not the thing itself, but the *sight*, the *colour*, the *idea* of it in the fancy; and when anything is *heard*, we reckon it not, but the *hearing* or *sound* only, which is our fancy or conception of it by the ear: and such are names of fancies.

18. Fourthly, we bring into account, consider, and give names to *names* themselves, and to *speeches*; for, *general, universal, special, equivocal*, are names of names. And *affirmation, interrogation, commandment, narration, syllogism, sermon, oration*, and many other such are names of speeches. And this is all the variety of names positive, which are put to mark somewhat which is in nature or may be feigned by the mind of man, as bodies that are or may be conceived to be, or of bodies, the properties that are, or may be feigned to be, or words and speech.

Use of names positive.

19. There be also other names, called *negative*; which are notes to signify that a word is not the name of the thing in question, as these words: *nothing, no man, infinite, indocible* [*unteachable*], *three want four*, and the like; which are nevertheless of use in reckoning, or in correcting of reckoning, and call to mind our past cogitations,

Negative names with their uses.

though they be not names of anything, because they make us refuse to admit of names not rightly used.

Words insignificant. 20. All other names are but insignificant sounds, and those of two sorts. One, when they are new and yet their meaning not [17] explained by definition, whereof there have been abundance coined by Schoolmen and puzzled philosophers.

21. Another, when men make a name of two names, whose significations are contradictory and inconsistent, as this name, an *incorporeal body*, or, which is all one, an *incorporeal substance*, and a great number more. For whensoever any affirmation is false, the two names of which it is composed, put together and made one, signify nothing at all. For example, if it be a false affirmation to say *a quadrangle is round*, the word *round quadrangle* signifies nothing, but is a mere sound. So likewise if it be false to say that virtue can be poured, or blown up and down, the words *inpoured virtue*, *inblown virtue*, are as absurd and insignificant as a *round quadrangle*. And therefore you shall hardly meet with a senseless and insignificant word that is not made up of some Latin or Greek names. A Frenchman seldom hears our Saviour called by the name of *Parole*, but by the name of *Verbe* often; yet *Verbe* and *Parole* differ no more but that one is Latin, the other French.

Understanding. 22. When a man upon the hearing of any speech hath those thoughts, which the words of that speech and their connexion were ordained and constituted to signify, then he is said to understand it, understanding being nothing else but conception caused by speech. And therefore if speech be peculiar to man, as for ought I know it is, then is understanding peculiar to him also. And therefore of absurd and false affirmations, in case they be universal, there can be no understanding, though many think they understand then, when they do but repeat the words softly, or con [examine] them in their mind.

23. What kinds of speeches signify the appetites, aversions, and passions of man's mind and of their use and abuse, I shall speak when I have spoken of the passions.

Inconstant names. 24. The names of such things as affect us, that is, which please and displease us, because all men be not alike affected with the same thing, nor the same man at all times, are in the common discourses of men of *inconstant* signification. For seeing all names are imposed to signify our conceptions and all our affections are but conceptions, when we conceive the same things differently, we can hardly avoid different naming of them. For though the nature of that we conceive be the same; yet the diversity of our reception of it, in respect of different constitutions of body and prejudices of opinion, gives everything a tincture of our different passions. And therefore in reasoning a man must take heed of words, which, besides the signification of what we imagine of their nature, have a signification also of the nature, disposition, and interest of the speaker; such as are the names of virtues and vices. For one man calleth *wisdom* what another calleth *fear*; and one *cruelty* what another *justice*; one *prodigality* what another *magnanimity*; and one *gravity* what another *stupidity*, etc.[1] And therefore such names can never be true grounds of any ratiocination. No more can metaphors and tropes of speech; but these are less dangerous because they profess their inconstancy, which the other do not.

## CHAPTER V [18]

## OF REASON AND SCIENCE

Reason what it is.

1. When a man *reasoneth*, he does nothing else but conceive a sum total from *addition* of parcels, or conceive a remainder, from *subtraction* of one sum from another; which (if it be done by words) is conceiving of the consequence of the names of all the parts to the name of the whole, or from the names of the whole and one part, to the name of the other part.[2] And though in some things (as in numbers), besides adding and subtracting, men name other operations, as *multiplying* and *dividing*; yet they are the same; for multiplication is but adding together of things equal, and division but

1 One person calls the death penalty justice, another calls it cruelty. See Hobbes's translation of Thucydides' *History of the Peloponnesian War* 3.82. Nonetheless, it is odd that Hobbes should include the words 'fear' and 'justice' among those names that "can never be true grounds of any ratiocination." What these words require in special contexts are explicit criteria for their application.

2 Reasoning is computation. Reason does not tell a person what to do; that is the job of desire; it only tells one how to do what one desires. Cf. 14.3, where Hobbes seems to say that reason forbids people to do what is destructive of their life.

subtracting of one thing, as often as we can. These operations are not incident to numbers only, but to all manner of things that can be added together and taken one out of another. For as arithmeticians teach to add and subtract in *numbers*, so the geometricians teach the same in *lines*, *figures* (solid and superficial), *angles*, *proportions*, *times*, degrees of *swiftness*, *force*, *power*, and the like. The logicians teach the same in *consequences of words*, adding together two *names* to make an *affirmation*, and two *affirmations* to make a *syllogism*, and *many syllogisms* to make a *demonstration*; and from the *sum* or *conclusion* of a *syllogism*, they subtract one *proposition* to find the other. Writers of politics add together *pactions* [contracts] to find men's *duties*, and lawyers, *laws* and *facts* to find what is *right* and *wrong* in the actions of private men. In sum, in what matter soever there is place for *addition* and *subtraction*, there also is place for *reason*; and where these have no place, there *reason* has nothing at all to do.

Reason defined.

2. Out of all which we may define (that is to say determine) what that is which is meant by this word *reason* when we reckon it amongst the faculties of the mind. For REASON, in this sense, is nothing but *reckoning* (that is, adding and subtracting) of the consequences of general names agreed upon for the *marking* and *signifying* of our thoughts; I say *marking* them, when we reckon by ourselves; and *signifying*, when we demonstrate or approve our reckonings to other men.

Right reason where.

3. And as in arithmetic, unpractised men must, and professors themselves may often, err and cast up false, so also in any other subject of reasoning, the ablest, most attentive, and most practised men may deceive themselves and infer false conclusions, not but that reason itself is always right reason, as well as arithmetic is a certain and infallible art. But no one man's reason nor the reason of any one number of men makes the certainty, no more than an account is therefore well cast up, because a great many men have unanimously approved it. And therefore, as when there is a con-
[19] troversy in an account, the parties must by their own accord set up for right reason the reason of some arbitrator or judge, to whose sentence they will both stand or their controversy must either come to blows or be undecided, for want of a right reason constituted by Nature, so is it also in all debates of what kind soever.

And when men that think themselves wiser than all others clamour and demand right reason for judge; yet seek no more but that things should be determined by no other men's reason but their own, it is as intolerable in the society of men, as it is in play after trump is turned, to use for trump on every occasion, that suit whereof they have most in their hand. For they do nothing else, that will have every of their passions, as it comes to bear sway in them, to be taken for right reason, and that in their own controversies, bewraying [revealing] their want of right reason by the claim they lay to it.

4. The use and end of reason is not the finding of the sum and truth of one or a few consequences, remote from the first definitions and settled significations of names, but to begin at these and proceed from one consequence to another. For there can be no certainty of the last conclusion without a certainty of all those affirmations and negations on which it was grounded and inferred. As when a master of a family, in taking an account, casteth up the sums of all the bills of expense into one sum, and not regarding how each bill is summed up, by those that give them in account, nor what it is he pays for, he advantages himself no more than if he allowed the account in gross, trusting to every of the accountant's skill and honesty. So also in reasoning of all other things, he that takes up conclusions on the trust of authors and doth not fetch them from the first items in every reckoning (which are the significations of names settled by definitions), loses his labour and does not know anything, but only believeth.

The use of reason.

5. When a man reckons without the use of words, which may be done in particular things (as when upon the sight of any one thing, we conjecture what was likely to have preceded or is likely to follow upon it); if that which he thought likely to follow follows not or that which he thought likely to have preceded it hath not preceded it, this is called error, to which even the most prudent men are subject. But when we reason in words of general signification and fall upon a general inference which is false, though it be commonly called *error*, it is indeed an absurdity or senseless speech. For error is but a deception in presuming that somewhat is past or to come, of which, though it were not past or not to come; yet there was no impossibility discoverable. But

Of error and absurdity.

when we make a general assertion, unless it be a true one, the possibility of it is inconceivable. And words whereby we conceive nothing but the sound are those we call *absurd*, *insignificant*, and *nonsense*. And therefore if a man should talk to me of a *round quadrangle*, or *accidents of bread in cheese*, or *immaterial substances*; or of a *free subject*; a *free will*, or any *free* but free from being hindered by opposition, I should not say he were in an error, but that his words were without meaning; that is to say, absurd.

[20] 6. I have said before (in the second chapter) that a man did excel all other animals in this faculty, that when he conceived anything whatsoever, he was apt to enquire the consequences of it and what effects he could do with it. And now I add this other degree of the same excellence, that he can by words reduce the consequences he finds to general rules, called *theorems* or aphorisms, that is, he can reason or reckon, not only in number, but in all other things whereof one may be added unto or subtracted from another.

7. But this privilege is allayed by another; and that is by the privilege of absurdity, to which no living creature is subject, but men only. And of men, those are of all most subject to it that profess philosophy. For it is most true that Cicero saith of them somewhere that there can be nothing so absurd but may be found in the books of philosophers. And the reason is manifest. For there is not one of them that begins his ratiocination from the definitions or explications of the names they are to use, which is a method that hath been used only in geometry, whose conclusions have thereby been made indisputable.

Causes of absurdity.

1. 8. The first cause of absurd conclusions I ascribe to the want of method, in that they begin not their ratiocination from definitions, that is, from settled significations of their words, as if they could cast account without knowing the value of the numeral words, *one*, *two*, and *three*.

9. And whereas all bodies enter into account upon divers considerations (which I have mentioned in the precedent chapter) these considerations being diversely named, diverse absurdities proceed from the confusion and unfit connexion of their names into assertions. And therefore

10. The second cause of absurd assertions, I ascribe to the giv- 2.
ing of names of *bodies* to *accidents,* or of *accidents* to *bodies*; as they
do that say, *faith is infused* or *inspired*, when nothing can be *poured*
or *breathed* into anything, but body, and that *extension* is *body*; that
*phantasms* are *spirits*, etc.

11. The third I ascribe to the giving of the names of the *acci-* 3.
*dents* of *bodies without us* to the *accidents* of our *own bodies,* as they
do that say, the *colour is in the body*; *the sound is in the air*, etc.

12. The fourth, to the giving of the names of *bodies* to *names*, or 4.
*speeches*; as they do that say that *there be things universal*; that *a living*
*creature is genus* or *a general thing*, etc.

13. The fifth, to the giving of the names of *accidents* to *names* 5.
and *speeches*; as they do that say, *the nature of a thing is its definition*; *a*
*man's command is his will*; and the like.

14. The sixth, to the use of metaphors, tropes, and other rhetor- 6.
ical figures, instead of words proper. For though it be lawful to say,
for example, in common speech, *the way goeth or leadeth hither or*
*thither*; *the proverb says this or that* (whereas ways cannot go, nor
proverbs speak); yet in reckoning and seeking of truth such
speeches are not to be admitted.

15. The seventh, to names that signify nothing, but are taken up 7.
and learned by rote from the Schools, as *hypostatical*, *transub-* [21]
*stantiate*, *consubstantiate*, *eternal-now*, and the like canting of Schoolmen.

16. To him that can avoid these things, it is not easy to fall into any absurdity, unless it be by the length of an account; wherein he may perhaps forget what went before. For all men by nature reason alike, and well, when they have good principles. For who is so stupid as both to mistake in geometry and also to persist in it when another detects his error to him?

17. By this it appears that reason is not, as sense and memory, Science.
born with us, nor gotten by experience only, as prudence is, but
attained by industry: first in apt imposing of names, and secondly
by getting a good and orderly method in proceeding from the elements,[1] which are names, to assertions made by connexion of one
of them to another, and so to syllogisms, which are the connexions

---

1 For Hobbes, like Descartes and some other early modern thinkers, the key to science is the right method. See also 7.4.

of one assertion to another, till we come to a knowledge of all the consequences of names appertaining to the subject in hand; and that is it, men call SCIENCE. And whereas sense and memory are but knowledge of fact, which is a thing past and irrevocable, *science* is the knowledge of consequences, and dependence of one fact upon another, by which, out of that we can presently do, we know how to do something else when we will or the like another time, because when we see how anything comes about, upon what causes, and by what manner, when the like causes come into our power, we see how to make it produce the like effects.

18. Children therefore are not endued with reason at all, till they have attained the use of speech, but are called reasonable creatures for the possibility apparent of having the use of reason in time to come. And the most part of men, though they have the use of reasoning a little way, as in numbering to some degree, yet it serves them to little use in common life, in which they govern themselves, some better, some worse, according to their differences of experience, quickness of memory, and inclinations to several ends, but specially according to good or evil fortune and the errors of one another. For as for *science* or certain rules of their actions, they are so far from it that they know not what it is. Geometry they have thought conjuring. But for other sciences, they who have not been taught the beginnings and some progress in them, that they may see how they be acquired and generated, are in this point like children that, having no thought of generation, are made believe by the women that their brothers and sisters are not born, but found in the garden.

19. But yet they that have no *science* are in better and nobler condition with their natural prudence than men that, by misreasoning or by trusting them that reason wrong, fall upon false and absurd general rules. For ignorance of causes and of rules does not set men so far out of their way as relying on false rules, and taking for causes of what they aspire to those that are not so, but rather causes of the contrary.

[22] 20. To conclude, the light of humane minds is perspicuous words, but by exact definitions first snuffed and purged from ambiguity; *reason* is the *pace*; increase of *science*, the way; and the benefit of mankind, the *end*. And, on the contrary, metaphors, and

senseless and ambiguous words are like *ignes fatui*;[1] and reasoning upon them is wandering amongst innumerable absurdities; and their end, contention and sedition, or contempt.

21. As much experience is *prudence*, so is much science *sapience*. For though we usually have one name of wisdom for them both; yet the Latins did always distinguish between *prudentia* and *sapientia*, ascribing the former to experience, the latter to science. But to make their difference appear more clearly, let us suppose one man endued with an excellent natural use and dexterity in handling his arms, and another to have added to that dexterity an acquired science of where he can offend or be offended by his adversary in every possible posture or guard. The ability of the former would be to the ability of the latter, as prudence to sapience; both useful, but the latter infallible. But they that, trusting only to the authority of books, follow the blind blindly, are like him that, trusting to the false rules of a master of fence, ventures presumptuously upon an adversary that either kills or disgraces him.

Prudence & sapience, with their difference.

22. The signs of science are some certain and infallible, some, uncertain. Certain, when he that pretendeth the science of anything can teach the same; that is to say, demonstrate the truth thereof perspicuously to another; uncertain, when only some particular events answer to his pretence and upon many occasions prove so as he says they must. Signs of prudence are all uncertain, because to observe by experience and remember all circumstances that may alter the success, is impossible. But in any business, whereof a man has not infallible science to proceed by, to forsake his own natural judgment and be guided by general sentences read in authors and subject to many exceptions is a sign of folly, and generally scorned by the name of pedantry. And even of those men themselves that in councils of the commonwealth love to show their reading of politics and history, very few do it in their domestic affairs where their particular interest is concerned, having prudence enough for their private affairs; but in public they study more the reputation of their own wit than the success of another's business.

Signs of science.

---

1 Literally, foolish fires. Something deceptive in experience.

[23]

# CHAPTER VI

## OF THE INTERIOUR BEGINNINGS OF VOLUNTARY MOTIONS, COMMONLY CALLED THE PASSIONS, AND THE SPEECHES BY WHICH THEY ARE EXPRESSED

Motion vital and animal.

1. There be in animals two sorts of *motions* peculiar to them: one called *vital*, begun in generation, and continued without interruption through their whole life, such as are the course of the blood, the pulse, the breathing, the concoction, nutrition, excretion, etc.; to which motions there needs no help of imagination; the other is *animal motion*, otherwise called *voluntary motion*; as to *go*, to *speak*, to *move* any of our limbs, in such manner as is first fancied in our minds. That sense is motion in the organs and interior parts of man's body, caused by the action of the things we see, hear, etc., and that fancy is but the relics of the same motion, remaining after sense, has been already said in the first and second chapters. And because *going*, *speaking*, and the like voluntary motions depend always upon a precedent thought of *whither*, *which way*, and *what*, it is evident that the imagination is the first internal beginning of all voluntary motion. And although unstudied men do not conceive any motion at all to be there where the thing moved is invisible or the space it is moved in is (for the shortness of it) insensible; yet that doth not hinder but that such motions are. For let a space be never so little, that which is moved over a greater space, whereof that little one is part, must first be moved over that. These small beginnings of motion within the body of man, before they appear in walking, speaking, striking, and other visible actions, are commonly called ENDEAVOUR.[1]

Endeavour.

Appetite. Desire. Hunger. Thirst.

2. This endeavour, when it is toward something which causes it, is called APPETITE or DESIRE, the latter being the general name, and the other oftentimes restrained to signify the desire of food, namely *hunger* and *thirst*. And when the endeavour is fromward

1 In animals, to try is to endeavour. In *De Corpore*, Hobbes says endeavour (*conatus*) is a motion smaller than can be measured; it is motion "through the length of a point" or "in an instant of time" (15.2).

something, it is generally called AVERSION.[1] These words *appetite* and *aversion* we have from the *Latins*; and they both of them signify the motions, one of approaching, the other of retiring. So also do the Greek words for the same, which are *orme* and *aphorme*. For Nature itself does often press upon men those truths which afterwards, when they look for somewhat beyond Nature, they stumble at. For the Schools find in mere appetite to go or move, no actual motion at all; but because some motion they must acknowledge, they call it metaphorical motion, which is but an absurd speech; for though words may be called metaphorical, bodies and motions cannot. Aversion.

3. That which men desire they are said to LOVE, and to HATE those things for which they have aversion. So that desire and love are the same thing, save that by desire, we signify the absence of the object; by love, most commonly the presence of the same. So also by aversion, we signify the absence; and by hate, the presence of the object. Love. Hate. [24]

4. Of appetites and aversions, some are born with men; as appetite of food, appetite of excretion, and exoneration (which may also and more properly be called aversions, from somewhat they feel in their bodies), and some other appetites, not many. The rest, which are appetites of particular things, proceed from experience and trial of their effects upon themselves or other men. For of things we know not at all or believe not to be, we can have no further desire than to taste and try. But aversion we have for things, not only which we know have hurt us, but also that we do not know whether they will hurt us, or not.

5. Those things which we neither desire nor hate, we are said to *contemn*: CONTEMPT being nothing else but an immobility or contumacy of the heart in resisting the action of certain things, and proceeding from that the heart is already moved otherwise by other more potent objects or from want of experience of them. Contempt.

6. And because the constitution of a man's body is in continual mutation, it is impossible that all the same things should always

---

1 Hobbes's goal in this chapter is to analyze or break down many seemingly irreducible and nonmaterialistic concepts into material components: complex motions of small bodies that move large bodies towards or away from something.

cause in him the same appetites and aversions; much less can all men consent in the desire of almost any one and the same object.

Good. Evil. 7. But whatsoever is the object of any man's appetite or desire, that is it which he for his part calleth *good;* and the object of his hate and aversion, *evil*; and of his contempt, *vile* and *inconsiderable*. For these words of *good*, *evil*, and *contemptible* are ever used with relation to the person that useth them, there being nothing simply and absolutely so, nor any common rule of good and evil to be taken from the nature of the objects themselves,[1] but from the person of the man (where there is no commonwealth) or (in a commonwealth) from the person that representeth it, or from an arbitrator or judge whom men disagreeing shall by consent set up and make his sentence the rule thereof.

Pulchrum. Turpe. 8. The Latin tongue has two words whose significations approach to those of good and evil, but are not precisely the same; and those are *pulchrum* and *turpe*. Whereof the former signifies that which by some apparent signs promiseth good, and the latter that which promiseth evil. But in our tongue we have not so general names to express them by. But for *pulchrum* we say, in some things, *fair*; in others, *beautiful*, or *handsome*, or *gallant*, or *honourable*, or *comely*, or *amiable*; and for *turpe*, *foul*, *deformed*, *ugly*, *base*, *nauseous*, and the like, as the subject shall require; all which words, in their proper places, signify nothing else but the *mien* or countenance that promiseth good and evil. So that of good there be three Delightful. Profitable. kinds: good in the promise, that is *pulchrum*; good in effect, as the end desired, which is called *jucundum*, *delightful*; and good as the
[25] means, which is called *utile*, *profitable*; and as many of evil: for evil Unpleasant. Unprofitable. in promise is that they call *turpe*; evil in effect and end is *molestum*, *unpleasant*, *troublesome*; and evil in the means, *inutile*, *unprofitable*, *hurtful*.

9. As in sense that which is really within us is (as I have said before) only motion, caused by the action of external objects (but in appearance, to the sight, light and colour; to the ear, sound; to the nostril, odour, etc.); so when the action of the same object is

---

1 What is good and evil is determined by each person only when there are no laws. Under a government, what is good or evil is determined by the commands of the sovereign, what he desires. See also 6.57.

continued from the eyes, ears, and other organs to the heart, the real effect there is nothing but motion or endeavour, which consisteth in appetite or aversion to or from the object moving. But the appearance or sense of that motion is that we either call DELIGHT or TROUBLE OF MIND. Delight. Displeasure.

10. This motion, which is called appetite and for the appearance of it *delight* and *pleasure*, seemeth to be a corroboration of vital motion and a help thereunto; and therefore such things as caused delight were not improperly called *jucunda* (*a juvando*, from helping or fortifying); and the contrary, *molesta*, *offensive*, from hindering and troubling the motion vital. Pleasure. Offence.

11. *Pleasure* therefore (or delight) is the appearance or sense of good; and *molestation* or *displeasure*, the appearance or sense of evil. And consequently all appetite, desire, and love is accompanied with some delight more or less; and all hatred and aversion with more or less displeasure and offence.

12. Of pleasures or delights, some arise from the sense of an object present; and those may be called *pleasures of sense* (the word *sensual*, as it is used by those only that condemn them, having no place till there be laws). Of this kind are all onerations and exonerations of the body, as also all that is pleasant, in the *sight*, *hearing*, *smell*, *taste*, or *touch*. Others arise from the expectation that proceeds from foresight of the end or consequence of things, whether those things in the sense please or displease; and these are *pleasures of the mind* of him that draweth in those consequences, and are generally called JOY. In the like manner, displeasures are some in the sense and called PAIN; others, in the expectation of consequences and are called GRIEF. Pleasures of sense. Pleasures of the mind. Joy. Pain. Grief.

13. These simple passions called *appetite*, *desire*, *love*, *aversion*, *hate*, *joy*, and *grief*, have their names for divers considerations diversified. As first, when they one succeed another, they are diversely called from the opinion men have of the likelihood of attaining what they desire. Secondly, from the object loved or hated. Thirdly, from the consideration of many of them together. Fourthly, from the alteration or succession itself.

14. For *appetite* with an opinion of attaining is called HOPE. Hope.

15. The same, without such opinion, DESPAIR. Despair.

16. *Aversion*, with opinion of *hurt* from the object, FEAR. Fear.

Courage.

17. The same, with hope of avoiding that hurt by resistance, COURAGE.

Anger.

18. Sudden *courage*, ANGER.

Confidence.

19. Constant *hope*, CONFIDENCE of ourselves.

Diffidence.

20. Constant *despair*, DIFFIDENCE of ourselves.

Indignation.

[26] 21. *Anger* for great hurt done to another, when we conceive the same to be done by injury, INDIGNATION.

Benevolence. Good nature.

22. *Desire* of good to another, BENEVOLENCE, GOOD WILL, CHARITY. If to man generally, GOOD NATURE.

Covetousness.

23. *Desire* of riches, COVETOUSNESS, a name used always in signification of blame, because men contending for them are displeased with one another's attaining them; though the desire in itself be to be blamed, or allowed, according to the means by which those riches are sought.

Ambition.

24. Desire of office or precedence, AMBITION, a name used also in the worse sense, for the reason before mentioned.

Pusillanimity.

25. *Desire* of things that conduce but a little to our ends, and fear of things that are but of little hindrance, PUSILLANIMITY.

Magnaminity.

26. *Contempt* of little helps and hindrances, MAGNANIMITY.

Valour.

27. *Magnanimity* in danger of death or wounds, Valour, FORTITUDE.

Liberality.

28. *Magnanimity* in the use of riches, LIBERALITY.

Miserableness.

29. *Pusillanimity*, in the same, WRETCHEDNESS, MISERABLENESS, or PARSIMONY, as it is liked or disliked.

Kindness.

30. *Love* of persons for society, KINDNESS.

Natural lust.

31. *Love* of persons for pleasing the sense only, NATURAL LUST.

Luxury.

32. *Love* of the same, acquired from rumination, that is, imagination of pleasure past, LUXURY.

The passion of love. Jealousy.

33. *Love* of one singularly, with desire to be singularly beloved, THE PASSION OF LOVE. The same, with fear that the love is not mutual, JEALOUSY.

Revengefulness.

34. *Desire* by doing hurt to another to make him condemn some fact of his own, REVENGEFULNESS.

Curiosity.

35. *Desire* to know why and how, CURIOSITY, such as is in no living creature but *man*; so that man is distinguished, not only by his reason, but also by this singular passion from other *animals*, in whom the appetite of food and other pleasures of sense by predominance, take away the care of knowing causes, which is a lust

of the mind, that by a perseverance of delight in the continual and indefatigable generation of knowledge, exceedeth the short vehemence of any carnal pleasure.

36. *Fear* of power invisible, feigned[1] by the mind, or imagined
from tales publicly allowed, RELIGION; not allowed, SUPER- Religion.
STITION.[2] And when the power imagined is truly such as we Superstition.
imagine, TRUE RELIGION. True religion.

37. *Fear* without the apprehension of why or what, PANIC TER- Panic. Terror.
ROR, called so from the fables that make Pan[3] the author of them; whereas in truth there is always in him that so feareth, first, some apprehension of the cause, though the rest run away by example, every one supposing his fellow to know why. And therefore this passion happens to none but in a throng, or multitude of people.

38. *Joy* from apprehension of novelty, ADMIRATION; proper to Admiration.
man because it excites the appetite of knowing the cause.

39. *Joy* arising from imagination of a man's own power and [27]
ability is that exultation of the mind which is called GLORYING; Glory.
which, if grounded upon the experience of his own former actions, is the same with *confidence*; but if grounded on the flattery of others or only supposed by himself for delight in the consequences of it, is called VAIN-GLORY; which name is properly Vain-glory.
given, because a well-grounded *confidence* begetteth attempt, whereas the supposing of power does not and is therefore rightly called *vain*.

40. *Grief* from opinion of want of power is called DEJECTION Dejection.
of mind.

41. The *vain-glory* which consisteth in the feigning or supposing of abilities in ourselves, which we know are not, is most incident to young men and nourished by the histories or fictions of gallant persons, and is corrected oftentimes by age and employment.

42. *Sudden glory* is the passion which maketh those *grimaces* Sudden glory.
called LAUGHTER, and is caused either by some sudden act of their Laughter.

1 'Feigned' usually means 'falsely invented' but it may mean simply 'composed by'. See e.g. 16.2.

2 It follows that a superstition (something not allowed) might be a true religion.

3 Pan is the Greek god of flocks and generally all things rural. The word 'panic' comes from the fact that Pan liked to scare travelers.

own that pleaseth them or by the apprehension of some deformed thing in another by comparison whereof they suddenly applaud themselves. And it is incident most to them that are conscious of the fewest abilities in themselves, who are forced to keep themselves in their own favour by observing the imperfections of other men. And therefore much laughter at the defects of others is a sign of pusillanimity. For of great minds one of the proper works is to help and free others from scorn, and compare themselves only with the most able.

Sudden dejection. Weeping. 43. On the contrary, *sudden dejection* is the passion that causeth WEEPING, and is caused by such accidents as suddenly take away some vehement hope or some prop of their power; and they are most subject to it that rely principally on helps external, such as are women and children. Therefore, some weep for the loss of friends, others for their unkindness, others for the sudden stop made to their thoughts of revenge by reconciliation. But in all cases both laughter and weeping are sudden motions, custom taking them both away. For no man laughs at old jests, or weeps for an old calamity.

Shame. Blushing. 44. *Grief* for the discovery of some defect of ability is SHAME or the passion that discovereth itself in blushing, and consisteth in the apprehension of something dishonourable, and in young men is a sign of the love of good reputation, and commendable; in old men it is a sign of the same; but because it comes too late, not commendable.

Impudence. 45. The *contempt* of good reputation is called IMPUDENCE.

Pity. 46. *Grief* for the calamity of another is PITY, and ariseth from the imagination that the like calamity may befall himself. And therefore is called also compassion, and in the phrase of this present time a fellow-feeling. And therefore for calamity arriving from great wickedness, the best men have the least pity; and for the same calamity those have least pity that think themselves least obnoxious to the same.

Cruelty. 47. *Contempt* or little sense of the calamity of others is that
[28] which men call CRUELTY, proceeding from security of their own fortune. For, that any man should take pleasure in other men's great harms, without other end of his own, I do not conceive it possible.

48. *Grief* for the success of a competitor in wealth, honour, or other good, if it be joined with endeavour to enforce our own abilities to equal or exceed him, is called EMULATION; but joined with endeavour to supplant or hinder a competitor, ENVY. Emulation. Envy.

49. When in the mind of man appetites and aversions, hopes and fears concerning one and the same thing arise alternately, and divers good and evil consequences of the doing or omitting the thing propounded come successively into our thoughts, so that sometimes we have an appetite to it, sometimes an aversion from it, sometimes hope to be able to do it, sometimes despair, or fear to attempt it, the whole sum of desires, aversions, hopes and fears, continued till the thing be either done or thought impossible, is that we call DELIBERATION. Deliberation.

50. Therefore of things past there is no *deliberation*, because manifestly impossible to be changed, nor of things known to be impossible, or thought so, because men know or think such deliberation vain. But of things impossible, which we think possible, we may deliberate, not knowing it is in vain. And it is called *deliberation*; because it is a putting an end to the *liberty* we had of doing or omitting, according to our own appetite or aversion.

51. This alternate succession of appetites, aversions, hopes and fears is no less in other living creatures than in man; and therefore beasts also deliberate.

52. Every *deliberation* is then said to *end* when that whereof they deliberate is either done or thought impossible, because till then we retain the liberty of doing or omitting, according to our appetite or aversion.

53. In *deliberation*, the last appetite, or aversion, immediately adhering to the action or to the omission thereof, is that we call the will; the act (not the faculty) of *willing*.[1] And beasts that have *deliberation* must necessarily also have *will*. The definition of the *will*, given commonly by the Schools, that it is a *rational appetite*, is not good. For if it were, then could there be no voluntary act against reason. For a *voluntary act* is that which proceedeth from The will.

---

1 Hobbes is a compatibilist. He believes that freedom is compatible with determinism, the doctrine that every event (including every human action) is caused by or determined by earlier events. He believes that human beings are free (when their actions are caused by a desire or appetite), but acts of will are not.

the *will* and no other. But if instead of a rational appetite, we shall say an appetite resulting from a precedent deliberation, then the definition is the same that I have given here. *Will*, therefore, *is the last appetite in deliberating*. And though we say in common discourse a man had a will once to do a thing that nevertheless he forbore to do; yet that is properly but an inclination, which makes no action voluntary, because the action depends not of it, but of the last inclination or appetite. For if the intervenient appetites make any action voluntary, then by the same reason all intervenient aversions should make the same action involuntary; and so one and the same action should be both voluntary and involuntary.

[29] 54. By this it is manifest that not only actions that have their beginning from covetousness, ambition, lust, or other appetites to the thing propounded, but also those that have their beginning from aversion or fear of those consequences that follow the omission, are *voluntary actions*.

Forms of speech in passion.

55. The forms of speech by which the passions are expressed are partly the same and partly different from those by which we express our thoughts. And first generally all passions may be expressed *indicatively*; as, *I love*, *I fear*, *I joy*, *I deliberate*, *I will*, *I command*; but some of them have particular expressions by themselves, which nevertheless are not affirmations, unless it be when they serve to make other inferences besides that of the passion they proceed from. Deliberation is expressed *subjunctively*, which is a speech proper to signify suppositions, with their consequences, as, *If this be done*, *then this will follow*, and differs not from the language of reasoning, save that reasoning is in general words, but deliberation for the most part is of particulars. The language of desire and aversion is *imperative*, as, *Do this*, *forbear that*; which when the party is obliged to do or forbear is *command*; otherwise *prayer* or else *counsel*. The language of vain-glory, of indignation, pity and revengefulness, *optative*; but of the desire to know, there is a peculiar expression called *interrogative*; as, *what is it*, *when shall it*, *how is it done*, and *why so*? Other language of the passions I find none: for cursing, swearing, reviling, and the like do not signify as speech, but as the actions of a tongue accustomed.

56. These forms of speech, I say, are expressions or voluntary

significations of our passions; but certain signs they be not, because they may be used arbitrarily, whether they that use them have such passions or not. The best signs of passions present are either in the countenance, motions of the body, actions, and ends, or aims, which we otherwise know the man to have.

57. And because in deliberation the appetites and aversions are raised by foresight of the good and evil consequences and sequels of the action whereof we deliberate, the good or evil effect thereof dependeth on the foresight of a long chain of consequences, of which very seldom any man is able to see to the end. But for so far as a man seeth, if the good in those consequences be greater than the evil, the whole chain is that which writers call *apparent* or *seeming good*. And contrarily, when the evil exceedeth the good, the whole is *apparent* or *seeming evil*; so that he who hath by experience or reason the greatest and surest prospect of consequences deliberates best himself, and is able, when he will, to give the best counsel unto others.

Good and evil apparent.

58. *Continual success* in obtaining those things which a man from time to time desireth, that is to say, continual prospering, is that men call FELICITY; I mean the felicity of this life. For there is no such thing as perpetual tranquillity of mind while we live here, because life itself is but motion and can never be without desire, [30] nor without fear no more than without sense. What kind of felicity God hath ordained to them that devoutly honour him a man shall no sooner know than enjoy, being joys that now are as incomprehensible as the word of Schoolmen, *beatifical vision*, is unintelligible.

Felicity.

59. The form of speech whereby men signify their opinion of the goodness of anything is PRAISE. That whereby they signify the power and greatness of anything is MAGNIFYING. And that whereby they signify the opinion they have of a man's felicity is by the Greeks called *makarismos*, for which we have no name in our tongue. And thus much is sufficient for the present purpose to have been said of the PASSIONS.

Praise. Magnification. *makarismos.*

# CHAPTER VII

## OF THE ENDS OR RESOLUTIONS OF DISCOURSE

1. Of all *discourse* governed by desire of knowledge, there is at last an *end*, either by attaining or by giving over. And in the chain of discourse, wheresoever it be interrupted, there is an end for that time.

2. If the discourse be merely mental, it consisteth of thoughts that the thing will be and will not be, or that it has been and has not been, alternately. So that wheresoever you break off the chain of a man's discourse, you leave him in a presumption of *it will be*, or *it will not be*; or *it has been*, or *has not been*. All which is *opinion*. And that which is alternate appetite, in deliberating concerning good and evil, the same is alternate opinion in the enquiry of the truth of *past* and *future*. And as the last appetite in deliberation is called the *will*, so the last opinion in search of the truth of past and future is called the JUDGEMENT or *resolute* and *final sentence* of him that *discourseth*. And as the whole chain of appetites alternate in the question of good or bad is called *deliberation*; so the whole chain of opinions alternate in the question of true or false is called DOUBT.

Judgement, or sentence final.

Doubt.

3. No discourse whatsoever can end in absolute knowledge of fact, past or to come. For, as for the knowledge of fact, it is originally sense, and ever after memory. And for the knowledge of consequence, which I have said before is called science, it is not absolute, but conditional. No man can know by discourse that this or that is, has been, or will be, which is to know absolutely; but only that if this be, that is; if this has been, [then] that has been; if this shall be, [then] that shall be; which is to know conditionally; and that not the consequence of one thing to another, but of one name of a thing to another name of the same thing.

4. And therefore, when the discourse is put into speech and begins with the definitions of words and proceeds by connection of the same into general affirmations and of these again into syllo- [31] gisms, the end or last sum is called the conclusion, and the thought of the mind by it signified is that conditional knowledge or knowledge of the consequence of words, which is commonly

called SCIENCE.[1] But if the first ground of such discourse be not definitions or if the definitions be not rightly joined together into syllogisms, then the end or conclusion is again OPINION, namely of the truth of somewhat said, though sometimes in absurd and senseless words, without possibility of being understood. When two or more men know of one and the same fact, they are said to be CONSCIOUS of it one to another; which is as much as to know it together. And because such are fittest witnesses of the facts of one another or of a third, it was and ever will be reputed a very evil act for any man to speak against his *conscience* or to corrupt or force another so to do, insomuch that the plea of conscience has been always hearkened unto very diligently in all times. Afterwards, men made use of the same word metaphorically for the knowledge of their own secret facts and secret thoughts; and therefore it is rhetorically said that the conscience is a thousand witnesses. And last of all, men vehemently in love with their own new opinions (though never so absurd) and obstinately bent to maintain them gave those their opinions also that reverenced name of conscience, as if they would have it seem unlawful to change or speak against them, and so pretend to know they are true, when they know at most but that they think so.

Science.

Opinion.

Conscience.

5. When a man's discourse beginneth not at definitions, it beginneth either at some other contemplation of his own, and then it is still called opinion; or it beginneth at some saying of another, of whose ability to know the truth and of whose honesty in not deceiving, he doubteth not; and then the discourse is not so much concerning the thing as the person; and the resolution is called BELIEF and FAITH; *faith in* the man, *belief* both *of* the man and *of* the truth of what he says. So that in belief are two opinions, one of the saying of the man, the other of his virtue.[2] To *have faith in*, or *trust to*, or *believe a man*, signify the same thing, namely, an

Belief. Faith.

1 See 5.17.

2 Hobbes might have said that belief or faith consists of three things. Consider this: "Ava believes that Beth is honest." (1) The word 'believes' expresses the psychological state that Ava is in. (Hobbes does not mention this element.) (2) The words 'that Beth is honest' expresses the content of the belief, that is, what is believed. (3) Ava has that belief because of her trust or faith in the person who told her that Beth is honest. This element of belief is usually implicit and not explicit.

opinion of the veracity of the man; but to *believe what is said* signifieth only an opinion of the truth of the saying. But we are to observe that this phrase, *I believe in*, as also the Latin, *credo in*, and the Greek, *pisteuo eis*, are never used but in the writings of divines. Instead of them, in other writings are put: *I believe him, I trust him, I have faith in him, I rely on him;* and in Latin, *credo illi*; *fido illi,* and in Greek, *pisteuo auto*, and that this singularity of the ecclesiastic use of the word hath raised many disputes about the right object of the Christian faith.

[32] 6. But *by believing in*, as it is in the Creed, is meant, not trust in the person, but confession and acknowledgement of the doctrine. For not only Christians, but all manner of men do so believe in God as to hold all for truth they hear him say, whether they understand it or not, which is all the faith and trust can possibly be had in any person whatsoever; but they do not all believe the doctrine of the Creed.

7. From whence we may infer that when we believe any saying, whatsoever it be, to be true, from arguments taken, not from the thing itself or from the principles of natural reason, but from the authority and good opinion we have of him that hath said it; then is the speaker or person we believe in or trust in and whose word we take, the object of our faith; and the honour done in believing is done to him only. And consequently, when we believe that the Scriptures are the word of God, having no immediate revelation from God himself, our belief, faith, and trust is in the Church, whose word we take and acquiesce therein. And they that believe that which a prophet relates unto them in the name of God, take the word of the prophet, do honour to him, and in him trust and believe, touching the truth of what he relateth, whether he be a true or a false prophet. And so it is also with all other history. For if I should not believe all that is written by historians of the glorious acts of Alexander or Caesar, I do not think the ghost of Alexander or Caesar had any just cause to be offended or anybody else but the historian. If Livy say the gods made once a cow speak and we believe it not, [then] we distrust not God therein, but Livy.[1] So that it is evident that whatsoever we believe, upon no

1 Livy (59 B.C.-A.D. 17) was a famous Roman historian. Here is the passage Hobbes is referring to: "Prodigies were reported that year [177 B.C.]: in the territory of

other reason than what is drawn from authority of men only and their writings, whether they be sent from God or not, is faith in men only.[1]

## CHAPTER VIII

## OF THE VIRTUES COMMONLY CALLED INTELLECTUAL, AND THEIR CONTRARY DEFECTS

Intellectual virtue, defined.

1. Virtue generally in all sorts of subjects is somewhat that is valued for eminence and consisteth in comparison. For if all things were equally in all men, nothing would be prized. And by *virtues* INTELLECTUAL are always understood such abilities of the mind as men praise, value, and desire should be in themselves, and go commonly under the name of a *good wit*; though the same word, wit, be used also to distinguish one certain ability from the rest.

Wit, natural, or acquired.

2. These *virtues* are of two sorts, *natural* and *acquired*. By natural, I mean not that which a man hath from his birth; for that is nothing else but sense, wherein men differ so little one from another and from brute beasts, as it is not to be reckoned amongst virtues. But I mean that *wit* which is gotten by use only and experience, without method, culture, or instruction. This NATURAL WIT consisteth principally in two things, *celerity of imagining* (that is, swift succession of one thought to another) and *steady direction* to some approved end. On the contrary, a slow imagination maketh that defect or fault of the mind, which is commonly called DULLNESS, *stupidity*, and sometimes by other names that signify slowness of motion or difficulty to be moved.

Natural wit.

---

Crustumerium they say that a bird, called *sangualis*, cut a sacred stone with its beak, that in Campania a cow spoke, that at Syracuse a brazen heifer was approached and impregnated by a wild bull which had strayed from its herd. ... [T]he cow was consigned to maintenance at the expense of the state" (*Livy*, tr. Evan T. Sage and Alfred C. Schlesinger, Cambridge: Harvard UP, 1938, p. 223). See also 32.5 and 42.46.

1 Christians, Jews and Muslims think that they have faith in God because they believe on the basis of the Bible or the Koran. In fact, Hobbes thinks that they have faith in the person who recommended the book to them, parent or clergyman or some other trusted person.

[33] 3. And this difference of quickness is caused by the difference of men's passions that love and dislike, some one thing, some another; and therefore some men's thoughts run one way, some another, and are held to and observe differently the things that pass through their imagination. And whereas in this succession of men's thoughts there is nothing to observe in the things they think on, but either in what they be *like one another* or in what they be *unlike* or *what they serve for* or *how they serve to such a purpose*, those that observe their similitudes, in case they be such as are but rarely observed by others, are said to have a *good wit*; by which, in this occasion, is meant a *good fancy*. But they that observe their differences and dissimilitudes, which is called *distinguishing* and *discerning* and *judging* between thing and thing, in case such discerning be not easy, are said to have a good judgement, and particularly in matter of conversation and business, wherein times, places, and persons are to be discerned, this virtue is called DISCRETION. The former, that is, fancy without the help of judgement, is not commended as a virtue; but the latter, which is judgement and discretion is commended for itself, without the help of fancy. Besides the discretion of times, places, and persons, necessary to a good fancy, there is required also an often application of his thoughts to their end, that is to say, to some use to be made of them. This done, he that hath this virtue will be easily fitted with similitudes that will please, not only by illustration of his discourse and adorning it with new and apt metaphors, but also by the rarity of their invention. But without steadiness and direction to some end, a great fancy is one kind of madness, such as they have that, entering into any discourse, are snatched from their purpose by everything that comes in their thought into so many and so long digressions and parentheses that they utterly lose themselves; which kind of folly I know no particular name for; but the cause of it is sometimes want of experience, whereby that seemeth to a man new and rare which doth not so to others, sometimes pusillanimity, by which that seems great to him which other men think a trifle, and whatsoever is new or great and therefore thought fit to be told withdraws a man by degrees from the intended way of his discourse.

Good wit, or fancy.

Good judgement.

Discretion.

4. In a good poem, whether it be *epic* or *dramatic*, as also in *sonnets*, *epigrams*, and other pieces, both judgement and fancy are required, but the fancy must be more eminent, because they please for the extravagancy, but ought not to displease by indiscretion.

5. In a good history, the judgement must be eminent, because the goodness consisteth in the method, in the truth, and in the choice of the actions that are most profitable to be known. Fancy has no place, but only in adorning the style.

6. In orations of praise and in invectives, the fancy is predominant, because the design is not truth, but to honour or dishonour, which is done by noble or by vile comparisons. The judgement does but suggest what circumstances make an action laudable or culpable.

7. In hortatives and pleadings, as truth or disguise serveth best [34] to the design in hand, so is the judgement or the fancy most required.

8. In demonstration, in council, and all rigorous search of truth, judgement does all, except sometimes the understanding have need to be opened by some apt similitude, and then there is so much use of fancy. But for metaphors, they are in this case utterly excluded. For seeing they openly profess deceit, to admit them into council or reasoning were manifest folly.

9. And in any discourse whatsoever, if the defect of discretion be apparent, how extravagant soever the fancy be, the whole discourse will be taken for a sign of want of wit; and so will it never when the discretion is manifest, though the fancy be never so ordinary.

10. The secret thoughts of a man run over all things holy, profane, clean, obscene, grave, and light, without shame or blame; which verbal discourse cannot do farther than the judgement shall approve of the time, place, and persons. An anatomist or physician may speak or write his judgement of unclean things, because it is not to please, but profit; but for another man to write his extravagant and pleasant fancies of the same is as if a man, from being tumbled into the dirt, should come and present himself before good company. And it is the want of discretion that makes the difference. Again, in professed remissness of mind and familiar

company, a man may play with the sounds and equivocal significations of words, and [do] that many times with encounters of extraordinary fancy; but in a sermon or in public or before persons unknown or whom we ought to reverence, there is no jingling of words that will not be accounted folly; and the difference is only in the want of discretion. So that where wit is wanting, it is not fancy that is wanting, but discretion. Judgement, therefore, without fancy is wit, but fancy without judgement, not.

11. When the thoughts of a man that has a design in hand, running over a multitude of things, observes how they conduce to that design or what design they may conduce unto, if his observations be such as are not easy or usual, this wit of his is called PRUDENCE and dependeth on much experience and memory of the like things and their consequences heretofore. In which there is not so much difference of men as there is in their fancies and judgements, because the experience of men equal in age is not much unequal as to the quantity, but lies in different occasions, every one having his private designs. To govern well a family and a kingdom are not different degrees of prudence but different sorts of business, no more than to draw a picture in little or as great or greater than the life are different degrees of art. A plain husbandman is more prudent in affairs of his own house than a Privy Counsellor in the affairs of another man.

Prudence.

12. To prudence, if you add the use of unjust or dishonest means, such as usually are prompted to men by fear or want, you have that crooked wisdom which is called CRAFT, which is a sign [35] of pusillanimity. For magnanimity is contempt of unjust or dishonest helps. And that which the Latins call *versutia* (translated into English, *shifting*) and is a putting off of a present danger or incommodity by engaging into a greater, as when a man robs one to pay another, is but a shorter-sighted craft, called *versutia*, from *versura*, which signifies taking money at usury for the present payment of interest.

Craft.

Acquired wit.

13. As for *acquired wit* (I mean acquired by method and instruction), there is none but reason, which is grounded on the right use of speech and produceth the sciences. But of reason and science, I have already spoken in the fifth and sixth chapters.

14. The causes of this difference of wits are in the passions; and the difference of passions proceedeth partly from the different constitution of the body and partly from different education. For if the difference proceeded from the temper of the brain and the organs of sense, either exterior or interior, there would be no less difference of men in their sight, hearing or other senses than in their fancies and discretions. It proceeds, therefore, from the passions, which are different, not only from the difference of men's complexions, but also from their difference of customs and education.

15. The passions that most of all cause the differences of wit are principally the more or less desire of power, of riches, of knowledge, and of honour. All which may be reduced to the first, that is, desire of power. For riches, knowledge and honour are but several sorts of power.

16. And therefore, a man who has no great passion for any of these things, but is as men term it indifferent; though he may be so far a good man as to be free from giving offence; yet he cannot possibly have either a great fancy or much judgement. For the thoughts are to the desires as scouts and spies to range abroad and find the way to the things desired; all steadiness of the mind's motion and all quickness of the same proceeding from thence. For as to have no desire is to be dead, so to have weak passions is dullness; and to have passions indifferently for everything, GIDDINESS and *distraction*; and to have stronger and more vehement passions for anything than is ordinarily seen in others is that which men call MADNESS.

Giddiness.

Madness.

17. Whereof there be almost as many kinds as of the passions themselves. Sometimes the extraordinary and extravagant passion proceedeth from the evil constitution of the organs of the body or harm done them; and sometimes the hurt and indisposition of the organs is caused by the vehemence or long continuance of the passion. But in both cases the madness is of one and the same nature.

18. The passion whose violence or continuance maketh madness is either great *vain-glory*, which is commonly called *pride* and *self-conceit*, or great *dejection* of mind.

Rage. 19. Pride subjecteth a man to anger, the excess whereof is the [36] madness called RAGE and FURY. And thus it comes to pass that excessive desire of revenge, when it becomes habitual, hurteth the organs and becomes rage; that excessive love with jealousy becomes also rage; excessive opinion of a man's own self for divine inspiration, for wisdom, learning, form, and the like, becomes distraction and giddiness; the same, joined with envy, rage; vehement opinion of the truth of anything, contradicted by others, rage.

20. Dejection subjects a man to causeless fears, which is a mad- Melancholy. ness commonly called MELANCHOLY, apparent also in divers manners, as in haunting of solitudes and graves, in superstitious behaviour and in fearing some one, some another, particular thing. In sum, all passions that produce strange and unusual behaviour are called by the general name of madness. But of the several kinds of madness, he that would take the pains might enroll a legion. And if the excesses be madness, there is no doubt but the passions themselves, when they tend to evil, are degrees of the same.

21. For example, though the effect of folly in them that are possessed of an opinion of being inspired be not visible always in one man by any very extravagant action that proceedeth from such passion; yet when many of them conspire together, the rage of the whole multitude is visible enough. For what argument of madness can there be greater than to clamour, strike, and throw stones at our best friends? Yet this is somewhat less than such a multitude will do. For they will clamour, fight against, and destroy those by whom all their lifetime before they have been protected and secured from injury. And if this be madness in the multitude, it is the same in every particular man. For as in the midst of the sea, though a man perceive no sound of that part of the water next him, yet he is well assured that part contributes as much to the roaring of the sea as any other part of the same quantity; so also, though we perceive no great unquietness in one or two men, yet we may be well assured that their singular passions are parts of the seditious roaring of a troubled nation. And [even] if there were nothing else that bewrayed [revealed] their madness, yet that very arrogating such inspiration to themselves is argument enough. If some man in Bedlam[1] should entertain you with sober discourse,

1 Bedlam was an asylum in London for the mentally ill.

and you desire in taking leave to know what he were that you might another time requite his civility, and he should tell you he were God the Father, I think you need expect no extravagant action for argument of his madness.

22. This opinion of inspiration, called commonly, private spirit, begins very often from some lucky finding of an error generally held by others; and not knowing or not remembering by what conduct of reason they came to so singular a truth, as they think it, though it be many times an untruth they light on, they presently admire themselves as being in the special grace of God Almighty, who hath revealed the same to them supernaturally by his Spirit.

23. Again, that madness is nothing else but too much appearing passion may be gathered out of the effects of wine, which are the same with those of the evil disposition of the organs. For the vari- [37]
ety of behaviour in men that have drunk too much is the same with that of madmen, some of them raging, others loving, others laughing, all extravagantly, but according to their several domineering passions. For the effect of the wine does but remove dissimulation and take from them the sight of the deformity of their passions. For (I believe) the most sober men, when they walk alone without care and employment of the mind, would be unwilling [that] the vanity and extravagance of their thoughts at that time should be publicly seen; which is a confession that passions unguided are for the most part mere madness.

24. The opinions of the world, both in ancient and later ages, concerning the cause of madness have been two. Some, deriving them from the passions, some, from demons[1] or spirits, either good or bad, which they thought might enter into a man, possess him, and move his organs in such strange and uncouth manner as madmen use to do. The former sort, therefore, called such men, madmen; but the latter called them sometimes *demoniacs* (that is, possessed with spirits), sometimes *energumeni* (that is, agitated or moved with spirits); and now in Italy they are called not only *pazzi*, madmen, but also *spiritati*, men possessed.

25. There was once a great conflux of people in Abdera, a city of the Greeks, at the acting of the tragedy of Andromeda,[2] upon

1 See also 12.16, 34.15, 34.18, 36.2.

2 In Greek mythology, Andromeda was to be sacrificed to a sea monster but was saved by Perseus. Euripides authored a play *Andromeda*, now lost.

an extreme hot day; whereupon a great many of the spectators, falling into fevers, had this accident from the heat and from the tragedy together that they did nothing but pronounce iambics with the names of Perseus and Andromeda; which, together with the fever, was cured by the coming on of winter; and this madness was thought to proceed from the passion imprinted by the tragedy. Likewise there reigned a fit of madness in another Grecian city which seized only the young maidens and caused many of them to hang themselves. This was by most then thought an act of the devil. But one that suspected that contempt of life in them might proceed from some passion of the mind and supposing they did not contemn also their honour, gave counsel to the magistrates to strip such as so hanged themselves and let them hang out naked. This, the story says, cured that madness. But on the other side, the same Grecians did often ascribe madness to the operation of the Eumenides or Furies, and sometimes of Ceres, Phoebus, and other gods; so much did men attribute to phantasms as to think them aerial living bodies and generally to call them spirits. And as the Romans in this held the same opinion with the Greeks, so also did the Jews, for they called madmen prophets, or (according as they thought the spirits good or bad) demoniacs; and some of them called both prophets and demoniacs madmen; and some called the same man both demoniac and madman. But for the Gentiles, it is no wonder, because diseases and health, vices and virtues, and many natural accidents were with them termed and worshipped as demons. So that a man was to understand by demon, as well (sometimes) an ague, as a devil. But for the Jews to
[38] have such opinion is somewhat strange. For neither Moses nor Abraham pretended to prophesy by possession of a spirit, but from the voice of God or by a vision or dream; nor is there anything in his law, moral or ceremonial, by which they were taught there was any such enthusiasm or any possession. When God is said (Num. 11:25) to take from the spirit that was in Moses and give to the seventy elders, the spirit of God (taking it for the substance of God) is not divided. The Scriptures, by the Spirit of God in man, mean a man's spirit, inclined to godliness. And where it is said, *Whom I have filled with the spirit of wisdom to make garments for Aaron* (Exod. 28:3), is not meant a spirit put into them that can make

garments, but the wisdom of their own spirits in that kind of work. In the like sense, the spirit of man, when it produceth unclean actions, is ordinarily called an unclean spirit; and so other spirits [are called], though not always, yet as often as the virtue or vice, so styled, is extraordinary and eminent. Neither did the other prophets of the Old Testament pretend enthusiasm or that God spoke in them, but to them by voice, vision, or dream; and the *burden of the Lord* was not possession, but command. How then could the Jews fall into this opinion of possession? I can imagine no reason but that which is common to all men, namely, the want of curiosity to search natural causes and their placing felicity in the acquisition of the gross pleasures of the senses and the things that most immediately conduce thereto. For they that see any strange and unusual ability or defect in a man's mind, unless they see withal from what cause it may probably proceed, can hardly think it natural; and if not natural, they must needs think it supernatural; and then what can it be, but that either God or the Devil is in him? And hence it came to pass, when our Saviour (Mark 3:21) was compassed about with the multitude, those of the house doubted he was mad and went out to hold him; but the Scribes said he had Beelzebub, and that was it by which he cast out devils, as if the greater madman had awed the lesser. And that some said, *He hath a devil and is mad*, whereas others, holding him for a prophet, said, *These are not the words of one that hath a devil* (John 10:20). So in the Old Testament he that came to anoint Jehu was a Prophet; but some of the company asked Jehu, *What came that madman for?* (2 Kings 9:11). So that, in sum, it is manifest that whosoever behaved himself in extraordinary manner was thought by the Jews to be possessed either with a good or evil spirit except by the Sadducees, who erred so far on the other hand as not to believe there were at all any spirits (which is very near to direct atheism), and thereby perhaps the more provoked others to term such men demoniacs rather than madmen.

26. But why then does our Saviour proceed in the curing of them, as if they were possessed and not as if they were mad? To which I can give no other kind of answer but that which is given to those that urge the Scripture in like manner against the opinion of the motion of the earth. The Scripture was written to show

unto men the kingdom of God and to prepare their minds to become his obedient subjects, leaving the world and the philosophy thereof to the disputation of men for the exercising of their natural reason. Whether the earth's or sun's motion make the day and night, or whether the exorbitant actions of men proceed from passion or from the Devil, so we worship him not, it is all one, as to our obedience and subjection to God Almighty; which is the thing for which the Scripture was written. As for that our Saviour speaketh to the disease as to a person, it is the usual phrase of all that cure by words only, as Christ did (and enchanters pretend to do, whether they speak to a devil or not). For is not Christ also said (Matt. 8:26) to have rebuked the winds? Is not he said also (Luke 4:39) to rebuke a fever? Yet this does not argue that a fever is a devil. And whereas many of those devils are said to confess Christ, it is not necessary to interpret those places otherwise than that those madmen confessed him. And whereas our Saviour (Matt. 12:43) speaketh of an unclean spirit that, having gone out of a man, wandereth through dry places, seeking rest, and finding none, and returning into the same man with seven other spirits worse than himself, it is manifestly a parable, alluding to a man that, after a little endeavour to quit his lusts, is vanquished by the strength of them and becomes seven times worse than he was. So that I see nothing at all in the Scripture that requireth a belief that demoniacs were any other thing but madmen.

[39]

Insignificant speech.

27. There is yet another fault in the discourses of some men, which may also be numbered amongst the sorts of madness, namely, that abuse of words, whereof I have spoken before in the fifth chapter by the name of absurdity. And that is when men speak such words as, put together, have in them no signification at all, but are fallen upon by some through misunderstanding of the words they have received and repeat by rote, by others from intention to deceive by obscurity. And this is incident to none but those that converse in questions of matters incomprehensible, as the Schoolmen, or in questions of abstruse philosophy. The common sort of men seldom speak insignificantly and are therefore, by those other egregious persons, counted idiots. But to be assured their words are without anything correspondent to them in the mind, there would need some examples; which if any man require,

let him take a Schoolman into his hands and see if he can translate any one chapter concerning any difficult point, as the Trinity, the Deity, the nature of Christ, transubstantiation, free will, etc., into any of the modern tongues, so as to make the same intelligible, or into any tolerable Latin, such as they were acquainted withal that lived when the Latin tongue was vulgar. What is the meaning of these words: *The first cause does not necessarily inflow anything into the second, by force of the essential subordination of the second causes, by which it may help it to work*? They are the translation of the title of the sixth chapter of *Suarez'*[1] first book, *Of the Concourse, Motion, and Help of God*. When men write whole volumes of such stuff, are they not mad or intend to make others so? And particularly in
the question of transubstantiation, where after certain words [40]
spoken they that say the white*ness*, round*ness*, magni*tude*, qual*ity*, corruptibil*ity*, all which are incorporeal, etc., go out of the wafer into the body of our blessed Saviour, do they not make those *nesses*, *tudes*, and *ties* to be so many spirits possessing his body? For by spirits they mean always things that, being incorporeal, are nevertheless movable from one place to another. So that this kind of absurdity may rightly be numbered amongst the many sorts of madness, and all the time that guided by clear thoughts of their worldly lust, they forbear disputing or writing thus, but lucid intervals. And thus much of the virtues and defects intellectual.

## CHAPTER IX

## OF THE SEVERAL SUBJECTS OF KNOWLEDGE

1. There are of KNOWLEDGE two kinds, whereof one is *knowledge of fact*; the other *knowledge of the consequence of one affirmation to another*. The former is nothing else but sense and memory and is *absolute* knowledge, as when we see a fact doing or remember it done; and this is the knowledge required in a witness. The latter is called *science* and is *conditional*, as when we know that: *if the figure*

1 Francisco Suarez (1584-1617), a Spanish Jesuit theologian and critic of Protestantism, was also known for his complex scholastic theories. Hobbes is referring to Suarez's *De Concursu, Motione, et Auxilio Dei* (II.1.6).

- SCIENCE, that is, knowledge of consequences; which is called also PHILOSOPHY.
  - Consequences from the accidents of bodies natural; which is called NATURAL PHILOSOPHY.
    - Consequences from the accidents common to all bodies natural; which are *quantity*, and *motion*. . . . . . . . . . .
    - PHYSICS or consequences from *qualities*.
      - Consequences from the qualities of bodies transient, such as sometimes appear, sometimes vanish, . . . . . . . . . . . . . . . . . . . . . . . .
      - Consequences from the qualities of bodies *permanent*.
        - Consequences from the qualities of the *stars*.
        - Consequences of the qualities from *liquid* bodies, that fill the space between the stars; such as are the *air*, or substance ethereal.
        - Consequences from the qualities of bodies *terrestrial*.
  - Consequences from the accidents of politic bodies; which is called POLITICS, and CIVIL PHILOSOPHY.
    - 1. Of consequences from the institution of COMMONWEALTHS, to the *rights*, and *duties* of the *body politic*, or *sovereign*.
    - 2. Of consequences from the same, to the duty and *right* of the *subjects*.

Consequences from quantity, and motion indeterminate; which being the principles or first foundation of philosophy, is called *Philosophia Prima*. — PHILOSOPHIA PRIMA

- Consequences from motion and quantity *etermined.*
  - Consequences from quantity, and motion determined.
    - By Figure / By Number — *Mathematics.*
      - GEOMETRY
      - ARITHMETIC
  - Consequences from the motion, and quantity of bodies in *special.*
    - Consequences from the motion and quantity of the greater parts of the world, as the *earth* and *stars.* — *Cosmography.*
      - ASTRONOMY
      - GEOGRAPHY
    - Consequences from the motions of special kinds, and figures of body. — *Mechanics.* Doctrine of *weight.*
      - *Science of* ENGINEERS
      - ARCHITECTURE
      - NAVIGATION

. . . . . . . . . . . . . . . . . . . . . . . . . . . . . . . . METEOROLOGY

Consequences from the *light* of the stars. Out of this, and the motion of the sun, is made the science of . . . . . . . . . . . . . . . . SCIOGRAPHY

Consequences from the influences of the stars . . . . . . . . . . . . . . . . ASTROLOGY

- Consequences om the parts f the earth at are *without nse.*
  - Consequences from the qualities of *minerals*, as *stones*, *metals*, &c.
  - Consequences from the qualities of *vegetables.*
- Consequences om the qualies of animals.
  - Consequences from the qualities of *animals in general.*
    - Consequences from *vision* . . . . . . . . . . OPTICS
    - Consequences from *sounds* . . . . . . . . . MUSIC
    - Consequences from the *rest of the senses.*
  - Consequences from the qualities of *men in special.*
    - Consequences from the *passions of men* ETHICS
    - Consequences from speech.
      - In *magnifying, vilifying,* &c. . . . . POETRY
      - In *persuading,* . . . . . . . RHETORIC
      - In *reasoning,* . . . . . . . . LOGIC
      - In *contracting,* . . . . . . . *The Science of* JUST and UNJUST

*shown be a circle, then any straight line through the center shall divide it into two equal parts.* And this is the knowledge required in a philosopher, that is to say, of him that pretends to reasoning.

2. The register of knowledge of fact is called *history*, whereof there be two sorts; one called *natural history*; which is the history of such facts or effects of nature as have no dependence on man's *will*, such as are the histories of metals, plants, animals, regions, and the like. The other is *civil history*, which is the history of the voluntary actions of men in commonwealths.

3. The registers of science are such books as contain the *demonstrations* of consequences of one affirmation to another; and are commonly called *books of philosophy*; whereof the sorts are many, according to the diversity of the matter, and may be divided in such manner as I have divided them in the following table.[1]

## CHAPTER X

## [41] OF POWER, WORTH, DIGNITY, HONOUR, AND WORTHINESS

1. The power of a man (to take it universally) is his present means to obtain some future apparent good and is either *original* or *instrumental.*

2. *Natural power* is the eminence of the faculties of body or mind, as extraordinary strength, form, prudence, arts, eloquence, liberality, nobility. *Instrumental* are those powers which, acquired by these or by fortune are means and instruments to acquire more, as riches, reputation, friends, and the secret working of God, which men call good luck. For the nature of power is in this point like to fame, increasing as it proceeds, or like the motion of heavy bodies, which, the further they go, make still the more haste.

---

1 As the table on pages 64–65 indicates, there are two basic parts of science: that of natural bodies (physics) and that of artificial bodies (politics). But Hobbes's complete system of science consists of three parts: *De Corpore* (*Of Body*), *De Homine* (*Of Man*) and *De Cive* (*Of the Citizen*). Human beings belong to natural science because they are bodies; insofar as they are parts of an artificial body, the civil state, they should be treated under politics. Notice that ethics and the science of just and unjust belong to natural, not civil, philosophy. Also notice the absence of theology from the table because it is not a science.

3. The greatest of human powers is that which is compounded of the powers of most men, united by consent, in one person, natural or civil, that has the use of all their powers depending on his will, such as is the power of a commonwealth;[1] or depending on the wills of each particular, such as is the power of a faction or of divers factions leagued. Therefore to have servants is power; to have friends is power; for they are strengths united.

4. Also, riches joined with liberality is power, because it procureth friends and servants; without liberality, not so, because in this case they defend not, but expose men to envy, as a prey.

5. Reputation of power is power, because it draweth with it the adherence of those that need protection.

6. So is reputation of love of a man's country called popularity, for the same reason.

7. Also, what quality soever maketh a man beloved or feared of many or the reputation of such quality is power, because it is a means to have the assistance and service of many.

8. Good success is power, because it maketh reputation of wisdom or good fortune, which makes men either fear him or rely on him.

9. Affability of men already in power is increase of power, because it gaineth love.

10. Reputation of prudence in the conduct of peace or war is power, because to prudent men we commit the government of ourselves more willingly than to others.

11. Nobility is power, not in all places, but only in those commonwealths where it has privileges; for in such privileges consisteth their power.

12. Eloquence is power, because it is seeming prudence.

13. Form is power, because being a promise of good, it recom- [42]
mendeth men to the favour of women and strangers.

14. The sciences are small powers, because not eminent, and therefore not acknowledged in any man; nor are at all, but in a few, and in them, but of a few things. For science is of that nature, as none can understand it to be, but such as in a good measure have attained it.

15. Arts of public use, as fortification, making of engines, and

---

1 See 14.21.

other instruments of war, because they confer to defense and victory, are power; and though the true mother of them be science, namely, the mathematics, yet, because they are brought into the light by the hand of the artificer, they be esteemed (the midwife passing with the vulgar for the mother) as his issue.

Worth.

16. The *value* or WORTH of a man is, as of all other things, his price, that is to say, so much as would be given for the use of his power and therefore is not absolute, but a thing dependent on the need and judgement of another. An able conductor of soldiers is of great price in time of war present or imminent but in peace not so. A learned and uncorrupt judge is much worth in time of peace, but not so much in war. And as in other things, so in men, not the seller, but the buyer determines the price. For let a man, as most men do, rate themselves at the highest value they can; yet their true value is no more than it is esteemed by others.

17. The manifestation of the value we set on one another is that which is commonly called honouring and dishonouring. To value a man at a high rate is to *honour* him, at a low rate is to *dishonour* him. But high and low in this case is to be understood by comparison to the rate that each man setteth on himself.

Dignity.

18. The public worth of a man, which is the value set on him by the commonwealth, is that which men commonly call DIGNITY. And this value of him by the commonwealth is understood by offices of command, judicature, public employment; or by names and titles introduced for distinction of such value.

To honour and dishonour.

19. To pray to another for aid of any kind is *to* HONOUR, because a sign we have an opinion he has power to help; and the more difficult the aid is, the more is the honour.

20. To obey is to honour, because no man obeys them who they think have no power to help or hurt them. And consequently to disobey is to *dishonour.*

21. To give great gifts to a man is to honour him, because it is buying of protection and acknowledging of power. To give little gifts is to dishonour, because it is but alms and signifies an opinion of the need of small helps.

22. To be sedulous in promoting another's good [and] also to flatter is to honour, as a sign we seek his protection or aid. To neglect is to dishonour.

23. To give way or place to another in any commodity is to honour, being a confession of greater power. To arrogate is to dishonour.

24. To show any sign of love or fear of another is honour, for both to love and to fear is to value. To contemn or less to love or fear than he expects is to dishonour, for it is undervaluing. [43]

25. To praise, magnify, or call happy is to honour, because nothing but goodness, power, and felicity is valued. To revile, mock, or pity is to dishonour.

26. To speak to another with consideration, to appear before him with decency and humility is to honour him, as signs of fear to offend. To speak to him rashly, to do anything before him obscenely, slovenly, impudently is to dishonour.

27. To believe, to trust, to rely on another is to honour him, sign of opinion of his virtue and power. To distrust or not believe is to dishonour.

28. To hearken to a man's counsel or discourse of what kind soever is to honour, as a sign we think him wise or eloquent or witty. To sleep or go forth or talk the while is to dishonour.

29. To do those things to another which he takes for signs of honour or which the law or custom makes so is to honour, because in approving the honour done by others, he acknowledgeth the power which others acknowledge. To refuse to do them is to dishonour.

30. To agree with in opinion is to honour, as being a sign of approving his judgement and wisdom. To dissent is dishonour and an upbraiding of error, and, if the dissent be in many things, of folly.

31. To imitate is to honour, for it is vehemently to approve. To imitate one's enemy is to dishonour.

32. To honour those another honours is to honour him, as a sign of approbation of his judgement. To honour his enemies is to dishonour him.

33. To employ in counsel or in actions of difficulty is to honour, as a sign of opinion of his wisdom or other power. To deny employment in the same cases to those that seek it is to dishonour.

34. All these ways of honouring are natural, and as well within as without commonwealths. But in commonwealths where he or

they that have the supreme authority can make whatsoever they please to stand for signs of honour, there be other honours.

35. A sovereign doth honour a subject with whatsoever title or office or employment or action that he himself will have taken for a sign of his will to honour him.

36. The king of Persia honoured Mordecai when he appointed [that] he should be conducted through the streets in the king's garment upon one of the king's horses with a crown on his head and a prince before him, proclaiming, *Thus shall it be done to him that the king will honour.*[1] And yet another king of Persia or the same another time to one that demanded for some great service to wear one of the king's robes, gave him leave so to do; but with this addition, that he should wear it as the king's fool, and then it was dishonour. So that of civil honour the fountain is in the person of the commonwealth and dependeth on the will of the sovereign and is therefore temporary and called *civil honour*, such as are mag-
[44] istracy, offices, titles, and in some places coats and scutcheons painted; and men honour such as have them, as having so many signs of favour in the Commonwealth, which favour is power.

Honourable. 37. *Honourable* is whatsoever possession, action, or quality is an argument and sign of power.

38. And therefore to be honoured, loved, or feared of many is honourable, as arguments of power. To be honoured of few or
Dishonourable. none, *dishonourable.*

39. Dominion and victory is honourable because acquired by power; and servitude, for need or fear, is dishonourable.

40. Good fortune (if lasting) honourable, as a sign of the favour of God. Ill fortune and losses, dishonourable. Riches are honourable, for they are power. Poverty, dishonourable. Magnanimity, liberality, hope, courage, [and] confidence are honourable; for they proceed from the conscience of power. Pusillanimity, parsimony, fear, diffidence, are dishonourable.

41. Timely resolution or determination of what a man is to do is honourable, as being the contempt of small difficulties and dangers. And irresolution dishonourable, as a sign of too much valuing of little impediments and little advantages, for when a man has

1 See Esther 1:1–12.

weighed things as long as the time permits and resolves not, the difference of weight is but little; and therefore if he resolve not, he overvalues little things, which is pusillanimity.

42. All actions and speeches that proceed or seem to proceed from much experience, science, discretion, or wit are honourable, for all these are powers. Actions or words that proceed from error, ignorance, or folly, dishonourable.

43. Gravity, as far forth as it seems to proceed from a mind employed on something else, is honourable, because employment is a sign of power. But if it seem to proceed from a purpose to appear grave, it is dishonourable. For the gravity of the former is like the steadiness of a ship laden with merchandise, but of the like the steadiness of a ship ballasted with sand and other trash.

44. To be conspicuous, that is to say, to be known, for wealth, office, great actions, or any eminent good is honourable, as a sign of the power for which he is conspicuous. On the contrary, obscurity is dishonourable.

45. To be descended from conspicuous parents is honourable, because they the more easily attain the aids and friends of their ancestors. On the contrary, to be descended from obscure parentage is dishonourable.

46. Actions proceeding from equity, joined with loss, are honourable, as signs of magnanimity, for magnanimity is a sign of power. On the contrary, craft, shifting, [and] neglect of equity is dishonourable.

47. Covetousness of great riches and ambition of great honours are honourable, as signs of power to obtain them. Covetousness and ambition of little gains or preferments is dishonourable.

48. Nor does it alter the case of honour whether an action (so it be great and difficult and consequently a sign of much power) [45] be just or unjust, for honour consisteth only in the opinion of power. Therefore, the ancient heathen did not think they dishonoured but greatly honoured the gods, when they introduced them in their poems committing rapes, thefts, and other great, but unjust or unclean acts, insomuch as nothing is so much celebrated in Jupiter as his adulteries, nor in Mercury as his frauds and thefts, of whose praises in a hymn of Homer the greatest is this, that being born in the morning, he had invented music at noon and before night stolen away the cattle of Apollo from his herdsmen.

49. Also amongst men, till there were constituted great commonwealths, it was thought no dishonour to be a pirate or a highway thief, but rather a lawful trade, not only amongst the Greeks, but also amongst all other nations, as is manifest by the histories of ancient time. And at this day, in this part of the world, private duels are and always will be honourable, though unlawful, till such time as there shall be honour ordained for them that refuse and ignominy for them that make the challenge. For duels also are many times effects of courage, and the ground of courage is always strength or skill, which are power, though for the most part they be effects of rash speaking and of the fear of dishonour in one or both the combatants, who, engaged by rashness, are driven into the lists to avoid disgrace.

Coats of arms.

50. Scutcheons and coats of arms hereditary, where they have any eminent privileges, are honourable; otherwise not; for their power consisteth either in such privileges or in riches or some such thing as is equally honoured in other men. This kind of honour, commonly called gentry, has been derived from the ancient Germans. For there never was any such thing known where the German customs were unknown. Nor is it now anywhere in use where the Germans have not inhabited. The ancient Greek commanders, when they went to war, had their shields painted with such devices as they pleased, insomuch as an unpainted buckler was a sign of poverty and of a common soldier; but they transmitted not the inheritance of them. The Romans transmitted the marks of their families; but they were the images, not the devices of their ancestors. Amongst the people of Asia, Africa, and America, there is not, nor was ever, any such thing. The Germans only had that custom, from whom it has been derived into England, France, Spain and Italy, when in great numbers they either aided the Romans or made their own conquests in these western parts of the world.

51. For Germany, being anciently, as all other countries in their beginnings, divided amongst an infinite number of little lords or masters of families that continually had wars one with another, those masters or lords, principally to the end they might, when they were covered with arms, be known by their followers and partly for ornament, both painted their armour or their scutcheon

or coat with the picture of some beast or other thing and also put some eminent and visible mark upon the crest of their helmets. [46] And this ornament both of the arms and crest descended by inheritance to their children to the eldest pure and to the rest with some note of diversity, such as the old master, that is to say in Dutch, the *Here-alt*, thought fit. But when many such families, joined together, made a greater monarchy, this duty of the herald to distinguish scutcheons was made a private office apart. And the issue of these lords is the great and ancient gentry, which for the most part bear living creatures noted for courage and rapine, or castles, battlements, belts, weapons, bars, palisades, and other notes of war; nothing being then in honour, but virtue military. Afterwards, not only kings but popular commonwealths gave divers manners of scutcheons to such as went forth to the war or returned from it for encouragement or recompense to their service. All which, by an observing reader, may be found in such ancient histories, Greek and Latin, as make mention of the German nation and manners in their times.[1]

Titles of honour.

52. Titles of honour, such as are duke, count, marquis, and baron, are honourable, as signifying the value set upon them by the sovereign power of the commonwealth; which titles were in old time titles of office and command derived some from the Romans, some from the Germans and French. Dukes, in Latin, *duces*, being generals in war; counts, *comites*, such as bore the general company out of friendship, and were left to govern and defend places conquered and pacified; marquises, *marchiones*, were counts that governed the marches or bounds of the Empire. Which titles of duke, count, and marquis came into the Empire about the time of Constantine the Great[2] from the customs of the German *militia*. But baron seems to have been a title of the Gauls and signifies a great man, such as were the kings' or princes' men whom they employed in war about their persons and seems to be derived from *vir* [Latin: man], to *ber*, and *bar*, that signified the same in the language of the Gauls, that *vir* in Latin, and thence to *bero* and *baro*, so

1 See Hobbes's translation of Thucydides, *History of the Peloponnesian War* 1.5-6.

2 Flavius Constantinus (274-337), Roman emperor who made Christianity the state religion. Constantine was praised by John Fox in his *Book of Martyrs* (English version, 1563) and Hobbes is similarly approving.

that such men were called *berones*, and after *barones*; and (in Spanish) *varones*. But he that would know more, particularly the original of titles of honour, may find it, as I have done this, in Mr. Selden's most excellent treatise of that subject.[1] In process of time these offices of honour, by occasion of trouble and for reasons of good and peaceable government, were turned into mere titles, serving for the most part to distinguish the precedence, place, and order of subjects in the commonwealth; and men were made dukes, counts, marquises, and barons of places, wherein they had neither possession nor command, and other titles also were devised to the same end.

Worthiness. 53. WORTHINESS is a thing different from the worth or value of a man and also from his merit or desert, and consisteth in a particular power or ability for that whereof he is said to be worthy;
Fitness. which particular ability is usually named FITNESS or *aptitude*.

54. For he is worthiest to be a commander, to be a judge, or to have any other charge, that is best fitted with the qualities required
[47] to the well discharging of it, and worthiest of riches that has the qualities most requisite for the well using of them, any of which qualities being absent, one may nevertheless be a worthy man and valuable for something else. Again, a man may be worthy of riches, office, and employment that nevertheless can plead no right to have it before another, and therefore cannot be said to merit or deserve it. For merit presupposeth a right, and that the thing deserved is due by promise, of which I shall say more hereafter when I shall speak of contracts.

1 John Selden, *Titles of Honour* (1614). Selden (1584-1654) was a friend of Hobbes during the early 1650s but they may have met at Great Tew in the 1630s.

# CHAPTER XI

## OF THE DIFFERENCE OF MANNERS

1. By MANNERS, I mean not here decency of behaviour, as how one man should salute another, or how a man should wash his mouth, or pick his teeth before company, and such other points of the *small morals,* but those qualities of mankind that concern their living together in peace and unity.[1] To which end we are to consider that the felicity of this life consisteth not in the repose of a mind satisfied. For there is no such *finis ultimus* (utmost aim) nor *summum bonum* (greatest good) as is spoken of in the books of the old moral philosophers. Nor can a man any more live whose desires are at an end than he whose senses and imaginations are at a stand.[2] Felicity is a continual progress of the desire from one object to another, the attaining of the former being still but the way to the latter. The cause whereof is that the object of man's desire is not to enjoy once only and for one instant of time, but to assure forever the way of his future desire. And therefore the voluntary actions and inclinations of all men tend not only to the procuring, but also to the assuring of a contented life and differ only in the way, which ariseth partly from the diversity of passions in divers men and partly from the difference of the knowledge or opinion each one has of the causes which produce the effect desired.

What is here meant by manners.

2. So that in the first place, I put for a general inclination of all mankind a perpetual and restless desire of power after power that ceaseth only in death. And the cause of this is not always that a man hopes for a more intensive delight than he has already attained to or that he cannot be content with a moderate power, but because he cannot assure the power and means to live well, which he hath present, without the acquisition of more. And from hence it is that kings, whose power is greatest, turn their endeavours to the assuring it at home by laws or abroad by wars; and

A restless desire of power in all men.

---

1 By 'manners', Hobbes does not mean etiquette but ethics.

2 In ancient Greek philosophy, to have a desire was a kind of imperfection, because it meant that one lacked (wanted) the thing desired. For Hobbes, desire is a necessary condition of life. See also 6.58.

when that is done, there succeedeth a new desire, in some, of fame from new conquest, in others, of ease and sensual pleasure, in others, of admiration or being flattered for excellence in some art or other ability of the mind.

Love of contention from competition.

3. Competition of riches, honour, command, or other power inclineth to contention, enmity, and war, because the way of one competitor to the attaining of his desire is to kill, subdue, supplant, [48] or repel the other. Particularly, competition of praise inclineth to a reverence of antiquity. For men contend with the living, not with the dead, to these ascribing more than due, that they may obscure the glory of the other.

Civil obedience from love of ease. From fear of death or wounds

4. Desire of ease and sensual delight disposeth men to obey a common power, because by such desires a man doth abandon the protection that might be hoped for from his own industry and labour. Fear of death and wounds disposeth to the same and for the same reason. On the contrary, needy men and hardy, not contented with their present condition, as also all men that are ambitious of military command, are inclined to continue the causes of war and to stir up trouble and sedition, for there is no honour military but by war nor any such hope to mend an ill game as by causing a new shuffle.

And from love of arts.

5. Desire of knowledge and arts of peace inclineth men to obey a common power, for such desire containeth a desire of leisure and consequently protection from some other power than their own.

Love of virtue from love of praise.

6. Desire of praise disposeth to laudable actions, such as please them whose judgement they value; for of those men whom we contemn, we contemn also the praises. Desire of fame after death does the same. And though after death there be no sense of the praise given us on earth, as being joys that are either swallowed up in the unspeakable joys of heaven or extinguished in the extreme torments of hell; yet is not such fame vain, because men have a present delight therein from the foresight of it and of the benefit that may redound thereby to their posterity, which though they now see not, yet they imagine; and anything that is pleasure in the sense the same also is pleasure in the imagination.[1]

---

1 What a person desires to happen after his death cannot make him happy at that time: the joys of heaven and the pain in hell overwhelm any earthly praise. But these desires for the future can make a person happy in the present.

Hate from difficulty of requiting great benefits.

7. To have received from one to whom we think ourselves equal greater benefits than there is hope to requite disposeth to counterfeit love, but really secret hatred, and puts a man into the estate of a desperate debtor that, in declining the sight of his creditor, tacitly wishes him there where he might never see him more. For benefits oblige; and obligation is thraldom; and unrequitable obligation, perpetual thraldom, which is to one's equal, hateful. But to have received benefits from one whom we acknowledge for superior inclines to love, because the obligation is no new depression; and cheerful acceptation (which men call *gratitude*) is such an honour done to the obliger as is taken generally for retribution. Also to receive benefits, though from an equal or inferior, as long as there is hope of requital, disposeth to love; for in the intention of the receiver the obligation is of aid and service mutual, from whence proceedeth an emulation of who shall exceed in benefiting, the most noble and profitable contention possible, wherein the victor is pleased with his victory, and the other revenged by confessing it.

And from conscience of deserving to be hated.[49]

8. To have done more hurt to a man than he can or is willing to expiate inclineth the doer to hate the sufferer. For he must expect revenge or forgiveness, both which are hateful.

Promptness to hurt from fear.

9. Fear of oppression disposeth a man to anticipate or to seek aid by society; for there is no other way by which a man can secure his life and liberty.

And from distrust of their own wit.

10. Men that distrust their own subtlety are in tumult and sedition better disposed for victory than they that suppose themselves wise or crafty. For these love to consult, the other (fearing to be circumvented) to strike first. And in sedition, men being always in the precincts of battle to hold together and use all advantages of force is a better stratagem than any that can proceed from subtlety of wit.

Vain undertaking from vain-glory.

11. Vain-glorious men, such as without being conscious to themselves of great sufficiency, delight in supposing themselves gallant men, are inclined only to ostentation, but not to attempt, because when danger or difficulty appears, they look for nothing but to have their insufficiency discovered.

12. Vain-glorious men, such as estimate their sufficiency by the flattery of other men or the fortune of some precedent action without assured ground of hope from the true knowledge of

themselves, are inclined to rash engaging, and in the approach of danger or difficulty to retire if they can, because not seeing the way of safety they will rather hazard their honour, which may be salved with an excuse than their lives, for which no salve is sufficient.

Ambition from opinion of sufficiency.

13. Men that have a strong opinion of their own wisdom in matter of government are disposed to ambition, because without public employment in counsel or magistracy, the honour of their wisdom is lost. And therefore eloquent speakers are inclined to ambition, for eloquence seemeth wisdom both to themselves and others.

Irresolution from too great valuing of small matters.

14. Pusillanimity disposeth men to irresolution and consequently to lose the occasions and fittest opportunities of action. For after men have been in deliberation till the time of action approach, if it be not then manifest what is best to be done, it is a sign [that] the difference of motives the one way and the other are not great; therefore not to resolve then is to lose the occasion by weighing of trifles, which is pusillanimity.

15. Frugality (though in poor men a virtue) maketh a man unapt to achieve such actions as require the strength of many men at once; for it weakeneth their endeavour, which is to be nourished and kept in vigour by reward.

Confidence in others from ignorance of the marks of wisdom and kindness.

16. Eloquence with flattery disposeth men to confide in them that have it, because the former is seeming wisdom, the latter seeming kindness. Add to them military reputation and it disposeth men to adhere and subject themselves to those men that have them. The two former, having given them caution against danger from him, the latter gives them caution against danger from others.

And from ignorance of natural causes.

17. Want of science, that is, ignorance of causes, disposeth or rather constraineth a man to rely on the advice and authority of others. For all men whom the truth concerns, if they rely not on their own, must rely on the opinion of some other whom they think wiser than themselves and see not why he should deceive them.

And from want of understanding.

[50] 18. Ignorance of the signification of words, which is want of understanding, disposeth men to take on trust, not only the truth they know not, but also the errors, and which is more, the non-

sense of them they trust; for neither error nor nonsense can without a perfect understanding of words be detected.

19. From the same it proceedeth that men give different names to one and the same thing from the difference of their own passions, as they that approve a private opinion call it opinion, but they that mislike it, heresy;[1] and yet heresy signifies no more than private opinion but has only a greater tincture of choler [anger].

20. From the same also it proceedeth that men cannot distinguish, without study and great understanding, between one action of many men and many actions of one multitude, as for example, between the one action of all the senators of Rome in killing Catiline and the many actions of a number of senators in killing Caesar, and therefore are disposed to take for the action of the people that which is a multitude of actions done by a multitude of men led perhaps by the persuasion of one.[2]

Adherence to custom from ignorance of the nature of right and wrong.

21. Ignorance of the causes and original constitution of right, equity, law, and justice disposeth a man to make custom and example the rule of his actions, in such manner as to think that unjust which it hath been the custom to punish and that just of the impunity and approbation whereof they can produce an example or (as the lawyers which only use this false measure of justice barbarously call it) a precedent,[3] like little children that have no other rule of good and evil manners but the correction they receive from their parents and masters, save that children are constant to their rule, whereas men are not so, because grown strong and stubborn, they appeal from custom to reason, and from reason to custom, as it serves their turn, receding from custom when their interest requires it and setting themselves against reason as oft as reason is against them; which is the cause that the doctrine of right and wrong is perpetually disputed both by the pen and the sword, whereas the doctrine of lines and figures is not so, because men care not in that subject what be truth, as a thing that crosses no man's ambition, profit, or lust. For I doubt not but if it had been a

---

1 See 42.130.

2 Hobbes may be alluding to the execution of King Charles I (1649) by the members of the Rump Parliament.

3 Hobbes is criticizing Edward Coke (1552–1634), who claimed the Common Law was independent of the king. See also note 1 on page 109.

thing contrary to any man's right of dominion or to the interest of men that have dominion *that the three angles of a triangle should be equal to two angles of a square*, that doctrine should [would] have been, if not disputed, yet by the burning of all books of geometry suppressed, as far as he whom it concerned was able.

Adherence to private men, from ignorance of the causes of peace.

22. Ignorance of remote causes disposeth men to attribute all events to the causes immediate and instrumental; for these are all the causes they perceive. And hence it comes to pass that in all places men that are grieved with payments to the public discharge their anger upon the publicans, that is to say, farmers, collectors, and other officers of the public revenue, and adhere to such as find fault with the public government, and thereby, when they have engaged themselves beyond hope of justification, fall also upon the
[51] supreme authority for fear of punishment or shame of receiving pardon.

Credulity from ignorance of nature.

23. Ignorance of natural causes disposeth a man to credulity, so as to believe many times impossibilities; for such [a man] knows nothing to the contrary but that they may be true, being unable to detect the impossibility. And credulity, because men love to be hearkened unto in company, disposeth them to lying, so that ignorance itself, without malice, is able to make a man both to believe lies and tell them and sometimes also to invent them.

Curiosity to know from care of future time.

24. Anxiety for the future time disposeth men to inquire into the causes of things, because the knowledge of them maketh men the better able to order the present to their best advantage.

Natural religion from the same.

25. Curiosity or love of the knowledge of causes draws a man from consideration of the effect to seek the cause, and again, the cause of that cause, till of necessity he must come to this thought at last that there is some cause whereof there is no former cause but is eternal; which is it men call God. So that it is impossible to make any profound inquiry into natural causes without being inclined thereby to believe there is one God eternal, though they cannot have any idea of him in their mind answerable to his nature.[1] For as a man that is born blind, hearing men talk of warming themselves by the fire and being brought to warm him-

1 Humans can know that God exists, but not what his nature is like, because they have no direct or unmediated knowledge of God. See also 3.12 and 12.6.

self by the same, may easily conceive and assure himself there is somewhat there which men call fire and is the cause of the heat he feels, but cannot imagine what it is like nor have an idea of it in his mind such as they have that see it, so also by the visible things of this world and their admirable order, a man may conceive there is a cause of them, which men call God, and yet not have an idea or image of him in his mind.

26. And they that make little or no inquiry into the natural causes of things, yet from the fear that proceeds from the ignorance itself of what it is that hath the power to do them much good or harm are inclined to suppose and feign unto themselves several kinds of powers invisible and to stand in awe of their own imaginations and in time of distress to invoke them, as also in the time of an expected good success, to give them thanks, making the creatures of their own fancy their gods. By which means it hath come to pass that from the innumerable variety of fancy, men have created in the world innumerable sorts of gods. And this fear of things invisible is the natural seed of that which every one in himself calleth religion, and in them that worship or fear that power otherwise than they do, superstition.

27. And this seed of religion, having been observed by many, some of those that have observed it have been inclined thereby to nourish, dress, and form it into laws, and to add to it of their own invention any opinion of the causes of future events by which they thought they should best be able to govern others and make unto themselves the greatest use of their powers.

## CHAPTER XII [52]

## OF RELIGION

1. Seeing there are no signs nor fruit of *religion* but in man only, there is no cause to doubt but that the seed of *religion* is also only in man[1] and consisteth in some peculiar quality or at least in some eminent degree thereof, not to be found in other living creatures. Religion in man only.

---

1 The seed of religion is curiosity. See 6.35.

First, from his desire of knowing causes.

2. And first, it is peculiar to the nature of man to be inquisitive into the causes of the events they see, some more, some less, but all men so much as to be curious in the search of the causes of their own good and evil fortune.

From the consideration of the beginning of things.

3. Secondly, upon the sight of anything that hath a beginning, to think also it had a cause which determined the same to begin then when it did, rather than sooner or later.

From his observation of the sequel of things.

4. Thirdly, whereas there is no other felicity of beasts but the enjoying of their quotidian food, ease, and lusts, as having little or no foresight of the time to come for want of observation and memory of the order, consequence, and dependence of the things they see, man observeth how one event hath been produced by another and remembereth in them antecedence and consequence, and when he cannot assure himself of the true causes of things (for the causes of good and evil fortune for the most part are invisible), he supposes causes of them either such as his own fancy suggesteth or trusteth to the authority of other men such as he thinks to be his friends and wiser than himself.

The natural cause of religion, the anxiety of the time to come.

5. The two first make anxiety. For being assured that there be causes of all things that have arrived hitherto or shall arrive hereafter, it is impossible for a man, who continually endeavoureth to secure himself against the evil he fears, and procure the good he desireth, not to be in a perpetual solicitude of the time to come, so that every man, especially those that are over-provident, are in an estate like to that of Prometheus. For as Prometheus (which, interpreted, is *the prudent man*) was bound to the hill Caucasus, a place of large prospect, where an eagle, feeding on his liver, devoured in the day as much as was repaired in the night, so that man, which looks too far before him in the care of future time, hath his heart all the day long gnawed on by fear of death, poverty, or other calamity and has no repose, nor pause of his anxiety, but in sleep.

Which makes them fear the power of invisible things.

6. This perpetual fear, always accompanying mankind in the ignorance of causes, as it were in the dark, must needs have for object something. And therefore when there is nothing to be seen, there is nothing to accuse either of their good or evil fortune but some *power* or agent *invisible*, in which sense perhaps it was that some of the old poets said that the gods were at first created by human fear, which, spoken of the gods (that is to say, of the many

gods of the Gentiles), is very true. But the acknowledging of one God, eternal, infinite, and omnipotent, may more easily be derived from the desire men have to know the causes of natural bodies and their several virtues and operations than from the fear of what was to befall them in time to come. For he that from any effect he seeth come to pass should reason to the next and immediate cause thereof and from thence to the cause of that cause and plunge himself profoundly in the pursuit of causes shall at last come to this, that there must be (as even the heathen philosophers confessed) one First Mover, that is, a first and an eternal cause of all things, which is that which men mean by the name of God, and all this without thought of their fortune, the solicitude whereof both inclines to fear and hinders them from the search of the causes of other things, and thereby gives occasion of feigning of as many gods as there be men that feign them. [53]

And suppose them incorporeal.

7. And for the matter or substance of the invisible agents, so fancied, they could not by natural cogitation fall upon any other concept but that it was the same with that of the soul of man, and that the soul of man was of the same substance with that which appeareth in a dream to one that sleepeth or in a looking-glass to one that is awake, which, men not knowing that such apparitions are nothing else but creatures of the fancy, think to be real and external substances and therefore call them ghosts, as the Latins called them *imagines* [images] and *umbrae* [shadows] and thought them spirits (that is, thin aerial bodies) and those invisible agents which they feared to be like them, save that they appear and vanish when they please. But the opinion that such spirits were incorporeal or immaterial could never enter into the mind of any man by nature, because though men may put together words of contradictory signification, as *spirit* and *incorporeal*; yet they can never have the imagination of anything answering to them; and therefore, men that by their own meditation arrive to the acknowledgement of one infinite, omnipotent, and eternal God choose rather to confess he is incomprehensible and above their understanding than to define his nature by *spirit incorporeal*,[1] and then confess their definition to be unintelligible; or if they give him such a title,

1 See 3.12.

it is not *dogmatically* with intention to make the Divine Nature understood, but *piously*, to honour him with attributes of significations as remote as they can from the grossness of bodies visible.

But know not the way how they effect anything.

8. Then, for the way by which they think these invisible agents wrought their effects, that is to say, what immediate causes they used in bringing things to pass, men that know not what it is that we call *causing* (that is, almost all men) have no other rule to guess by but by observing and remembering what they have seen to precede the like effect at some other time or times before, without seeing between the antecedent and subsequent event any dependence or connexion at all; and therefore from the like things past, they expect the like things to come and hope for good or evil luck superstitiously from things that have no part at all in the causing
[54] of it, as the Athenians did for their Lepanto demand another Phormio, the Pompeian faction for their war in Africa another Scipio,[1] and others have done in divers other occasions since. In like manner they attribute their fortune to a stander by, to a lucky or unlucky place, to words spoken, especially if the name of God be amongst them, as charming, and conjuring (the liturgy of witches), insomuch as to believe they have power to turn a stone into bread, bread into a man, or anything into anything.

But honour them as they honour men.

9. Thirdly, for the worship which naturally men exhibit to powers invisible, it can be no other but such expressions of their reverence as they would use towards men, [namely,] gifts, petitions, thanks, submission of body, considerate addresses, sober behaviour, premeditated words, swearing (that is, assuring one another of their promises) by invoking them. Beyond that, reason suggesteth nothing but leaves them either to rest there or for further ceremonies to rely on those they believe to be wiser than themselves.

And attribute to them all extraordinary events.

10. Lastly, concerning how these invisible powers declare to men the things which shall hereafter come to pass, especially concerning their good or evil fortune in general or good or ill success in any particular undertaking, men are naturally at a stand, save that using to conjecture of the time to come by the time past, they are very apt, not only to take casual things, after one or two encounters, for prognostics of the like encounter ever after, but

---

1 See Thucydides, *History of the Peloponnesian War* iii.7; and Plutarch, *Lives*, "Cato the Younger."

also to believe the like prognostics from other men of whom they have once conceived a good opinion.

11. And in these four things, opinion of ghosts, ignorance of second causes, devotion towards what men fear, and taking of things casual for prognostics, consisteth the natural seed of *religion,* which, by reason of the different fancies, judgements, and passions of several men, hath grown up into ceremonies so different that those which are used by one man are for the most part ridiculous to another.

Four things, natural seeds of religion.

12. For these seeds have received culture from two sorts of men. One sort have been they that have nourished and ordered them, according to their own invention. The other have done it by God's commandment and direction. But both sorts have done it with a purpose to make those men that relied on them the more apt to obedience, laws, peace, charity, and civil society. So that the religion of the former sort is a part of human politics and teacheth part of the duty which earthly kings require of their subjects. And the religion of the latter sort is divine politics and containeth precepts to those that have yielded themselves subjects in the kingdom of God. Of the former sort were all the founders of commonwealths, and the lawgivers of the Gentiles, of the latter sort were Abraham, Moses, and our blessed Saviour, by whom have been derived unto us the laws of the kingdom of God.

Made different by culture.

13. And for that part of religion which consisteth in opinions concerning the nature of powers invisible, there is almost nothing that has a name that has not been esteemed amongst the Gentiles in one place or another, a god or devil, or by their poets feigned to be animated, inhabited, or possessed by some spirit or other.

The absurd opinion of gentilism.

[55]

14. The unformed matter of the world was a god by the name of Chaos.

15. The heaven, the ocean, the planets, the fire, the earth, the winds, were so many gods.

16. Men, women, a bird, a crocodile, a calf, a dog, a snake, an onion, a leek, were deified. Besides that, they filled almost all places with spirits called *demons*;[1] the plains with Pan and Panises or Satyrs, the woods with Fauns and Nymphs, the sea, with Tri-

1 See also 8.25, 34.15, 34.18, and 36.2.

tons and other Nymphs, every river and fountain with a ghost of his name and with Nymphs, every house, with its *Lares* or familiars, every man with his *Genius*; hell with ghosts and spiritual officers, as Charon, Cerberus, and the Furies, and in the night time, all places with *larvae*, *lemures*, ghosts of men deceased and a whole kingdom of fairies and bugbears. They have also ascribed divinity and built temples to mere accidents and qualities, such as are time, night, day, peace, concord, love, contention, virtue, honour, health, rust, fever, and the like, which when they prayed for or against, they prayed to as if there were ghosts of those names hanging over their heads and letting fall or withholding that good or evil for or against which they prayed. They invoked also their own wit by the name of Muses, their own ignorance by the name of Fortune, their own lust by the name of Cupid, their own rage by the name Furies, their own privy members by the name of Priapus, and attributed their pollutions to *incubi* and *succubae*, insomuch as there was nothing which a poet could introduce as a person in his poem which they did not make either a *god* or a *devil*.[1]

17. The same authors of the religion of the Gentiles, observing the second ground for religion, which is men's ignorance of causes, and thereby their aptness to attribute their fortune to causes on which there was no dependence at all apparent, took occasion to obtrude on their ignorance, instead of second causes, a kind of second and ministerial gods, ascribing the cause of fecundity to Venus, the cause of arts to Apollo, of subtlety and craft to Mercury, of tempests and storms to Aeolus, and of other effects to other gods, insomuch as there was amongst the heathen almost as great variety of gods as of business.

18. And to the worship which naturally men conceived fit to be used towards their gods, namely, oblations, prayers, thanks, and the rest formerly named, the same legislators of the Gentiles have added their images both in picture and sculpture, that the more ignorant sort (that is to say, the most part or generality of the people), thinking the gods for whose representation they were made were really included and as it were housed within them, might so much the more stand in fear of them, and endowed them with

1 See also 38.6, 44.3, 45.33, and 45.38.

lands and houses and officers and revenues, set apart from all other human uses, that is, consecrated, made holy to those their idols, as caverns, groves, woods, mountains, and whole islands, and have [56] attributed to them, not only the shapes, some of men, some of beasts, some of monsters, but also the faculties and passions of men and beasts, as sense, speech, sex, lust, generation, and this not only by mixing one with another to propagate the kind of gods, but also by mixing with men and women to beget mongrel gods and but inmates of heaven, as Bacchus, Hercules, and others, besides anger, revenge, and other passions of living creatures and the actions proceeding from them, as fraud, theft, adultery, sodomy, and any vice that may be taken for an effect of power or a cause of pleasure, and all such vices as amongst men are taken to be against law rather than against honour.

19. Lastly, to the prognostics of time to come, which are naturally but conjectures upon the experience of time past, and supernaturally divine revelation, the same authors of the religion of the Gentiles, partly upon pretended experience, partly upon pretended revelation, have added innumerable other superstitious ways of divination and made men believe they should find their fortunes, sometimes in the ambiguous or senseless answers of the priests at Delphi, Delos, Ammon, and other famous oracles, which answers were made ambiguous by design, to own the event both ways, or absurd by the intoxicating vapour of the place, which is very frequent in sulphurous caverns, sometimes in the leaves of the Sibyls, of whose prophecies (like those perhaps of Nostradamus;[1] for the fragments now extant seem to be the invention of later times), there were some books in reputation in the time of the Roman republic. Sometimes [the authors of the religion of the Gentiles made men believe they should find their fortunes] in the insignificant speeches of madmen, supposed to be possessed with a divine spirit, which possession they called enthusiasm; and these kinds of foretelling events were accounted theomancy or prophecy. Sometimes [the authors of the religion of the Gentiles made men believe they should find their fortunes] in the aspect of the stars at their nativity, which was called horoscopy and esteemed a part of

1 Michel de Nostredama (1503-66), French physician, whose obscure prognostications in *Centuries* are still believed by some people today.

judiciary astrology; sometimes in their own hopes and fears, called *thumomancy* or *presage*; sometimes in the prediction of witches that pretended conference with the dead, which is called necromancy, conjuring, and witchcraft, and is but juggling and confederate knavery; sometimes in the casual flight or feeding of birds, called augury; sometimes in the entrails of a sacrificed beast, which was *aruspicina*, sometimes in dreams; sometimes in croaking of ravens or chattering of birds; sometimes in the lineaments of the face, which was called metoposcopy, or by palmistry in the lines of the hand in casual words called *omina;* sometimes in monsters or unusual accidents, as eclipses, comets, rare meteors, earthquakes, inundations, uncouth births, and the like, which they called *portenta* and *ostenta*, because they thought them to portend or foreshow some great calamity to come; [and] sometimes in mere lottery, as cross and pile, counting holes in a sieve, dipping of verses in Homer and Virgil, and innumerable other such vain conceits. So easy are men to be drawn to believe anything from such men as have gotten credit with them; and can with gentleness, and dexterity, take hold of their fear and ignorance.

[57] The designs of the authors of the religion of the heathen.

20. And therefore the first founders and legislators of commonwealths amongst the Gentiles, whose ends were only to keep the people in obedience and peace, have in all places taken care first to imprint their minds a belief that those precepts which they gave concerning religion might not be thought to proceed from their own device, but from the dictates of some god or other spirit, or else that they themselves were of a higher nature than mere mortals that their laws might the more easily be received; so Numa Pompilius pretended to receive the ceremonies he instituted amongst the Romans from the nymph Egeria and the first king and founder of the kingdom of Peru pretended himself and his wife to be the children of the sun; and Mahomet,[1] to set up his new religion, pretended to have conferences with the Holy Ghost in form of a dove. Secondly, they have had a care to make it believed that the same things were displeasing to the gods which were forbidden by the laws. Thirdly, to prescribe ceremonies, supplications, sacrifices, and festivals by which they were to believe

1 Mohammed (570-632), founder of Islam and author of the *Koran*, which was dictated to him by the angel Gabriel.

the anger of the gods might be appeased, and that ill success in war, great contagions of sickness, earthquakes, and each man's private misery came from the anger of the gods, and their anger from the neglect of their worship or the forgetting or mistaking some point of the ceremonies required. And though amongst the ancient Romans men were not forbidden to deny that which in the poets is written of the pains and pleasures after this life, which divers of great authority and gravity in that state have in their harangues openly derided; yet that belief was always more cherished than the contrary.

21. And by these and such other institutions, they obtained in order to their end, which was the peace of the commonwealth, that the common people in their misfortunes, laying the fault on neglect or error in their ceremonies or on their own disobedience to the laws, were the less apt to mutiny against their governors. And being entertained with the pomp and pastime of festivals and public games made in honour of the gods, needed nothing else but bread to keep them from discontent, murmuring, and commotion against the state. And therefore the Romans, that had conquered the greatest part of the then known world, made no scruple of tolerating any religion whatsoever in the city of Rome itself, unless it had something in it that could not consist with their civil government, nor do we read that any religion was there forbidden but that of the Jews, who (being the peculiar kingdom of God) thought it unlawful to acknowledge subjection to any mortal king or state whatsoever. And thus you see how the religion of the Gentiles was a part of their policy.

The true religion and the laws of God's kingdom the same.

22. But where God himself by supernatural revelation planted religion, there he also made to himself a peculiar kingdom and gave laws, not only of behaviour towards himself but also towards one another; and thereby in the kingdom of God the policy and laws civil are a part of religion; and therefore the distinction of temporal and spiritual domination hath there no place. It is true [58] that God is king of all the earth; yet may he be king of a peculiar and chosen nation. For there is no more incongruity therein than that he that hath the general command of the whole army should have withal a peculiar regiment or company of his own. God is king of all the earth by his power, but of his chosen people, he is

king by covenant. But to speak more largely of the kingdom of God, both by nature and covenant, I have in the following discourse assigned another place.

Chap. 35.[1] The causes of change in religion.

23. From the propagation of religion, it is not hard to understand the causes of the resolution of the same into its first seeds or principles, which are only an opinion of a deity and powers invisible and supernatural, that can never be so abolished out of human nature but that new religions may again be made to spring out of them by the culture of such men as for such purpose are in reputation.

24. For seeing all formed religion is founded at first upon the faith which a multitude hath in some one person, whom they believe not only to be a wise man and to labour to procure their happiness, but also to be a holy man to whom God himself vouchsafeth to declare his will supernaturally; it followeth necessarily, when they that have the government of religion shall come to have either the wisdom of those men, [or] their sincerity, or their love suspected, or that they shall be unable to show any probable token of divine revelation, that the religion which they desire to uphold must be suspected likewise and (without the fear of the civil sword) [will be] contradicted and rejected.

Enjoining belief of impossibilities.

25. That which taketh away the reputation of wisdom in him that formeth a religion or addeth to it when it is already formed is the enjoining of a belief of contradictories; for both parts of a contradiction cannot possibly be true; and therefore to enjoin the belief of them is an argument of ignorance, which detects the author in that and discredits him in all things else he shall propound as from revelation supernatural; which revelation a man may indeed have of many things above, but of nothing against natural reason.

Doing contrary to the religion they establish.

26. That which taketh away the reputation of sincerity is the doing or saying of such things as appear to be signs that what they require other men to believe is not believed by themselves; all which doings or sayings are therefore called scandalous because they be stumbling-blocks that make men to fall in the way of religion, as injustice, cruelty, profaneness, avarice, and luxury. For who

1 Hobbes means chapter 32, as Edwin Curley pointed out in his edition of *Leviathan*.

can believe that he that doth ordinarily such actions, as proceed from any of these roots, believeth there is any such invisible power to be feared as he affrighteth other men withal for lesser faults?

27. That which taketh away the reputation of love is the being detected of private ends, as when the belief they require of others conduceth or seemeth to conduce to the acquiring of dominion, riches, dignity, or secure pleasure to themselves only or specially. [59] For that which men reap benefit by to themselves they are thought to do for their own sakes, and not for love of others.

Want of the testimony of miracles.

28. Lastly, the testimony that men can render of divine calling can be no other than the operation of miracles or true prophecy (which also is a miracle) or extraordinary felicity. And therefore, to those points of religion which have been received from them that did such miracles, those that are added by such as approve not their calling by some miracle obtain no greater belief than what the custom and laws of the places in which they be educated have wrought into them. For as in natural things men of judgement require natural signs and arguments, so in supernatural things they require signs supernatural (which are miracles) before they consent inwardly and from their hearts.

29. All which causes of the weakening of men's faith do manifestly appear in the examples following. First, we have the example of the children of Israel, who when Moses that had approved his calling to them by miracles and by the happy conduct of them out of Egypt, was absent but forty days, revolted from the worship of the true God recommended to them by him, and, setting up a golden calf for their god, relapsed into the idolatry of the Egyptians from whom they had been so lately delivered. And again, after Moses, Aaron, Joshua, and that generation which had seen the great works of God in Israel were dead, another generation arose and served Baal. So that miracles failing, faith also failed.

Exodus 32:1-2.

Judges 2:11.

I Samuel 8:3.

30. Again, when the sons of Samuel, being constituted by their father Judges in Beer-sheba, received bribes and judged unjustly, the people of Israel refused any more to have God to be their king in other manner than he was king of other people and therefore cried out to Samuel to choose them a king after the manner of the nations. So that justice failing, faith also failed, insomuch as they deposed their God from reigning over them.

31. And whereas in the planting of Christian religion the oracles ceased in all parts of the Roman Empire and the number of Christians increased wonderfully every day and in every place by the preaching of the Apostles and Evangelists, a great part of that success may reasonably be attributed to the contempt into which the priests of the Gentiles of that time had brought themselves by their uncleanness, avarice, and juggling between princes. Also the religion of the Church of Rome was partly for the same cause abolished in England and many other parts of Christendom, insomuch as the failing of virtue in the pastors maketh faith fail in the people and partly from bringing of the philosophy and doctrine of Aristotle into religion by the Schoolmen, from whence there arose so many contradictions and absurdities as brought the clergy into a reputation both of ignorance and of fraudulent intention and inclined people to revolt from them either against the will of their own princes as in France and Holland or with their will as in England.[1]

[60] 32. Lastly, amongst the points by the Church of Rome declared necessary for salvation, there be so many manifestly to the advantage of the Pope, so many of his spiritual subjects residing in the territories of other Christian princes that, were it not for the mutual emulation of those princes, they might without war or trouble exclude all foreign authority, as easily as it has been excluded in England. For who is there that does not see to whose benefit it conduceth to have it believed that a king hath not his authority from Christ unless a bishop crown him? That a king, if he be a priest, cannot marry? That whether a prince be born in lawful marriage or not, must be judged by authority from Rome? That subjects may be freed from their allegiance if by the court of Rome the king be judged a heretic? That a king, as Childeric[2] of France, may be deposed by a Pope, as Pope Zachary, for no cause, and his kingdom given to one of his subjects? That the clergy and regulars, in what country soever, shall be exempt from the jurisdiction of their king in cases criminal? Or

1 A criticism of Roman Catholicism.

2 Childeric, last of the Merovingian kings in France, was deposed in 751 by Pepin, the Mayor of the Palace. Pope Zachary [Zacharias] held that the deposition was permissible. In 1651 editions of *Leviathan*, Childeric's name is spelled 'Chilperique'.

who does not see to whose profit redound the fees of private Masses and vales of purgatory,[1] with other signs of private interest enough to mortify the most lively faith, if, as I said, the civil magistrate and custom did not more sustain it than any opinion they have of the sanctity, wisdom, or probity of their teachers? So that I may attribute all the changes of religion in the world to one and the same cause, and that is unpleasing priests; and those not only amongst catholics, but even in that Church that hath presumed most of reformation.[2]

## CHAPTER XIII

## OF THE NATURAL CONDITION OF MANKIND AS CONCERNING THEIR FELICITY AND MISERY

Men by nature equal.

1. Nature hath made men so equal in the faculties of body and mind, as that, though there be found one man sometimes manifestly stronger in body or of quicker mind than another; yet when all is reckoned together, the difference between man and man is not so considerable as that one man can thereupon claim to himself any benefit to which another may not pretend as well as he. For as to the strength of body, the weakest has strength enough to kill the strongest, either by secret machination or by confederacy with others that are in the same danger with himself.

2. And as to the faculties of the mind, setting aside the arts grounded upon words, and especially that skill of proceeding upon general and infallible rules, called science, which very few have and but in few things, as being not a native faculty born with us, nor attained, as prudence, while we look after somewhat else, I find yet a greater equality amongst men than that of strength. For prudence is but experience, which equal time equally bestows on all men in those things they equally apply themselves unto. That [61]

1 See also 43.14, 43.17, 44.16, 44.30–40, 46.21, 46.27, and 47.14.

2 Edward Hyde, the earl of Clarendon, thought that Hobbes was refering to the Church of England. I, like most commentators, think he was referring to the Presbyterian Church

which may perhaps make such equality incredible is but a vain conceit of one's own wisdom, which almost all men think they have in a greater degree than the vulgar, that is, than all men but themselves and a few others, whom by fame or for concurring with themselves, they approve. For such is the nature of men that howsoever they may acknowledge many others to be more witty or more eloquent or more learned, they will hardly believe there be many so wise as themselves; for they see their own wit at hand and other men's at a distance. But this proveth rather that men are in that point equal, than unequal. For there is not ordinarily a greater sign of the equal distribution of anything than that every man is contented with his share.

From equality proceeds diffidence.

3. From this equality of ability ariseth equality of hope in the attaining of our ends. And therefore if any two men desire the same thing, which nevertheless they cannot both enjoy, they become enemies; and in the way to their end (which is principally their own conservation, and sometimes their delectation only) endeavour to destroy or subdue one another. And from hence it comes to pass that where an invader hath no more to fear than another man's single power, if one plant, sow, build, or possess a convenient seat, others may probably be expected to come prepared with forces united to dispossess and deprive him, not only of the fruit of his labour, but also of his life or liberty. And the invader again is in the like danger of another.

From diffidence war.

4. And from this diffidence of one another, there is no way for any man to secure himself so reasonable as anticipation, that is, by force or wiles, to master the persons of all men he can so long till he see no other power great enough to endanger him; and this is no more than his own conservation requireth, and is generally allowed. Also, because there be some that, taking pleasure in contemplating their own power in the acts of conquest, which they pursue farther than their security requires, if others, that otherwise would be glad to be at ease within modest bounds, should not by invasion increase their power, they would not be able, long time, by standing only on their defence, to subsist. And by consequence, such augmentation of dominion over men being necessary to a man's conservation, it ought to be allowed him.

5. Again, men have no pleasure (but on the contrary a great

deal of grief) in keeping company where there is no power able to overawe them all. For every man looketh that his companion should value him at the same rate he sets upon himself, and upon all signs of contempt or undervaluing naturally endeavours, as far as he dares (which amongst them that have no common power to keep them in quiet is far enough to make them destroy each other), to extort a greater value from his contemners, by damage; and from others, by the example.

6. So that in the nature of man, we find three principal causes of quarrel. First, competition; secondly, diffidence; thirdly, glory.

7. The first maketh men invade for gain; the second, for safety; [62] and the third, for reputation. The first use violence to make themselves masters of other men's persons, wives, children, and cattle; the second, to defend them; the third, for trifles, as a word, a smile, a different opinion, and any other sign of undervalue, either direct in their persons or by reflection in their kindred, their friends, their nation, their profession, or their name.

Out of civil states there is always war of every one against every one.

8. Hereby it is manifest that during the time men live without a common power to keep them all in awe, they are in that condition which is called war; and such a war as is of every man against every man. For WAR consisteth not in battle only, or the act of fighting, but in a tract of time, wherein the will to contend by battle is sufficiently known; and therefore the notion of *time* is to be considered in the nature of war, as it is in the nature of weather. For as the nature of foul weather lieth not in a shower or two of rain, but in an inclination thereto of many days together, so the nature of war consisteth not in actual fighting, but in the known disposition thereto during all the time there is no assurance to the contrary. All other time is PEACE.

The incommodities of such a war.

9. Whatsoever therefore is consequent to a time of war, where every man is enemy to every man, the same consequent to the time wherein men live without other security than what their own strength and their own invention shall furnish them withal. In such condition there is no place for industry, because the fruit thereof is uncertain; and consequently no culture of the earth; no navigation, nor use of the commodities that may be imported by sea; no commodious building; no instruments of moving and removing such things as require much force; no knowledge of the

face of the earth; no account of time; no arts; no letters; no society; and which is worst of all, continual fear, and danger of violent death; and the life of man, solitary, poor, nasty, brutish, and short.

10. It may seem strange to some man that has not well weighed these things that nature should thus dissociate and render men apt to invade and destroy one another; and he may therefore, not trusting to this inference, made from the passions, desire perhaps to have the same confirmed by experience. Let him therefore consider with himself; when taking a journey, he arms himself and seeks to go well accompanied; when going to sleep, he locks his doors; when even in his house he locks his chests; and this when he knows there be laws and public officers, armed to revenge all injuries shall be done him; what opinion he has of his fellow subjects, when he rides armed; of his fellow citizens, when he locks his doors; and of his children, and servants, when he locks his chests. Does he not there as much accuse mankind by his actions as I do by my words? But neither of us accuse man's nature in it. The desires and other passions of man are in themselves no sin. No more are the actions that proceed from those passions till they know a law that forbids them; which, till laws be made, they cannot know; nor can any law be made till they have agreed upon the person that shall make it.

[63] 11. It may peradventure be thought there was never such a time nor condition of war as this; and I believe it was never generally so, over all the world; but there are many places where they live so now. For the savage people in many places of America, except the government of small families, the concord whereof dependeth on natural lust, have no government at all, and live at this day in that brutish manner, as I said before. Howsoever, it may be perceived what manner of life there would be, where there were no common power to fear, by the manner of life which men that have formerly lived under a peaceful government use to degenerate into a civil war.

12. But though there had never been any time wherein particular men were in a condition of war one against another; yet in all times kings and persons of sovereign authority, because of their independency, are in continual jealousies, and in the state and posture of gladiators, having their weapons pointing and their eyes

fixed on one another, that is, their forts, garrisons, and guns upon the frontiers of their kingdoms, and continual spies upon their neighbours, which is a posture of war. But because they uphold thereby the industry of their subjects, there does not follow from it that misery which accompanies the liberty of particular men.

In such a war nothing is unjust.

13. To this war of every man against every man, this also is consequent; that nothing can be unjust. The notions of right and wrong, justice and injustice, have there no place. Where there is no common power, there is no law; where no law, no injustice.[1] Force and fraud are in war the two cardinal virtues. Justice and injustice are none of the faculties neither of the body nor mind. If they were, they might be in a man that were alone in the world, as well as his senses and passions. They are qualities that relate to men in society, not in solitude. It is consequent also to the same condition that there be no propriety, no dominion, no *mine* and *thine* distinct; but only that to be every man's that he can get, and for so long as he can keep it. And thus much for the ill condition which man by mere nature is actually placed in; though with a possibility to come out of it, consisting partly in the passions, partly in his reason.

The passions that incline men to peace.

14. The passions that incline men to peace are fear of death,[2] desire of such things as are necessary to commodious living, and a hope by their industry to obtain them. And reason suggesteth convenient articles of peace upon which men may be drawn to agreement. These articles are they which otherwise are called the laws of nature, whereof I shall speak more particularly in the two following chapters.

---

1 Cf. 14.7.

2 See also 27.19.

[64]

# CHAPTER XIV

## OF THE FIRST AND SECOND NATURAL LAWS, AND OF CONTRACTS

Right of nature what.

1. The right of nature, which writers commonly call *jus naturale*, is the liberty each man hath to use his own power as he will himself for the preservation of his own nature; that is to say, of his own life; and consequently, of doing anything which, in his own judgement and reason, he shall conceive to be the aptest means thereunto.

Liberty what.

2. By LIBERTY is understood, according to the proper signification of the word, the absence of external impediments; which impediments may oft take away part of a man's power to do what he would, but cannot hinder him from using the power left him according as his judgement and reason shall dictate to him.[1]

A law of nature what.

3. A LAW OF NATURE (*lex naturalis*) is a precept or general rule,[2] found out by reason, by which a man is forbidden to do that which is destructive of his life, or taketh away the means of preserving the same, and to omit that by which he thinketh it may be best preserved. For though they that speak of this subject use to confound *jus* and *lex*, *right* and *law*; yet they ought to be distinguished, because right consisteth in liberty to do or to forbear; whereas law determineth and bindeth to one of them; so that law and right differ as much as obligation and liberty,[3] which in one and the same matter are inconsistent.[4]

Difference of right and law.

Naturally every man has right to every thing.

4. And because the condition of man (as hath been declared in the precedent chapter) is a condition of war of every one against every one, in which case every one is governed by his own reason, and there is nothing he can make use of that may not be a help unto him in preserving his life against his enemies; it followeth that in such a condition every man has a right to every thing, even to one another's body. And therefore, as long as this natural right of every man to every thing endureth, there can be no security to any man, how strong or wise soever he be, of living out the time

---

1 See also 21.1.

2 See also 25.1.

3 See also 26.43.

4 Cf. 21.10.

which nature ordinarily alloweth men to live. And consequently it is a precept, or general rule of reason *that every man ought to endeavour peace, as far as he has hope of obtaining it; and when he cannot obtain it, that he may seek and use all helps and advantages of war.*[1] The first branch of which rule containeth the first and fundamental law of nature, which is *to seek peace and follow it.* The second, the sum of the right of nature, which is *by all means we can to defend ourselves.*

The fundamental law of nature, to seek peace.

5. From this fundamental law of nature, by which men are commanded to endeavour peace, is derived this second law: *that a man be willing, when others are so too, as far forth as for peace and defense of himself he shall think it necessary, to lay down this right to all things; and be contented with so much liberty against other men as he would allow other men against himself.* For as long as every man holdeth this right of doing anything he liketh, so long are all men in the condition of war. But if other men will not lay down their right, as well as he, then there is no reason for anyone to divest himself of his, for that were to expose himself to prey, which no man is bound to, rather than to dispose himself to peace. This is that law of the gospel: *Whatsoever you require that others should do to you, that do ye to them.*[2] And that law of all men, *quod tibi fieri non vis, alteri ne feceris [What you do not want done to you, do not do to another].*

The second law of nature. Contract in way of peace.

[65]

6. To *lay down* a man's *right* to anything is to *divest* himself of the *liberty* of hindering another of the benefit of his own right to the same. For he that renounceth or passeth away his right giveth not to any other man a right which he had not before, because there is nothing to which every man had not right by nature, but only standeth out of his way that he may enjoy his own original right without hindrance from him, not without hindrance from another. So that the effect which redoundeth to one man by another man's defect of right is but so much diminution of impediments to the use of his own right original.

What it is to lay down a right.

7. Right is laid aside either by simply renouncing it or by transferring it to another. By *simply* RENOUNCING, when he cares not

Renouncing a right what it is.

---

1 The fundamental precept or general rule consists of two parts: the first part is the first or fundamental law of nature; the second part is the right of nature.

2 Hobbes is wrong about what is "the law of the gospel." The gospel recommends, "Whatsoever you wish others to do to you, that do ye to them" (Matt. 7:12). At 15.35, Hobbes gives the so-called negative Golden Rule: "*Do not that to another which thou wouldest not have done to thyself.*"

Transferring right what. to whom the benefit thereof redoubeth. By TRANSFERRING, when he intendeth the benefit thereof to some certain person or persons. And when a man hath in either manner abandoned or Obligation. granted away his right, then is he said to be OBLIGED or BOUND, not to hinder those to whom such right is granted, or abandoned, Duty. from the benefit of it; and that he *ought*, and it is DUTY, not to make void that voluntary act of his own; and that such hindrance Injustice. is INJUSTICE and INJURY, as being *sine jure*; the right being before renounced or transferred. So that *injury* or *injustice*, in the controversies of the world, is somewhat like to that which in the disputations of scholars is called *absurdity*. For as it is there called an absurdity to contradict what one maintained in the beginning, so in the world it is called injustice and injury voluntarily to undo that which from the beginning he had voluntarily done. The way by which a man either simply renounceth or transferreth his right is a declaration or signification by some voluntary and sufficient sign or signs that he doth so renounce or transfer or hath so renounced or transferred the same to him that accepteth it. And these signs are either words only, or actions only; or, as it happeneth most often, both words and actions. And the same are the BONDS, by which men are bound and obliged, bonds that have their strength, not from their own nature (for nothing is more easily broken than a man's word), but from fear of some evil consequence upon the rupture.

8. Whensoever a man transferreth his right, or renounceth it, it is either in consideration of some right reciprocally transferred to [66] himself, or for some other good he hopeth for thereby. For it is a voluntary act; and of the voluntary acts of every man, the object is some *good to himself*. And therefore there be some rights which no Not all rights are alienable. man can be understood by any words, or other signs, to have abandoned or transferred. As first a man cannot lay down the right of resisting them that assault him by force to take away his life, because he cannot be understood to aim thereby at any good to himself. The same may be said of wounds, and chains, and imprisonment, both because there is no benefit consequent to such patience, as there is to the patience of suffering another to be wounded or imprisoned, as also because a man cannot tell when

he seeth men proceed against him by violence whether they intend his death or not. And lastly the motive and end for which this renouncing and transferring of right is introduced is nothing else but the security of a man's person in his life, and in the means of so preserving life as not to be weary of it. And therefore if a man by words, or other signs, seem to despoil himself of the end for which those signs were intended, he is not to be understood as if he meant it, or that it was his will, but that he was ignorant of how such words and actions were to be interpreted.

9. The mutual transferring of right is that which men call CONTRACT. Contract what.

10. There is difference between transferring of right to the thing, and transferring or tradition, that is, delivery of the thing itself. For the thing may be delivered together with the translation of the right, as in buying and selling with ready money, or exchange of goods or lands; and it may be delivered some time after.

11. Again, one of the contractors may deliver the thing contracted for on his part, and leave the other to perform his part at some determinate time after, and in the meantime be trusted; and then the contract on his part is called PACT or COVENANT; or both parts may contract now to perform hereafter, in which cases he that is to perform in time to come, being trusted, his performance is called *keeping of promise*, or faith, and the failing of performance, if it be voluntary, *violation of faith*. Covenant what.

12. When the transferring of right is not mutual, but one of the parties transferreth in hope to gain thereby friendship or service from another or from his friends; or in hope to gain the reputation of charity or magnanimity; or to deliver his mind from the pain of compassion; or in hope of reward in heaven; this is not contract, but GIFT, FREE GIFT, GRACE; which words signify one and the same thing. Free gift.

13. Signs of contract are either *express* or *by inference*. Express are words spoken with understanding of what they signify; and such words are either of the time *present* or *past*, as, *I give*, *I grant*, *I have given*, *I have granted*, *I will that this be yours*; or of the future, as, *I will give*, *I will grant*, which words of the future are called PROMISE. Signs of contract express.

Signs of contract by inference.

14. Signs by inference are sometimes the consequence of words, sometimes the consequence of silence, sometimes the consequence of actions, sometimes the consequence of forbearing an
[67] action, and generally a sign by inference, of any contract, is whatsoever sufficiently argues the will of the contractor.

Free gift passeth by words of the present or past.

15. Words alone, if they be of the time to come, and contain a bare promise, are an insufficient sign of a free gift and therefore not obligatory. For if they be of the time to come, as, *tomorrow I will give*, they are a sign I have not given yet, and consequently that my right is not transferred, but remaineth till I transfer it by some other act. But if the words be of the time present or past, as, *I have given*, or *do give to be delivered tomorrow*, then is my tomorrow's right given away today; and that by the virtue of the words, though there were no other argument of my will. And there is a great difference in the signification of these words, *volo hoc tuum esse cras*, and *cras dabo*; that is, between *I will that this be thine tomorrow*, and, *I will give it thee tomorrow*, for the word *I will*, in the former manner of speech, signifies an act of the will present; but in the latter, it signifies a promise of an act of the will to come; and therefore the former words, being of the present, transfer a future right; the latter, that be of the future, transfer nothing. But if there be other signs of the will to transfer a right besides words, then, though the gift be free, yet may the right be understood to pass by words of the future, as if a man propound a prize to him that comes first to the end of a race, the gift is free; and though the words be of the future, yet the right passeth, for if he would not have his words so be understood, he should not have let them run.

Signs of contract are words both of the past, present, and future.

16. In contracts the right passeth, not only where the words are of the time present or past, but also where they are of the future, because all contract is mutual translation or change of right; and therefore he that promiseth only, because he hath already received the benefit for which he promiseth, is to be understood as if he intended the right should pass, for unless he had been content to have his words so understood, the other would not have performed his part first. And for that cause, in buying and selling, and other acts of contract, a promise is equivalent to a covenant, and therefore obligatory.

17. He that performeth first in the case of a contract is said to MERIT that which he is to receive by the performance of the other, and he hath it as *due*. Also when a prize is propounded to many, which is to be given to him only that winneth, or money is thrown amongst many to be enjoyed by them that catch it, though this be a free gift; yet so to win or so to catch is to *merit*, and to have it as DUE. For the right is transferred in the propounding of the prize and in throwing down the money, though it be not determined to whom, but by the event of the contention. But there is between these two sorts of merit this difference, that in contract I merit by virtue of my own power and the contractor's need, but in this case of free gift I am enabled to merit only by the benignity of the giver; in contract I merit at the contractor's hand that he should depart with his right; in this case of gift, I merit not [68] that the giver should part with his right, but that when he has parted with it, it should be mine rather than another's. And this I think to be the meaning of that distinction of the Schools between *meritum congrui* and *meritum condigni*. For God Almighty, having promised paradise to those men, hoodwinked with carnal desires, that can walk through this world according to the precepts and limits prescribed by him, they say he that shall so walk shall merit paradise *ex congruo* [*from its appropriateness*]. But because no man can demand a right to it by his own righteousness, or any other power in himself, but by the free grace of God only, they say no man can merit paradise *ex condigno [from being deserved]*. This, I say, I think is the meaning of that distinction; but because disputers do not agree upon the signification of their own terms of art longer than it serves their turn, I will not affirm anything of their meaning; only this I say; when a gift is given indefinitely, as a prize to be contended for, he that winneth meriteth, and may claim the prize as due.

Merit what.

18. If a covenant be made wherein neither of the parties perform presently, but trust one another, in the condition of mere nature (which is a condition of war of every man against every man) upon any reasonable suspicion, it is void; but if there be a common power set over them both, with right and force sufficient to compel performance, it is not void. For he that performeth first has no assurance the other will perform after, because the bonds of

Covenants of mutual trust, when invalid.

words are too weak to bridle men's ambition, avarice, anger, and other passions, without the fear of some coercive power; which in the condition of mere nature, where all men are equal, and judges of the justness of their own fears, cannot possibly be supposed. And therefore he which performeth first does but betray himself to his enemy, contrary to the right he can never abandon of defending his life and means of living.

19. But in a civil estate, where there a power set up to constrain those that would otherwise violate their faith, that fear is no more reasonable; and for that cause, he which by the covenant is to perform first is obliged so to do.

20. The cause of fear, which maketh such a covenant invalid, must be always something arising after the covenant made, as some new fact or other sign of the will not to perform, else it cannot make the covenant void. For that which could not hinder a man from promising ought not to be admitted as a hindrance of performing.

Right to the end, containeth right to the means.

21. He that transferreth any right transferreth the means of enjoying it, as far as lieth in his power. As he that selleth land is understood to transfer the herbage and whatsoever grows upon it; nor can he that sells a mill turn away the stream that drives it. And they that give to a man the right of government in sovereignty are understood to give him the right of levying money to maintain soldiers, and of appointing magistrates for the administration of justice.

No covenant with beasts.

22. To make covenants with brute beasts is impossible, because not understanding our speech, they understand not, nor accept of
[69] any translation of right, nor can translate any right to another; and without mutual acceptation, there is no covenant.

Nor with God without special revelation.

23. To make covenant with God is impossible but by mediation of such as God speaketh to either by revelation supernatural or by his lieutenants that govern under him and in his name; for otherwise we know not whether our covenants be accepted or not. And therefore they that vow anything contrary to any law of nature, vow in vain, as being a thing unjust to pay such vow. And if it be a thing commanded by the law of nature, it is not the vow, but the law that binds them.

24. The matter or subject of a covenant is always something that falleth under deliberation; for to covenant is an act of the will, that is to say, an act, and the last act, of deliberation, and is therefore always understood to be something to come, and which judged possible for him that covenanteth to perform.

No covenant, but of possible and future.

25. And therefore, to promise that which is known to be impossible is no covenant. But if that prove impossible afterwards, which before was thought possible, the covenant is valid and bindeth, though not to the thing itself, yet to the value; or, if that also be impossible, to the unfeigned endeavour of performing as much as is possible, for to more no man can be obliged.

26. Men are freed of their covenants two ways, by performing or by being forgiven. For performance is the natural end of obligation, and forgiveness the restitution of liberty, as being a retransferring of that right in which the obligation consisted.

Covenants, how made void.

27. Covenants entered into by fear, in the condition of mere nature, are obligatory.[1] For example, if I covenant to pay a ransom or service for my life to an enemy, I am bound by it. For it is a contract, wherein one receiveth the benefit of life, the other is to receive money or service for it; and consequently, where no other law (as in the condition of mere nature) forbiddeth the performance, the covenant is valid. Therefore prisoners of war, if trusted with the payment of their ransom, are obliged to pay it; and if a weaker prince make a disadvantageous peace with a stronger, for fear, he is bound to keep it, unless (as hath been said before) there ariseth some new and just cause of fear to renew the war. And even in commonwealths, if I be forced to redeem myself from a thief by promising him money, I am bound to pay it, till the civil law discharge me. For whatsoever I may lawfully do without obligation, the same I may lawfully covenant to do through fear; and what I lawfully covenant, I cannot lawfully break.

Covenants extorted by fear are valid.

28. A former covenant makes void a later. For a man that hath passed away his right to one man today hath it not to pass tomorrow to another; and therefore the later promise passeth no right, but is null.

The former covenant to one makes void the later to another.

1 See also 21.3.

*A man's covenant not to defend himself is void.*

[70]

29. A covenant not to defend myself from force, by force, is always void. For (as I have shown before) no man can transfer or lay down his right to save himself from death, wounds, and imprisonment, the avoiding whereof is the only end of laying down any right; and therefore the promise of not resisting force, in no covenant transferreth any right, nor is obliging. For though a man may covenant thus, *unless I do so, or so, kill me*; he cannot covenant thus, *unless I do so, or so, I will not resist you when you come to kill me.* For man by nature chooseth the lesser evil, which is danger of death in resisting, rather than the greater, which is certain and present death in not resisting. And this is granted to be true by all men in that they lead criminals to execution and prison with armed men, notwithstanding that such criminals have consented to the law by which they are condemned.

*No man obliged to accuse himself.*

30. A covenant to accuse oneself, without assurance of pardon, is likewise invalid. For in the condition of nature where every man is judge, there is no place for accusation; and in the civil state the accusation is followed with punishment, which, being force, a man is not obliged not to resist. The same is also true of the accusation of those by whose condemnation a man falls into misery, as of a father, wife, or benefactor. For the testimony of such an accuser, if it be not willingly given, is presumed to be corrupted by nature, and therefore not to be received; and where a man's testimony is not to be credited, he is not bound to give it. Also accusations upon torture are not to be reputed as testimonies. For torture is to be used but as means of conjecture and light in the further examination and search of truth; and what is in that case confessed tendeth to the ease of him that is tortured, not to the informing of the torturers, and therefore ought not to have the credit of a sufficient testimony, for whether he deliver himself by true or false accusation, he does it by the right of preserving his own life.

*The end of an oath.*

31. The force of words being (as I have formerly noted) too weak to hold men to the performance of their covenants, there are in man's nature but two imaginable helps to strengthen it. And those are either a fear of the consequence of breaking their word or a glory or pride in appearing not to need to break it. This latter is a generosity too rarely found to be presumed on, especially in the pursuers of wealth, command, or sensual pleasure, which are

the greatest part of mankind. The passion to be reckoned upon is fear; whereof there be two very general objects: one, the power of spirits invisible; the other, the power of those men they shall therein offend. Of these two, though the former be the greater power; yet the fear of the latter is commonly the greater fear. The fear of the former is in every man his own religion, which hath place in the nature of man before civil society. The latter hath not so, at least not place enough to keep men to their promises, because in the condition of mere nature, the inequality of power is not discerned, but by the event of battle. So that before the time of civil society, or in the interruption thereof by war, there is nothing can strengthen a covenant of peace agreed on against the temptations of avarice, ambition, lust, or other strong desire, but the fear of that invisible power which they every one worship as God, and fear as a revenger of their perfidy. All therefore that can be done between two men not subject to civil power is to put one another to swear [71] by the God he feareth; which *swearing*, or OATH, is a *form of speech, added to a promise, by which he that promiseth signifieth that unless he perform he renounceth the mercy of his God, or calleth to him for vengeance on himself.* Such was the heathen form, *Let Jupiter kill me else, as I kill this beast.* So is our form, *I shall do thus, and thus, so help me God.* And this, with the rites and ceremonies which every one useth in his own religion, that the fear of breaking faith might be the greater.

The form of an oath.

No oath, but by God.

32. By this it appears that an oath taken according to any other form or rite than his that sweareth is in vain and no oath; and that there is no swearing by anything which the swearer thinks not God. For though men have sometimes used to swear by their kings, for fear, or flattery; yet they would have it thereby understood they attributed to them divine honour. And that swearing unnecessarily by God is but profaning of his name; and swearing by other things, as men do in common discourse, is not swearing, but an impious custom, gotten by too much vehemence of talking.

An oath adds nothing to the obligation.

33. It appears also that the oath adds nothing to the obligation. For a covenant, if lawful, binds in the sight of God, without the oath, as much as with it; if unlawful, bindeth not at all, though it be confirmed with an oath.

## CHAPTER XV

## OF OTHER LAWS OF NATURE

The third law of nature, Justice.

1. From that law of nature by which we are obliged to transfer to another such rights as, being retained, hinder the peace of mankind, there followeth a third, which is this; *that men perform their covenants made*; without which, covenants are in vain and but empty words; and the right of all men to all things remaining, we are still in the condition of war.

Justice and injustice what.

2. And in this law of nature consisteth the fountain and original of JUSTICE. For where no covenant hath preceded, there hath no right been transferred; and every man has right to everything; and consequently, no action can be unjust. But when a covenant is made, then to break it is *unjust* and the definition of INJUSTICE is no other than *the not performance of covenant*. And whatsoever is not unjust is *just*.[1]

Justice and propriety begin with the constitution of the commonwealth.

3. But because covenants of mutual trust, where there is a fear of not performance on either part (as hath been said in the former chapter), are invalid, though the original of justice be the making of covenants; yet injustice actually there can be none till the cause of such fear be taken away; which, while men are in the natural condition of war, cannot be done. Therefore before the names of *just* and *unjust* can have place, there must be some coercive power to compel men equally to the performance of their covenants by the terror of some punishment greater than the benefit they [72] expect by the breach of their covenant, and to make good that propriety which by mutual contract men acquire in recompense of the universal right they abandon; and such power there is none before the erection of a commonwealth. And this is also to be gathered out of the ordinary definition of justice in the Schools, for they say that *justice is the constant will of giving to every man his own*. And therefore where there is no *own*, that is, no propriety [property], there is no injustice; and where there is no coercive

1 'Just' and 'unjust' are normally contraries, not contradictories. However, Hobbes defines 'just' in such a way that it becomes the contradictory of 'unjust'. Taking his definitions strictly, anyone in the state of nature who makes no covenants is just, because he is not unjust.

power erected, that is, where there is no commonwealth, there is no propriety, all men having right to all things; therefore where there is no commonwealth, there nothing is unjust. So that the nature of justice consisteth in keeping of valid covenants; but the validity of covenants begins not but with the constitution of a civil power sufficient to compel men to keep them; and then it is also that propriety begins.

Justice not contrary to reason.

4. The fool hath said in his heart, there is no such thing as justice; and sometimes also with his tongue, seriously alleging that every man's conservation and contentment being committed to his own care, there could be no reason why every man might not do what he thought conduced thereunto; and therefore also to make or not make, keep or not keep covenants was not against reason when it conduced to one's benefit. He does not therein deny that there be covenants; and that they are sometimes broken, sometimes kept; and that such breach of them may be called injustice, and the observance of them justice; but he questioneth whether injustice, taking away the fear of God (for the same fool hath said in his heart there is no God), not sometimes stand with that reason which dictateth to every man his own good; and particularly then, when it conduceth to such a benefit as shall put a man in a condition to neglect not only the dispraise and revilings, but also the power of other men. The kingdom of God is gotten by violence; but what if it could be gotten by unjust violence? Were it against reason so to get it, when it is impossible to receive hurt by it? And if it be not against reason, it is not against justice; or else justice is not to be approved for good. From such reasoning as this, successful wickedness hath obtained the name of virtue; and some that in all other things have disallowed the violation of faith, yet have allowed it when it is for the getting of a kingdom. And the heathen that believed that Saturn was deposed by his son Jupiter believed nevertheless the same Jupiter to be the avenger of injustice, somewhat like to a piece of law in Coke's[1] *Commentaries on Littleton*, where he says, if the right heir of the crown be

---

1 Edward Coke (1552-1634) was England's leading theorist of the common law. This sometimes put him into opposition to King James I and later Charles I. His commentaries on the *Tenures* of Sir Thomas Littleton (c. 1422-81), an English jurist, are among his most famous works.

attainted of treason, yet the crown shall descend to him, and *eo instante* the attainder be void; from which instances a man will be very prone to infer that when the heir apparent of a kingdom shall kill him that is in possession, though his father, you may call it injustice or by what other name you will; yet it can never be against reason, seeing all the voluntary actions of men tend to the benefit of themselves; and those actions are most reasonable that
[73] conduce most to their ends. This specious reasoning is nevertheless false.

5. For the question is not of promises mutual, where there is no security of performance on either side, as when there is no civil power erected over the parties promising, for such promises are no covenants; but either where one of the parties has performed already or where there is a power to make him perform, there is the question whether it be against reason, that is, against the benefit of the other to perform or not. And I say it is not against reason. For the manifestation whereof we are to consider, first, that when a man doth a thing, which notwithstanding anything can be foreseen and reckoned on tendeth to his own destruction, howsoever some accident, which he could not expect, arriving may turn it to his benefit; yet such events do not make it reasonably or wisely done. Secondly, that in a condition of war, wherein every man to every man, for want of a common power to keep them all in awe, is an enemy, there is no man can hope by his own strength or wit to himself from destruction without the help of confederates, where every one expects the same defence by the confederation that any one else does; and therefore he which declares he thinks it reason to deceive those that help him can in reason expect no other means of safety than what can be had from his own single power. He, therefore, that breaketh his covenant and consequently declareth that he thinks he may with reason do so, cannot be received into any society that unite themselves for peace and defence but by the error of them that receive him; nor when he is received be retained in it without seeing the danger of their error; which errors a man cannot reasonably reckon upon as the means of his security; and therefore if he be left or cast out of society, he perisheth; and if he live in society, it is by the errors of other men, which he could not foresee nor reckon upon, and consequently

against the reason of his preservation; and so, as all men that contribute not to his destruction forbear him only out of ignorance of what is good for themselves.

6. As for the instance of gaining the secure and perpetual felicity of heaven by any way, it is frivolous; there being but one way imaginable, and that is not breaking, but keeping of covenant.

7. And for the other instance of attaining sovereignty by rebellion, it is manifest that, though the event follow; yet because it cannot reasonably be expected, but rather the contrary, and because, by gaining it so, others are taught to gain the same in like manner, the attempt thereof is against reason. Justice therefore, that is to say, keeping of covenant, is a rule of reason by which we are forbidden to do anything destructive to our life, and consequently a law of nature.

8. There be some that proceed further and will not have the law of nature to be those rules which conduce to the preservation of man's life on earth, but to the attaining of an eternal felicity after death, to which [felicity] they think the breach of covenant may conduce and consequently be just and reasonable; such are they that think it a work of merit to kill or depose or rebel against [74] the sovereign power constituted over them by their own consent. But because there is no natural knowledge of man's estate after death, much less of the reward that is then to be given to breach of faith, but only a belief grounded upon other men's saying that they know it supernaturally or that they know those that knew them that knew others that knew it supernaturally, breach of faith cannot be called a precept of reason or nature.

Covenants not discharged by the vice of the person to whom they are made.

9. Others, that allow for a law of nature the keeping of faith, do nevertheless make exception of certain persons, as heretics, and such as use not to perform their covenant to others; and this also is against reason. For if any fault of a man be sufficient to discharge our covenant made, the same ought in reason to have been sufficient to have hindered the making of it.

Justice of men, & justice of actions what.

10. The names of *just* and *unjust*, when they are attributed to men, signify one thing, and, when they are attributed to actions, another. When they are attributed to men, they signify conformity or inconformity of manners to reason. But when they are attributed to action they signify the conformity or inconformity

to reason, not of manners, or manner of life, but of particular actions. A just man therefore is he that taketh all the care he can that his actions may be all just; and an unjust man is he that neglecteth it. And such men are more often in our language styled by the names of righteous and unrighteous than just and unjust though the meaning be the same. Therefore a righteous man does not lose that title by one or a few unjust actions that proceed from sudden passion or mistake of things or persons; nor does an unrighteous man lose his character for such actions as he does or forbears to do for fear, because his will is not framed by the justice, but by the apparent benefit of what he is to do. That which gives to human actions the relish of justice is a certain nobleness or gallantness of courage, rarely found, by which a man scorns to be beholding for the contentment of his life to fraud or breach of promise. This justice of the manners is that which is meant where justice is called a virtue; and injustice, a vice.

11. But the justice of actions denominates men, not just, but *guiltless*; and the injustice of the same (which is also called injury) gives them but the name of *guilty*.

Justice of manners and justice of actions.

12. Again, the injustice of manners is the disposition or aptitude to do injury, and is injustice before it proceed to act and without supposing any individual person injured. But the injustice of an action (that is to say, injury) supposeth an individual person injured; namely him to whom the covenant was made; and therefore many times the injury is received by one man when the damage redoundeth to another. As when the master commandeth his servant to give money to a stranger; if it be not done, the injury is done to the master, whom he had before covenanted to obey; but the damage redoundeth to the stranger, to whom he had no obligation, and therefore could not injure him. And so also in [75] commonwealths private men may remit to one another their debts, but not robberies or other violences, whereby they are endamaged, because the detaining of debt is an injury to themselves; but robbery and violence are injuries to the person of the commonwealth.

Nothing done to a man by his own consent can be injury.

13. Whatsoever is done to a man, conformable to his own will signified to the doer, is not injury to him. For if he that doeth it hath not passed away his original right to do what he please by some antecedent covenant, there is no breach of covenant, and

therefore no injury done him. And if he have, then his will to have it done, being signified, is a release of that covenant, and so again there is no injury done him.

14. Justice of actions is by writers divided into *commutative* and *distributive*; and the former they say consisteth in proportion arithmetical; the latter in proportion geometrical. Commutative, therefore, they place in the equality of value of the things contracted for; and distributive, in the distribution of equal benefit to men of equal merit. As if it were injustice to sell dearer than we buy, or to give more to a man than he merits. The value of all things contracted for is measured by the appetite of the contractors, and therefore the just value is that which they be contented to give. And merit (besides that which is by covenant, where the performance on one part meriteth the performance of the other part, and falls under justice commutative, not distributive) is not due by justice, but is rewarded of grace only. And therefore this distinction, in the sense wherein it useth to be expounded, is not right. To speak properly, commutative justice is the justice of a contractor; that is, a performance of covenant in buying and selling, hiring and letting to hire, lending and borrowing, exchanging, bartering, and other acts of contract.

Justice commutative and distributive.

15. And distributive justice [is] the justice of an arbitrator, that is to say, the act of defining what is just. Wherein, being trusted by them that make him arbitrator, if he perform his trust, he is said to distribute to every man his own; and this is indeed just distribution, and may be called, though improperly, distributive justice, but more properly equity, which also is a law of nature, as shall be shown in due place.

16. As justice dependeth on antecedent covenant, so does GRATITUDE depend on antecedent grace, that is to say, antecedent free gift, and is the fourth law of nature, which may be conceived in this form: *that a man which receiveth benefit from another of mere grace endeavour that he which giveth it have no reasonable cause to repent him of his good will.* For no man giveth but with intention of good to himself, because gift is voluntary; and of all voluntary acts, the object is to every man his own good; of which, if men see [that] they shall be frustrated, there will be no beginning of benevolence or trust, nor consequently of mutual help, nor of reconciliation of one man to another; and therefore they are to remain still in the

The fourth law of nature, gratitude.

[76]

condition of *war*, which is contrary to the first and fundamental law of nature which commandeth men to *seek peace*. The breach
[76] of this law is called *ingratitude* and hath the same relation to grace that injustice hath to obligation by covenant.

The fifth, mutual accommodation or complaisance.

17. A fifth law of nature is COMPLAISANCE; that is to say, *that every man strive to accommodate himself to the rest*. For the understanding whereof we may consider that there is in men's aptness to society a diversity of nature, rising from their diversity of affections, not unlike to that we see in stones brought together for building of an edifice. For as that stone which by the asperity and irregularity of figure takes more room from others than itself fills, and for hardness cannot be easily made plain, and thereby hindereth the building, is by the builders cast away as unprofitable and troublesome; so also, a man that by asperity of nature will strive to retain those things which to himself are superfluous and to others necessary, and for the stubbornness of his passions cannot be corrected, is to be left or cast out of society as cumbersome thereunto. For seeing every man, not only by right, but also by necessity of nature, is supposed to endeavour all he can to obtain that which is necessary for his conservation, he that shall oppose himself against it for things superfluous is guilty of the war that thereupon is to follow, and therefore doth that which is contrary to the fundamental law of nature, which commandeth *to seek peace*. The observers of this law may be called SOCIABLE, (the Latins call them *commodi*); the contrary, *stubborn*, *insociable*, *forward*, *intractable*.

The sixth, facility to pardon.

18. A sixth law of nature is this: *that upon caution of the future time, a man ought to pardon the offences past of them that, repenting, desire it*. For PARDON is nothing but granting of peace, which though granted to them that persevere in their hostility, be not peace, but fear; yet not granted to them that give caution of the future time is sign of an aversion to peace and therefore contrary to the law of nature.

The seventh, that in revenges men respect on the future good.

19. A seventh is, *that in revenges* (that is, retribution of evil for evil), *men look not at the greatness of the evil past, but the greatness of the good to follow*. Whereby we are forbidden to inflict punishment with any other design than for correction of the offender or direction of others. For this law is consequent to the next before it, that commandeth pardon upon security of the future time. Besides,

revenge without respect to the example and profit to come is a triumph or glorying in the hurt of another, tending to no end (for the end is always somewhat to come); and glorying to no end is vain-glory and contrary to reason; and to hurt without reason tendeth to the introduction of war, which is against the law of nature, and is commonly styled by the name of *cruelty*.

The eighth, against contumely.

20. And because all signs of hatred or contempt provoke to fight, insomuch as most men choose rather to hazard their life than not to be revenged, we may in the eighth place, for a law of nature, set down this precept; *that no man by deed, word, countenance, or gesture, declare hatred or contempt of another.* The breach of which law is commonly called *contumely*.

The ninth, against pride. [77]

21. The question who is the better man has no place in the condition of mere nature, where (as has been shown before) all men are equal. The inequality that now is has been introduced by the laws civil. I know that Aristotle in the first book of his *Politics*, for a foundation of his doctrine, maketh men by nature, some more worthy to command, meaning the wiser sort, such as he thought himself to be for his philosophy; others to serve, meaning those that had strong bodies, but were not philosophers as he, as master and servant were not introduced by consent of men, but by difference of wit; which is not only against reason, but also against experience. For there are very few so foolish that had not rather govern themselves than be governed by others; nor when the wise, in their own conceit, contend by force with them who distrust their own wisdom, do they always, or often, or almost at any time, get the victory. If nature therefore have made men equal, that equality is to be acknowledged; or if nature have made men unequal, yet because men that think themselves equal will not enter into conditions of peace, but upon equal terms, such equality must be admitted. And therefore for the ninth law of nature, I put this, *that every man acknowledge another for his equal by nature.* The breach of this precept is *pride*.

The tenth, against arrogance.

22. On this law dependeth another, *that at the entrance into conditions of peace, no man require to reserve to himself any right which he is not content should be reserved to every one of the rest.* As it is necessary for all men that seek peace to lay down certain rights of nature, that is to say, not to have liberty to do all they list, so is it necessary

for man's life to retain some, as right to govern their own bodies, enjoy air, water, motion, ways to go from place to place, and all things else without which a man cannot live or not live well. If in this case, at the making of peace, men require for themselves that which they would not have to be granted to others, they do contrary to the precedent law that commandeth the acknowledgement of natural equality, and therefore also against the law of nature. The observers of this law are those we call *modest*, and the breakers *arrogant* men. The Greeks call the violation of this law *pleonexia,* that is, a desire of more than their share.

The eleventh, equity.

23. Also, if *a man be trusted to judge between man and man,* it is a precept of the law of nature *that he deal equally between them.* For without that, the controversies of men cannot be determined but by war. He therefore that is partial in judgement doth what in him lies to deter men from the use of judges and arbitrators, and consequently (against the fundamental law of nature) is the cause of war.

24. The observance of this law, from the equal distribution to each man of that which in reason belonged to him, is called EQUITY, and (as I have said before) distributive justice; the violation, *acception of persons, prosopolepsia.*

The twelfth, equal use of things common.

25. And from this followeth another law: *that such things as cannot be divided be enjoyed in common, if it can be; and if the quantity of the thing permit, without stint; otherwise proportionably to the number of them that have right.* For otherwise the distribution is unequal, and contrary to equity.

The thirteenth, of lot.

26. But some things there be that can neither be divided nor enjoyed in common. Then, the law of nature which prescribeth
[78] equity requireth, *that the entire right, or else (making the use alternate) the first possession, be determined by lot.* For equal distribution is of the law of nature; and other means of equal distribution cannot be imagined.

The fourteenth, of primogeniture, and first seizing.

27. Of *lots* there be two sorts, *arbitrary* and *natural.* Arbitrary is that which is agreed on by the competitors; natural is either *primogeniture* (which the Greek calls *klerovomia,* which signifies, *given by lot*) or *first seizure.*

28. And therefore those things which cannot be enjoyed in common, nor divided, ought to be adjudged to the first possessor; and in some cases to the first born, as acquired by lot.

29. It is also a law of nature, *that all men that mediate peace be allowed safe conduct.* For the law that commandeth peace, as the *end*, commandeth intercession, as the *means*; and to intercession the means is safe conduct.

The fifteenth, of mediators.

30. And because, though men be never so willing to observe these laws, there may nevertheless arise questions concerning a man's action; first, whether it were done or not done; secondly, if done, whether against the law or not against the law; the former whereof is called a question *of fact*, the latter a question *of right*; therefore unless the parties to the question covenant mutually to stand to the sentence of another, they are as far from peace as ever. This other, to whose sentence they submit, is called an ARBITRATOR. And therefore it is of the law of nature *that they that are at controversy submit their right to the judgement of an arbitrator.*

The sixteenth, of submission to arbitrement.

31. And seeing every man is presumed to do all things in order to his own benefit, no man is a fit arbitrator in his own cause; and if he were never so fit, yet equity allowing to each party equal benefit, if one be admitted to be judge, the other is to be admitted also; and so the controversy, that is, the cause of war, remains, against the law of nature.

The seventeenth, no man is his own judge.

32. For the same reason no man in any cause ought to be received for arbitrator to whom greater profit or honour or pleasure apparently ariseth out of the victory of one party than of the other, for he hath taken (though an unavoidable bribe, yet) a bribe; and no man can be obliged to trust him. And thus also the controversy and the condition of war remaineth, contrary to the law of nature.

The eighteenth, no man is to be judge that has in him a natural cause of partiality.

33. And in a controversy of *fact*, the judge being to give no more credit to one than to the other, if there be no other arguments, must give credit to a third; or to a third and fourth; or more, for else the question is undecided, and left to force, contrary to the law of nature.

The nineteenth, of witnesses.

34. These are the laws of nature, dictating peace, for a means of the conservation of men in multitudes; and which only concern the doctrine of civil society. There be other things tending to the destruction of particular men, as drunkenness, and all other parts of intemperance, which may therefore also be reckoned amongst those things which the law of nature hath forbidden, but are

[79] not necessary to be mentioned, nor are pertinent enough to this place.

A rule by which the laws of nature may easily be examined.

35. And though this may seem too subtle a deduction of the laws of nature to be taken notice of by all men, whereof the most part are too busy in getting food, and the rest too negligent to understand; yet to leave all men inexcusable, they have been contracted into one easy sum, intelligible even to the meanest capacity; and that is: *Do not that to another which thou wouldest not have done to thyself;* which showeth him that he has no more to do in learning the laws of nature but, when weighing the actions of other men with his own they seem too heavy, to put them into the other part of the balance, and his own into their place, that his own passions and self-love may add nothing to the weight; and then there is none of these laws of nature that will not appear unto him very reasonable.

The laws of nature oblige in conscience always, but in effect then only where there is security.

36. The laws of nature oblige *in foro interno*, that is to say, they bind to a desire they should take place;[1] but *in foro externo*; that is, to the putting them in act, not always. For he that should be modest and tractable, and perform all he promises in such time and place where no man else should do so, should but make himself a prey to others, and procure his own certain ruin, contrary to the ground of all laws of nature which tend to nature's preservation. And again, he that having sufficient security that others shall observe the same laws towards him, observes them not himself, seeketh not peace, but war, and consequently the destruction of his nature by violence.

37. And whatsoever laws bind *in foro interno* may be broken, not only by a fact contrary to the law, but also by a fact according to it, in case a man think it contrary. For though his action in this case be according to the law; yet his purpose was against the law; which, where the obligation is *in foro interno*, is a breach.

The laws of nature are eternal;

38. The laws of nature are immutable and eternal, for injustice, ingratitude, arrogance, pride, iniquity, acception of persons, and the rest can never be made lawful. For it can never be that war shall preserve life, and peace destroy it.

And yet easy.

39. The same laws, because they oblige only to a desire and

---

1 See also 30.30.

endeavour, mean an unfeigned and constant endeavour, are easy to be observed. For in that they require nothing but endeavour, he that endeavoureth their performance fulfilleth them; and he that fulfilleth the law is just.

The science of these laws is the true moral philosophy.

40. And the science of them is the true and only moral philosophy. For moral philosophy is nothing else but the science of what is *good* and *evil* in the conversation [interactions] and society of mankind. *Good* and *evil* are names that signify our appetites and aversions, which in different tempers, customs, and doctrines of men are different; and divers men differ not only in their judgement on the senses of what is pleasant and unpleasant to the taste, smell, hearing, touch, and sight; but also of what is conformable or disagreeable to reason in the actions of common life. Nay, the same man, in divers times, differs from himself; and one time praiseth, that is, calleth *good*, what another time he dispraiseth, and calleth *evil*. From whence arise disputes, controversies, and at last [80] war. And therefore so long a man is in the condition of mere nature (which is a condition of war), as private appetite is the measure of good and evil; and consequently all men agree on this, that peace is good, and therefore also the way or means of peace, which (as I have shown before) are *justice*, *gratitude*, *modesty*, *equity*, *mercy*, and the rest of the laws of nature, are good; that is to say, *moral virtues*; and their contrary *vices*, evil. Now the science of virtue and vice is moral philosophy; and therefore the true doctrine of the laws of nature is the true moral philosophy. But the writers of moral philosophy, though they acknowledge the same virtues and vices; yet, not seeing wherein consisted their goodness, nor that they come to be praised as the means of peaceable, sociable, and comfortable living, place them in a mediocrity of passions, as if not the cause, but the degree of daring, made fortitude, or not the cause, but the quantity of a gift, made liberality.

41. These dictates of reason men used to call by the name of laws, but improperly; for they are but conclusions or theorems concerning what conduceth to the conservation and defence of themselves; whereas law, properly, is the word of him that by right hath command over others. But yet if we consider the same theorems as delivered in the word of God that by right commandeth all things, then are they properly called *laws*.

# CHAPTER XVI

## OF PERSONS, AUTHORS, AND THINGS PERSONATED

A person what.

1. A person is he *whose words or actions are considered, either as his own, or as representing the words or actions of another man, or of any other thing to whom they are attributed, whether truly or by fiction.*[1]

Person natural, and artificial.

2. When they are considered as his own, then is he called a *natural person*; and when they are considered as representing the words and actions of another, then is he a *feigned* or *artificial* person.

The word *person*, whence.

3. The word person is Latin, instead whereof the Greeks have *prosopon*, which signifies the *face*, as *persona* in Latin signifies the *disguise* or *outward appearance* of a man, counterfeited on the stage; and sometimes more particularly that part of it which disguiseth the face, as a mask or vizard; and from the stage hath been translated to any representer of speech and action, as well in tribunals as theatres. So that a *person* is the same that an *actor* is, both on the stage and in common conversation; and to *personate* is to *act* or *represent* himself or another; and he that acteth another is said to bear his person or act in his name (in which sense Cicero useth it where he says, *Unus sustineo tres personas: mei, adversarii, et judicis*; I bear three persons: my own, my adversary's, and the judge's), and is
[81] called in divers occasions, diversely, as a *representer*, or *representative*, a *lieutenant*, a *vicar*, an *attorney*, a *deputy*, a *procurator*, an *actor*, and the like.

Actor, author.

4. Of persons artificial, some have their words and actions *owned* by those whom they represent. And then the person is the *actor*; and he that owneth his words and actions is the AUTHOR, in which case the actor acteth by authority. For that which in speaking of goods and possessions is called an *owner*, and in Latin *dominus* in Greek *kurios*; speaking of actions, is called author. And as the right of possession is called dominion, so the right of doing any

Authority

action is called AUTHORITY and sometimes *warrant*. So that by authority is always understood a right of doing any act; and *done by*

---

1 See also 23.2 and 42.3.

*authority*, done by commission or license from him whose right it is.

5. From hence it followeth that when the actor maketh a covenant by authority, he bindeth thereby the author no less than if he had made it himself, and no less subjecteth him to all the consequences of the same. And therefore all that hath been said formerly (Chapter 14) of the nature of covenants between man and man in their natural capacity is true also when they are made by their actors, representers, or procurators, that have authority from them, so far forth as is in their commission, but no further.

Covenants by authority bind the author.

6. And therefore he that maketh a covenant with the actor, or representer, not knowing the authority he hath, doth it at his own peril. For no man is obliged by a covenant whereof he is not author, nor consequently by a covenant made against or beside the authority he gave.

7. When the actor doth anything against the law of nature by command of the author, if he be obliged by former covenant to obey him, not he, but the author breaketh the law of nature, for though the action be against the law of nature, yet it is not his; but, contrarily, to refuse to do it is against the law of nature that forbiddeth breach of covenant.

But not the actor.

8. And he that maketh a covenant with the author by mediation of the actor, not knowing what authority he hath, but only takes his word, in case such authority be not made manifest unto him upon demand, is no longer obliged; for the covenant made with the author is not valid without his counter-assurance. But if he that so covenanteth knew beforehand he was to expect no other assurance than the actor's word, then is the covenant valid, because the actor in this case maketh himself the author. And therefore, as when the authority is evident, the covenant obligeth the author, not the actor, so when the authority is feigned, it obligeth the actor only, there being no author but himself.

The authority is to be shown.

9. There are few things that are incapable of being represented by fiction. Inanimate things, as a church, a hospital, a bridge, may be personated by a rector, master, or overseer. But things inanimate cannot be authors, nor therefore give authority to their actors. Yet the actors may have authority to procure their maintenance, given them by those that are owners or governors of those [82]

Things personated, inanimate.

things. And therefore such things cannot be personated before there be some state of civil government.

Irrational. 10. Likewise children, fools, and madmen that have no use of reason may be personated by guardians or curators, but can be no authors during that time of any action done by them, longer than (when they shall recover the use of reason) they shall judge the same reasonable. Yet during the folly he that hath right of governing them may give authority to the guardian. But this again has no place but in a state civil, because before such estate there is no dominion of persons.

False gods. 11. An idol or mere figment of the brain may be personated, as were the gods of the heathen, which, by such officers as the state appointed, were personated and held possessions and other goods and rights, which men from time to time dedicated and consecrated unto them. But idols cannot be authors; for an idol is nothing. The authority proceeded from the state; and therefore before introduction of civil government the gods of the heathen could not be personated.

The true God. 12. The true God may be personated. As he was, first, by Moses, who governed the Israelites (that were not his, but God's people), not in his own name (with *hoc dicit Moses* [*thus Moses says*], but in God's name, with (*hoc dicit Dominus* [*thus the Lord says*]). Secondly, by the Son of Man, his own son, our blessed Saviour Jesus Christ, that came to reduce the Jews and induce all nations into the kingdom of his Father; not as of himself, but as sent from his Father. And thirdly, by the Holy Ghost or Comforter, speaking and working in the Apostles; which Holy Ghost was a Comforter that came not of himself, but was sent and proceeded from them both on the day of Pentecost.

A multitude of men, how one person. 13. A multitude of men are made *one* person when they are by one man, or one person, represented, so that it be done with the consent of every one of that multitude in particular. For it is the *unity* of the representer, not the *unity* of the represented, that maketh the person *one*. And it is the representer that beareth the person, and but one person; and *unity* cannot otherwise be understood in multitude.

Every one is author. 14. And because the multitude naturally is not *one*, but *many*, they cannot be understood for one, but in any authors, of everything their representative saith or doth in their name, every man giving their common representer authority from himself in particular, and owning all the actions the representer doth, in case they give him authority without stint; otherwise, when they limit him in what, and [in] how far, he shall represent them, none of them owneth more than they gave him commission to act.

An actor may be many men made one by plurality of voices.

15. And if the representative consist of many men, the voice of the greater number must be considered as the voice of them all. For if the lesser number pronounce (for example) in the affirmative, and the greater in the negative, there will be negatives more than enough to destroy the affirmatives; and thereby the excess of negatives, standing uncontradicted, are the only voice the repre- [83]
sentative hath.

Representatives, when the number is even, unprofitable.

16. And a representative of even number, especially when the number is not great, whereby the contradictory voices are oftentimes equal, is therefore oftentimes mute and incapable of action. Yet in some cases contradictory voices, equal in number, may determine a question (as [for example] in condemning or absolving, equality of votes, even in that they condemn not, do absolve) but not on the contrary condemn, in that they absolve not. For when a cause is heard, not to condemn is to absolve; but on the contrary to say that not absolving is condemning is not true. The like it is in deliberation of executing presently or deferring till another time; for when the voices are equal, the not decreeing execution is a decree of dilation.

Negative voice

17. Or if the number be odd, as three or more men or assemblies, whereof every one has, by a negative voice, authority to take away the effect of all the affirmative voices of the rest, this number is no representative; by the diversity of opinions and interests of men, it becomes oftentimes, and in cases of the greatest consequence, a mute person and unapt, as for many things else, so for the government of a multitude, especially in time of war.

18. Of authors there be two sorts. The first simply so called, which I have before defined to be him that owneth the action of another simply. The second is he that owneth an action or covenant of another conditionally; that is to say, he undertaketh to do it, if the other doth it not, at or before a certain time. And these authors conditional are generally called SURETIES, in Latin, *fidejussores* and *sponsores*; and particularly for debt, *praedes*; and for appearance before a judge or magistrate, *vades*.

# PART II

[85]

# OF COMMONWEALTH

## CHAPTER XVII

## OF THE CAUSES, GENERATION, AND DEFINITION OF A COMMONWEALTH

The end of commonwealth, particular security.

1. The final cause, end, or design of men (who naturally love liberty, and dominion over others) in the introduction of that restraint upon themselves (in which we see them live in commonwealths) is the foresight of their own preservation and of a more contented life thereby, that is to say, of getting themselves out from that miserable condition of war which is necessarily consequent (as hath been shown) to the natural passions of men, when there is no visible power to keep them in awe and tie them by fear of punishment[1] to the performance of their covenants and observation of those laws of nature set down in the fourteenth and fifteenth chapters.

Chap 13.

Which is not to be had from the law of nature.

2. For the laws of nature (as *justice, equity, modesty, mercy,* and, in sum, *doing to others as we would be done to*) of themselves, without the terror of some power to cause them to be observed, are contrary to our natural passions that carry us to partiality, pride, revenge, and the like. And covenants without the sword are but words and of no strength to secure a man at all.[2] Therefore, notwithstanding the laws of nature (which every one hath then kept, when he has the will to keep them, when he can do it safely), if there be no power erected or not great enough for our security, every man will and may lawfully rely on his own strength and art for caution against all other men. And in all places, where men have lived by small families, to rob and spoil one another has been

1 See also 14.7 and 15.31.

2 See also 15.31 and 18.4.

a trade, and so far from being reputed against the law of nature, that the greater spoils they gained, the greater was their honour; and men observed no other laws therein but the laws of honour, that is, to abstain from cruelty, leaving to men their lives and instruments of husbandry. And as small families did then, so now do cities and kingdoms, which are but greater families[1] (for their own security), enlarge their dominions, upon all pretences of danger and fear of invasion or assistance that may be given to invaders, endeavour as much as they can to subdue or weaken their neighbours by open force and secret arts, for want of other caution, justly, and are remembered for it in after ages with honour.

Nor from the conjunction of a few men or families.

3. Nor is it the joining together of a small number of men that gives them this security, because in small numbers, small additions on the one side or the other make the advantage of strength so great as is sufficient to carry the victory, and therefore gives
[86] encouragement to an invasion. The multitude sufficient to confide in for our security is not determined by any certain number, but by comparison with the enemy we fear; and [it] is then sufficient, when the odds of the enemy is not of so visible and conspicuous moment, to determine the event of war, as to move him to attempt.

Nor from a great multitude, unless directed by one judgment.

4. And be there never so great a multitude; yet if their actions be directed according to their particular judgements and particular appetites, they can expect thereby no defence nor protection, neither against a common enemy nor against the injuries of one another. For being distracted in opinions concerning the best use and application of their strength, they do not help but hinder one another; and [they] reduce their strength by mutual opposition to nothing, whereby they are easily not only subdued by a very few that agree together, but also, when there is no common enemy, they make war upon each other for their particular interests. For if we could suppose a great multitude of men to consent in the observation of justice and other laws of nature, without a common power to keep them all in awe, we might as well suppose all

1 Cf. 20.15. One way to make Hobbes's doctrine consistent is to maintain that when a family is big enough to withstand raids from others and when the members have covenanted to make one or more members the sovereign, then a family is a commonwealth and not otherwise.

mankind to do the same; and then there neither would be nor need to be any civil government or commonwealth at all, because there would be peace without subjection.

And that continually.

5. Nor is it enough for the security which men desire should last all the time of their life, that they be governed and directed by one judgement for a limited time, as in one battle or one war. For though they obtain a victory by their unanimous endeavour against a foreign enemy; yet afterwards, when either they have no common enemy, or he that by one part is held for an enemy is by another part held for a friend, they must needs by the difference of their interests dissolve and fall again into a war amongst themselves.

Why certain creatures without reason or speech do nevertheless live in society, without any coercive power.

6. It is true that certain living creatures, as bees and ants, live sociably one with another (which are therefore by Aristotle numbered amongst political creatures), and yet have no other direction than their particular judgements and appetites, nor [do they have] speech, whereby one of them can signify to another what he thinks expedient for the common benefit; and therefore some man may perhaps desire to know why mankind cannot do the same. To which I answer,

7. First, that men are continually in competition for honour and dignity, which these creatures are not; and consequently amongst men there ariseth on that ground envy and hatred and finally war; but amongst these not so.

8. Secondly, that amongst these creatures the common good differeth not from the private; and being by nature inclined to their private, they procure thereby the common benefit. But man, whose joy consisteth in comparing himself with other men, can relish nothing but what is eminent.

9. Thirdly, that these creatures, having not, as man, the use of reason, do not see, nor think they see, any fault in the administration of their common business; whereas amongst men there are [87] very many that think themselves wiser and abler to govern the public better than the rest; and these strive to reform and innovate, one this way, another that way, and thereby bring it into distraction and civil war.

10. Fourthly, that these creatures, though they have some use of voice in making known to one another their desires and other

affections; yet they want that art of words by which some men can represent to others that which is good in the likeness of evil and evil in the likeness of good, and augment or diminish the apparent greatness of good and evil, discontenting men and troubling their peace at their pleasure.

11. Fifthly, irrational creatures cannot distinguish between *injury* and *damage*; and therefore as long as they be at ease, they are not offended with their fellows; whereas man is then most troublesome when he is most at ease; for then it is that he loves to show his wisdom, and control the actions of them that govern the commonwealth.

12. Lastly, the agreement of these creatures is natural; that of men is by covenant only, which is artificial; and therefore it is no wonder if there be somewhat else required, besides covenant, to make their agreement constant and lasting, which is a common power to keep them in awe and to direct their actions to the common benefit.

The generation of a commonwealth.

13. The only way to erect such a common power as may be able to defend them from the invasion of foreigners and the injuries of one another, and thereby to secure them in such sort as that by their own industry and by the fruits of the earth they may nourish themselves and live contentedly, is to confer all their power and strength[1] upon one man or upon one assembly of men, that may reduce all their wills by plurality of voices unto one will; which is as much as to say, to appoint one man or assembly of men to bear their person; and every one to own and acknowledge himself to be author of whatsoever he that so beareth their person shall act or cause to be acted in those things which concern the common peace and safety; and therein to submit their wills, every one to his will, and their judgements to his judgement.[2] This is more than consent or concord; it is a real unity of them all in one and the same person, made by covenant of every man with every man in such manner as if every man should say to every man, *I*

---

1 If citizens confer all of their power and strength on the sovereign, it would appear that they would have none left for themselves.

2 Each person wills to will what the sovereign wills and to judge as the sovereign judges.

*authorize and give up my right of governing myself to this man,*[1] *or to this assembly of men, on this condition: that thou give up thy right to him, and authorize all his actions in like manner.*[2] This done, the multitude so united in one person is called a COMMONWEALTH; in Latin, CIVITAS. This is the generation of that great LEVIATHAN,[3] or rather, to speak more reverently, of that *mortal god* to which we owe, under the *immortal God*, our peace and defense. For by this authority, given him by every particular man in the commonwealth, he hath the use of so much power and strength conferred [88] on him that, by terror thereof, he is enabled to conform[4] the wills of them all to peace at home and mutual aid against their enemies abroad. And in him consisteth the essence of the commonwealth, which, to define it, is *one person, of whose acts a great multitude, by mutual covenants one with another, have made themselves every one the author, to the end he may use the strength and means of them all as he shall think expedient for their peace and common defense.*

The definition of a commonwealth.

14. And he that carryeth this person is called SOVEREIGN, and said to have *sovereign power*; and every one besides, his SUBJECT.

Sovereign, and subject, what.

15. The attaining to this sovereign power is by two ways. One, by natural force, as when a man maketh his children to submit themselves and their children to his government, as being able to destroy them if they refuse, or by war subdueth his enemies to his will, giving them their lives on that condition. The other is when men agree amongst themselves to submit to some man, or assembly of men, voluntarily, on confidence to be protected by him against all others. This latter may be called a political commonwealth or commonwealth by *institution*, and the former [may be called] a commonwealth by *acquisition*. And first, I shall speak of a commonwealth by institution.

---

1 Is authorization consistent with alienation (giving up the right of governing oneself)?

2 See also 14.8, 18.1, 20.13, and 21.10.

3 See Job 41, Psalms 74.15-17, and Is. 27.1. In the Bible, Leviathan, sometimes pictured as a whale and sometimes as a crocodile, is a principle of chaos and an enemy of God, whom God defeats. For Hobbes, Leviathan saves people from the state of nature. At 28.27, Hobbes quotes the book of Job, which says at 41:34 that Leviathan is "king of all the children of pride." Christian theologians often identified pride as the cause of sin.

4 Many editions have 'conform' and there is some textual support for 'form'. But 'conform' makes more sense.

## CHAPTER XVIII

## OF THE RIGHTS OF SOVEREIGNS BY INSTITUTION

The act of instituting a commonwealth, what.

1. A *commonwealth* is said to be *instituted* when a *multitude* of men do agree and *covenant, every one with every one*, that to whatsoever *man* or *assembly of men* shall be given by the major part the *right* to *present* the person of them all, that is to say, to be their *representative*, every one, as well he that *voted for it* as he that *voted against it*, shall *authorize* all the actions[1] and judgements of that man, or assembly of men, in the same manner as if they were his own, to the end to live peaceably amongst themselves and be protected against other men.[2]

The consequences to such institutions, are:

2. From this institution of a commonwealth are derived all the *rights* and *faculties* of him or them, on whom the sovereign power is conferred by the consent of the people assembled.[3]

1. The subjects cannot change the form of government.

3. First, because they covenant, it is to be understood they are not obliged by former covenant to anything repugnant hereunto. And consequently they that have already instituted a commonwealth, being thereby bound by covenant to own the actions and judgements of one, cannot lawfully make a new covenant amongst themselves to be obedient to any other, in anything whatsoever, without his permission. And therefore, they that are subjects to a monarch cannot without his leave cast off monarchy and return to the confusion of a disunited multitude nor transfer their person

---

1 This seems to be hyperbolic. If a subject authorizes all of the sovereign's actions, then he would authorize the sovereign's killing or punishing of him, even though no one can ever lay down his right of self-preservation. Hobbes sometimes says that a criminal punishes himself because he has authorized all of his sovereign's actions (18.3).

2 See also 22.9. Hobbes gives the impression that there are two stages to instituting a commonwealth. First, people agree to have a vote on the kind of commonwealth and then they vote on who will be the sovereign. In his *The Elements of Law, Natural and Politic* (1640), Hobbes said that democracy is the first kind of commonwealth (although it is the least stable). What Hobbes says in *Leviathan* may be a remnant of that doctrine. See also18.5.

3 The sovereign is the artificial person who governs his subjects. The sovereign is a single human being in a monarchy. In an aristocracy, the sovereign is the group of people who rule. In a democracy, the sovereign is the entire citizenry, considered as a unity, not in the multiplicity of each subject.

from him that beareth it to another man or other assembly of men;[1] for they are bound, every man to every man, to own and be [89] reputed author of all that he that already is their sovereign shall do and judge fit to be done; so that any one man dissenting, all the rest should break their covenant made to that man, which is injustice; and they have also every man given the sovereignty to him that beareth their person; and therefore if they depose him, they take from him that which is his own, and so again it is injustice. Besides, if he that attempteth to depose his sovereign be killed or punished by him for such attempt, he is author of his own punishment, as being, by the institution, author of all his sovereign shall do;[2] and because it is injustice for a man to do anything for which he may be punished by his own authority, he is also upon that title unjust. And whereas some men have pretended for their disobedience to their sovereign a new covenant, made, not with men but with God, this also is unjust; for there is no covenant with God but by mediation of somebody that representeth God's person, which none doth but God's lieutenant who hath the sovereignty under God.[3] But this pretence of covenant with God is so evident a lie, even in the pretenders' own consciences, that it is not only an act of an unjust, but also of a vile and unmanly disposition.

2. Sovereign power cannot be forfeited.

4. Secondly, because the right of bearing the person of them all is given to him [whom] they make sovereign by covenant only of one to another and not of him to any of them, there can happen no breach of covenant on the part of the sovereign;[4] and consequently none of his subjects, by any pretence of forfeiture, can be freed from his subjection. That he which is made sovereign maketh no covenant with his subjects beforehand is manifest,[5] because either he must make it with the whole multitude, as one party to the covenant, or he must make a several covenant with

---

1 Hobbes is probably criticizing the Scots, who in the National Covenant (1638) made a covenant that appeared to supercede one that Hobbes thought they already had with the king, and criticizing the English who, with the Scots, did the same in the Solemn League and Covenant (1643).

2 See also 18.5.

3 See note 1.

4 The sovereign is not a party of the covenant, as Hobbes says in the next sentence.

5 King James I wrote, "I deny any such contract to be made [between the king and the people]" ("The Trew Law of Free Monarchies," 1598).

every man. With the whole, as one party, it is impossible, because as yet they are not one person; and if he make so many several covenants as there be men, those covenants after he hath the sovereignty are void, because what act soever can be pretended by any one of them for breach thereof is the act both of himself and of all the rest, because done in the person and by the right of every one of them in particular. Besides, if any one or more of them pretend a breach of the covenant made by the sovereign at his institution, and others or one other of his subjects or himself alone pretend there was no such breach, [then] there is in this case no judge to decide the controversy, [and] it returns therefore to the sword again, and every man recovereth the right of protecting himself by his own strength, contrary to the design they had in the institution. It is therefore in vain to grant sovereignty by way of precedent covenant. The opinion that any monarch receiveth his power by covenant, that is to say, on condition, proceedeth from want of understanding this easy truth: that covenants being but words[1] and breath, have no force to oblige, contain, constrain, or protect any man, but what it has from the public sword,[2] that is, from the untied hands of that man or assembly of men that hath the sovereignty, [90] and whose actions are avouched by them all, and performed by the strength of them all in him united. But when an assembly of men is made sovereign, then no man imagineth any such covenant to have passed in the institution; for no man is so dull as to say, for example, the people of Rome made a covenant with the Romans to hold the sovereignty on such or such conditions, which not performed, the Romans might lawfully depose the Roman people. That men see not the reason to be alike in a monarchy and in a popular government proceedeth from the ambition of some that are kinder to the government of an assembly, whereof they may hope to participate, than of monarchy, which they despair to enjoy.

3. No man can without injustice

5. Thirdly, because the major part hath by consenting voices declared a sovereign, he that dissented must now consent with the rest, that is, be contented to avow all the actions he shall do, or else

1 See also 14.31 and 17.2.

2 See also 14.31 and 17.2.

justly be destroyed by the rest.[1] For if he voluntarily entered into the congregation of them that were assembled, [then] he sufficiently declared thereby his will and therefore tacitly covenanted to stand to what the major part should ordain; and therefore if he refuse to stand thereto or make protestation against any of their decrees, [then] he does contrary to his covenant and therefore unjustly. And whether he be of the congregation or not and whether his consent be asked or not, he must either submit to their decrees or be left in the condition of war he was in before, wherein he might without injustice be destroyed by any man whatsoever.

protest against the institution of the sovereign declared by the major part.

4. The sovereign's actions cannot be justly accused by the subject.

6. Fourthly, because every subject is by this institution author of all the actions and judgements of the sovereign instituted, it follows that whatsoever he doth can be no injury to any of his subjects nor ought he to be by any of them accused of injustice. For he that doth anything by authority from another doth therein no injury to him by whose authority he acteth; but by this institution of a commonwealth every particular man is author of all the sovereign doth; and consequently he that complaineth of injury from his sovereign complaineth of that whereof he himself is author; and therefore [he] ought not to accuse any man but himself; no, nor himself, of injury, because to do injury to oneself is impossible. It is true that they that have sovereign power may commit iniquity, but not injustice or injury[2] in the proper signification.

5. Whatsoever the sovereign doth is unpunishable by the subject.

7. Fifthly, and consequently to that which was said last, no man that hath sovereign power can justly be put to death or otherwise in any manner by his subjects punished. For seeing every subject is author of the actions of his sovereign, he punisheth another for the actions committed by himself.

6. The sovereign is judge of what is necessary for the peace and

8. And because the end of this institution is the peace and defence of them all, and whosoever has right to the end has right to the means, it belongs of right to whatsoever man or assembly that hath the sovereignty to be judge both of the means of peace

1 See also 18.1.

1 Hobbes is playing on the etymology of the Latin word for 'right,' '*jus*' (genitive '*juris*'). Injustice and injury is what is done without *jus* because the wrongdoer has laid down or given up his *jus*. *Iniquity* is merely harm done; the word comes from the Latin '*in* + *aequus*': not equal.

defence of his subjects.

and defence and also of the hindrances and disturbances of the same; and to do whatsoever he shall think necessary to be done, both beforehand, for the preserving of peace and security, by pre-
[91] vention of discord at home, and hostility from abroad; and when peace and security are lost, for the recovery of the same. And therefore,

And judge of what doctrines are fit to be taught them.

9. Sixthly, it is annexed to the sovereignty to be judge of what opinions and doctrines are averse, and what [opinions and doctrines are] conducing to peace; and consequently on what occasions, how far, and what men are to be trusted withal in speaking to multitudes of people, and who shall examine the doctrines of all books before they be published. For the actions of men proceed from their opinions, and in the well governing of opinions consisteth the well governing of men's actions in order to their peace and concord. And though in matter of doctrine nothing ought to be regarded but the truth; yet this is not repugnant to regulating of the same by peace. For doctrine repugnant to peace can no more be true than peace and concord can be against the law of nature. It is true that in a commonwealth, where by the negligence or unskillfulness of governors and teachers false doctrines are by time generally received, the contrary truths may be generally offensive. Yet the most sudden and rough bustling in of a new truth that can be does never break the peace, but only sometimes awake the war. For those men that are so remissly governed that they dare take up arms to defend or introduce an opinion are still in war; and their condition not peace, but only a cessation of arms for fear of one another; and they live, as it were, in the precincts of battle continually. It belongeth therefore to him that hath the sovereign power to be judge, or constitute all judges of opinions and doctrines, as a thing necessary to peace, thereby to prevent discord and civil war.

7. The right of making rules, whereby the subjects may every man know what is so his own, as no other subject can

10. Seventhly, is annexed to the sovereignty the whole power of prescribing the rules whereby every man may know what goods he may enjoy and what actions he may do without being molested by any of his fellow subjects; and this is it men call *propriety [property]*. For before constitution of sovereign power, as hath already been shown, all men had right to all things, which necessarily causeth war; and therefore this propriety, being necessary to peace and depending on sovereign power, is the act of that power, in order to the public peace. These rules of propriety (or *meum* and

*tuum*) and of *good*, *evil*, *lawful*, and *unlawful* in the actions of subjects are the civil laws, that is to say, the laws of each commonwealth in particular; though the name of civil law be now restrained to the ancient civil laws of the city of Rome, which being the head of a great part of the world, her laws at that time were in these parts the civil law.

without injustice take it from him.

11. Eighthly, is annexed to the sovereignty the right of judicature, that is to say, of hearing and deciding all controversies which may arise concerning law, either civil or natural, or concerning fact. For without the decision of controversies there is no protection of one subject against the injuries of another, the laws concerning *meum* and *tuum* are in vain, and to every man remaineth, from the natural and necessary appetite of his own conservation, the right of protecting himself by his private strength, which is the condition of war and contrary to the end for which every com- [92]
monwealth is instituted.

8. To him also belongeth the right of judicature and decision of controversy.

12. Ninthly, is annexed to the sovereignty the right of making war and peace with other nations and commonwealths, that is to say, of judging when it is for the public good, and how great forces are to be assembled, armed, and paid for that end, and to levy money upon the subjects to defray the expenses thereof. For the power by which the people are to be defended consisteth in their armies, and the strength of an army in the union of their strength under one command; which command the sovereign instituted, therefore hath, because the command of the *militia*, without other institution, maketh him that hath it sovereign. And therefore, whosoever is made general of an army, he that hath the sovereign power is always generalissimo.

9. And of making war, and peace, as he shall think best.

13. Tenthly, is annexed to the sovereignty the choosing of all counsellors, ministers, magistrates, and officers, both in peace and war. For seeing the sovereign is charged with the end, which is the common peace and defence, he is understood to have power to use such means as he shall think most fit for his discharge.

10. And of choosing all counsellors and ministers, both of peace and war.

14. Eleventhly, to the sovereign is committed the power of rewarding with riches or honour and of punishing with corporal or pecuniary punishment or with ignominy [disgrace], every subject according to the law he hath formerly made; or if there be no

11. And of rewarding and punishing, and that (where no

former law hath determined the measure of it) arbitrary.

law made, according as he shall judge most to conduce to the encouraging of men to serve the commonwealth or deterring of them from doing disservice to the same.

12. And of honour and order.

15. Lastly, considering what values men are naturally apt to set upon themselves, what respect they look for from others, and how little they value other men, from whence continually arise amongst them emulation, quarrels, factions, and at last war, to the destroying of one another and diminution of their strength against a common enemy, it is necessary that there be laws of honour and a public rate of the worth of such men as have deserved or are able to deserve well of the commonwealth, and that there be force in the hands of some or other to put those laws in execution. But it hath already been shown that not only the whole militia or forces of the commonwealth, but also the judicature of all controversies is annexed to the sovereignty. To the sovereign therefore it belongeth also to give titles of honour and to appoint what order of place and dignity each man shall hold and what signs of respect in public or private meetings they shall give to one another.

These rights are indivisible.

16. These are the rights which make the essence of sovereignty and which are the marks whereby a man may discern in what man or assembly of men the sovereign power is placed and resideth. For these are incommunicable and inseparable. The power to coin money, to dispose of the estate and persons of infant heirs, to have preemption in markets, and all other statute prerogatives may be transferred by the sovereign, and yet the power to protect his subjects be retained. But if he transfer the militia, he retains the judi-
[93] cature in vain, for want of execution of the laws; or if he grant away the power of raising money, the militia is in vain; or if he give away the government of doctrines, men will be frighted into rebellion with the fear of spirits. And so if we consider any one of the said rights, we shall presently see that the holding of all the rest will produce no effect in the conservation of peace and justice, the end for which all commonwealths are instituted. And this division is it whereof it is said, *A kingdom divided in itself cannot stand*; for unless this division precede, division into opposite armies can never happen. If there had not first been an opinion received of the greatest part of England that these powers were divided between the King and the Lords and the House of Commons, the

people had never been divided and fallen into this Civil War, first between those that disagreed in politics and after between the dissenters about the liberty of religion; which have so instructed men in this point of sovereign right that there be few now (in England) that do not see that these rights are inseparable and will be so generally acknowledged at the next return of peace; and so [they will] continue [to see this] till their miseries are forgotten; and [it will be seen] no longer, except the vulgar be better taught than they have hitherto been.[1]

And can by no grant pass away without direct renouncing of the sovereign power.

17. And because they are essential and inseparable rights, it follows necessarily that in whatsoever words any of them seem to be granted away, yet if the sovereign power itself be not in direct terms renounced and the name of sovereign no more given by the grantees to him that grants them, [then] the grant is void; for when he has granted all he can, if we grant back the sovereignty, all is restored, as inseparably annexed thereunto.

The power and honour of subjects vanisheth in the presence of the power sovereign.

18. This great authority being indivisible and inseparably annexed to the sovereignty, there is little ground for the opinion of them that say of sovereign kings, though they be *singulis majores*, of greater power than every one of their subjects; yet they be *universis minores*, of less power than them all together. For if by *all together* they mean not the collective body as one person, then *all together* and *every one* signify the same and the speech is absurd. But if by *all together* they understand them as one person (which person the sovereign bears), then the power of all together is the same with the sovereign's power and so again the speech is absurd, which absurdity they see well enough when the sovereignty is in an assembly of the people; but in a monarch they see it not, and yet the power of sovereignty is the same in whomsoever it be placed.

19. And as the power, so also the honour of the sovereign ought to be greater than that of any or all the subjects. For in the sovereignty is the fountain of honour. The dignities of lord, earl, duke, and prince are his creatures. As in the presence of the master the servants are equal and without any honour at all, so are the subjects in the presence of the sovereign. And though they shine some more, some less, when they are out of his sight; yet in his presence they shine no more than the stars in presence of the sun.

1 Better teaching would include teaching *Leviathan*, according to Hobbes.

[94] Sovereign power not so hurtful as the want of it, and the hurt proceeds for the greatest part from not submitting readily to a less.

20. But a man may here object that the condition of subjects is very miserable, as being obnoxious to the lusts and other irregular passions of him or them that have so unlimited a power in their hands. And commonly they that live under a monarch think it the fault of monarchy; and they that live under the government of democracy or other sovereign assembly attribute all the inconvenience to that form of commonwealth; whereas the power in all forms, if they be perfect enough to protect them, is the same; [and they are] not considering that the estate of man can never be without some incommodity or other, and that the greatest that in any form of government can possibly happen to the people in general is scarce sensible in respect of the miseries and horrible calamities that accompany a civil war or that dissolute condition of masterless men without subjection to laws and a coercive power to tie their hands from rapine and revenge; nor [are they] considering that the greatest pressure of sovereign governors proceedeth not from any delight or profit they can expect in the damage or weakening of their subjects (in whose vigour consisteth their own strength and glory), but in the restiveness of themselves that, unwillingly contributing to their own defense, make it necessary for their governors to draw from them what they can in time of peace, [in order] that they may have means on any emergent occasion or sudden need to resist or take advantage on their enemies. For all men are by nature provided of notable multiplying glasses (that is their passions and self-love) through which every little payment appeareth a great grievance, but are destitute of those prospective glasses (namely moral and civil science) to see afar off the miseries that hang over them and cannot without such payments be avoided.

# CHAPTER XIX

## OF THE SEVERAL KINDS OF COMM WEALTH BY INSTITUTION AND ( SUCCESSION TO THE SOVEREIGN PC

The different forms of commonwealths but three.

1. The difference of commonwealths consisteth in the difference of the sovereign or the person representative of all and every one of the multitude. And because the sovereignty is either in one man or in an assembly of more than one, and into that assembly either every man hath right to enter or not every one, but certain men distinguished from the rest; it is manifest there can be but three kinds of commonwealth. For the representative must needs be one man or more; and if more, then it is the assembly of all, or but of a part. When the representative is one man, then is the commonwealth a MONARCHY; when an assembly of all that will come together, then it is a DEMOCRACY or popular commonwealth; when an assembly of a part only, then it is called an ARISTOCRACY. Other kind of commonwealth there can be none; for either one, or more, or all, must have the sovereign power (which I have shown to be indivisible) entire.

Tyranny and oligarchy, but different names of monarchy, and aristocracy.

2. There be other names of government in the histories and [95]
books of policy, as *tyranny* and *oligarchy*; but they are not the names of other forms of government, but of the same forms misliked. For they that are discontented under *monarchy* call it *tyranny*[1] and they that are displeased with *aristocracy* call it *oligarchy*; so also, they which find themselves grieved under a *democracy* call it *anarchy*,[2] which signifies want of government; and yet I think no man believes that want of government is any new kind of government; nor by the same reason ought they to believe that the government is of one kind when they like it and another when they mislike it or are oppressed by the governors.

---

1 See also 46.35 and "A Review and Conclusion," 9.

2 The word 'tyranny' means monarchy but has a negative connotation. 'Oligarchy' means aristocracy but has a negative connotation. 'Anarchy' means democracy but has a negative connotation, according to Hobbes. Almost everyone else, all those who think there is a difference between a good government and a very bad government, would claim that 'tyranny' does not mean the same thing as 'monarchy' and so on.

te atives angerous.

3. It is manifest that men who are in absolute liberty may, if they please, give authority to one man to represent them every one, as well as give such authority to any assembly of men whatsoever; and consequently [they] may subject themselves, if they think good, to a monarch as absolutely as to any other representative. Therefore, where there is already erected a sovereign power, there can be no other representative of the same people, but only to certain particular ends by the sovereign limited. For that [that is, to erect a representative in addition to the sovereign power] were to erect two sovereigns and every man to have his person represented by two actors that, by opposing one another, must needs divide that power which (if men will live in peace) is indivisible, and thereby reduce the multitude into the condition of war, contrary to the end for which all sovereignty is instituted.[1] And therefore as it is absurd to think that a sovereign assembly, inviting the people of their dominion to send up their deputies with power to make known their advice or desires, should therefore hold such deputies, rather than themselves, for the absolute representative of the people, so it is absurd also to think the same in a monarchy. And I know not how this so manifest a truth should of late be so little observed, that in a monarchy he that had the sovereignty from a descent of six hundred years,[2] was alone called sovereign, had the title of Majesty from every one of his subjects, and was unquestionably taken by them for their king, was notwithstanding never considered as their representative, that name without contradiction passing for the title of those men which at his command were sent up by the people to carry their petitions and give him, if he permitted it, their advice.[3] Which may serve as an admonition for those that are the true and absolute representative of a people to instruct men in the nature of that office, and to take heed how

---

1 Hobbes thinks that genuine separation of powers, as the United States claims for its government, leads to civil war. He was thinking in particular of the English Civil Wars (1642-9), which pitted the king and his followers against a majority of the parliament and their followers.

2 The Stuart monarchs traced their lineage back to William I (the Conqueror), who conquered England in 1066.

3 Hobbes believed that Parliament had no political power independent of the monarch. He thought it was a purely advisory body, as the French etymology of 'parliament' suggests: to talk.

they admit of any other general representation upon any occasion whatsoever, if they mean to discharge the trust committed to them.

Comparison of monarchy, with sovereign assemblies.

4. The difference between these three kinds of commonwealth consisteth not in the difference of power,[1] but in the difference of convenience or aptitude to produce the peace and security of the people, which end they were instituted. And to compare monarchy with the other two, we may observe; first, that whosoever beareth the person of the people or is one of that assembly that bears it beareth also his own natural person. And though he be careful in his politic person to procure the common interest; yet [96] he is more, or no less, careful to procure the private good of himself, his family, kindred and friends; and for the most part, if the public interest chance to cross the private, he prefers the private, for the passions of men are commonly more potent than their reason. From whence it follows that where the public and private interest are most closely united, there is the public most advanced. Now in monarchy the private interest is the same with the public. The riches, power, and honour of a monarch arise only from the riches, strength, and reputation of his subjects. For no king can be rich nor glorious nor secure, whose subjects are either poor or contemptible or too weak through want or dissension to maintain a war against their enemies; whereas in a democracy or aristocracy, the public prosperity confers not so much to the private fortune of one that is corrupt or ambitious, as doth many times a perfidious advice, a treacherous action, or a civil war.

5. Secondly, that a monarch receiveth counsel of whom, when, and where he pleaseth; and consequently may hear the opinion of men versed in the matter about which he deliberates, of what rank or quality soever, and as long before the time of action and with as much secrecy as he will. But when a sovereign assembly has need of counsel, none are admitted but such as have a right thereto from the beginning, which for the most part are of those who have been versed more in the acquisition of wealth than of knowledge and are to give their advice in long discourses which may,

---

1 All three forms of government are equally sovereign. But Hobbes thinks that monarchy is the most stable form of government; democracy the least. See also 20.2 and 20.3.

and do commonly, excite men to action, but not govern them in it. For the *understanding* is by the flame of the passions never enlightened, but dazzled; nor is there any place or time wherein an assembly can receive counsel with secrecy, because of their own multitude.

6. Thirdly, that the resolutions of a monarch are subject to no other inconstancy than that of human nature; but in assemblies, besides that of nature, there ariseth an inconstancy from the number. For the absence of a few that would have the resolution, once taken, continue firm (which may happen by security, negligence, or private impediments), or the diligent appearance of a few of the contrary opinion, undoes today all that was concluded yesterday.

7. Fourthly, that a monarch cannot disagree with himself out of envy or interest, but an assembly may, and that to such a height as may produce a civil war.

8. Fifthly, that in monarchy there is this inconvenience: that any subject, by the power of one man, for the enriching of a favorite or flatterer, may be deprived of all he possesseth, which I confess is a great and inevitable inconvenience. But the same may as well happen where the sovereign power is in an assembly; for their power is the same, and they are as subject to evil counsel and to be seduced by orators as a monarch by flatterers; and becoming one another's flatterers, serve one another's covetousness and ambition by turns. And whereas the favorites of monarchs are few and they have none else to advance but their own kindred, the favorites of
[97] an assembly are many, and the kindred much more numerous than of any monarch. Besides, there is no favorite of a monarch which cannot as well succour his friends as hurt his enemies; but orators, that is to say favorites of sovereign assemblies, though they have great power to hurt, have little to save. For to accuse requires less eloquence (such is man's nature) than to excuse; and condemnation, than absolution, more resembles justice.

9. Sixthly, that it is an inconvenience in monarchy that the sovereignty may descend upon an infant or one that cannot discern between good and evil, and [the inconvenience] consisteth in this: that the use of his power must be in the hand of another man or of some assembly of men, which are to govern by his right and in his name as curators and protectors of his person and authority. But to

say there is inconvenience in putting the use of the sovereign power into the hand of a man or an assembly of men is to say that all government is more inconvenient than confusion and civil war. And therefore all the danger that can be pretended must arise from the contention of those that, for an office of so great honour and profit, may become competitors. To make it appear that this inconvenience proceedeth not from that form of government we call monarchy, we are to consider that the precedent monarch hath appointed who shall have the tuition of his infant successor, either expressly by testament or tacitly by not controlling the custom in that case received; and then such inconvenience, if it happen, is to be attributed not to the monarchy, but to the ambition and injustice of the subjects, which in all kinds of government where the people are not well instructed in their duty and the rights of sovereignty, is the same. Or else the precedent monarch hath not at all taken order for such tuition; and then the law of nature hath provided this sufficient rule, that the tuition shall be in him that hath by nature most interest in the preservation of the authority of the infant, and to whom least benefit can accrue by his death or diminution. For seeing every man by nature seeketh his own benefit and promotion, to put an infant into the power of those that can promote themselves by his destruction or damage is not tuition but treachery. So that sufficient provision being taken against all just quarrel about the government under a child, if any contention arise to the disturbance of the public peace, it is not to be attributed to the form of monarchy but to the ambition of subjects and ignorance of their duty. On the other side, there is no great commonwealth, the sovereignty whereof is in a great assembly, which is not, as to consultations of peace and war and making of laws, in the same condition as if the government were in a child. For as a child wants the judgement to dissent from counsel given him and is thereby necessitated to take the advice of them or him to whom he is committed; so an assembly wanteth the liberty to dissent from the counsel of the major part, be it good or bad. And as a child has need of a tutor or protector to preserve his person and authority, so also in great commonwealths the sovereign assembly, in all great dangers and troubles, have need of *custodes libertatis*, that is, of dictators or protectors of their authority, [98] which are as much as temporary monarchs, to whom for a time they may commit the entire exercise of their power; and have (at the end of that time) been oftener deprived thereof than infant kings by their protectors, regents, or any other tutors.

10. Though the kinds of sovereignty be, as I have now shown, but three; that is to say, monarchy, where one man has it; or democracy, where the general assembly of subjects hath it; or aristocracy, where it is in an assembly of certain persons nominated or otherwise distinguished from the rest; yet he that shall consider the particular commonwealths that have been and are in the world will not perhaps easily reduce them to three, and may thereby be inclined to think there be other forms arising from these mingled together. As for example elective kingdoms, where kings have the sovereign power put into their hands for a time, or kingdoms wherein the king hath a power limited, which governments are nevertheless by most writers called monarchy. Likewise if a popular or aristocratical commonwealth subdue an enemy's country and govern the same by a president, procurator, or other magistrate, this may seem perhaps, at first sight, to be a democratical or aristocratical government. But it is not so. For elective kings are not sovereigns, but ministers of the sovereign; nor limited kings sovereigns, but ministers of them that have the sovereign power; nor are those provinces which are in subjection to a democracy or aristocracy of another commonwealth democratically or aristocratically governed, but monarchically.[1]

11. And first, concerning an elective king whose power is limited to his life, as it is in many places of Christendom at this day, or to certain years or months, as the dictator's power amongst the Romans, if he have right to appoint his successor he is no more elective but hereditary. But if he have no power to elect his successor, then there is some other man or assembly known, which after his decease may elect a new; or else the commonwealth dieth and dissolveth with him, and returneth to the condition of war. If

1 A government may appear to be of one form but really be of another. Constitutional monarchies, like the United Kingdom and Canada, are not monarchies at all, but representative democracies. When a province, like first-century Palestine, is ruled by a foreign conqueror, like Rome, the form of government is monarchy. The people of Rome as sovereign, is an artificial person and in that capacity governed Palestine. See also 19.13.

it be known who have the power to give the sovereignty after his death, it is known also that the sovereignty was in them before; for none have right to give that which they have not right to possess, and keep to themselves, if they think good. But if there be none that can give the sovereignty after the decease of him that was first elected, then has he power, nay he is obliged by the law of nature, to provide, by establishing his successor, to keep to those that had trusted him with the government from relapsing into the miserable condition of civil war. And consequently he was, when elected, a sovereign absolute.

12. Secondly, that king whose power is limited is not superior to him or them that have the power to limit it; and he that is not superior is not supreme, that is to say, not sovereign. The sovereignty therefore was always in that assembly which had the right to limit him, and by consequence the government [was] not [99] monarchy, but either democracy or aristocracy, as of old time in Sparta, where the kings had a privilege to lead their armies, but the sovereignty was in the Ephori.[1]

13. Thirdly, whereas heretofore the Roman people governed the land of Judea, for example, by a president; yet was not Judea therefore a democracy, because they were not governed by any assembly into which any of them had right to enter, nor by an aristocracy, because they were not governed by any assembly into which any man could enter by their election; but they were governed by one person, which though as to the people of Rome was an assembly of the people, or democracy; yet as to the people of Judea, which had no right at all of participating in the government, was a monarch. For though where the people are governed by an assembly chosen by themselves out of their own number, the government is called a democracy or aristocracy; yet when they are governed by an assembly not of their own choosing, it is a monarchy, not of one man over another man, but of one people over another people.

Of the right of succession.

14. Of all these forms of government, the matter being mortal, so that not only monarchs but also whole assemblies die, it is necessary for the conservation of the peace of men that as there was

---

1 The Ephori were five senior government officials, elected annually, who advised the king.

order taken for an artificial man, so there be order also taken for an artificial eternity of life, without which men that are governed by an assembly should return into the condition of war in every age, and they that are governed by one man as soon as their governor dieth. This artificial eternity is that which men call the right of *succession.*

15. There is no perfect form of government, where the disposing of the succession is not in the present sovereign. For if it be in any other particular man or private assembly, it is in a person subject, and may be assumed by the sovereign at his pleasure; and consequently the right is in himself. And if it be in no particular man, but left to a new choice, then is the commonwealth dissolved, and the right is in him that can get it, contrary to the intention of them that did institute the commonwealth for their perpetual, and not temporary, security.

16. In a democracy, the whole assembly cannot fail unless the multitude that are to be governed fail. And therefore questions of the right of succession have in that form of government no place at all.

17. In an aristocracy when any of the assembly dieth, the election of another into his room belonged to the assembly, as the sovereign, to whom belonged the choosing of all counsellors and officers. For that which the representative doth as actor, every one of the subjects doth as author. And though the sovereign assembly may give power to others to elect new men for supply of their court; yet it is still by their authority that the election is made; and by the same it may, when the public shall require it, be recalled.

The present monarch hath right to dispose of the succession.

[100] 18. The greatest difficulty about the right of succession is in monarchy; and the difficulty ariseth from this, that at first sight it is not manifest who is to appoint the successor nor many times who it is whom he hath appointed. For in both these cases there is required a more exact ratiocination than every man is accustomed to use. As to the question who shall appoint the successor of a monarch that hath the sovereign authority, that is to say, who shall determine of the right of inheritance (for elective kings and princes have not the sovereign power in propriety, but in use only), we are to consider that either he that is in possession has

right to dispose of the succession or else that right is again in the dissolved multitude. For the death of him that hath the sovereign power in propriety leaves the multitude without any sovereign at all, that is, without any representative in whom they should be united and be capable of doing any one action at all. And therefore they are incapable of election of any new monarch, every man having equal right to submit himself to such as he thinks best able to protect him, or, if he can, protect himself by his own sword, which is a return to confusion and to the condition of a war of every man against every man, contrary to the end for which monarchy had its first institution. Therefore it is manifest that by the institution of monarchy the disposing of the successor is always left to the judgement and will of the present possessor.

19. And for the question (which may arise sometimes), *who it is that the monarch in possession hath designed to the succession and inheritance of his power*, it is determined by his express words and testament, or by other tacit signs sufficient.

Succession passeth by express words.

20. By express words or testament, when it is declared by him in his lifetime, *viva voce*, or by writing, as the first emperors of Rome declared who should be their heirs. For the word *heir* does not of itself imply the children or nearest kindred of a man, but whomsoever a man shall any way declare he would have to succeed him in his estate. If therefore a monarch declare expressly that such a man shall be his heir, either by word or writing, then is that man immediately after the decease of his predecessor invested in the right of being monarch.

Or, by not controlling a custom.

21. But where testament and express words are wanting, other natural signs of the will are to be followed, whereof the one is custom. And therefore where the custom is that the next of kindred absolutely succeedeth, there also the next of kindred hath right to the succession that, if the will of him that was in possession had been otherwise, he might easily have declared the same in his lifetime. And likewise where the custom is that the next of the male kindred succeedeth, there also the right of succession is in the next of the kindred male, for the same reason. And so it is if the custom were to advance the female. For whatsoever custom a man may by a word control and does not, it is a natural sign he would have that custom stand.

Or, by presumption of natural affection. [101]

22. But where neither custom nor testament hath preceded, there it is to be understood: first, that a monarch's will is that the government remain monarchical, because he hath approved that government in himself. Secondly, that a child of his own, male or female, be preferred before any other, because men are presumed to be more inclined by nature to advance their own children than the children of other men; and of their own, rather a male than a female, because men are naturally fitter than women for actions of labour and danger. Thirdly, where his own issue faileth, rather a brother than a stranger, and so still the nearer in blood rather than the more remote, because it is always presumed that the nearer of kin is the nearer in affection and it is evident that a man receives always, by reflection, the most honour from the greatness of his nearest kindred.

To dispose of the succession, though to a king of another nation, not unlawful.

23. But if it be lawful for a monarch to dispose of the succession by words of contract or testament, men may perhaps object a great inconvenience; for he may sell or give his right of governing to a stranger, which, because strangers (that is, men not used to live under the same government, nor speaking the same language) do commonly undervalue one another, may turn to the oppression of his subjects, which is indeed a great inconvenience; but it proceedeth not necessarily from the subjection to a stranger's government, but from the unskillfulness of the governors ignorant of the true rules of politics. And therefore the Romans, when they had subdued many nations, to make their government digestible were wont to take away that grievance as much as they thought necessary by giving sometimes to whole nations, and sometimes to principal men of every nation they conquered, not only the privileges but also the name of Romans, and took many of them into the Senate and offices of charge, even in the Roman city. And this was it our most wise king, King James, aimed at in endeavouring the union of his two realms of England and Scotland.[1] Which, if he could have obtained, had in all likelihood prevented the civil wars which make both those kingdoms, at this present, miserable. It is not therefore any injury to the people for a monarch to dis-

1 James I and VI was separately king of Scotland (hence VI) and king of England and Wales (I). His attempt to unite the two realms failed, and was achieved only in 1717 by the Act of Union.

pose of the succession by will, though by the fault of many princes it hath been sometimes found inconvenient. Of the lawfulness of it, this also is an argument: that whatsoever inconvenience can arrive by giving a kingdom to a stranger may arrive also by so marrying with strangers, as the right of succession may descend upon them; yet this by all men is accounted lawful.

# CHAPTER XX

## OF DOMINION PATERNAL AND DESPOTICAL

A common-wealth by acquisition. [102]

1. A commonwealth *by acquisition* is that where the sovereign power is acquired by force; and it is acquired by force when men singly, or many together by plurality of voices, for fear of death or bonds, do authorize all the actions of that man or assembly that hath their lives and liberty in his power.

Wherein different from a common-wealth by institution.

2. And this kind of dominion or sovereignty differeth from sovereignty by institution only in this, that men who choose their sovereign do it for fear of one another and not of him whom they institute; but in this case, they subject themselves to him they are afraid of. In both cases they do it for fear; which is to be noted by them that hold all such covenants, as proceed from fear of death or violence, void; which, if it were true, no man in any kind of commonwealth could be obliged to obedience. It is true that in a commonwealth once instituted or acquired, promises proceeding from fear of death or violence are no covenants nor obliging when the thing promised is contrary to the laws; but the reason is not because it was made upon fear, but because he that promiseth hath no right in the thing promised. Also, when he may lawfully perform and doth not, it is not the invalidity of the covenant that absolveth him, but the sentence of the sovereign. Otherwise, whensoever a man lawfully promiseth, he unlawfully breaketh; but when the sovereign, who is the actor, acquitteth him, then he is acquitted by him that extorted the promise, as by the author of such absolution.

The rights of sovereignty the same in both.

3. But the rights and consequences of sovereignty are the same in both. His power cannot without his consent be transferred to another; he cannot forfeit it; he cannot be accused by any of his subjects of injury; he cannot be punished by them; he is judge of what is necessary for peace and judge of doctrines; he is sole legislator and supreme judge of controversies and of the times and occasions of war and peace; to him it belonged to choose magistrates, counselors, commanders, and all other officers and ministers, and to determine of rewards and punishments, honour and order. The reasons whereof are the same which are alleged in the precedent chapter for the same rights and consequences of sovereignty by institution.

Dominion paternal how attained. Not by generation, but by contract;

4. Dominion is acquired two ways, by generation and by conquest. The right of dominion by generation is that which the parent hath over his children and is called PATERNAL. And is not so derived from the generation, as if therefore the parent had dominion over his child because he begat him, but from the child's consent, either express or by other sufficient arguments declared. For as to the generation, God hath ordained to man a helper, and there be always two that are equally parents; the dominion therefore over the child should belong equally to both and he be equally subject to both, which is impossible; for no man can obey two masters. And whereas some have attributed the dominion to the man only, as being of the more excellent sex, they misreckon in it. For there is not always that difference of strength or prudence between the man and the woman as that the right can be determined without war. In commonwealths this controversy is decided by the civil law; and for the most part (but not always) the sentence is in favour of the father, because for the most part com-
[103] monwealths have been erected by the fathers, not by the mothers of families. But the question lieth now in the state of mere nature where there are supposed no laws of matrimony, no laws for the education of children but the law of nature and the natural inclination of the sexes, one to another, and to their children. In this condition of mere nature either the parents between themselves dispose of the dominion over the child by contract or do not dispose thereof at all. If they dispose thereof, the right passeth according to the contract. We find in history that the Amazons

contracted with the men of the neighbouring countries, to whom they had recourse for issue, that the issue male should be sent back, but the female remain with themselves; so that the dominion of the females was in the mother.

5. If there be no contract, the dominion is in the mother. For in the condition of mere nature, where there are no matrimonial laws, it cannot be known who is the father unless it be declared by the mother; and therefore the right of dominion over the child dependeth on her will, and is consequently hers. Again, seeing the infant is first in the power of the mother, so as she may either nourish or expose it, if she nourish it, it oweth its life to the mother, and is therefore obliged to obey her rather than any other; and by consequence the dominion over it is hers. But if she expose it, and another find and nourish it, dominion is in him that nourisheth it. For it ought to obey him by whom it is preserved, because preservation of life being the end for which one man becomes subject to another, every man is supposed to promise obedience to him in whose power it is to save or destroy him.

Or education;

6. If the mother be the father's subject, the child is in the father's power; and if the father be the mother's subject (as when a sovereign queen marrieth one of her subjects), the child is subject to the mother, because the father also is her subject.

Or precedent subjection of one of the parents to the other.

7. If a man and a woman, monarchs of two several kingdoms, have a child, and contract concerning who shall have the dominion of him, the right of the dominion passeth by the contract. If they contract not, the dominion followeth the dominion of the place of his residence. For the sovereign of each country hath dominion over all that reside therein.

8. He that hath the dominion over the child hath dominion also over the children of the child, and over their children's children. For he that hath dominion over the person of a man hath dominion over all that is his, without which dominion were but a title without the effect.

9. The right of succession to paternal dominion proceedeth in the same manner as doth the right of succession to monarchy, of which I have already sufficiently spoken in the precedent chapter.

The right of succession followeth the rules of the right of possession.

Despotical dominion how attained.

10. Dominion acquired by conquest or victory in war is that which some writers call DESPOTICAL from *Despotes*, which signifieth a *lord* or *master* and is the dominion of the master over his servant. And this dominion is then acquired to the victor [104] when the vanquished, to avoid the present stroke of death, covenanteth either in express words or by other sufficient signs of the will that so long as his life and the liberty of his body is allowed him, the victor shall have the use thereof at his pleasure. And after such covenant made, the vanquished is a SERVANT, and not before; for by the word *servant* (whether it be derived from [the Latin] *servire*, to serve, or from *servare*, to save, which I leave to grammarians to dispute) is not meant a captive, which is kept in prison or bonds, till the owner of him that took him or bought him of one that did, shall consider what to do with him; for such men, commonly called slaves, have no obligation at all, but may break their bonds or the prison and kill or carry away captive their master, justly; but one that, being taken, hath corporal liberty allowed him, and upon promise not to run away nor to do violence to his master, is trusted by him.

Not by the victory, but by the consent of the vanquished.

11. It is not therefore the victory that giveth the right of dominion over the vanquished, but his own covenant. Nor is he obliged because he is conquered, that is to say, beaten and taken or put to flight, but because he cometh in and submitteth to the victor; nor is the victor obliged by an enemy's rendering himself, without promise of life, to spare him for this his yielding to discretion, which obliges not the victor longer than in his own discretion he shall think fit.

12. And that which men do when they demand, as it is now called, *quarter* (which the Greeks called *Zogria, taking alive*) is to evade the present fury of the victor by submission and to compound for their life with ransom or service; and therefore he that hath quarter hath not his life given, but deferred till further deliberation; for it is not a yielding on condition of life, but to discretion. And then only is his life in security, and his service due, when the victor hath trusted him with his corporal liberty. For slaves that work in prisons or fetters do it not of duty, but to avoid the cruelty of their task-masters.

13. The master of the servant is master also of all he hath and

may exact the use thereof; that is to say, of his goods, of his labour, of his servants, and of his children, as often as he shall think fit. For he holdeth his life of his master by the covenant of obedience, that is, of owning and authorizing whatsoever the master shall do. And in case the master, if he refuse, kill him or cast him into bonds, or otherwise punish him for his disobedience, he is himself the author of the same and cannot accuse him of injury.

14. In sum, the rights and consequences of both *paternal* and *despotical* dominion are the very same with those of a sovereign by institution, and for the same reasons, which reasons are set down in the precedent chapter. So that for a man that is monarch of divers nations, whereof he hath in one the sovereignty by institution of the people assembled, and in another by conquest, that is, by the submission of each particular to avoid death or bonds, to demand of one nation more than of the other, from the title of conquest, as being a conquered nation, is an act of ignorance of the rights of sovereignty. For the sovereign is absolute over both [105] alike or else there is no sovereignty at all, and so every man may lawfully protect himself, if he can, with his own sword, which is the condition of war.

Difference between a family and a kingdom.

15. By this it appears that a great family, if it be not part of some commonwealth, is of itself, as to the rights of sovereignty, a little monarchy, whether that family consist of a man and his children, or of a man and his servants, or of a man and his children and servants together, wherein the father or master is the sovereign. But yet a family is not properly a commonwealth unless it be of that power by its own number or by other opportunities,[1] as not to be subdued without the hazard of war. For where a number of men are manifestly too weak to defend themselves united, every one may use his own reason in time of danger to save his own life either by flight or by submission to the enemy, as he shall think best; in the same manner as a very small company of soldiers, surprised by an army, may cast down their arms and demand quarter or run away rather than be put to the sword. And thus much shall suffice concerning what I find by speculation and deduction of sovereign rights, from the nature, need, and designs of men in

1 See also 17.2.

erecting of commonwealths and putting themselves under monarchs or assemblies entrusted with power enough for their protection.

The rights of monarchy from Scripture.

16. Let us now consider what the Scripture teacheth in the
same point. To Moses the children of Israel say thus: *Speak thou to*
*us, and we will hear thee; but let not God speak to us, lest we die*. This is
Exod. 20:19. absolute obedience to Moses. Concerning the right of kings, God
himself, by the mouth of Samuel, saith, *This shall be the right of the*
*king you will have to reign over you. He shall take your sons, and set them*
*to drive his chariots and to be his horsemen, and to run before his chariots,*
*and gather in his harvest, and to make his engines of war, and instruments*
*of his chariots; and [he] shall take your daughters to make perfumes, to be*
*his cooks, and bakers. He shall take your fields, your vineyards, and your*
*olive-yards, and give them to his servants. He shall take the tithe of your*
*corn and wine, and give it to the men of his chamber, and to his other ser-*
*vants. He shall take your man-servants, and your maidservants, and the*
*choice of your youth, and employ them in his business. He shall take the*
1 Sam. *tithe of your flocks; and you shall be his servants.* This is absolute
8:11-17. power, and summed up in the last words, *you shall be his servants.*[1]
Again, when the people heard what power their king was to have;
yet they consented thereto, and say thus: *We will be as all other*
1 Sam. *nations, and our king shall judge our causes, and go before us, to conduct*
8:19-20. *our wars*. Here is confirmed the right that sovereigns have, both to
the *militia* and to all *judicature*, in which is contained as absolute
power as one man can possibly transfer to another. Again, the
prayer of King Solomon to God was this: *Give to thy servant under-*
1 Kings 3:9. *standing, to judge thy people, and to discern between good and evil.* It
[106] belonged therefore to the sovereign to be *judge* and to prescribe
the rules of *discerning good and evil*, which rules are laws; and therefore in him is the legislative power. Saul sought the life of David;
yet when it was in his power to slay Saul, and his servants would
have done it, David forbade them, saying, *God forbid I should do*
1 Sam. 24:9. *such an act against my Lord, the anointed of God*. For obedience of
servants St. Paul saith, *Servants obey your masters in all things.* and
Col. 3:20. *Children obey your parents in all things*. There is simple obedience in

1 It is ironic that Hobbes uses this passage to support absolute sovereignty since the passage clearly is warning the Israelites against establishing a monarchy.

those that are subject to paternal or despotical dominion. Again, *The scribes and Pharisees sit in Moses' chair, and therefore all that they shall bid you observe, that observe and do.* There again is simple obedience. And St. Paul, *Warn them that they subject themselves to princes, and to those that are in authority, and obey them.* This obedience is also simple. Lastly, our Saviour himself acknowledges that men ought to pay such taxes as are by kings imposed where he says, *Give to Caesar that which is Caesar's* and paid such taxes himself. And that the king's word is sufficient to take anything from any subject, when there is need; and that the king is judge of that need; for he himself, as king of the Jews, commanded his Disciples to take the ass and ass's colt to carry him into Jerusalem, saying, *Go into the village over against you, and you shall find a she ass tied, and her colt with her; untie them, and bring them to me. And if any man ask you, what you mean by it, say the Lord hath need of them; and they will let them go.* They will not ask whether his necessity be a sufficient title nor whether he be judge of that necessity, but acquiesce in the will of the Lord.

Col. 3:22.

Matt. 23:2-3.

Titus 3:2.

Matt. 21:2-3.

17. To these places may be added also that of Genesis, *You shall be as gods, knowing good and evil.* And, *Who told thee that thou wast naked? Hast thou eaten of the tree, of which I commanded thee thou shouldest not eat?* [Gen. 3:11]. For the cognizance or judicature of good and evil, being forbidden by the name of the fruit of the tree of knowledge, as a trial of Adam's obedience, the devil to inflame the ambition of the woman, to whom that fruit already seemed beautiful, told her that by tasting it they should be as gods, knowing good and evil. Whereupon having both eaten, they did indeed take upon them God's office, which is judicature of good and evil, but acquired no new ability to distinguish between them aright. And whereas it is said that having eaten, they saw they were naked, no man hath so interpreted that place as if they had been formerly blind and saw not their own skins, the meaning is plain that it was then they first judged their nakedness (wherein it was God's will to create them) to be uncomely, and by being ashamed did tacitly censure God himself. And thereupon God saith, *Hast thou eaten*, etc., as if he should say, doest thou that owest me obedience take upon thee to judge of my commandments? Whereby it is clearly, though allegorically, signified that the commands of them that

Gen. 3:5.

have the right to command are not by their subjects to be censured nor disputed.

Sovereign power ought in all commonwealths to be absolute. [107]

18. So that it appeareth plainly, to my understanding, both from reason and Scripture, that the sovereign power, whether placed in one man, as in monarchy, or in one assembly of men, as in popular and aristocratical commonwealths, is as great as possibly men can be imagined to make it. And though of so unlimited a power men may fancy many evil consequences; yet the consequences of the want of it, which is perpetual war of every man against his neighbour, are much worse.[1] The condition of man in this life shall never be without inconveniences; but there happeneth in no commonwealth any great inconvenience but what proceeds from the subjects' disobedience and breach of those covenants from which the commonwealth hath its being. And whosoever thinking sovereign power too great will seek to make it less must subject himself to the power that can limit it, that is to say, to a greater.

19. The greatest objection is that of the practice when men ask where and when such power has by subjects been acknowledged. But one may ask them again, when or where has there been a kingdom long free from sedition and civil war? In those nations whose commonwealths have been long-lived and not been destroyed but by foreign war the subjects never did dispute of the sovereign power. But howsoever, an argument from the practice of men that have not sifted to the bottom, and with exact reason weighed the causes and nature of commonwealths, and suffer daily those miseries that proceed from the ignorance thereof, is invalid. For though in all places of the world men should lay the foundation of their houses on the sand, it could not thence be inferred that so it ought to be. The skill of making and maintaining commonwealths consisteth in certain rules, as doth arithmetic and geometry, not, as tennis play, on practice only; which rules neither poor men have the leisure, nor men that have

---

1 King James I wrote, "For a king cannot be imagined to be so unruly and tyrannous, but the commonwealth will be kept in better order, notwithstanding thereof by him than it can be by his way-taking. ... [I]t is better to live in a commonwealth where nothing is lawful, than [a commonwealth] where all things are lawful to all men" ("The Trew Law of Free Monarchies").

had the leisure have hitherto had the curiosity or the method, to find out.

# CHAPTER XXI

## OF THE LIBERTY OF SUBJECTS

1. LIBERTY or FREEDOM signifieth properly the absence of opposition (by opposition I mean external impediments of motion) and may be applied no less to irrational and inanimate creatures than to rational. For whatsoever is so tied or environed, as it cannot move but within a certain space, which space is determined by the opposition of some external body, we say it hath not liberty to go further. And so of all living creatures, whilst they are imprisoned or restrained with walls or chains, and of the water, whilst it is kept in by banks or vessels that otherwise would spread itself into a larger space, we use to say they are not at liberty to move in such manner as without those external impediments they would. But when the impediment of motion is in the constitution of the thing itself, we use not to say it wants the liberty, but the power, to move, as when a stone lieth still or a man is fastened to his bed by sickness.[1]

Liberty, what.

2. And according to this proper and generally received meaning of the word, a FREEMAN *is he that, in those things which by his strength and wit he is able to do, is not hindered to do what he has a will to.* But when the words *free* and *liberty* are applied to anything but *bodies*, they are abused; for that which is not subject to motion is not subject to impediment; and therefore, when it is said, for example, the way is free, no liberty of the way is signified, but of those that walk in it without stop. And when we say a gift is free, there is not meant any liberty of the gift, but of the giver, that was not bound by any law or covenant to give it. So when we *speak freely*, it is not the liberty of voice or pronunciation, but of the man whom no law hath obliged to speak otherwise than he did. Lastly,

[108]

What it is to be free.

1 Liberty or freedom relates to the absence of *external* impediments to motion. Power relates to the *internal* constitution of a thing that makes it able to do things.

from the use of the words *free will*, no liberty can be inferred of the will, desire, or inclination, but the liberty of the man, which consisteth in this, that he finds no stop in doing what he has the will, desire, or inclination to do.[1]

Fear and liberty consistent.

3. Fear and liberty are consistent, as when a man throweth his goods into the sea for *fear* the ship should sink, he doth it nevertheless very willingly,[2] and may refuse to do it if he will; it is therefore the action of one that was *free*; so a man sometimes pays his debt only for *fear* of imprisonment, which, because no body hindered him from detaining, was the action of a man at *liberty*. And generally all actions which men do in commonwealths for *fear* of the law are actions which the doers had *liberty* to omit.[3]

Liberty and necessity consistent.

4. *Liberty* and *necessity* are consistent, as in the water that hath not only *liberty* but a *necessity* of descending by the channel; so likewise in the actions which men voluntarily do, which, because they proceed from their will, proceed from *liberty*; and yet because every act of man's will and every desire and inclination proceedeth from some cause, and that from another cause, in a continual chain (whose first link is in the hand of God, the first of all causes), proceed from *necessity*.[4] So that to him that could see the connection of those causes, the *necessity* of all men's voluntary actions would appear manifest. And therefore God, that seeth and disposeth all things, seeth also that the *liberty* of man in doing what he will is accompanied with the *necessity* of doing that which God will and no more nor less. For though men may do many things which God does not command nor is therefore author of them;[5] yet they can have no passion nor appetite to anything of which appetite

1 The concept of free will is incoherent because freedom applies only to bodies. A will is the last desire a body has before it acts; that is, it is the desire that causes the motion.

2 Cf. Aristotle, *Nicomachean Ethics* 3.1.

3 Hobbes needs freedom to be consistent with fear, because fear motivates people to institute a sovereign. See 20.2.

4 Liberty concerns absence of external impediments. Necessity concerns what must occur because there is a cause of it.

5 Hobbes agrees with Calvin that God is the cause of sin. Many of Hobbes's contemporaries did not like the fine line he drew when proposing that God is the cause of everything but not the author of everything, because he does not command people to sin.

God's will is not the cause. And did not his will assure the *necessity* of man's will, and consequently of all that on man's will dependeth, the *liberty* of men would be a contradiction and impediment to the omnipotence and *liberty* of God. And this shall suffice, as to the matter in hand, of that natural *liberty*, which only is properly called *liberty*.

Artificial bonds, or covenants.

5. But as men, for the attaining of peace and conservation of themselves thereby, have made an artificial man, which we call a commonwealth, so also have they made artificial chains, called *civil laws*, which they themselves by mutual covenants have fastened at [109] one end to the lips of that man or assembly to whom they have given the sovereign power and at the other to their own ears. These bonds, in their own nature but weak, may nevertheless be made to hold by the danger, though not by the difficulty, of breaking them.

Liberty of subjects consisteth in liberty from covenants.

6. In relation to these bonds only it is that I am to speak now of the *liberty of subjects*. For seeing there is no commonwealth in the world wherein there be rules enough set down for the regulating of all the actions and words of men (as being a thing impossible); it followeth necessarily that in all kinds of actions by the laws pretermitted,[1] men have the liberty of doing what their own reasons shall suggest for the most profitable to themselves. For if we take liberty in the proper sense, for corporal liberty, that is to say, freedom from chains and prison, it were very absurd for men to clamour as they do for the liberty they so manifestly enjoy. Again, if we take liberty for an exemption from laws, it is no less absurd for men to demand as they do that liberty by which all other men may be masters of their lives. And yet as absurd as it is, this is it they demand, not knowing that the laws are of no power to protect them without a sword in the hands of a man or men to cause those laws to be put in execution. The liberty of a subject lieth therefore only in those things which, in regulating their actions, the sovereign hath pretermitted, such as is the liberty to buy, and sell, and otherwise contract with one another, to choose their own abode, their own diet, their own trade of life, and institute their children as they themselves think fit, and the like.

---

1 Liberty is what is left over after the sovereign has issued all of his laws or commands. See also 21.18.

Liberty of the subject consistent with the unlimited power of the sovereign.

7. Nevertheless we are not to understand that by such liberty the sovereign power of life and death is either abolished or limited. For it has been already shown that nothing the sovereign representative can do to a subject, on what pretence soever, can properly be called injustice or injury, because every subject is author of every act the sovereign doth, so that he never wanteth right to any thing, otherwise than as he himself is the subject of God and bound thereby to observe the laws of nature. And therefore it may and doth often happen in commonwealths that a subject may be put to death by the command of the sovereign power and yet neither do the other wrong, as when Jephthah caused his daughter to be sacrificed; in which, and the like cases, he that so dieth had liberty to do the action for which he is nevertheless, without injury, put to death. And the same holdeth also in a sovereign prince that putteth to death an innocent subject. For though the action be against the law of nature, as being contrary to equity, as was the killing of Uriah by David; yet it was not an injury to Uriah, but to God. Not to Uriah, because the right to do what he pleased was given him by Uriah himself; and yet to God, because David was God's subject and prohibited all iniquity by the law of nature, which distinction David himself, when he repented the fact, evidently confirmed, saying, *To thee only have I sinned.* In the same
[110] manner the people of Athens, when they banished the most potent of their commonwealth for ten years, thought they committed no injustice; and yet they never questioned what crime he had done, but what hurt he would do; nay, they commanded the banishment of they knew not whom; and every citizen bringing his oyster shell into the market place, written with the name of him he desired should be banished, without actually accusing him sometimes banished an Aristides, for his reputation of justice, and sometimes a scurrilous jester, as Hyperbolus, to make a jest of it. And yet a man cannot say the sovereign people of Athens wanted right to banish them, or an Athenian the liberty to jest, or to be just.

The liberty which writers praise, is the

8. The liberty whereof there is so frequent and honourable mention in the histories and philosophy of the ancient Greeks and Romans and in the writings and discourse of those that from them

have received all their learning in the politics is not the liberty of particular men, but the liberty of the commonwealth,[1] which is the same with that which every man then should have if there were no civil laws nor commonwealth at all. And the effects of it also be the same. For as amongst masterless men there is perpetual war of every man against his neighbour, no inheritance to transmit to the son nor to expect from the father, no propriety of goods or lands, no security, but a full and absolute liberty in every particular man, so in states and commonwealths not dependent on one another every commonwealth (not every man) has an absolute liberty to do what it shall judge (that is to say, what that man or assembly that representeth it shall judge) most conducing to their benefit. But withal they live in the condition of a perpetual war and upon the confines of battle, with their frontiers armed and cannons planted against their neighbours round about. The Athenians and Romans were free, that is, free commonwealths; not that any particular men had the liberty to resist their own representative, but that their representative had the liberty to resist, or invade, other people. There is written on the turrets of the city of Luca in great characters at this day the word LIBERTAS; yet no man can thence infer that a particular man has more liberty or immunity from the service of the commonwealth there than in Constantinople. Whether a commonwealth be monarchical or popular, the freedom is still the same.

liberty of sovereigns; not of private men.

9. But it is an easy thing for men to be deceived by the specious name of liberty and (for want of judgement to distinguish) mistake that for their private inheritance and birthright which is the right of the public only. And when the same error is confirmed by the authority of men in reputation for their writings on this subject, it is no wonder if it produce sedition and change of government. In these western parts of the world we are made to receive our opinions concerning the institution and rights of commonwealths from Aristotle, Cicero, and other men, Greeks and Romans, that, living under popular states, derived those rights not from the principles of nature, but transcribed them into their books out of the [111]

1 Hobbes is criticizing the neo-Roman or republican theory of government in 21.8-15.

practice of their own commonwealths, which were popular, as the grammarians describe the rules of language out of the practice of the time or the rules of poetry out of the poems of Homer and Virgil. And because the Athenians were taught (to keep them from desire of changing their government) that they were freemen, and all that lived under monarchy were slaves, therefore Aristotle puts it down in his *Politics, In democracy*, LIBERTY *is to be supposed; for it is commonly held that no man is* FREE *in any other government* (Bk. VI: Ch.2). And as Aristotle, so Cicero and other writers have grounded their civil doctrine on the opinions of the Romans, who were taught to hate monarchy, at first by them that, having deposed their sovereign, shared amongst them the sovereignty of Rome, and afterwards by their successors. And by reading of these Greek and Latin authors men from their childhood have gotten a habit, under a false show of liberty, of favouring tumults, and of licentious controlling the actions of their sovereigns, and again of controlling those controllers, with the effusion of so much blood as I think I may truly say there was never anything so dearly bought as these western parts have bought the learning of the Greek and Latin tongues.

Liberty of subjects, how to be measured.

10. To come now to the particulars of the true liberty of a subject, that is to say, what are the things which, though commanded by the sovereign, he may nevertheless without injustice refuse to do, we are to consider what rights we pass away when we make a commonwealth or, which is all one, what liberty we deny ourselves by owning all the actions, without exception, of the man or assembly we make our sovereign. For in the act of our *submission* consisteth both our *obligation* and our *liberty*, which must therefore be inferred by arguments taken from thence; there being no obligation on any man which ariseth not from some act of his own; for all men equally are by nature free. And because such arguments must either be drawn from the express words, *I authorize all his actions*, or from the intention of him that submitteth himself to his power (which intention is to be understood by the end for which he so submitteth), the obligation and liberty of the subject is to be derived either from those words or others equivalent, or else from the end of the institution of sovereignty; namely, the peace of the

subjects within themselves and their defense against a common enemy.[1]

11. First therefore, seeing sovereignty by institution is by covenant of every one to every one, and sovereignty by acquisition by covenants of the vanquished to the victor or child to the parent, it is manifest that every subject has liberty in all those things the right whereof cannot by covenant be transferred. I have shown before, in the fourteenth chapter, that covenants not to defend a man's own body are void. Therefore,

Subjects have liberty to defend their own bodies, even against them that lawfully invade them.

12. If the sovereign command a man (though justly condemned) to kill, wound, or maim himself, or not to resist those that assault him, or to abstain from the use of food, air, medicine, or any other thing without which he cannot live; yet hath that man the liberty to disobey.

Are not bound to hurt themselves.

[112]

13. If a man be interrogated by the sovereign or his authority, concerning a crime done by himself, [then] he is not bound (without assurance of pardon) to confess it, because no man, as I have shown in the same chapter, can be obliged by covenant to accuse himself.

14. Again, the consent of a subject to sovereign power is contained in these words, *I authorize, or take upon me, all his actions*, in which there is no restriction at all of his own former natural liberty; for by allowing him to *kill me*, I am not bound to kill myself when he commands me.[2] It is one thing to say, *Kill me, or my fellow, if you please*, another thing to say, *I will kill myself, or my fellow*.[3] It followeth, therefore, that

15. No man is bound by the words themselves either to kill

---

1 Hobbes is emphasizing his theory of authorization in this and the following paragraphs and suppressing his theory of alienation. (See 17.13.) Hobbes is claiming here that authorization preserves the complete liberty of a subject and that political obligation arises from the subject's intention in entering a civil state. See 21.15, 21.17 and 21.21.

2 Authorizing the sovereign to kill me does not impose any obligation on me. So if the sovereign tried to 'command' me to kill myself, I would be under no obligation to do so.

3 The sentence 'Kill me, or my fellow, if you please' authorizes the addressee to kill me or my fellow. The sentence, "I will kill myself, or my fellow' would impose an obligation on me (in virtue of the future tense) if it were possible for a person to lay down his right to self-preservation. But it is not. See also 14.16.

himself or any other man; and consequently, that the obligation a man may sometimes have, upon the command of the sovereign, to execute any dangerous or dishonourable office, dependeth not on the words of our submission, but on the intention, which is to be understood by the end thereof. When therefore our refusal to obey frustrates the end for which the sovereignty was ordained, then there is no liberty to refuse; otherwise, there is.[1]

Nor to warfare, unless they voluntarily undertake it.

16. Upon this ground a man that is commanded as a soldier to fight against the enemy, though his sovereign have right enough to punish his refusal with death, may nevertheless in many cases refuse without injustice, as when he substituteth a sufficient soldier in his place; for in this case he deserteth not the service of the commonwealth. And there is allowance to be made for natural timorousness, not only to women (of whom no such dangerous duty is expected) but also to men of feminine courage. When armies fight, there is on one side or both a running away; yet when they do it not out of treachery, but fear, they are not esteemed to do it unjustly, but dishonourably. For the same reason to avoid battle is not injustice but cowardice. But he that enrolleth himself a soldier, or taketh impressed money, taketh away the excuse of a timorous nature and is obliged, not only to go to the battle but also not to run from it without his captain's leave. And when the defence of the commonwealth requireth at once the help of all that are able to bear arms, every one is obliged, because otherwise the institution of the commonwealth, which they have not the purpose or courage to preserve, was in vain.

17. To resist the sword of the commonwealth in defence of another man, guilty or innocent, no man hath liberty, because such liberty takes away from the sovereign the means of protecting us and is therefore destructive of the very essence of government. But in case a great many men together have already resisted the sovereign power unjustly or committed some capital crime for which every one of them expecteth death, whether have they not the liberty then to join together, and assist, and defend one another? Certainly they have; for they but defend their lives, which
[113] the guilty man may as well do as the innocent. There was indeed

1 See 21.10 and 21.17.

injustice in the first breach of their duty; their bearing of arms subsequent to it, though it be to maintain what they have done, is no new unjust act. And if it be only to defend their persons, it is not unjust at all. But the offer of pardon taketh from them to whom it is offered the plea of self-defence, and maketh their perseverance in assisting or defending the rest unlawful.

The greatest liberty of subjects, dependeth on the silence of the law.

18. As for other liberties, they depend on the silence of the law. In cases where the sovereign has prescribed no rule, there the subject hath the liberty to do or forbear, according to his own discretion. And therefore such liberty is in some places more and in some less, and in some times more, in other times less, according as they that have the sovereignty shall think most convenient. As for example, there was a time when in England a man might enter into his own land (and dispossess such as wrongfully possessed it) by force. But in after times that liberty of forcible entry was taken away by a statute made (by the king) in parliament. And in some places of the world men have the liberty of many wives; in other places, such liberty is not allowed.

19. If a subject have a controversy with his sovereign of debt, or of right of possession of lands or goods, or concerning any service required at his hands, or concerning any penalty, corporal or pecuniary, grounded on a precedent law, he hath the same liberty to sue for his right as if it were against a subject, and before such judges as are appointed by the sovereign. For seeing the sovereign demandeth by force of a former law and not by virtue of his power, he declareth thereby that he requireth no more than shall appear to be due by that law. The suit therefore is not contrary to the will of the sovereign, and consequently the subject hath the liberty to demand the hearing of his cause, and sentence according to that law. But if he demand or take anything by pretence of his power, there lieth, in that case, no action of law; for all that is done by him in virtue of his power is done by the authority of every subject, and consequently, he that brings an action against the sovereign brings it against himself.

20. If a monarch or sovereign assembly grant a liberty to all or any of his subjects, [and if] which grant standing, he is disabled to provide for their safety, [then] the grant is void, unless he directly renounce or transfer the sovereignty to another. For in that he

might openly (if it had been his will) and in plain terms have renounced or transferred it and did not, it is to be understood it was not his will, but that the grant proceeded from ignorance of the repugnancy between such a liberty and the sovereign power; and therefore the sovereignty is still retained, and consequently all those powers which are necessary to the exercising thereof, such as are the power of war and peace, of judicature, of appointing officers and counselors, of levying money, and the rest named in the eighteenth chapter.

In what cases subjects are absolved of their obedience to their sovereign.

[114] 21. The obligation of subjects to the sovereign is understood to last as long [as] and no longer than the power lasteth by which he is able to protect them. For the right men have by nature to protect themselves, when none else can protect them, can by no covenant be relinquished.[1] The sovereignty is the soul of the commonwealth, which, once departed from the body, the members do no more receive their motion from it. The end of obedience is protection, which, wheresoever a man seeth it either in his own or in another's sword, nature applieth his obedience to it and his endeavour to maintain it. And though sovereignty, in the intention of them that make it, be immortal; yet is it in its own nature not only subject to violent death by foreign war, but also through the ignorance and passions of men, it hath in it from the very institution many seeds of a natural mortality, by intestine discord.

In case of captivity.

22. If a subject be taken prisoner in war or his person or his means of life be within the guards of the enemy, and hath his life and corporal liberty given him on condition to be subject to the victor, [then] he hath liberty to accept the condition; and, having accepted it, is the subject of him that took him, because he had no other way to preserve himself. The case is the same if he be detained on the same terms in a foreign country. But if a man be held in prison or bonds or is not trusted with the liberty of his body, he cannot be understood to be bound by covenant to subjection and therefore may, if he can, make his escape by any means whatsoever.

In case the sovereign cast off

23. If a monarch shall relinquish the sovereignty, both for himself and his heirs, his subjects return to the absolute liberty of

1 See also 'Review and Conclusion' 7.

nature, because, though nature may declare who are his sons and who are the nearest of his kin; yet it dependeth on his own will, as hath been said in the precedent chapter, who shall be his heir. If therefore he will have no heir, there is no sovereignty, nor subjection. The case is the same if he die without known kindred and without declaration of his heir. For then there can no heir be known, and consequently no subjection be due.

the government from himself and his heirs.

In case of banishment.

24. If the sovereign banish his subject, [then] during the banishment he is not subject. But he that is sent on a message or hath leave to travel is still subject, but it is by contract between sovereigns, not by virtue of the covenant of subjection. For whosoever entereth into another's dominion is subject to all the laws thereof, unless he have a privilege by the amity of the sovereigns or by special license.

In case the sovereign render himself subject to another.

25. If a monarch subdued by war render himself subject to the victor, his subjects are delivered from their former obligation and become obliged to the victor. But if he be held prisoner or have not the liberty of his own body, he is not understood to have given away the right of sovereignty; and therefore his subjects are obliged to yield obedience to the magistrates formerly placed, governing not in their own name, but in his. For, his right remaining, the question is only of the administration, that is to say, of the magistrates and officers, which if he have not means to name, he is [115] supposed to approve those which he himself had formerly appointed.

# CHAPTER XXII

## OF SYSTEMS SUBJECT, POLITICAL AND PRIVATE

The diverse sorts of systems of people.

1. Having spoken of the generation, form, and power of a commonwealth, I am in order to speak next of the parts thereof. And first of systems, which resemble the similar parts or muscles of a body natural. By SYSTEMS I understand any numbers of men joined in one interest or one business. Of which some are *regular* and some *irregular*. *Regular* are those where one man or assembly

of men is constituted representative of the whole number. All other are *irregular.*

2. Of regular, some are *absolute* and *independent*, subject to none but their own representative; such are only commonwealths, of which I have spoken already in the five last precedent chapters. Others are dependent, that is to say, subordinate to some sovereign power, to which every one, as also their representative, is *subject.*

3. Of systems subordinate, some are *political* and some *private. Political* (otherwise called *bodies politic* and *persons in law*) are those which are made by authority from the sovereign power of the commonwealth. *Private* are those which are constituted by subjects amongst themselves or by authority from a stranger. For no authority derived from foreign power, within the dominion of another, is public there, but private.

4. And of private systems, some are *lawful*, some *unlawful*; *lawful* are those which are allowed by the commonwealth; all other are *unlawful. Irregular* systems are those which, having no representative, consist only in concourse of people, which if not forbidden by the commonwealth nor made on evil design (such as are conflux of people to markets, or shows, or any other harmless end) are lawful. But when the intention is evil or (if the number be considerable) unknown, they are unlawful.

In all bodies politic the power of the representative is limited.

5. In bodies politic, the power of the representative is always limited; and that which prescribeth the limits thereof is the power sovereign. For power unlimited is absolute sovereignty. And the sovereign in every commonwealth is the absolute representative of all the subjects; and therefore no other can be representative of any part of them but so far forth as he shall give leave; and to give leave to a body politic of subjects to have an absolute representative, to all intents and purposes were to abandon the government of so much of the commonwealth, and to divide the dominion, contrary to their peace and defence, which the sovereign cannot be understood to do by any grant that does not plainly and directly
[116] discharge them of their subjection. For consequences of words are not the signs of his will, when other consequences are signs of the contrary, but rather signs of error and misreckoning to which all mankind is too prone.

6. The bounds of that power which is given to the representa-

tive of a body politic are to be taken notice of from two things. One is their writ or letters from the sovereign; the other is the law of the commonwealth.

By letters patents.

7. For though in the institution or acquisition of a commonwealth, which is independent, there needs no writing, because the power of the representative has there no other bounds but such as are set out by the unwritten law of nature; yet in subordinate bodies there are such diversities of limitation necessary concerning their businesses, times, and places, as can neither be remembered without letters nor taken notice of unless such letters be patent, that they may be read to them, and withal sealed or testified with the seals or other permanent signs of the authority sovereign.

And the laws.

8. And because such limitation is not always easy or perhaps possible to be described in writing, the ordinary laws common to all subjects must determine what the representative may lawfully do in all cases where the letters themselves are silent. And therefore

When the representative is one man, his unwarranted acts are his own only.

9. In a body politic, if the representative be one man, whatsoever he does in the person of the body which is not warranted in his letters nor by the laws is his own act and not the act of the body, nor of any other member thereof besides himself; because further than his letters or the laws limit, he representeth no man's person but his own. But what he does according to these is the act of every one; for of the act of the sovereign every one is author,[1] because he is their representative unlimited; and the act of him that recedes not from the letters of the sovereign is the act of the sovereign, and therefore every member of the body is author of it.

When it is an assembly, it is the act of them that assented only.

10. But if the representative be an assembly, whatsoever that assembly shall decree, not warranted by their letters or the laws, is the act of the assembly or body politic; and [it is] the act of every one by whose vote the decree was made, but not the act of any man that being present voted to the contrary, nor of any man absent, unless he voted it by procuration [proxy]. It is the act of the assembly because voted by the major part; and if it be a crime, [then] the assembly may be punished as far forth as it is capable, as by dissolution or forfeiture of their letters (which is to such arti-

1 See also 18.1.

ficial and fictitious bodies, capital); or, if the assembly have a common stock wherein none of the innocent members have propriety, [then they may be punished] by pecuniary mulct [fine]. For from corporal penalties nature hath exempted all bodies politic. But they that gave not their vote are therefore innocent, because the assembly cannot represent any man in things unwarranted by their letters, and consequently are not involved in their votes.

When the representative is one man, if he borrow money, or owe it, by contract, he is liable only, the members not.

11. If the person of the body politic, being in one man, borrow money of a stranger, that is, of one that is not of the same body (for no letters need limit borrowing, seeing it is left to men's own inclinations to limit lending), the debt is the representative's. For if he should have authority from his letters to make the members pay what he borroweth, he should have by consequence the sovereignty of them; and therefore the grant were either void, as proceeding from error, commonly incident to human nature, and an insufficient sign of the will of the granter; or if it be avowed by [117] him, then is the representer sovereign, and falleth not under the present question, which is only of bodies subordinate. No member therefore is obliged to pay the debt so borrowed but the representative himself, because he that lendeth it, being a stranger to the letters and to the qualification of the body, understandeth those only for his debtors that are engaged; and seeing the representer can engage himself, and none else, has him only for debtor, who must therefore pay him out of the common stock, if there be any, or, if there be none, out of his own estate.

12. If he come into debt by contract or mulct, the case is the same.

When it is an assembly, they only are liable that have assented.

13. But when the representative is an assembly and the debt to a stranger, all they, and only they, are responsible for the debt that gave their votes to the borrowing of it or to the contract that made it due or to the fact for which the mulct was imposed, because every one of those in voting did engage himself for the payment; for he that is author of the borrowing is obliged to the payment, even of the whole debt, though when paid by any one, he be discharged.

If the debt be to one of the assembly, the

14. But if the debt be to one of the assembly, the assembly only is obliged to the payment out of their common stock (if they have any); for having liberty of vote, if he vote [that] the money shall be

borrowed, [then] he votes it shall be paid; if he vote it shall not be borrowed or be absent; yet because in lending he voteth the borrowing, he contradicteth his former vote and is obliged by the latter, and becomes both borrower and lender, and consequently cannot demand payment from any particular man, but from the common treasury only; which failing, he hath no remedy nor complaint but against himself, that being privy to the acts of the assembly, and to their means to pay, and not being enforced, did nevertheless through his own folly lend his money.

body only is obliged.

15. It is manifest by this that in bodies politic subordinate and subject to a sovereign power, it is sometimes not only lawful but expedient for a particular man to make open protestation against the decrees of the representative assembly and cause their dissent to be registered, or to take witness of it, because otherwise they may be obliged to pay debts contracted and be responsible for crimes committed by other men. But in a sovereign assembly that liberty is taken away, both because he that protesteth there denies their sovereignty and also because whatsoever is commanded by the sovereign power is as to the subject (though not so always in the sight of God) justified by the command; for of such command every subject is the author.

Protestation against the decrees of bodies politic sometimes lawful, but against sovereign power never.

16. The variety of bodies politic is almost infinite; for they are not only distinguished by the several affairs for which they are constituted, wherein there is an unspeakable diversity, but also by the times, places, and numbers, subject to many limitations. And as to their affairs, some are ordained for government; as first, the government of a province may be committed to an assembly of men, wherein all resolutions shall depend on the votes of the major part; and then this assembly is a body politic, and their power limited by commission. This word *province* signifies a charge or care of business, which he whose it is committeth to another man to be administered for and under him; and therefore when in one commonwealth there be divers countries that have their laws distinct one from another or are far distant in place, the administration of the government being committed to divers persons, those countries where the sovereign is not resident, but governs by commission, are called provinces. But of the government of a province by an assembly residing in the province itself there be few examples.

[118]

Bodies politic for government of a province, colony, or town.

The Romans, who had the sovereignty of many provinces; yet governed them always by presidents and praetors and not by assemblies, as they governed the city of Rome and territories adjacent. In like manner, when there were colonies sent from England to plant Virginia,[1] and Sommer-islands [the Bermudas], though the government of them here were committed to assemblies in London; yet did those assemblies never commit the government under them to any assembly there, but did to each plantation send one governor; for though every man, where he can be present by nature, desires to participate of government; yet where they cannot be present, they are by nature also inclined to commit the government of their common interest rather to a monarchical, than a popular, form of government; which is also evident in those men that have great private estates, who, when they are unwilling to take the pains of administering the business that belongs to them, choose rather to trust one servant than an assembly either of their friends or servants. But howsoever it be in fact; yet we may suppose the government of a province or colony committed to an assembly; and when it is, that which in this place I have to say is this: that whatsoever debt is by that assembly contracted, or whatsoever unlawful act is decreed, is the act only of those that assented, and not of any that dissented or were absent, for the reasons before alleged. Also that an assembly residing out of the bounds of that colony whereof they have the government cannot execute any power over the persons or goods of any of the colony, to seize on them for debt or other duty in any place without the colony itself, as having no jurisdiction nor authority elsewhere, but are left to the remedy which the law of the place alloweth them. And though the assembly have right to impose mulct upon any of their members that shall break the laws they make; yet out of the colony itself they have no right to execute the same. And that which is said here of the rights of an assembly for the government of a province or a colony is applicable also to an assembly for the government of a town, a university, or a college, or a church, or for any other government over the persons of men.

[119] 17. And generally, in all bodies politic, if any particular member

1 Hobbes had owned one share of stock in the Virginia Company, a gift from his employer, the earl of Devonshire.

conceive himself injured by the body itself, the cognizance of his cause belonged to the sovereign and those the sovereign hath ordained for judges in such causes or shall ordain for that particular cause, and not to the body itself. For the whole body is in this case his fellow subject, which in a sovereign assembly, is otherwise; for there, if the sovereign be not judge, though in his own cause, there can be no judge at all.

Bodies politic for ordering of trade.

18. In a body politic, for the well ordering of foreign traffic, the most commodious representative is an assembly of all the members, that is to say, such a one as every one that adventureth his money may be present at all the deliberations and resolutions of the body, if they will themselves. For proof whereof we are to consider the end for which men that are merchants, and may buy and sell, export, and import their merchandise according to their own discretions, do nevertheless bind themselves up in one corporation. It is true there be few merchants that with the merchandise they buy at home can freight a ship to export it, or with that they buy abroad to bring it home; and [they] have therefore need to join together in one society, where every man may either participate of the gain according to the proportion of his adventure, or take his own and sell what he transports or imports at such prices as he thinks fit. But this is no body politic, there being no common representative to oblige them to any other law than that which is common to all other subjects. The end of their incorporating is to make their gain the greater, which is done two ways, by sole buying and sole selling, both at home and abroad. So that to grant to a company of merchants to be a corporation or body politic is to grant them a double monopoly, whereof one is to be sole buyers, another to be sole sellers. For when there is a company incorporate for any particular foreign country, they only export the commodities vendible in that country, which is sole buying at home and sole selling abroad. For at home there is but one buyer and abroad but one that selleth, both which is gainful to the merchant, because thereby they buy at home at lower and sell abroad at higher rates; and abroad there is but one buyer of foreign merchandise and but one that sells them at home, both which again are gainful to the adventurers.

19. Of this double monopoly one part is disadvantageous to the

people at home, the other to foreigners. For at home by their sole exportation they set what price they please on the husbandry and handiworks of the people, and by the sole importation what price they please on all foreign commodities the people have need of, both which are ill for the people. On the contrary, by the sole selling of the native commodities abroad and sole buying the foreign commodities upon the place, they raise the price of those and abate the price of these, to the disadvantage of the foreigner; for
[120] where but one selleth the merchandise is the dearer and where but one buyeth, the cheaper; such corporations therefore are no other than monopolies, though they would be very profitable for a commonwealth, if being bound up into one body in foreign markets they were at liberty at home, every man to buy and sell at what price he could.

20. The end then of these bodies of merchants, being not a common benefit to the whole body (which have in this case no common stock, but what is deducted out of the particular adventures for building, buying, victualling [supplying food] and manning of ships), but the particular gain of every adventurer, it is reason that every one be acquainted with the employment of his own, that is, that every one be of the assembly that shall have the power to order the same and be acquainted with their accounts. And therefore the representative of such a body must be an assembly, where every member of the body may be present at the consultations, if he will.

21. If a body politic of merchants contract a debt to a stranger by the act of their representative assembly, every member is liable by himself for the whole. For a stranger can take no notice of their private laws, but considereth them as so many particular men, obliged every one to the whole payment till payment made by one dischargeth all the rest; but if the debt be to one of the company, the creditor is debtor for the whole to himself, and cannot therefore demand his debt, but only from the common stock, if there be any.

22. If the commonwealth impose a tax upon the body, it is understood to be laid upon every member proportionably to his particular adventure in the company. For there is in this case no

other common stock, but what is made of their particular adventures.

23. If a mulct be laid upon the body for some unlawful act, they only are liable by whose votes the act was decreed or by whose assistance it was executed; for in none of the rest is there any other crime but being of the body, which if a crime (because the body was ordained by the authority of the commonwealth) is not his.

24. If one of the members be indebted to the body, he may be sued by the body, but his goods cannot be taken nor his person imprisoned by the authority of the body, but only by authority of the commonwealth; for if they can do it by their own authority, they can by their own authority give judgement that the debt is due, which is as much as to be judge in their own cause.

A body politic for counsel to be given to the sovereign.

25. Those bodies made for the government of men or of traffic be either perpetual or for a time prescribed by writing. But there be bodies also whose times are limited, and that only by the nature of their business. For example, if a sovereign monarch or a sovereign assembly shall think fit to give command to the towns and other several parts of their territory to send to him their deputies to inform him of the condition and necessities of the [121] subjects, or to advise with him for the making of good laws, or for any other cause, as with one person representing the whole country, [then] such deputies, having a place and time of meeting assigned them, are there and at that time a body politic, representing every subject of that dominion; but it is only for such matters as shall be propounded unto them by that man or assembly, that by the sovereign authority sent for them; and when it shall be declared that nothing more shall be propounded nor debated by them, the body is dissolved. For if they were the absolute representative of the people, then were it the sovereign assembly; and so there would be two sovereign assemblies or two sovereigns over the same people, which cannot consist [be consistent] with their peace. And therefore where there is once a sovereignty, there can be no absolute representation of the people but by it. And for the limits of how far such a body shall represent the whole people, they are set forth in the writing by which they were sent for. For the people cannot choose their deputies to other

intent than is in the writing directed to them from their sovereign expressed.

A regular private body, lawful, as a family.

26. Private bodies regular and lawful are those that are constituted without letters or other written authority, saving the laws common to all other subjects. And because they be united in one person representative, they are held for regular, such as are all families in which the father or master ordereth the whole family. For he obligeth his children and servants as far as the law permitteth, though not further, because none of them are bound to obedience in those actions which the law hath forbidden to be done. In all other actions during the time they are under domestic government, they are subject to their fathers and masters as to their immediate sovereigns. For the father and master being before the institution of commonwealth absolute sovereigns in their own families, they lose afterward no more of their authority than the law of the commonwealth taketh from them.

Private bodies regular, but unlawful.

27. Private bodies regular, but unlawful, are those that unite themselves into one person representative without any public authority at all, such as are the corporations of beggars, thieves and gipsies, the better to order their trade of begging and stealing; and [such as] the corporations of men that by authority from any foreign person unite themselves in another's dominion for the easier propagation of doctrines and for making a party against the power of the commonwealth.

Systems irregular, such as are private leagues.

28. Irregular systems, in their nature but leagues, or sometimes mere concourse of people without union to any particular design, not[1] by obligation of one to another, but proceeding only from a similitude of wills and inclinations, become lawful or unlawful according to the lawfulness or unlawfulness of every particular man's design therein; and his design is to be understood by the occasion.

29. The leagues of subjects (because leagues are commonly made for mutual defense) are in a commonwealth (which is no more than a league of all the subjects together) for the most part
[122] unnecessary and savour of unlawful design and are for that cause unlawful, and go commonly by the name of factions or conspiracies. For a league being a connection of men by covenants, if there

1 Some editions delete this 'not'.

be no power given to any one man or assembly (as in the condition of mere nature) to compel them to performance, is so long only valid as there ariseth no just cause of distrust; and therefore leagues between commonwealths, over whom there is no human power established to keep them all in awe, are not only lawful but also profitable for the time they last. But leagues of the subjects of one and the same commonwealth, where every one may obtain his right by means of the sovereign power, are unnecessary to the maintaining of peace and justice, and in case the design of them be evil or unknown to the commonwealth, unlawful. For all uniting of strength by private men is, if for evil intent, unjust; if for intent unknown, dangerous to the public and unjustly concealed.

Secret cabals.

30. If the sovereign power be in a great assembly and a number of men, part of the assembly, without authority, consult a part to contrive the guidance of the rest, this is a faction or conspiracy unlawful, as being a fraudulent seducing of the assembly for their particular interest. But if he whose private interest is to be debated and judged in the assembly make as many friends as he can, in him it is no injustice, because in this case he is no part of the assembly. And though he hire such friends with money (unless there be an express law against it); yet it is not injustice. For sometimes (as men's manners are) justice cannot be had without money, and every man may think his own cause just till it be heard and judged.

Feuds of private families.

31. In all commonwealths, if private men entertain more servants than the government of his estate and lawful employment he has for them requires, it is faction, and unlawful. For having the protection of the commonwealth, he needeth not the defence of private force. And whereas in nations not thoroughly civilized, several numerous families have lived in continual hostility and invaded one another with private force; yet it is evident enough that they have done unjustly, or else that they had no commonwealth.

Factions for government.

32. And as factions for kindred, so also factions for government of religion, as of Papists, Protestants, etc., or of state, as patricians and plebeians of old time in Rome and of aristocraticals and democraticals of old time in Greece, are unjust, as being contrary to the peace and safety of the people and a taking of the sword out of the hand of the sovereign.

33. Concourse of people is an irregular system, the lawfulness or unlawfulness whereof dependeth on the occasion and on the number of them that are assembled. If the occasion be lawful and manifest, the concourse is lawful as the usual meeting of men at church or at a public show, in usual numbers; for if the numbers be extraordinarily great, the occasion is not evident, and consequently he that cannot render a particular and good account of his being amongst them is to be judged conscious of an unlawful and tumultuous design. It may be lawful for a thousand men to join in
[123] a petition to be delivered to a judge or magistrate; yet if a thousand men come to present it, it is a tumultuous assembly, because there needs but one or two for that purpose. But in such cases as these it is not a set number that makes the assembly unlawful, but such a number as the present officers are not able to suppress and bring to justice.

34. When an unusual number of men assemble against a man whom they accuse, the assembly is an unlawful tumult, because they may deliver their accusation to the magistrate by a few or by one man. Such was the case of St. Paul at Ephesus, where Demetrius and a great number of other men brought two of Paul's companions before the magistrate, saying with one voice, *Great is Diana of the Ephesians*, which was their way of demanding justice against them for teaching the people such doctrine as was against their religion and trade. The occasion here, considering the laws of that people, was just; yet was their assembly judged unlawful, and the magistrate reprehended them for it in these words, *If Demetrius and the other workmen can accuse any man of any thing, there be pleas, and deputies; let them accuse one another. And if you have any*
Acts 19:40. *other thing to demand, your case may be judged in an assembly lawfully called. For we are in danger to be accused for this day's sedition, because there is no cause by which any man can render any reason of this concourse of people.* Where he calleth an assembly whereof men can give no just account, a sedition, and such as they could not answer for. And this is all I shall say concerning *systems* and assemblies of people, which may be compared, as I said [in the Introduction], to the similar parts of man's body, such as be lawful to the muscles, such as are unlawful to wens [tumors], biles, and apostems [a large, deep abscess] engendered by the unnatural conflux of evil humours.

# CHAPTER XXIII

## OF THE PUBLIC MINISTERS OF SOVEREIGN POWER

Public minister, who.

1. In the last chapter I have spoken of the similar parts of a commonwealth; in this I shall speak of the parts organical, which are public ministers.

2. A PUBLIC MINISTER is he that by the sovereign, whether a monarch or an assembly, is employed in any affairs with authority to represent in that employment the person of the commonwealth. And whereas every man or assembly that hath sovereignty representeth two persons, or (as the more common phrase is) has two capacities, one natural and another politic (as a monarch hath the person not only of the commonwealth but also of a man, and a sovereign assembly hath the person not only of the commonwealth but also of the assembly),[1] they that be servants to them in their natural capacity are not public ministers, but those only that serve them in the administration of the public business. And [124] therefore neither ushers nor sergeants nor other officers that wait on the assembly for no other purpose but for the commodity of the men assembled in an aristocracy or democracy, nor stewards, chamberlains, cofferers, or any other officers of the household of a monarch, are public ministers in a monarchy.

Ministers for the general administration.

3. Of public ministers, some have charge committed to them of a general administration, either of the whole dominion or of a part thereof. Of the whole, as to a protector or regent, may be committed by the predecessor of an infant king during his minority the whole administration of his kingdom. In which case, every subject is so far obliged to obedience, as the ordinances he shall make and the commands he shall give be in the king's name, and not inconsistent with his sovereign power. Of a part or province, as when either a monarch or a sovereign assembly shall give the general charge thereof to a governor, lieutenant, prefect, or viceroy, and in this case also every one of that province is obliged to all he shall do in the name of the sovereign and that is not incompatible with the

1 The doctrine of the king's two bodies was well-established in seventeenth-century England. The regicides claimed that they were executing the man Charles Stuart, not the king of England.

sovereign's right. For such protectors, viceroys, and governors have no other right but what depends on the sovereign's will; and no commission that can be given them can be interpreted for a declaration of the will to transfer the sovereignty without express and perspicuous words to that purpose. And this kind of public ministers resembleth the nerves and tendons that move the several limbs of a body natural.

For special administration, as for economy.

4. Others have special administration, that is to say, charges of some special business either at home or abroad; as at home, first, for the economy of a commonwealth, they that have authority concerning the *treasure*, as tributes, impositions, rents, fines, or whatsoever public revenue, to collect, receive, issue, or take the accounts thereof, are public ministers; ministers, because they serve the person representative and can do nothing against his command nor without his authority; public, because they serve him in his political capacity.

5. Secondly, they that have authority concerning the *militia* to have the custody of arms, forts, ports, to levy, pay, or conduct soldiers, or to provide for any necessary thing for the use of war either by land or sea, are public ministers. But a soldier without command, though he fight for the commonwealth, does not therefore represent the person of it, because there is none to represent it to. For every one that hath command represents it to them only whom he commandeth.

For instruction of the people.

6. They also that have authority to teach or to enable others to teach the people their duty to the sovereign power and instruct them in the knowledge of what is just and unjust, thereby to render them more apt to live in godliness and in peace amongst themselves and resist the public enemy, are public ministers; ministers, in that they do it not by their own authority but by another's;
[125] and public, because they do it (or should do it) by no authority but that of the sovereign. The monarch or the sovereign assembly only hath immediate authority from God to teach and instruct the people, and no man but the sovereign receiveth his power *Dei gratia* simply, that is to say from the favour of none but God;[1] all other

1 Hobbes is using the language of the theory of the divine right of kings here even though it does not fit his theory, according to which sovereigns are instituted by their subjects.

receive theirs from the favour and providence of God and their sovereigns, as in a monarchy *Dei gratia et regis* [by the grace of God and king] or *Dei providentia et voluntate regis* [by the providence of God and the will of the king].

7. They also to whom jurisdiction is given are public ministers. For in their seats of justice they represent the person of the sovereign; and their sentence is his sentence; for as hath been before declared, all judicature is essentially annexed to the sovereignty, and therefore all other judges are but ministers of him or them that have the sovereign power. And as controversies are of two sorts, namely of *fact* and of *law*, so are judgements, some of fact, some of law; and consequently in the same controversy there may be two judges, one of fact, another of law.

For judicature.

8. And in both these controversies, there may arise a controversy between the party judged and the judge, which, because they be both subjects to the sovereign, ought in equity to be judged by men agreed on by consent of both, for no man can be judge in his own cause. But the sovereign is already agreed on for judge by them both, and is therefore either to hear the cause and determine it himself or appoint for judge such as they shall both agree on. And this agreement is then understood to be made between them divers ways; as first, if the defendant be allowed to except [object] against such of his judges whose interest maketh him suspect them (for as to the complainant, he hath already chosen his own judge), those which he excepteth not against are judges he himself agrees on. Secondly, if he appeal to any other judge, he can appeal no further, for his appeal is his choice. Thirdly, if he appeal to the sovereign himself, and he by himself or by delegates which the parties shall agree on give sentence, that sentence is final; for the defendant is judged by his own judges, that is to say, by himself.

9. These properties of just and rational judicature considered, I cannot forbear to observe the excellent constitution of the courts of justice established both for common and also for public pleas in England. By common pleas I mean those where both the complainant and defendant are subjects and by public (which are also called pleas of the crown) those where the complainant is the sovereign. For whereas there were two orders of men, whereof one was lords, the other commons, the lords had this privilege, to

have for judges in all capital crimes none but lords, and of them, as many as would be present; which being ever acknowledged as a privilege of favour, their judges were none but such as they had themselves desired. And in all controversies every subject (as also in civil controversies the lords) had for judges men of the country where the matter in controversy lay, against which he might make

[126] his exceptions, till at last twelve men without exception being agreed on, they were judged by those twelve. So that having his own judges, there could be nothing alleged by the party why the sentence should not be final. These public persons, with authority from the sovereign power either to instruct or judge the people, are such members of the commonwealth as may fitly be compared to the organs of voice in a body natural.

For execution.

10. Public ministers are also all those that have authority from the sovereign to procure the execution of judgements given, to publish the sovereign's commands, to suppress tumults, to apprehend and imprison malefactors, and other acts tending to the conservation of the peace. For every act they do by such authority is the act of the commonwealth and their service answerable to that of the hands in a body natural.

11. Public ministers abroad are those that represent the person of their own sovereign to foreign states. Such are ambassadors, messengers, agents, and heralds sent by public authority and on public business.

12. But such as are sent by authority only of some private party of a troubled state, though they be received, are neither public nor private ministers of the commonwealth, because none of their actions have the commonwealth for author. Likewise, an ambassador, sent from a prince to congratulate, condole, or to assist at a solemnity, though the authority be public; yet because the business is private and belonging to him in his natural capacity, is a private person. Also if a man be sent into another country, secretly to explore their counsels and strength, though both the authority and the business be public; yet because there is none to take notice of any person in him but his own, he is but a private minister, but yet a minister of the commonwealth, and may be compared to an eye in the body natural. And those that are appointed to receive the

petitions or other informations of the people and are, as it were, the public ear, are public ministers and represent their sovereign in that office.

Counselors without other employment than to advise are not public ministers.

13. Neither a counselor (nor a council of state, if we consider it with no authority of judicature or command, but only of giving advice to the sovereign when it is required or of offering it when it is not required) is a public person. For the advice is addressed to the sovereign only, whose person cannot in his own presence be represented to him by another. But a body of counselors are never without some other authority, either of judicature or of immediate administration. As in a monarchy, they represent the monarch in delivering his commands to the public ministers. In a democracy, the council or senate propounds the result of their deliberations to the people as a council; but when they appoint judges or hear causes, or give audience to ambassadors, it is in the quality of a minister of the people. And in an aristocracy the council of state is the sovereign assembly itself and gives counsel to none but themselves.

## CHAPTER XXIV

[127]

## OF THE NUTRITION AND PROCREATION OF A COMMONWEALTH

The nourishment of a commonwealth consisteth in the commodities of sea and land:

1. The NUTRITION of a commonwealth consisteth in the plenty and distribution of materials conducing to life in concoction (or preparation) and (when concocted) in the conveyance of it by convenient conduits to the public use.

2. As for the plenty of matter, it is a thing limited by nature to those commodities which from (the two breasts of our common mother) land and sea, God usually either freely giveth or for labour selleth to mankind.

3. For the matter of this nutriment, consisting in animals, vegetables, and minerals, God hath freely laid them before us in or near to the face of the earth, so as there needeth no more but the labour and industry of receiving them. Insomuch as plenty depen-

deth, (next to God's favour) merely on the labour and industry of men.

4. This matter, commonly called commodities, is partly *native* and partly *foreign*; *native*, that which is to be had within the territory of the commonwealth; *foreign*, that which is imported from without. And because there is no territory under the dominion of one commonwealth (except it be of very vast extent) that produceth all things needful for the maintenance and motion of the whole body and few that produce not something more than necessary, the superfluous commodities to be had within become no more superfluous, but supply these wants at home by importation of that which may be had abroad, either by exchange or by just war or by labour; for a man's labour also is a commodity exchangeable for benefit as well as any other thing; and there have been commonwealths that, having no more territory than hath served them for habitation, have nevertheless not only maintained but also increased their power, partly by the labour of trading from one place to another and partly by selling the manufactures, whereof the materials were brought in from other places.

And the right distribution of them.

5. The distribution of the materials of this nourishment is the constitution of *mine* and *thine* and *his*, that is to say in one word, *propriety [property]*, and belongeth in all kinds of commonwealth to the sovereign power.[1] For where there is no commonwealth there is, as hath been already shown, a perpetual war of every man against his neighbour, and therefore everything is his that getteth it and keepeth it by force, which is neither *propriety* nor *community*, but *uncertainty*. Which is so evident that even Cicero, a passionate defender of liberty, in a public pleading attributeth all propriety to the law civil; *Let the civil law*, saith he, *be once abandoned, or but negli-*
[128] *gently guarded (not to say oppressed), and there is nothing that any man can be sure to receive from his ancestor, or leave to his children*. And again,

1 Hobbes seems to be taking the republican theorists of the 1640s (and earlier) head on. The republicans, that is, those inspired by certain ancient authors, especially Romans such as Cicero and Livy, claimed that if citizens did not have an absolute right in their property, then they were servants or slaves. Hobbes said that subjects do not have such a right and they were servants of the sovereign (chapter 20). See also Quentin Skinner, "John Milton and the Politics of Slavery," *Prose Studies* 23 (2000), 1-23.

*Take away the civil law, and no man knows what is his own, and what another man's.* Seeing therefore the introduction of propriety is an effect of commonwealth, which can do nothing but by the person that represents it, it is the act only of the sovereign and consisteth in the laws, which none can make that have not the sovereign power. And this they well knew of old, who called that *nomos* (that is to say, *distribution*) which we call law, and defined justice, by *distributing* to every man *his own.*

All private estates of land proceed originally from the arbitrary distribution of the sovereign.

6. In this distribution, the first law is for division of the land itself, wherein the sovereign assigneth to every man a portion according as he, and not according as any subject or any number of them, shall judge agreeable to equity and the common good. The children of Israel were a commonwealth in the wilderness, but wanted the commodities of the earth till they were masters of the Land of Promise, which afterward was divided amongst them not by their own discretion but by the discretion of Eleazar the priest and Joshua their general; who when there were twelve tribes, making them thirteen by subdivision of the tribe of Joseph, made nevertheless but twelve portions of the land and ordained for the tribe of Levi no land, but assigned them the tenth part of the whole fruits, which division was therefore arbitrary. And though a people coming into possession of a land by war do not always exterminate the ancient inhabitants as did the Jews, but leave to many or most or all of them their estates; yet it is manifest they hold them afterwards as of the victor's distribution, as the people of England held all theirs of William the Conqueror.

Propriety of a subject excludes not the dominion of the sovereign, but only of another subject.

7. From whence we may collect that the propriety which a subject hath in his lands consisteth in a right to exclude all other subjects from the use of them, and not to exclude their sovereign, be it an assembly or a monarch. For seeing the sovereign, that is to say, the commonwealth (whose person he representeth), is understood to do nothing but in order to the common peace and security, this distribution of lands is to be understood as done in order to the same; and consequently, whatsoever distribution he shall make in prejudice thereof is contrary to the will of every subject that committed his peace and safety to his discretion and conscience, and therefore by the will of every one of them is to be

reputed void. It is true that a sovereign monarch, or the greater part of a sovereign assembly, may ordain the doing of many things in pursuit of their passions, contrary to their own consciences, which is a breach of trust and of the law of nature; but this is not enough to authorize any subject either to make war upon or so much as to accuse of injustice or any way to speak evil of their sovereign, because they have authorized all his actions, and in bestowing the sovereign power made them their own.[1] But in what cases the commands of sovereigns are contrary to equity and the law of nature is to be considered hereafter in another place.

The public is not to be dieted. [129]

8. In the distribution of land, the commonwealth itself may be conceived to have a portion, and possess and improve the same by their representative, and that such portion may be made sufficient to sustain the whole expense to the common peace and defense necessarily required; which were very true, if there could be any representative conceived free from human passions and infirmities. But the nature of men being as it is, the setting forth of public land or of any certain revenue for the commonwealth is in vain and tendeth to the dissolution of government, to the condition of mere nature and war, as soon as ever the sovereign power falleth into the hands of a monarch or of an assembly that are either too negligent of money or too hazardous in engaging the public stock into long or costly war. Commonwealths can endure no diet; for seeing their expense is not limited by their own appetite but by external accidents and the appetites of their neighbours, the public riches cannot be limited by other limits than those which the emergent occasions shall require. And whereas in England there were, by the Conqueror, divers lands reserved to his own use (besides forests and chases, either for his recreation or for preservation of woods), and divers services reserved on the land he gave his subjects; yet it seems they were not reserved for his maintenance in his public but in his natural capacity; for he and his successors did,

---

1 In *Eikonoklastes* (1649), John Milton wrote that Charles I had aspired to make all Britain "ty'd and chain'd to the conscience, judgement, and reason of one Man" and thereby to put his subjects "into the condition of Slaves" (quoted from Skinner, "John Milton and the Politics of Slavery," p. 12). Hobbes takes this position head on and says that the king's reason and conscience should be that of all of his subjects. See also 18.1 and 22.9.

for all that, lay arbitrary taxes on all subjects' land when they judged it necessary. Or if those public lands and services were ordained as a sufficient maintenance of the commonwealth, it was contrary to the scope of the institution, being (as it appeared by those ensuing taxes) insufficient and (as it appears by the late small revenue of the Crown) subject to alienation and diminution. It is therefore in vain to assign a portion to the commonwealth, which may sell or give it away, and does sell and give it away when it is done by their representative.

The places and matter of traffic depend, as their distribution, on the sovereign.

9. As the distribution of lands at home, so also to assign in what places and for what commodities the subject shall traffic abroad belongeth to the sovereign. For if it did belong to private persons to use their own discretion therein, some of them would be drawn for gain, both to furnish the enemy with means to hurt the commonwealth and hurt it themselves by importing such things as, pleasing men's appetites, be nevertheless noxious or at least unprofitable to them. And therefore it belongeth to the commonwealth (that is, to the sovereign only) to approve or disapprove both of the places and matter of foreign traffic.

The laws of transferring propriety belong also to the sovereign.

10. Further, seeing it is not enough to the sustentation of a commonwealth that every man have a propriety in a portion of land or in some few commodities, or a natural property in some useful art, and that there is no art in the world but is necessary either for the being or well-being almost of every particular man, it is necessary that men distribute that which they can spare and transfer their propriety therein mutually one to another by exchange and mutual contract. And therefore it belongeth to the commonwealth (that is to say, to the sovereign) to appoint in what [130] manner all kinds of contract between subjects (as buying, selling, exchanging, borrowing, lending, letting, and taking to hire) are to be made, and by what words and signs they shall be understood for valid. And for the matter and distribution of the nourishment to the several members of the commonwealth, thus much, considering the model of the whole work, is sufficient.

Money the blood of a commonwealth.

11. By concoction, I understand the reducing of all commodities which are not presently consumed but reserved for nourishment in time to come to something of equal value, and withal so portable as not to hinder the motion of men from place to

place, to the end a man may have in what place soever such nourishment as the place affordeth. And this is nothing else but gold, and silver, and money. For gold and silver, being, as it happens, almost in all countries of the world highly valued, is a commodious measure of the value of all things else between nations; and money, of what matter soever coined by the sovereign of a commonwealth, is a sufficient measure of the value of all things else between the subjects of that commonwealth. By the means of which measures all commodities, movable and immovable, are made to accompany a man to all places of his resort within and without the place of his ordinary residence; and the same passeth from man to man within the commonwealth and goes round about, nourishing (as it passeth) every part thereof, in so much as this concoction is as it were the sanguification of the commonwealth; for natural blood is in like manner made of the fruits of the earth, and circulating, nourisheth by the way every member of the body of man.

12. And because silver and gold have their value from the matter itself, they have first this privilege, that the value of them cannot be altered by the power of one nor of a few commonwealths, as being a common measure of the commodities of all places. But base money may easily be enhanced or abased. Secondly, they have the privilege to make commonwealths move and stretch out their arms, when need is, into foreign countries, and supply not only private subjects that travel but also whole armies with provision. But that coin, which is not considerable for the matter, but for the stamp of the place, being unable to endure change of air, hath its effect at home only, where also it is subject to the change of laws, and thereby to have the value diminished to the prejudice many times of those that have it.

The conduits and way of money to the public use.

13. The conduits and ways by which it is conveyed to the public use are of two sorts: one, that conveyeth it to the public coffers; the other, that issueth the same out again for public payments. Of the first sort are collectors, receivers, and treasurers; of the second are the treasurers again and the officers appointed for payment of several public or private ministers. And in this also the artificial man maintains his resemblance with the natural, whose veins
[131] receiving the blood from the several parts of the body carry it to

the heart, where being made vital, the heart by the arteries sends it out again to enliven and enable for motion all the members of the same.[1]

14. The procreation or children of a commonwealth are those we call *plantations* or *colonies*, which are numbers of men sent out from the commonwealth under a conductor or governor to inhabit a foreign country either formerly void of inhabitants or made void then by war. And when a colony is settled, they are either a commonwealth of themselves, discharged of their subjection to their sovereign that sent them (as hath been done by many commonwealths of ancient time), in which case the commonwealth from which they went was called their metropolis or mother, and requires no more of them than fathers require of the children whom they emancipate and make free from their domestic government, which is honour and friendship, or else they remain united to their metropolis, as were the colonies of the people of Rome; and then they are no commonwealths themselves, but provinces, and parts of the commonwealth that sent them. So that the right of colonies, saving honour and league with their metropolis, dependeth wholly on their license or letters, by which their sovereign authorized them to plant.

The children of a commonwealth colonies.

## CHAPTER XXV

## OF COUNSEL

1. How fallacious it is to judge of the nature of things by the ordinary and inconstant use of words appeareth in nothing more than in the confusion of counsels and commands, arising from the imperative manner of speaking in them both, and in many other occasions besides. For the words *do this* are the words not only of him that commandeth, but also of him that giveth counsel and of him that exhorteth; and yet there are but few that see not that these are very different things or that cannot distinguish between

Counsel what.

1 Hobbes's friend William Harvey had discovered the way blood circulates in the body and explained it in *De Motu Cordis et Sanguinis* (1628). Hobbes is showing off his scientific knowledge.

them when they perceive who it is that speaketh and to whom the speech is directed and upon what occasion. But finding those phrases in men's writings and being not able or not willing to enter into a consideration of the circumstances, they mistake sometimes the precepts of counsellors for the precepts[1] of them that command, and sometimes the contrary, according as it best agreeth with the conclusions they would infer or the actions they approve. To avoid which mistakes and render to those terms of commanding, counselling, and exhorting, their proper and distinct significations, I define them thus.

Differences between command and counsel.

[132]

2. COMMAND is where a man saith, *Do this* or *Do not this*, without expecting other reason than the will of him that says it.[2] From this it followeth manifestly that he that commandeth pretendeth thereby his own benefit; for the reason of his command is his own will only, and the proper object of every man's will is some good to himself.[3]

3. COUNSEL is where a man saith, *Do* or *Do not this*, and deduceth his reasons from the benefit that arriveth by it to him to whom he saith it. And from this it is evident that he that giveth counsel pretendeth only (whatsoever he intendeth) the good of him to whom he giveth it.[4]

4. Therefore between counsel and command, one great difference is that command is directed to a man's own benefit and counsel to the benefit of another man. And from this ariseth another difference, that a man may be obliged to do what he is commanded, as when he hath covenanted to obey: but he cannot be obliged to do as he is counselled, because the hurt of not

---

1 A precept is a proposition that aims at guiding action. Hobbes talks about two kinds of precepts: counsels and commands (or laws). See also 14.3 and 26.2.

2 See also 26.44.

3 According to Hobbes, an imperative sentence is used as a command when the speaker intends the addressee's action to benefit himself, the speaker, rather than the addressee. In the next paragraph, he says that an imperative sentence is used as advice "counsel" when the speaker intends the addressee to benefit from his own action. What would Hobbes say about the cases in which a parent says to her child, "Eat your carrots," or a sergeant during combat says to his soldiers, "Get down!"? What would he say about the salesman who says, "Buy this vacuum cleaner"? See also 25.4, 25.9 and 25.10.

4 See also 42.45, 42.101, 42.104–9.

following it is his own; or if he should covenant to follow it, then is the counsel turned into the nature of a command. A third difference between them is that no man can pretend a right to be of another man's counsel, because he is not to pretend benefit by it to himself, but to demand right to counsel another argues a will to know his designs or to gain some other good to himself, which, as I said before, is of every man's will the proper object.

5. This also is incident to the nature of counsel, that whatsoever it be, he that asketh it cannot in equity accuse or punish it; for to ask counsel of another is to permit him to give such counsel as he shall think best; and consequently, he that giveth counsel to his sovereign (whether a monarch or an assembly) when he asketh it, cannot in equity be punished for it,[1] whether the same be conformable to the opinion of the most or not, so it be to the proposition in debate. For if the sense of the assembly can be taken notice of, before the debate be ended, they should neither ask nor take any further counsel; for sense of the assembly is the resolution of the debate and end of all deliberation. And generally he that demandeth counsel is author of it and therefore cannot punish it; and what the sovereign cannot, no man else can.[2] But if one subject giveth counsel to another to do anything contrary to the laws, whether that counsel proceed from evil intention or from ignorance only, it is punishable by the commonwealth, because ignorance of the law is no good excuse, where every man is bound to take notice of the laws to which he is subject.

Exhortation and dehortation, what.

6. EXHORTATION and DEHORTATION is counsel, accompanied with signs in him that giveth it of vehement desire to have it followed, or, to say it more briefly, counsel vehemently pressed. For he that exhorteth doth not deduce the consequences of what he adviseth to be done and tie himself therein to the rigor of true reasoning, but encourages him he counselleth to action, as he that dehorteth deterreth him from it. And therefore they have in their speeches a regard to the common passions and

1 The king's counselors sometimes were punished for the advice they gave. Hobbes is defending counselors against the actual practice of kings.

2 Hobbes may be giving a belated defense of Lord Strafford, who was executed by a bill of attainder in Parliament for doing the king's business.

opinions of men in deducing their reasons, and [they] make use of similitudes, metaphors, examples, and other tools of oratory, to persuade their hearers of the utility, honour, or justice of following their advice.

[133] 7. From whence may be inferred, first, that exhortation and dehortation is directed to the good of him that giveth the counsel, not of him that asketh it, which is contrary to the duty of a counsellor, who, by the definition of counsel, ought to regard, not his own benefit, but his whom he adviseth. And that he directeth his counsel to his own benefit is manifest enough by the long and vehement urging or by the artificial giving thereof, which being not required of him and consequently proceeding from his own occasions, is directed principally to his own benefit and but accidentally to the good of him that is counselled, or not at all.

8. Secondly, that the use of exhortation and dehortation lieth only where a man is to speak to a multitude, because when the speech is addressed to one, he may interrupt him and examine his reasons more rigorously than can be done in a multitude, which are too many to enter into dispute and dialogue with him that speaketh indifferently to them all at once.

9. Thirdly, that they that exhort and dehort, where they are required to give counsel, are corrupt counsellors and, as it were, bribed by their own interest. For though the counsel they give be never so good; yet he that gives it is no more a good counsellor than he that giveth a just sentence for a reward is a just judge. But where a man may lawfully command, as a father in his family or a leader in an army, his exhortations and dehortations are not only lawful, but also necessary and laudable; but when they are no more counsels, but commands, which when they are for execution of sour [disagreeable] labour, sometimes necessity and always humanity, requireth to be sweetened in the delivery by encouragement and in the tune and phrase of counsel rather than in harsher language of command.

10. Examples of the difference between command and counsel we may take from the forms of speech that express them in Holy Scripture. *Have no other Gods but me; Make to thyself no graven image; Take not God's name in vain; Sanctify the Sabbath; Honour thy parents; Kill not; Steal not, etc.* are commands, because the reason for which we are to obey them is drawn from the will of God our

King,[1] whom we are obliged to obey. But these words, *Sell all thou hast; give it to the poor; and follow me*, are counsel, because the reason for which we are to do so is drawn from our own benefit, which is this; that we shall have *treasure in Heaven*. These words, *Go into the village over against you, and you shall find an ass tied, and her colt; loose her, and bring her to me*, are a command; for the reason of their fact is drawn from the will of their master; but these words, *Repent, and be baptized in the name of Jesus*, are counsel, because the reason why we should so do tendeth not to any benefit of God Almighty, who shall still be King in what manner soever we rebel, but of ourselves, who have no other means of avoiding the punishment hanging over us for our sins.

Differences of fit and unfit counsellors.

[134]

11. As the difference of counsel from command hath been now deduced from the nature of counsel, consisting in a deducing of the benefit or hurt that may arise to him that is to be counselled, by the necessary or probable consequences of the action he propoundeth; so may also the differences between apt and inept counsellors be derived from the same. For experience, being but memory of the consequences of like actions formerly observed, and counsel but the speech whereby that experience is made known to another, the virtues and defects of counsel are the same with the virtues and defects intellectual; and to the person of a commonwealth, his counsellors serve him in the place of memory and mental discourse. But with this resemblance of the commonwealth to a natural man, there is one dissimilitude joined of great importance, which is that a natural man receiveth his experience from the natural objects of sense, which work upon him without passion or interest of their own; whereas they that give counsel to the representative person of a commonwealth may have, and have often, their particular ends and passions that render their counsels always suspected, and many times unfaithful. And therefore we may set down for the first condition of a good counsellor, *that his ends and interest be not inconsistent with the ends and interest of him he counselleth*.

12. Secondly, because the office of a counsellor, when an action comes into deliberation, is to make manifest the consequences of

1 Hobbes's view differs from the usual one according to which God's commands are for our own benefit. Again against the usual view, Hobbes claims that the precepts of Jesus are counsels, precepts for our benefit.

it in such manner as he that is counselled may be truly and evidently informed, he ought to propound his advice in such form of speech as may make the truth most evidently appear, that is to say, with as firm ratiocination, as significant and proper language and as briefly as the evidence will permit. And therefore *rash and unevident inferences* (such as are fetched only from examples or authority of books and are not arguments of what is good or evil, but witnesses of fact or of opinion), *obscure, confused, and ambiguous expressions, also all metaphorical speeches tending to the stirring up of passion* (because such reasoning and such expressions are useful only to deceive or to lead him we counsel towards other ends than his own), *are repugnant to the office of a counsellor.*

13. Thirdly, because the ability of counselling proceedeth from experience and long study and no man is presumed to have experience in all those things that to the administration of a great commonwealth are necessary to be known, *no man is presumed to be a good counsellor but in such business as he hath not only been much versed in, but hath also much meditated on and considered.* For seeing the business of a commonwealth is this, to preserve the people in peace at home and defend them against foreign invasion, we shall find it requires great knowledge of the disposition of mankind, of the rights of government, and of the nature of equity, law, justice, and honour, not to be attained without study; and of the strength, commodities, places, both of their own country and their neighbours', as also of the inclinations and designs of all nations that may [in] any way annoy them. And this is not attained to without
[135] much experience. Of which things, not only the whole sum, but every one of the particulars requires the age and observation of a man in years and of more than ordinary study. The wit required for counsel, as I have said before (Chapter 8), is judgement. And the differences of men in that point come from different education, of some, to one kind of study or business, and of others, to another. When for the doing of anything there be infallible rules (as in engines and edifices, the rules of geometry), all the experience of the world cannot equal his counsel that has learned or found out the rule. And when there is no such rule, he that hath most experience in that particular kind of business has therein the best judgement and is the best counsellor.

14. Fourthly, to be able to give counsel to a commonwealth in a business that hath reference to another commonwealth, *it is necessary to be acquainted with the intelligences and letters that come from thence and with all the records of treaties and other transactions of state* between them, which none can do but such as the representative shall think fit. By which we may see that they who are not called to counsel can have no good counsel in such cases to obtrude.

15. Fifthly, supposing the number of counsellors equal, a man is better counselled by hearing them apart than in an assembly, and that for many causes. First, in hearing them apart, you have the advice of every man; but in an assembly many of them deliver their advice with aye or no or with their hands or feet, not moved by their own sense, but by the eloquence of another, or for fear of displeasing some that have spoken, or the whole by contradiction, or for fear of appearing duller in apprehension than those that have applauded the contrary opinion. Secondly, in an assembly of many there cannot choose but be some whose interests are contrary to that of the public; and these their interests make passionate, and passion eloquent, and eloquence draws others into the same advice. For the passions of men, which asunder are moderate, as the heat of one brand, in assembly are like many brands that inflame one another (especially when they blow one another with orations) to the setting of the commonwealth on fire, under pretence of counselling it. Thirdly, in hearing every man apart, one may examine, when there is need, the truth or probability of his reasons and of the grounds of the advice he gives, by frequent interruptions and objections; which cannot be done in an assembly, where in every difficult question a man is rather astonied [bewildered] and dazzled with the variety of discourse upon it, than informed of the course he ought to take. Besides, there cannot be an assembly of many, called together for advice, wherein there be not some that have the ambition to be thought eloquent and also learned in the politics; and [they] give not their advice with care of the business propounded, but of the applause of their motley orations, made of the divers colored threads or shreds of authors; which is an impertinence, at least, that takes away the time of serious consultation and in the secret way of counseling apart is easily avoided. Fourthly, in deliberations that ought to be kept [136]

secret, whereof there be many occasions in public business, the counsels of many and especially in assemblies, are dangerous; and therefore great assemblies are necessitated to commit such affairs to lesser numbers and of such persons as are most versed and in whose fidelity they have most confidence.

16. To conclude, who is there that so far approves the taking of counsel from a great assembly of counsellors, that wisheth for or would accept of their pains, when there is a question of marrying his children, disposing of his lands, governing his household, or managing his private estate, especially if there be amongst them such as wish not his prosperity? A man that doth his business by the help of many prudent counsellors, with every one consulting apart in his proper element, does it best, as he that useth able seconds at tennis play, placed in their proper stations. He does next best that useth his own judgement only, as he that has no second at all. But he that is carried up and down to his business in a framed counsel, which cannot move but by the plurality of consenting opinions, the execution whereof is commonly, out of envy or interest, retarded by the part dissenting, does it worst of all, and like one that is carried to the ball, though by good players; yet in a wheelbarrow or other frame, heavy of itself, and retarded also by the inconcurrent [conflicting] judgements and endeavours of them that drive it, and so much the more, as they be more that set their hands to it, and most of all, when there is one or more amongst them that desire to have him lose. And though it be true that many eyes see more than one; yet it is not to be understood of many counsellors, but then only when the final resolution is in one man. Otherwise, because many eyes see the same thing in divers lines and are apt to look asquint towards their private benefit; they that desire not to miss their mark, though they look about with two eyes; yet they never aim but with one; and therefore no great popular commonwealth was ever kept up, but either by a foreign enemy that united them, or by the reputation of some one eminent man amongst them, or by the secret counsel of a few, or by the mutual fear of equal factions, and not by the open consultations of the assembly. And as for very little commonwealths, be they popular or monarchical, there is no human wisdom can uphold them longer than the jealousy lasteth of their potent neighbours.

# CHAPTER XXVI

## OF CIVIL LAWS

1. By CIVIL LAWS, I understand the laws that men are therefore bound to observe, because they are members, not of this or that commonwealth in particular, but of a commonwealth. For the knowledge of particular laws belongeth to them that profess the study of the laws of their several countries; but the knowledge of civil law in general to any man. The ancient law of Rome was called their *civil law* from the word *civitas*, which signifies a commonwealth; and those countries which, having been under the Roman Empire and governed by that law, retain still such part thereof as they think fit, call that part the civil law to distinguish it from the rest of their own civil laws. But that is not it I intend to speak of here, my design being not to show what is law here and there, but what is law, as Plato, Aristotle, Cicero, and divers others have done, without taking upon them the profession of the study of the law. Civil law, what. [137]

2. And first it is manifest that law in general is not counsel, but command, nor a command of any man to any man, but only of him whose command is addressed to one formerly obliged to obey him. And as for civil law, it addeth only the name of the person commanding, which is *persona civitatis*, the person of the commonwealth.

3. Which considered, I define civil law in this manner. CIVIL LAW *is to every subject those rules which the commonwealth hath commanded him (by word, writing, or other sufficient sign of the will) to make use of, for the distinction of right and wrong, that is to say, of what is contrary and what is not contrary to the rule.*

4. In which definition there is nothing that is not at first sight evident. For every man seeth that some laws are addressed to all the subjects in general, some to particular provinces, some to particular vocations, and some to particular men; and are therefore laws to every of those to whom the command is directed, and to none else. As also, that laws are the rules of just and unjust, nothing being reputed unjust that is not contrary to some law. Likewise, that none can make laws but the commonwealth, because our subjection is to the commonwealth only; and that

commands are to be signified by sufficient signs, because a man knows not otherwise how to obey them. And therefore, whatsoever can from this definition by necessary consequence be deduced, ought to be acknowledged for truth. Now I deduce from it this that followeth.

1. The sovereign is legislator.

5. The legislator in all commonwealths is only the sovereign, be he one man, as in a monarchy, or one assembly of men, as in a democracy or aristocracy. For the legislator is he that maketh the law. And the commonwealth only prescribes and commandeth the observation of those rules which we call law; therefore the commonwealth is the legislator. But the commonwealth is no person, nor has capacity to do anything but by the representative, that is, the sovereign; and therefore the sovereign is the sole legislator.[1] For the same reason, none can abrogate a law made, but the sovereign, because a law is not abrogated but by another law that forbiddeth it to be put in execution.

2. And not subject to civil law.

6. The sovereign of a commonwealth, be it an assembly or one man, is not subject to the civil laws. For having power to make and repeal laws, he may, when he pleaseth, free himself from that
[138] subjection by repealing those laws that trouble him and making of new, and consequently he was free before. For he is free that can be free when he will; nor is it possible for any person to be bound to himself, because he that can bind can release; and therefore he that is bound to himself only is not bound.

3. Use, a law not by virtue of time, but of the sovereign's consent.

7. When long use obtaineth the authority of a law, it is not the length of time that maketh the authority, but the will of the sovereign signified by his silence (for silence is sometimes an argument of consent);[2] and it is no longer law, than the sovereign shall be silent therein. And therefore if the sovereign shall have a question of right grounded, not upon his present will, but upon the laws formerly made, the length of time shall bring no prejudice to his right; but the question shall be judged by equity. For many unjust actions and unjust sentences go uncontrolled a longer time than

1 Since England had been a monarchy prior to 1649, Hobbes thought that parliament had no part in the sovereignty and that the belief that it did contributed to the English Civil War.

2 Hobbes is probably criticizing Edward Coke, the great advocate of Common Law. Hobbes criticized his views at more length in *A Dialogue Between a Philosopher and a Student of the Common Laws of England*. See also 26.7.

any man can remember. And our lawyers account no customs law but such as are reasonable, and that evil customs are to be abolished; but the judgement of what is reasonable and of what is to be abolished, belonged to him that maketh the law, which is the sovereign assembly or monarch.

4. The law of nature and the civil law contain each other.

8. The law of nature and the civil law contain each other and are of equal extent.[1] For the laws of nature, which consist in equity, justice, gratitude, and other moral virtues on these depending, in the condition of mere nature (as I have said before in the end of the fifteenth Chapter), are not properly laws, but qualities that dispose men to peace and to obedience.[2] When a commonwealth is once settled, then are they actually laws, and not before, as being then the commands of the commonwealth; and therefore also civil laws; for it is the sovereign power that obliges men to obey them. For the differences of private men to declare what is equity, what is justice, and is moral virtue, and to make them binding, there is need of the ordinances of sovereign power; and punishments to be ordained for such as shall break them, which ordinances are therefore part of the civil law. The law of nature therefore is a part of the civil law in all commonwealths of the world. Reciprocally also, the civil law is a part of the dictates of nature. For justice, that is to say, performance of covenant and giving to every man his own is a dictate of the law of nature. But every subject in a commonwealth hath covenanted to obey the civil law; either one with another, as when they assemble to make a common representative, or with the representative itself one by one when, subdued by the sword, they promise obedience that they may receive life; and therefore obedience to the civil law is part also of the law of nature. Civil and natural law are not different kinds, but different parts of law, whereof one part, being written, is called civil, the other unwritten, natural. But the right of nature, that is, the natural liberty of man, may by the civil law be abridged and restrained, nay, the end of making laws is no other but such restraint, without which there cannot possibly be any peace. And law was brought

1 Hobbes must be speaking metaphorically since the relation 'x contains y' is asymmetric: if x contains y, then y cannot contain x. Hobbes certainly thought that civil laws entail the laws of nature. It is harder to see the converse.

2 This sentence is strong evidence that the laws of nature are not genuine laws.

[139] into the world for nothing else but to limit the natural liberty of particular men in such manner as they might not hurt, but assist one another, and join together against a common enemy.

5. Provincial laws are not made by custom, but by the sovereign power.

9. If the sovereign of one commonwealth subdue a people that have lived under other written laws and afterwards govern them by the same laws by which they were governed before; yet those laws are the civil laws of the victor and not of the vanquished commonwealth. For the legislator is he, not by whose authority the laws were first made, but by whose authority they now continue to be laws. And therefore where there be divers provinces within the dominion of a commonwealth and in those provinces diversity of laws, which commonly are called the customs of each several province, we are not to understand that such customs have their force only from length of time, but that they were anciently laws written or otherwise made known for the constitutions and statutes of their sovereigns, and are now laws, not by virtue of the prescription of time, but by the constitutions of their present sovereigns.[1] But if an unwritten law in all the provinces of a dominion shall be generally observed and no iniquity appear in the use thereof, that law can be no other but a law of nature, equally obliging all mankind.

6. Some foolish opinions of lawyers concerning the making of laws.

10. Seeing then all laws, written and unwritten, have their authority and force from the will of the commonwealth, that is to say, from the will of the representative, which in a monarchy is the monarch and in other commonwealths the sovereign assembly, a man may wonder from whence proceed such opinions as are found in the books of lawyers of eminence in several commonwealths, directly or by consequence making the legislative power depend on private men or subordinate judges. As for example, *that the common law hath no controller but the parliament,* which is true only where a parliament has the sovereign power and cannot be assembled nor dissolved, but by their own discretion.[2] For if there be a right in any else to dissolve them, there is a right also to control them and consequently to control their controllings. And if there be no such right, then the controller of laws is not *parla-*

1 See also 26.7.

2 The English parliament was assembled at the command of the monarch and dissolved at his command.

*mentum*, but *rex in parlamento* [the king in parliament]. And where a parliament is sovereign, if it should assemble never so many or so wise men from the countries subject to them for whatsoever cause; yet there is no man will believe that such an assembly hath thereby acquired to themselves a legislative power. *Item* [also], that the two arms of a commonwealth are *force and justice, the first whereof is in the king, the other deposited in the hands of the parliament.*[1] As if a commonwealth could consist where the force were in any hand which justice had not the authority to command and govern.

11. That law can never be against reason, our lawyers are 7.
agreed, and that not the letter (that is, every construction of it), but that which is according to the intention of the legislator is the law.[2] And it is true; but the doubt is of whose reason it is that shall be received for law. It is not meant of any private reason; for then [140]
there would be as much contradiction in the laws as there is in the Schools; nor yet, as Sir Edward Coke makes it, an *artificial perfection of reason, gotten by long study, observation, and experience*, as his was. For it is possible long study may increase and confirm erroneous sentences; and where men build on false grounds, the more they build, the greater is the ruin; and of those that study and observe with equal time and diligence, the reasons and resolutions are and must remain discordant; and therefore it is not that *juris prudentia* or wisdom of subordinate judges, but the reason of this our artificial man the commonwealth and his command that maketh law; and the commonwealth being in their representative but one person, there cannot easily arise any contradiction in the laws; and when there doth [arise contradiction], the same reason is able, by interpretation or alteration, to take it away. In all courts of justice, the sovereign (which is the person of the commonwealth) is he that judgeth; the subordinate judge ought to have regard to the reason which moved his sovereign to make such law, that his sentence may be according thereunto, which then is his sovereign's sentence; otherwise it is his own, and an unjust one.

Sir Edw. Coke upon Littleton, lib. 2, ch. 6, fol. 97, b.

1 Hobbes is criticizing various actions by parliament in the early 1640s. For example, parliament organized a military force independent of the king.

2 What Hobbes gives with the first clause, "the law can never be against reason," he effectively takes back with the last, "that which is according to the intention of the legislator is the law."

8. Law made, if not also made known, is no law.

12. From this, that the law is a command, and a command consisteth in declaration or manifestation of the will of him that commandeth by voice, writing, or some other sufficient argument of the same, we may understand that the command of the commonwealth is law only to those that have means to take notice of it. Over natural fools, children, or madmen there is no law, no more than over brute beasts; nor are they capable of the title of just or unjust, because they had never power to make any covenant or to understand the consequences thereof, and consequently never took upon them to authorize the actions of any sovereign, as they must do that make to themselves a commonwealth. And as those from whom nature or accident hath taken away the notice of all laws in general, so also every man, from whom any accident not proceeding from his own default, hath taken away the means to take notice of any particular law, is excused if he observe it not; and to speak properly, that law is no law to him. It is therefore necessary to consider in this place what arguments and signs be sufficient for the knowledge of what is the law, that is to say, what is the will of the sovereign, as well in monarchies as in other forms of government.

Unwritten laws are all of them laws of nature.

13. And first, if it be a law that obliges all the subjects without exception and is not written nor otherwise published in such places as they may take notice thereof, it is a law of nature. For whatever men are to take knowledge of for law, not upon other men's words, but every one from his own reason, must be such as is agreeable to the reason of all men; which no law can be, but the law of nature. The laws of nature therefore need not any publishing nor proclamation, as being contained in this one sentence, approved by all the world, *Do not that to another which thou thinkest unreasonable to be done by another to thyself.*

[141] 14. Secondly, if it be a law that obliges only some condition of men or one particular man and be not written nor published by word, then also it is a law of nature and known by the same arguments and signs that distinguish those in such a condition from other subjects. For whatsoever law is not written or some way published by him that makes it law can be known no way but by the reason of him that is to obey it; and is therefore also a law not

only civil, but natural. For example, if the sovereign employ a public minister, without written instructions what to do, [then] he is obliged to take for instructions the dictates of reason, as, if he make a judge, the judge is to take notice that his sentence ought to be according to the reason of his sovereign (which being always understood to be equity), he is bound to it by the law of nature; or if an ambassador, he is (in all things not contained in his written instructions), to take for instruction that which reason dictates to be most conducing to his sovereign's interest, and so of all other ministers of the sovereignty, public and private. All which instructions of natural reason may be comprehended under one name of *fidelity*, which is a branch of natural justice.

15. The law of nature excepted, it belonged to the essence of all other laws to be made known to every man that shall be obliged to obey them, either by word or writing or some other act known to proceed from the sovereign authority. For the will of another cannot be understood but by his own word or act or by conjecture taken from his scope and purpose, which in the person of the commonwealth is to be supposed always consonant to equity and reason. And in ancient time, before letters were in common use, the laws were many times put into verse, [in order] that the rude people, taking pleasure in singing or reciting them, might the more easily retain them in memory. And for the same reason Solomon adviseth a man to bind the Ten Commandments upon his ten fingers. And for the Law which Moses gave to the people of Israel at the renewing of the Covenant, he biddeth them to teach it their children by discoursing of it both at home and upon the way at going to bed and at rising from bed; and to write it upon the posts and doors of their houses and to assemble the people, man, woman, and child, to hear it read.

Prov. 7:3.

Deut. 11:19.

Deut. 31:12.

Nothing is law where the legislator cannot be known.

16. Nor is it enough the law be written and published, but also that there be manifest signs that it proceedeth from the will of the sovereign. For private men, when they have or think they have force enough to secure their unjust designs and convoy them safely to their ambitious ends, may publish for laws what they please, without or against the legislative authority. There is therefore requisite not only a declaration of the law, but also sufficient signs of

the author and authority.[1] The author or legislator is supposed in every commonwealth to be evident, because he is the sovereign, who, having been constituted by the consent of every one, is supposed by every one to be sufficiently known. And though the ignorance and security of men be such, for the most part, as that [142] when the memory of the first constitution of their commonwealth is worn out, they do not consider by whose power they use to be defended against their enemies and to have their industry protected and to be righted when injury is done them; yet because no man that considers can make question of it, no excuse can be derived from the ignorance of where the sovereignty is placed. And it is a dictate of natural reason and consequently an evident law of nature that no man ought to weaken that power, the protection whereof he hath himself demanded or wittingly received against others. Therefore of who is sovereign, no man but by his own fault (whatsoever evil men suggest), can make any doubt. The difficulty consisteth in the evidence of the authority derived from him, the removing whereof dependeth on the knowledge of the public registers, public counsels, public ministers, and public seals, by which all laws are sufficiently verified; verified, I say, not authorized; for the verification is but the testimony and record, not the authority of the law, which consisteth in the command of the sovereign only.

Difference between verifying and authorizing.

The law verified by the subordinate judge.

17. If therefore a man have a question of injury, depending on the law of nature, that is to say, on common equity, the sentence of the judge, that by commission hath authority to take cognizance of such causes, is a sufficient verification of the law of nature in that individual case. For though the advice of one that professeth the study of the law be useful for the avoiding of contention; yet it is but advice; it is the judge must tell men what is law, upon the hearing of the controversy.

By the public registers.

18. But when the question is of injury or crime upon a written law, every man by recourse to the registers by himself or others may, if he will, be sufficiently informed before he do such injury or commit the crime whether it be an injury or not; nay, he ought to do so; for when a man doubts whether the act he goeth about be just or unjust, and may inform himself if he will, the doing is

1 In traditional terms, this is the requirement that a law must be promulgated.

unlawful. In like manner, he that supposeth himself injured in a case determined by the written law, which he may by himself or others see and consider; if he complain before he consults with the law, he does unjustly, and bewrayeth [betrays] a disposition rather to vex other men than to demand his own right.

19. If the question be of obedience to a public officer, to have seen his commission (with the public seal) and heard it read, or to have had the means to be informed of it, if a man would, is a sufficient verification of his authority. For every man is obliged to do his best endeavour to inform himself of all written laws that may concern his own future actions.

By letters patent and by public seal.

20. The legislator [being] known, and the laws either by writing or by the light of nature sufficiently published, there wanteth yet another very material circumstance to make them obligatory. For it is not the letter, but the intendment or meaning, that is to say, the authentic interpretation of the law (which is the sense of the legislator), in which the nature of the law consisteth; and therefore the interpretation of all laws dependeth on the authority sovereign; and the interpreters can be none but those which the sovereign, to whom only the subject oweth obedience, shall appoint. For else, by the craft of an interpreter, the law may be made to bear a sense contrary to that of the sovereign, by which means the interpreter becomes the legislator.

The interpretation of the law dependeth on the sovereign power.

[143]

21. All laws, written and unwritten, have need of interpretation. The unwritten law of nature, though it be easy to such as without partiality and passion make use of their natural reason and therefore leaves the violators thereof without excuse; yet considering there be very few, perhaps none, that in some cases are not blinded by self-love or some other passion, it is now become of all laws the most obscure and has consequently the greatest need of able interpreters. The written laws, if laws, if they be short, are easily misinterpreted, for the divers significations of a word or two; if long, they be more obscure by the divers significations of many words, insomuch as no written law, delivered in few or many words, can be well understood without a perfect understanding of the final causes for which the law was made, the knowledge of which final causes is in the legislator. To him therefore there cannot be any knot in the law insoluble either by finding out the ends

All laws need interpretation.

to undo it by or else by making what ends he will (as Alexander did with his sword in the Gordian knot)[1] by the legislative power; which no other interpreter can do.

The authentical interpretation of law is not that of writers.

22. The interpretation of the laws of nature in a commonwealth dependeth not on the books of moral philosophy. The authority of writers without the authority of the commonwealth maketh not their opinions law, be they never so true. That which I have written in this treatise concerning the moral virtues and of their necessity for the procuring and maintaining peace, though it be evident truth, is not therefore presently law, but because in all commonwealths in the world it is part of the civil law. For though it be naturally reasonable; yet it is by the sovereign power that it is law; otherwise, it were a great error to call the laws of nature unwritten law, whereof we see so many volumes published and in them so many contradictions of one another and of themselves.

The interpreter of the law is the judge giving sentence *viva voce* [orally] in every particular case.

23. The interpretation of the law of nature is the sentence of the judge constituted by the sovereign authority to hear and determine such controversies as depend thereon, and consisteth in the application of the law to the present case. For in the act of judicature the judge doth no more but consider whether the demand of the party be consonant to natural reason and equity; and the sentence he giveth is therefore the interpretation of the law of nature; which interpretation is authentic, not because it is his private sentence, but because he giveth it by authority of the sovereign, whereby it becomes the sovereign's sentence; which is law for that time to the parties pleading.

[144] The sentence of a judge does not bind him or another judge to give like sentence in like cases ever after.

24. But because there is no judge subordinate nor sovereign, but may err in a judgement of equity, if afterward in another like case he find it more consonant to equity to give a contrary sentence, he is obliged to do it. No man's error becomes his own law nor obliges him to persist in it. Neither, for the same reason, becomes it a law to other judges, though sworn to follow it. For though a wrong sentence given by authority of the sovereign, if he know and allow it, in such laws as are mutable, be a constitution of a new law in cases in which every little circumstance is the same;

---

1 According to legend, whoever untied the Gordian knot would rule Asia. Supposedly, Alexander the Great 'untied' the knot by cutting it with his sword. He went on to capture much of Asia.

yet in laws immutable, such as are the laws of nature, they are no laws to the same or other judges in the like cases for ever after. Princes succeed one another; and one judge passeth, another cometh; nay, heaven and earth shall pass; but not one tittle of the law of nature shall pass; for it is the eternal law of God. Therefore all the sentences of precedent judges that have ever been cannot all together make a law contrary to natural equity. Nor any examples of former judges can warrant an unreasonable sentence or discharge the present judge of the trouble of studying what is equity (in the case he is to judge) from the principles of his own natural reason. For example sake, it is against the law of nature to punish the innocent; and innocent is he that acquitteth himself judicially and is acknowledged for innocent by the judge. Put the case now that a man is accused of a capital crime, and seeing the power and malice of some enemy and the frequent corruption and partiality of judges, runneth away for fear of the event and afterwards is taken and brought to a legal trial and maketh it sufficiently appear he was not guilty of the crime and being thereof acquitted is nevertheless condemned to lose his goods; this is a manifest condemnation of the innocent. I say therefore that there is no place in the world where this can be an interpretation of a law of nature or be made a law by the sentences of precedent judges that had done the same. For he that judged it first judged unjustly; and no injustice can be a pattern of judgement to succeeding judges. A written law may forbid innocent men to fly, and they may be punished for flying; but that flying for fear of injury should be taken for presumption of guilt after a man is already absolved of the crime judicially is contrary to the nature of a presumption, which hath no place after judgement given. Yet this is set down by a great lawyer[1] for the common law of England: *If a man*, saith he, *that is innocent be accused of felony, and for fear flyeth for the same; albeit he judicially acquitteth himself of the felony; yet if it be found that he fled for the felony, he shall, notwithstanding his innocency, forfeit all his goods, chattels, debts, and duties. For as to the forfeiture of them, the law will admit no proof against the presumption in law, grounded upon his flight*. Here you see *an innocent man, judicially acquitted, notwithstanding his innocency*

---

1 Sir Edward Coke (1522–1634), whose theories Hobbes often attacked.

(when no written law forbade him to fly) after his acquittal, *upon a presumption in law*, condemned to lose all the goods he hath. If the law ground upon his flight a presumption of the fact (which was
[145] capital), the sentence ought to have been capital: if the presumption were not of the fact, for what then ought he to lose his goods? This therefore is no law of England;[1] nor is the condemnation grounded upon a presumption of law, but upon the presumption of the judges. It is also against law to say that no proof shall be admitted against a presumption of law. For all judges, sovereign and subordinate, if they refuse to hear proof, refuse to do justice; for though the sentence be just; yet the judges that condemn, without hearing the proofs offered, are unjust judges; and their presumption is but prejudice; which no man ought to bring with him to the seat of justice whatsoever precedent judgements or examples he shall pretend to follow. There be other things of this nature, wherein men's judgements have been perverted by trusting to precedents; but this is enough to show that though the sentence of the judge be a law to the party pleading; yet it is no law to any judge that shall succeed him in that office.

25. In like manner, when question is of the meaning of written laws, he is not the interpreter of them that writeth a commentary upon them. For commentaries are commonly more subject to cavil than the text, and therefore need other commentaries; and so there will be no end of such interpretation. And therefore unless there be an interpreter authorized by the sovereign, from which the subordinate judges are not to recede, the interpreter can be no other than the ordinary judges, in the same manner as they are in cases of the unwritten law; and their sentences are to be taken by them that plead for laws in that particular case, but not to bind other judges in like cases to give like judgements. For a judge may err in the interpretation even of written laws; but no error of a subordinate judge can change the law, which is the general sentence of the sovereign.

The difference between the letter and the

26. In written laws men use to make a difference between the letter and the sentence of the law; and when by the letter is meant whatsoever can be gathered from the bare words, it is well distin-

1 Hobbes is declaring what is the law of England. Recall that he said the law is whatever the sovereign wills it to be (26.7).

guished. For the significations of almost all are either in themselves or in the metaphorical use of them ambiguous; and [the words] may be drawn in argument to make many senses; but there is only one sense of the law. But if by the letter be meant the literal sense,[1] then the letter and the sentence or intention of the law is all one. For the literal sense is that which the legislator intended should by the letter of the law be signified. Now the intention of the legislator is always supposed to be equity; for it were a great contumely for a judge to think otherwise of the sovereign. He ought therefore, if the word of the law do not fully authorize a reasonable sentence, to supply it with the law of nature; or if the case be difficult, to respite judgement till he have received more ample authority. For example, a written law ordaineth that he which is thrust out of his house by force shall be restored by force. It happens that a man by negligence leaves his house empty and returning is kept out by force, in which case there is no special law ordained. It is evident that this case is contained in the same law; [146]
for else there is no remedy for him at all, which is to be supposed against the intention of the legislator. Again, the word of the law commandeth to judge according to the evidence. A man is accused falsely of a fact which the judge himself saw done by another, and not by him that is accused. In this case neither shall the letter of the law be followed to the condemnation of the innocent, nor shall the judge give sentence against the evidence of the witnesses, because the letter of the law is to the contrary; but [the judge] procure of the sovereign that another be made judge and himself witness. So that the incommodity that follows the bare words of a written law may lead him to the intention of the law, whereby to interpret the same the better; though no incommodity can warrant a sentence against the law. For every judge of right and wrong is not judge of what is commodious or incommodious to the commonwealth.

sentence of the law.

The abilities required in a judge.

27. The abilities required in a good interpreter of the law, that is to say, in a good judge, are not the same with those of an advocate, namely, the study of the laws. For a judge, as he ought to take

1 Traditionally, the literal sense meant the sense intended by the author, not, as it is today, the 'dictionary meaning'. The literal sense of the law is the sense intended by the sovereign.

notice of the fact from none but the witnesses, so also he ought to take notice of the law from nothing but the statutes and constitutions of the sovereign, alleged in the pleading or declared to him by some that have authority from the sovereign power to declare them; and [the judge] need not take care beforehand what he shall judge; for it shall be given him what he shall say concerning the fact, by witnesses; and what he shall say in point of law, from those that shall in their pleadings show it and by authority interpret it upon the place. The Lords of Parliament in England were judges; and most difficult causes have been heard and determined by them; yet few of them were much versed in the study of the laws, and fewer had made profession of them; and though they consulted with lawyers that were appointed to be present there for that purpose; yet they alone had the authority of giving sentence. In like manner, in the ordinary trials of right, twelve men of the common people are the judges and give sentence, not only of the fact, but of the right; and pronounce simply for the complainant or for the defendant; that is to say, are judges not only of the fact, but also of the right; and in a question of crime, not only determine whether done or not done, but also whether it be *murder, homicide, felony, assault,* and the like, which are determinations of law; but because they are not supposed to know the law of themselves, there is one that hath authority to inform them of it in the particular case they are to judge of. But yet if they judge not according to that he tells them, they are not subject thereby to any penalty, unless it be made appear they did it against their consciences or had been corrupted by reward.

28. The things that make a good judge or good interpreter of the laws are, first, *a right understanding* of that principal law of nature called *equity*, which, depending not on the reading of other men's writings, but on the goodness of a man's own natural reason
[147] and meditation, is presumed to be in those most that have had most leisure and had the most inclination to meditate thereon. Secondly, *contempt of unnecessary riches and preferments*. Thirdly, *to be able in judgement to divest himself of all fear, anger, hatred, love, and compassion*. Fourthly, and lastly, *patience to hear, diligent attention in hearing, and memory to retain, digest, and apply what he hath heard.*

29. The difference and division of the laws has been made in Divisions of law.
divers manners, according to the different methods of those men
that have written of them. For it is a thing that dependeth not on
nature, but on the scope of the writer, and is subservient to every
man's proper method. In the *Institutions* of Justinian, we find seven
sorts of civil laws: The *edicts, constitutions*, and *epistles of the prince*, 1.
that is, of the emperor, because the whole power of the people was
in him. Like these are the proclamations of the kings of England.

30. *The decrees of the whole people of Rome* (comprehending the 2.
Senate), when they were put to the question by the *Senate*. These
were laws, at first, by the virtue of the sovereign power residing in
the people; and such of them as by the emperors were not abrogated
remained laws by the authority imperial. For all laws that
bind are understood to be laws by his authority that has power to
repeal them. Somewhat like to these laws are the Acts of Parliament in England.

31. *The decrees of the common people* (excluding the Senate), 3.
when they were put to the question by the *tribune* of the people.
For such of them as were not abrogated by the emperors,
remained laws by the authority imperial. Like to these were the
orders of the House of Commons in England.

32. *Senatus consulta*, the *orders of the Senate,* because when the 4.
people of Rome grew so numerous as it was inconvenient to
assemble them, it was thought fit by the emperor that men should
consult the Senate instead of the people: and these have some
resemblance with the Acts of Council.

33. *The edicts of praetors*, and (in some cases) of the *aediles*,[1] such 5.
as are the chief justices in the courts of England.

34. *Responsa prudentum*, which were the sentences and opinions 6.
of those lawyers to whom the emperor gave authority to interpret
the law, and to give answer to such as in matter of law demanded
their advice; which answers the judges in giving judgement were
obliged by the constitutions of the emperor to observe, and should
be like the reports of cases judged, if other judges be by the law of

---

1 Praetors and aediles were two kinds of magistrates of ancient Rome. The praetors held the higher rank.

England bound to observe them. For the judges of the common law of England are not properly judges, but *juris consulti*,[1] of whom the judges, who are either the lords or twelve men of the country, are in point of law to ask advice.

35. Also, *unwritten customs* (which in their own nature are an imitation of law), by the tacit consent of the emperor, in case they be not contrary to the law of nature, are very laws.

36. Another division of laws is into *natural* and *positive*.[2] Natur-
[148] al are those which have been laws from all eternity, and are called not only natural, but also moral laws, consisting in the moral virtues, as justice, equity, and all habits of the mind that conduce to peace and charity, of which I have already spoken in the fourteenth and fifteenth chapters.

37. *Positive* are those which have not been from eternity, but have been made laws by the will of those that have had the sovereign power over others, and are either written or made known to men by some other argument of the will of their legislator.

Another division of law.

38. Again, of positive laws some are *human*, some *divine*; and of human positive laws, some are *distributive*, some *penal*. *Distributive* are those that determine the rights of the subjects, declaring to every man what it is by which he acquireth and holdeth a propriety in lands or goods, and a right or liberty of action; and these speak to all the subjects. *Penal* are those which declare what penalty shall be inflicted on those that violate the law; and [they] speak to the ministers and officers ordained for execution. For though every one ought to be informed of the punishments ordained beforehand for their transgression, nevertheless the command is not addressed to the delinquent (who cannot be supposed will faithfully punish himself), but to public ministers appointed to see the penalty executed. And these penal laws are for the most part written together with the laws distributive, and are sometimes called judgements. For all laws are general judgements, or sentences of the legislator, as also every particular judgement is a law to him whose case is judged.

---

1 *Juris consulti* means lawyers.

2 If the laws of nature are not genuine laws, then the division of laws into natural and positive is analogous to the division of horses into sawhorses and biological horses.

39. *Divine positive laws* (for natural laws, being eternal and universal, are all divine[1]) are those which, being the commandments of God, not from all eternity, nor universally addressed to all men, but only to a certain people or to certain persons, are declared for such by those whom God hath authorized to declare them. But this authority of man to declare what be these positive laws of God, how can it be known? God may command a man by a supernatural way to deliver laws to other men. But because it is of the essence of law that he who is to be obliged be assured of the authority of him that declareth it, which we cannot naturally take notice to be from God, *how can a man without supernatural revelations be assured of the revelation received by the declarer?* and *how can he be bound to obey them?* For the first question, how a man can be assured of the revelation of another without a revelation particularly to himself, it is evidently impossible; for though a man may be induced to believe such revelation from the miracles they see him do or from seeing the extraordinary sanctity of his life or from seeing the extraordinary wisdom or extraordinary felicity of his actions, all which are marks of God's extraordinary favour; yet they are not assured evidences of special revelation. Miracles are marvellous works; but that which is marvellous to one may not be so to another. Sanctity may be feigned; and the visible felicities of this world are most often the work of God by natural and ordinary [149] causes. And therefore no man can infallibly know by natural reason that another has had a supernatural revelation of God's will but only a belief; every one, as the signs thereof shall appear greater or lesser, a firmer or a weaker belief.[2]

Divine positive law how made known to be law.

40. But for the second,[3] how he can be bound to obey them, it is not so hard. For if the law declared be not against the law of nature (which is undoubtedly God's law) and he undertake to obey it, he is bound by his own act; bound I say to obey it, but not

1 Are divine (natural) laws genuine laws or not? If they are, then natural laws are genuine laws. If they are not, then God's command has no force.

2 Hobbes draws a sharp line between belief and knowledge. People can believe or have faith in some person who claims to have had a revelation from God. But this is never knowledge. Hobbes does not commit himself here about whether the person who purportedly has the revelation knows that he had it. Cf. Chapter 36.

3 This was the second question posed about halfway through 26.39.

bound to believe it;[1] for men's belief and interior cogitations are not subject to the commands, but only to the operation of God, ordinary or extraordinary. Faith of supernatural law is not a fulfilling, but only an assenting to the same and not a duty that we exhibit to God, but a gift which God freely giveth to whom he pleaseth, as also unbelief is not a breach of any of his laws, but a rejection of them all, except the laws natural. But this that I say will be made yet clearer by the examples and testimonies concerning this point in Holy Scripture. The covenant God made with Abraham in a supernatural manner was thus, *This is the covenant which thou shalt observe between me and thee and thy seed after thee.*
Gen. 17:10 Abraham's seed had not this revelation, nor were yet in being; yet they are a party to the covenant and bound to obey what Abraham should declare to them for God's law; which they could not be but in virtue of the obedience they owed to their parents, who (if they be subject to no other earthly power, as here in the case of Abraham) have sovereign power over their children and servants. Again, where God saith to Abraham, *In thee shall all nations of the earth be blessed; for I know thou wilt command thy children and thy house after thee to keep the way of the Lord, and to observe righteousness and judgement,* it is manifest the obedience of his family, who had no revelation, depended on their former obligation to obey their sovereign. At Mount Sinai Moses only went up to God; the people were forbidden to approach on pain of death; yet were they bound to obey all that Moses declared to them for God's law. Upon what ground, but on this submission of their own, *Speak thou to us, and we will hear thee; but let not God speak to us, lest we die*? By which two places it sufficiently appeareth that in a commonwealth a subject that has no certain and assured revelation particularly to himself concerning the will of God is to obey for such the command of the commonwealth; for if men were at liberty to take for God's commandments their own dreams and fancies or the dreams and fancies of private men, scarce two men would agree upon what is God's commandment; and yet in respect of them every man

1 Hobbes's conventionalist answer—one is required to obey laws about religion commanded by the sovereign, but one is not required to believe them—drove his contemporaries to consternation and has delighted cynics and some atheists since the eighteenth century.

would despise the commandments of the commonwealth. I conclude, therefore, that in all things not contrary to the moral law (that is to say, to the law of nature), all subjects are bound to obey that for divine law which is declared to be so by the laws of the commonwealth.[1] Which also is evident to any man's reason; for whatsoever is not against the law of nature may be made law in the name of them that have the sovereign power; there is no rea- [150] son men should be the less obliged by it when it is propounded in the name of God. Besides, there is no place in the world where men are permitted to pretend other commandments of God than are declared for such by the commonwealth. Christian states punish those that revolt from Christian religion; and all other states, those that set up any religion by them forbidden. For in whatsoever is not regulated by the commonwealth, it is equity (which is the law of nature, and therefore an eternal law of God) that every man equally enjoy his liberty.

Another division of laws.

41. There is also another distinction of laws into *fundamental* and *not fundamental*: but I could never see in any author what a fundamental law signifieth. Nevertheless one may very reasonably distinguish laws in that manner.

A fundamental law, what?

42. For a fundamental law in every commonwealth is that which, being taken away, the commonwealth faileth and is utterly dissolved, as a building whose foundation is destroyed. And therefore a fundamental law is that by which subjects are bound to uphold whatsoever power is given to the sovereign, whether a monarch or a sovereign assembly, without which the commonwealth cannot stand; such as is the power of war and peace, of judicature, of election of officers, and of doing whatsoever he shall think necessary for the public good. Not fundamental is that, the abrogating whereof draweth not with it the dissolution of the commonwealth; such as are the laws concerning controversies between subject and subject. Thus much of the division of laws.

Difference between law and right.

43. I find the words *lex civilis* and *jus civile*, that is to say, *law* and *right civil*, promiscuously used for the same thing, even in the most learned authors; which nevertheless ought not to be so. For *right* is liberty, namely that liberty which the civil law leaves us; but *civil*

1 Hobbes wants to preserve the status quo. Allowing each person to judge what God has revealed is politically destabilizing and hence dangerous.

*law* is an *obligation*, and takes from us the liberty which the law of nature gave us. Nature gave a right to every man to secure himself by his own strength and to invade a suspected neighbour by way of prevention; but the civil law takes away that liberty, in all cases where the protection of the law may be safely stayed for. Insomuch as *lex* and *jus* are as different as *obligation* and *liberty*.[1]

And between a law and a charter.

44. Likewise laws and charters are taken promiscuously for the same thing. Yet charters are donations of the sovereign; and not laws, but exemptions from law. The phrase of a law is *jubeo, injungo*; *I command,* and *enjoin*: the phrase of a charter is *dedi, concessi*; *I have given, I have granted*: but what is given or granted to a man is not forced upon him by a law.[2] A law may be made to bind all the subjects of a commonwealth; a liberty or charter is only to one man or some one part of the people. For to say all the people of a commonwealth have liberty in any case whatsoever is to say that, in such case, there hath been no law made; or else, having been made, is now abrogated.

[151]

## CHAPTER XXVII

## OF CRIMES, EXCUSES, AND EXTENUATIONS

Sin what.

1. A SIN is not only a transgression of a law, but also any contempt of the legislator. For such contempt is a breach of all his laws at once, and therefore may consist, not only in the *commission* of a fact or in the speaking of words by the laws forbidden or in the *omission* of what the law commandeth, but also in the intention or purpose to transgress. For the purpose to break the law is some degree of contempt of him to whom it belonged to see it executed. To be delighted in the imagination only of being possessed of another man's goods, servants, or wife, without any intention to take them from him by force or fraud, is no breach of the law, that saith, *Thou shalt not covet;* nor is the pleasure a man may have in

1 See also 14.3.

2 See also 25.2–5.

imagining or dreaming of the death of him from whose life he expecteth nothing but damage and displeasure a sin, but the resolving to put some act in execution that tendeth thereto. For to be pleased in the fiction of that which would please a man if it were real is a passion so adherent to the nature both of man and every other living creature, as to make it a sin were to make sin of being a man. The consideration of this has made me think them too severe, both to themselves and others, that maintain that the first motions of the mind, though checked with the fear of God, be sins. But I confess it is safer to err on that hand than on the other.

A crime, what.

2. A CRIME is a sin consisting in the committing by deed or word of that which the law forbiddeth, or the omission of what it hath commanded. So that every crime is a sin; but not every sin a crime. To intend to steal or kill is a sin, though it never appear in word or fact; for God that seeth the thought of man can lay it to his charge; but till it appear by something done or said, by which the intention may be argued by a human judge, it hath not the name of crime; which distinction the Greeks observed in the word *hamartema* and *egklema* or *aitia*; whereof the former (which is translated *sin*) signifieth any swerving from the law whatsoever; but the two latter (which are translated *crime*) signify that sin only whereof one man may accuse another. But of intentions which never appear by any outward act there is no place for human accusation. In like manner the Latins by *peccatum*, which is sin, signify all manner of deviation from the law; but by *crimen* (which word they derive from *cerno*, which signifies *to perceive*) they mean only such sins as may be made appear before a judge, and therefore are not mere intentions.

Where no civil law is, there is no crime.

3. From this relation of sin to the law and of crime to the civil law, may be inferred, first, that where law ceaseth, sin ceaseth.[1] But because the law of nature is eternal, violation of covenants, ingratitude, arrogance, and all facts contrary to any moral virtue can [152]

1 In the state of nature, considered as having no law of any kind, there can be no sin (and no crime). It is a mistake to think of Adam and Eve as being in the state of nature. They were under God's law, namely, not to eat of the fruit of the tree in the middle of the garden.

never cease to be sin.[1] Secondly, that the civil law ceasing, crimes cease; for there being no other law remaining but that of nature, there is no place for accusation, every man being his own judge and accused only by his own conscience and cleared by the uprightness of his own intention. When therefore his intention is right, his fact is no sin; if otherwise, his fact is sin, but not crime. Thirdly, that when the sovereign power ceaseth, crime also ceaseth; for where there is no such power, there is no protection to be had from the law; and therefore everyone may protect himself by his own power; for no man in the institution of sovereign power can be supposed to give away the right of preserving his own body, for the safety whereof all sovereignty was ordained. But this is to be understood only of those that have not themselves contributed to the taking away of the power that protected them; for that was a crime from the beginning.

Ignorance of the law of nature excuseth no man.

4. The source of every crime is some defect of the understanding or some error in reasoning or some sudden force of the passions. Defect in the understanding is *ignorance*; in reasoning, *erroneous opinion*. Again, ignorance is of three sorts: of the *law,* and of the *sovereign,* and of the *penalty*. Ignorance of the law of nature excuseth no man, because every man that hath attained to the use of reason is supposed to know he ought not to do to another what he would not have done to himself. Therefore into what place soever a man shall come, if he do anything contrary to that law, it is a crime. If a man come from the Indies hither and persuade men here to receive a new religion or teach them anything that tendeth to disobedience of the laws of this country, though he be never so well persuaded of the truth of what he teacheth, he commits a crime and may be justly punished for the same, not only because his doctrine is false, but also because he does that which he would not approve in another, namely, that coming from hence, he should endeavour to alter the religion there. But ignorance of the civil law shall excuse a man in a strange country till it be declared to him, because till then no civil law is binding.

---

1 In the state of nature, considered as regulated by the laws of nature, sin is possible. If the laws of nature are not genuine laws, it would seem that sin would be impossible. Hobbes must be thinking of the laws of nature here as genuine divine laws.

Ignorance of the civil law excuseth sometimes.

5. In the like manner, if the civil law of a man's own country be not so sufficiently declared as he may know it if he will, nor the action against the law of nature, [then] the ignorance is a good excuse; in other cases ignorance of the civil law excuseth not.

Ignorance of the sovereign excuseth not.

6. Ignorance of the sovereign power in the place of a man's ordinary residence excuseth him not, because he ought to take notice of the power by which he hath been protected there.

Ignorance of penalty excuseth not.

7. Ignorance of the penalty, where the law is declared, excuseth no man; for in breaking the law, which without a fear of penalty to follow were not a law, but vain words, he undergoeth the penalty, though he know not what it is, because whosoever voluntarily doth any action, accepteth all the known consequences of it; but punishment is a known consequence of the violation of the laws in every commonwealth; which punishment, if it be determined [153] already by the law, he is subject to that; if not, then is he subject to arbitrary punishment. For it is reason [reasonable] that he which does injury, without other limitation than that of his own will, should suffer punishment without other limitation than that of his will whose law is thereby violated.

Punishments declared before the fact excuse from greater punishments after it.

8. But when a penalty is either annexed to the crime in the law itself or hath been usually inflicted in the like cases, there the delinquent is excused from a greater penalty. For the punishment foreknown, if not great enough to deter men from the action, is an invitement to it, because when men compare the benefit of their injustice with the harm of their punishment, by necessity of nature they choose that which appeareth best for themselves; and therefore when they are punished more than the law had formerly determined or more than others were punished for the same crime, it is the law that tempted and deceiveth them.

Nothing can be made a crime by a law made after the fact.

9. No law made after a fact done can make it a crime, because if the fact be against the law of nature, the law was before the fact; and a positive law cannot be taken notice of before it be made and therefore cannot be obligatory. But when the law that forbiddeth a fact is made before the fact be done; yet he that doth the fact is liable to the penalty ordained after, in case no lesser penalty were made known before, neither by writing nor by example, for the reason immediately before alleged.

False principles of right and wrong causes of crime.

10. From defect in reasoning (that is to say, from error), men are prone to violate the laws three ways. First, by presumption of false principles, as when men, from having observed how in all places and in all ages unjust actions have been authorized by the force and victories of those who have committed them; and that, potent men breaking through the cobweb laws of their country, the weaker sort and those that have failed in their enterprises have been esteemed the only criminals, have thereupon taken for principles and grounds of their reasoning *that justice is but a vain word, that whatsoever a man can get by his own industry and hazard is his own, that the practice of all nations cannot be unjust, that examples of former times are good arguments of doing the like again*, and many more of that kind; which being granted, no act in itself can be a crime, but must be made so (not by the law, but) by the success of them that commit it; and the same fact be virtuous or vicious, as fortune pleaseth; so that what Marius makes a crime, Sylla shall make meritorious, and Caesar (the same laws standing) turn again into a crime, to the perpetual disturbance of the peace of the commonwealth.

False teachers misinterpreting the law of nature.

11. Secondly, by false teachers that either misinterpret the law of nature, making it thereby repugnant to the law civil, or by teaching for laws such doctrines of their own, or traditions of former times, as are inconsistent with the duty of a subject.

And false inferences from true principles by teachers.

12. Thirdly, by erroneous inferences from true principles; which happens commonly to men that are hasty and precipitate in [154] concluding and resolving what to do; such as are they that have both a great opinion of their own understanding and believe that things of this nature require not time and study, but only common experience and a good natural wit, whereof no man thinks himself unprovided; whereas the knowledge of right and wrong, which is no less difficult, there is no man will pretend to without great and long study.[1] And of those defects in reasoning, there is none that can excuse, though some of them may extenuate, a crime in any man that pretendeth to the administration of his own private busi-

1 Everyone knows that the knowledge of right and wrong requires great and long study; nonetheless, people think that drawing the right conclusions from the laws requires only common experience and a good natural wit, even though getting this knowledge is as difficult as getting that of right and wrong.

ness; [it excuses] much less in them that undertake a public charge, because they pretend to the reason upon the want whereof they would ground their excuse.

13. Of the passions that most frequently are the causes of crime, one is vainglory or a foolish overrating of their own worth, as if difference of worth were an effect of their wit or riches or blood or some other natural quality, not depending on the will of those that have the sovereign authority. From whence proceedeth a presumption that the punishments ordained by the laws and extended generally to all subjects ought not to be inflicted on them with the same rigor they are inflicted on poor, obscure, and simple men, comprehended under the name of the *vulgar*.

By their passions.

14. Therefore it happeneth commonly that such as value themselves by the greatness of their wealth adventure on crimes, upon hope of escaping punishment by corrupting public justice or obtaining pardon by money or other rewards.

Presumption of riches.

15. And that such as have a multitude of potent kindred and popular men that have gained reputation amongst the multitude take courage to violate the laws from a hope of oppressing the power to whom it belonged to put them in execution.

And friends.

16. And that such as have a great and false opinion of their own wisdom take upon them to reprehend the actions and call in question the authority of them that govern and so to unsettle the laws with their public discourse, as that nothing shall be a crime but what their own designs require should be so. It happeneth also to the same men to be prone to all such crimes as consist in craft and in deceiving of their neighbours, because they think their designs are too subtle to be perceived. These I say are effects of a false presumption of their own wisdom. For of them that are the first movers in the disturbance of commonwealth (which can never happen without a civil war), very few are left alive long enough to see their new designs established; so that the benefit of their crimes redoundeth to posterity and such as would least have wished it; which argues they were not so wise as they thought they were. And those that deceive upon hope of not being observed do commonly deceive themselves (the darkness in which they believe they lie hidden being nothing else but their own blindness), and are no wiser than children that think all hid by hiding their own eyes.

Wisdom.

17. And generally all vainglorious men (unless they be withal [155] timorous) are subject to anger, as being more prone than others to interpret for contempt the ordinary liberty of conversation; and there are few crimes that may not be produced by anger.

Hatred, lust, ambition, covetousness, causes of crime.

18. As for the passions of hate, lust, ambition, and covetousness, what crimes they are apt to produce is so obvious to every man's experience and understanding, as there needeth nothing to be said of them, saving that they are infirmities so annexed to the nature both of man and all other living creatures, as that their effects cannot be hindered but by extraordinary use of reason or a constant severity in punishing them. For in those things men hate, they find a continual and unavoidable molestation, whereby either a man's patience must be everlasting or he must be eased by removing the power of that which molesteth him; the former is difficult; the latter is many times impossible without some violation of the law. Ambition and covetousness are passions also that are perpetually incumbent and pressing; whereas reason is not perpetually present to resist them; and therefore whensoever the hope of impunity appears, their effects proceed. And for lust, what it wants in the lasting it hath in the vehemence, which sufficeth to weigh down the apprehension of all easy or uncertain punishments.

Fear sometimes cause of crime, as when the danger is neither present nor corporeal.

19. Of all passions, that which inclineth men least to break the laws is fear.[1] Nay, excepting some generous natures, it is the only thing (when there is appearance of profit or pleasure by breaking the laws) that makes men keep them. And yet in many cases a crime may be committed through fear.

20. For not every fear justifies the action it produceth, but the fear only of corporeal hurt, which we call bodily fear and from which a man cannot see how to be delivered but by the action. A man is assaulted [and] fears present death, from which he sees not how to escape but by wounding him that assaulteth him; if he wound him to death, this is no crime, because no man is supposed at the making of a commonwealth to have abandoned the defense of his life or limbs, where the law cannot arrive time enough to his assistance. But to kill a man because from his actions or his threatenings I may argue he will kill me when he can (seeing I

1 Hobbes could be called the philosopher of fear. See also 13.14.

have time and means to demand protection from the sovereign power) is a crime.[1] Again, a man receives words of disgrace or some little injuries (for which they that made the laws had assigned no punishment, nor thought it worthy of a man that hath the use of reason to take notice of) and is afraid unless he revenge it, he shall fall into contempt and consequently be obnoxious to the like injuries from others; and to avoid this, [he] breaks the law and protects himself for the future by the terror of his private revenge. This is a crime; for the hurt is not corporeal, but fantastical, and (though, in this corner of the world, made sensible by a custom not many years since begun, amongst young and vain men) so light as a gallant man and one that is assured of his own courage, cannot take notice of. Also a man may stand in fear of spirits, either through his own superstition or through too much credit given to other men that tell him of strange dreams and [156]
visions; and thereby be made believe they will hurt him for doing or omitting divers things which, nevertheless, to do or omit is contrary to the laws; and that which is so done or omitted is not to be excused by this fear, but is a crime. For, as I have shown before in the second chapter, dreams be naturally but the fancies remaining in sleep after the impressions our senses had formerly received waking; and, when men are by any accident unassured they have slept, [they] seem to be real visions; and therefore he that presumes to break the law upon his own or another's dream or pretended vision or upon other fancy of the power of invisible spirits than is permitted by the commonwealth leaveth the law of nature, which is a certain offence, and followeth the imagery of his own or another private man's brain, which he can never know whether it signifieth anything or nothing, nor whether he that tells his dream say true or lie; which if every private man should have leave to do (as they must, by the law of nature, if any one have it), there could no law be made to hold, and so all commonwealth would be dissolved.

---

1 Hobbes does not discuss intermediate cases, such as when a person knows that his enemy is about to set in motion a complex plan to kill him and that the only way to stop the plan is to kill the enemy before the plan is begun. Another intermediate case is that in which a person knows an enemy will kill him some time in the future and has good reason to believe that the sovereign cannot protect him from that attack.

Crimes not equal.

21. From these different sources of crimes, it appears already that all crimes are not, as the Stoics of old time maintained,[1] of the same alloy. There is place, not only for EXCUSE, by which that which seemed a crime is proved to be none at all; but also for EXTENUATION, by which the crime, that seemed great, is made less. For though all crimes do equally deserve the name of injustice, as all deviation from a straight line is equally crookedness, which the Stoics rightly observed; yet it does not follow that all crimes are equally unjust, no more than that all crooked lines are equally crooked; which the Stoics, not observing, held it as great a crime to kill a hen, against the law, as to kill one's father.

Total excuses.

22. That which totally excuseth a fact and takes away from it the nature of a crime can be none but that which, at the same time, taketh away the obligation of the law. For the fact committed once against the law, if he that committed it be obliged to the law, can be no other than a crime.

23. The want of means to know the law totally excuseth; for the law whereof a man has no means to inform himself is not obligatory. But the want of diligence to enquire shall not be considered as a want of means; nor shall any man that pretendeth to reason enough for the government of his own affairs be supposed to want means to know the laws of nature, because they are known by the reason he pretends to; only children and madmen are excused from offences against the law natural.

24. Where a man is captive, or in the power of the enemy (and he is then in the power of the enemy when his person, or his means of living, is so), if it be without his own fault, the obligation of the law ceaseth, because he must obey the enemy or die, and consequently such obedience is no crime; for no man is obliged (when the protection of the law faileth) not to protect himself by the best means he can.

[157] 25. If a man by the terror of present death be compelled to do a fact against the law, he is totally excused, because no law can oblige a man to abandon his own preservation. And supposing such a law were obligatory; yet a man would reason thus: *If I do it not, I die presently; if I do it, I die afterwards; therefore by doing it, there is time of life gained.* Nature therefore compels him to the fact.

1 See for example, Cicero, *De Finibus* IV. 23 and 28.

26. When a man is destitute of food or other thing necessary for his life and cannot preserve himself any other way but by some fact against the law, as if in a great famine he take the food by force or stealth, which he cannot obtain for money nor charity; or in defence of his life, snatch away another man's sword; he is totally excused for the reason next before alleged.

Excuses against the author.

27. Again, facts done against the law by the authority of another are by that authority excused against the author, because no man ought to accuse his own fact in another that is but his instrument;[1] but it is not excused against a third person thereby injured, because in the violation of the law both the author and actor are criminals. From hence it followeth that when that man or assembly that hath the sovereign power commandeth a man to do that which is contrary to a former law, the doing of it is totally excused; for he ought not to condemn it himself, because he is the author; and what cannot justly be condemned by the sovereign cannot justly be punished by any other. Besides, when the sovereign commandeth anything to be done against his own former law, the command, as to that particular fact, is an abrogation of the law.

28. If that man or assembly that hath the sovereign power disclaim any right essential to the sovereignty, whereby there accrueth to the subject any liberty inconsistent with the sovereign power, that is to say, with the very being of a commonwealth; if the subject shall refuse to obey the command in anything, contrary to the liberty granted, [then] this is nevertheless a sin and contrary to the duty of the subject; for he ought to take notice of what is inconsistent with the sovereignty, because it was erected by his own consent and for his own defence, and that such liberty as is inconsistent with it was granted through ignorance of the evil consequence thereof. But if he not only disobey, but also resist a public minister in the execution of it, then it is a crime, because he might have been righted, without any breach of the peace, upon complaint.

---

1 In 1640 and earlier, an agent of the monarch could be convicted of doing something that the king had commanded even though the king could not be. Hobbes may be thinking of the famous case of Lord Strafford, who was executed for supposedly breaking the law, even though he was acting for the king.

29. The degrees of crime are taken on divers scales and measured, first, by the malignity of the source or cause; secondly, by the contagion of the example; thirdly, by the mischief of the effect; and fourthly, by the concurrence of times, places, and persons.

Presumption of power aggravateth.

30. The same fact done against the law, if it proceed from presumption of strength, riches, or friends to resist those that are to execute the law, is a greater crime than if it proceed from hope of not being discovered or of escape by flight; for presumption of
[158] impunity by force is a root from whence springeth at all times and upon all temptations a contempt of all laws; whereas in the latter case the apprehension of danger that makes a man fly renders him more obedient for the future. A crime which we know to be so is greater than the same crime proceeding from a false persuasion that it is lawful; for he that committeth it against his own conscience presumeth on his force or other power, which encourages him to commit the same again, but he that doth it by error, after the error [is] shown him, is conformable to the law.

Evil teachers extenuate.

31. He whose error proceeds from the authority of a teacher or an interpreter of the law publicly authorized is not so faulty as he whose error proceedeth from a peremptory pursuit of his own principles and reasoning; for what is taught by one that teacheth by public authority, the commonwealth teacheth and hath a resemblance of law, till the same authority controlleth it; and in all crimes that contain not in them a denial of the sovereign power nor are against an evident law excuseth totally; whereas he that groundeth his actions on his private judgement ought, according to the rectitude or error thereof, to stand or fall.

Examples of impunity extenuate.

32. The same fact, if it have been constantly punished in other men, is a greater crime than if there have been many precedent examples of impunity. For those examples are so many hopes of impunity, given by the sovereign himself; and because he which furnishes a man with such a hope and presumption of mercy, as encourageth him to offend, hath his part in the offence, he cannot reasonably charge the offender with the whole.

Premeditation aggravateth.

33. A crime arising from a sudden passion is not so great as when the same ariseth from long meditation; for in the former case there is a place for extenuation in the common infirmity of human nature; but he that doth it with premeditation has used cir-

cumspection and cast his eye on the law, on the punishment, and on the consequence thereof to human society; all which in committing the crime he hath contemned and postponed to his own appetite. But there is no suddenness of passion sufficient for a total excuse; for all the time between the first knowing of the law and the commission of the fact, shall be taken for a time of deliberation, because he ought, by meditation of the law, to rectify the irregularity of his passions.

34. Where the law is publicly and with assiduity before all the people read and interpreted, a fact done against it is a greater crime than where men are left without such instruction to inquire of it with difficulty, uncertainty, and interruption of their callings, and be informed by private men; for in this case, part of the fault is discharged upon common infirmity; but in the former there is apparent negligence, which is not without some contempt of the sovereign power.

Tacit approbation of the sovereign extenuates.

35. Those facts which the law expressly condemneth, but the lawmaker by other manifest signs of his will tacitly approveth, are less crimes than the same facts condemned both by the law and lawmaker. For seeing the will of the lawmaker is a law, there appear in this case two contradictory laws; which would totally [159] excuse, if men were bound to take notice of the sovereign's approbation, by other arguments than are expressed by his command. But because there are punishments consequent, not only to the transgression of his law, but also to the observing of it, he is in part a cause of the transgression and therefore cannot reasonably impute the whole crime to the delinquent. For example, the law condemneth duels; the punishment is made capital; on the contrary part, he that refuseth duel is subject to contempt and scorn, without remedy; and sometimes by the sovereign himself thought unworthy to have any charge or preferment in war; if thereupon he accept duel, considering all men lawfully endeavour to obtain the good opinion of them that have the sovereign power, he ought not in reason to be rigorously punished, seeing part of the fault may be discharged on the punisher; which I say, not as wishing liberty of private revenges or any other kind of disobedience, but a care in governors not to countenance anything obliquely which directly they forbid. The examples of princes, to those that see

them, are and ever have been more potent to govern their actions than the laws themselves. And though it be our duty to do, not what they do, but what they say; yet will that duty never be performed till it please God to give men an extraordinary and supernatural grace to follow that precept.

Comparison of crimes from their effects.

36. Again, if we compare crimes by the mischief of their effects; first, the same fact when it redounds to the damage of many is greater than when it redounds to the hurt of few. And therefore when a fact hurteth, not only in the present, but also by example in the future, it is a greater crime than if it hurt only in the present; for the former is a fertile crime and multiplies to the hurt of many; the latter is barren. To maintain doctrines contrary to the religion established in the commonwealth is a greater fault in an authorized preacher than in a private person; so also is it to live profanely, incontinently, or do any irreligious act whatsoever. Likewise in a professor of the law to maintain any point or do any act that tendeth to the weakening of the sovereign power is a greater crime than in another man; also in a man that hath such reputation for wisdom, as that his counsels are followed or his actions imitated by many, his fact against the law is a greater crime than the same fact in another; for such men not only commit crime, but teach it for law to all other men. And generally all crimes are the greater by the scandal they give, that is to say, by becoming stumbling-blocks to the weak, that look not so much upon the way they go in, as upon the light that other men carry before them.

*Laesa majestas.*

37. Also facts of hostility against the present state of the commonwealth are greater crimes than the same acts done to private men; for the damage extends itself to all; such are the betraying of the strengths or revealing of the secrets of the commonwealth to an enemy; also all attempts upon the representative of the commonwealth, be it a monarch or an assembly; and all endeavours by [160] word or deed to diminish the authority of the same either in the present time or in succession; which crimes the Latins understand by *crimina laesae majestatis*,[1] and consist in design or act contrary to a fundamental law.

---

1 Latin: Crimes against the sovereignty of the state.

38. Likewise those crimes which render judgements of no effect are greater crimes than injuries done to one or a few persons; as to receive money to give false judgement or testimony is a greater crime than otherwise to deceive a man of the like or a greater sum, because not only he has wrong that falls by such judgements, but [also] all judgements are rendered useless and occasion ministered to force and private revenges. Bribery and false testimony.

39. Also robbery and depeculation [embezzlement] of the public treasury or revenues is a greater crime than the robbing or defrauding of a private man, because to rob the public is to rob many at once. Depeculation.

40. Also the counterfeit usurpation of public ministry, the counterfeiting of public seals or public coin [is a greater crime] than counterfeiting of a private man's person or his seal, because the fraud thereof extendeth to the damage of many. Counterfeiting authority.

41. Of facts against the law done to private men, the greater crime is that where the damage, in the common opinion of men, is most sensible. And therefore: Crimes against private men compared.

42. To kill against the law is a greater crime than any other injury, life preserved.

43. And to kill with torment, greater than simply to kill.

44. And mutilation of a limb, greater than the spoiling a man of his goods.

45. And the spoiling a man of his goods by terror of death or wounds, than by clandestine surreption [theft].

46. And by clandestine surreption, than by consent fraudulently obtained.

47. And the violation of chastity by force, greater than by flattery.

48. And of a woman married, than of a woman not married.

49. For all these things are commonly so valued, though some men are more, and some less, sensible of the same offence. But the law regardeth not the particular, but the general inclination of mankind.

50. And therefore the offence men take from contumely [insult] in words or gesture, when they produce no other harm than the present grief of him that is reproached, hath been neglected in the laws of the Greeks, Romans, and other both

ancient and modern commonwealths, supposing the true cause of such grief to consist, not in the contumely (which takes no hold upon men conscious of their own virtue), but in the pusillanimity [pettiness] of him that is offended by it.

51. Also a crime against a private man is much aggravated by the person, time, and place. For to kill one's parent is a greater crime than to kill another; for the parent ought to have the honour of a sovereign (though he have surrendered his power to the civil law), because he had it originally by nature. And to rob a
[161] poor man is a greater crime than to rob a rich man, because it is to the poor a more sensible damage.[1]

52. And a crime committed in the time or place appointed for devotion is greater than if committed at another time or place; for it proceeds from a greater contempt of the law.

53. Many other cases of aggravation and extenuation might be added; but by these I have set down, it is obvious to every man to take the altitude of any other crime proposed.

Public crimes, what.

54. Lastly, because in almost all crimes there is an injury done, not only to some private men, but also to the commonwealth, the same crime, when the accusation is in the name of the commonwealth, is called public crime; and when in the name of a private man, a private crime; and the pleas according thereupon called public, *judicia publica*, Pleas of the Crown; or Private Pleas. As in an accusation of murder, if the accuser be a private man, the plea is a private plea; if the accuser be the sovereign, the plea is a public plea.

## CHAPTER XXVIII

## OF PUNISHMENTS AND REWARDS

The definition of punishment.

1. A PUNISHMENT *is an evil inflicted by public authority on him that hath done or omitted that which is judged by the same authority to be a transgression of the law, to the end that the will of men may thereby the better be disposed to obedience.*[2]

---

1 This is Hobbes at his best.

2 Cf. 20.13, 30.23.

2. Before I infer anything from this definition, there is a question to be answered of much importance; which is, by what door the right or authority of punishing, in any case, came in. For by that which has been said before, no man is supposed bound by covenant not to resist violence;[1] and consequently it cannot be intended that he gave any right to another to lay violent hands upon his person. In the making of a commonwealth every man giveth away the right of defending another, but not of defending himself.[2] Also he obligeth himself to assist him that hath the sovereignty in the punishing of another, but of himself not. But to covenant to assist the sovereign in doing hurt to another, unless he that so covenanteth have a right to do it himself, is not to give him a right to punish. It is manifest therefore that the right which the commonwealth (that is, he or they that represent it) hath to punish is not grounded on any concession or gift of the subjects.[3] But I have also shown formerly that before the institution of commonwealth, every man had a right to everything and to do whatsoever he thought necessary to his own preservation, subduing, hurting, or killing any man in order thereunto. And this is the foundation of that right of punishing which is exercised in every commonwealth. [162] For the subjects did not give the sovereign that right, but only, in laying down theirs, strengthened him to use his own as he should think fit for the preservation of them all; so that it was not given, but left to him and to him only, and, excepting the limits set him by natural law, as entire as in the condition of mere nature and of war of everyone against his neighbour.

Right to punish whence derived.

3. From the definition of punishment, I infer, first, that neither private revenges nor injuries of private men can properly be styled punishment, because they proceed not from public authority.[4]

Private injuries and revenges, no punishments.

4. Secondly, that to be neglected and unpreferred by the public favour is not a punishment, because no new evil is thereby on any man inflicted; he is only left in the estate he was in before.

Nor denial of preferment.

---

1 See 14.30.

2 See also 27.20.

3 See also 18.2, 20.1, 21.14.

4 Hobbes is commenting on the concept of punishment. It is part of the concept of punishment that if x is a punishment, then x was administered by a public authority. If someone says, "Ali punished Liston in the fourth round of the boxing match" either the use is metaphorical or the sentence is false. See also 28.22.

Nor pain inflicted without public hearing.

5. Thirdly, that the evil inflicted by public authority, without precedent public condemnation, is not to be styled by the name of punishment, but of a hostile act, because the fact for which a man is punished ought first to be judged by public authority to be a transgression of the law.

Nor pain inflicted by usurped power

6. Fourthly, that the evil inflicted by usurped power and judges without authority from the sovereign is not punishment, but an act of hostility, because the acts of power usurped have not for author the person condemned, and therefore are not acts of public authority.

Nor pain inflicted by usurped power.

7. Fifthly, that all evil which is inflicted without intention or possibility of disposing the delinquent or, by his example, other men to obey the laws is not punishment, but an act of hostility, because without such an end no hurt done is contained under that name.

Natural evil consequences, no punishments.

8. Sixthly, whereas to certain actions there be annexed by nature divers hurtful consequences, as when a man in assaulting another is himself slain or wounded or when he falleth into sickness by the doing of some unlawful act; such hurt, though in respect of God, who is the author of nature, it may be said to be inflicted and therefore a punishment divine;[1] yet it is not contained in the name of punishment in respect of men, because it is not inflicted by the authority of man.

Hurt inflicted, if less than the benefit of transgressing is not punishment, but hostility.

9. Seventhly, if the harm inflicted be less than the benefit of contentment that naturally followeth the crime committed, that harm is not within the definition and is rather the price or redemption than the punishment of a crime, because it is of the nature of punishment to have for end the disposing of men to obey the law; which end (if it be less than the benefit of the transgression) it attaineth not, but worketh a contrary effect.

Where the punishment is annexed to the law, a greater hurt is not punishment, but hostility.

10. Eighthly, if a punishment be determined and prescribed in the law itself and after the crime committed there be a greater punishment inflicted, the excess is not punishment, but an act of hostility. For seeing the aim of punishment is not a revenge, but terror, and the terror of a great punishment unknown is taken away by the declaration of a less, the unexpected addition is no part of the punishment. But where there is no punishment at all

1 See also 31.40.

determined by the law, there whatsoever is inflicted hath the nature of punishment. For he that goes about the violation of a law, wherein no penalty is determined, expecteth an indeterminate, that is to say, an arbitrary punishment. [163]

Hurt inflicted for a fact done before the law, no punishment.

11. Ninthly, harm inflicted for a fact done before there was a law that forbade it is not punishment, but an act of hostility; for before the law, there is no transgression of the law; but punishment supposeth a fact judged to have been a transgression of the law; therefore harm inflicted before the law made is not punishment, but an act of hostility.

The representative of the commonwealth unpunishable.

12. Tenthly, hurt inflicted on the representative of the commonwealth is not punishment, but an act of hostility, because it is of the nature of punishment to be inflicted by public authority, which is the authority only of the representative itself.

Hurt to revolted subjects is done by right of war, not by way of punishment.

13. Lastly, harm inflicted upon one that is a declared enemy falls not under the name of punishment, because seeing they were either never subject to the law and therefore cannot transgress it or having been subject to it and professing to be no longer so, by consequence deny they can transgress it, all the harms that can be done them must be taken as acts of hostility. But in declared hostility all infliction of evil is lawful. From whence it followeth that if a subject shall by fact or word wittingly and deliberately deny the authority of the representative of the commonwealth (whatsoever penalty hath been formerly ordained for treason), he may lawfully be made to suffer whatsoever the representative will; for in denying subjection, he denies such punishment as by the law hath been ordained, and therefore suffers as an enemy of the commonwealth, that is, according to the will of the representative. For the punishments set down in the law are to subjects, not to enemies; such as are they that, having been by their own act subjects, deliberately revolting, deny the sovereign power.

14. The first and most general distribution of punishments is into *divine* and *human*. Of the former I shall have occasion to speak in a more convenient place hereafter.[1]

15. *Human* are those punishments that be inflicted by the commandment of man; and are either corporal or pecuniary or ignominy or imprisonment or exile or mixed of these.

---

1 See 31.40.

Punishments corporal.

16. *Corporal punishment* is that which is inflicted on the body directly and according to the intention of him that inflicteth it; such as are stripes or wounds or deprivation of such pleasures of the body as were before lawfully enjoyed.

Capital.

17. And of these, some be *capital*, some *less* than *capital*. Capital is the infliction of death, and that either simply or with torment. Less than capital are stripes, wounds, chains, and any other corporal pain not in its own nature mortal. For if upon the infliction of a punishment death follow, not in the intention of the inflicter, the punishment is not to be esteemed capital, though the harm prove [164] mortal by an accident not to be foreseen; in which case death is not inflicted, but hastened.

18. *Pecuniary punishment* is that which consisteth not only in the deprivation of a sum of money, but also of lands or any other goods which are usually bought and sold for money. And in case the law that ordaineth such a punishment be made with design to gather money from such as shall transgress the same, it is not properly a punishment, but the price of privilege and exemption from the law, which doth not absolutely forbid the fact but only to those that are not able to pay the money, except where the law is natural or part of religion; for in that case it is not an exemption from the law, but a transgression of it. As where a law exacteth a pecuniary mulct [fine] of them that take the name of God in vain, the payment of the mulct is not the price of a dispensation to swear, but the punishment of the transgression of a law indispensable. In like manner if the law impose a sum of money to be paid to him that has been injured, this is but a satisfaction for the hurt done him and extinguisheth the accusation of the party injured, not the crime of the offender.

Ignominy.

19. *Ignominy* is the infliction of such evil as is made dishonourable or the deprivation of such good as is made honourable by the commonwealth. For there be some things honourable by nature, as the effects of courage, magnanimity, strength, wisdom, and other abilities of body and mind, others made honourable by the commonwealth, as badges, titles, offices, or any other singular mark of the sovereign's favour. The former (though they may fail by nature or accident) cannot be taken away by a law; and therefore the loss of them is not punishment. But the latter may be

taken away by the public authority that made them honourable, and are properly punishments; such are, degrading men condemned of their badges, titles, and offices, or declaring them incapable of the like in time to come.

20. *Imprisonment* is when a man is by public authority deprived of liberty and may happen from two divers ends, whereof one is the safe custody of a man accused, the other is the inflicting of pain on a man condemned. The former is not punishment, because no man is supposed to be punished before he be judicially heard and declared guilty. And therefore whatsoever hurt a man is made to suffer by bonds or restraint before his cause be heard, over and above that which is necessary to assure his custody, is against the law of nature. But the latter is punishment because evil and inflicted by public authority for somewhat that has by the same authority been judged a transgression of the law. Under this word imprisonment, I comprehend all restraint of motion caused by an external obstacle, be it a house, which is called by the general name of a prison, or an island, as when men are said to be confined to it, or a place where men are set to work, as in old time men have been condemned to quarries, and in these times to galleys, or be it a chain or any other such impediment. Imprisonment.

21. *Exile* (banishment) is when a man is for a crime condemned to depart out of the dominion of the commonwealth or out of a certain part thereof, and during a prefixed time or forever not to return into it, and seemeth not in its own nature, without other circumstances, to be a punishment, but rather an escape or a public commandment to avoid punishment by flight. And Cicero[1] says there was never any such punishment ordained in the city of Rome; but calls it a refuge of men in danger. For if a man banished be nevertheless permitted to enjoy his goods and the revenue of his lands, the mere change of air is no punishment; nor does it tend to that benefit of the commonwealth for which all punishments are ordained, that is to say, to the forming of men's wills to the observation of the law; but many times to the damage of the commonwealth. For a banished man is a lawful enemy of the commonwealth that banished him, as being no more a member of the same. But if he be withal deprived of his lands or goods, Exile. [165]

1 *Pro Caecina*, #100.

then the punishment lieth not in the exile, but is to be reckoned amongst punishments pecuniary.

The punishment of innocent subjects is contrary to the law of nature.

22. All punishments of innocent subjects, be they great or little, are against the law of nature; for punishment is only for transgression of the law; and therefore there can be no punishment of the innocent.[1] It is therefore a violation, first, of that law of nature which forbiddeth all men in their revenges to look at anything but some future good; for there can arrive no good to the commonwealth by punishing the innocent. Secondly, of that which forbiddeth ingratitude; for seeing all sovereign power is originally given by the consent of everyone of the subjects, to the end they should as long as they are obedient be protected thereby, the punishment of the innocent is a rendering of evil for good. And thirdly, of the law that commandeth equity, that is to say, an equal distribution of justice, which in punishing the innocent is not observed.

But the harm done to innocents in war, not so.

23. But the infliction of what evil soever on an innocent man that is not a subject, if it be for the benefit of the commonwealth and without violation of any former covenant, is no breach of the law of nature. For all men that are not subjects are either enemies or else they have ceased from being so by some precedent covenants. But against enemies, whom the commonwealth judgeth capable to do them hurt, it is lawful by the original right of nature to make war, wherein the sword judgeth not; nor doth the victor make distinction of nocent [guilty] and innocent as to the time past, nor has other respect of mercy than as it conduceth to the good of his own people. And upon this ground it is that also in subjects who deliberately deny the authority of the commonwealth established, the vengeance is lawfully extended, not only to the fathers, but also to the third and fourth generation not yet in being, and consequently innocent of the fact for which they are afflicted, because the nature of this offence consisteth in the renouncing of subjection, which is a relapse into the condition of war commonly called rebellion; and they that so offend, suffer not [166] as subjects, but as enemies. For rebellion is but war renewed.

Nor that which is done to declared rebels.

1 Hobbes is making a logical point. It is part of the meaning of the word 'punishment' that whoever is punished is guilty. If an innocent person is wrongly convicted of a crime she did not do and imprisoned, fined or executed, that person surely suffers and her suffering appears to be *punishment*, but is in fact, harm, not punishment. See also 17.11 and 28.3.

24. Reward is either of gift or by contract. When by contract, it is called salary and wages, which is benefit due for service performed or promised. When of gift, it is benefit proceeding from the grace of them that bestow it, to encourage or enable men to do them service. And therefore when the sovereign of a commonwealth appointeth a salary to any public office, he that receiveth it is bound in justice to perform his office; otherwise, he is bound only in honour to acknowledgement and an endeavour of requital. For though men have no lawful remedy when they be commanded to quit their private business to serve the public, without reward or salary; yet they are not bound thereto by the law of nature nor by the institution of the commonwealth, unless the service cannot otherwise be done, because it is supposed the sovereign may make use of all their means, insomuch as the most common soldier may demand the wages of his warfare as a debt.

Reward is either salary or grace.

25. The benefits which a sovereign bestoweth on a subject for fear of some power and ability he hath to do hurt to the commonwealth are not properly rewards; for they are not salaries, because there is in this case no contract supposed, every man being obliged already not to do the commonwealth disservice; nor are they graces, because they be extorted by fear, which ought not to be incident to the sovereign power; but [they] are rather sacrifices, which the sovereign, considered in his natural person and not in the person of the commonwealth, makes for the appeasing the discontent of him he thinks more potent than himself; and [such actions] encourage not to obedience, but, on the contrary, to the continuance and increasing of further extortion.

Benefits bestowed for fear are not rewards.

26. And whereas some salaries are certain and proceed from the public treasury, and others uncertain and casual, proceeding from the execution of the office for which the salary is ordained, the latter is in some cases hurtful to the commonwealth, as in the case of judicature. For where the benefit of the judges and ministers of a court of justice ariseth for the multitude of causes that are brought to their cognizance, there must needs follow two inconveniences: one is the nourishing of suits (for the more suits, the greater benefit); and another that depends on that, which is contention which is about jurisdiction (each court drawing to itself as many causes as it can). But in offices of execution there are not

Salaries certain and casual.

those inconveniences, because their employment cannot be increased by any endeavour of their own. And thus much shall suffice for the nature of punishment and reward; which are, as it were, the nerves and tendons that move the limbs and joints of a commonwealth.

27. Hitherto I have set forth the nature of man, whose pride and other passions have compelled him to submit himself to government, together with the great power of his governor, whom I compared to Leviathan, taking that comparison out of the two last verses of the one-and-fortieth of Job where God, having set forth the great power of Leviathan,[1] calleth him king of the proud.
[167] *There is nothing*, saith he, *on earth to be compared with him. He is made so as not to be afraid. He seeth every high thing below him; and is king of all the children of pride.* But because he is mortal and subject to decay, as all other earthly creatures are, and because there is that in heaven, though not on earth, that he should stand in fear of and whose laws he ought to obey, I shall in the next following chapters speak of his diseases and the causes of his mortality, and of what laws of nature he is bound to obey.

# CHAPTER XXIX

## OF THOSE THINGS THAT WEAKEN OR TEND TO THE DISSOLUTION OF A COMMONWEALTH

Dissolution of commonwealths proceedeth from their imperfect institution.

1. Though nothing can be immortal which mortals make; yet, if men had the use of reason they pretend to, their commonwealths might be secured, at least, from perishing by internal diseases. For by the nature of their institution, they are designed to live as long as mankind or as the laws of nature or as justice itself, which gives them life. Therefore when they come to be dissolved, not by external violence, but intestine disorder, the fault is not in men as

---

1 See also 17.13; and Psalms 74:13-14, 104:26, Job 3:8, 41:1-34. In *A Midsummer Night's Dream*, Shakespeare used 'Leviathan' to express speed and strength (2.1. 174). In "Anniversary of the Government under O.C. [Oliver Cromwell]," Andrew Marvell used 'Leviathan' to refer to a large ship.

they are the matter, but as they are the makers and orderers of them. For men, as they become at last weary of irregular jostling and hewing one another and desire with all their hearts to conform themselves into one firm and lasting edifice, so for want both of the art of making fit laws to square their actions by and also of humility and patience to suffer the rude and cumbersome points of their present greatness to be taken off, they cannot without the help of a very able architect be compiled into any other than a crazy building, such as, hardly lasting out their own time, must assuredly fall upon the heads of their posterity.

2. Amongst the *infirmities* therefore of a commonwealth, I will reckon in the first place those that arise from an imperfect institution and resemble the diseases of a natural body, which proceed from a defectuous [defective] procreation.

Want of absolute power.

3. Of which this is one: *that a man to obtain a kingdom is sometimes content with less power than to the peace and defence of the commonwealth is necessarily required.* From whence it cometh to pass that when the exercise of the power laid by is for the public safety to be resumed, it hath the resemblance of an unjust act, which disposeth great numbers of men, when occasion is presented, to rebel, in the same manner as the bodies of children, gotten by diseased parents, are subject either to untimely death or to purge the ill quality derived from their vicious conception, by breaking out into biles and scabs. And when kings deny themselves some such necessary power, it is not always (though sometimes) out of ignorance of what is necessary to the office they undertake, but many times out of a hope to recover the same again at their pleasure;[1] [168]
wherein they reason not well, because such as will hold them to their promises shall be maintained against them by foreign commonwealths, who in order to the good of their own subjects let slip few occasions to weaken the estate of their neighbours. So was Thomas Becket,[2] Archbishop of Canterbury, supported against

1 Hobbes may be thinking of Charles I, who made concessions to Parliament in his "Reply to the Nineteen Propositions," which he probably intended to retract once he had sufficient power to do so.

2 Thomas à Becket (1118-1170), English martyr. King Henry II appointed Becket Archbishop of Canterbury with the expectation that he would support the king's position on the church. Becket did not and when Henry in anger said, "Will none of those who live off my bounty relieve me of this troublesome clerk?" four of Henry's knights went off and murdered Becket in his cathedral.

Henry the Second by the Pope, the subjection of ecclesiastics to the commonwealth having been dispensed with by William the Conqueror at his reception, when he took an oath not to infringe the liberty of the Church. And so were the barons, whose power was by William Rufus,[1] to have their help in transferring the succession from his elder brother to himself, increased to a degree inconsistent with the sovereign power, maintained in their rebellion against King John by the French.

4. Nor does this happen in monarchy only. For whereas the style of the ancient Roman commonwealth was, *The Senate and People of Rome*, neither Senate nor people pretended to the whole power; which first caused the seditions of Tiberius Gracchus, Caius Gracchus, Lucius Saturninus, and others, and afterwards the wars between the Senate and the people under Marius and Sylla, and again under Pompey and Caesar to the extinction of their democracy and the setting up of monarchy.

5. The people of Athens bound themselves but from one only action, which was that no man on pain of death should propound the renewing of the war for the island of Salamis; and yet thereby, if Solon[2] had not caused to be given out he was mad, and afterwards in gesture and habit of a madman, and in verse, propounded it to the people that flocked about him, they had had an enemy perpetually in readiness, even at the gates of their city; such damage or shifts are all commonwealths forced to that have their power never so little limited.

Private judgement of good and evil.

6. In the second place, I observe the diseases of a commonwealth that proceed from the poison of seditious doctrines, whereof one is that every private man is judge of good and evil actions.[3] This is true in the condition of mere nature, where there are no civil laws, and also under civil government in such cases as are not determined by the law. But otherwise, it is manifest that the measure of good and evil actions is the civil law; and the judge [is] the

1 William Rufus, King William II, (c. 1060-1100) was son of William the Conqueror (c. 1027-1087) and fought with Anselm of Canterbury over the issue of lay investiture. William was not well-liked. He was shot in the back with an arrow on a hunting party; no one was prosecuted for the crime.

2 Solon (c. 639-559 B.C.) was an Athenian reformer, statesman, and lawgiver. The rich opposed Solon's reforms.

3 See also 6.7.

legislator, who is always representative of the commonwealth. From this false doctrine, men are disposed to debate with themselves and dispute the commands of the commonwealth, and afterwards to obey or disobey them as in their private judgements they shall think fit, whereby the commonwealth is distracted and weakened.

7. Another doctrine repugnant to civil society is that whatsoever a man does against his conscience is sin; and it dependeth on the presumption of making himself judge of good and evil. For a man's conscience and his judgement is the same thing; and as the judgement, so also the conscience may be erroneous.[1] Therefore, though he that is subject to no civil law sinneth in all he does [169] against his conscience, because he has no other rule to follow but his own reason; yet it is not so with him that lives in a commonwealth, because the law is the public conscience by which he hath already undertaken to be guided. Otherwise in such diversity as there is of private consciences, which are but private opinions, the commonwealth must needs be distracted, and no man dare to obey the sovereign power farther than it shall seem good in his own eyes.

Erroneous conscience.

8. It hath been also commonly taught that faith and sanctity are not to be attained by study and reason, but by supernatural inspiration or infusion. Which granted, I see not why any man should render a reason of his faith, or why every Christian should not be also a prophet; or why any man should take the law of his country rather than his own inspiration for the rule of his action. And thus we fall again into the fault of taking upon us to judge of good and evil, or to make judges of it such private men as pretend to be supernaturally inspired, to the dissolution of all civil government. Faith comes by hearing,[2] and hearing by those accidents which guide us into the presence of them that speak to us; which accidents are all contrived by God Almighty, and yet are not supernatural, but only, for the great number of them that concur to every effect, unobservable. Faith and sanctity are indeed not very frequent; but yet they are not miracles, but brought to pass by education, discipline, correction, and other natural ways by which

Pretence of inspiration.

1 See also 7.4 and 30.14.

2 A reference to the Epistle to the Romans 10:17. See also 43.8.

God worketh them in his elect, at such time as he thinketh fit. And these three opinions, pernicious to peace and government, have in this part of the world proceeded chiefly from tongues and pens of unlearned divines, who, joining the words of Holy Scripture together otherwise is agreeable to reason, do what they can to make men think that sanctity and natural reason cannot stand together.

Subjecting the sovereign power to civil laws.

9. A fourth opinion repugnant to the nature of a commonwealth is this: *that he that hath the sovereign power is subject to the civil laws*. It is true that sovereigns are all subject to the laws of nature, because such laws be divine and cannot by any man or commonwealth be abrogated. But to those laws which the sovereign himself, that is, which the commonwealth, maketh, he is not subject. For to be subject to laws is to be subject to the commonwealth, that is, to the sovereign representative, that is, to himself which is not subjection, but freedom from the laws. Which error, because it setteth the laws above the sovereign, setteth also a judge above him, and a power to punish him; which is to make a new sovereign; and again for the same reason a third, to punish the second; and so continually without end, to the confusion and dissolution of the commonwealth.

Attributing of absolute propriety to subjects.

10. A fifth doctrine that tendeth to the dissolution of a commonwealth is that every private man has an absolute propriety in his goods, such as excludeth the right of the sovereign. Every man has indeed a propriety that excludes the right of every other subject; and he has it only from the sovereign power, without the protection whereof every other man should have right to the same. [170] But the right of the sovereign also be excluded, he cannot perform the office they have put him into, which is to defend them both from foreign enemies and from the injuries of one another, and consequently there is no longer a commonwealth.

11. And if the propriety of subjects exclude not the right of the sovereign representative to their goods, [then] much less to their offices of judicature or execution in which they represent the sovereign himself.

Dividing of the sovereign power.

12. There is a sixth doctrine, plainly and directly against the essence of a commonwealth, and it is this: *that the sovereign power may be divided*. For what is it to divide the power of a common-

wealth, but to dissolve it; for powers divided mutually destroy each other. And for these doctrines men are chiefly beholding to some of those that, making profession of the laws, endeavour to make them depend upon their own learning, and not upon the legislative power.

13. And as false doctrine, so also oftentimes the example of different government in a neighbouring nation disposeth men to alteration of the form already settled. So the people of the Jews were stirred up to reject God and to call upon the prophet Samuel for a king after the manner of the nations;[1] so also the lesser cities of Greece were continually disturbed with seditions of the aristocratical and democratical factions, one part of almost every commonwealth desiring to imitate the Lacedaemonians, the other, the Athenians. And I doubt not but many men have been contented to see the late troubles in England out of an imitation of the Low Countries, supposing there needed no more to grow rich than to change, as they had done, the form of their government. For the constitution of man's nature is of itself subject to desire novelty; when therefore they are provoked to the same by the neighbourhood also of those that have been enriched by it, it is almost impossible to be content with those that solicit them to change, and love the first beginnings, though they be grieved with the continuance of disorder, like hot bloods that, having gotten the itch, tear themselves with their own nails till they can endure the smart no longer.

Imitation of neighbor nations.

14. And as to rebellion in particular against monarchy, one of the most frequent causes of it is the reading of the books of policy and histories of the ancient Greeks and Romans,[2] from which young men and all others that are unprovided of the antidote of

Imitation of the Greeks and Romans.

---

1 "Then all the elders of Israel gathered themselves together, and came to Samuel unto Ramah, And said unto him, 'Behold, thou are old, and thy sons walk not in thy ways. Now make us a king to judge us, like all the nations'. But the thing displeased Samuel, when they said, 'Give us a king to judge us'; and Samuel prayed unto the Lord. And the Lord said unto Samuel, 'Hearken unto the voice of the people in all that they say unto thee; for they have not rejected thee, but they have rejected me, that I should not reign over them'." (I Sam. 8:4-7, Authorized Version.)

2 Hobbes genuinely hated the political views of such thinkers as Aristotle, as represented by his *Politics,* not his *Rhetoric,* and Cicero, who was a republican. See also 46.11-14 and 47.16. Hobbes approved of other ancient Greek and Latin authors, such as Thucydides, whose history of the Peloponnesian war he translated.

solid reason, receiving a strong and delightful impression of the great exploits of war achieved by the conductors of their armies, receive withal a pleasing idea of all they have done besides; and [they] imagine their great prosperity not to have proceeded from the emulation of particular men, but from the virtue of their popular form of government, not considering the frequent seditions and civil wars produced by the imperfection of their policy. From the reading, I say, of such books, men have undertaken to kill their kings, because the Greek and Latin writers in their books and dis-
[171] courses of policy make it lawful and laudable for any man so to do, provided before he do it he call him tyrant. For they say not *regicide*, that is, killing of a king, but *tyrannicide*, that is, killing of a tyrant, is lawful. From the same books they that live under a monarch conceive an opinion that the subjects in a popular commonwealth enjoy liberty, but that in a monarchy they are all slaves. I say, they that live under a monarchy conceive such an opinion, not they that live under a popular government, for they find no such matter. In sum, I cannot imagine how anything can be more prejudicial to a monarchy than the allowing of such books to be publicly read, without present applying such correctives of discreet masters as are fit to take away their venom; which venom I will not doubt to compare to the biting of a mad dog, which is a disease that physicians call *hydrophobia* or *fear of water*. For as he that is so bitten has a continual torment of thirst and yet abhorreth water; and [he] is in such an estate as if the poison endeavoured to convert him into a dog; so when a monarchy is once bitten to the quick by those democratical writers that continually snarl at that estate, it wanteth nothing more than a strong monarch, which nevertheless out of a certain *tyrannophobia* or fear of being strongly governed, when they have him, they abhor.

15. As there have been doctors that hold there be three souls in a man, so there be [doctors] also that think there may be more souls, that is, more sovereigns, than one in a commonwealth; and [they] set up a *supremacy* against the *sovereignty*, *canons* against *laws*, and a *ghostly authority* against the *civil*, working on men's minds with words and distinctions that of themselves signify nothing, but bewray, by their obscurity, that there walketh (as some think invisibly) another kingdom, as it were a kingdom of fairies, in the dark.

Now seeing it is manifest that the civil power and the power of the commonwealth is the same thing; and that supremacy and the power of making canons and granting faculties, implieth a commonwealth; it followeth that where one is sovereign, another supreme; where one can make laws and another make canons, there must needs be two commonwealths, of one and the same subjects; which is a kingdom divided in itself and cannot stand. For notwithstanding the insignificant distinction of *temporal* and *ghostly*, they are still two kingdoms,[1] and every subject is subject to two masters.[2] For seeing the *ghostly* power challengeth the right to declare what is sin, it challengeth by consequence to declare what is law, sin being nothing but the transgression of the law; and again, the civil power challenging to declare what is law, every subject must obey two masters, who both will have their commands be observed as law, which is impossible. Or, if it be but one kingdom, [then] either the civil, which is the power of the commonwealth, must be subordinate to the ghostly, and then there is no sovereignty but the ghostly; or the ghostly must be subordinate to the temporal, and then there is no supremacy but the temporal. When therefore these two powers oppose one another, the commonwealth cannot but be in great danger of civil war and dissolu- [172] tion. For the civil authority being more visible, and standing in the clearer light of natural reason, cannot choose but draw to it in all times a very considerable part of the people; and the spiritual, though it stand in the darkness of School distinctions and hard words; yet, because the fear of darkness and ghosts is greater than other fears, [the spiritual] cannot want a party sufficient to trouble and sometimes to destroy a commonwealth. And this is a disease which not unfitly may be compared to the epilepsy or falling sickness (which the Jews took to be one kind of possession by spirits) in the body natural. For as in this disease there is an unnatural spirit or wind in the head that obstructeth the roots of the nerves and, moving them violently, taketh the motion which naturally they should have from the power of the soul in the brain, thereby

1 Hobbes insisted that every citizen is subject to only one kingdom. This is one reason that he maintained that the kingdom of God did not exist at the present but would exist sometime in the indefinite future, with Christ as the sovereign.

2 Matt. 5:24: "No man can serve two masters." Hobbes applied this biblical aphorism to politics. See 42.102 and 42.123.

causeth violent and irregular motions, which men call convulsions in the parts, insomuch as he that is seized therewith falleth down sometimes into the water and sometimes into the fire, as a man deprived of his senses; so also in the body politic, when the spiritual power moveth the members of a commonwealth by the terror of punishments and hope of rewards, which are the nerves of it, otherwise than by the civil power, which is the soul of the commonwealth, they ought to be moved; and [when] by strange and hard words suffocates their understanding, it must needs thereby distract the people and either overwhelm the commonwealth with oppression or cast it into the fire of a civil war.

Mixed government.

16. Sometimes also in the merely civil government there be more than one soul, as when the power of levying money, which is the nutritive faculty, has depended on a general assembly;[1] the power of conduct and command, which is the motive faculty, on one man;[2] and the power of making laws, which is the rational faculty, on the accidental consent, not only of those two, but also of a third;[3] this endangereth the commonwealth, sometimes for want of consent to good laws, but most often for want of such nourishment as is necessary to life and motion. For although few perceive that such government is not government, but division of the commonwealth into three factions, and call it mixed monarchy; yet the truth is that it is not one independent commonwealth, but three independent factions; nor one representative person, but three. In the kingdom of God there may be three persons independent, without breach of unity in God that reigneth; but where men reign, that be subject to diversity of opinions, it cannot be so. And therefore if the king bear the person of the people, and the general assembly bear also the person of the people, and another assembly bear the person of a part of the people, they are not one person, nor one sovereign, but three persons and three sovereigns.

17. To what disease in the natural body of man I may exactly compare this irregularity of a commonwealth, I know not. But I have seen a man that had another man growing out of his side, with a head, arms, breast, and stomach of his own; if he had had

1 The monarch depended on the House of Commons to approve funds.

2 Hobbes is thinking of the monarch of England.

3 I believe Hobbes is thinking of the House of Lords as the third faculty.

another man growing out of his other side, the comparison might then have been exact. [173]

18. Hitherto I have named such diseases of a commonwealth as are of the greatest and most present danger. There be other, not so great, which nevertheless are not unfit to be observed. As first, the difficulty of raising money for the necessary uses of the commonwealth, especially in the approach of war.[1] This difficulty ariseth from the opinion that every subject hath of a propriety in his lands and goods exclusive of the sovereign's right to the use of the same. From whence it cometh to pass that the sovereign power, which foreseeth the necessities and dangers of the commonwealth (finding the passage of money to the public treasury obstructed by the tenacity of the people), whereas it ought to extend itself, to encounter and prevent such dangers in their beginnings, contracteth itself as long as it can; and when it cannot longer, [the sovereign power] struggles with the people by stratagems of law to obtain little sums, which, not sufficing, he is fain [required] at last violently to open the way for present supply or perish; and, being put often to these extremities, at last reduceth the people to their due temper or else the commonwealth must perish.[2] Insomuch as we may compare this distemper very aptly to an ague, wherein, the fleshy parts being congealed or by venomous matter obstructed, the veins which by their natural course empty themselves into the heart, are not (as they ought to be) supplied from the arteries, whereby there succeedeth at first a cold contraction and trembling of the limbs, and afterwards a hot and strong endeavour of the heart to force a passage for the blood; and before it can do that, contenteth itself with the small refreshments of such things as cool for a time, till, if nature be strong enough, it break at last the contumacy of the parts obstructed and dissipateth the venom into sweat; or, if nature be too weak, the patient dieth.

Want of money.

---

1 Charles had trouble getting money from Parliament for his entire reign, beginning with his first year of rule, 1625, when, contrary to tradition, Parliament refused to grant him the right to levy tonnage and poundage (customs duties). His imposition of Ship Money in 1634 was legal but extremely unpopular. Charles called his first Parliament since 1629 for the spring of 1640 in order to have funds approved to fight a second Bishops' War. When the members refused to consider levying money until after their grievances had been resolved, Charles dissolved Parliament.

2 Although this looks like a prediction or generalization, Hobbes is thinking specifically of the English Civil War.

Monopolies and abuses of publicans.

19. Again, there is sometimes in a commonwealth a disease which resembleth the pleurisy; and that is when the treasury of the commonwealth, flowing out of its due course, is gathered together in too much abundance in one or a few private men, by monopolies or by farms of the public revenues; in the same manner as the blood in a pleurisy, getting into the membrane of the breast, breedeth there an inflammation, accompanied with a fever and painful stitches.

Popular men.

20. Also, the popularity of a potent subject, unless the commonwealth have very good caution of his fidelity, is a dangerous disease, because the people, which should receive their motion from the authority of the sovereign, by the flattery and by the reputation of an ambitious man, are drawn away from their obedience to the laws to follow a man of whose virtues and designs they have no knowledge. And this is commonly of more danger in a popular government than in a monarchy, because an army is of so great force and multitude as it may easily be made believe they are the
[174] people. By this means it was that Julius Caesar, who was set up by the people against the Senate, having won to himself the affections of his army, made himself master both of Senate and people. And this proceeding of popular and ambitious men is plain rebellion, and may be resembled to the effects of witchcraft.

Excessive greatness of a town or multitude of corporations.

21. Another infirmity of a commonwealth is the immoderate greatness of a town,[1] when it is able to furnish out of its own circuit the number and expense of a great army, as also the great number of corporations, which are as it were many lesser commonwealths in the bowels of a greater, like worms in the entrails of a natural man. To which may be added, the liberty of disputing against absolute power by pretenders to political prudence; which though bred for the most part in the lees [dregs] of the people; yet animated by false doctrines are perpetually meddling with the fundamental laws, to the molestation of the commonwealth, like the little worms which physicians call *ascarides*.

Liberty of disputing against sovereign power.

22. We may further add the insatiable appetite or *bulimia* of enlarging dominion, with the incurable *wounds* thereby many

1 Hobbes is thinking of London, which on the one hand, often opposed the king, and on the other, sometimes opposed Parliament. London raised its own army during the Civil War to protect against parliamentary troops.

times received from the enemy, and the *wens* [lumps] of ununited conquests, which are many times a burden, and with less danger lost than kept, as also the lethargy of ease, and consumption of riot and vain expense.

Dissolution of the commonwealth.

23. Lastly, when in a war, foreign or intestine, the enemies get a final victory, so as, the forces of the commonwealth keeping the field no longer, there is no further protection of subjects in their loyalty, then is the commonwealth DISSOLVED, and every man at liberty to protect himself by such courses as his own discretion shall suggest unto him. For the sovereign is the public soul, giving life and motion to the commonwealth, which expiring, the members are governed by it no more than the carcass of a man by his departed, though immortal, soul. For though the right of a sovereign monarch cannot be extinguished by the act of another; yet the obligation of the members may. For he that wants protection may seek it anywhere; and, when he hath it, is obliged (without fraudulent pretence of having submitted himself out of fear) to protect his protection as long as he is able. But when the power of an assembly is once suppressed, the right of the same perisheth utterly, because the assembly itself is extinct; and consequently, there is no possibility for sovereignty to re-enter.

## CHAPTER XXX

[175]

## OF THE OFFICE OF THE SOVEREIGN REPRESENTATIVE

The procuration of the good of the people.

1. The OFFICE of the sovereign (be it a monarch or an assembly) consisteth in the end for which he was trusted with the sovereign power, namely the procuration of the safety of the people, to which he is obliged by the law of nature, and to render an account thereof to God, the Author of that law, and to none but him. But by safety here is not meant a bare preservation, but also all other contentments of life, which every man by lawful industry, without danger or hurt to the commonwealth, shall acquire to himself.

By instruction and laws.

2. And this is intended should be done, not by care applied to individuals, further than their protection from injuries when they

shall complain, but by a general providence, contained in public instruction, both of doctrine and example; and in the making and executing of good laws to which individual persons may apply their own cases.

Against the duty of a sovereign to relinquish any essential right of sovereignty.

3. And because, if the essential rights of sovereignty (specified before in the eighteenth chapter) be taken away, the commonwealth is thereby dissolved, and every man returneth into the condition and calamity of a war with every other man, which is the greatest evil that can happen in this life; it is the office of the sovereign to maintain those rights entire, and consequently against his duty, first, to transfer to another or to lay from himself any of them. For he that deserteth the means deserteth the ends; and he deserteth the means that, being the sovereign, acknowledgeth himself subject to the civil laws, and renounceth the power of supreme judicature; or of making war or peace by his own authority; or of judging of the necessities of the commonwealth; or of levying money and soldiers when and as much as in his own conscience he shall judge necessary; or of making officers and ministers both of war and peace; or of appointing teachers and examining what doctrines are conformable or contrary to the defence, peace, and good of the people. Secondly, it is against his duty to let the people be ignorant or misinformed of the grounds and reasons of those his essential rights, because thereby men are easy to be seduced and drawn to resist him when the commonwealth shall require their use and exercise.

4. And the grounds of these rights have the rather [greater] need to be diligently and truly taught, because they cannot be maintained by any civil law or terror of legal punishment. For a civil law that shall forbid rebellion (and such is all resistance to the
[176] essential rights of sovereignty) is not (as a civil law) any obligation but by virtue only of the law of nature that forbiddeth the violation of faith;[1] which natural obligation, if men know not, they cannot know the right of any law the sovereign maketh. And for the punishment, they take it but for an act of hostility; which

1 The obligation not to rebel is more basic than any obligation in civil laws. It exists in virtue of the laws of nature, certainly the first, since rebellion is war, and obviously also the third, that people are to keep their covenants (15.1).

when they think they have strength enough, they will endeavour, by acts of hostility, to avoid.

Objection of those that say there are no principles of reason for absolute sovereignty.

5. As I have heard some say that justice is but a word, without substance, and that whatsoever a man can by force or art acquire to himself (not only in the condition of war, but also in a commonwealth) is his own, which I have already shown to be false; so there be also [some] that maintain that there are no grounds nor principles of reason to sustain those essential rights which make sovereignty absolute. For if there were, they would have been found out in some place or other; whereas we see there has not hitherto been any commonwealth where those rights have been acknowledged or challenged. Wherein they argue as ill, as if the savage people of America should deny there were any grounds or principles of reason so to build a house as to last as long as the materials, because they never yet saw any so well built. Time and industry produce every day new knowledge. And as the art of well building is derived from principles of reason, observed by industrious men that had long studied the nature of materials and the divers effects of figure and proportion, long after mankind began, though poorly, to build; so, long time after men have begun to constitute commonwealths, imperfect and apt to relapse into disorder, there may principles of reason be found out by industrious meditation, to make their constitution, excepting by external violence, everlasting. And such are those which I have in this discourse set forth; which, whether they come not into the sight of those that have power to make use of them or be neglected by them or not, concerneth my particular interest, at this day, very little. But supposing that these of mine are not such principles of reason; yet I am sure they are principles from authority of Scripture, as I shall make it appear when I shall come to speak of the kingdom of God, administered by Moses, over the Jews, his peculiar people by covenant.

Objection from the incapacity of the vulgar.

6. But they say again that though the principles be right; yet common people are not of capacity enough to be made to understand them. I should be glad that the rich and potent subjects of a kingdom, or those that are accounted the most learned, were no less incapable than they. But all men know that the obstructions to this kind of doctrine proceed not so much from the difficulty of

the matter, as from the interest of them that are to learn. Potent men digest hardly anything that setteth up a power to bridle their affections; and learned men, anything that discovereth their errors, and thereby their authority; whereas the common people's minds, unless they be tainted with dependence on the potent or scribbled over with the opinions of their doctors are like clean paper, fit to receive whatsoever by public authority shall be imprinted in them.
[177] Shall whole nations be brought to acquiesce in the great mysteries of Christian religion, which are above reason, and millions of men be made believe that the same body may be in innumerable places at one and the same time, which is against reason; and shall not men be able by their teaching and preaching, protected by the law, to make that received which is so consonant to reason that any unprejudicated man needs no more to learn it than to hear it?[1] I conclude therefore that in the instruction of the people in the essential rights which are the natural and fundamental laws of sovereignty, there is no difficulty, whilst a sovereign has his power entire, but what proceeds from his own fault or the fault of those whom he trusteth in the administration of the commonwealth; and consequently, it is his duty to cause them so to be instructed; and not only his duty, but his benefit also and security against the danger that may arrive to himself in his natural person from rebellion.

Subjects are to be taught not to affect change of government.

7. And (to descend to particulars) the people are to be taught, first, that they ought not to be in love with any form of government they see in their neighbour nations, more than with their own, nor, (whatsoever present prosperity they behold in nations that are otherwise governed than they) to desire change. For the prosperity of a people ruled by an aristocratical or democratical assembly cometh not from aristocracy nor from democracy, but from the obedience and concord of the subjects; nor do the people flourish in a monarchy because one man has the right to rule them, but because they obey him. Take away in any kind of state the obedience (and consequently the concord of the people) and they shall not only not flourish, but in short time be dissolved. And they that go about by disobedience to do no more than

1 Since people have been taught to believe Christian mysteries and even some absurd doctrines, they certainly can be taught to believe the reasonable principles of political obedience.

reform the commonwealth shall find they do thereby destroy it, like the foolish daughters of Peleus, in the fable, which desiring to renew the youth of their decrepit father, did by the counsel of Medea cut him in pieces and boil him, together with strange herbs, but made not of him a new man. This desire of change is like the breach of the first of God's commandments; for there God says, *Non habebis Deos alienos*:[1] Thou shalt not have the Gods of other nations; and in another place concerning *kings*, that they are *gods* [Psalm 82:6].

Nor adhere (against the sovereign) to popular men.

8. Secondly, they are to be taught that they ought not to be led with admiration of the virtue of any of their fellow subjects, how high soever he stand nor how conspicuously soever he shine in the commonwealth; nor [of any admiration of the virtue] of any assembly (except the sovereign assembly), so as to defer to them any obedience or honour appropriate to the sovereign only, whom (in their particular stations) they represent; nor to receive any influence from them, but such as is conveyed by them from the sovereign authority. For that sovereign cannot be imagined to love his people as he ought that is not jealous of them, but suffers [allows] them by the flattery of popular men to be seduced from their loyalty, as they have often been, not only secretly, but openly, so as to proclaim marriage with them *in facie ecclesiae*[2] by preachers, and by publishing the same in the open streets; which may fitly be [178] compared to the violation of the second of the Ten Commandments.

Nor to dispute the sovereign power.

9. Thirdly, in consequence to this, they ought to be informed how great a fault it is to speak evil of the sovereign representative (whether one man or an assembly of men) or to argue and dispute his power or any way to use his name irreverently, whereby he may be brought into contempt with his people and [with] their obedience (in which the safety of the commonwealth consisteth) slackened. Which doctrine the third Commandment by resemblance pointeth to.

And to have days set apart to learn their duty.

10. Fourthly, seeing people cannot be taught this, nor, when it is taught, remember it, nor after one generation past so much as know in whom the sovereign power is placed, without setting

1 See also 42.37 and 45.10.

2 Latin: "In the appearance, that is, the presence of the church."

apart from their ordinary labour some certain times in which they may attend those that are appointed to instruct them; it is necessary that some such times be determined wherein they may assemble together, and (after prayers and praises given to God, the Sovereign of sovereigns), hear those their duties told them, and the positive laws, such as generally concern them all, read and expounded, and be put in mind of the authority that maketh them laws. To this end had the Jews every seventh day a Sabbath, in which the law was read and expounded; and in the solemnity whereof they were put in mind that their king was God; that having created the world in six days, he rested on the seventh day; and by their resting on it from their labour, that that God was their king, which redeemed them from their servile and painful labour in Egypt, and gave them a time, after they had rejoiced in God, to take joy also in themselves, by lawful recreation. So that the first table of the commandments is spent all in setting down the sum of God's absolute power, not only as God, but as King by pact (in peculiar) of the Jews; and [the first table] may therefore give light to those that have sovereign power conferred on them by the consent of men, to see what doctrine they ought to teach their subjects.

And to honour their parents.

11. And because the first instruction of children dependeth on the care of their parents, it is necessary that they should be obedient to them whilst they are under their tuition; and not only so, but that also afterwards (as gratitude requireth) they acknowledge the benefit of their education by external signs of honour. To which end they are to be taught that originally the father of every man was also his sovereign lord, with power over him of life and death; and that the fathers of families, when by instituting a commonwealth they resigned that absolute power; yet it was never intended they should lose the honour due unto them for their education. For to relinquish such right was not necessary to the institution of sovereign power; nor would there be any reason why any man should desire to have children or take the care to nourish and instruct them, if they were afterwards to have no other benefit from them than from other men. And this accordeth with the fifth Commandment.

12. Again, every sovereign ought to cause justice to be taught, which (consisting in taking from no man what is his) is as much as to say, to cause men to be taught not to deprive their neighbours by violence or fraud of anything which by the sovereign authority is theirs. Of things held in propriety, those that are dearest to a man are his own life and limbs; and in the next degree (in most men) those that concern conjugal affection; and after them riches and means of living. Therefore the people are to be taught to abstain from violence to one another's person by private revenges, from violation of conjugal honour, and from forcible rapine and fraudulent surreption of one another's goods. For which purpose also it is necessary they be shown the evil consequences of false judgement, by corruption either of judges or witnesses, whereby the distinction of propriety is taken away, and justice becomes of no effect; all which things are intimated in the sixth, seventh, eighth, and ninth commandments. [179]

And to avoid doing of injury.

13. Lastly, they are to be taught that not only the unjust facts [actions], but the designs and intentions to do them (though by accident hindered) are injustice; which consisteth in the [depravity] of the will, as well as in the irregularity of the act. And this is the intention of the tenth commandment and the sum of the second table; which is reduced all to this one commandment of mutual charity, *Thou shalt love thy neighbour as thy self*, as the sum of the first table is reduced to *the love of God*; whom they had then newly received as their king.

And to do all this sincerely from the heart.

14. As for the means and conduits by which the people may receive this instruction, we are to search by what means so many opinions contrary to the peace of mankind, upon weak and false principles, have nevertheless been so deeply rooted in them. I mean those which I have in the precedent chapter specified, as that men shall judge of what is lawful and unlawful, not by the law itself, but by their own consciences, that is to say, by their own private judgements;[1] that subjects sin in obeying the commands of the commonwealth, unless they themselves have first judged them to be lawful; that their propriety in their riches is such as to

The use of universities.

1 See also 29.7.

exclude the dominion which the commonwealth hath the same; that it is lawful for subjects to kill such as they call tyrants; that the sovereign power may be divided,[1] and the like; which come to be instilled into the people by this means. They whom necessity or covetousness keepeth attent on their trades and labour, and they, on the other side, whom superfluity or sloth carrieth after their sensual pleasures (which two sorts of men take up the greatest part of mankind), being diverted from the deep meditation which the learning of truth, not only in the matter of natural justice, but also of all other sciences necessarily requireth, receive the notions of their duty chiefly from divines in the pulpit, and partly from such of their neighbours or familiar acquaintance as having the faculty of discoursing readily and plausibly seem wiser and better learned in cases of law and conscience than themselves. And the divines
[180] and such others as make show of learning derive their knowledge from the universities and from the schools of law or from the books which by men eminent in those schools and universities have been published. It is therefore manifest that the instruction of the people dependeth wholly on the right teaching of youth in the universities. But are not (may some man say) the universities of England learned enough already to do that? Or is it you [who] will undertake to teach the universities? Hard questions. Yet to the first, I doubt not to answer, that till towards the latter end of Henry the Eighth, the power of the Pope was always upheld against the power of the commonwealth principally by the universities; and that the doctrines by so many preachers against the sovereign power of the king and by so many lawyers and others that had their education there, is a sufficient argument that, though the universities were not authors of those false doctrines, yet they knew not how to plant the true. For in such a contradiction of opinions, it is most certain that they have not been sufficiently instructed; and it is no wonder, if they yet retain a relish of that subtle liquor wherewith they were first seasoned against the civil authority. But to the latter question, it is not fit nor needful for me to say either aye or no; for any man that sees what I am doing may easily perceive what I think.

1 Many supporters of Parliament in the 1640s, and some royalists, thought that political authority in England was divided between the monarch and Parliament.

15. The safety of the people requireth further from him or them that have the sovereign power, that justice be equally administered to all degrees of people, that is, that as well the rich and mighty, as poor and obscure persons, may be righted of the injuries done them, so as the great may have no greater hope of impunity, when they do violence, dishonour or any injury to the meaner sort, than when one of these does the like to one of them; for in this consisteth equity; to which, as being a precept of the law of nature, a sovereign is as much subject as any of the meanest of his people. All breaches of the law are offences against the commonwealth; but there be some that are also against private persons. Those that concern the commonwealth only may without breach of equity be pardoned; for every man may pardon what is done against himself, according to his own discretion. But an offence against a private man cannot in equity be pardoned without the consent of him that is injured, or reasonable satisfaction.

16. The inequality of subjects proceedeth from the acts of sovereign power and therefore has no more place in the presence of the sovereign, that is to say, in a court of justice, than the inequality between kings and their subjects in the presence of the King of kings.[1] The honour of great persons is to be valued for their beneficence and the aids they give to men of inferior rank, or not at all. And the violences, oppressions, and injuries they do are not extenuated, but aggravated, by the greatness of their persons, because they have least need to commit them. The consequences of this partiality towards the great proceed in this manner. Impunity maketh insolence; insolence, hatred; and hatred, an endeavour to pull down all oppressing and contumelious greatness, though with the ruin of the commonwealth.

17. To equal justice appertaineth also the equal imposition of taxes; the equality whereof dependeth not on the equality of riches, but on the equality of the debt that every man oweth to the commonwealth for his defence. It is not enough for a man to labour for the maintenance of his life, but also to fight (if need be) [181]

Equal taxes.

1 Hobbes's assertion of the equality of all subjects is surprising since he had lived off nobility for most of his life. The surprise is moderated somewhat by the fact that the House of Commons abolished the House of Lords on 19 March 1649, the same day that it declared England to be a "Commonwealth and Free State," and two days after abolishing the office of king. See also chapter 21 and 30.25.

for the securing of his labour. They must either do as the Jews did after their return from captivity in re-edifying the Temple, [namely, to] build with one hand and hold the sword in the other, or else they must hire others to fight for them. For the impositions that are laid on the people by the sovereign power are nothing else but the wages due to them that hold the public sword to defend private men in the exercise of several trades and callings. Seeing then the benefit that every one receiveth thereby is the enjoyment of life, which is equally dear to poor and rich; the debt which a poor man oweth them that defend his life is the same which a rich man oweth for the defence of his, saving that the rich, who have the service of the poor, may be debtors not only for their own persons, but for many more. Which considered, the equality of imposition consisteth rather in the equality of that which is consumed than of the riches of the persons that consume the same. For what reason is there that he which laboureth much and, sparing the fruits of his labour, consumeth little should be more charged than he that, living idly, getteth little and spendeth all he gets, seeing the one hath no more protection from the commonwealth than the other? But when the impositions are laid upon those things which men consume, every man payeth equally for what he useth; nor is the commonwealth defrauded by the luxurious waste of private men.

Public charity.

18. And whereas many men, by accident inevitable, become unable to maintain themselves by their labour, they ought not to be left to the charity of private persons, but to be provided for, as far forth as the necessities of nature require, by the laws of the commonwealth. For as it is uncharitableness in any man to neglect the impotent; so it is in the sovereign of a commonwealth, to expose them to the hazard of such uncertain charity.

Prevention of idleness.

19. But for such as have strong bodies the case is otherwise; they are to be forced to work; and to avoid the excuse of not finding employment, there ought to be such laws as may encourage all manner of arts, as navigation, agriculture, fishing, and all manner of manufacture that requires labour. The multitude of poor and yet strong people still increasing, they are to be transplanted into countries not sufficiently inhabited; where nevertheless they are not to exterminate those they find there, but constrain them to

inhabit closer together, and not range a great deal of ground to snatch what they find, but to court each little plot with art and labour, to give them their sustenance in due season. And when all the world is overcharged with inhabitants, then the last remedy of all is war, which provideth for every man, by victory or death.

Good laws, what.

20. To the care of the sovereign belongeth the making of good laws. But what is a good law? By a good law, I mean not a just law; for no law can be unjust. The law is made by the sovereign power; [182] and all that is done by such power is warranted and owned by every one of the people; and that which every man will have so, no man can say is unjust. It is in the laws of a commonwealth, as in the laws of gaming: whatsoever the gamesters all agree on is injustice to none of them. A good law is that which is *needful*, for the *good of the people*, and withal *perspicuous*.

Such as are necessary.

21. For the use of laws (which are but rules authorized) is not to bind the people from all voluntary actions, but to direct and keep them in such a motion as not to hurt themselves by their own impetuous desires, rashness, or indiscretion, as hedges are set, not to stop travellers, but to keep them in the way. And therefore a law that is not needful, having not the true end of a law, is not good. A law may be conceived to be good when it is for the benefit of the sovereign, though it be not necessary for the people, but it is not so. For the good of the sovereign and people cannot be separated. It is a weak sovereign that has weak subjects, and a weak people whose sovereign wanteth power to rule them at his will. Unnecessary laws are not good laws, but traps for money which, where the right of sovereign power is acknowledged, are superfluous; and where it is not acknowledged, insufficient to defend the people.

Such as are perspicuous.

22. The perspicuity consisteth not so much in the words of the law itself, as in a declaration of the causes and motives for which it was made. That is it that shows us the meaning of the legislator; and the meaning of the legislator known, the law is more easily understood by few than many words. For all words are subject to ambiguity; and therefore multiplication of words in the body of the law is multiplication of ambiguity; besides it seems to imply (by too much diligence) that whosoever can evade the words is without the compass of the law. And this is a cause of many

unnecessary processes. For when I consider how short were the laws of ancient times, and how they grew by degrees still longer, methinks I see a contention between the penners and pleaders of the law; the former seeking to circumscribe the latter and the latter to evade their circumscriptions; and that the pleaders have got the victory. It belongeth therefore to the office of a legislator (such as is in all commonwealths the supreme representative, be it one man or an assembly) to make the reason perspicuous why the law was made, and the body of the law itself as short, but in as proper and significant terms, as may be.

Punishments. 23. It belongeth also to the office of the sovereign to make a right application of punishments and rewards. And seeing the end of punishing is not revenge and discharge of choler [anger], but correction either of the offender or of others by his example,[1] the severest punishments are to be inflicted for those crimes that are of most danger to the public; such as are those which proceed from malice to the government established; those that spring from contempt of justice; those that provoke indignation in the multitude; [183] and those which, unpunished, seem authorized, as when they are committed by sons, servants, or favourites of men in authority; for indignation carrieth men, not only against the actors and authors of injustice, but against all power that is likely to protect them, as in the case of Tarquin, when for the insolent act of one of his sons he was driven out of Rome and the monarchy itself dissolved.[2] But crimes of infirmity, such as are those which proceed from great provocation, from great fear, great need, or from ignorance whether the fact be a great crime or not, there is place many times for lenity, without prejudice to the commonwealth; and lenity, when there is such place for it, is required by the law of nature. The punishment of the leaders and teachers in a commotion, not the poor seduced people, when they are punished, can profit the commonwealth by their example. To be severe to people is to punish ignorance which may in great part be imputed to the sovereign, whose fault it was they were no better instructed.

Rewards. 24. In like manner it belongeth to the office and duty of the

1 Hobbes's views about punishment are enlightened. See 28.1 and 28.9.

2 The monarchy was abolished after Tarquin's son (Sextus Tarquinus) raped Lucretia, the wife of his cousin Cullatinus. The entire Tarquin family was exiled.

sovereign to apply his rewards always so as there may arise from them benefit to the commonwealth; wherein consisteth their use and end; and is then done when they that have well served the commonwealth are, with as little expense of the common treasury as is possible, so well recompensed as others thereby may be encouraged, both to serve the same as faithfully as they can and to study the arts by which they may be enabled to do it better. To buy with money or preferment from a popular ambitious subject [his agreement] to be quiet and desist from making ill impressions in the minds of the people, has nothing of the nature of reward (which is ordained not for disservice, but for service past); nor a sign of gratitude, but of fear; nor does it tend to the benefit, but to the damage of the public. It is a contention with ambition, like that of Hercules with the monster Hydra, which, having many heads, for every one that was vanquished there grew up three. For in like manner, when the stubbornness of one popular man is overcome with reward, there arise many more by the example, that do the same mischief in hope of like benefit; and as all sorts of manufacture, so also malice increaseth by being vendible. And though sometimes a civil war may be deferred by such ways as that; yet the danger grows still the greater, and the public ruin more assured. It is therefore against the duty of the sovereign, to whom the public safety is committed, to reward those that aspire to greatness by disturbing the peace of their country, and not rather to oppose the beginnings of such men with a little danger, than after a longer time with greater.

25. Another business of the sovereign is to choose good counsellors; I mean such whose advice he is to take in the government of the commonwealth. For this word counsel (*consilium*, corrupted from *considium*) is of a large signification and comprehendeth all assemblies of men that sit together, not only to deliberate what is to be done hereafter, but also to judge of facts past and of law for the present. I take it here in the first sense only; and in this sense, there is no choice of counsel, neither in a democracy nor aristocracy, because the persons counselling are members of the person counselled. The choice of counsellors therefore is proper to monarchy, in which the sovereign that endeavoureth not to make choice of those that in every kind are the most able, dischargeth

Counsellors.

[184]

not his office as he ought to do. The most able counsellors are they that have least hope of benefit by giving evil counsel and most knowledge of those things that conduce to the peace and defence of the commonwealth. It is a hard matter to know who expecteth benefit from public troubles; but the signs that guide to a just suspicion is the soothing of the people in their unreasonable or irremediable grievances by men whose estates are not sufficient to discharge their accustomed expenses, and may easily be observed by any one whom it concerns to know it. But to know who has most knowledge of the public affairs is yet harder; and they that know them need them a great deal the less. For to know who knows the rules almost of any art is a great degree of the knowledge of the same art, because no man can be assured of the truth of another's rules but he that is first taught to understand them. But the best signs of knowledge of any art are much conversing in it and constant good effects of it. Good counsel comes not by lot nor by inheritance; and therefore there is no more reason to expect good advice from the rich or noble in matter of state,[1] than in delineating the dimensions of a fortress; unless we shall think there needs no method in the study of the politics (as there does in the study of geometry) but only to be lookers on; which is not so. For the politics is the harder study of the two. Whereas in these parts of Europe it hath been taken for a right of certain persons to have place in the highest council of state by inheritance, it derived from the conquests of the ancient Germans; wherein many absolute lords, joining together to conquer other nations, would not enter into the confederacy without such privileges as might be marks of difference in time following between their posterity and the posterity of their subjects; which privileges being inconsistent with the sovereign power, by the favour of the sovereign they may seem to keep; but contending for them as their right, they must needs by degrees let them go and have at last no further honour than adhereth naturally to their abilities.

26. And how able soever be the counsellors in any affair, the benefit of their counsel is greater when they give every one his advice and the reasons of it apart, than when they do it in an assembly by way of orations, and when they have premeditated,

1 Another attack on the nobles. See also 30.16.

than when they speak on the sudden, both because they have more time to survey the consequences of action and are less subject to be carried away to contradiction through envy, emulation, or other passions arising from the difference of opinion.

27. The best counsel in those things that concern not other nations, but only the ease and benefit the subjects may enjoy, by laws that look only inward, is to be taken from the general informations and complaints of the people of each province, who are best acquainted with their own wants, and ought therefore, when they demand nothing in derogation of the essential rights of sovereignty, to be diligently taken notice of. For without those essential rights, as I have often before said, the commonwealth cannot at all subsist. [185]

Commanders.

28. A commander of an army in chief, if he be not popular, shall not be beloved, nor feared as he ought to be by his army, and consequently cannot perform that office with good success. He must therefore be industrious, valiant, affable, liberal and fortunate, that he may gain an opinion both of sufficiency and of loving his soldiers. This is popularity and breeds in the soldiers both desire and courage to recommend themselves to his favour; and protects the severity of the general in punishing, when need is, the mutinous or negligent soldiers. But this love of soldiers, if caution be not given of the commander's fidelity, is a dangerous thing to sovereign power, especially when it is in the hands of an assembly not popular. It belongeth therefore to the safety of the people, both that they be good conductors and faithful subjects, to whom the sovereign commits his armies.

29. But when the sovereign himself is popular, that is, reverenced and beloved of his people, there is no danger at all from the popularity of a subject. For soldiers are never so generally unjust as to side with their captain, though they love him, against their sovereign, when they love not only his person, but also his cause. And therefore those who by violence have at any time suppressed the power of their lawful sovereign before they could settle themselves in his place, have been always put to the trouble of contriving their titles to save the people from the shame of receiving them. To have a known right to sovereign power is so popular a quality as he that has it needs no more for his own part, to turn the hearts of

his subjects to him, but that they see him able absolutely to govern his own family: nor, on the part of his enemies, but a disbanding of their armies. For the greatest and most active part of mankind has never hitherto been well contented with the present.

30. Concerning the offices of one sovereign to another, which are comprehended in that law which is commonly called the law of nations, I need not say anything in this place, because the law of nations and the law of nature is the same thing. And every sovereign hath the same right in procuring the safety of his people, that any particular man can have in procuring the safety of his own body. And the same law that dictateth to men that have no civil government what they ought to do, and what to avoid in regard of one another, dictateth the same to commonwealths, that is, to the consciences of sovereign princes and sovereign assemblies; there being no court of natural justice, but in the conscience only,[1] where not man, but God reigneth, whose laws, such of them as
[186] oblige all mankind, in respect of God, as he is the author of nature, are *natural*;[2] and in respect of the same God, as he is King of kings, are *laws*. But of the kingdom of God, as King of kings, and as King also of a peculiar people, I shall speak in the rest of this discourse.

## CHAPTER XXXI

## OF THE KINGDOM OF GOD BY NATURE

The scope of the following chapters.

1. That the condition of mere nature, that is to say, of absolute liberty, such as is theirs that neither are sovereigns nor subjects, is anarchy and the condition of war; that the precepts by which men are guided to avoid that condition, are the laws of nature; that a commonwealth without sovereign power is but a word without substance and cannot stand; that subjects owe to sovereigns simple obedience in all things wherein their obedience is not repugnant to the laws of God, I have sufficiently proved in that which I have already written. There wants only for the entire knowledge of

---

1 See also 14.36.

2 This is evidence that the laws of nature are genuine laws. If they are not, sovereigns seem to have less motive for obeying the laws of nature.

civil duty to know what are those laws of God. For without that, a man knows not when he is commanded anything by the civil power, whether it be contrary to the law of God or no; and so, either by too much civil obedience offends the Divine Majesty, or, through fear of offending God, transgresses the commandments of the commonwealth. To avoid both these rocks, it is necessary to know what are the laws divine.[1] And seeing the knowledge of all law dependeth on the knowledge of the sovereign power, I shall say something in that which followeth of the KINGDOM OF GOD.

2. *God is King, let the earth rejoice*, saith the psalmist. And again, *God is King though the nations be angry; and he that sitteth on the cherubim, though the earth be moved*. Whether men will or not, they must be subject always to the divine power. By denying the existence or providence of God, men may shake off their ease, but not their yoke. But to call this power of God, which extendeth itself not only to man, but also to beasts and plants and bodies inanimate, by the name of kingdom, is but a metaphorical use of the word. For he only is properly said to reign that governs his subjects by his word and by promise of rewards to those that obey it, by threatening them with punishment that obey it not. Subjects therefore in the kingdom of God are not bodies inanimate, nor creatures irrational, because they understand no precepts as his, nor atheists,[2] nor they that believe not that God has any care of the actions of mankind, because they acknowledge no word for his, nor have hope of his rewards, or fear of his threatenings. They therefore that believe there is a God that governeth the world and hath given [187] precepts and propounded rewards and punishments to mankind are God's subjects; all the rest are to be understood as enemies.

Ps. 97:1.

Ps. 99:1. Who are subjects in the kingdom of God.

3. To rule by words requires that such words be manifestly made known; for else they are no laws; for to the nature of laws belongeth a sufficient and clear promulgation, such as may take away the excuse of ignorance; which in the laws of men is but of one only kind, and that is, proclamation or promulgation by the

A threefold word of God, reason, revelation, and prophecy.

---

1 To know what the sovereign, in this case, God, commands is to know what his laws are.

2 Hobbes was criticized for excluding atheists from the kingdom of God, because it meant that atheists could not sin. Hobbes's reply, adequate I think, is that atheists will be punished as enemies of God because they do not acknowledge him. (See also 31.5.)

voice of man. But God declareth his laws three ways: by the dictates of *natural reason*, by *revelation*, and by the *voice* of some *man* to whom, by the operation of miracles, he procureth credit with the rest. From hence there ariseth a triple word of God, *rational*, *sensible*, and *prophetic*; to which correspondeth a triple hearing: *right reason*, *sense supernatural*, and *faith*. As for sense supernatural, which consisteth in revelation or inspiration, there have not been any universal laws so given, because God speaketh not in that manner but to particular persons and to divers men divers things.

A twofold kingdom of God, natural and prophetic.

4. From the difference between the other two kinds of God's word, rational and prophetic, there may be attributed to God a twofold kingdom, *natural* and *prophetic*: natural, wherein he governeth as many of mankind as acknowledge his providence by the natural dictates of right reason; and prophetic, wherein having chosen out one peculiar nation, the Jews, for his subjects, he governed them, and none but them, not only by natural reason, but by positive laws, which he gave them by the mouths of his holy prophets. Of the natural kingdom of God I intend to speak in this chapter.

The right of God's sovereignty is derived from his omnipotence.

5. The right of nature whereby God reigneth over men and punisheth those that break his laws is to be derived, not from his creating them, as if he required obedience as of gratitude for his benefits, but from his *irresistible power*. I have formerly shown how the sovereign right ariseth from pact; to show how the same right may arise from nature requires no more but to show in what case it is never taken away. Seeing all men by nature had right to all things, they had right every one to reign over all the rest. But because this right could not be obtained by force, it concerned the safety of everyone, laying by that right, to set up men (with sovereign authority) by common consent, to rule and defend them; whereas if there had been any man of power irresistible, there had been no reason why he should not by that power have ruled and defended both himself and them, according to his own discretion. To those therefore whose power is irresistible, the dominion of all men adhereth naturally by their excellence of power; and consequently it is from that power that the kingdom over men and the
[188] right of afflicting men at his pleasure belongeth naturally to God Almighty, not as Creator and gracious, but as omnipotent. And

though punishment be due for sin only, because by that word is understood affliction for sin; yet the right of afflicting is not always derived from men's sin, but from God's power.

6. This question, *why evil men often prosper; and good men suffer adversity*, has been much disputed by the ancient, and is the same with this of ours, *by what right God dispenseth the prosperities and adversities of this life*, and is of that difficulty, as it hath shaken the faith, not only of the vulgar, but of philosophers and, which is more, of the saints, concerning the Divine Providence. *How good*, saith David, *is the God of Israel to those that are upright in heart; and yet my feet were almost gone, my treadings had well-nigh slipped; for I was grieved at the wicked, when I saw the ungodly in such prosperity.* And Job, how earnestly does he expostulate with God for the many afflictions he suffered, notwithstanding his righteousness? This question in the case of Job is decided by God himself, not by arguments derived from Job's sin, but his own power.[1] For whereas the friends of Job drew their arguments from his affliction to his sin, and he defended himself by the conscience of his innocence; God himself taketh up the matter and, having justified the affliction by arguments drawn from his power, such as this, *Where wast thou when I laid the foundations of the earth,*[2] and the like, both approved Job's innocence and reproved the erroneous doctrine of his friends. Conformable to this doctrine is the sentence of our Saviour concerning the man that was born blind, in these words, *Neither hath this man sinned, nor his fathers; but that the works of God might be made manifest in him.*[3] And though it be said, *that death entered into the world by sin* (by which is meant that if Adam had never sinned, he had never died, that is, never suffered any separation of his soul from his body), it follows not thence that God

Sin not the cause of all affliction.

Ps. 72:1-3.

Job 38:4.

1 The book of Job proposes many solutions to the problem of evil. Hobbes's preferred solution might be called 'The God-Above-Justice Solution'. Almighty God has a natural authority over humans, that is, he is sovereign over them, hence cannot be unjust to them.

2 This verse contains a solution to the problem of evil that might be called 'The Unanswerable-Question Solution'. Humans do not have enough information to be able to answer the question. This solution is different from The God-Above-Justice Solution.

3 This verse from the gospel of John 9:3 expresses still another solution, different from those mentioned above. It does not occur in Job.

could not justly have afflicted him, though he had not sinned, as well as he afflicteth other living creatures that cannot sin.

Divine laws.

7. Having spoken of the right of God's sovereignty as grounded only on nature, we are to consider next what are the divine laws, or dictates of natural reason; which laws concern either the natural duties of one man to another, or the honour naturally due to our Divine Sovereign. The first are the same laws of nature, of which I have spoken already in the fourteenth and fifteenth chapters of this treatise, namely, equity, justice, mercy, humility, and the rest of the moral virtues. It remaineth therefore that we consider what precepts are dictated to men by their natural reason only, without other word of God, touching the honour and worship of the Divine Majesty.

Honour and worship what.

8. Honour consisteth in the inward thought and opinion of the power and goodness of another; and therefore to honour God is to think as highly of his power and goodness as is possible. And of that opinion, the external signs appearing in the words and actions of men are called *worship*;[1] which is one part of that which the Latins understand by the word *cultus*; for *cultus* signifieth properly and constantly that labour which a man bestows on anything with
[189] a purpose to make benefit by it. Now those things whereof we make benefit are either subject to us, and the profit they yield followeth the labour we bestow upon them as a natural effect; or they are not subject to us, but answer our labour according to their own wills. In the first sense the labour bestowed on the earth is called *culture*; and the education of children, a *culture* of their minds. In the second sense, where men's wills are to be wrought to our purpose, not by force, but by complaisance, it signifieth as much as courting, that is, winning of favour by good offices, as by praises, by acknowledging their power, and by whatsoever is pleasing to them from whom we look for any benefit. And this is properly *worship*; in which sense *publicola* is understood for a worshipper of the people; and *cultus Dei*, for the worship of God.

Several signs of honour.

9. From internal honour, consisting in the opinion of power and goodness, arise three passions: *love*, which hath reference to

1 Notice that Hobbes distinguishes between honour and worship on the basis of what is internal and external. This contrast is continued in 31.9.

goodness; and *hope*, and *fear*, that relate to power; and three parts of external worship: *praise*, *magnifying*, and *blessing*; the subject of praise being goodness; the subject of magnifying and blessing being power; and the effect thereof felicity. Praise and magnifying are signified both by words and actions: by words, when we say a man is good or great; by actions, when we thank him for his bounty and obey his power. The opinion of the happiness of another can only be expressed by words.

Worship natural and arbitrary.

10. There be some signs of honour (both in attributes and actions) that be naturally so, as amongst attributes, *good*, *just*, *liberal*, and the like; and amongst actions, *prayers*, *thanks*, and *obedience*. Others are so by institution or custom of men; and in some times and places are honourable; in others, dishonourable; in others, indifferent; such as are the gestures in salutation, prayer, and thanksgiving, in different times and places, differently used. The former is *natural*; the latter *arbitrary* worship.

Worship commanded and free.

11. And of arbitrary worship, there be two differences; for sometimes it is *commanded*, sometimes a *voluntary* worship: commanded, when it is such as he requireth who is worshipped; free, when it is such as the worshipper thinks fit. When it is commanded, not the words or gesture, but the obedience is the worship. But when free, the worship consists in the opinion of the beholders; for if to them the words or actions by which we intend honour seem ridiculous and tending to contumely, [then] they are no worship, because no signs of honour; and [they are] no signs of honour, because a sign is not a sign to him that giveth it, but to him to whom it is made, that is, to the spectator.

Worship public and private.

12. Again there is a *public* and a *private* worship. Public is the worship that a commonwealth performeth, as one person. Private is that which a private person exhibiteth. Public, in respect of the whole commonwealth, is free; but in respect of particular men it is not so. Private is in secret free; but in the sight of the multitude it is never without some restraint either from the laws or from the opinion of men; which is contrary to the nature of liberty.

The end of worship.

13. The end of worship amongst men is power. For where a man seeth another worshipped, he supposeth him powerful and is the readier to obey him; which makes his power greater. But God [190]
has no ends; the worship we do him proceeds from our duty and is

directed according to our capacity by those rules of honour that reason dictateth to be done by the weak to the more potent men, in hope of benefit, for fear of damage or in thankfulness for good already received from them.

Attributes of divine honour.

14. That we may know what worship of God is taught us by the light of nature, I will begin with his attributes. Where, first, it is manifest, we ought to attribute to him *existence*;[1] for no man can have the will to honour that which he thinks not to have any being.

15. Secondly, that those philosophers who said the world, or the soul of the world, was God spake unworthily of him, and denied his existence; for by God is understood the cause of the world; and to say the world is God[2] is to say there is no cause of it, that is, no God.

16. Thirdly, to say the world was not created, but eternal (seeing that which is eternal has no cause) is to deny there is a God.

17. Fourthly, that they who, attributing (as they think) ease to God, take from him the care of mankind, take from him his honour; for it takes away men's love and fear of him, which is the root of honour.

18. Fifthly, in those things that signify greatness and power, to say he is *finite* is not to honour him; for it is not a sign of the will to honour God to attribute to him less than we can, because to finite, it is easy to add more.

19. Therefore to attribute *figure* to him is not honour; for all figure is finite:

20. Nor to say we conceive, and imagine, or have an *idea* of him in our mind; for whatsoever we conceive is finite:

21. Nor to attribute to him *parts* or *totality*; which are the attributes only of things finite:

22. Nor to say he is in this or that *place*; for whatsoever is in place is bounded and finite:

---

1 In this and the following paragraphs, Hobbes is saying what "we ought to attribute" to God and not necessarily what is literally true of God. It happens to be the case that God exists and that we ought to attribute existence to him, but God is literally in some place because he is a body and all bodies are in some place, but we are not to attribute being in a place to him because it suggests that he is finite and that dishonours him. See 31.22 and 31.33.

2 If the world is defined as the totality of bodies, God is part of the world since God is a body. But he is not identical with the world. Cf. 34.2.

23. Nor that he is *moved* or *resteth*; for both these attributes ascribe to him place:

24. Nor that there be more gods than one, because it implies them all finite; for there cannot be more than one infinite:

25. Nor to ascribe to him (unless metaphorically, meaning not the passion, but the effect) passions that partake of grief, as *repentance*, *anger*, mercy; or of want, as *appetite*, *hope*, *desire*; or of any passive faculty; for passion is power limited by somewhat else.

26. And therefore when we ascribe to God a *will*, it is not to be understood, as that of man, for a *rational appetite*; but as the power by which he effecteth everything.

27. Likewise when we attribute to him *sight*, and other acts of sense, as also *knowledge* and *understanding,* which in us is nothing else but a tumult of the mind, raised by external things that press the organical parts of man's body; for there is no such thing in God, and, being things that depend on natural causes, cannot be attributed to him.

28. He that will attribute to God nothing but what is warranted by natural reason must either use such negative attributes [191] as *infinite*, *eternal*, *incomprehensible*;[1] or superlatives, as *most high*, *most great*, and the like; or indefinite, as *good*, *just*, *holy*, *creator*, and in such sense as if he meant not to declare what he is (for that were to circumscribe him within the limits of our fancy), but how much we admire him, and how ready we would be to obey him; which is a sign of humility and of a will to honour him as much as we can;[2] for there is but one name to signify our conception of his nature, and that is I AM;[3] and but one name of his relation to us, and that is God, in which is contained father, king, and lord.

Actions that are signs of divine honour.

29. Concerning the actions of divine worship, it is a most general precept of reason that they be signs of the intention to honour God; such as are, first, *prayers*; for not the carvers, when they made

1 These attributes are negative because 'infinite' means not finite, 'eternal' means not temporal and 'incomprehensible' means not comprehensible.

2 Most philosophers have been insensitive to the fact that language is used to do many more things that just state the facts. Even indicative sentences can be used for nondescriptive purposes. Hobbes's point is that a sentence such as 'God is good' is not describing God but worshipping him. See also 36.9.

3 'I am' is a translation from the Greek of the name God gave as his own to Moses, which in Hebrew is 'Yahweh'.

images, were thought to make them gods, but the people that prayed to them.

30. Secondly, *thanksgiving,* which differeth from prayer in divine worship no otherwise than that prayers precede, and thanks succeed, the benefit, the end both of the one and the other being to acknowledge God for author of all benefits as well past as future.

31. Thirdly, *gifts*; that is to say, sacrifices and oblations (if they be of the best) are signs of honour; for they are thanksgivings.

32. Fourthly, *not to swear* by any but God is naturally a sign of honour; for it is a confession that God only knoweth the heart and that no man's wit or strength can protect a man against God's vengeance on the perjured.

33. Fifthly, it is a part of rational worship to speak considerately of God; for it argues a fear of him, and fear is a confession of his power. Hence followeth, that the name of God is not to be used rashly and to no purpose; for that is as much as in vain; and it is to no purpose unless it be by way of oath and by order of the commonwealth, to make judgements certain; or between commonwealths, to avoid war. And that disputing of God's nature is contrary to his honour; for it is supposed that in this natural kingdom of God, there is no other way to know anything but by natural reason, that is, from the principles of natural science, which are so far from teaching us anything of God's nature, as they cannot teach us our own nature, nor the nature of the smallest creature living.[1] And therefore, when men out of the principles of natural reason dispute of the attributes of God, they but dishonour him; for in the attributes which we give to God, we are not to consider the signification of philosophical truth, but the signification of pious intention to do him the greatest honour we are able.[2] From the want of which consideration have proceeded the volumes of disputation about the nature of God that tend not to his honour, but to the honour of our own wits and learning; and are nothing else but inconsiderate and vain abuses of his sacred name.

34. Sixthly, in *prayers*, *thanksgivings*, *offerings* and *sacrifices*, it is a

---

1 Hobbes is putting God beyond the ken of science. Some scholars think this is a sign of his reverence for God; others think that this is a sign of his atheism or agnosticism.

2 See also 31.14.

dictate of natural reason that they be every one in his kind the best and most significant of honour. As, for example, that prayers and thanksgiving be made in words and phrases not sudden, nor light, nor plebeian, but beautiful and well composed; for else we do not God as much honour as we can. And therefore the heathens did absurdly to worship images for gods, but their doing it in verse and with music, both of voice and instruments, was reasonable. Also that the beasts they offered in sacrifice, and the gifts they offered, and their actions in worshipping, were full of submission and commemorative of benefits received, was according to reason, as proceeding from an intention to honour him. [192]

35. Seventhly, reason directeth not only to worship God in secret, but also and especially in public and in the sight of men; for without that, that which in honour is most acceptable, the procuring others to honour him is lost.

36. Lastly, obedience to his laws (that is, in this case to the laws of nature) is the greatest worship of all. For as obedience is more acceptable to God than sacrifice, so also to set light by his commandments is the greatest of all contumelies.[1] And these are the laws of that divine worship which natural reason dictateth to private men.

Public worship consisteth in uniformity.

37. But seeing a commonwealth is but one person, it ought also to exhibit to God but one worship; which then it doth when it commandeth it to be exhibited by private men, publicly. And this is public worship, the property whereof is to be uniform;[2] for those actions that are done differently by different men cannot said to be a public worship. And therefore, where many sorts of worship be allowed, proceeding from the different religions of private men, it cannot be said there is any public worship, nor that the commonwealth is of any religion at all.

All attributes depend on the laws civil.

38. And because words (and consequently the attributes of God) have their signification by agreement and constitution of

1 Hobbes may have in mind Amos 5:21–24, where God says, "I hate, I despise your feast days … Though ye offer me burnt offerings and your offerings, I will not accept them," because the Israelites were not obeying him.

2 Cf. 47.20. Since the Commonwealth did not have any uniform public worship, Hobbes is indicating that England no longer has any religion. I take him to be criticizing the Commonwealth.

men, those attributes are to be held significative of honour that men intend shall so be; and whatsoever may be done by the wills of particular men, where there is no law but reason, may be done by the will of the commonwealth by laws civil. And because a commonwealth hath no will nor makes no laws but those that are made by the will of him or them that have the sovereign power; it followeth that those attributes which the sovereign ordaineth in the worship of God for signs of honour ought to be taken and used for such by private men in their public worship.

Not all actions.

39. But because not all actions are signs by constitution, but some are naturally signs of honour, others of contumely, these latter, which are those that men are ashamed to do in the sight of them they reverence, cannot be made by human power a part of divine worship; nor the former, such as are decent, modest, humble behaviour, ever be separated from it. But whereas there be an infinite number of actions and gestures of an indifferent nature, such of them as the commonwealth shall ordain to be publicly and universally in use, as signs of honour and part of God's worship, are
[193] to be taken and used for such by the subjects. And that which is said in the Scripture, *It is better to obey God than man*, hath place in the kingdom of God by pact, and not by nature.

Natural punishments.

40. Having thus briefly spoken of the natural kingdom of God, and his natural laws, I will add only to this chapter a short declaration of his natural punishments. There is no action of man in this life that is not the beginning of so long a chain of consequences as no human providence is high enough to give a man a prospect to the end. And in this chain there are linked together both pleasing and unpleasing events; in such manner as he that will do anything for his pleasure, must engage himself to suffer all the pains annexed to it; and these pains are the natural punishments of those actions which are the beginning of more harm than good. And hereby it comes to pass that intemperance is naturally punished with diseases; rashness, with mischances; injustice, with the violence of enemies; pride, with ruin; cowardice, with oppression; negligent government of princes, with rebellion; and rebellion, with slaughter. For seeing punishments are consequent to the breach of laws, natural punishments must be naturally consequent to the breach of

the laws of nature, and therefore follow them as their natural, not arbitrary, effects.[1]

41. And thus far concerning the constitution, nature, and right of sovereigns, and concerning the duty of subjects, derived from the principles of natural reason. And now, considering how different this doctrine is from the practice of the greatest part of the world, especially of these western parts that have received their moral learning from Rome and Athens, and how much depth of moral philosophy is required in them that have the administration of the sovereign power, I am at the point of believing this my labour as useless as the commonwealth of Plato; for he also is of opinion that it is impossible for the disorders of state and change of governments by civil war, ever to be taken away till sovereigns be philosophers. But when I consider again that the science of natural justice is the only science necessary for sovereigns and their principal ministers, and that they need not be charged with the sciences mathematical, as by Plato they are, further than by good laws to encourage men to the study of them; and that neither Plato nor any other philosopher hitherto hath put into order and sufficiently or probably proved all the theorems of moral doctrine, that men may learn thereby both how to govern and how to obey, I recover some hope that one time or other this writing of mine may fall into the hands of a sovereign who will consider it himself (for it is short, and I think clear) without the help of any interested or envious interpreter; and by the exercise of entire sovereignty, in protecting the public teaching of it, convert this truth of speculation into the utility of practice.

The conclusion of the second part.

1 See also 28.8.

# PART III

[195]

# OF A CHRISTIAN COMMONWEALTH

## CHAPTER XXXII

## OF THE PRINCIPLES OF CHRISTIAN POLITICS

The word of God delivered by prophets is the main principle of Christian politics.

1. I have derived the rights of sovereign power and the duty of subjects hitherto from the principles of nature only, such as experience has found true or consent concerning the use of words has made so, that is to say, from the nature of men, known to us by experience and from definitions of such words as are essential to all political reasoning, universally agreed on. But in that I am next to handle, which is the nature and rights of a CHRISTIAN COMMONWEALTH, whereof there dependeth much upon supernatural revelations of the will of God, the ground of my discourse must be not only the natural word of God, but also the prophetical.

Yet is not natural reason to be renounced.

2. Nevertheless, we are not to renounce our senses and experience, nor that which is the undoubted word of God, our natural reason. For they are the talents which he hath put into our hands to negotiate till the coming again of our blessed Saviour, and therefore not to be folded up in the napkin of an implicit faith, but employed in the purchase of justice, peace, and true religion. For though there be many things in God's word above reason, that is to say, which cannot by natural reason be either demonstrated or confuted; yet there is nothing contrary to it; but when it seemeth so, the fault is either in our unskillful interpretation, or erroneous ratiocination.[1]

1 It was not unusual in the seventeenth century to distinguish between faith and reason and to maintain that there is no conflict between the two. William Chillingworth in *The Faith of Protestants* (1638) was probably most famous for this position.

3. Therefore, when anything therein written is too hard for our examination, we are bidden to captivate our understanding to the words,[1] and not to labour in sifting out a philosophical truth by logic of such mysteries as are not comprehensible nor fall under any rule of natural science. For it is with the mysteries of our religion as with wholesome pills for the sick, which swallowed whole have the virtue to cure, but chewed, are for the most part cast up again without effect.[2]

[196] What it is to captivate the understanding.

4. But by the captivity of our understanding is not meant a submission of the intellectual faculty to the opinion of any other man, but of the will to obedience where obedience is due. For sense, memory, understanding, reason, and opinion are not in our power to change, but always and necessarily such, as the things we see, hear, and consider suggest unto us, and therefore are not effects of our will, but our will of them. We then captivate our understanding and reason when we forbear contradiction, when we so speak as (by lawful authority) we are commanded, and when we live accordingly, which, in sum, is trust and faith reposed in him that speaketh, though the mind be incapable of any notion at all from the words spoken.

How God speaketh to man.

5. When God speaketh to man, it must be either immediately or by mediation of another man, to whom he had formerly spoken by himself immediately. How God speaketh to a man immediately may be understood by those well enough to whom he hath so spoken; but how the same should be understood by another is hard, if not impossible, to know. For if a man pretend to me that God hath spoken to him supernaturally and immediately, and I make doubt of it, I cannot easily perceive what argument he can produce to oblige me to believe it.[3] It is true that if he be my sovereign, he may oblige me to obedience, so as not by act or word to declare [that] I believe him not; but not to think any otherwise than my reason persuades me. But if one that hath not such

---

1 2 Corinthians 10:5: "Casting down imaginations and every high thing that exalteth it selfe against the knowledge of God, and bring into captivitie every thought to the obedience of Christ" (Authorized Version).

2 Such imagery was not unusual or offensive in the seventeenth century. See also "A Review and Conclusion," 15.

3 See also 7.7 and 42.46.

authority over me shall pretend the same, there is nothing that exacteth either belief or obedience.

6. For to say that God hath spoken to him in the Holy Scripture is not to say God hath spoken to him immediately, but by mediation of the prophets or of the Apostles or of the Church, in such manner as he speaks to all other Christian men. To say he hath spoken to him in a dream is no more than to say he dreamed that God spake to him; which is not of force to win belief from any man that knows dreams are for the most part natural and may proceed from former thoughts and such dreams as that, from self-conceit and foolish arrogance and false opinion of a man's own goodliness or virtue, by which he thinks he hath merited the favour of extraordinary revelation. To say he hath seen a vision or heard a voice is to say that he dreamed between sleeping and waking; for in such manner a man doth many times naturally take his dream for a vision, as not having well observed his own slumbering. To say he speaks by supernatural inspiration is to say he finds an ardent desire to speak or some strong opinion of himself, for which he can allege no natural and sufficient reason. So that though God Almighty can speak to a man by dreams, visions, voice, and inspiration; yet he obliges no man to believe he hath so done to him that pretends it, who, being a man, may err and, which is more, may lie.

By what marks prophets are known.

7. How then can he to whom God hath never revealed his will immediately (saving by the way of natural reason) know when he is to obey or not to obey his word, delivered by him that says he is a prophet? Of four hundred prophets, of whom the King of Israel, asked counsel concerning the war he made against Ramoth [197] Gilead, only Micaiah was a true one.[1] The prophet that was sent to prophesy against the altar set up by Jeroboam, though a true prophet, and that by two miracles done in his presence appears to be a prophet sent from God, was yet deceived by another old prophet that persuaded him, as from the mouth of God, to eat and drink with him.[2] If one prophet deceive another, what certainty is

1 Kings 22.

1 Kings 13.

---

1 See also 36.19.

2 Hobbes's use of biblical stories to disparage Christians who used the Bible for their own purposes is effective in this and next several chapters.

there of knowing the will of God by other way than that of reason? To which I answer out of the Holy Scripture that there be two marks by which together, not asunder, a true prophet is to be known. One is the doing of miracles; the other is the not teaching any other religion than that which is already established. Asunder, I say, neither of these is sufficient. *If a prophet rise amongst you, or a dreamer of dreams, and shall pretend the doing of a miracle,*[1] *and the miracle come to pass; if he say, Let us follow strange gods, which thou hast not known, thou shalt not hearken to him, etc. But that prophet and dreamer of dreams shall be put to death, because he hath spoken to you to revolt*
Deut. 13:1-5. *from the Lord your God.* In which words two things are to be observed: first, that God will not have miracles alone serve for arguments to approve the prophet's calling; but (as it is in the third verse) for an experiment of the constancy of our adherence to himself. For the works of the Egyptian sorcerers, though not so great as those of Moses, yet were great miracles.[2] Secondly, that how great soever the miracle be, yet if it tend to stir up revolt against the king or him that governeth by the king's authority, he that doth such miracle is not to be considered otherwise than as sent to make trial of their allegiance. For these words, *revolt from the Lord your God*, are in this place equivalent to *revolt from your king*. For they had made God their king by pact at the foot of Mount Sinai, who ruled them by Moses only; for he only spake with God and from time to time declared God's commandments to the people. In like manner, after our Saviour Christ had made his Disciples acknowledge him for the Messiah (that is to say, for God's anointed, whom the nation of the Jews daily expected for their king, but refused when he came), he omitted not to advertise them of the danger of miracles. *There shall arise*, saith he, *false Christs, and false prophets, and shall do great wonders and miracles,*[3] *even*
Matt. 24:24. *to the seducing (if it were possible) of the very elect.* By which it appears that false prophets may have the power of miracles, yet are we not

1 The Authorized Version of the Bible has "signe, or a wonder" where Hobbes has "miracle."

2 Hobbes is using 'miracle' to mean something impressive, unusual, and without a natural explanation. This does not quite fit his explicit treatment of miracles in chapter 37.

3 The Authorized Version has "great signes and wonders" where Hobbes has 'great wonders and miracles'.

to take their doctrine for God's word. St. Paul says further to the Galatians that *if himself or an angel from heaven preach another Gospel to them than he had preached, let him be accursed.* That Gospel was that Christ was King, so that all preaching against the power of the king received, in consequence to these words, is by St. Paul accursed. For his speech is addressed to those who by his preaching had already received Jesus for the Christ, that is to say, for King of the Jews.

Gal. 1:8.

8. And as miracles without preaching that doctrine which God hath established, so preaching the true doctrine, without the doing of miracles, is an insufficient argument of immediate revelation. For if a man that teacheth not false doctrine should pretend to be [198] a prophet without showing any miracle, he is never the more to be regarded for his pretence, as is evident by Deut. 18:21–22: *If thou say in thy heart, How shall we know that the word* (of the prophet) *is not that which the Lord hath spoken? When the prophet shall have spoken in the name of the Lord, that which shall not come to pass, that is the word which the Lord hath not spoken, but the prophet has spoken it out of the pride of his own heart, fear him not.* But a man may here again ask: When the prophet hath foretold a thing, how shall we know whether it will come to pass or not? For he may foretell it as a thing to arrive after a certain long time, longer than the time of man's life, or indefinitely, that it will come to pass one time or other; in which case this mark of a prophet is unuseful and therefore the miracles that oblige us to believe a prophet ought to be confirmed by an immediate or a not long deferred event. So that it is manifest that the teaching of the religion which God hath established and the showing of a present miracle, joined together, were the only marks whereby the Scripture would have a true prophet, that is to say, immediate revelation, to be acknowledged, of them being singly sufficient to oblige any other man to regard what he saith.

The marks of a prophet in the old law, miracles, and doctrine conformable to the law.

9. Seeing therefore miracles now cease,[1] we have no sign left whereby to acknowledge the pretended revelations or inspirations of any private man, nor obligation to give ear to any doctrine, farther than it is conformable to the Holy Scriptures, which since the

Miracles ceasing, prophets cease, and the Scripture supplies their place.

---

1 It was not unusual for a Protestant to hold this view, against the Roman Catholic Church. Miracles are unnecessary since revelation is complete in the Bible.

time of our Saviour supply the place and sufficiently recompense the want of all other prophecy and from which, by wise and learned interpretation and careful ratiocination, all rules and precepts necessary to the knowledge of our duty both to God and man, without enthusiasm or supernatural inspiration, may easily be deduced. And this Scripture is it out of which I am to take the principles of my discourse concerning the rights of those that are the supreme governors on earth of Christian commonwealths and of the duty of Christian subjects towards their sovereigns. And to that end, I shall speak, in the next chapter, of the books, writers, scope and authority of the Bible.

[199]

## CHAPTER XXXIII

## OF THE NUMBER, ANTIQUITY, SCOPE, AUTHORITY, AND INTERPRETERS OF THE BOOKS OF HOLY SCRIPTURE

Of the books of Holy Scripture.

1. By the books of Holy SCRIPTURE are understood those which ought to be the *canon*, that is to say, the rules of Christian life. And because all rules of life, which men are in conscience bound to observe, are laws, the question of the Scripture is the question of what is law throughout all Christendom, both natural and civil. For though it be not determined in Scripture what laws every Christian king shall constitute in his own dominions; yet it is determined what laws he shall not constitute. Seeing therefore I have already proved that sovereigns in their own dominions are the sole legislators, those books only are canonical, that is, law, in every nation, which are established for such by the sovereign authority. It is true that God is the Sovereign of all sovereigns and therefore, when he speaks to any subject, he ought to be obeyed, whatsoever any earthly potentate command to the contrary. But the question is not of obedience to God, but of *when* and *what* God hath said; which, to subjects that have no supernatural revelation, cannot be known but by that natural reason which guided them for the obtaining of peace and justice to obey the authority of their several commonwealths, that is to say, of their lawful

sovereigns.[1] According to this obligation, I can acknowledge no other books of the Old Testament to be Holy Scripture but those which have been commanded to be acknowledged for such by the authority of the Church of England. What books these are is sufficiently known without a catalogue of them here, and they are the same that are acknowledged by St. Jerome, who holdeth the rest, namely, the Wisdom of Solomon, Ecclesiasticus, Judith, Tobias, the first and the second of Maccabees (though he had seen the first in Hebrew) and the third and fourth of Esdras, for Apocrypha. Of the canonical, Josephus, a learned Jew, that wrote in the time of the Emperor Domitian, reckoneth *twenty-two*, making the number agree with the Hebrew alphabet. St. Jerome does the same, though they reckon them in different manner. For Josephus numbers five books of Moses, thirteen of prophets that writ the history of their own times (which how it agrees with the prophets writings contained in the Bible we shall see hereafter), and four of Hymns and moral precepts. But St. Jerome reckons five Books of Moses, eight of prophets, and nine of other Holy Writ which he calls of Hagiographa. The Septuagint, who were seventy learned men of the Jews, sent for by Ptolemy, king of Egypt, to translate the Jewish law out of the Hebrew into the Greek, have left us no [200] other for Holy Scripture in the Greek tongue but the same that are received in the Church of England.

2. As for the books of the New Testament, they are equally acknowledged for canon by all Christian churches and by all sects of Christians that admit any books at all for canonical.

Their antiquity.

3. Who were the original writers of the several books of Holy Scripture has not been made evident by any sufficient testimony of other history, which is the only proof of matter of fact, nor can be by any arguments of natural reason; for reason serves only to convince the truth, not of fact, but of consequence. The light therefore that must guide us in this question must be that which is held out unto us from the books themselves; and this light, though it show us not the writer of every book; yet it is not unuseful to give us knowledge of the time wherein they were written.

4. And first, for the *Pentateuch*, it is not argument enough that

---

1 See also 36.20.

they were written by Moses, because they are called the five Books of Moses, no more than these titles, the Book of Joshua, the Book of Judges, the Book of Ruth, and the Books of the Kings, are arguments sufficient to prove that they were written by Joshua, by the Judges, by Ruth, and by the Kings. For in titles of books, the subject is marked as often as the writer. The History of Livy denotes the writer; but the History of Scanderberg is denominated from the subject. We read in the last chapter of Deut., verse 6, concerning the sepulchre of Moses, *that no man knoweth of his sepulchre to this day*, that is, to the day wherein those words were written. It is therefore manifest that those words were written after his interment. For it were a strange interpretation to say Moses spake of his own sepulchre (though by prophecy), that it was not found to that day wherein he was yet living. But it may perhaps be alleged that the last chapter only, not the whole *Pentateuch*, was written by some other man, but the rest not. Let us therefore consider that which we find in the Book of Genesis (12:6), *And Abraham passed through the land to the place of Sichem, unto the plain of Moreh, and the Canaanite was then in the land*, which must needs be the words of one that wrote when the Canaanite was not in the land, and consequently, not of Moses, who died before he came into it. Likewise Numbers, 21:14, the writer citeth another more ancient book, entitled, *The Book of the Wars of the Lord*, wherein were registered the acts of Moses, at the Red Sea, and at the brook of Arnon. It is therefore sufficiently evident that the five Books of Moses were written after his time; though how long after, it be not so manifest.

The Pentateuch not written by Moses.

5. But though Moses did not compile those books entirely, and in the form we have them; yet he wrote all that which he is there said to have written, as for example, the volume of the law, which is contained, as it seemeth, in the eleventh of Deuteronomy, and the following chapters to the 27th, which was also commanded to be written on stones, in their entry into the land of Canaan. And this did Moses himself write and deliver to the priests and elders of Israel, to be read every seventh year to all Israel, at their assembling in the feast of tabernacles. And this is that law which God commanded that their kings (when they should have established that form of government) should take a copy of from the priests

Deut. 31:9.

[201]

and Levites, and which Moses commanded the priests and Levites to lay in the side of the Ark, and the same which, having been lost, was long time after found again by Hilkiah and sent to King Josias, who, causing it to be read to the people, renewed the covenant between God and them.

Deut. 31:26.
2 Kings 22:8, & 23:1-3.

6. That the Book of Joshua was also written long after the time of Joshua may be gathered out of many places of the book itself. Joshua had set up twelve stones in the midst of Jordan for a monument of their passage, of which the writer saith thus, *They are there unto this day*, for *unto this day* is a phrase that signifieth a time past, beyond the memory of man. In like manner, upon the saying of the Lord that he had rolled off from the people the reproach of Egypt, the writer saith, *The place is called Gilgal unto this day*, which to have said in the time of Joshua had been improper. So also the name of the valley of Achor from the trouble that Achan raised in the camp, the writer saith, *remaineth unto this day*, which must needs be therefore long after the time of Joshua. Arguments of this kind there be many other, as Josh. 8:29, 13:13, 14:14, 15:63.

The book of Joshua written after his time.
Josh. 4:9.
Josh. 5:9.
Josh. 7:26.

7. The same is manifest by like arguments of the Book of Judges 1:21, 1:26, 4:24, 10:4, 15:19, 18:6, and Ruth 1:1, but especially Judges 18:30, where it said that *Jonathan and his sons were priests to the tribe of Dan, until the day of the captivity of the land.*

The books of Judges and Ruth written long after the captivity.

8. That the Books of Samuel were also written after his own time, there are the like arguments, 1 Samuel 5:5, 7:13, 7:15, 27:6, and 30:25, where, after David had adjudged equal part of the spoils to them that guarded the ammunition with them that fought, the writer saith, *He made it a statute and an ordinance to Israel to this day.* Again, when David (displeased that the Lord had slain Uzzah for putting out his hand to sustain the Ark) called the place Perez-uzzah, the writer saith it is called so *to this day* the time therefore of the writing of that book must be long after the time of the fact; that is, long after the time of David.

The like of the books of Samuel.
2 Sam. 6:4.

9. As for the two Books of the Kings and the two Books of the Chronicles, besides the places which mention such monuments, as the writer saith remained till his own days, such as are 1 Kings 9:13, 9:21, 10:12, 12:19; 2 Kings 2:22, 10:27, 14:7, 16:6, 17:23, 17:34, 17:41; and 1 Chron. 4:41, 5:26. It is argument sufficient they were written after the captivity in Babylon that the history of

them is continued till that time. For the facts registered are always more ancient than the register and much more ancient than such books as make mention of and quote the register, as these books do in divers places, referring the reader to the chronicles of the Kings of Judah, to the chronicles of the Kings of Israel, to the books of the prophet Samuel, of the prophet Nathan, of the prophet Ahijah, to the vision of Jehdo, to the books of the prophet Serveiah, and of the prophet Addo.

[202] Ezra and Nehemiah. 10. The Books of Esdras and Nehemiah were written certainly after their return from captivity, because their return, the re-edification of the walls and houses of Jerusalem, the renovation of the covenant, and ordination of their policy are therein contained.

Esther. 11. The history of Queen Esther is of the time of the Captivity, and therefore the writer must have been of the same time, or after it.

Job. 12. The Book of Job hath no mark in it of the time wherein it was written; and though it appear sufficiently that he was no feigned person (Ezek. 14:14 and James 5:11); yet the book itself seemeth not to be a history, but a treatise concerning a question in ancient time much disputed: *why wicked men have often prospered in this world, and good men have been afflicted*, and it is the more probable, because from the beginning to the third verse of the third chapter, where the complaint of Job beginneth, the Hebrew is (as St. Jerome testifies) in prose, and from thence to the sixth verse of the last chapter in hexameter verses, and the rest of that chapter again in prose. So that the dispute is all in verse, and the prose is added, as a preface in the beginning and an epilogue in the end. But verse is no usual style of such as either are themselves in great pain, as Job, or of such as come to comfort them, as his friends; but in philosophy, especially moral philosophy, in ancient time frequent.

The Psalter. 13. The Psalms were written the most part by David, for the use of the choir. To these are added some songs of Moses and other holy men, and some of them after the return from the Captivity, as the 137 and the 126, whereby it is manifest that the Psalter was compiled and put into the form it now hath after the return of the Jews from Babylon.

The Proverbs. 14. The Proverbs, being a collection of wise and godly sayings, partly of Solomon, partly of Agur the son of Jakeh, and partly of the mother of King Lemuel, cannot probably be thought to have been collected by Solomon, rather than by Agur or the mother of Lemuel, and that, though the sentences be theirs, yet the collection or compiling them into this one book was the work of some other godly man that lived after them all.

Ecclesiastes and the Canticles.

15. The Books of Ecclesiastes and the Canticles have nothing that was not Solomon's, except it be the titles or inscriptions. For *The Words of the Preacher, the Son of David, King in Jerusalem*, and *The Song of Songs*, which is Solomon's, seem to have been made for distinction's sake, then, when the books of Scripture were gathered into one body of the law, to the end that not the doctrine only, but the authors also might be extant.

The Prophets.

16. Of the prophets, the most ancient are Zephaniah, Jonas, Amos, Hosea, Isaiah, and Micaiah [Micah], who lived in the time of Amaziah and Azariah, otherwise Ozias, Kings of Judah. But the Book of Jonah is not properly a register of his prophecy; for that is contained in these few words, *Forty days and Nineveh shall be destroyed* [Jonah 3:4], but a history or narration of his frowardness and disputing God's commandments, so that there is small probability he should be the author, seeing he is the subject of it. But the Book of Amos is his prophecy.

17. Jeremiah, Obadiah, Nahum, and Habakkuk prophesied in [203] the time of Josiah.

18. Ezekiel, Daniel, Haggai, and Zechariah, in the Captivity.

19. When Joel and Malachi prophesied is not evident by their writings. But considering the inscriptions or titles of their books, it is manifest enough that the whole Scripture of the Old Testament was set forth, in the form we have it, after the return of the Jews from their Captivity in Babylon, and before the time of Ptolemaeus Philadelphus, that caused it to be translated into Greek by seventy men, which were sent him out of Judea for that purpose.[1] And if the books of Apocrypha (which are recommended to us by the Church, though not for canonical; yet for profitable books for our instruction) may in this point be credited,

1 About 250 B.C. There is some mythology in this story. In fact, the Hebrew Bible was translated into Greek over a long period of time by some indeterminate number of translators. Jews of the Diaspora usually did not know Hebrew, and Greek was the language of the literate.

the Scripture was set forth in the form we have it in by Esdras, as may appear by that which he himself saith, in the second book, chapter 14, verses 21, 22, etc., where, speaking to God, he saith thus, *Thy law is burnt; therefore no man knoweth the things which thou hast done or the works that are to begin. But if I have found grace before thee, send down the holy spirit into me, and I shall write all that hath been done in the world, since the beginning, which were written in thy law, that men may find thy path, and that they which will live in the latter days, may live.* And verse 45: *And it came to pass, when the forty days were fulfilled, that the Highest spake, saying, The first that thou hast written publish openly, that the worthy and unworthy may read it; but keep the seventy last, that thou mayst deliver them only to such as be wise among the people.* And thus much concerning the time of the writing of the books of the Old Testament.

The New Testament.

20. The writers of the New Testament lived all in less than an age after Christ's ascension and had all of them seen our Saviour or been his Disciples, except St. Paul and St. Luke, and consequently whatsoever was written by them is as ancient as the time of the Apostles. But the time wherein the books of the New Testament were received and acknowledged by the Church to be of their writing is not altogether so ancient. For, as the books of the Old Testament are derived to us from no higher time than that of Esdras, who by the direction of God's spirit retrieved them when they were lost, those of the New Testament, of which the copies were not many nor could easily be all in any one private man's hand, cannot be derived from a higher time than that wherein the governors of the Church collected, approved, and recommended them to us as the writings of those Apostles and disciples under whose names they go. The first enumeration of all the books, both of the Old and New Testament, is in the Canons of the Apostles, supposed to be collected by Clement the First (after St. Peter), Bishop of Rome. But because that is but supposed and by many questioned, the Council of Laodicea is the first we know that recommended the Bible to the then Christian churches for the writings of the prophets and Apostles; and this Council was held in the 364th year after Christ. At which time, though ambition had so far
[204] prevailed on the great doctors of the Church as no more to esteem emperors, [even] though Christian, for the shepherds of the

people, but for sheep, and emperors not Christian, for wolves, and endeavoured to pass their doctrine, not for counsel and information, as preachers, but for laws, as absolute governors, and thought such frauds as tended to make the people the more obedient to Christian doctrine to be pious; yet I am persuaded they did not therefore falsify the Scriptures, though the copies of the books of the New Testament were in the hands only of the ecclesiastics, because if they had had an intention so to do, they would surely have made them more favorable to their power over Christian princes and civil sovereignty than they are.[1] I see not therefore any reason to doubt but that the Old and New Testament, as we have them now, are the true registers of those things which were done and said by the prophets and Apostles. And so perhaps are some of those books which are called Apocrypha, if left out of the Canon, not for inconformity of doctrine with the rest, but only because they are not found in the Hebrew. For after the conquest of Asia by Alexander the Great, there were few learned Jews that were not perfect in the Greek tongue. For the seventy interpreters that converted the Bible into Greek were all of them Hebrews; and we have extant the works of Philo and Josephus, both Jews, written by them eloquently in Greek. But it is not the writer but the authority of the Church that maketh a book canonical.[2] And although these books were written by divers men, yet it is manifest the writers were all endued with one and the same spirit, in that they conspire to one and the same end, which is the setting forth of the rights of the kingdom of God, the Father, Son, and Holy Ghost. For the book of Genesis deriveth the genealogy of God's people from the creation of the world to the going into Egypt; the other four Books of Moses contain the election of God for their King, and the laws which he prescribed for their government: the Books of Joshua, Judges, Ruth, and Samuel, to the time of Saul describe the acts of God's people till the time they cast off God's yoke and called for a king after the manner of their neighbour nations; the rest of the history of the Old Testament derives the succession of the line of David to the Captivity, of which line was to spring the

Their scope.

1 This is known as a backhanded compliment.

2 Roman Catholics would agree with this, but not with Hobbes's belief about who has the authority of the Church, namely, the sovereign. By the Act of Sovereignty, the English monarch was declared head of the English Church.

restorer of the kingdom of God, even our blessed Saviour, God the Son, whose coming was foretold in the books of the prophets, after whom the Evangelists wrote his life and actions, and his claim to the kingdom, whilst he lived on earth; and lastly, the Acts and Epistles of the Apostles declare the coming of God, the Holy Ghost, and the authority he left with them and their successors for the direction of the Jews and for the invitation of the Gentiles. In sum, the histories and the prophecies of the Old Testament and the gospels and epistles of the New Testament have had one and the same scope, to convert men to the obedience of God: 1. in Moses and the priests; 2. in the man Christ; and 3. in the Apostles and the successors to apostolical power. For these three at several times did represent the person of God: Moses and his successors [205] the high priests, and kings of Judah, in the Old Testament; Christ himself in the time he lived on earth; and the Apostles and their successors from the day of Pentecost (when the Holy Ghost descended on them) to this day.

The question of the authority of Scripture stated.

21. It is a question much disputed between the divers sects of Christian religion, *from whence the Scriptures derive their authority*; which question is also propounded sometimes in other terms, as, *how we know them to be the word of God*, or, *why we believe them to be so*, and the difficulty of resolving it ariseth chiefly from the improperness of the words wherein the question itself is couched. For it is believed on all hands that the first and original author of them is God, and consequently the question disputed is not that. Again, it is manifest that none can know they are God's word (though all true Christians believe it) but those to whom God himself hath revealed it supernaturally, and therefore the question is not rightly moved, of our *knowledge* of it.[1] Lastly, when the question is propounded of our *belief*; because some are moved to believe for one, and others for other reasons, there can be rendered no one general answer for them all. The question truly stated is: *by what authority they are made law.*

Their authority and interpretation.

22. As far as they differ not from the laws of nature, there is no doubt but they are the law of God and carry their authority with them, legible to all men that have the use of natural reason; but this

1 Hobbes is using his distinction between faith and reason to put "God's word" into the category of things believed by faith, not known by reason

is no other authority than that of all other moral doctrine consonant to reason; the dictates whereof are laws, not *made*, but *eternal*.

23. If they be made law by God himself, they are of the nature of written law, which are laws to them only to whom God hath so sufficiently published them as no man can excuse himself by saying he knew not they were his.

24. He therefore to whom God hath not supernaturally revealed that they are his, nor that those that published them were sent by him, is not obliged to obey them by any authority but his whose commands have already the force of laws, that is to say, by any other authority than that of the commonwealth, residing in the sovereign, who only has the legislative power.[1] Again, if it be not the legislative authority of the commonwealth that giveth them the force of laws, it must be some other authority derived from God, either private or public: if private, it obliges only him to whom in particular God hath been pleased to reveal it. For if every man should be obliged to take for God's law what particular men, on pretence of private inspiration or revelation, should obtrude upon him (in such a number of men that out of pride and ignorance take their own dreams and extravagant fancies and madness for testimonies of God's spirit, or, out of ambition, pretend to such divine testimonies falsely and contrary to their own consciences), it were impossible that any divine law should be acknowledged. If public, it is the authority of the commonwealth or of the Church.[2] But the Church, if it be one person, is the same thing with a commonwealth of Christians, called a common- [206]
wealth because it consisteth of men united in one person, their sovereign, and a *Church*, because it consisteth in Christian men, united in one Christian sovereign. But if the Church be not one person, then it hath no authority at all; it can neither command nor do any action at all nor is capable of having any power or right to anything; nor has any will, reason, nor voice; for all these qualities are personal. Now if the whole number of Christians be not contained in one commonwealth, they are not one person; nor is there a universal Church that hath any authority over them; and therefore the Scriptures are not made laws by the universal

---

1 See also 42.41.

2 See also chapter 39.

Church; or if it be one commonwealth, then all Christian monarchs and states are private persons and subject to be judged, deposed, and punished by a universal sovereign of all Christendom. So that the question of the authority of the Scriptures is reduced to this: *Whether Christian kings, and the sovereign assemblies in Christian commonwealths be absolute in their own territories, immediately under God, or subject to one Vicar of Christ, constituted over the universal Church, to be judged condemned, deposed, and put to death, as he shall think expedient or necessary for the common good.*

25. Which question cannot be resolved without a more particular consideration of the kingdom of God; from whence also, we are to judge of the authority of interpreting the Scripture. For, whosoever hath a lawful power over any writing, to make it law, hath the power also to approve or disapprove the interpretation of the same.

[207]

## CHAPTER XXXIV

## OF THE SIGNIFICATION OF SPIRIT, ANGEL, AND INSPIRATION IN THE BOOKS OF HOLY SCRIPTURE

Body and spirit how taken in the Scripture.

1. Seeing the foundation of all true ratiocination is the constant signification of words, which, in the doctrine following, dependeth not (as in natural science) on the will of the writer nor (as in common conversation) on vulgar use, but on the sense they carry in the Scripture, it is necessary, before I proceed any further, to determine, out of the Bible, the meaning of such words as by their ambiguity may render what I am to infer upon them obscure or disputable. I will begin with the words Body and Spirit, which in the language of the Schools are termed *substances, corporeal* and *incorporeal.*[1]

2. The word *body*, in the most general acceptation, signifieth

1 Hobbes is about to give a linguistic analysis of the words 'body' and 'spirit' as part of his argument that all substances are bodies and either the word 'spirit' is meaningless or means some kind of body. He will give linguistic analyses of several words in this and the next two chapters. See also 34.2. Cf. 31.15.

that which filleth or occupieth some certain room or imagined place and dependeth not on the imagination, but is a real part of that we call the *universe*. For the *universe*, being the aggregate of all bodies, there is no real part thereof that is not also *body* nor anything properly a *body* that is not also part of that aggregate of all *bodies*, the *universe*. The same also, because bodies are subject to change, that is to say, to variety of appearance to the sense of living creatures, is called *substance*, that is to say, *subject* to various accidents, as sometimes to be moved, sometimes to stand still, and to seem to our senses sometimes hot, sometimes cold; sometimes of one colour, smell, taste, or sound, sometimes of another. And this diversity of seeming, produced by the diversity of the operation of bodies on the organs of our sense, we attribute to alterations of the bodies that operate and call them *accidents* of those bodies. And according to this acceptation of the word, *substance* and *body* signify the same thing; and therefore *substance incorporeal* are words which, when they are joined together, destroy one another, as if a man should say, an *incorporeal body*.

3. But in the sense of common people, not all the universe is called body, but only such parts thereof as they can discern by the sense of feeling to resist their force, or, by the sense of their eyes to hinder them from a farther prospect. Therefore in the common language of men, *air* and *aerial substances* use not to be taken for *bodies*, but, as often as men are sensible of their effects, are called *wind*, or *breath*, or (because the same are called in the Latin *spiritus*) *spirits*, as when they call that aerial substance which in the body of any living creature gives it life and motion, *vital* and *animal spirits*. But for those idols of the brain which represent bodies to us where they are not, as in a looking-glass, in a dream, or to a distempered brain waking, they are (as the Apostle saith generally of all idols) nothing; nothing at all, I say, there where they seem to be, and in the brain itself, nothing but tumult, proceeding either from the action of the objects or from the disorderly agitation of the organs of our sense.[1] And men that are otherwise employed than to search into their causes know not of themselves what to call them and may therefore easily be persuaded, by those whose [208]

1 See also 1.1-4.

knowledge they much reverence, some to call them *bodies*, and think them made of air compacted by a power supernatural, because the sight judges them corporeal, and some to call them *spirits*, because the sense of touch discerneth nothing, in the place where they appear, to resist their fingers, so that the proper signification of *spirit* in common speech is either a subtle, fluid, and invisible body, or a ghost, or other idol or phantasm of the imagination. But for metaphorical significations there be many; for sometimes it is taken for disposition or inclination of the mind, as when for the disposition to control the sayings of other men, we say, *a spirit of contradiction;* for a disposition to uncleanness [we say] *an unclean spirit*; for perverseness, *a froward spirit*; for sullenness, *a dumb spirit*, and for inclination to godliness and God's service, *the Spirit of God*; sometimes for any eminent ability or extraordinary passion or disease of the mind, as when great wisdom is called *the spirit of wisdom*, and madmen are said to be *possessed with a spirit.*

4. Other signification of *spirit* I find nowhere any, and where none of these can satisfy the sense of that word in Scripture, the place falleth not under human understanding; and our faith therein consisteth, not in our opinion, but in our submission, as in all places where God is said to be a *Spirit*, or where by the *Spirit of God* is meant God himself. For the nature of God is incomprehensible;[1] that is to say, we understand nothing of *what he is*, but only *that he is*,[2] and therefore the attributes we give him are not to tell one another *what he is* nor to signify our opinion of his nature, but our desire to honour him with such names as we conceive most honourable amongst ourselves.[3]

The spirit of God taken in the Scripture

5. Gen. 1:2: *The Spirit of God moved upon the face of the waters.* Here if by the *spirit of God* be meant God himself, then is *motion* attributed to God, and consequently *place*, which are intelligible

1 It was not unusual to say that God was incomprehensible in the seventeenth century, especially among Calvinists. See also 12.7, 46.23, 46.31.

2 Scholastic philosophers distinguished between the questions 'Does it exist?' and 'What is it?' If something does not exist, then it has no nature. The latter question asks what the nature of an existent thing is. The nature (*natura*) of a thing is its essence (*essentia*): what makes it to be what it is. The nature of a human being is to be a rational animal. Few other examples were given. (One is that an angel is a finite being that has will and intellect, that is, can make decisions and know things.)

3 See also 31.33.

only of bodies and not of substances incorporeal; and so the place is above our understanding that can conceive nothing moved that changes not place or that has not dimension, and whatsoever has dimension is body. But the meaning of those words is best understood by the like place, where when the earth was covered with waters, as in the beginning, God intending to abate them, and again to discover the dry land, useth the like words, *I will bring my Spirit upon the earth, and the waters shall be diminished* (Gen. 8:1), in which place by *Spirit* is understood a wind (that is an air or *spirit moved*), which might be called, as in the former place, the *Spirit of God*, because it was God's work.[1]

sometimes for a wind or breath.

6. Gen. 41:38: Pharaoh calleth the wisdom of Joseph the *Spirit of God*. For Joseph having advised him to look out a wise and discreet man, and to set him over the land of Egypt, he saith thus, *Can we find such a man as this is, in whom is the Spirit of God*? And Exod., 28:3, *Thou shalt speak*, saith God, *to all that are wise hearted, whom I have filled with the spirit of wisdom, to make Aaron garments, to consecrate him*. Where extraordinary understanding, though but in making garments, as being the *gift* of God, is called the *Spirit of God*. The same is found again, Exod. 31:3–6 and 35:31. And Isaiah 11:2–3, where the prophet, speaking of the Messiah, saith, *The Spirit of the Lord shall abide upon him the spirit of wisdom and understanding, the spirit of counsel and fortitude, and the spirit of the fear of the Lord*. Where manifestly is meant, not so many ghosts, but so many eminent *graces* that God would give him. [209]

Secondly, for extraordinary gifts of the understanding.

7. In the Book of Judges, an extraordinary zeal and courage in the defence of God's people is called the *Spirit* of God, as when it excited Othniel, Gideon, Jephtha, and Samson to deliver them from servitude, Judges, 3:10, 6:34, 11:29, 13:25, 14:6, [and] 14:19. And of Saul, upon the news of the insolence of the Ammonites towards the men of Jabesh Gilead, it is said that *The Spirit of God came upon Saul, and his anger* (or, as it is in the Latin, *his fury*) *was kindled greatly* (1 Sam. 11:6). Where it is not probable was meant a ghost but an extraordinary *zeal* to punish the cruelty of the Ammonites. In like manner by the *Spirit* of God that came upon Saul, when he was amongst the prophets that praised God in songs

Thirdly, for extraordinary affections.

1 By 'spirit', the phrase 'spirit of God' means either that God has a body, or, as is more likely, that God is working or acting.

and music (1 Sam. 19:20) is to be understood, not a ghost, but an unexpected and sudden *zeal* to join with them in their devotion.

Fourthly, for the gift of prediction by dreams and visions.

8. The false prophet Zedekiah saith to Micaiah, *Which way went the Spirit of the Lord from me to speak to thee?* (1 Kings 22:24). Which cannot be understood of a ghost; for Micaiah declared before the kings of Israel and Judah the event of the battle as from a *vision* and not as from a *spirit* speaking in him.

9. In the same manner it appeareth in the books of the Prophets that though they spake by the *Spirit* of God, that is to say, by a special grace of prediction; yet their knowledge of the future was not by a ghost within them, but by some supernatural *dream* or *vision*.

Fifthly, for life.

10. Gen. 2:7: It is said, *God made man of the dust of the earth, and breathed into his nostrils* (spiraculum vitae) *the breath of life, and man was made a living soul.* There the *breath of life* inspired by God signifies no more but that God gave him life, and *as long as the spirit of God is in my nostrils* is no more than to say, *as long as I live.* So in Ezek. 1:20, *the spirit of life was in the wheels*, is equivalent to, *the wheels were alive.* And *the spirit entered into me, and me, and set me on my feet* (Ezek. 2:30), that is, *I recovered my vital strength*, not that any ghost or incorporeal substance entered into and possessed his body.

Sixthly, for a subordination to authority.

11. In the eleventh chapter of Numbers, verse 17, *I will take*, saith God, *of the spirit which is upon thee, and will put it upon them, and they shall bear the burden of the people with thee*, that is, upon the
[210] seventy elders; whereupon two of the seventy are said to prophesy in the camp, of whom some complained, and Joshua desired Moses to forbid them, which Moses would not do. Whereby it appears that Joshua knew not they had received authority so to do and prophesied according to the mind of Moses, that is to say, by a *spirit* or *authority* subordinate to his own.

12. In the like sense we read that *Joshua was full of the spirit of wisdom, because Moses had laid his hands upon him* (Deut. 34:9), that is, because he was *ordained* by Moses to prosecute the work he had himself begun (namely, the bringing of God's people into the promised land) but, prevented by death, could not finish.

13. In the like sense it is said, *If any man have not the Spirit of Christ, he is none of his* (Rom. 8:9), not meaning thereby the *ghost*

of Christ, but a *submission* to his doctrine. As also, *Hereby you shall know the Spirit of God: every spirit that confesseth that Jesus Christ is come in the flesh is of God* (1 John 4:2), by which is meant the spirit of unfeigned Christianity, or *submission* to that main article of Christian faith, that Jesus is the Christ; which cannot be interpreted of a ghost.

14. Likewise these words, *And Jesus full of the Holy Ghost* (Luke 4:1), (that is, as it is expressed, Matt. 4:1 and Mark 1:12, *of the Holy Spirit*) may be understood for *zeal* to do the work for which he was sent by God the Father; but to interpret it of a ghost is to say that God himself (for so our Saviour was)[1] was filled with God, which is very improper and insignificant. How we came to translate *spirits* by the word *ghosts*, which signifieth nothing, neither in heaven nor earth, but the imaginary inhabitants of man's brain, I examine not; but this I say, the word *spirit* in the text signifieth no such thing, but either properly a real *substance* or, metaphorically, some extraordinary *ability* or *affection* of the mind or of the body.

Seventhly, for aerial bodies.

15. The Disciples of Christ, seeing him walking upon the sea (Matt. 14:26 and Mark 6:49) supposed him to be a *spirit*, meaning thereby an aerial *body*, and not a phantasm; for it is said they all saw him; which cannot be understood of the delusions of the brain (which are not common to many at once, as visible bodies are, but singular, because of the differences of fancies), but of bodies only. In like manner, where he was taken for a *spirit* by the same Apostles (Luke 24:3, 24:7), so also when St. Peter was delivered out of prison, it would not be believed; but when the maid said he was at the door, they said it was his *angel* (Acts 12:15) by which must be meant a corporeal substance; or we must say the disciples themselves did follow the common opinion of both Jews and Gentiles that some such apparitions were not imaginary, but real, and such as needed not the fancy of man for their existence; these the Jews called *spirits* and *angels*, good or bad, as the Greeks called the same by the name of *demons*.[2] And some such apparitions may be real [211] and substantial, that is to say, subtle bodies, which God can form by the same power by which he formed all things and make use of as ministers and messengers (that is to say, angels), to declare his

1 See also 45.24.

1 See also 8.25, 12.16, 34.18, 36.2.

will and execute the same when he pleaseth in extraordinary and supernatural manner. But when he hath so formed them they are substances, endued with dimensions, and take up room and can be moved from place to place, which is peculiar to bodies; and therefore [they] are not ghosts *incorporeal*, that is to say, ghosts that are in *no place*, that is to say, that are *nowhere*, that is to say, that, seeming to be *somewhat*, are *nothing*. But if corporeal be taken in the most vulgar manner, for such substances as are perceptible by our external senses, then is substance incorporeal a thing not imaginary, but real, namely, a thin substance invisible, but that hath the same dimensions that are in grosser bodies.

Angel what.

16. By the name of ANGEL is signified, generally, a *messenger*[1] and most often, a *messenger of God*; and by a messenger of God is signified anything that makes known his extraordinary presence, that is to say, the extraordinary manifestation of his power, especially by a dream or vision.

17. Concerning the creation of *angels*, there is nothing delivered in the Scriptures.[2] That they are spirits is often repeated; but by the name of spirit is signified both in Scripture and vulgarly, both amongst Jews and Gentiles, sometimes thin bodies, as the air, the wind, the spirits vital and animal of living creatures, and sometimes the images that rise in the fancy in dreams and visions, which are not real substances nor last any longer than the dream or vision they appear in; which apparitions, though no real substances, but accidents of the brain; yet when God raiseth them supernaturally, to signify his will, they are not improperly termed God's messengers, that is to say, his *angels*.

18. And as the Gentiles did vulgarly conceive the imagery of the brain for things really subsistent without them and not dependent on the fancy, and out of them framed their opinions of *demons*,[3] good and evil, which because they seemed to subsist really, they called *substances*, and because they could not feel them with their hands, *incorporeal*;[4] so also the Jews upon the same ground,

1 The Latin word for a messenger is '*angelus*'.

2 Many of the beliefs that Christians have about angels stem either from neoplatonic views or John Milton's *Paradise Lost* (1667).

3 See also 8.25, 12.16, 34.15, 36.2.

4 Hobbes blames much of the corruption in Christianity to importations from paganism. The Roman Catholic Church is the worst offender, but in this para-

without anything in the Old Testament that constrained them thereunto, had generally an opinion (except the sect of the Sadducees) that those apparitions, which it pleased God sometimes to produce in the fancy of men for his own service and therefore called them his *angels*, were substances, not dependent on the fancy, but permanent creatures of God, whereof those which they thought were good to them, they esteemed the *angels of God*, and those they thought would hurt them, they called *evil angels* or evil spirits; such as was the spirit of Python, and the spirits of madmen, of lunatics and epileptics; for they esteemed such as were troubled with such diseases, *demoniacs*.

19. But if we consider the places of the Old Testament where angels are mentioned, we shall find that in most of them, there can nothing else be understood by the word *angel*, but some image [212] raised supernaturally in the fancy, to signify the presence of God in the execution of some supernatural work, and therefore in the rest, where their nature is not expressed, it may be understood in the same manner.

20. For we read that the same apparition is called not only an *angel*, but *God*, where that which is called the *angel* of the Lord, saith to Hagar, *I will multiply thy seed exceedingly* (Gen. 16:7), that is, speaketh in the person of God. Neither was this apparition a fancy figured, but a voice. By which it is manifest that *angel* signifieth there nothing but *God* himself, that caused Hagar supernaturally to apprehend a voice from heaven or rather, nothing else but a voice supernatural, testifying God's special presence there. Why therefore may not the angels that appeared to Lot, and are called *men* (Gen. 19:12) and to whom, though they were two, Lot speaketh as but to one and that one as God (for the words are, *Lot said unto them, Oh not so my Lord* (Gen. 19:18)), be understood of images of men, supernaturally formed in the fancy, as well as before by *angel* was understood a fancied voice? When the angel called to Abraham out of heaven, to stay his hand from slaying Isaac (Gen. 22:11), there was no apparition, but a voice, which nevertheless was called properly enough a messenger or *angel* of God, because it declared God's will supernaturally and saves the

---

graph he also puts some blame on the Sadducees, a Jewish group mentioned in the gospels.

labour of supposing any permanent ghosts. The angels which Jacob saw on the ladder of heaven (Gen. 28:12) were a vision of his sleep; therefore only fancy and a dream; yet being supernatural, and signs of God's special presence, those apparitions are not improperly called *angels*. The same is to be understood where Jacob saith thus, *The angel of the Lord appeared to me in my sleep* (Gen. 31:11). For an apparition made to a man in his sleep is that which all men call a dream, whether such dream be natural or supernatural: and that which there Jacob calleth an *angel* was God himself; for the same angel saith, *I am the God of Bethel* (Gen. 31:13).

21. Also the angel that went before the army of Israel to the Red Sea and then came behind it is the Lord himself (Exod. 14:19); and he appeared not in the form of a beautiful man, but in form, by day, of a *pillar of cloud*, and, by night, in form of a *pillar of fire* and yet this pillar was all the apparition and *angel* promised to Moses for the army's guide (Exod. 14:9); for this cloudy pillar is said to have descended and stood at the door of the tabernacle, and to have talked with Moses.

22. There you see motion and speech, which are commonly attributed to angels, attributed to a cloud, because the cloud served as a sign of God's presence and was no less an angel than if it had had the form of a man or child of never so great beauty, or wings, as usually they are painted, for the false instruction of common people. For it is not the shape, but their use,[1] that makes them angels. But their use is to be significations of God's presence in
[213] supernatural operations, as when Moses had desired God to go along with the camp, as he had done always before the making of the golden calf, God did not answer, *I will go*, nor *I will send an angel in my stead*; but thus, *My presence shall go with thee* (Exod. 33:14).

23. To mention all the places of the Old Testament where the name of angel is found would be too long. Therefore to comprehend them all at once, I say there is no text in that part of the Old Testament which the Church of England holdeth for canonical from which we can conclude there is or hath been created any

1 By 'use' Hobbes means their function as messengers.

permanent thing (understood by the name of *spirit* or *angel*) that hath not quantity and that may not be by the understanding divided, that is to say, considered by parts, so as one part may be in one place, and the next part in the next place to it, and, in sum, which is not (taking body for that which is somewhat or somewhere) corporeal; but in every place the sense will bear the interpretation of angel for messenger, as John Baptist is called an angel and Christ the Angel of the Covenant, and as (according to the same analogy) the dove and the fiery tongues, in that they were signs of God's special presence, might also be called angels. Though we find in Daniel two names of angels, Gabriel and Michael; yet it is clear out of the text itself that by Michael is meant Christ, not as an angel, but as a prince (Dan. 12:1), and that Gabriel (as the like apparitions made to other holy men in their sleep) was nothing but a supernatural phantasm, by which it seemed to Daniel in his dream that two saints being in talk, one of them said to the other, *Gabriel, let us make this man understand his vision*; for God needeth not to distinguish his celestial servants by names, which are useful only to the short memories of mortals. Nor in the New Testament is there any place out of which it can be proved that angels (except when they are put for such men as God hath made the messengers and ministers of his word or works) are things permanent, and withal [also] incorporeal. That they are permanent may be gathered from the words of our Saviour himself where he saith it shall be said to the wicked in the last day, *Go ye cursed into everlasting fire prepared for the Devil and his angels* (Matt. 25:41); which place is manifest for the permanence of evil angels (unless we might think the name of Devil and his angels may be understood of the Church's adversaries and their ministers); but then it is repugnant to their immateriality, because everlasting fire is no punishment to impatible substances, such as are all things incorporeal. Angels therefore are not thence proved to be incorporeal. In like manner where St. Paul says, *Know ye not that we shall judge the angels?* (1 Cor. 6:3), and (2 Peter 2:4) *For if God spared not the angels that sinned, but cast them down into hell.* And (Jude 1:6) *And the angels that kept not their first estate, but left their own habitation, he hath reserved in everlasting chains under darkness unto the judgement of the last day* though it prove the permanence of angelical nature, it

[214] confirmeth also their materiality. And, (Matt. 22:30) *In the resurrection men do neither marry, nor give in marriage, but are as the angels of God in heaven*; but in the resurrection men shall be permanent, and not incorporeal; so therefore also are the angels.

24. There be divers other places out of which may be drawn the like conclusion. To men that understand the signification of these words, *substance* and *incorporeal* (as *incorporeal* is taken not for subtle body, but for *not body*), they imply a contradiction, insomuch as to say, an angel or spirit is in that sense an incorporeal substance is to say, in effect, there is no angel nor spirit at all. Considering therefore the signification of the word *angel* in the Old Testament and the nature of dreams and visions that happen to men by the ordinary way of nature, I was inclined to this opinion, that angels were nothing but supernatural apparitions of the fancy, raised by the special and extraordinary operation of God, thereby to make his presence and commandments known to mankind, and chiefly to his own people. But the many places of the New Testament and our Saviour's own words and in such texts wherein is no suspicion of corruption of the Scripture have extorted from my feeble reason an acknowledgement and belief that there be also angels substantial and permanent.[1] But to believe they be in no place, that is to say, nowhere, that is to say, nothing, as they, though indirectly, say that will have them incorporeal, cannot by Scripture be evinced.

Inspiration what.

25. On the signification of the word *spirit* dependeth that of the word INSPIRATION, which must either be taken properly and then it is nothing but the blowing into a man some thin and subtle air or wind in such manner as a man filleth a bladder with his breath; or if spirits be not corporeal, but have their existence only in the fancy, it is nothing but the blowing in of a phantasm, which is improper to say and impossible; for phantasms[2] are not, but only seem to be, somewhat. That word therefore is used in the Scripture metaphorically only, as where it is said that God *inspired* into man the breath of life (Gen. 2:7), no more is meant than that God

---

1 This is an interesting admission on Hobbes's part. Some scholars who think Hobbes is an atheist claim that Hobbes intends this statement to strike people as so obviously false that he must intend his readers to know that he is an atheist. (I take Hobbes at his word here.)

2 See also 36.2, 44.1, 44.13, 44.16, 44.21, 45.2, 45.4, 45.8, 45.10, and 45.14.

gave unto him vital motion. For we are not to think that God made first a living breath, and then blew it into Adam after he was made, whether that breath were real or seeming, but only as it is *that he gave him life, and breath* (Acts 17:25), that is, made him a living creature. And where it is said *all Scripture is given by inspiration from God* (2 Tim. 3:13), speaking there of the Scripture of the Old Testament, it is an easy metaphor to signify that God inclined the spirit or mind of those writers to write that which should be useful in teaching, reproving, correcting, and instructing men in the way of righteous living. But where St. Peter saith that *Prophecy came not in old time by the will of man, but the holy men of God spake as they were moved by the Holy Spirit* (2 Pet. 1:21), by the Holy Spirit is meant the voice of God in a dream or vision supernatural, which is not *inspiration*; nor when our Saviour, breathing on his disciples, said, *Receive the Holy Spirit*, was that breath the Spirit, but a sign of the spiritual graces he gave unto them. And though it be said of [215]
many and of our Saviour himself, that he was full of the Holy Spirit; yet that fullness is not to be understood for *infusion* of the substance of God, but for accumulation of his gifts, such as are the gift of sanctity of life, of tongues, and the like, whether attained supernaturally or by study and industry; for in all cases they are the gifts of God. So likewise where God says, *I will pour out my Spirit upon all flesh, and your sons and your daughters shall prophesy, your old men shall dream dreams, and your young men shall see visions* (Joel 2:28) we are not to understand it in the proper sense, as if his Spirit were like water, subject to effusion or infusion, but as if God had promised to give them prophetical dreams and visions. For the proper use of the word *infused*, in speaking of the graces of God, is an abuse of it; for those graces are virtues, not bodies to be carried hither and thither, and to be poured into men as into barrels.

26. In the same manner, to take *inspiration* in the proper sense or to say that good spirits entered into men to make them prophesy, or evil spirits into those that became phrenetic, lunatic, or epileptic, is not to take the word in the sense of the Scripture; for the spirit there is taken for the power of God, working by causes to us unknown. As also the wind that is there said to fill the house wherein the Apostles were assembled on the day of Pentecost is not to be understood for the *Holy Spirit*, which is the Deity itself,

but for an external sign of God's special working on their hearts to effect in them the internal graces and holy virtues he thought requisite for the performance of their apostleship (Acts 2:2).

[216]

# CHAPTER XXXV

## OF THE SIGNIFICATION IN SCRIPTURE OF THE KINGDOM OF GOD, OF HOLY, SACRED, AND SACRAMENT

The kingdom of God taken by divines metaphorically, but in the Scriptures properly.

1. The *kingdom of God* in the writings of divines and specially in sermons and treatises of devotion is taken most commonly for eternal felicity after this life in the highest heaven, which they also call the kingdom of glory and sometimes (for the earnest of that felicity) sanctification, which they term the kingdom of grace, but never for the monarchy, that is to say, the sovereign power of God over any subjects acquired by their own consent, which is the proper signification of kingdom.

2. To the contrary, I find the KINGDOM OF GOD to signify in most places of Scripture a *kingdom properly so named*, constituted by the votes of the people of Israel in peculiar manner, wherein they chose God for their king by covenant made with him, upon God's promising them the possession of the land of Canaan and but seldom metaphorically, and then it is taken for *dominion over sin* (and only in the New Testament), because such a dominion as that every subject shall have in the kingdom of God, and without prejudice to the sovereign.

3. From the very creation, God not only reigned over all men *naturally* by his might,[1] but also had *peculiar* subjects, whom he commanded by a voice, as one man speaketh to another. In which manner he *reigned* over Adam and gave him commandment to abstain from the tree of cognizance of good and evil; which when he obeyed not, but tasting thereof took upon him to be as God, judging between good and evil, not by his Creator's commandment, but by his own sense, his punishment was a privation of the

1 Hobbes discussed this kingdom in chapter 31.

estate of eternal life, wherein God had at first created him. And afterwards God punished his posterity for their vices, all but eight persons,[1] with a universal deluge, and in these eight did consist the then *kingdom of God*.

4. After this, it pleased God to speak to Abraham, and to make a covenant with him[2] in these words, *I will establish my covenant between me and thee and thy seed after thee in their generations for an everlasting covenant, to be a God to thee, and to thy seed after thee; And I will give unto thee, and to thy seed after thee, the land wherein thou art a stranger, all the land of Canaan, for an everlasting possession* (Gen. 17:7-8). In this covenant Abraham promiseth for himself and his posterity to obey, as God, the Lord that spake to him,[3] and God on his part promiseth to Abraham the land of Canaan for an everlasting possession. And for a memorial and a token of this covenant, he ordaineth the *sacrament of circumcision* (Gen. 17:11). This is it which is called the *Old Covenant* or *Testament*, and containeth a contract between God and Abraham, by which Abraham obligeth himself and his posterity in a peculiar manner to be subject to God's positive law; for to the law moral he was obliged before, as by an oath of allegiance. And though the name of *King* be not yet given to God, nor of *kingdom* to Abraham and his seed; yet the thing is the same, namely, an institution by pact of God's peculiar sovereignty over the seed of Abraham, which in the renewing of the same covenant by Moses at Mount Sinai is expressly called a peculiar *kingdom of God* over the Jews;[4] and it is of Abraham, not of Moses, St. Paul saith that he is the *father of the faithful* (Rom. 4:11), that is, of those that are loyal and do not violate their allegiance sworn to God, then by circumcision, and afterwards in the *New Covenant* by baptism.

The original of the kingdom of God.

[217]

5. This covenant at the foot of Mount Sinai was renewed by Moses where the Lord commandeth Moses to speak to the people

That the kingdom of God is

1 Hobbes is referring to Noah, his wife, their three children and their wives.

2 It is odd for Hobbes to say that God made a covenant with Abraham because this covenant made God a sovereign over Abraham and the sovereign is not supposed to be a contracting-party (18.4).

3 See also 40.1-4.

4 It is not clear what the force of "the renewing of the same covenant" is. One difference between the covenant involving Abraham and the one involving Moses is that Abraham was a sovereign over his extended family and Moses only became one when the Israelites covenanted to make him their sovereign (35.5).

properly his civil sovereignty over a peculiar people by pact.

in this manner, *If you will obey my voice indeed, and keep my covenant, then ye shall be a peculiar people to me, for all the earth is mine; and ye shall be unto me a sacerdotal kingdom, and an holy nation*[1] (Exod. 19:5). For a *peculiar people*, the vulgar Latin hath, *peculium de cunctis populis*, the English translation made in the beginning of the reign of King James hath, a *peculiar treasure unto me above all nations*, and the Geneva French, *the most precious jewel of all nations*. But the truest translation is the first, because it is confirmed by St. Paul himself where he saith, alluding to that place, that our blessed Saviour *gave himself for us, that he might purify us to himself, a peculiar* (that is, an extraordinary) *people* (Titus 2:14); for the word is in the Greek *periousios*, which is opposed commonly to the word *epiousios*; and as this signifieth *ordinary, quotidian*, or, as in the Lord's Prayer, *of daily use,* so the other signifieth that which is *overplus* and *stored up* and *enjoyed in a special manner*; which the Latins call *peculium,* and this meaning of the place is confirmed by the reason God rendereth of it, which followeth immediately, in that he addeth, *For all the earth is mine*, as if he should say, *All the nations of the world are mine*; but it is not so that you are mine, but in a *special manner*; for they are all mine, by reason of my power; but you shall be mine by your own consent and covenant, which is an addition to his ordinary title to all nations.

6. The same is again confirmed in express words in the same text, *Ye shall be to me a sacerdotal kingdom, and an holy nation*. The vulgar Latin hath it, *regnum sacerdotale*, to which agreeth the translation of that place, *sacerdotium regale, a regal priesthood* (1 Peter 2:9), as also the institution itself, by which no man might enter into the *sanctum sanctorum*, that is to say, no man might enquire God's will immediately of God himself, but only the high priest. The English translation before mentioned, following that of Geneva, has, *a king-*
[218] *dom of priests*; which is either meant of the succession of one high priest after another or else it accordeth not with St. Peter, nor with the exercise of the high priesthood. For there was never any but the high priest only that was to inform the people of God's will; nor any convocation of priests ever allowed to enter into the *sanctum sanctorum*.

1 Hobbes is rightly mystified about the meaning of a "sarcedotal [priestly] kingdom." It may well mean simply "holy nation," as he suggests at 35.7. See also 35.16.

7. Again, the title of a *holy nation* confirms the same; for *holy* signifies that which is God's by special, not by general, right. All the earth, as is said in the text, is God's; but all the earth is not called *holy*, but that only which is set apart for his especial service, as was the nation of the Jews. It is therefore manifest enough by this one place that by the *kingdom of God* is properly meant a commonwealth,[1] instituted (by the consent of those which were to be subject thereto) for their civil government and the regulating of their behaviour, not only towards God their king, but also towards one another in point of justice and towards other nations both in peace and war; which properly was a kingdom wherein God was king, and the high priest was to be, after the death of Moses, his sole viceroy, or lieutenant.

8. But there be many other places that clearly prove the same. As first when the elders of Israel (grieved with the corruption of the sons of Samuel) demanded a king, Samuel, displeased therewith, prayed unto the Lord, and the Lord answering said unto him, *Hearken unto the voice of the people, for they have not rejected thee, but they have rejected me, that I should not reign over them* (1 Samuel 8:7). Out of which it is evident that God himself was then their king; and Samuel did not command the people, but only delivered to them that which God from time to time appointed him.

9. Again, where Samuel saith to the people, *When ye saw that Nahash, king of the children of Ammon, came against you, ye said unto me, Nay, but a king shall reign over us; when the Lord your God was your king* (1 Sam. 12:12), it is manifest that God was their king, and governed the civil state of their commonwealth.

10. And after the Israelites had rejected God, the prophets did foretell his restitution, as, *Then the moon shall be confounded, and the sun ashamed, when the Lord of hosts shall reign in Mount Zion, and in Jerusalem* (Is. 24:23), where he speaketh expressly of his reign in Zion and Jerusalem, that is, on earth. And, *And the Lord shall reign over them in Mount Zion* (Mic. 4:7), this Mount Zion is in

1 Hobbes wants the kingdom of God to be understood literally, that is, to be a commonwealth, for two reasons. First, he wants to argue that a subject of any commonwealth owes the sovereign the same kind of obedience that the Israelites owed to God. Second, he wants to argue that God will not have an earthly kingdom again until the Second Coming. This makes the kingdom of God functionally irrelevant for the present. See also 35.13 and 41.3.

Jerusalem upon the earth. And, *As I live, saith the Lord God, surely with a mighty hand, and a stretched out arm, and with fury poured out, I will rule over you* (Ezek. 20:33), and, *I will cause you to pass under the rod, and I will bring you into the bond of the covenant* (Ezek. 20:37), that is, I will reign over you,[1] and make you to stand to that covenant which you made with me by Moses and broke in your rebellion against me in the days of Samuel, and in your election of another king.

11. And in the New Testament the angel Gabriel saith of our Saviour, *He shall be great, and be called the Son of the most High, and*
[219] *the Lord shall give him the throne of his father David; and he shall reign over the house of Jacob for ever; and of his kingdom there shall be no end* (Luke 1:32–33). This is also a kingdom upon earth, for the claim whereof, as an enemy to Caesar, he was put to death; the title of his cross was *Jesus of Nazareth, King of the Jews*; he was crowned in scorn with a crown of thorns; and for the proclaiming of him, it is said of the Disciples *That they did all of them contrary to the decrees of Caesar, saying there was another King, one Jesus* (Acts 17:17). The kingdom therefore of God is a real, not a metaphorical kingdom, and so taken, not only in the Old Testament, but the New. When we say, *For thine is the kingdom, the power, and glory*, it is to be understood of God's kingdom, by force of our covenant, not by the right of God's power; for such a kingdom God always hath, so that it were superfluous to say in our prayer, *Thy kingdom come*, unless it be meant of the restoration of that kingdom of God by Christ[2] which by revolt of the Israelites had been interrupted in the election of Saul.[3] Nor had it been proper to say, *The kingdom of heaven is at hand*; or to pray, *Thy kingdom come*, if it had still continued.

12. There be so many other places that confirm this interpretation that it were a wonder there is no greater notice taken of it, but that it gives too much light to Christian kings to see their right of ecclesiastical government. This they have observed, that instead of a *sacerdotal kingdom*, translate, *a kingdom of priests*; for they may as well translate a *royal priesthood*, as it is in St. Peter, into a

---

1 According to Hobbes, God was the sovereign of the Israelites either from the time of Abraham or Moses until they chose Saul to be their king. God will have another kingdom on earth at the Second Coming of Christ.

2 See 35.13 and 40.1.

3 See 35.10.

*priesthood of kings*. And whereas, for a *peculiar people*, they put a *precious jewel* or *treasure*, a man might as well call the special regiment or company of a general the general's precious jewel or his treasure.

13. In short, the kingdom of God is a civil kingdom, which consisted first, in the obligation of the people of Israel to those laws which Moses should bring unto them from Mount Sinai and which afterwards the high priest, for the time being, should deliver to them from before the cherubim in the *sanctum sanctorum*, and which kingdom having been cast off in the election of Saul, the prophets foretold, should be restored by Christ, and the restoration whereof we daily pray for when we say in the Lord's Prayer, *Thy kingdom come*, and the right whereof we acknowledge when we add, *For thine is the kingdom, the power, and glory, for ever and ever, Amen*, and the proclaiming whereof was the preaching of the Apostles, and to which men are prepared by the teachers of the Gospel[1] to embrace which Gospel (that is to say, to promise obedience to God's government) is to be in the *kingdom of grace*, because God hath *gratis* given to such the power to be the subjects (that is, children) of God hereafter when Christ shall come in majesty to judge the world and actually to govern his own people, which is called *the kingdom of glory*. If the kingdom of God (called also the kingdom of heaven, from the gloriousness and admirable height of that throne) were not a kingdom which God by his lieutenants or vicars, who deliver his commandments to the people, did exercise [220] on earth, there would not have been so much contention and war about who it is by whom God speaketh to us, neither would many priests have troubled themselves with spiritual jurisdiction, nor any king have denied it them.

Holy, what.

14. Out of this literal interpretation of the *kingdom of God* ariseth also the true interpretation of the word HOLY. For it is a word which in God's kingdom answereth to that which men in their kingdoms use to call *public* or the *king's*.

15. The king of any country is the *public* person or representative of all his own subjects. And God the king of Israel was the

1 Because the kingdom of God will be restored at the Second Coming, the Apostles and other ministers of the Church are only teachers and have no authority to make laws.

*Holy One* of Israel. The nation which is subject to one earthly sovereign is the nation of that sovereign, that is, of the public person. So the Jews, who were God's nation, were called *a holy nation* (Exod. 19:6). For by *holy* is always understood either God himself or that which is God's in propriety, as by public is always meant either the person of the commonwealth itself, or something that is so the commonwealth's as no private person can claim any propriety therein.

16. Therefore the Sabbath (God's day) is a *holy day*; the Temple (God's house), *a holy house*; sacrifices, tithes, and offerings (God's tribute), *holy duties*; priests, prophets, and anointed kings, under Christ (God's ministers), *holy men*; the celestial ministering spirits (God's messengers), *holy angels*, and the like; and wheresoever the word *holy* is taken properly, there is still something signified of propriety gotten by consent. In saying *Hallowed be thy name*, we do but pray to God for grace to keep the first Commandment of *having no other Gods but him*. Mankind is God's nation in propriety; but the Jews only were a *holy nation*. Why, but because they became his propriety by covenant?

17. And the word *profane* is usually taken in the Scripture for the same with *common*, and consequently their contraries, *holy* and *proper*, in the kingdom of God must be the same also. But figuratively, those men also are called *holy* that led such godly lives, as if they had forsaken all worldly designs and wholly devoted and given themselves to God. In the proper sense, that which is made *holy* by God's appropriating or separating it to his own use is said to be *sanctified* by God, as the seventh day in the fourth Commandment, and as the elect in the New Testament were said to be *sanctified* when they were endued with the spirit of godliness. And that which is made *holy* by the dedication of men and given to God, so as to be used only in his public service, is called also

Sacred, what.

SACRED, and said to be consecrated, as temples, and other houses of public prayer, and their utensils, priests, and ministers, victims, offerings, and the external matter of sacraments.

Degrees of sanctity.

18. Of *holiness* there be degrees; for of those things that are set apart for the service of God, there may be some set apart again for a nearer and more especial service. The whole nation of the Israelites were a people holy to God, yet the tribe of Levi was

amongst the Israelites a holy tribe and amongst the Levites the priests were yet more holy and amongst the priests the high priest was the most holy. So the land of Judea was the Holy Land, but the Holy City wherein God was to be worshipped was more holy, and again, the Temple more holy than the city, and the *sanctum sanctorum* more holy than the rest of the Temple. [221]

19. A SACRAMENT is a separation of some visible thing from common use and a consecration of it to God's service for a sign either of our admission into the kingdom of God, to be of the number of his peculiar people or for a commemoration of the same. In the Old Testament the sign of admission was *circumcision*, in the New Testament, *baptism*. The commemoration of it in the Old Testament was the *eating* (at a certain time, which was anniversary) of the Paschal Lamb, by which they were put in mind of the night wherein they were delivered out of their bondage in Egypt, and in the New Testament, the celebrating of the Lord's Supper, by which we are put in mind of our deliverance from the bondage of sin by our blessed Saviour's death upon the cross. The sacraments of admission are but once to be used, because there needs but one admission;[1] but because we have need of being often put in mind of our deliverance and of our allegiance, the sacraments of commemoration have need to be reiterated. And these are the principal sacraments and, as it were, the solemn oaths we make of our allegiance. There be also other consecrations that may be called sacraments, as the word implieth only consecration to God's service; but as it implies an oath or promise of allegiance to God, there were no other in the Old Testament but *circumcision* and the *Passover*; nor are there any other in the New Testament but *baptism* and the *Lord's Supper*. Sacrament.

1 Hobbes affirms the orthodox view of one baptism.

[222]

# CHAPTER XXXVI

## OF THE WORD OF GOD, AND OF PROPHETS

Word, what.

1. When there is mention of the *word of God* or of *man*, it doth not signify a part of speech, such as grammarians call a noun or a verb or any simple voice without a contexture with other words to make it significative; but a perfect speech or discourse, whereby the speaker *affirmeth, denieth, commandeth, promiseth, threateneth, wisheth, or interrogateth.* In which sense it is not *vocabulum* that signifies a *word*, but *sermo* (in Greek *logos*) that is, some *speech, discourse*, or *saying*.[1]

The words spoken by God and concerning God both are called God's word in Scripture.

2. Again, if we say the *word of God* or of *man*, it may be understood sometimes of the speaker (as the words that God hath spoken) or that a man hath spoken; in which sense, when we say the Gospel of St. Matthew, we understand St. Matthew to be the writer of it, and sometimes of the subject; in which sense, when we read in the Bible, *The words of the days of the kings of Israel, or Judah*, it is meant the acts that were done in those days were the subject of those words; and in the Greek, which (in the Scripture) retaineth many Hebraisms, by the word of God is oftentimes meant, not that which is spoken by God, but concerning God and his government, that is to say, the doctrine of religion,[2] insomuch as it is all one to say *logos theou* and *theologia*; which is that doctrine which we usually call *divinity*, as is manifest by the places following: *Then Paul and Barnabas waxed bold, and said, it was necessary that the word of God should first have been spoken to you, but seeing you put it from you, and judge yourselves unworthy of everlasting life, lo, we turn to the Gentiles* (Acts 13:46). That which is here called the word of God was the doctrine of Christian religion, as it appears evidently by that which goes before. And where it is said to the Apostles by an angel, *Go stand and speak in the Temple, all the words of this life*

---

1 Hobbes gives a linguistic analysis of the phrase 'word of God' in order to deflate the idea to some extent.

2 'The word of God' can mean either the words God actually uttered, say, 'Let there be light' or words spoken about God, say, 'God created the heavens and the earth'. The latter is usually about his commandments or the doctrine of the Christian religion. See also 36.3.

(Acts 5:20), by the words of this life is meant the doctrine of the Gospel, as is evident by what they did in the Temple and is expressed in the last verse of the same chapter. *Daily in the Temple, and in every house, they ceased not to teach and preach Christ Jesus*, in which place it is manifest that Jesus Christ was the subject of this *word of life*, or (which is all one) the subject of the *words of this life eternal* that our Saviour offered them. So the word of God is called *the word of the Gospel* (Acts 15:7), because it containeth the doctrine of the kingdom of Christ, and the same word is called *the word of faith* (Romans 10:8-9), that is, as is there expressed, the doctrine of Christ come and raised from the dead. Also, *When any one* [223] *heareth the word of the kingdom* (Matt. 13:19), that is the doctrine of the kingdom taught by Christ. Again, the same word is said *to grow and to be multiplied* (Acts 12:24), which to understand of the evangelical doctrine is easy, but of the voice or speech of God, hard and strange. In the same sense the *doctrine of devils* signifieth not the words of any devil, but the doctrine of heathen men concerning *demons*,[1] and those phantasms[2] which they worshipped as gods. 1 Tim. 4:1.

3. Considering these two significations of the WORD OF GOD, as it is taken in Scripture, it is manifest in this latter sense (where it is taken for the doctrine of Christian religion) that the whole Scripture is the word of God, but in the former sense, not so. For example, though these words, *I am the Lord thy God*, etc., to the end of the Ten Commandments, were spoken by God to Moses, yet the preface, *God spake these words and said*, is to be understood for the words of him that wrote the holy history. The *word of God*, as it is taken for that which he hath spoken, is understood sometimes *properly*, sometimes *metaphorically*. *Properly*, as the words he hath spoken to his prophets; *metaphorically*, for his wisdom, power, and eternal decree, in making the world; in which sense, those fiats, *Let there be light, Let there be a firmament, Let us make man* (Gen. 1), etc. are the word of God.[3] And in the same sense it is said, *All things were made by it, and without it was nothing made that was made* (John 1:3) and *He upholdeth all things by the word of his power* (Heb.

1 See also 8.25, 12.16, 34.15, 34.18, 45.2.

2 See also 34.25, 44.1, 44.13, 44.16, 44.21, 45.2, 45.4, 45.8, 45.10, and 45.14.

3 God only metaphorically and not literally spoke the words of creation. He literally spoke to prophets.

1:3), that is, by the power of his word; that is, by his power; and *The worlds were framed by the word of God* (Heb. 11:3) and many other places to the same sense, as also amongst the Latins, the name of *fate*, which signifieth properly *the word spoken*, is taken in the same sense.

Secondly, for the effect of his word.

4. Secondly, for the effect of his word, that is to say, for the thing itself, which by his word is affirmed, commanded, threatened, or promised, as where Joseph is said to have been kept in prison, *till his word was come* (Psalm 105:19), that is, till that was come to pass which he had foretold to Pharoah's butler concerning his being restored to his office; for there, by *his word was come*, is meant the thing itself was come to pass (Gen. 40:13). So also, Elijah saith to God, *I have done all these thy words* (1 Kings 18:36) instead of *I have done all these things at thy word* or commandment. And, *Where is the word of the Lord* (Jer. 17:15) is put for *Where is the evil he threatened*. And, *There shall none of my words be prolonged any more* (Ezek. 12:28), by *words* are understood those *things* which God promised to his people. And in the New Testament, *heaven and earth shall pass away, but my words shall not pass away* (Matt. 24:35), that is, there is nothing that I have promised or foretold that shall not come to pass. And in this sense it is that St. John the Evangelist, and, I think, St. John only, calleth our Saviour himself as in the flesh *the Word of God, And the Word was made flesh* (John 1:14), that is to say, the word or promise that Christ should come into the world, *who in the beginning was with God*; that is to say, it
[224] was in the purpose of God the Father to send God the Son into the world to enlighten men in the way of eternal life; but it was not till then put in execution, and actually incarnate, so that our Saviour is there called the *Word*, not because he was the promise, but the thing promised. They that taking occasion from this place do commonly call him the Verb of God do but render the text more obscure. They might as well term him the Noun of God; for as by *noun*, so also by *verb*, men understand nothing but a part of speech, a voice, a sound, that neither affirms nor denies nor commands nor promiseth nor is any substance corporeal or spiritual, and therefore it cannot be said to be either God or man; whereas our Saviour is both. And this *Word* which St. John in his Gospel saith was with God is, in his first Epistle, called the *Word of life*

(1 John 1) and *the Eternal Life, which was with the Father* (1 John 1), so that he can be in no other sense called the *Word* than in that wherein he is called Eternal Life, that is, *he that hath procured us eternal life* by his coming in the flesh. So also the Apostle, speaking of Christ clothed in a garment dipped in blood, saith his name is *the Word of God* (Apocalypse [Revelation] 19:13), which is to be understood as if he had said his name had been *he that was come according to the purpose of God from the beginning, and according to his word and promises delivered by the prophets.* So that there is nothing here of the incarnation of a word, but of the incarnation of God the Son, therefore called *the Word,* because his incarnation was the performance of the promise; in like manner as the Holy Ghost is called *the Promise.* Acts 1:4. Luke 24:49.

Thirdly, for the words of reason and equity.

5. There are also places of the Scripture where by the *Word of God* is signified such words as are consonant to reason and equity, though spoken sometimes neither by prophet nor by a holy man. For Pharaoh Necho was an idolater, yet his words to the good King Josiah, in which he advised him by messengers not to oppose him in his march against Carchemish, are said to have proceeded from the mouth of God, and that Josiah, not hearkening to them, was slain in the battle, as is to be read 2 Chron. 35:21–23. It is true that as the same history is related in the first Book of Esdras,[1] not Pharaoh, but Jeremiah, spake these words to Josiah from the mouth of the Lord. But we are to give credit to the canonical Scripture whatsoever be written in the Apocrypha.

6. The *Word of God* is then also to be taken for the dictates of reason and equity, when the same is said in the Scriptures to be written in man's heart, as Ps. 37:31, Jer. 31:33, Deut. 30:11, 30:14, and many other like places.

Diverse acceptions of the word prophet.

7. The name of PROPHET signifieth in Scripture sometimes *prolocutor,* that is, he that speaketh from God to man,[2] or from man to God; and sometimes *predictor* or a foreteller of things to come; and sometimes one that speaketh incoherently, as men that are distracted. It is most frequently used in the sense speaking from God to the people. So Moses, Samuel, Elijah, Isaiah, Jeremiah, and others

---

1 This is an apocryphal book but is included in the Authorized (King James) Version of the Bible.

2 See also 31.3.

were *prophets*. And in this sense the high priest was a *prophet*; for he only went into the *sanctum sanctorum* to enquire of God and was to [225] declare his answer to the people. And therefore when Caiaphas said it was expedient that one man should die for the people, St. John (11:51) saith that *He spake not this of himself, but being high priest that year, he prophesied that one man should die for the nation.* Also they that in Christian congregations taught the people are said to prophesy (1 Cor. 14:13). In the like sense it is that God saith to Moses concerning Aaron, *He shall be thy spokesman to the people; and he shall be to thee a mouth, and thou shalt be to him instead of God* (Exod. 4:13), that which here is *spokesman* is (Exod. 7:1) interpreted prophet: *See*, saith God, *I have made thee a god to Pharaoh, and Aaron thy brother shall be thy prophet.* In the sense of speaking from man to God, Abraham is called a prophet where God in a dream speaketh to Abimelech in this manner, *Now therefore restore the man his wife, for he is a prophet, and shall pray for thee* (Gen. 20:7), whereby may be also gathered that the name of prophet may be given not unproperly to them that in Christian churches have a calling to say public prayers for the congregation. In the same sense, the prophets that came down from the high place or hill of god with a psaltery and a tabret [a small drum] and a pipe and a harp, Saul amongst them, are said to prophesy, in that they praised God in that manner publicly (1 Sam. 10:5–6, 10:10). In the like sense is Miriam called a prophetess (Exod. 15:20). So is it also to be taken where St. Paul saith, *Every man that prayeth or prophesieth with his head covered, etc., and every woman that prayeth or prophesieth with her head uncovered* (1 Cor. 11:4–5), for prophecy in that place signifieth no more but praising God in psalms and holy songs, which women might do in the church, though it were not lawful for them to speak to the congregation.[1] And in this signification it is that the poets of the heathen, that composed hymns and other sorts of poems in the honor of their gods, were called *vates* (prophets), as is well enough known by all that are versed in the books of the Gentiles, and as is evident where St. Paul saith of the Cretans that a prophet of their own said they were liars (Titus 1:12), not that St. Paul held their poets for prophets, but acknow-

1 Hobbes's linguistic analysis of 'prophet' is intended to deflate the pretensions of self-proclaimed prophets.

ledgeth that the word *prophet* was commonly used to signify them that celebrated the honour of God in verse.

8. When by prophecy is meant prediction or foretelling of future contingents, not only they were prophets who were God's spokesmen and foretold those things to others which God had foretold to them, but also all those impostors that pretend by the help familiar spirits or by superstitious divination of events past, from false causes, to foretell the like events in time to come; of which (as I have declared already in the twelfth Chapter of this discourse) there be many kinds who gain in the opinion of the common sort of men a greater reputation of prophecy by one casual event that may be but wrested to their purpose than can be lost again by never so many failings. Prophecy is not an art, nor, when it is taken for prediction, a constant vocation, but an extraordinary and temporary employment from God, most often of good men, but sometimes also of the wicked. The woman of [226] Endor, who is said to have had a familiar spirit and thereby to have raised a phantasm of Samuel and foretold Saul his death, was not therefore a prophetess; for neither had she any science whereby she could raise such a phantasm, nor does it appear that God commanded the raising of it, but only guided that imposture to be a means of Saul's terror and discouragement, and by consequent, of the discomfiture by which he fell. And for incoherent speech, it was amongst the Gentiles taken for one sort of prophecy, because the prophets of their oracles, intoxicated with a spirit or vapor from the cave of the Pythian Oracle at Delphi, were for the time really mad and spake like madmen; of whose loose words a sense might be made to fit any event, in such sort as all bodies are said to be made of *materia prima*. In the Scripture I find it also so taken in these words, *And the evil spirit came upon Saul, and he prophesied in the midst of the house* (1 Sam. 18:10).

Prediction of future contingents.

9. And although there be so many significations in Scripture of the word *prophet*, yet is that the most frequent in which it is taken for him to whom God speaketh immediately that which the prophet is to say from him to some other man or to the people. And hereupon a question may be asked, in what manner God speaketh to such a prophet. Can it, may some say, be properly said that God hath voice and language, when it cannot be properly said

The manner how God hath spoken to the prophets.

he hath a tongue or other organs as a man? The Prophet David argueth thus, *Shall he that made the eye, not see? or he that made the ear, not hear?* (Psalm 94:9). But this may be spoken, not, as usually, to signify God's nature, but to signify our intention to honour him.[1] For to *see* and *hear* are honourable attributes and may be given to God to declare as far as capacity can conceive his almighty power. But if it were to be taken in the strict and proper sense, one might argue from his making of all other parts of man's body that he had also the same use of them which we have; which would be many of them so uncomely as it would be the greatest contumely in the world to ascribe them to him. Therefore we are to interpret God's speaking to men immediately for that way, whatsoever it be, by which God makes them understand his will; and the ways whereby he doth this are many and to be sought only in the Holy Scripture, where though many times it be said that God spake to this and that person, without declaring in what manner, yet there be again many places that deliver also the signs by which they were to acknowledge his presence and commandment, and by these may be understood how he spake to many of the rest.

To the extraordinary prophets of the Old Testament he spake by dreams, or visions.

10. In what manner God spake to Adam and Eve and Cain and Noah is not expressed; nor how he spake to Abraham, till such time as he came out of his own country to Sichem in the land of Canaan, and then God is said to have *appeared* to him (Gen. 12:7). So there is one way whereby God made his presence manifest, that is, by an *apparition* or *vision*. And again, *the word of the Lord came to Abraham in a vision* (Gen. 15:1), that is to say, somewhat, as a sign of God's presence, appeared as God's messenger to speak to him. [227] Again, the Lord appeared to Abraham by an apparition of three angels (Gen. 18:1) and to Abimelech in a dream (Gen. 20:3), to Lot by an apparition of two angels (Gen. 19:1) and to Hagar by the apparition of one angel (Gen. 21:17) and to Abraham again by the apparition of a voice from heaven (Gen. 22:11), and to Isaac in the night (Gen. 26:24) (that is, in his sleep, or by dream), and to Jacob in a dream (Gen. 18:12), that is to say (as are the words of the text), *Jacob dreamed that he saw a ladder*, etc. And in a vision of

1 See also 31.28.

angels (Gen. 32:1) and to Moses in the apparition of a flame of fire out of the midst of a bush (Exod. 3:2), and after the time of Moses (where the manner how God spake immediately to man in the Old Testament is expressed) he spake always by a vision or by a dream, as to Gideon, Samuel, Eliah, Elisha, Isaiah, Ezekiel, and the rest of the prophets, and often in the New Testament, as to Joseph, to St. Peter, to St. Paul, and to St. John the Evangelist in the Apocalypse.

11. Only to Moses he spake in a more extraordinary manner in Mount Sinai and in the Tabernacle and to the high priest in the Tabernacle and in the *sanctum sanctorum* of the Temple. But Moses and after him the high priests were prophets of a more eminent place and degree in God's favour; and God himself in express words declareth that to other prophets he spake in dreams and visions, but to his servant Moses in such manner as a man speaketh to his friend. The words are these: *If there be a prophet among you, I the Lord will make myself known to him in a vision, and will speak unto him in a dream. My servant Moses is not so, who is faithful in all my house; with him I will speak mouth to mouth, even apparently, not in dark speeches; and the similitude of the Lord shall he behold* (Num. 21:6–8). And, *The Lord spake to Moses face to face, as a man speaketh to his friend* (Exod. 33:11).[1] And yet this speaking of God to Moses was by mediation of an angel or angels, as appears expressly, Acts 7:35 and 53, and Gal. 3:19, and was therefore a vision, though a more clear vision than was given to other prophets. And conformable hereunto, where God saith, *If there arise amongst you a prophet, or dreamer of dreams* (Deut. 13:1), the latter word is but the interpretation of the former. And, *Your sons and your daughters shall prophesy; your old men shall dream dreams, and your young men shall see visions* (Joel 2:28), where again, the word *prophesy* is expounded by *dream* and *vision*. And in the same manner it was that God spake to Solomon, promising him wisdom, riches, and honour; for the text saith, *And Solomon awoke, and behold it was a dream* (1 Kings 3:15), so that generally the prophets extraordinary in the Old Testament took notice of the word of God no otherwise than from their dreams or visions, that is to say, from the imaginations which they

---

1 This is contradicted at Exodus 33.20.

had in their sleep or in an ecstasy; which imaginations in every true prophet were supernatural, but in false prophets were either natural or feigned.

12. The same prophets were nevertheless said to speak by the
[228] spirit, as where the prophet, speaking of the Jews, saith, *They made their hearts hard as adamant, lest they should hear the law, and the words which the Lord of Hosts hath sent in his Spirit by the former prophets* (Zech. 7:12). By which it is manifest that speaking by the *spirit* or *inspiration* was not a particular manner of God's speaking, different from vision, when they that were said to speak by the Spirit were extraordinary prophets, such as for every new message were to have a particular commission or, which is all one, a new dream or vision.

To prophets of perpetual calling, and supreme, God spake in the Old Testament from the mercy-seat, in a manner not expressed in the Scripture.

13. Of prophets that were so by a perpetual calling in the Old Testament, some were *supreme* and some *subordinate*; supreme were first Moses and after him the high priests, every one for his time, as long the priesthood was royal, and after the people of the Jews had rejected God, that he should no more reign over them, those kings which submitted themselves to God's government were also his chief prophets, and the high priest's office became ministerial. And when God was to be consulted, they put on the holy vestments and enquired of the Lord as the king commanded them and were deprived of their office when the king thought fit. For King Saul commanded the burnt offering to be brought (1 Sam. 13:9); and he commands the priest to bring the Ark near him (1 Sam. 14:18); and, again, to let it alone, because he saw an advantage upon his enemies (1 Sam. 14:19). And in the same chapter Saul asketh counsel of God. In like manner King David, after his being anointed, though before he had possession of the kingdom, is said to *enquire of the Lord* whether he should fight against the Philistines at Keilah (1 Sam. 23:2); and David commandeth the priest to bring him the ephod, to enquire whether he should stay in Keilah or not (1 Sam. 23:10). And King Solomon took the priesthood from Abiathar (1 Kings 2:27), and gave it to Zadok (1 Kings 2:35). Therefore Moses and the high priests and the pious kings who enquired of God on all extraordinary occasions how they were to carry themselves or what event they were to have were all sovereign prophets. But in what manner God spake unto them is not

manifest. To say that when Moses went up to God in Mount Sinai it was a dream or vision, such as other prophets had, is contrary to that distinction which God made between Moses and other prophets (Num. 12:6–8). To say God spake or appeared as he is in his own nature is to deny his infiniteness, invisibility, incomprehensibility.[1] To say he spake by inspiration or infusion of the Holy Spirit, as the Holy Spirit signifieth the Deity, is to make Moses equal with Christ, in whom only the Godhead, as St. Paul speaketh, dwelleth bodily (Col. 2:9). And lastly, to say he spake by the Holy Spirit, as it signifieth the graces or gifts of the Holy Spirit, is to attribute nothing to him supernatural. For God disposeth men to piety, justice, mercy, truth, faith, and all manner of virtue, both moral and intellectual, by doctrine, example, and by several occasions, natural and ordinary.

14. And as these ways cannot be applied to God in his speaking to Moses at Mount Sinai, so also they cannot be applied to him in his speaking to the high priests from the mercy-seat. Therefore in [229]
what manner God spake to those sovereign prophets of the Old Testament, whose office it was to enquire of him, is not intelligible. In the time of the New Testament there was no sovereign prophet but our Saviour, who was both God that spake and the prophet to whom he spake.

To prophets of perpetual calling, but subordinate, God spake by the spirit.

15. To subordinate prophets of perpetual calling, I find not any place that proveth God spake to them supernaturally, but only in such manner as naturally he inclineth men to piety, to belief, to righteousness, and to other virtues all other Christian men. Which way, though it consist in constitution, instruction, education, and the occasions and invitements men have to Christian virtues; yet it is truly attributed to the operation of the Spirit of God or Holy Spirit, which we in our language call the Holy Ghost; for there is no good inclination that is not of the operation of God. But these operations are not always supernatural. When therefore a prophet is said to speak in the spirit or by the Spirit of God, we are to understand no more but that he speaks according to God's will, declared by the supreme prophet. For the most common acceptation of the word *spirit* is in the signification of a man's intention, mind, or disposition.

---

1 See also "A Review and Conclusion," 12.

16. In the time of Moses, there were seventy men besides himself that *prophesied* in the camp of the Israelites. In what manner God spake to them is declared in the eleventh Chapter of Numbers, verse 25: *The Lord came down in a cloud, and spake unto Moses, and took of the spirit that was upon him, and gave it to the seventy elders. And it came to pass, when the spirit rested upon them, they prophesied, and did not cease.* By which it is manifest, first, that their prophesying to the people was subservient and subordinate to the prophesying of Moses; for that God took of the spirit of Moses put upon them, so that they prophesied as Moses would have them; otherwise they had not been suffered to prophesy at all. For there was a complaint made against them to Moses (Num. 11:27), and Joshua would have Moses to have forbidden them; which he did not, but said to Joshua *Be not jealous in my behalf.* Secondly, that the Spirit of God in that place signifieth nothing but the mind and disposition to obey and assist Moses in the administration of the government. For if it were meant they had the substantial Spirit of God, that is, the divine nature, inspired into them, then they had it in no less manner than Christ himself, in whom only the Spirit of God dwelt bodily. It is meant therefore of the gift and grace of God that guided them to co-operate with Moses, from whom their spirit was derived. And it appeareth that they were such as Moses himself should appoint for elders and officers of the people (Num. 11:16), for the words are, *Gather unto me seventy men, whom thou knowest to be elders and officers of the people*, where, *thou knowest*, is the same with *thou appointest*, or *hast appointed to be such.* For we are told before that Moses, following the counsel of Jethro his father-in-law, did appoint judges and officers over the people such as [230] feared God (Exod. 18:24), and of these were those seventy whom God, by putting upon them Moses' spirit, inclined to aid Moses in the administration of the kingdom; and in this sense the spirit of God is said presently upon the anointing of David to have come upon David, and left Saul (1 Sam. 16:13–14), God giving his graces to him [whom] he chose to govern his people, and taking them away from him he rejected. So that by the spirit is meant inclination to God's service, and not any supernatural revelation.

God sometimes also

17. God spake also many times by the event of lots, which were ordered by such as he had put in authority over his people. So we

read that God manifested by the lots which Saul caused to be drawn the fault that Jonathan had committed in eating a honeycomb, contrary to the oath taken by the people (1 Sam. 14:43). And God divided the land of Canaan amongst the Israelites by the *lots that Joshua did cast before the Lord in Shiloh* (Josh. 18:10). In the same manner it seemeth to be that God discovered the crime of Achan (Josh. 7:16, &c.). And these are the ways whereby God declared his will in the Old Testament.

spake by lots.

18. All which ways he used also in the New Testament. To the Virgin Mary, by a vision of an angel; to Joseph, in a dream; again to Paul, in the way to Damascus in a vision of our Saviour; and to Peter in the vision of a sheet let down from heaven with divers sorts of flesh of clean and unclean beasts, and in prison by vision of an angel, and to all the Apostles and writers of the New Testament by the graces of his Spirit, and to the Apostles again at the choosing of Matthias in the place of Judas Iscariot by lot.

Every man ought to examine the probability of a pretended prophet's calling.

19. Seeing then all prophecy supposeth vision or dream (which two, when they be natural, are the same), or some especial gift of God so rarely observed in mankind as to be admired where observed, and seeing as well such gifts as the most extraordinary dreams and visions may proceed from God, not only by his supernatural and immediate, but also by his natural operation and by mediation of second causes, there is need of reason and judgement to discern between natural and supernatural gifts and between natural and supernatural visions or dreams. And consequently men had need to be very circumspect and wary in obeying the voice of man that, pretending himself to be a prophet, requires us to obey God in that way which he in God's name telleth us to be the way to happiness. For he that pretends to teach men the way of so great felicity pretends to govern them, that is to say, rule and reign over them; which is a thing that all men naturally desire and is therefore worthy to be suspected of ambition and imposture and consequently ought be examined and tried by every man before he yield them obedience, unless he have yielded it them already in the institution of a commonwealth, as when the prophet is the civil sovereign or by the civil sovereign authorized. And if this examination of prophets and spirits were not allowed to every one of the people, it had been to no purpose to set out the marks by

which every man might be able to distinguish between those
[231] whom they ought, and those whom they ought not to follow. Seeing therefore such marks are set out to know a prophet by (Deut. 13:1, &c.) and to know a spirit by (1 John 4:1 &c.), and seeing there is so much prophesying in the Old Testament and so much preaching in the New Testament against prophets and so much greater a number ordinarily of false prophets than of true, every one is to beware of obeying their directions at their own peril. And first, that there were many more false than true prophets appears by this, that when Ahab consulted four hundred prophets, they were all false impostors, but only one [true prophet] Micaiah (1 Kings 12).[1] And a little before the time of the Captivity the prophets were generally liars. *The prophets*, saith the Lord by Jeremiah (14:14), *prophesy lies in my name. I sent them not, neither have I commanded them, nor spake unto them; they prophesy to you a false vision, a thing of naught, and the deceit of their heart.* Insomuch as God commanded the people by the mouth of the prophet Jeremiah (23:16) not to obey them. *Thus saith the Lord of Hosts, hearken not unto the words of the prophets that prophesy to you. They make you vain: they speak a vision of their own heart, and not out of the mouth of the Lord.*

All prophecy but of the sovereign prophet is to be examined by every subject.

20. Seeing then there was in the time of the Old Testament such quarrels amongst the visionary prophets, one contesting with another, and asking, *When departed the spirit from me, to go to thee?* as between Micaiah and the rest of the four hundred, and such giving of the lie to one another, as in Jeremiah, 14:14, and such controversies in the New Testament this day amongst the spiritual prophets; every man then was, and now is, bound to make use of his natural reason to apply to all prophecy those rules which God hath given us to discern the true from the false.[2] Of which rules, in the Old Testament, one was conformable doctrine to that which Moses the sovereign prophet had taught them, and the other the miraculous power of foretelling what God would bring to pass, as I have already shown out of Deut. 13:1, etc. And in the New Testament there was but one only mark, and that was the preaching of this doctrine *that Jesus is the Christ*, that is, the King of

1 See also 32.7.
2 See also 32.7, 33.1 and 37.13.

the Jews, promised in the Old Testament. Whosoever denied that article, he was a false prophet, whatsoever miracles he might seem to work, and he that taught it was a true prophet. For St. John, speaking expressly of the means to examine spirits, whether they be of God or not, after he had told them that there would arise false prophets, saith thus, *Hereby know ye the Spirit of God. Every spirit that confesseth that Jesus Christ is come in the flesh, is of God* (1 John 4:2), that is, is approved and allowed as a prophet of God, not that he is a godly man or one of the elect for this that he confesseth, professeth, or preacheth Jesus to be the Christ, but for that he is a prophet avowed. For God sometimes speaketh by prophets whose persons he hath not accepted, as he did by Baalam, and as he foretold Saul of his death by the Witch of Endor. Again in the next verse, *Every spirit that confesseth not that Jesus Christ is come in the flesh, is not of Christ. And this is the spirit of Antichrist.* So that the rule is perfect on both sides; that he is a true prophet which [232] preacheth the Messiah already come in the person of Jesus, and he a false one that denieth him come and looketh for him in some future impostor that shall take upon him that honour falsely, whom the Apostle there properly calleth Antichrist. Every man therefore ought to consider who is the sovereign prophet, that is to say, who it is that is God's vicegerent on earth and hath next under God the authority of governing Christian men, and to observe for a rule that doctrine which in the name of God he hath commanded to be taught, and thereby to examine and try out the truth of those doctrines which pretended prophets, with miracle or without, shall at any time advance; and if they find it contrary to that rule, to do as they did that came to Moses and complained that there were some that prophesied in the camp whose authority so to do they doubted of, and leave to the sovereign, as they did to Moses, to uphold or to forbid them, as he should see cause, and if he disavow them, then no more to obey their voice, or if he approve them, then to obey them as men to whom God hath given a part of the spirit of their sovereign. For when Christian men take not their Christian sovereign for God's prophet, they must either take their own dreams for the prophecy they mean to be governed by and the tumour of their own hearts for the Spirit of God; or they must suffer themselves to be lead by some strange prince or by some of their fellow subjects that can bewitch them by slander of the government into rebellion, without other miracle to confirm their calling than sometimes an extraordinary success and impunity, and by this means destroying all laws, both divine and human, reduce all order, government, and society to the first chaos of violence and civil war.

[233]

# CHAPTER XXXVII

## OF MIRACLES, AND THEIR USE

A miracle is a work that causeth admiration.

1. By *miracles* are signified the admirable works of God: and therefore they are also called *wonders*. And because they are for the most part done for a signification of his commandment in such occasions as, without them, men are apt to doubt (following their private natural reasoning) what he hath commanded and what not, they are commonly, in Holy Scripture, called *signs*, in the same sense as they are called by the Latins *ostenta* and *portenta*, from showing and foresignifying that which the Almighty is about to bring to pass.[1]

And must therefore be rare, and whereof there is no natural cause known.

2. To understand therefore what is a miracle, we must first understand what works they are which men wonder at and call admirable. And there be but two things which make men wonder at any event: the one is if it be strange, that is to say, such as the like of it hath never or very rarely been produced; the other is if when it is produced, we cannot imagine it to have been done by natural means, but only by the immediate hand of God. But when we see some possible natural cause of it, how rarely soever the like has been done, or if the like have been often done, how impossible soever it be to imagine a natural means thereof, we no more wonder nor esteem it for a miracle.

3. Therefore, if a horse or cow should speak, it were a miracle, because both the thing is strange and the natural cause difficult to imagine; so also were it to see a strange deviation of nature in the production of some new shape of a living creature. But when a

1 Cf. 37.7.

man or other animal engenders his like, though we know no more how this is done than the other; yet because it is usual, it is no miracle. In like manner, if a man be metamorphosed into a stone or into a pillar, it is a miracle, because strange; but if a piece of wood be so changed, because we see it often it is no miracle and yet we know no more by what operation of God the one is brought to pass than the other.

4. The first rainbow that was seen in the world was a miracle, because the first, and consequently strange, and served for a sign from God, placed in heaven to assure his people there should be no more a universal destruction of the world by water.[1] But at this day, because they are frequent, they are not miracles, neither to them that know their natural causes nor to them who know them not. Again, there be many rare works produced by the art of man; yet when we know they are done, because thereby we know also the means how they are done, we count them not for miracles, because not wrought by the immediate hand of God, but by [234] mediation of human industry.

That which seemeth a miracle to one man may seem otherwise to another.

5. Furthermore, seeing admiration and wonder is consequent to the knowledge and experience wherewith men are endued, some more, some less; it followeth that the same thing may be a miracle to one and not to another. And thence it is that ignorant and superstitious men make great wonders of those works which other men, knowing to proceed from nature (which is not the immediate, but the ordinary work of God), admire not at all, as when eclipses of the sun and moon have been taken for supernatural works by the common people, when nevertheless there were others could from their natural causes have foretold the very hour they should arrive;[2] or, as when a man, by confederacy and secret intelligence, getting knowledge of the private actions of an ignorant, unwary man, thereby tells him what he has done in former time, it seems to him a miraculous thing; but amongst wise and

1 This is a nice example in part because the physics of the rainbow was figured out in the seventeenth century. Hobbes is trying to reconcile modern science and religion. In analogy with immediate and mediate revelation, there are immediate and mediate miracles. Noah experienced an immediate miracle. Those who believe that the story about Noah was a revelation of God accept a mediate miracle.

2 Hobbes wants both to be able to admit the existence of miracles and to discourage people from claiming to see them by exploiting their pride. People do not like to admit their ignorance.

cautelous [cautious] men, such miracles as those cannot easily be done.

The end of miracles. 6. Again, it belongeth to the nature of a miracle that it be wrought for the procuring of credit to God's messengers, ministers, and prophets, that thereby men may know they are called, sent, and employed by God, and thereby be the better inclined to obey them. And therefore, though the creation of the world and after that the destruction of all living creatures in the universal deluge, were admirable works; yet because they were not done to procure credit to any prophet or other minister of God, they use not to be called miracles. For how admirable soever any work be, the admiration consisteth not in that could be done, because men naturally believe the Almighty can do all things, but because he does it at the prayer or word of a man. But the works of God in Egypt by the hand of Moses were properly miracles, because they were done with intention to make the people of Israel believe that Moses came unto them, not out of any design of his own interest, but as sent from God. Therefore after God had commanded him to deliver the Israelites from the Egyptian bondage, when he said, *They will not believe me, but will say the Lord hath not appeared unto me* [Exod. 4:1], God gave him power to turn the rod he had in his hand into a serpent, and again to return it into a rod, and by putting his hand into his bosom, to make it leprous and again by pulling it out to make it whole, to make the children of Israel believe (as it is in verse 5) that the God of their fathers had appeared unto him. And if that were not enough, he gave him power to turn their waters into blood. And when he had done these miracles before the people, it is said (verse 41) that *they believed him.* (Exod. 4:1, etc.) Nevertheless, for fear of Pharaoh, they durst [dared] not yet obey him. Therefore the other works which were done to plague Pharaoh and the Egyptians tended all to make the Israelites believe in Moses, and were properly miracles. In like manner if we consider all the miracles done by the hand of Moses and all the rest of the prophets till the Captivity, and those of our Saviour and his Apostles afterwards, we shall find their end was always to beget
[235] or confirm belief that they came not of their own motion, but were sent by God. We may further observe in Scripture that the end of miracles was to beget belief, not universally in all men, elect

and reprobate, but in the elect only, that is to say, in such as God had determined should become his subjects.[1] For those miraculous plagues of Egypt had not for end the conversion of Pharaoh; for God had told Moses before that he would harden the heart of Pharaoh, that he should not let the people go; and when he let them go at last, not the miracles persuaded him, but the plagues forced him to it. So also of our Saviour it is written that he wrought not many miracles in his own country, because of their unbelief; and instead of, *He wrought not many*, it is, *He could work none* (Mark 6:5). It was not because he wanted power; which, to say, were blasphemy against God, nor that the end of miracles was not to convert incredulous men to Christ; for the end of all the miracles of Moses, of the prophets, of our Saviour and of his Apostles was to add men to the Church; but it was because the end of their miracles was to add to the Church, not all men, but such as should be saved, that is to say, such as God had elected. Seeing therefore our Saviour was sent from his Father, he could not use his power in the conversion of those whom his Father had rejected. They that, expounding this place of St. Mark, say that this word, *He could not*, is put for, *He would not*, do it without example in the Greek tongue (where *would not* is put sometimes for *could not*, in things inanimate that have no will, but *could not*, for *would not*, never), and thereby lay a stumbling block before weak Christians, as if Christ could do no miracles but amongst the credulous.

The definition of a miracle.

7. From that which I have here set down of the nature and use of a miracle, we may define it thus: *a* MIRACLE *is a work of God (besides his operation by the way of nature, ordained in the Creation) done for the making manifest to his elect the mission of an extraordinary minister for their salvation.*[2]

8. And from this definition, we may infer: first, that in all miracles the work done is not the effect of any virtue in the prophet, because it is the effect of the immediate hand of God; that is to say, God hath done it, without using the prophet therein as a subordinate cause.

---

1 This remark is related to the Protestant debate about whether Jesus died for all humans or only for the elect. The Bible says that he died for all. But if this were taken literally, then since not all are saved, some of God's work would be ineffective. So Calvinists, like Hobbes, held that Jesus died only for the elect.

2 Cf. 37.1.

9. Secondly, that no devil, angel, or other created spirit can do a miracle. For it must either be by virtue of some natural science or by incantation, that is, virtue of words. For if the enchanters do it by their own power independent, there is some power that proceedeth not from God, which all men deny, and if they do it by power given them, then is the work not from the immediate hand of God, but natural, and consequently no miracle.

10. There be some texts of Scripture that seem to attribute the
power of working wonders, equal to some of those immediate
miracles wrought by God himself, to certain arts of magic and
incantation. As, for example, when we read that after the rod of
[236] Moses being cast on the ground became a serpent, *the magicians of*
Exod. 7:11 *Egypt did the like by their enchantments*, and that after Moses had
turned the waters of the Egyptian streams, rivers, ponds, and pools
of water into blood, *the magicians of Egypt did so likewise, with their*
Exod. 7:22. *enchantments*, and that after Moses had by the power of God
brought frogs upon the land, *the magicians also did so with their*
Exod. 8:7. *enchantments, and brought up frogs upon the land of Egypt*, will not
man be apt to attribute miracles to enchantments, that is to say, to the efficacy of the sound of words, and think the same very well proved out of this and other such places? And yet there is no place of Scripture that telleth us what an enchantment is. If therefore enchantment be not, as many think it, a working of strange effects by spells and words, but imposture and delusion wrought by ordinary means and so far from supernatural, as the impostors need not the study so much of natural causes, but the ordinary ignorance, stupidity, and superstition of mankind, to do them, those texts that seem to countenance the power of magic, witchcraft, and enchantment must needs have another sense than at first sight they seem to bear.

That men are apt to be deceived by false miracles.

11. For it is evident enough that words have no effect but on those that understand them, and then they have no other but to signify the intentions or passions of them that speak, and thereby produce hope, fear, or other passions or conceptions in the hearer. Therefore when a rod seemeth a serpent or the waters blood or any other miracle seemeth done by enchantment, if it be not to the edification of God's people, not the rod nor the water nor any other thing is enchanted, that is to say, wrought upon by the

words, but the spectator. So that all the miracle consisteth in this, that the enchanter has deceived a man; which is no miracle, but a very easy matter to do.

12. For such is the ignorance and aptitude to error generally of all men, but especially of them that have not much knowledge of natural causes and of the nature and interests of men, as by innumerable and easy tricks to be abused. What opinion of miraculous power, before it was known there was a science of the course of the stars, might a man have gained that should have told the people, this hour, or day, the sun should be darkened? A juggler, by the handling of his goblets and other trinkets, if it were not now ordinarily practised, would be thought to do his wonders by the power at least of the Devil. A man that hath practised to speak by drawing in of his breath (which kind of men in ancient time were called *ventriloqui*) and so make the weakness of his voice seem to proceed, not from the weak impulsion of the organs of speech, but from distance of place, is able to make very many men believe it is a voice from heaven, whatsoever he please to tell them. And for a crafty man that hath enquired into the secrets and familiar confessions that one man ordinarily maketh to another of his actions and adventures past, to tell them him again is no hard matter, and yet there be many that by such means as that obtain the reputation of being conjurers. But it is too long a business to reckon up the sev- [237] eral sorts of those men which the Greeks called *Thaumaturgi*, that is to say, workers of things wonderful; and yet these do all they do by their own single dexterity. But if we look upon the impostures wrought by confederacy, there is nothing how impossible soever to be done that is impossible to be believed. For two men conspiring, one to seem lame, the other to cure him with a charm, will deceive many; but many conspiring, one to seem lame, another so to cure him, and all the rest to bear witness, will deceive many more.

Cautions against the imposture of miracles.

13. In this aptitude of mankind to give too hasty belief to pretended miracles, there can be no better nor I think any other caution than that which God hath prescribed, first by Moses (as I have said before in the precedent chapter), in the beginning of the thirteenth and end of the eighteenth of Deut.; that we take not any for prophets that teach any other religion than that which God's

lieutenant, which at that time was Moses, hath established, nor any, though he teach the same religion, whose prediction we do not see come to pass.[1] Moses therefore in his time, and Aaron and his successors in their times, and the sovereign governor of God's people next under God himself, that is to say, the head of the Church in all times, are to be consulted what doctrine he hath established before we give credit to a pretended miracle or prophet. And when that is done, the thing they pretend to be a miracle, we must both see it done and use all means possible to consider whether it be really done, and not only so, but whether it be such as no man can do the like by his natural power, but that it requires the immediate hand of God. And in this also we must have recourse to God's lieutenant, to whom in all doubtful cases we have submitted our private judgements. For example, if a man pretend that after certain words spoken over a piece of bread, that presently God hath made it not bread, but a god or a man or both, and nevertheless it looketh still as like bread as ever it did, there is no reason for any man to think it really done,[2] nor consequently to fear him till he enquire of God by his vicar or lieutenant whether it be done or not. If he say not, then followeth that which Moses, saith *he hath spoken it presumptuously; thou shalt not fear him* (Deut. 18:22). If he say it is done, then he is not to contradict it. So also if we see not, but only hear tell of a miracle, we are to consult the lawful Church, that is to say, the lawful head thereof, how far we are to give credit to the relators of it. And this is chiefly the case of men that in these days live under Christian sovereigns. For in these times I do not know one man that ever saw any such wondrous work, done by the charm or at the word or prayer of a man, that a man endued but with a mediocrity of reason would think supernatural; and the question is no more whether what we see done be a miracle, whether the miracle we hear or read of were a real work and not the act of a tongue or pen, but in plain terms, whether the report be true or a lie. In which question we are not every one to make our own private reason or conscience, but the public reason, that is, the reason of God's supreme lieutenant, judge; and indeed

---

1 See also 32.7, 33.1 and 36.20.

2 Hobbes is criticizing the Roman Catholic doctrine of transubstantiation, according to which bread and wine become the body and blood of Jesus at the consecration of the Mass. See also 44.11.

we have made him judge already, if we have given him a sovereign power to do all that is necessary for our peace and defense. A private man has always the liberty (because thought is free) to believe or not believe in his heart those acts that have been given out for miracles, according as he shall see what benefit can accrue, by men's belief, to those that pretend or countenance them and thereby conjecture whether they be miracles or lies. But when it comes to confession of that faith, the private reason must submit to the public, that is to say, to God's lieutenant. But who is this lieutenant of God, and head of the Church, shall be considered in its proper place hereafter. [238]

## CHAPTER XXXVIII

## OF THE SIGNIFICATION IN SCRIPTURE OF ETERNAL LIFE, HELL, SALVATION, THE WORLD TO COME, AND REDEMPTION

1. The maintenance of civil society depending on justice, and justice on the power of life and death, and other less rewards and punishments residing in them that have the sovereignty of the commonwealth, it is impossible a commonwealth should stand where any other than the sovereign hath a power of giving greater rewards than life, and of inflicting greater punishments than death. Now seeing *eternal life* is a greater reward than the *life present*, and *eternal torment* a greater punishment than the *death of nature*, it is a thing worthy to be well considered of all men that desire by obeying authority to avoid the calamities of confusion and civil war, what is meant in Holy Scripture by *life eternal* and *torment eternal*, and for what offences and against whom committed, men are to be *eternally tormented*, and for what actions they are to obtain *eternal life*.

The place of Adam's eternity if he had not sinned had

2. And first we find that Adam was created in such a condition of life as, had he not broken the commandment of God, he had enjoyed it in the Paradise of Eden everlastingly. For there was the *tree of life*, whereof he was so long allowed to eat as he should for-

been the terrestrial paradise.

Gen. 3:22.

bear to eat of the tree of knowledge of good and evil, which was not allowed him. And therefore as soon as he had eaten of it, God thrust him out of Paradise, *lest he should put forth his hand, and take also of the tree of life, and live forever.*[1] By which it seemeth to me (with submission nevertheless both in this and in all questions whereof the determination dependeth on the Scriptures to the interpretation of the Bible authorized by the commonwealth whose subject I am) that Adam, if he had not sinned, had had an eternal life on earth, and that mortality entered upon himself and his posterity by his first sin. Not that actual death then entered, for Adam then could never have had children, whereas he lived long after and saw a numerous posterity ere he died. But where it is said, *In the day that thou eatest thereof, thou shalt surely die*, it must needs be meant of his mortality and certitude of death. Seeing then eternal life was lost by Adam's forfeiture, in committing sin, he that should cancel that forefeiture was to recover thereby that
[239] life again. Now Jesus Christ hath satisfied for the sins of all that believe in him[2] and therefore recovered to all believers that ETERNAL LIFE which was lost by the sin of Adam. And in this sense it is that the comparison of St. Paul holdeth: *As by the offence of one, judgement came upon all men to condemnation; even so by the righteousness of one, the free gift came upon all men to justification of life* (Romans 5:18-19). Which is again more perspicuously delivered in these words, *For since by man came death, by man came also the resurrection of the dead. For as in Adam all die, even so in Christ shall all be made alive* (Corinthians 15:21-22).

Texts concerning the place of life eternal for believers.

3. Concerning the place wherein men shall enjoy that eternal life which Christ hath obtained for them, the texts next before alleged seem to make it on earth.[3] For if, as in Adam, all die, that is, have forfeited paradise and eternal life on earth, even so in Christ all shall be made alive, then all men shall be made to live on earth; for else the comparison were not proper. Hereunto seemeth to agree that of the Psalmist, *Upon Zion God commanded the blessing, even life for evermore* (Psalm 133:3); for Zion is in Jerusalem upon

1 See also 44.14.

2 Hobbes holds the Calvinist view that Jesus died only for the elect. He is not moved by the quotations in the rest of the paragraph. See also 37.6-7, 41.8, and 44.29.

3 It is no longer unusual for Christian theologians to hold that heaven will be on earth.

earth, as also that of St. John, *To him that overcometh I will give to eat of the tree of life, which is in the midst of the Paradise of God* (Rev. 2:7). This was the tree of Adam's eternal life; but his life was to have been on earth. The same seemeth to be confirmed again by St. John, where he saith, *I John saw the holy city, new Jerusalem, coming down from God out of heaven, prepared as a bride adorned for her husband* (Rev. 21:2),[1] and again, verse 10, to the same effect, as if he should say, the new Jerusalem, the Paradise of God, at the coming again of Christ, should come down to God's people from heaven, and not they go up to it from earth. And this differs nothing from that which the two men in white clothing (that is, the two angels) said to the Apostles that were looking upon Christ ascending: *This same Jesus, who is taken up from you into heaven, shall so come, as you have seen him go up into heaven* (Acts 1:1). Which soundeth as if they had said he should come down to govern them under his Father eternally here and not take them up to govern them in heaven and is conformable to the restoration of the kingdom of God, instituted under Moses, which was a political government of the Jews on earth. Again, that saying of our Saviour, *that in the resurrection they neither marry, nor are given in marriage, but are as the angels of God in heaven* (Matt. 22:30) is a description of an eternal life, resembling that which we lost in Adam in the point of marriage. For seeing Adam and Eve, if they had not sinned, had lived on earth eternally in their individual persons, it is manifest they should not continually have procreated their kind. For if immortals should have generated, as mankind doth now, the earth in a small time would not have been able to afford them place to stand on. The Jews that asked our Saviour the question, whose wife the woman that had married many brothers should be in the resurrection, knew not what were the consequences of life eternal; and therefore our Savior puts them in mind of this consequence of immortality, that there shall be no generation and consequently no marriage, no more than there is marriage or generation among the angels. The comparison between that eternal life which Adam lost and our Saviour by his victory over death hath recovered holdeth [240]
also in this, that as Adam lost eternal life by his sin, and yet lived after it for a time, so the faithful Christian hath recovered eternal

1 Since the New Jerusalem is descending from heaven, it must be coming to earth.

life by Christ's passion, though he die a natural death and remain dead for a time, namely, till the resurrection. For as death is reckoned from the condemnation of Adam, not from the execution, so life is reckoned from the absolution, not from the resurrection of them that are elected in Christ.

Ascension into heaven.

4. That the place wherein men are to live eternally after the resurrection is the heavens, meaning by heaven those parts of the world which are the most remote from earth, as where the stars are or above the stars, in another higher heaven called *coelum empyreum* (whereof there is no mention in Scripture, nor ground in reason), is not easily to be drawn from any text that I can find. By the Kingdom of Heaven is meant the kingdom of the King that dwelleth in heaven, and his kingdom was the people of Israel, whom he ruled by the prophets, his lieutenants; first Moses, and after him Eleazar, and the sovereign priests, till in the days of Samuel they rebelled and would have a mortal man for their king after the manner of other nations. And when our Saviour Christ by the preaching of his ministers shall have persuaded the Jews to return and called the Gentiles to his obedience, then shall there be a new king of heaven, because our King shall then be God, whose *throne* is heaven, without any necessity evident in the Scripture that man shall ascend to his happiness any higher than God's *footstool* the earth. On the contrary, we find written that *no man hath ascended into heaven, but he that came down from heaven, even the Son of Man, that is in heaven* (John 3:13). Where I observe, by the way, that these words are not, as those which go immediately before, the words of our Saviour, but of St. John himself; for Christ was then not in heaven, but upon the earth. The like is said of David (Acts 2:34) where St. Peter, to prove the Ascension of Christ, using the words of the Psalmist, *Thou wilt not leave my soul in hell, nor suffer thine Holy One to see corruption* (Psalm 16:10), saith they were spoken, not of David, but of Christ, and to prove it, addeth this reason, *For David is not ascended into heaven.* But to this a man may easily answer and say that, though their bodies were not to ascend till the general day of judgement; yet their souls were in heaven as soon as they were departed from their bodies, which also seemeth to be confirmed by the words of our Saviour, who, proving the resurrection out of the words of Moses, saith thus, *That the dead are*

*raised, even Moses shewed at the bush, when he calleth the Lord, the God of Abraham, and the God of Isaac, and the God of Jacob. For he is not a God of the dead, but of the living; for they all live to him* (Luke 20:37–38). But if these words be to be understood only of the immortality of the soul, they prove not at all that which our Saviour intended to prove, which was the resurrection of the body, that is to say, the immortality of the man. Therefore our Saviour meaneth that those patriarchs were immortal, not by a property consequent to the essence and nature of mankind, but by the will of God, that was pleased of his mere grace to bestow *eternal life* upon the faithful. And though at that time the patriarchs and many other faithful [241] men were *dead*; yet as it is in the text, they *lived to God*; that is, they were written in the Book of Life with them that were absolved of their sins and ordained to life eternal at the resurrection. That the soul of man is in its own nature eternal and a living creature independent on the body, or that any mere man is immortal, otherwise than by the resurrection in the last day, except Enos and Elias, is a doctrine not apparent in Scripture. The whole fourteenth Chapter of Job, which is the speech not of his friends, but of himself, is a complaint of this mortality of nature, and yet no contradiction of the immortality at the resurrection.[1] *There is hope of a tree*, saith he, *if it be cast down. Though the root thereof wax old, and the stock thereof die in the ground, yet when it scenteth the water it will bud, and bring forth boughs like a plant. But man dieth, and wasteth away, yea, man giveth up the ghost, and where is he?* [Job 14:7]. And, verse 12, *man lieth down, riseth not, till the heavens be no more.* But when is it that the heavens shall be no more? St. Peter tells us that it is at the general resurrection. For in his second Epistle, third Chapter, verse 7, he saith that *the heavens and the earth that are now, are reserved unto fire against the day of judgement and perdition of ungodly men*, and, verse 12, *looking for and hasting to the coming of God, wherein the heavens shall be on fire, and shall be dissolved, and the elements shall melt with fervent heat. Nevertheless, we according to the promise look for new heavens and a new earth, wherein dwelleth righteousness.* Therefore where

1 Hobbes is right in holding that there is no doctrine of the immortality of the soul in the Book of Job. There is also no idea of good people going to heaven after death. These doctrines came into the religion of Israel after the Babylonian Captivity. See also 44.15 and 44.24–5.

Job saith, *man riseth not till the heavens be no more*, it is all one, as if he had said the immortal life (and *soul* and *life* in the Scripture do usually signify the same thing) beginneth not in man till the resurrection and day of judgement and hath for cause, not his specifical nature and generation, but the promise. For St. Peter says not, *We look for new heavens, and a new earth*, but *from promise.*

5. Lastly, seeing it hath been already proved out of diverse evident places of Scripture, in the thirty-fifth chapter of this book, that the kingdom of God is a civil commonwealth, where God himself is sovereign, by virtue first of the *Old*, and since of the *New*, Covenant, wherein he reigneth by his vicar or lieutenant; the same places do therefore also prove that after the coming again of our Saviour in his majesty and glory to reign actually and eternally, the kingdom of God is to be on earth.[1] But because this doctrine, though proved out of places of Scripture not few nor obscure, will appear to most men a novelty, I do but propound it, maintaining nothing in this or any other paradox of religion, but attending the end of that dispute of the sword concerning the authority (not yet amongst my countrymen decided), by which all sorts of doctrine are to be approved or rejected, and whose commands, both in speech and writing, whatsoever be the opinions of private men, must by all men that mean to be protected by their laws, be obeyed. For the points of doctrine concerning the king-
[242] dom of God have so great influence on the kingdom of man as not to be determined but by them that under God have the sovereign power.

The place after judgment of those who were never in the kingdom of God or having been in are case out.

6. As the kingdom of God and eternal life, so also God's enemies and their torments after judgement appear by the Scripture to have their place on earth. The name of the place where all men remain till the resurrection, that were either buried or swallowed up of the earth, is usually called in Scripture by words that signify *under ground*, which the Latins read generally *infernus* and *inferi*, and the Greeks *hades* (that is to say, a place where men cannot see) and containeth as well the grave as any other deeper place. But for the place of the damned after the resurrection, it is not determined, neither in the Old nor New Testament, by any note of situation, but only by the company: as that it shall be where such wicked

1 See also 35.11 and 38.17.

men were, as God in former times in extraordinary and miraculous manner had destroyed from off the face of the earth (as for example, that they are in *Inferno*, in *Tartarus*, or in the bottomless pit, because Corah, Dathan, and Abiram were swallowed up alive into the earth). Not that the writers of the Scripture would have us believe there could be in the globe of the earth, which is not only finite, but also, compared to the height of the stars, of no considerable magnitude, a pit without a bottom, that is, a hole of infinite depth, such as the Greeks in their *demonology* (that is to say in their doctrine concerning *demons*), and after them the Romans, called *Tartarus*; of which Virgil says, *Bis patet in praeceps, tantum tenditque sub umbras, Quantus ad aethereum coeli suspectus Olympum [It opens and extends beneath the shades twice as far as its ascent to the aetherial height of heaven (Aeneid VI. 578-79)]*; for that is a thing the proportion of earth to heaven cannot bear,[1] but that we should believe them there, indefinitely, where those men are, on whom God inflicted that exemplary punishment. Tartarus.

7. Again, because those mighty men of the earth that lived in the time of Noah before the flood (which the Greeks called *heroes* and the Scripture *giants*, and both say were begotten by copulation of the children of God with the children of men), were for their wicked life destroyed by the general deluge, the place of the damned is therefore also sometimes marked out by the company of those deceased giants, as Proverbs 21:16, *The man that wandereth out of the way of understanding shall remain in the congregation of the giants*, and Job 26:5, *Behold the giants groan under water, and they that dwell with them*, here the place of the damned is under the water. And Isaiah 14:9: *Hell is troubled how to meet thee* (that is, the King of Babylon) *and will displace the giants for thee*; and here again the place of the damned, if the sense be literal, is to be under water. The congregation of giants.

8. Thirdly, because the cities of Sodom and Gomorrah, by the extraordinary wrath of God, were consumed for their wickedness with fire and brimstone and together with them the country about made a stinking bituminous lake, the place of the damned is sometimes expressed by fire and a fiery lake, as in the Apocalypse Lake of fire.

---

1 Hobbes believes that many importations from pagan religions into Christianity corrupted it (44.3 and 45.33). He points out an absurdity in Virgil's conception of hell.

[Rev.] 21:8, *But the timorous, incredulous, and abominable, and murder-*
[243] *ers, and whoremongers, and sorcerers, and idolaters, and all liars, shall have their part in the lake that burneth with fire and brimstone; which is the second death.* So that it is manifest that hell fire, which is here expressed by metaphor, from the real fire of Sodom, signifieth not any certain kind or place of torment, but is to be taken indefinitely for destruction, as it is in the 20 chapter at the fourteenth verse, where it is said that *Death and hell were cast into the lake of fire*, that is to say, were abolished and destroyed, as if after the day of judgement there shall be no more dying, nor no more going into hell; that is, no more going to Hades (from which word perhaps our word hell is derived), which is the same with no more dying.

Utter darkness.

9. Fourthly, from the plague of darkness inflicted on the Egyptians, of which it is written, *They saw not one another, neither rose any man from his place for three days; but all the children of Israel had light in their dwellings* (Exod. 10:23); the place of the wicked after judgement is called *utter darkness*, or, as it is in the original, *darkness without.* And so it is expressed where the king commandeth his servants, *to bind hand and foot the man that had not on his wedding garment and to cast him into, eis to skotos to ezoteron* eis, *into external darkness* (Matt. 22:13) or *darkness without*, which, though translated *utter darkness*, does not signify how great, but *where* that darkness is to be, namely, *without the habitation* of God's elect.

Gehenna and Tophet.

10. Lastly, whereas there was a place near Jerusalem called the Valley of the Children of Hinnon in a part whereof called *Tophet* the Jews had committed most grievous idolatry, sacrificing their children to the idol Moloch, and wherein also God had afflicted his enemies with most grievous punishments and wherein Josiah had burnt the priests of Moloch upon their own altars, as appeareth at large in 2 Kings, Chapter 23, the place served afterwards to receive the filth and garbage which was carried thither out of the city; and there used to be fires made, from time to time, to purify the air and take away the stench of carrion. From this abominable place, the Jews used ever after to call the place of the damned by the name of *Gehenna* or Valley of Hinnon. And this *Gehenna* is that word which is usually now translated HELL, and from the fires from time to time there burning, we have the notion of *everlasting* and *unquenchable fire*.

11. Seeing now there is none that so interprets the Scripture as that after the day of judgement the wicked are all eternally to be punished in the Valley of Hinnon, or that they shall so rise again as to be ever after underground or underwater, or that after the resurrection they shall no more see one another, nor stir from one place to another; it followeth, methinks, very necessarily, that which is thus said concerning hell fire is spoken metaphorically and that therefore there is a proper sense to be enquired after (for of all metaphors there is some real ground, that may be expressed in proper words), both of the *place of hell*, and the nature of *hellish torments* and *tormenters*.

Of the literal sense of the Scripture concerning hell.

12. And first for the tormenters, we have their nature and properties exactly and properly delivered by the names of *the enemy* or Satan; the Accuser or *Diabolus*; the Destroyer, or *Abaddon*. Which significant names, Satan, Devil, *Abaddon*, set not forth to us any individual person, as proper names use to do, but only an office or quality and are therefore appellatives; which ought not to have been left untranslated,[1] as they are in the Latin and modern Bibles, because thereby they seem to be the proper names of *demons*, and men are more easily seduced to believe the doctrine of devils, which at that time was the religion of the Gentiles, and contrary to that of Moses and of Christ.

[244]

Satan, Devil, not proper names, but appellatives.

13. And because by the Enemy, the Accuser, and Destroyer is meant the enemy of them that shall be in the kingdom of God, therefore if the kingdom of God after the resurrection be upon the earth (as in the former chapter I have shown by Scripture it seems to be), the enemy and his kingdom must be on earth also. For so also was it in the time before the Jews had deposed God. For God's kingdom was in Palestine, and the nations round about were the kingdoms of the Enemy, and consequently by *Satan* is meant any earthly enemy of the Church.

14. The torments of hell are expressed sometimes by *weeping and gnashing of teeth*, as Matt. 8:12; sometimes by the *worm of conscience*, as Isaiah, 66:24 and Mark 9:44, 9:46, 9:48; sometimes by fire,

Torments of hell.

1 Hobbes is right about the word 'satan', which is a common noun that means something like the accuser. It should not be translated, as it usually is, as a proper noun ('Satan'). Also the identification of 'Satan' with the serpent in the Garden of Eden comes relatively late in the history of the Hebrew Bible. See also 42.24, 44.2, 44.27, and 45.7.

as in the place now quoted, *where the worm dieth not, and the fire is not quenched*, and many places besides; sometimes by *shame, and contempt*, as, *And many of them that sleep in the dust of the earth shall awake; some to everlasting life; and some to shame, and everlasting contempt* (Daniel 12:2). All which places design metaphorically a grief and discontent of mind from the sight of that eternal felicity in others which they themselves through their own incredulity and disobedience have lost. And because such felicity in others is not sensible but by comparison with their own actual miseries; it followeth that they are to suffer such bodily pains and calamities as are incident to those who not only live under evil and cruel governors, but have also for enemy the eternal king of the saints, God Almighty. And amongst these bodily pains is to be reckoned also to every one of the wicked a second death.[1] For though the Scripture be clear for a universal resurrection; yet we do not read that to any of the reprobate is promised an eternal life. For whereas St. Paul, to the question concerning what bodies men shall rise with again, saith that *the body is sown in corruption, and is raised in incorruption; it is sown in dishonour, it is raised in glory; it is sown in weakness, it is raised in power* (1 Cor. 15:42-43). Glory and power cannot be applied to the bodies of the wicked; nor can the name of *second death* be applied to those that can never die but once. And although in metaphorical speech a calamitous life everlasting may be called an everlasting death, yet it cannot well be understood of
[245] a *second death*. The fire prepared for the wicked is an everlasting fire; that is to say, the estate wherein no man can be without torture, both of body and mind, after the resurrection, shall endure for ever; and in that sense the fire shall be unquenchable and the torments everlasting; but it cannot thence be inferred that he who shall be cast into that fire or be tormented with those torments shall endure and resist them so as be eternally burnt and tortured, and yet never be destroyed nor die. And though there be many places that affirm everlasting fire and torments into which men may be cast successively one after another for ever;[2] yet I find

1 Hobbes wants to take 'second death' literally, just as he took 'kingdom of God' literally. This allows him to offer the relatively merciful doctrine that the wicked suffer for a finite period of time.

2 Hobbes's idea that the fires of hell are eternal but not the suffering of any one person is clever. His idea that an infinite number of wicked people will keep the fires

none that affirm there shall be an eternal life therein of any individual person, but to the contrary, an everlasting death, which is the second death: For *after death and the grave shall have delivered up the dead which were in them, and every man be judged according to his works; death and the grave shall also be cast into the lake of fire. This is the second death.* Whereby it is evident that there is to be a second death of every one that shall be condemned at the day judgement, after which he shall die no more.

Apoc. [Revelation] 20:13-14.

The joys of life eternal and salvation, the same thing.

15. The joys of life eternal are in Scripture comprehended all under the name of SALVATION or *being saved*. To be saved is to be secured, either respectively against special evils or absolutely against all evil, comprehending want, sickness, and death itself. And because man was created in a condition immortal, not subject to corruption, and consequently to nothing that tendeth to the dissolution of his nature, and fell from that happiness by the sin of Adam; it followeth that to be *saved* from sin is to be saved from all the evil and calamities that sin hath brought upon us. And therefore in the Holy Scripture, remission of sin and salvation from death and misery is the same thing,[1] as it appears by the words of our Saviour, who, having cured a man sick of the palsy, by saying, *Son be of good cheer thy sins be forgiven thee* (Matt. 9:2), and knowing that the scribes took for blasphemy that a man should pretend to forgive sins, asked them (verse 5) *whether it were easier to say, Thy sins be forgiven thee, or, Arise and walk*, signifying thereby that it was all one, as to the saving of the sick, to say, *Thy sins are forgiven*, and *Arise and walk*, and that he used that form of speech only to show he had power to forgive sins. And it is besides evident in reason that since death and misery were the punishments of sin, the discharge of sin must also be a discharge of death and misery, that is to say, salvation absolute, such as the faithful are to enjoy after the day of judgement, by the power and favour of Jesus Christ, who that cause is called our Saviour.

Salvation from sin and from misery, all one.

16. Concerning particular salvations, such as are understood, *as*

---

going was unfortunate, and he did not espouse this idea in the Latin version. See also 44.26.

1 The civil state is the saviour for human beings because it literally saves humans from the death and misery they would otherwise meet in the state of nature. Those nations of the twenty-first century known as welfare states are especially good examples of secular saviours since they protect people from birth until death.

*the Lord liveth that saveth Israel* (1 Sam. 14:29), that is, from their temporary enemies, and, *Thou art my Saviour, thou savest me from violence* (2 Sam. 22:4) and, *God gave the Israelites a Saviour, and so they were delivered from the hand of the Assyrians* (2 Kings 13:5), and
[246] the like, I need say nothing, there being neither difficulty nor interest to corrupt the interpretation of texts of that kind.

The place of eternal salvation.

17. But concerning the general salvation, because it must be in the kingdom of heaven, there is great difficulty concerning the place. On one side, by *kingdom*, which is an estate ordained by men for their perpetual security against enemies and want, it seemeth that this salvation should be on earth.[1] For by salvation is set forth unto us a glorious reign of our king by conquest, not a safety by escape; and therefore there where we look for salvation, we must look also for triumph, and before triumph for victory, and before victory for battle; which cannot well be supposed shall be in heaven. But how good soever this reason may be, I will not trust to it without very evident places of Scripture. The state of salvation is described at large, Isaiah, 33:20–24:

18. *Look upon Zion, the city of our solemnities; thine eyes shall see Jerusalem a quiet habitation, a tabernacle that shall not be taken down; not one of the stakes thereof shall ever be removed, neither shall any of the cords thereof be broken.*

19. *But there the glorious Lord will be unto us a place of broad rivers and streams; wherein shall go no galley with oars, neither shall gallant ship pass thereby.*

20. *For the Lord is our judge, the Lord is our lawgiver, the Lord is our king, he will save us.*

21. *Thy tacklings are loosed; they could not well strengthen their mast; they could not spread the sail: then is the prey of a great spoil divided; the lame take the prey.*

22. *And the inhabitant shall not say, I am sick; the people that shall dwell therein shall be forgiven their iniquity.*

23. In which words we have the place from whence salvation is to proceed, *Jerusalem, a quiet habitation*; the eternity of it, *a tabernacle that shall not be taken down*, etc.; the Saviour of it, *the Lord, their judge, their lawgiver, their king, he will save us*; the salvation, *the Lord shall be to them as a broad moat of swift waters*, etc.; the condition of

---

1 See also 35.11, 38.5 and 38.23.

their enemies, *their tacklings are loose, their masts weak, the lame shall take the spoil of them*; the condition of the saved, *The inhabitant shall not say, I am sick*, and lastly, all this is comprehended in forgiveness of sin, *the people that dwell therein shall be forgiven their iniquity*. By which it is evident that salvation shall be on earth,[1] then, when God shall reign at the coming again of Christ, in Jerusalem, and from Jerusalem shall proceed the salvation of the Gentiles that shall be received into God's kingdom, as is also more expressly declared by the same prophet, *And they* (that is, the Gentiles who had any Jew in bondage) *shall bring all your brethren for an offering to the Lord, out of all nations, upon horses, and in chariots and in litters, and upon mules and upon swift beasts, to my holy mountain, Jerusalem, saith the Lord, as the children of Israel bring an offering in a clean vessel into the house of the Lord. And I will also take of them for priests and for Levites, saith the Lord* (Is. 65:20-21). Whereby it is manifest that the chief seat of God's kingdom (which is the place from whence the salva- [247]
tion of us that were Gentiles shall proceed) shall be Jerusalem; and the same is also confirmed by our Saviour in his discourse with the woman of Samaria concerning the place of God's worship; to whom he saith that the Samaritans worshipped they knew not what, but the Jews worshipped what they knew, *for salvation is of the Jews* (John 4:22) (*ex Judaeis*, that is, begins at the Jews). [It is] as if he should say, you worship God, but know not by whom he will save you, as we do, that know it shall be by one of the tribe of Judah, a Jew, not a Samaritan. And therefore also the woman not impertinently answered him again, *We know the Messiah shall come*. So that which our Saviour saith, *Salvation is from the Jews*, is the same that Paul says, *The gospel is the power of God to salvation to every one that believeth: to the Jew first, and also to the Greek. For therein is the righteousness of God revealed from faith to faith* (Rom. 1:16-17), from the faith of the Jew to the faith of the Gentile. In the like sense the prophet Joel, describing the day of judgement, that God would *shew wonders in heaven, and in earth, blood, and fire, and pillars of smoke. The sun should be turned to darkness, and the moon into blood, before the great and terrible day of the Lord come* (Joel 2:30-31). He addeth, *and it shall come to pass, that whosoever shall call upon the name of the Lord shall be saved. For in Mount Zion and in Jerusalem shall be*

---

1 See also 35.11, 38.5 and 38.17.

*salvation* (verse 32). And Obadiah, verse 17, saith the same, *Upon Mount Zion shall be deliverance; and there shall be holiness, and the house of Jacob shall possess their possessions*, that is, the possessions of the *heathen*, which *possessions* he expresseth more particularly in the following verses, by the *mount of Esau*, the *land of the Philistines*, the *fields of Ephraim*, of *Samaria*, *Gilead*, and the *cities of the South*, and concludes with these words, *the kingdom shall be the Lord's*. All these places are for salvation, and the kingdom of God, after the day of judgement, upon earth. On the other side, I have not found any text that can probably be drawn to prove any ascension of the saints into heaven, that is to say, into any *coelum empyreum* or other ethereal region, saving that it is called the kingdom of heaven; which name it may have because God, that was king of the Jews, governed them by his commands sent to Moses by angels from heaven, and after their revolt sent his Son from heaven to reduce them to their obedience and shall send him thence again to rule both them and all other faithful men from the day of judgement, everlastingly, or from that, that the throne of this our Great King is in heaven, whereas the earth is but his footstool. But that the subjects of God should have any place as high as his throne or higher than his footstool, it seemeth not suitable to the dignity of a king, nor can I find any evident text for it in Holy Scripture.

24. From this that hath been said of the kingdom of God, and of salvation, it is not hard to interpret what is meant by the World to Come. There are three worlds mentioned in the Scripture: the *old world*, the *present world*, and the *world to come*. Of
2 Peter 2:5. the first, St. Peter speaks, *If God spared not the old world, but saved Noah the eighth person, a preacher of righteousness, bringing the flood*
[248] *upon the world of the ungodly*, etc. So the *first world* was from Adam to the general flood. Of the present world, our Saviour speaks, *My kingdom is not of this world* (John 18:36). For he came only to teach men the way of salvation and to renew the kingdom of his Father by his doctrine. Of the world to come, St. Peter speaks, *Neverthe-*
2 Peter 3:13. *less we according to his promise look for new heavens, and a new earth.* This is that World wherein Christ coming down from heaven in the clouds, with great power and glory, shall send his angels and shall gather together his elect from the four winds and from the uttermost parts of the earth and thenceforth reign over them, under his Father, everlastingly.

25. *Salvation* of a sinner supposeth a precedent REDEMPTION; for he that is once guilty of sin is obnoxious to the penalty of the same, and must pay, or some other for him, such ransom as he that is offended and has him in his power, shall require. And seeing the person offended is Almighty God, in whose power are all things, such ransom is to be paid before salvation can be acquired, as God hath been pleased to require. By this ransom is not intended a satisfaction for sin equivalent to the offence,[1] which no sinner for himself nor righteous man can ever be able to make for another; the damage a man does to another he may make amends for by restitution or recompense, but sin cannot be taken away by recompense; for that were to make the liberty to sin a thing vendible. But sins may be pardoned to the repentant either *gratis* or upon such penalty as God is pleased to accept. That which God usually accepted in the Old Testament was some sacrifice or oblation. To forgive sin is not an act of injustice, though the punishment have been threatened. Even amongst men, though the promise of good bind the promiser, yet threats, that is to say, promises of evil, bind them not, much less shall they bind God, who is infinitely more merciful than men. Our Saviour Christ therefore to *redeem* us did not in that sense satisfy for the sins of men, as that his death, of its own virtue, could make it unjust in God to punish sinners with eternal death; but [he] did make that sacrifice and oblation of himself at his first coming, which God was pleased to require for the salvation at his second coming, of such as in the meantime should repent and believe in him. And though this act of our *redemption* be not always in Scripture called a *sacrifice* and *oblation*, but sometimes a *price*; yet by *price* we are not to understand anything by the

Redemption.

1 There are two dominant theories of redemption: the Ransom theory, supported by Hobbes but found in many Church Fathers, e.g., Augustine of Hippo, and the Satisfaction Theory, originated by Anselm of Canterbury. According to the Satisfaction Theory, when Adam sinned, humans incurred a debt to God that had to be repaid. A human being had to repay it because humans owed it. But no purely human being had anything of his own since each is completely dependent on God. Only God had the wherewithal to repay the debt. Thus, Anselm concludes that it was necessary for a human being who was also divine to repay the debt. This explains the necessity of the Incarnation, God becoming a human being. Hobbes's objection to the Satisfaction Theory is that it makes sin a commodity, "a thing vendible," that can be bought. Jesus paid the 'price' of the sin. Hobbes's instincts are good. According to his own theory, Jesus made a sacrifice on behalf of the elect. God, in his mercy, accepted this sacrifice and thereby the elect were redeemed.

value whereof he could claim to a pardon for us from his offended Father; but that price which God the Father was pleased in mercy to demand.[1]

[247]

# CHAPTER XXXIX

## OF THE SIGNIFICATION IN SCRIPTURE OF THE WORD *CHURCH*

Church the Lord's house.

1. The word *church* (*ecclesia*) signifieth in the books of Holy Scripture divers things. Sometimes, though not often, it is taken for *God's house*, that is to say, for a temple wherein Christians assemble to perform holy duties publicly, as, *Let your women keep silence in the churches* (1 Cor. 14:34); but this is metaphorically put for the congregation there assembled and hath been since used for the edifice itself to distinguish between the temples of Christians and idolaters. The Temple of Jerusalem was *God's house* and the house of prayer, and so is any edifice dedicated by Christians to the worship of Christ, *Christ's house*; and therefore the Greek Fathers call it *Kuriake, the Lord's house*, and thence in our language it came to be called *kirk*, and *church*.

*Ecclesia*, properly what.

2. *Church* (when not taken for a house) signifieth the same that *ecclesia* signified in the Grecian commonwealths, that is to say, a congregation, or an assembly of citizens, called forth to hear the magistrate speak unto them, and which in the commonwealth of Rome was called *concio*, as he that spake was called *ecclesiastes*, and *concionator*. And when they were called forth by lawful authority, it

Acts 19:39.

was *ecclesia legitima*, a *lawful Church*, *ennomos ekklesia*. But when they were excited by tumultuous and seditious clamour, then it was a confused Church, *ekklesia sugkexumene*.

3. It is taken also sometimes for the men that have right to be of the congregation, though not actually assembled, that is to say, for the whole multitude of Christian men, how far soever they be dispersed, as where it is said that *Saul made havoc of the church* (Acts 8:3); and in this sense is Christ said to be Head of the Church. And sometimes for a certain part of Christians, as, *Salute the Church*

1 Redemption occurs because of God's mercy, not his justice. See also 41.2.

*that is in his house* (Col. 4:15). Sometimes also for the elect only, as, *A glorious Church, without spot or wrinkle, holy and without blemish* (Eph. 5:27); which is meant of the *Church triumphant* or *Church to come.* Sometimes, for a congregation assembled of professors of Christianity, whether their profession be true or counterfeit, as it is understood where it is said, *Tell it to the Church, and if he neglect to hear the Church, let him be to thee as a Gentile, or publican* (Matt. 18:17).

In what sense the Church is one person.

4. And in this last sense only it is that the *Church* can be taken for one person;[1] that is to say, that it can be said to have power to will, to pronounce, to command, to be obeyed, to make laws, or to do any other action whatsoever; for without authority from a lawful congregation, whatsoever act be done in a concourse of people, it is the particular act of every one of those that were present, [248] and gave their aid to the performance of it, and not the act of them all in gross, as of one body; much less the act of them that were absent, or that, being present, were not willing it should be done. According to this sense, I define a CHURCH to be: *a company of men professing Christian religion, united in the person of one sovereign; at whose command they ought to assemble, and without whose authority they ought not to assemble.* And because in all commonwealths that assembly which is without warrant from the civil sovereign is unlawful; that Church also which is assembled in any commonwealth that hath forbidden them to assemble is an unlawful assembly.

Church defined.

A Christian commonwealth, and a church all one.

5. It followeth also that there is on earth no such universal Church as all Christians are bound to obey, because there is no power on earth to which all other commonwealths are subject.[2] There are Christians in the dominions of several princes and states, but every one of them is subject to that commonwealth whereof he is himself a member, and consequently cannot be subject to the commands of any other person. And therefore a Church, such a one as is capable to command, to judge, absolve, condemn, or do any other act, is the same thing with a civil commonwealth consisting of Christian men, and is called a *civil state,*

1 See also 33.24.

2 This is an attack on the Roman Catholic doctrine of one Church. Many Protestants understood the doctrine of one Church to mean being united in Christ and not to be under some earthly universal authority.

for that the subjects of it are *men*, and a *Church*, for that the subjects thereof are *Christians*. *Temporal* and *spiritual* government are but two words brought into the world to make men see double and mistake their *lawful sovereign*.[1] It is true that the bodies of the faithful, after the resurrection, shall be not only spiritual, but eternal; but in this life they are gross and corruptible. There is therefore no other government in this life, neither of state nor religion, but temporal; nor teaching of any doctrine lawful to any subject which the governor both of the state and of the religion forbiddeth to be taught. And that governor must be one; or else there must needs follow faction and civil war in the commonwealth between the *Church* and *State*; between *spiritualists* and *temporalists*; between the *sword of justice* and the *shield of faith*; and (which is more) in every Christian man's own breast between the *Christian* and the *man*. The doctors of the Church are called pastors; so also are civil sovereigns. But if pastors be not subordinate one to another, so as that there may be one chief pastor, men will be taught contrary doctrines, whereof both may be, and one must be, false. Who that one chief pastor is, according to the law of nature, hath been already shown; namely, that it is the civil sovereign. And to whom the Scripture hath assigned that office, we shall see in the chapters following.

[249]

## CHAPTER XL

## OF THE RIGHTS OF THE KINGDOM OF GOD, IN ABRAHAM, MOSES, THE HIGH PRIESTS, AND THE KINGS OF JUDAH

The sovereign rights of Abraham

1. The father of the faithful, and first in the kingdom of God by covenant, was Abraham.[2] For with him was the covenant first made; wherein he obliged himself and his seed after him to acknowledge and obey the commands of God, not only such as he

---

1 An attack on the Roman Catholic doctrine of "the two swords," one wielded by the secular governor, the other wielded by the Pope.

2 See also 35.4.

could take notice of (as moral laws) by the light of nature, but also such as God should in special manner deliver to him by dreams and visions. For as to the moral law, they were already obliged, and needed not have been contracted withal by promise of the land of Canaan. Nor was there any contract that could add to or strengthen the obligation by which both they and all men else were bound naturally to obey God Almighty; and therefore the covenant which Abraham made with God was to take for the commandment of God that which in the name of God was commanded him in a dream or vision, and to deliver it to his family and cause them to observe the same.

2. In this contract of God with Abraham, we may observe three points of important consequence in the government of God's people. First, that at the making of this covenant God spoke only to Abraham, and therefore contracted not with any of his family or seed otherwise than as their wills (which make the essence of all covenants) were before the contract involved in the will of Abraham, who was therefore supposed to have had a lawful power to make them perform all that he covenanted for them.[1] According whereunto God saith, *All the nations of the earth shall be blessed in him, for I know him that he will command his children and his household after him, and they shall keep the way of the Lord* (Genesis 18:18–19). From whence may be concluded this first point, that they to whom God hath not spoken immediately are to receive the positive commandments of God from their sovereign, as the family and seed of Abraham did from Abraham, their father and lord and civil sovereign. And consequently in every commonwealth, they who have no supernatural revelation to the contrary ought to obey the laws of their own sovereign in the external acts and profession of religion. As for the inward *thought* and *belief* of men, which human governors can take no notice of (for God only knoweth the heart), they are not voluntary, nor the effect of the

Abraham had the sole power of ordering the religion of his own people.

1 Hobbes could have said that by his doctrine of authorization, all of Abraham's subjects covenanted among themselves to obey God's special commands. But Hobbes has a different purpose in mind in this passage. He wants to claim that no subject, e.g., no Englishman or Scotsman, is justified in claiming that God has given him a special commandment, such as to oppose the sovereign. See also 40.3.

[250] laws, but of the unrevealed will and of the power of God, and consequently fall not under obligation.[1]

No pretence of private spirit against the religion of Abraham.

3. From whence proceedeth another point; that it was not unlawful for Abraham, when any of his subjects should pretend private vision or spirit, or other revelation from God, for the countenancing of any doctrine which Abraham should forbid, or when they followed or adhered to any such pretender, to punish them; and consequently that it is lawful now for the sovereign to punish any man that shall oppose his private spirit against the laws; for he hath the same place in the commonwealth that Abraham had in his own family.

Abraham sole judge and interpreter of what God spake.

4. There ariseth also from the same a third point, [namely,] that as none but Abraham in his family, so none but the sovereign in a Christian commonwealth, can take notice what is or what is not the word of God. For God spoke only to Abraham, and it was he only that was able to know what God said and to interpret the same to his family; and therefore also, they that have the place of Abraham in a commonwealth are the only interpreters of what God hath spoken.

The authority of Moses, whereon grounded.

5. The same covenant was renewed with Isaac and afterwards with Jacob, but afterwards no more till the Israelites were freed from the Egyptians and arrived at the foot of Mount Sinai; and then it was renewed by Moses (as I have said before, Chapter 35 [paragraph 5]), in such manner as they became from that time forward the peculiar kingdom of God, whose lieutenant was Moses for his own time; and the succession to that office was settled upon Aaron and his heirs after him to be to God a sacerdotal kingdom forever.

6. By this constitution, a kingdom is acquired to God. But seeing Moses had no authority to govern the Israelites as a successor to the right of Abraham, because he could not claim it by inheritance, it appeareth not as yet that the people were obliged to take him for God's lieutenant longer than they believed that God spoke unto him. And therefore his authority, notwithstanding the covenant they made with God, depended yet merely upon the

1 Hobbes's defense of 'freedom of conscience' is not freedom of conscience as it is ordinarily understood to be, since it does not allow one to act against the sovereign on the basis of one's conscience.

opinion they had of his sanctity, and of the reality of his conferences with God, and the verity of his miracles; which opinion coming to change, they were no more obliged to take anything for the law of God which he propounded to them in God's name. We are therefore to consider what other ground there was of their obligation to obey him. For it could not be the commandment of God that could oblige them, because God spoke not to them immediately, but by the mediation of Moses himself; and our Saviour saith of himself, *If I bear witness of myself, my witness is not true,* much less if Moses bear witness of himself, especially in a claim of kingly power over God's people, ought his testimony to be received. His authority therefore, as the authority of all other princes, must be grounded on the consent of the people and their promise to obey him. And so it was; for *the people when they saw the thunderings, and the lightnings, and the noise of the trumpet, and the mountain smoking, removed and stood afar off. And they said unto Moses, Speak thou with us, and we will hear, but let not God speak with us lest we die* (Exodus 20:18-19). Here was their promise of obedience; and by this it was they obliged themselves to obey whatsoever he should deliver unto them for the commandment of God.

John 5:31

[251]

Moses was (under God) sovereign of the Jews all his own time, though Aaron had the priesthood.

7. And notwithstanding the covenant constituteth a sacerdotal kingdom, that is to say, a kingdom hereditary to Aaron; yet that is to be understood of the succession after Moses should be dead. For whosoever ordereth and establisheth the policy as first founder of a commonwealth, be it monarchy, aristocracy or democracy, must needs have sovereign power over the people all the while he is doing of it. And that Moses had that power all his own time is evidently affirmed in the Scripture. First, in the text last before cited, because the people promised obedience, not to Aaron, but to him. Secondly, *And God said unto Moses, Come up unto the Lord, thou and Aaron, Nadab and Abihu, and seventy of the elders of Israel. And Moses alone shall come near the Lord, but they shall not come nigh, neither shall the people go up with him* (Exodus 24:1-2). By which it is plain that Moses, who was alone called up to God (and not Aaron, nor the other priests, nor the seventy elders, nor the people who were forbidden to come up), was alone he that represented to the Israelites the person of God; that is to say, was their sole sovereign under God. And though afterwards it be said, *Then went up*

*Moses and Aaron, Nadab and Abihu, and seventy of the elders of Israel, and they saw the God of Israel, and there was under his feet as it were a paved work of sapphire stone* etc. (Exodus 24:9); yet this was not till after Moses had been with God before and had brought to the people the words which God had said to him. He only went for the business of the people; the others, as the nobles of his retinue, were admitted for honour to that special grace which was not allowed to the people; which was (as in the verse after appeareth) to see God and live. *God laid not his hand upon them, they saw God, and did eat and drink* (that is, did live), but did not carry any commandment from him to the people. Again, it is everywhere said, *The Lord spake unto Moses,* as in all other occasions of government, so also in the ordering of the ceremonies of religion, contained in the 25th, 26th, 27th, 28th, 29th, 30th, and 31st chapters of Exodus, and throughout Leviticus; to Aaron, seldom. The calf that Aaron made, Moses threw into the fire. Lastly, the question of the authority of Aaron, by occasion of his and Miriam's mutiny against Moses, was judged by God himself for Moses (Numbers 12). So also in the question between Moses and the people, who had the right of governing the people, when Korah, Dathan, and Abiram, and two hundred and fifty princes of the assembly *gathered themselves together against Moses and against Aaron, and said unto them, ye take too much upon you, seeing all the congregation are holy, every one of them, and the Lord is amongst them, why lift you up yourselves above the congregation of the Lord?* (Numbers 16:3). God caused the earth to
[252] swallow Korah, Dathan, and Abiram, with their wives and children, alive, and consumed those two hundred and fifty princes with fire. Therefore neither Aaron, nor the people, nor any aristocracy of the chief princes of the people, but Moses alone had next under God the sovereignty over the Israelites, and that not only in causes of civil policy but also of religion; for Moses only spoke with God and therefore only could tell the people what it was that God required at their hands. No man upon pain of death might be so presumptuous as to approach the mountain where God talked with Moses. *Thou shalt set bounds,* saith the Lord, *to the people round about, and say, Take heed to yourselves that you go not up into the Mount, or touch the border of it; whosoever toucheth the Mount*

*shall surely be put to death* (Exodus 19:12). And again, *Go down, charge the people, lest they break through unto the Lord to gaze* (verse 21). Out of which we may conclude that whosoever in Christian commonwealth holdeth the place of Moses is the sole messenger of God and interpreter of his commandments. And according hereunto, no man ought in the interpretation of the Scripture to proceed further than the bounds which are set by their several sovereigns. For the Scriptures, since God now speaketh in them, are the Mount Sinai, the bounds whereof are the laws of them that represent God's person on earth. To look upon them, and therein to behold the wondrous works of God, and learn to fear him, is allowed; but to interpret them, that is, to pry into what God saith to him whom he appointeth to govern under him, and [to] make themselves judges whether he govern as God commandeth him or not, is to transgress the bounds God hath set us, and to gaze upon God irreverently.

All spirits were subordinate to the spirit of Moses.

8. There was no prophet in the time of Moses, nor pretender to the spirit of God, but such as Moses had approved and authorized. For there were in his time but seventy men that are said to prophesy by the spirit of God, and these were all of Moses his election, concerning whom God said to Moses, *Gather to me seventy of the elders of Israel, whom thou knowest to be the elders of the people* (Numbers 11:16). To these God imparted his spirit; but it was not a different spirit from that of Moses; for it is said, *God came down in a cloud, and took of the spirit that was upon Moses, and gave it to the seventy elders* (verse 25). But as I have shown before (chapter thirty-six) by *spirit* is understood the *mind*; so that the sense of the place is no other than this, [namely,] that God endued them with a mind conformable and subordinate to that of Moses, [in order] that they might prophesy, that is to say, speak to the people in God's name in such manner as to set forward (as ministers of Moses, and by his authority) such doctrine as was agreeable to Moses his doctrine. For they were but ministers; and when two of them prophesied in the camp, it was thought a new and unlawful thing; and as it is in the 27th and 28th verses of the same chapter [11], they were accused of it, and Joshua advised Moses to forbid them, as not knowing that it was by Moses his spirit that they prophesied. By

which it is manifest that no subject ought to pretend to prophecy, [253] or to the spirit, in opposition to the doctrine established by him whom God hath set in the place of Moses.

After Moses the sovereignty was in the high priest.

9. Aaron being dead, and after him also Moses, the kingdom, as being a sacerdotal kingdom, descended by virtue of the covenant to Aaron's son, Eleazar the high priest; and God declared him, next under himself, for sovereign, at the same time that he appointed Joshua for the general of their army. For thus God saith expressly concerning Joshua; *He shall stand before Eleazar the priest, who shall ask counsel for him before the Lord; at his word shall they go out, and at his word they shall come in, both he, and all the children of Israel with him* (Numbers 27:21); therefore the supreme power of making war and peace was in the priest. The supreme power of judicature belonged also to the high priest; for the Book of the Law was in their keeping, and the priests and Levites only were the subordinate judges in causes civil, as appears in Deuteronomy 17:8-10. And for the manner of God's worship, there was never doubt made but that the high priest, till the time of Saul, had the supreme authority. Therefore the civil and ecclesiastical power were both joined together in one and the same person, the high priest; and ought to be so, in whosoever governeth by divine right; that is, by authority immediate from God.

Of the sovereign power between the time of Joshua and Saul.

10. After the death of Joshua, till the time of Saul, the time between is noted frequently in the Book of Judges, that there was in those days no king in Israel; and sometimes with this addition, that *every man did that which was right in his own eyes*. By which is to be understood that where it is said, *there was no king*, is meant, *there was no sovereign power*, in Israel. And so it was, if we consider the act and exercise of such power. For after the death of Joshua and Eleazar, *there arose another generation that knew not the Lord, nor the works which he had done for Israel, but did evil in the sight of the Lord and served Baalim* (Judges 2:10-11). And the Jews had that quality which St. Paul noteth, *to look for a sign*, not only before they would submit themselves to the government of Moses, but also after they had obliged themselves by their submission. Whereas signs and miracles had for end to procure faith, not to keep men from violating it when they have once given it; for to that men are obliged by the law of nature. But if we consider not the exercise, but the

right of governing, the sovereign power was still in the high priest. Therefore whatsoever obedience was yielded to any of the judges (who were men chosen by God extraordinarily to save his rebellious subjects out of the hands of the enemy), it cannot be drawn into argument against the right the high priest had to the sovereign power in all matters both of policy and religion. And neither the judges nor Samuel himself had an ordinary, but extraordinary, calling to the government, and [they] were obeyed by the Israelites, not out of duty, but out of reverence to their favour with God, appearing in their wisdom, courage, or felicity. Hitherto therefore the right of regulating both the policy and the religion were inseparable.

11. To the judges succeeded kings; and whereas before all authority, both in religion and policy, was in the high priest; so now it was all in the king. For the sovereignty over the people which was before, not only by virtue of the divine power, but also by a particular pact of the Israelites in God, and next under him, in the high priest, as his vicegerent [deputy] on earth, was cast off by the people, with the consent of God himself. For when they said to Samuel, *make us a king to judge us, like all the nations* (1 Sam. 8:5), they signified that they would no more be governed by the commands that should be laid upon them by the priest, in the name of God; but by one that should command them in the same manner that all other nations were commanded; and consequently in deposing the high priest of royal authority, they deposed that peculiar government of God. And yet God consented to it, saying to Samuel, *Hearken unto the voice of the people, in all that they shall say unto thee; for they have not rejected thee; but they have rejected me, that I should not reign over them* (1 Sam. 8:7). Having therefore rejected God, in whose right the priests governed, there was no authority left to the priests but such as the king was pleased to allow them; which was more or less, according as the kings were good or evil. And for the government of civil affairs, it is manifest, it was all in the hands of the king. For in the same chapter (verse 20) they say *they will be like all the nations; that their king shall be their judge, and go before them, and fight their battles*, that is, he shall have the whole authority, both in peace and war. In which is continued also the ordering of religion; for there was no other word of God in that

[254] Of the rights of the kings of Israel.

time by which to regulate religion but the Law of Moses, which was their civil law. Besides, we read that Solomon *thrust out Abiathar from being priest before the Lord* (1 Kings 2:27); he had therefore authority over the high priest, as over any other subject, which is a great mark of supremacy in religion. And we read also that he dedicated the Temple; that he blessed the people; and that he himself in person made that excellent prayer, used in the consecrations of all churches and houses of prayer (1 Kings 8); which is another great mark of supremacy in religion. Again, we read that when there was question concerning the Book of the Law found in the Temple, the same was not decided by the high priest, but Josiah sent both and others to enquire concerning it, of Huldah, the prophetess (2 Kings 22); which is another mark of the supremacy in religion. Lastly, we read that David made Hashabiah and his brethren, Hebronites, officers of Israel among them westward, *in all business of the Lord, and in the service of the king* (1 Chron. 26:30). Likewise (verse 32), that he made other Hebronites *rulers over the Reubenites, the Gadites, and the half tribe of Manasseh* (these were the rest of Israel that dwelt beyond Jordan) *for every matter pertaining to God, and affairs of the king.* Is not this full power, both temporal and spiritual, as they call it that would divide it? To con-
[255] clude; from the first institution of God's kingdom, to the Captivity, the supremacy of religion was in the same hand with that of the civil sovereignty; and the priest's office, after the election of Saul, was not magisterial, but ministerial.[1]

*The practice of supremacy in religion was not in the time of the kings according to the right thereof.*

12. Notwithstanding the government both in policy and religion were joined, first in the high priests and afterwards in the kings, so far forth as concerned the right; yet it appeareth by the same holy history that the people understood it not; but there being amongst them a great part, and probably the greatest part, that no longer than they saw great miracles, or (which is equivalent to a miracle) great abilities or great felicity in the enterprises of their governors, gave sufficient credit either to the fame of Moses or to the colloquies between God and the priests, they took

1 Hobbes is suggesting that if Israel had the temporal and spiritual components united in the sovereign, then it is appropriate for England to have them united in the same way. In the kingdom of God, priests were ministers, that is, they rendered service to the people, but were not magisterial, that is, had no independent authority over the people. See also 40.13–14.

occasion, as oft as their governors displeased them, by blaming sometimes the policy, sometimes the religion, to change the government or revolt from their obedience at their pleasure; and from thence proceeded from time to time the civil troubles, divisions, and calamities of the nation. As for example, after the death of Eleazar and Joshua, the next generation, which had not seen the wonders of God, but were left to their own weak reason, not knowing themselves obliged by the covenant of a sacerdotal kingdom, regarded no more the commandment of the priest, nor any law of Moses, but did every man that which was right in his own eyes; and [every man] obeyed in civil affairs such men as from time to time they thought able to deliver them from the neighbour nations that oppressed them; and [they] consulted not with God, as they ought to do, but with such men or women, as they guessed to be prophets by their predictions of things to come; and though they had an idol in their chapel, yet if they had a Levite for their chaplain, they made account they worshipped the God of Israel.

13. And afterwards when they demanded a king, after the manner of the nations; yet it was not with a design to depart from the worship of God their King; but despairing of the justice of the sons of Samuel, they would have a king to judge them in civil actions; but not that they would allow their king to change the religion which they thought was recommended to them by Moses. So that they always kept in store a pretext, either of justice or religion, to discharge themselves of their obedience whensoever they had hope to prevail. Samuel was displeased with the people, for that they desired a king (for God was their King already, and Samuel had but an authority under him); yet did Samuel, when Saul observed not his counsel in destroying Agag as God had commanded, anoint another king, namely, David, to take the succession from his heirs. Rehoboam was no idolater; but when the people thought him an oppressor, that civil pretence carried from him ten tribes to Jeroboam an idolater. And generally through the whole history of the kings, as well of Judah as of Israel, there were prophets that always controlled the kings for
transgressing the religion, and sometimes also for errors of state; as 2 Chron. 19:2.
Jehoshaphat was reproved by the prophet Jehu for aiding the King [256]
of Israel against the Syrians; and Hezekiah, by Isaiah, for showing

his treasures to the ambassadors of Babylon. By all which it appeareth that though the power both of state and religion were in the kings; yet none of them were uncontrolled in the use of it but such as were gracious for their own natural abilities or felicities. So that from the practice of those times, there can no argument be drawn that the right of supremacy in religion was not in the kings, unless we place it in the prophets, and conclude that because Hezekiah, praying to the Lord before the cherubim, was not answered from thence, nor then, but afterwards by the prophet Isaiah, therefore Isaiah was supreme head of the Church; or because Josiah consulted Huldah the prophetess, concerning the Book of the Law, that therefore neither he nor the high priest, but Huldah the prophetess had the supreme authority in matter of religion, which I think is not the opinion of any doctor.

After the captivity, the Jews had no settled commonwealth.

14. During the Captivity the Jews had no commonwealth at all; and after their return, though they renewed their covenant with God, yet there was no promise made of obedience, neither to Esdras nor to any other; and presently after they became subjects to the Greeks (from whose customs and demonology,[1] and from the doctrine of the Cabalists, their religion became much corrupted); in such sort as nothing can be gathered from their confusion, both in state and religion, concerning the supremacy in either. And therefore so far forth as concerneth the Old Testament, we may conclude that whosoever had the sovereignty of the commonwealth amongst the Jews, the same had also the supreme authority in matter of God's external worship and represented God's person; that is, the person of God the Father; though he were not called by the name of Father till such time as he sent into the world his Son Jesus Christ to redeem mankind from their sins and [to] bring them into his everlasting kingdom, to be saved for evermore. Of which we are to speak in the chapter following.

1 See also 44.3, 44.16, 45.2, and 47.15.

# CHAPTER XLI

[261][1]

## OF THE OFFICE OF OUR BLESSED SAVIOUR

Three parts of the office of Christ.

1. We find in Holy Scripture three parts of the office of the Messiah; the first of a *Redeemer* or *Saviour*; the second of a *Pastor*, *Counsellor* or *Teacher*, that is, of a prophet sent from God to convert such as God hath elected to salvation; the third of a *King*, an *eternal king*, but under his Father, as Moses and the high priests were in their several times. And to these three parts are correspondent three times. For, our redemption he wrought at his first coming by the sacrifice wherein he offered up himself for our sins upon the cross; our conversion he wrought partly then in his own person and partly worketh now by his ministers, and [he] will continue to work till his coming again. And after his coming again shall begin that his glorious reign over his elect which is to last eternally.

His office as Redeemer.

2. To the office of a redeemer, that is, of one that payeth the ransom of sin[2] (which ransom is death) it appertaineth that he was sacrificed, and thereby bore upon his own head and carried away from us our iniquities, in such sort as God had required. Not that the death of one man, though without sin, can satisfy for the offences of all men, in the rigour of justice, but in the mercy of God, that ordained such sacrifices for sin as he was pleased in his mercy to accept. In the old law (as we may read, Leviticus, 16) the Lord required that there should, every year once, be made an atonement for the sins of all Israel, both priests and others; for the doing whereof Aaron alone was to sacrifice for himself and the priests a young bullock, and for the rest of the people he was to receive from them two young goats, of which he was to *sacrifice* one; but as for the other, which was the *scapegoat*, he was to lay his hands on the head thereof, and by a confession of the iniquities of the people, to lay them all on that head, and then by some opportune man to cause the goat to be led into the wilderness, and there to *escape* and carry away with him the iniquities of the people. As the sacrifice of the one goat was a sufficient, because an accept-

1 The Head edition, which I am using, does not have page numbers 257-260.

2 See also 38.25.

able, price for the ransom of all Israel; so the death of the Messiah is a sufficient price for the sins of all mankind, because there was no more required. Our Saviour Christ's sufferings seem to be here figured as clearly as in the oblation of Isaac or in any other type of him in the Old Testament. He was both the sacrificed goat and the scapegoat; *He was oppressed, and he was afflicted; he opened not his*
[262] *mouth; he is brought as a lamb to the slaughter, and as a sheep is dumb before the shearer, so opened he not his mouth* (Isaiah 53:7); here is the sacrificed goat. *He hath borne our griefs and carried our sorrows* (verse 4); and again, *the Lord hath laid upon him the iniquities of us all* (verse 6) and so he is the *scapegoat. He was cut off from the land of the living for the transgression of my people* (verse 8); there again he is the *sacrificed goat*. And again, *he shall bear their sins* (verse 11); he is the *scapegoat*. Thus is the Lamb of God equivalent to both those goats; sacrificed, in that he died; and escaping, in his resurrection; being raised opportunely by his Father, and removed from the habitation of men in his ascension.

Christ's kingdom not of this world.

3. For as much therefore as he that *redeemeth* hath no title to the *thing redeemed*, before *the redemption* and ransom paid; and this ransom was the death of the redeemer; it is manifest that our Saviour, as man, was not king of those that he redeemed before he suffered death, that is, during that time he conversed bodily on the earth. I say he was not then king in present by virtue of the pact which the faithful make with him in baptism; nevertheless, by the renewing of their pact with God in baptism, they were obliged to obey him for king, under his Father, whensoever he should be pleased to take the kingdom upon him. According whereunto, our Saviour himself expressly saith, *My kingdom is not of this world*[1] (John 18:36). Now seeing the Scripture maketh mention but of two worlds since the flood; this that is now and shall remain to the day of judgement (which is therefore also called the *last day*), and that which shall be after the day of judgement, when there shall be a new heaven and a new earth; the kingdom of Christ is not to begin till the general resurrection. And that is it which our Saviour saith, *The Son of Man shall come in the glory of his Father, with his angels; and then he shall reward every man according to his works*

1 See also 35.7 and 35.13. Cf. 44.4.

(Matthew 16:27). To reward every man according to his works is to execute the office of a king; and this is not to be till he come in the glory of his Father, with his angels. When our Saviour saith, *The Scribes and Pharisees sit in Moses' seat; all therefore whatsoever they bid you do, that observe and do* (Matthew 23:2), he declareth plainly that he ascribeth kingly power, for that time, not to himself, but to them. And so he doth also, where he saith, *Who made me a judge or divider over you?* (Luke 12:14). And, *I came not to judge the world, but to save the world* (John 12:47). And yet our Saviour came into this world that he might be a king and a judge in the world to come; for he was the Messiah, that is, the Christ, that is, the anointed priest and the sovereign prophet of God; that is to say, he was to have all the power that was in Moses the prophet, in the high priests that succeeded Moses, and in the kings that succeeded the priests. And St. John says expressly, *The Father judgeth no man, but hath committed all judgement to the Son* (John 5:22). And this is not repugnant to that other place, *I came not to judge the world*; for this is [263] spoken of the world present, the other of the world to come; as also where it is said that at the second coming of Christ, *Ye that have followed me, in the regeneration when the Son of man shall sit in the throne of his glory, ye shall also sit on twelve thrones, judging the twelve tribes of Israel* (Matthew 19:28).

The end of Christ's coming was to renew the Covenant of the Kingdom of God, and to persuade the elect to embrace it, which was the second part of his office.

4. If then Christ, whilst he was on earth, had no kingdom in this world, to what end was his first coming? It was to restore unto God by a new covenant the kingdom which, being his by the old covenant, had been cut off by the rebellion of the Israelites in the election of Saul. Which to do, he was to preach unto them that he was the *Messiah*, that is, the king promised to them by the prophets, and to offer himself in sacrifice for the sins of them that should by faith submit themselves thereto; and in case the nation generally should refuse him, to call to his obedience such as should believe in him amongst the Gentiles. So that there are two parts of our Saviour's office during his abode upon the earth: one to proclaim himself the Christ, and another by teaching and by working of miracles to persuade and prepare men to live so as to be worthy of the immortality believers were to enjoy, at such time as he should come in majesty to take possession of his Father's kingdom. And therefore it is that the time of his preaching is often by him-

self called the *regeneration*, which is not properly a kingdom, and thereby a warrant to deny obedience to the magistrates that then were; for he commanded to obey those that sat then in Moses' chair and to pay tribute to Caesar; but only an earnest of the kingdom of God that was to come to those to whom God had given the grace to be his disciples and to believe in him; for which cause the godly are said to be already in the *kingdom of grace*, as naturalized in that heavenly kingdom.

The preaching of Christ not contrary to the then law of the Jews nor of Caesar.

5. Hitherto therefore there is nothing done or taught by Christ that tendeth to the diminution of the civil right of the Jews or of Caesar. For as touching the commonwealth which then was amongst the Jews, both they that bore rule amongst them and they that were governed did all expect the Messiah and kingdom of God; which they could not have done if their laws had forbidden him, when he came, to manifest and declare himself. Seeing therefore he did nothing, but by preaching and miracles go about to prove himself to be that Messiah, he did therein nothing against their laws. The kingdom he claimed was to be in another world; he taught all men to obey in the meantime them that sat in Moses' seat; he allowed them to give Caesar his tribute, and refused to take upon himself to be a judge. How then could his words or actions be seditious, or tend to the overthrow of their then civil government? But God having determined his sacrifice for the reduction of his elect to their former covenanted obedience, for the means, whereby he would bring the same to effect, made use
[264] of their malice and ingratitude. Nor was it contrary to the laws of Caesar. For though Pilate himself, to gratify the Jews, delivered him to be crucified; yet before he did so, he pronounced openly that he found no fault in him; and put for title of his condemnation, not as the Jews required, *that he pretended to be king*, but simply, *that he was King of the Jews*; and notwithstanding their clamour, refused to alter it, saying, *What I have written, I have written.*

The third part of his office was to be King (under his Father) of the elect.

6. As for the third part of his office, which was to be *king*, I have already shown that his kingdom was not to begin till the resurrection. But then he shall be king, not only as God, in which sense he is king already and ever shall be of all the earth, in virtue of his omnipotence;[1] but also peculiarly of his own elect, by virtue of the

1 See also chapter 31.

pact they make with him in their baptism. And therefore it is that our Saviour saith that his Apostles should sit upon twelve thrones, judging the twelve tribes of Israel, *When the Son of Man shall sit in the throne of his glory* (Matthew 19:28), whereby he signified that he should reign then in his human nature; and *The Son of Man shall come in the glory of his Father, with his angels, and then he shall reward every man according to his works* (Matthew 16:27). The same we may read, Mark 13:26 and 14:62, and more expressly for the time, Luke 22:29–30, *I appoint unto you a kingdom, as my Father hath appointed to me, that you may eat and drink at my table in my kingdom, and sit on thrones judging the twelve tribes of Israel.* By which it is manifest that the kingdom of Christ appointed to him by his Father is not to be before the Son of Man shall come in glory, and make his Apostles judges of the twelve tribes of Israel. But a man may here ask, seeing there is no marriage in the kingdom of heaven, whether men shall then eat and drink. What eating therefore is meant in this place? This is expounded by our Saviour where he saith, *Labour not for the meat which perisheth, but for that meat which endureth unto everlasting life, which the Son of Man shall give you* (John 6:27). So that by eating at Christ's table is meant the eating of the tree of life; that is to say, the enjoying of immortality, in the kingdom of the Son of Man. By which places, and many more, it is evident that our Saviour's kingdom is to be exercised by him in his human nature.

Christ's authority in the kingdom of God subordinate to that of his Father.

7. Again, he is to be king then no otherwise than as subordinate or vicegerent of God the Father, as Moses was in the wilderness and as the high priests were before the reign of Saul and as the kings were after it. For it is one of the prophecies concerning Christ that he be like, in office, to Moses; *I will raise them up a prophet*, saith the Lord, *from amongst their brethren like unto thee, and will put my words into his mouth* (Deut. 18:18); and this similitude with Moses is also apparent in the actions of our Saviour himself, whilst he was conversant on earth. For as Moses chose twelve princes of the tribes to govern under him, so did our Saviour choose twelve Apostles, who shall sit on twelve thrones and judge [265]
the twelve tribes of Israel; and as Moses authorized seventy elders to receive the Spirit of God and to prophesy to the people, that is, as I have said before, to speak unto them in the name of God; so

our Saviour also ordained seventy disciples to preach his kingdom and salvation to all nations. And as when a complaint was made to Moses against those of the seventy that prophesied in the camp of Israel, he justified them in it as being subservient therein to his government; so also our Saviour, when St. John complained to him of a certain man that cast out devils in his name, justified him therein, saying, *Forbid him not, for he that is not against us is on our part* (Luke 9:50).

8. Again, our Saviour resembled Moses in the institution of *sacraments*, both of *admission* into the kingdom of God and of *commemoration* of his deliverance of his elect from their miserable condition. As the children of Israel had for sacrament of their reception into the kingdom of God, before the time of Moses, the rite of *circumcision*, which rite, having been omitted in the wilderness, was again restored as soon as they came into the Land of Promise; so also the Jews, before the coming of our Saviour, had a rite of *baptizing*, that is, of washing with water all those that, being Gentiles, embraced the God of Israel. This rite St. John the Baptist used in the reception of all them that gave their names to the Christ, whom he preached to be already come into the world; and our Saviour instituted the same for a sacrament to be taken by all that believed in him. For what cause the rite of baptism first proceeded is not expressed formally in the Scripture, but it may be probably thought to be an imitation of the law of Moses concerning leprosy; wherein the leprous man was commanded to be kept out of the camp of Israel for a certain time; after which time, being judged by the priest to be clean, he was admitted into the camp after a solemn washing. And this may therefore be a type of the washing in baptism, wherein such men as are cleansed of the leprosy of sin by faith are received into the Church with the solemnity of baptism. There is another conjecture drawn from the ceremonies of the Gentiles, in a certain case that rarely happens; and that is, when a man that was thought dead chanced to recover, other men made scruple to converse with him, as they would do to converse with a ghost, unless he were received again into the number of men by washing, as children new born were washed from the uncleanness of their nativity, which was a kind of new birth. This ceremony of the Greeks, in the time that Judaea was

under the dominion of Alexander and the Greeks his successors, may probably enough have crept into the religion of the Jews. But seeing it is not likely our Saviour would countenance a heathen rite, it is most likely it proceeded from the legal ceremony of washing after leprosy. And for the other sacrament, of eating the [266] *Paschal Lamb*, it is manifestly imitated in the sacrament of the *Lord's Supper*, in which the breaking of the bread and the pouring out of the wine do keep in memory our deliverance from the misery of sin by Christ's Passion, as the eating of the Paschal Lamb kept in memory the deliverance of the Jews out of the bondage of Egypt. Seeing therefore the authority of Moses was but subordinate, and he but a lieutenant to God, it followeth that Christ, whose authority, as man, was to be like that of Moses, was no more but subordinate to the authority of his Father. The same is more expressly signified by that that he teacheth us to pray, *Our Father, let thy kingdom come*; and, *For thine is the kingdom, the power, and the glory*; and by that it is said that *he shall come in the glory of his Father*; and by that which St. Paul saith, *then cometh the end, when he shall have delivered up the kingdom to God, even the Father* (1 Corinthians 15:24), and by many other most express places.

One and the same God is the person represented by Moses and by Christ.

9. Our Saviour therefore, both in teaching and reigning, representeth, as Moses did, the person God; which God from that time forward, but not before, is called *the Father*; and, being still one and the same substance, is one person as represented by Moses, and another person as represented by his Son the Christ. For *person* being a relative to a *representer*, it is consequent to plurality of representers that there be a plurality of persons, though of one and the same substance.

# CHAPTER XLII [267]

## OF POWER ECCLESIASTICAL

1. For the understanding of Power Ecclesiastical, what and in whom it is, we are to distinguish the time from the ascension of our Saviour into two parts; one before the conversion of kings and men endued with sovereign civil power; the other after their con-

version. For it was long after the ascension before any king or civil sovereign embraced and publicly allowed the teaching of Christian religion.

Of the Holy Spirit that fell on the Apostles.

2. And for the time between, it is manifest that the *power ecclesiastical* was in the Apostles; and after them in such as were by them ordained to preach the gospel and to convert men to Christianity and to direct them that were converted in the way of salvation; and after these the power was delivered again to others by these ordained, and this was done by imposition of hands upon such as were ordained; by which was signified the giving of the Holy Spirit or Spirit of God to those whom they ordained ministers of God, to advance his kingdom. So that imposition of hands was nothing else but the seal of their commission to preach Christ and teach his doctrine; and the giving of the Holy Ghost by that ceremony of imposition of hands was an imitation of that which Moses did. For Moses used the same ceremony to his minister Joshua, as we read, Deuteronomy 34:9, *And Joshua the son of Nun was full of the spirit of wisdom; for Moses had laid his hands upon him.* Our Saviour therefore between his resurrection and ascension gave his spirit to the Apostles; first, by *breathing on them, and saying, Receive ye the Holy Spirit* (John 20:22), and after his ascension by sending down upon them a *mighty wind, and cloven tongues of fire* (Acts 2:2–3) and not by imposition of hands; as neither did God lay his hands on Moses; and his Apostles afterward transmitted the same spirit by imposition of hands, as Moses did to Joshua. So that it is manifest hereby in whom the power ecclesiastical continually remained in those first times where there was not any Christian commonwealth, namely, in them that received the same from the Apostles, by successive laying on of hands.

Of the Trinity.

3. Here we have the person of God born now the third time. For Moses and the high priests were God's representative in the Old Testament; and our Saviour himself, as man, during his abode on earth; so the Holy Ghost, that is to say, the Apostles and their
[268] successors, in the office of preaching and teaching, that had received the Holy Spirit, have represented him ever since. But a person (as I have shown before, Chapter [16]) is he that is represented, as often as he is represented; and therefore God, who has been represented (that is, personated) thrice, may properly enough

be said to be three persons; though neither the word *Person* nor *Trinity* be ascribed to him in the Bible. St. John indeed saith, *There be three that bear witness in heaven, the Father, the Word, and the Holy Spirit; and these three are one* (1 John 5:7). But this disagreeth not, but accordeth fitly with three persons in the proper signification of persons; which is, [namely] that which is represented by another. For so God the Father, as represented by Moses, is one person; and as represented by his Son, another person; and as represented by the Apostles, and by the doctors that taught by authority from them derived, is a third person; and yet every person here is the person of one and the same God.[1] But a man may here ask what it was whereof these three bore witness. St. John therefore tells us (verse 11) that they bear witness that *God hath given us eternal life in his Son.* Again, if it should be asked wherein that testimony appeareth, the answer is easy; for he hath testified the same by the miracles he wrought, first by Moses; secondly, by his Son himself; and lastly by his Apostles that had received the Holy Spirit; all which in their times represented the person of God, and either prophesied or preached Jesus Christ. And as for the Apostles, it was the character of the apostleship, in the twelve first and great Apostles, to bear witness of his resurrection, as appeareth expressly where St. Peter, when a new Apostle was to be chosen in the place of Judas Iscariot, useth these words, *Of these men which have companied with us all the time that the Lord Jesus went in and out amongst us, beginning at the baptism of John, unto that same day that he was taken up from us, must one be ordained to be a witness with us of his resurrection* (Acts 1: 21-22), which words interpret the *bearing of witness* mentioned by St. John. There is in the same place mentioned another Trinity of witnesses in earth. For he saith, *there are three that bear witness in earth; the Spirit, and the water, and the blood; and these three agree in one* (1 John 5:8); that is to say, the graces of God's Spirit and the two sacraments, baptism and the Lord's Supper, which all agree in one testimony to assure the consciences of believers of eternal life; of which testimony he saith (verse 10), *He*

---

1 Hobbes's theory of the Trinity was a form of Sabellianism; that is, his theory that a person of the Trinity is constituted by there being a human representative of God does not make each person sufficiently distinct from the others to satisfy the requirement that there be three persons that are God. Hobbes's theory was soon criticized, and he abandoned it.

*that believeth on the Son of Man hath the witness in himself.* In this Trinity on earth, the unity is not of the thing; for the spirit, the water, and the blood are not the same substance, though they give the same testimony. But in the Trinity of heaven, the persons are the persons of one and the same God, though represented in three different times and occasions. To conclude, the doctrine of the Trinity, as far as can be gathered directly from the Scripture, is in substance this: that God, who is always one and the same, was the [269] person represented by Moses; the person represented by his Son incarnate; and the person represented by the Apostles. As represented by the Apostles, the Holy Spirit by which they spoke is God; as represented by his Son (that was God and man), the Son is that God. As represented by Moses and the high priests, the Father, that is to say, the Father of our Lord Jesus Christ, is that God. From whence we may gather the reason those names *Father, Son,* and *Holy Spirit,* in the signification of the godhead, are never used in the Old Testament. For they are persons, that is, they have their names from representing; which could not be till divers men had represented God's person in ruling or in directing under him.

4. Thus we see how the power ecclesiastical was left by our Saviour to the Apostles; and how they were (to the end they might the better exercise that power) endued with the Holy Spirit, which is therefore called sometimes in the New Testament *paracletus,* which signifieth an *assister* or one called to for help, though it be commonly translated a *comforter.* Let us now consider the power itself, what it was, and over whom.

The power ecclesiastical is but the power to teach.

5. Cardinal Bellarmine,[1] in his third general controversy, hath handled a great many questions concerning the ecclesiastical power of the Pope of Rome; and [he] begins with this, whether it ought to be monarchical, aristocratical, or democratical. All which sorts of power are sovereign and coercive. If now it should appear that there is no coercive power left them by our Saviour, but only a power to proclaim the kingdom of Christ, and to persuade men to submit themselves there unto; and, by precepts and good coun-

1 Robert Bellarmine (1542-1621) was a prominent Roman Catholic theologian during the Counter-Reformation. Hobbes is referring to the third disputation of Bellarmine's *Disputationes de Controversiis Christianae Fidei Adversus Huius Temporis Haereticos* [*Disputations on Controversies of the Christian Faith Against the Heretics of this Time*] (1590).

sel, to teach them that have submitted what they are to do, [in order] that they may be received into the kingdom of God when it comes; and that the Apostles and other ministers of the Gospel are our schoolmasters, and not our commanders, and their precepts not laws, but wholesome counsels; then were all that dispute in vain.

6. I have shown already (in the last chapter)[1] that the kingdom of Christ is not of this world; therefore neither can his ministers, unless they be kings, require obedience in his name. For if the Supreme King have not his regal power in this world; by what authority can obedience be required to his officers? *As my Father sent me* (so saith our Saviour) *I send you* [John 20:21]. But our Saviour was sent to persuade the Jews to return to, and to invite the Gentiles to receive, the kingdom of his Father, and not to reign in majesty, no not as his Father's lieutenant till the day of judgement.

An argument thereof from the power of Christ himself;

7. The time between the ascension and the general resurrection is called, not a reigning, but a regeneration, that is, a preparation of men for the second and glorious coming of Christ at the day of judgement, as appeareth by the words of our Saviour, *You that have followed me in the regeneration, when the Son of man shall sit in the throne of his glory, you shall also sit upon twelve thrones* (Matt. 19:28), and of St. Paul, *Having your feet shod with the preparation of the gospel of peace* (Ephesians 6:15).

From the name of regeneration;

[270]

8. And is compared by our Saviour to fishing; that is, to winning men to obedience, not by coercion and punishing, but by persuasion. And therefore he said not to his Apostles he would make them so many Nimrods, hunters of men; but fishers of men. It is compared also to leaven, to sowing of seed, and to the multiplication of a grain of mustard-seed; by all which compulsion is excluded; and consequently there can in that time be no actual reigning. The work of Christ's ministers is evangelization; that is, a proclamation of Christ, and a preparation for his second coming; as the evangelization of John the Baptist was a preparation to his first coming.

From the comparison of it with fishing, leaven, seed;

9. Again, the office of Christ's ministers in this world is to make men believe and have faith in Christ; but faith hath no relation to, nor dependence at all upon, compulsion or commandment; but

From the nature of faith;

---

1 Especially 41.3-5.

only upon certainty, or probability of arguments drawn from reason, or from something men believe already. Therefore the ministers of Christ in this world have no power by that title to punish any man for not believing or for contradicting what they say; they have, I say, no power by that title of Christ's ministers to punish such; but if they have sovereign civil power, by politic institution, then they may indeed lawfully punish any contradiction to their laws whatsoever; and St. Paul, of himself and [of] other [of]the then preachers of the Gospel, saith in express words, *We have no dominion over your faith, but are helpers of your joy.*

Cor. 1:24

From the authority Christ hath left to civil princes.

10. Another argument, that the ministers of Christ in this present world have no right of commanding, may be drawn from the lawful authority which Christ hath left to all princes, as well Christians as infidels. St. Paul saith, *Children, obey your parents in all things; for this is well pleasing to the Lord* (Colossians 3:20). And, *Servants, obey in all things your masters according to the flesh, not with eye-service, as men-pleasers, but in singleness of heart, as fearing the Lord* (Colossians 3:22); this is spoken to them whose masters were infidels; and yet they are bidden to obey them *in all things.* And again, concerning obedience to princes, exhorting *to be subject to the higher powers*, he saith, *that all power is ordained of God*; and *that we ought to subject to them not only for* fear of incurring their *wrath, but also for conscience sake* (Romans 13:1–6). And St. Peter, *Submit yourselves to every ordinance of man, for the Lord's sake, whether it be to the king, as supreme, or unto governors, as to them that be sent by him for the punishment of evildoers, and for the praise of them that do well; for so is the will of God* (1 Peter, 2:13–15). And again St. Paul, *Put men in mind to be subject to principalities, and powers, and to obey magistrates* (Titus 3:1). These princes and powers whereof St. Peter and St. [271] Paul here speak were all infidels; much more therefore we are to obey those Christians whom God hath ordained to have sovereign power over us. How then can we be obliged to obey any minister of Christ if he should command us to do anything contrary to the command of the king or other sovereign representant of the commonwealth whereof we are members, and by whom we look to be protected? It is therefore manifest that Christ hath not left to his ministers in this world, unless they be also endued with civil authority, any authority to command other men.

11. But what (may some object) if a king or a senate or other sovereign person forbid us to believe in Christ? To this I answer that such forbidding is of no effect; because belief and unbelief never follow men's commands. Faith is a gift of God which man can neither give nor take away by promise of rewards or menaces of torture. And, if it be further asked, what if we be commanded by our lawful prince to say with our tongue we believe not; must we obey such command? Profession with the tongue is but an external thing and no more than any other gesture whereby we signify our obedience; and wherein a Christian, holding firmly in his heart the faith of Christ, hath the same liberty which the prophet Elisha allowed to Naaman the Syrian. Naaman was converted in his heart to the God of Israel, for he saith, *Thy servant will henceforth offer neither burnt offering nor sacrifice unto other gods, but unto the Lord. In this thing the Lord pardon thy servant, that when my master goeth into the house of Rimmon to worship there, and he leaneth on my hand, and I bow myself in the house of Rimmon; when I bow myself in the house of Rimmon, the Lord pardon thy servant in this thing*[1] (2 Kings 5:17). This the Prophet approved, and bid him *Go in peace.* Here Naaman believed in his heart; but by bowing before the idol Rimmon, he denied the true God in effect as much as if he had done it with his lips. But then what shall we answer to our Saviour's saying, *Whosoever denieth me before men, I will deny him before my Father which is in heaven?* (Matt. 10:33). This we may say, that whatsoever a subject, as Naaman was, is compelled to in obedience to his sovereign, and doth it not in order to his own mind, but in order to the laws of his country, that action is not his, but his sovereign's;[2] nor is it he that in this case denieth Christ before men, but his governor, and the law of his country. If any man shall accuse this doctrine as repugnant to true and unfeigned Christianity, I ask him, in case there should be a subject in any Christian commonwealth that should be inwardly in his heart of the Mahomedan religion, whether if his sovereign command him to be present at the divine service of the Christian church, and that on pain of death, he think that Mahomedan obliged in conscience

What Christians may do to escape persecution.

---

1 See also 43.23.

2 Whatever a subject does because he is commanded to do it is the action of the sovereign. However, by his theory of authorization, whatever the sovereign does the subject does. Hobbes suppresses this latter point when it does not suit his purposes.

to suffer death for that cause, rather than to obey that command of his lawful prince. If he say he ought rather to suffer death, then he authorizeth all private men to disobey their princes in mainte-
[272] nance of their religion, true or false; if he say he ought to be obedient, then he alloweth to himself that which he denieth to another, contrary to the words of our Saviour, *Whatsoever you would that men should do unto you, that do ye unto them*; and contrary to the law of nature (which is the indubitable everlasting law of God), *Do not to another that which thou wouldest not he should do unto thee.*

Of martyrs.

12. But what then shall we say of all those martyrs we read of in the history of the Church, that they have needlessly cast away their lives? For answer hereunto, we are to distinguish the persons that have been for that cause put to death; whereof some have received a calling to preach and profess the kingdom of Christ openly; others have had no such calling, nor more has been required of them than their own faith. The former sort, if they have been put to death for bearing witness to this point, that Jesus Christ is risen from the dead, were true martyrs; for a *martyr* is, to give the true definition of the word, a witness of the resurrection of Jesus the Messiah; which none can be but those that conversed with him on earth, and saw him after he was risen; for a witness must have seen what he testifieth, or else his testimony is not good. And that none but such can properly be called martyrs of Christ is manifest out of the words of St. Peter, *Wherefore of these men which have companied with us all the time that the Lord Jesus went in and out amongst us, beginning from the baptism of John unto that same day he was taken up from us, must one be ordained to be a martyr* (that is, a witness) *with us of his resurrection* (Acts 1:21-22): where we may observe that he which is to be a witness of truth of the resurrection of Christ, that is to say, of the truth of this fundamental article of Christian religion, that Jesus was the Christ, must be some Disciple that conversed with him, and saw him before and after his resurrection; and consequently must be one of his original Disciples; whereas they which were not so can witness no more, but that their antecessors said it, and are therefore but witnesses of other men's testimony, and are but second martyrs, or martyrs of Christ's witnesses.

13. He that to maintain every doctrine which he himself

draweth out of the history of our Saviour's life and of the Acts or Epistles of the Apostles (or which he believeth, upon the authority of a private man) will oppose the laws and authority of the civil state is very far from being a martyr of Christ or a martyr of his martyrs. It is one article only, which to die for meriteth so honourable a name, and that article is this, that *Jesus is the Christ*;[1] that is to say, he that hath redeemed us, and shall come again to give us salvation, and eternal life in his glorious kingdom. To die for every tenet that serveth the ambition or profit of the clergy is not required; nor is it the death of the witness, but the testimony itself that makes the martyr; for the word signifieth nothing else but the man that beareth witness whether he be put to death for his testimony, or not.

14. Also he that is not sent to preach this fundamental article, but taketh it upon him of his private authority, though he be a [273] witness, and consequently a martyr, either primary of Christ or secondary of his Apostles, Disciples, or their successors; yet is he not obliged to suffer death for that cause, because being not called thereto, it is not required at his hands; nor ought he to complain if he loseth the reward he expecteth from those that never set him on work. None therefore can be a martyr, neither of the first nor second degree, that have not a warrant to preach Christ come in the flesh; that is to say, none but such as are sent to the conversion of infidels. For no man is a witness to him that already believeth, and therefore needs no witness; but to them that deny or doubt or have not heard it. Christ sent his Apostles and his seventy Disciples with authority to preach; he sent not all that believed. And he sent them to unbelievers; *I send you*, saith he, *as sheep amongst wolves* (Matt. 10:16); not as sheep to other sheep.

Arguments from the points of their commission.

15. Lastly, the points of their commission, as they are expressly set down in the gospel, contain none of them any authority over the congregation.

1 Hobbes's goal is to make belief in Christianity easy and also to make esoteric theological disputes irrelevant. However, he is also committed by the Thirty-Nine Articles of the English Church to believe everything asserted in the Nicene and Apostles' Creeds. So he sometimes says that "Jesus is the Christ" entails all of these assertions (43.18). Hobbes wants to have things both ways: both very simple and not very simple. See also 42.13, 42.34, and 43.11.

To preach;

16. We have first that the twelve Apostles were sent *to the lost sheep of the house of Israel*, and commanded to preach *that the kingdom of God was at hand* (Matt. 10:6-7). Now preaching, in the original, is that act which a crier, herald, or other officer useth to do publicly in proclaiming of a king. But a crier hath not right to command any man. And the seventy Disciples are sent out as *Labourers, not as lords of the harvest* (Luke 10:2); and are bidden to say, *The kingdom of God is come nigh unto you* (verse 9); and by kingdom here is meant, not the kingdom of grace, but the kingdom of glory; for they are bidden to denounce it to those cities which shall not receive them, as a threatening, that it shall be more tolerable in that day for Sodom than for such a city (verse 11). And our Saviour telleth his Disciples, that sought priority of place, [that] their office was to minister, even as the Son of Man came, not to be ministered unto, but to minister (Matt. 20:28). Preachers therefore have not magisterial, but ministerial power; *Be not called masters*, saith our Saviour, *for one is your master, even Christ* (Matt. 23:10).

And teach;

17. Another point of their commission is to *teach all nations*; as it is in Matthew 28:19, or as in St. Mark 16:15, *Go into all the world, and preach the gospel to every creature*. Teaching, therefore, and preaching is the same thing. For they that proclaim the coming of a king must withal make known by what right he cometh, if they mean men shall submit themselves unto him; as St. Paul did to the Jews of Thessalonica, when *three Sabbath days he reasoned with them out of the Scriptures, opening and alleging that Christ must needs have suffered, and risen again from the dead, and that this Jesus is Christ* (Acts 17:2-3). But to teach out of the Old Testament that Jesus was Christ (that is to say, king) and risen from the dead, is not to say that men are bound, after they believe it, to obey those that tell them so, against the laws and commands of their sovereigns; but [274] that they shall do wisely to expect the coming of Christ hereafter, in patience and faith, with obedience to their present magistrates.

To baptize;

18. Another point of their commission is to *baptize, in the name of the Father, and of the Son, and of the Holy Ghost*. What is baptism? Dipping into water. But what is it to dip a man into the water in the name of anything? The meaning of these words of baptism is this. He that is baptized is dipped or washed as a sign of becoming

a new man and a loyal subject to that God whose person was represented in old time by Moses and the high priests when he reigned over the Jews; and to Jesus Christ, his Son, God and Man, that hath redeemed us and shall in his human nature represent his Father's person in his eternal kingdom after the resurrection; and to acknowledge the doctrine of the Apostles, who, assisted by the Spirit of the Father and of the Son, were left for guides to bring us into that kingdom, to be the only and assured way thereunto. This being our promise in baptism, and the authority of earthly sovereigns being not to be put down till the day of judgement (for that is expressly affirmed by St. Paul, where he saith, *As in Adam all die, so in Christ all shall be made alive. But every man in his own order, Christ the first fruits, afterward they that are Christ's at his coming; then cometh the end, when he shall have delivered up the kingdom to God, even the Father, when he shall have put down all rule, and all authority and power* (1 Cor. 15:22-24)) it is manifest that we do not in baptism constitute over us another authority by which our external actions are to be governed in this life, but promise to take the doctrine of the Apostles for our direction in the way to life eternal.

19. The power of *remission and retention of sins*, called also the power of *loosing* and *binding*, and sometimes the *keys of the kingdom of heaven* is a consequence of the authority to baptize or refuse to baptize. For baptism is the sacrament of allegiance of them that are to be received into the kingdom of God; that is to say, into eternal life; that is to say, to remission of sin; for as eternal life was lost by the committing, so it is recovered by the remitting of men's sins. The end of baptism is remission of sins; therefore St. Peter, when they that were converted by his sermon on the day of Pentecost asked what they were to do, advised them to *repent, and be baptized in the name of Jesus, for the remission of sins* (Acts 2:38). And therefore, seeing to baptize is to declare the reception of men into God's kingdom and to refuse to baptize is to declare their exclusion, it followeth that the power to declare them cast out, or retained in it, was given to the same Apostles and their substitutes and successors. And therefore after our Saviour had breathed upon them, saying, *Receive the Holy Ghost* (John 20:22), he addeth in the next verse, *Whosesoever sins ye remit, they are remitted unto them; and whosesoever sins ye retain, they are retained.* By which words is not

And to forgive and to retain sins.

granted an authority to forgive or retain sins simply and absolute-
[275] ly, as God forgiveth or retaineth them, who knoweth the heart of man and truth of his penitence and conversion, but conditionally, to the penitent; and this forgiveness or absolution, in case the absolved have but a feigned repentance, is thereby, without other act or sentence of the absolved, made void, and hath no effect at all to salvation, but, on the contrary, to the aggravation of his sin. Therefore the Apostles and their successors are to follow but the outward marks of repentance; which appearing, they have no authority to deny absolution; and if they appear not, they have no authority to absolve. The same also is to be observed in baptism; for to a converted Jew or Gentile, the Apostles had not the power to deny baptism, nor to grant it to the unpenitent. But seeing no man is able to discern the truth of another man's repentance, further than by external marks taken from his words and actions, which are subject to hypocrisy, another question will arise, Who is it that is constituted judge of those marks? And this question is decided by our Saviour himself; *If thy brother*, saith he, *shall trespass against thee, go and tell him his fault between thee and him alone; if he shall hear thee, thou hast gained thy brother. But if he will not hear thee, then take with thee one or two more. And if he shall neglect to hear them, tell it unto the Church; but if he neglect to hear the Church, let him be*
Matt. 18: *unto thee as an heathen man and a publican.* By which it is manifest
15-17 that the judgement concerning the truth of repentance belonged not to any one man, but to the Church, that is, to the assembly of the faithful or to them that have authority to be their representant. But besides the judgement, there is necessary also the pronouncing of sentence; and this belonged always to the Apostle or some pastor of the Church as prolocutor; and of this our Saviour speaketh in the eighteenth verse, *Whatsoever ye shall bind on earth shall be bound in heaven; and whatsoever ye shall loose on earth shall be loosed in heaven.* And conformable hereunto was the practice of St. Paul where he saith, *For I verily, as absent in body, but present in spirit, have determined already, as though I were present, concerning him that hath so done this deed; in the name of our Lord Jesus Christ, when ye are gathered together, and my spirit, with the power of our Lord Jesus Christ, to deliver such a one to Satan* (1 Cor. 5:3-5); that is to say, to cast him out of the Church, as a man whose sins are not forgiven. Paul here pro-

nounceth the sentence, but the assembly was first to hear the cause (for St. Paul was absent), and by consequence to condemn him. But in the same chapter [verses 11–12] the judgement in such a case is more expressly attributed to the assembly; *But now I have written unto you not to keep company, if any man that is called a brother be a fornicator*, etc., *with such a one no not to eat. For what have I to do to judge them that are without? Do not ye judge them that are within?*. The sentence therefore by which a man was put out of the Church was pronounced by the Apostle or pastor; but the judgement concerning the merit of the cause was in the Church; that is to say (as the times were before the conversion of kings and men that had sovereign authority in the commonwealth), the assembly of the Christians dwelling in the same city; as in Corinth, in the [276] assembly of the Christians of Corinth.

Of excommunication.

20. This part of the power of the keys by which men were thrust out from the kingdom of God is that which is called *excommunication* and to *excommunicate* is, in the original, *aposunagogon poiein, to cast out of the synagogue*; that is, out of the place of divine service, a word drawn from the custom of the Jews to cast out of their synagogues such as they thought in manners or doctrine contagious, as lepers were by the law of Moses separated from the congregation of Israel till such time as they should be by the priest pronounced clean.[1]

The use of excommunication without civil power,

21. The use and effect of excommunication, whilst it was not yet strengthened with the civil power, was no more than that they who were not excommunicate were to avoid the company of them that were. It was not enough to repute them as heathen, that never had been Christians; for with such they might eat and drink, which with excommunicate persons they might not do, as appeareth by the words of St. Paul where he telleth them he had formerly forbidden them to *company with fornicators* (1 Cor. 5:9–10); but, because that could not be without going out of the world, he restraineth it to such fornicators and otherwise vicious persons as were of the brethren; *with such a one*, he saith, they ought not to keep company, *no not to eat*. And this is no more than our Saviour saith, *Let him be to thee as a heathen, and as a publican* (Matt.

1 Hobbes's goal is to take the teeth out of excommunication, as the following several paragraphs make clear.

18:17). For publicans (which signifieth farmers and receivers of the revenue of the commonwealth) were so hated and detested by the Jews that were to pay it, as that *publican* and *sinner* were taken amongst them for the same thing; insomuch as when our Saviour accepted the invitation of Zacchaeus a publican, though it were to convert him, yet it was objected to him as a crime. And therefore, when our Saviour, to *heathen*, added *publican*, he did forbid them to eat with a man excommunicate.

22. As for keeping them out of their synagogues or places of assembly, they had no power to do it but that of the owner of the place, whether he were Christian or heathen. And because all places are by right in the dominion of the commonwealth, as well he that was excommunicated as he that never was baptized, might enter into them by commission from the civil magistrate (as Paul before his conversion entered into their synagogues at Damascus, to apprehend Christians, men and women, and to carry them bound to Jerusalem, by commission from the high priest (Acts (9:2)).

Of no effect upon an apostate.

23. By which it appears that upon a Christian that should become an apostate, in a place where the civil power did persecute (or not assist the Church) the effect of excommunication had nothing in it, neither of damage in this world nor of terror; not of terror, because of their unbelief; nor of damage, because they returned thereby into the favour of the world; and in the world to come were to be in no worse estate than they which never had believed. The damage redounded rather to the Church, by provo-
[277] cation of them they cast out to a freer execution of their malice.

But upon the faithful only.

24. Excommunication therefore had its effect only upon those that believed that Jesus Christ was to come again in glory to reign over and to judge both the quick and the dead, and should therefore refuse entrance into his kingdom to those whose sins were retained; that is, to those that were excommunicated by the Church. And thence it is that St. Paul calleth excommunication a delivery of the excommunicate person to Satan.[1] For without the kingdom of Christ, all other kingdoms after judgement are comprehended in the kingdom of Satan. This is it that the faithful stood in fear of as long as they stood excommunicate, that is to say,

1 See also 38.12–13, 44.2, 44.27, and 45.7.

in an estate wherein their sins were not forgiven. Whereby we may understand that excommunication in the time that Christian religion was not authorized by the civil power was used only for a correction of manners, not of errors in opinion; for it is a punishment whereof none could be sensible but such as believed and expected the coming again of our Saviour to judge the world; and they who so believed needed no other opinion, but only uprightness of life, to be saved.

For what fault lieth excommunication.

25. There lieth excommunication for injustice; as, if thy brother offend thee, tell it him privately, then with witnesses; lastly, tell the Church, and then if he obey not, *Let him be to thee as an heathen man, and a publican* (Matt. 8:15–17). And there lieth excommunication for a scandalous life, as *If any man that is called a brother be a fornicator, or covetous, or an idolater, or a drunkard, or an extortioner, with such a one ye are not to eat* (1 Corinthian 5:11). But to excommunicate a man that held this foundation, that *Jesus was the Christ*, for difference of opinion in other points by which that foundation was not destroyed, there appeareth no authority in the Scripture, nor example in the Apostles. There is indeed in St. Paul a text that seemeth to be to the contrary; *A man that is an heretic, after the first and second admonition, reject* (Titus 3:10). For a *heretic* is he that, being a member of the Church, teacheth nevertheless some private opinion which the Church has forbidden; and such a one, St. Paul adviseth Titus after the first and second admonition, to *reject*. But to *reject* (in this place) is not to *excommunicate* the man; but to *give over admonishing him, to let him alone, to set by disputing with him*, as one that is to be convinced only by himself. The same Apostle saith, *Foolish and unlearned questions avoid* (2 Timothy 2:23). The word *avoid* in this place, and *reject* in the former, is the same in the original, *paraitou*; but foolish questions may be set by without excommunication. And again, *Avoid foolish questions* (Titus 3:9), where the original *periistaso* (set them by) is equivalent to the former word, *reject*. There is no other place that can so much as colourably be drawn to countenance the casting out of the Church faithful men, such as believed the foundation, only for a singular superstructure of their own, proceeding perhaps from a good and pious conscience. But, on the contrary, all such places as command avoiding such disputes are written for a lesson to pastors [278]

(such as Timothy and Titus were) not to make new articles of faith by determining every small controversy, which oblige men to a needless burden of conscience, or provoke them to break the union of the Church. Which lesson the Apostles themselves observed well. St. Peter and St. Paul, though their controversy were great (as we may read in Galatians 2:11); yet they did not cast one another out of the Church. Nevertheless, during the Apostles' times, there were other pastors that observed it not; as Diotrephes who cast out of the Church such as St. John himself thought fit to be received into it, out of a pride he took in pre-eminence (3 John 9 etc.), so early it was that vainglory and ambition had found entrance into the Church of Christ.

Of persons liable to excommunication.

26. That a man be liable to excommunication, there be many conditions requisite; as first, that he be a member of some commonalty, that is to say, of some lawful assembly, that is to say, of some Christian Church that hath power to judge of the cause for which he is to be excommunicated. For where there is no community, there can be no excommunication; nor where there is no power to judge, can there be any power to give sentence.

27. From hence it followeth that one Church cannot be excommunicated by another; for either they have equal power to excommunicate each other, in which case excommunication is not discipline, nor an act of authority, but schism, and dissolution of charity; or one is so subordinate to the other as that they both have but one voice, and then they be but one Church; and the part excommunicated is no more a Church, but a dissolute number of individual persons.

28. And because the sentence of excommunication importeth an advice not to keep company nor so much as to eat with him that is excommunicate, if a sovereign prince or assembly be excommunicate, the sentence is of no effect. For all subjects are bound to be in the company and presence of their own sovereign, when he requireth it, by the law of nature; nor can they lawfully either expel him from any place of his own dominion, whether profane or holy; nor go out of his dominion without his leave; much less, if he call them to that honour, refuse to eat with him. And as to other princes and states, because they are not parts of one and the same congregation, they need not any other sentence

to keep them from keeping company with the state excommunicate; for the very institution, as it uniteth many men into one community, so it dissociateth one community from another; so that excommunication is not needful for keeping kings and states asunder; nor has any further effect than is in the nature of policy itself, unless it be to instigate princes to war upon one another.

29. Nor is the excommunication of a Christian subject that obeyeth the laws of his own sovereign, whether Christian or heathen, of any effect. For if he believe that *Jesus is the Christ,*[1] *he hath the Spirit of God* (1 John 4:1), *and God dwelleth in him, and he in God* [279] (1 John 4:15). But he that hath the Spirit of God; he that dwelleth in God; he in whom God dwelleth, can receive no harm by the excommunication of men. Therefore, he that believeth Jesus to be the Christ is free from all the dangers threatened to persons excommunicate. He that believeth it not is no Christian. Therefore a true and unfeigned Christian is not liable to excommunication; nor he also that is a professed Christian, till his hypocrisy appear in his manners; that is, till his behaviour be contrary to the law of his sovereign, which is the rule of manners, and which Christ and his Apostles have commanded us to be subject to. For the Church cannot judge of manners but by external actions, which actions can never be unlawful but when they are against the law of the commonwealth.

30. If a man's father, or mother, or master be excommunicate, yet are not the children forbidden to keep them company nor to eat with them; for that were, for the most part, to oblige them not to eat at all, for want of means to get food; and to authorize them to disobey their parents and masters, contrary to the precept of the Apostles.

31. In sum, the power of excommunication cannot be extended further than to the end for which the Apostles and pastors of the Church have their commission from our Saviour; which is not to rule by command and coercion, but by teaching and direction of men in the way of salvation in the world to come. And as a master in any science may abandon his scholar when he obstinately neglecteth the practice of his rules, but not accuse him of injustice, because he was never bound to obey him; so a teacher of

1 42.13, 42.34, and 43.11.

Christian doctrine may abandon his disciples that obstinately continue in an unchristian life; but he cannot say they do him wrong, because they are not obliged to obey him; for to a teacher that shall so complain may be applied the answer of God to Samuel in the like place, *They have not rejected thee, but me* (1 Samuel 8:7). Excommunication therefore, when it wanteth the assistance of the civil power, as it doth when a Christian state or prince is excommunicate by a foreign authority, is without effect, and consequently ought to be without terror. The name of *fulmen excommunicationis* (that is, *the thunderbolt of excommunication*) proceeded from an imagination of the Bishop of Rome, which first used it, that he was king of kings, as the heathen made Jupiter king of the gods; and assigned him, in their poems and pictures, a thunderbolt wherewith to subdue and punish the giants that should dare to deny his power; which imagination was grounded on two errors; one, that the kingdom of Christ is of this world, contrary to our Saviour's own words, *My kingdom is not of this world* (John 18:36); the other, that he is Christ's vicar, not only over his own subjects, but over all the Christians of the world; whereof there is no
[280] ground in Scripture, and the contrary shall be proved in its due place.

*Of the interpreter of the Scriptures before civil sovereigns became Christians.*

32. St. Paul coming to Thessalonica, where was a synagogue of the Jews, *as his manner was, went in unto them, and three Sabbath days reasoned with them out of the Scriptures, opening and alleging, that Christ must needs have suffered, and risen again from the dead; and that this Jesus whom he preached was the Christ* (Acts 17:2-3). The Scriptures here mentioned were the Scriptures of the Jews, that is, the Old Testament. The men to whom he was to prove that Jesus was the Christ and risen again from the dead were also Jews, and [they] did believe already that they were the word of God. Hereupon, as it is in the fourth verse some of them believed, and, as it is in the fifth verse, some believed not. What was the reason, when they all believed the Scripture, that they did not all believe alike, but that some approved, others disapproved, the interpretation of St. Paul that cited them, and every one interpreted them to himself? It was this; St. Paul came to them without any legal commission, and in the manner of one that would not command, but persuade; which he must needs do either by miracles, as Moses did to the Israelites

in Egypt, that they might see his authority in God's works, or by reasoning from the already received Scripture, [in order] that they might see the truth of his doctrine in God's word. But whosoever persuadeth by reasoning from principles written maketh him to whom he speaketh judge, both of the meaning of those principles and also of the force of his inferences upon them. If these Jews of Thessalonica were not, who else was the judge of what St. Paul alleged out of Scripture? If St. Paul, what needed he to quote any places to prove his doctrine? It had been enough to have said, *I find it so in Scripture; that is to say, in your laws, of which I am interpreter, as sent by Christ.* The interpreter therefore of the Scripture, to whose interpretation the Jews of Thessalonica were bound to stand, could be none; every one might believe or not believe, according as the allegations seemed to himself to be agreeable or not agreeable to the meaning of the places alleged. And generally in all cases of the world he that pretendeth any proof maketh judge of his proof him to whom he addresseth his speech. And as to the case of the Jews in particular, they were bound by express words to receive the determination of all hard questions from the priests and judges of Israel for the time being (Deuteronomy 17:8-13). But this is to be understood of the Jews that were yet unconverted.

33. For the conversion of the Gentiles, there was no use of alleging the Scriptures, which they believed not. The Apostles therefore laboured by reason to confute their idolatry; and that done, to persuade them to the faith of Christ by their testimony of his life and resurrection. So that there could not yet be any controversy concerning the authority to interpret Scripture; seeing no man was obliged during his infidelity to follow any man's interpretation of any Scripture except his sovereign's interpretation of the laws of his country.

34. Let us now consider the conversion itself, and see what [281]
there was therein that could be cause of such an obligation. Men were converted to no other thing than to the belief of that which the Apostles preached; and the Apostles preached nothing but that Jesus was the Christ, that is to say, the King that was to save them and reign over them eternally in the world to come; and consequently that he was not dead, but risen again from the dead and

gone up into heaven and should come again one day to judge the world (which also should rise again to be judged) and reward every man according to his works. None of them preached that himself or any other Apostle was such an interpreter of the Scripture as all that became Christians ought to take their interpretation for law. For to interpret the laws is part of the administration of a present kingdom, which the Apostles had not. They prayed then, and all other pastors since, *Let thy kingdom come*, and exhorted their converts to obey their then ethnic princes. The New Testament was not yet published in one body. Every of the evangelists was interpreter of his own gospel, and every Apostle of his own epistle; and of the Old Testament our Saviour himself saith to the Jews, *Search the Scriptures; for in them ye think to have eternal life, and they are they that testify of me* (John 5:39). If he had not meant they should interpret them, he would not have bidden them take thence the proof of his being the Christ; he would either have interpreted them himself, or referred them to the interpretation of the priests.

35. When a difficulty arose, the Apostles and elders of the Church assembled themselves together and determined what should be preached and taught and how they should interpret the Scriptures to the people, but took not from the people the liberty to read and interpret them to themselves. The Apostles sent divers letters to the Churches and other writings for their instruction; which had been in vain if they had not allowed them to interpret, that is, to consider the meaning of them. And as it was in the Apostles' time, it must be till such time as there should be pastors that could authorize an interpreter whose interpretation should generally be stood to; but that could not be till kings were pastors, or pastors kings.

Of the power to make Scripture law.

36. There be two senses wherein a writing may be said to be *canonical*; for *canon* signifieth a *rule*; and a rule is a precept by which a man is guided and directed in any action whatsoever. Such precepts, though given by a teacher to his disciple or a counsellor to his friend without power to compel him to observe them are nevertheless canons, because they are rules. But when they are given by one whom he that receiveth them is bound to obey, then are those canons not only rules, but laws; the question therefore here is of the power to make the Scriptures, which are the rules of Christian faith, laws.

37. That part of the Scripture which was first law was the Ten Commandments, written in two tables of stone and delivered by God himself to Moses, and by Moses made known to the people. Before that time there was no written law of God, who, as yet having not chosen any people to be his peculiar kingdom, had given no law to men, but the law of nature, that is to say, the precepts of natural reason, written in every man's own heart. Of these two tables, the first containeth the law of sovereignty; 1. That they should not obey nor honour the gods of other nations, in these words, *Non habebis deos alienos coram me*;[1] that is, *Thou shalt not have for gods, the gods that other nations worship, but only me*; whereby they were forbidden to obey or honour as their king and governor any other God than him that spake unto them by Moses, and afterwards by the high priest. 2. That they *should not make any image to represent him*; that is to say, they were not to choose to themselves, neither in heaven nor in earth, any representative of their own fancying, but obey Moses and Aaron, whom he had appointed to that office. 3. That *they should not take the name of God in vain*; that is, they should not speak rashly of their King, nor dispute his right, nor the commissions of Moses and Aaron, his lieutenants. 4. That *they should every seventh day abstain from their ordinary labour*, and employ that time in doing him public honour. The second table containeth the duty of one man towards another, as *To honour parents*; *Not to kill*; *Not to commit adultery*; *Not to steal*; *Not to corrupt judgement by false witness*; and finally, *Not so much as to design in their heart the doing of any injury one to another*. The question now is who it was that gave to these written tables the obligatory force of laws. There is no doubt but they were made laws by God himself; but because a law obliges not, nor is law to any but to them that acknowledge it to be the act of the sovereign, how could the people of Israel, that were forbidden to approach the mountain to hear what God said to Moses, be obliged to obedience to all those laws which Moses propounded to them? Some of them were indeed the laws of nature, as all the second table, and therefore to be acknowledged for God's laws, not to the Israelites alone, but to all people; but of those that were peculiar to the Israelites, as those of the first table, the question remains, saving that they had obliged

Of the Ten Commandments.

[282]

1 See also 30.7 and 48.10.

themselves, presently after the propounding of them, to obey Moses, in these words, *Speak thou to us, and we will hear thee; but let not God speak to us, lest we die* (Exod. 20:19). It was therefore only Moses then, and after him the high priest, whom, by Moses, God declared should administer this his peculiar kingdom, that had on earth the power to make this short Scripture of the Decalogue to be law in the commonwealth of Israel. But Moses, and Aaron, and the succeeding high priests were the civil sovereigns. Therefore hitherto the canonizing, or making of the Scripture law, belonged to the civil sovereign.

Of the judicial and levitical law.

38. The judicial law, that is to say, the laws that God prescribed to the magistrates of Israel for the rule of their administration of justice, and of the sentences or judgements they should pronounce
[283] in pleas between man and man) and the Levitical law, that is to say, the rule that God prescribed touching the rites and ceremonies of the priests and Levites, were all delivered to them by Moses only; and therefore also became laws by virtue of the same promise of obedience to Moses. Whether these laws were then written, or not written, but dictated to the people by Moses (after his forty days being with God in the Mount) by word of mouth, is not expressed in the text; but they were all positive laws and equivalent to Holy Scripture and made canonical by Moses the civil sovereign.

The second law.

39. After the Israelites were come into the plains of Moab over against Jericho and ready to enter into the Land of Promise, Moses to the former laws added divers others; which therefore are called *Deuteronomy*; that is, *Second Laws*; and are (as it is written) *the words of a covenant which the Lord commanded Moses to make with the children of Israel, besides the covenant which he made with them in Horeb* (Deut. 29:1). For having explained those former laws, in the beginning of the Book of Deuteronomy, he addeth others, that begin at the twelfth Chapter and continue to the end of the twenty-sixth of the same book. This law they were commanded to write upon great stones plastered over, at their passing over Jordan: this law also was written by Moses himself in a book, and delivered into the hands of the *priests, and to the elders of Israel* (Deut. 31:9), and commanded *to be put in the side of the Ark*; for in the Ark itself was nothing but the *Ten Commandments*. This was the law which

Moses commanded the kings of Israel should keep a copy of (Deut. 17:18); and this is the law which, having been long time lost, was found again in the Temple in the time of Josiah, and by his authority received for the law of God. But both Moses at the writing and Josiah at the recovery thereof had both of them the civil sovereignty. Hitherto therefore the power of making Scripture canonical was in the civil sovereign.

40. Besides this Book of the Law, there was no other book from the time of Moses till after the Captivity received amongst the Jews for the law of God. For the prophets, except a few, lived in the time of the Captivity itself; and the rest lived but a little before it, and were so far from having their prophecies generally received for laws as that their persons were persecuted, partly by false prophets and partly by the kings were seduced by them. And this book itself, which was confirmed by Josiah for the law of God, and with it all the history of the works of God, was lost in the Captivity, and sack of the city of Jerusalem, as appears by that of 2 Esdras 14:21, *Thy law is burnt; therefore no man knoweth the things that are done of Thee, or the works that shall begin.* And before the Captivity, between the time when the law was lost (which is not mentioned in the Scripture, but may probably be thought to be the time of Rehoboam when Shishak, King of Egypt, took the spoil of the Temple) and the time of Josiah, when it was found again, they had no written word of God, but ruled according to their own discretion or by the direction of such as each of them esteemed prophets.

1 Kings 14:26.

[284]

The Old Testament when made canonical.

41. From hence we may infer that the Scriptures of the Old Testament, which we have at this day, were not canonical nor a law unto the Jews till the renovation of their covenant with God at their return from the Captivity and restoration of their commonwealth under Esdras. But from that time forward they were accounted the law of the Jews, and for such translated into Greek by seventy elders of Judaea, and put into the library of Ptolemy at Alexandria, and approved for the word of God. Now seeing Esdras was the high priest, and the high priest was their civil sovereign, it is manifest that the Scriptures were never made laws, but by the sovereign civil power.[1]

1 See also 33.24.

The New Testament began to be canonical under Christian sovereigns.

42. By the writings of the Fathers that lived in the time before that Christian religion was received and authorized by Constantine the Emperor,[1] we may find that the books we now have of the New Testament were held by the Christians of that time (except a few, in respect of whose paucity the rest were called the Catholic Church, and others heretics) for the dictates of the Holy Ghost; and consequently for the canon or rule of faith; such was the reverence and opinion they had of their teachers; as generally the reverence that the disciples bear to their first masters in all manner of doctrine they receive from them is not small. Therefore there is no doubt but when St. Paul wrote to the churches he had converted, or any other Apostle or Disciple of Christ, to those which had then embraced Christ, they received those their writings for the true Christian doctrine. But in that time when not the power and authority of the teacher, but the faith of the hearer, caused them to receive it, it was not the Apostles that made their own writings canonical, but every convert made them so to himself.

43. But the question here is not what any Christian made a law or canon to himself, which he might again reject by the same right he received it, but what was so made a canon to them as without injustice they could not do anything contrary thereunto. That the New Testament should in this sense be canonical, that is to say, a law in any place where the law of the commonwealth had not made it so, is contrary to the nature of a law. For a law, as hath been already shown, is the commandment of that man, or assembly, to whom we have given sovereign authority to make such rules for the direction of our actions as he shall think fit, and to punish us when we do anything contrary to the same. When therefore any other man shall offer unto us any other rules, which the sovereign ruler hath not prescribed, they are but counsel and advice; which, whether good or bad, he that is counselled may
[285] without injustice refuse to observe; and when contrary to the laws already established, without injustice cannot observe, how good

1 Emperor Constantine, the first ruler to make Christianity a state religion, was a favorite of Protestants. In John Foxe's *Book of Martyrs*, chapter 2, Constantine, "a second Moses," is said to have "established the peace of the Church, that for the space of a thousand years we read of no persecutions against the Christians."

soever he conceiveth it to be. I say he cannot in this case observe the same in his actions, nor in his discourse with other men, though he may without blame believe his private teachers and wish he had the liberty to practise their advice, and that it were publicly received for law. For internal faith is in its own nature invisible and consequently exempted from all human jurisdiction; whereas the words and actions that proceed from it, as breaches of our civil obedience, are injustice both before God and man. Seeing then our Saviour hath denied his kingdom to be in this world, seeing he hath said he came not to judge, but to save the world, he hath not subjected us to other laws than those of the commonwealth, that is, the Jews to the law of Moses (which he saith) he came not to destroy, but to fulfil (Matt. 5:17); and [he subjecteth] other nations to the laws of their several sovereigns, and all men to the laws of nature, the observing whereof, both he himself and his Apostles have in their teaching recommended to us as a necessary condition of being admitted by him in the last day into his eternal kingdom, wherein shall be protection and life everlasting. Seeing then our Saviour and his Apostles left not new laws to oblige us in this world, but new doctrine to prepare us for the next, the books of the New Testament, which contain that doctrine, until obedience to them was commanded by them that God had given power to on earth to be legislators, were not obligatory canons, that is, laws, but only good and safe advice for the direction of sinners in the way to salvation, which every man might take and refuse at his own peril, without injustice.

44. Again, our Saviour Christ's commission to his Apostles and Disciples was to proclaim his kingdom (not present, but) to come; and [his commission was] to teach all nations and to baptize them that should believe, and to enter into the houses of them that should receive them; and where they were not received, to shake off the dust of their feet against them, but not to call for fire from heaven to destroy them, nor to compel them to obedience by the sword. In all which there is nothing of power, but of persuasion. He sent them out as sheep unto wolves, not as kings to their subjects. They had not in commission to make laws; but to obey and teach obedience to laws made; and consequently they could not make their writings obligatory canons, without the help of the

sovereign civil power. And therefore the Scripture of the New Testament is there only law where the lawful civil power hath made it so. And there also the king, or sovereign, maketh it a law to himself, by which [law] he subjecteth himself, not to the doctor or Apostle that converted him, but to God himself, and his Son Jesus Christ, as immediately as did the Apostles themselves.

Of the power of Councils to make the Scriptures law. [286]

45. That which may seem to give the New Testament, in respect of those that have embraced Christian doctrine, the force of laws, in the times and places of persecution, is the decrees they made amongst themselves in their synods. For we read the style of the council[1] of the Apostles, the elders, and the whole Church, in this manner, *It seemed good to the Holy Ghost, and to us, to lay upon you no greater burden than these necessary things*, (Acts 15:28) etc., which is a style that signifieth a power to lay a burden on them that had received their doctrine. Now *to lay a burden on another* seemeth the same as *to oblige*; and therefore the acts of that council were laws to the then Christians. Nevertheless, they were no more laws than are these other precepts, *Repent*; *Be baptized*; *Keep the Commandments*; *Believe the Gospel*; *Come unto me*; *Sell all that thou hast*; *Give it to the poor*; and *Follow me*; which are not commands, but invitations and callings of men to Christianity (like that of Isaiah 55:1), *Ho, every man that thirsteth, come ye to the waters, come, and buy wine and milk without money*. For first, the Apostles' power was no other than that of our Saviour, to invite men to embrace the kingdom of God; which they themselves acknowledged for a kingdom, not present, but to come; and they that have no kingdom can make no laws. And secondly, if their acts of council were laws, they could not without sin be disobeyed. But we read not anywhere that they who received not the doctrine of Christ did therein sin, but that they died in their sins; that is, that their sins against the laws to which they owed obedience were not pardoned. And those laws were the laws of nature, and the civil laws of the state, whereto every Christian man had by pact submitted himself. And therefore by the burden which the Apostles might lay on such as they had converted are not to be understood laws, but conditions, proposed to those that sought salvation; which they might accept or refuse at their own peril, without a new sin,

1 See also 25.3.

though not without the hazard of being condemned and excluded out of the kingdom of God for their sins past. And therefore of infidels, St. John saith not, the wrath of God shall *come* upon them, but *the wrath of God remaineth upon them*; and not that they shall he condemned, but that *they are condemned already*. Nor can it be conceived that the benefit of faith *is remission of sins*, unless we conceive withal that the damage of infidelity *is the retention of the same sins*. John 3:36. John 3:18.

46. But to what end is it (may some man ask) that the Apostles and other pastors of the Church, after their time, should meet together to agree upon what doctrine should be taught both for faith and manners, if no man were obliged to observe their decrees? To this may be answered that the Apostles and elders of that council were obliged, even by their entrance into it, to teach the doctrine therein concluded and decreed to be taught, so far forth as no precedent law, to which they were obliged to yield obedience, was to the contrary; but not that all other Christians should be obliged to observe what they taught. For though they might deliberate what each of them should teach; yet they could not deliberate what others should do, unless their assembly had had a legislative power, which none could have but civil sovereigns. For though God be the sovereign of all the world, we are not bound to take for his law whatsoever is propounded by every man in his name; nor anything contrary to the civil law, which [287] God hath expressly commanded us to obey.[1]

47. Seeing then the acts of council of the Apostles were then no laws, but counsels; much less are laws the acts of any other doctors or councils since, if assembled without the authority of the civil sovereign. And consequently, the books of the New Testament, though most perfect rules of Christian doctrine, could not be made laws by any other authority than that of kings or sovereign assemblies.

48. The first council that made the Scriptures we now have canon is not extant; for that collection of the canons of the Apostles, attributed to Clement, the first bishop of Rome after St. Peter, is subject to question; for though the canonical books be there reckoned up; yet these words, *Sint vobis omnibus Clericis &*

1 See also 7.7, 32.5, and 43.6.

*Laicis Libri venerandi*, etc., contain a distinction of clergy and laity that was not in use so near St. Peter's time. The first council for settling the canonical Scripture that is extant is that of Laodicea, *Canon* 59, which forbids the reading of other books than those in the churches; which is a mandate that is not addressed to every Christian, but to those only that had authority to read anything publicly in the Church; that is, to ecclesiastics only.

Of the right of constituting ecclesiastical officers in the time of the Apostles.

49. Of ecclesiastical officers in the time of the Apostles, some were magisterial, some ministerial. Magisterial were the offices of preaching of the gospel of the kingdom of God to infidels; of administering the sacraments and divine service; and of teaching the rules of faith and manners to those that were converted. Ministerial was the office of deacons, that is, of them that were appointed to the administration of the secular necessities of the Church, at such time as they lived upon a common stock of money, raised out of the voluntary contributions of the faithful.

50. Amongst the officers magisterial, the first and principal were the Apostles, whereof there were at first but twelve; and these were chosen and constituted by our Saviour himself; and their office was not only to preach, teach, and baptize, but also to be martyrs (witnesses of our Saviour's resurrection). This testimony was the specifical and essential mark whereby the apostleship was distinguished from other magistracy ecclesiastical, as being necessary for an Apostle either to have seen our Saviour after his resurrection or to have conversed with him before, and seen his works, and other arguments of his divinity, whereby they might be taken for sufficient witnesses. And therefore at the election of a new Apostle in the place of Judas Iscariot, St. Peter saith, *Of these men that have companied with us, all the time that the Lord Jesus went in and out among us, beginning from the baptism of John unto that same day that he was taken up from us, must one be ordained to be a witness with us of his resurrection* (Acts 1:21-22), where by this word *must* is implied a
[288] necessary property of an Apostle, to have companied with the first and prime Apostles in the time that our Saviour manifested himself in the flesh.

Matthias made Apostle by the Congregations.

51. The first Apostle of those which were not constituted by Christ in the time he was upon the earth was Matthias, chosen in this manner; there were assembled together in Jerusalem about

one hundred and twenty Christians (Acts 1:15). These appointed two, Joseph the Just and Matthias (Acts 1:23), and caused lots to be drawn; *and the lot fell on Matthias, and he was numbered with the apostles* (Acts 1:26). So that here we see the ordination of this Apostle was the act of the congregation, and not of St. Peter, nor of the eleven, otherwise than as members of the assembly.

Paul and Barnabas made Apostles by the Church of Antioch.

52. After him there was never any other Apostle ordained, but Paul and Barnabas, which was done (as we read Acts, 13:1–3), in this manner: *There were in the church that was at Antioch, certain prophets and teachers; as Barnabas, and Simeon that was called Niger, and Lucius of Cyrene, and Manaen; which had been brought up with Herod the Tetrarch, and Saul. As they ministered unto the Lord, and fasted, the Holy Ghost said, Separate me Barnabas and Saul for the work whereunto I have called them. And when they had fasted, and prayed, and laid their hands on them, they sent them away.*

53. By which it is manifest that though they were called by the Holy Ghost, their calling was declared unto them, and their mission authorized by the particular church of Antioch. And that this their calling was to the apostleship is apparent by that, that they are both called Apostles (Acts 14:14); and that it was by virtue of this act of the church of Antioch that they were Apostles, St. Paul declareth plainly in that he useth the word, which the Holy Ghost used at his calling, for he styleth himself, *An apostle separated unto the gospel of God* (Romans 1:1), alluding to the words of the Holy Ghost, *Separate me Barnabas and Saul*, etc. But seeing the work of an Apostle was to be a witness of the resurrection of Christ, a man may here ask how St. Paul, that conversed not with our Saviour before his Passion, could know he was risen. To which is easily answered that our Saviour himself appeared to him in the way to Damascus, from heaven, after his ascension; *and chose him for a vessel to bear his name before the Gentiles, and kings, and children of Israel*; and consequently, having seen the Lord after his Passion, was a competent witness of his resurrection; and as for Barnabas, he was a disciple before the Passion. It is therefore evident that Paul and Barnabas were Apostles, and yet chosen and authorized, not by the first Apostles alone, but by the Church of Antioch, as Matthias was chosen and authorized by the Church of Jerusalem.

What offices in the Church are magisterial.

54. *Bishop*, a word formed in our language out of the Greek *episcopus*, signifieth an overseer or superintendent of any business, and particularly a pastor or shepherd; and thence by metaphor was taken, not only amongst the Jews that were originally shepherds, [289] but also amongst the heathen, to signify the office of a king, or any other ruler or guide of people, whether he ruled by laws or doctrine. And so the Apostles were the first Christian bishops,[1] instituted by Christ himself; in which sense the apostleship of Judas is called *his bishoprick* (Acts 1:20). And afterwards, when there were constituted elders in the Christian churches, with charge to guide Christ's flock by their doctrine and advice, these elders were also called bishops. Timothy was an elder (which word *elder*, in the New Testament, is a name of office as well as of age); yet he was also a bishop. And bishops were then content with the title of elders. Nay, St. John himself, the Apostle beloved of our Lord, beginneth his Second Epistle with these words, *The elder to the elect lady*. By which it is evident that *bishop*, *pastor*, *elder*, *doctor*, that is to say, *teacher*, were but so many divers names of the same office in the time of the Apostles. For there was then no government by coercion, but only by doctrine and persuading. The kingdom of God was yet to come, in a new world; so that there could be no authority to compel in any church till the commonwealth had embraced the Christian faith; and consequently no diversity of authority, though there were diversity of employments.

55. Besides these magisterial employments in the Church; namely, apostles, bishops, elders, pastors, and doctors, whose calling was to proclaim Christ to the Jews and infidels, and to direct and teach those that believed, we read in the New Testament of no other. For by the names of *evangelists* and *prophets* is not signified any office, but several gifts by which several men were profitable to the Church; as evangelists, by writing the life and acts of our Saviour; such as were St. Matt. and St. John Apostles, and St. Mark and St. Luke Disciples, and whosoever else wrote of that subject (as St. Thomas and St. Barnabas are said to have done, though the Church have not received the books that have gone under their names); and as prophets, by the gift of interpreting the Old Testament, and sometimes by declaring their special revelations to the

1 Hobbes's point is that the episcopacy was not of divine institution. See also 42.110.

Church. For neither these gifts, nor the gifts of languages, nor the gift of casting out devils, nor of curing other diseases, nor anything else did make an officer in the Church, save only the due calling and election to the charge of teaching.

Ordination of teachers.

56. As the Apostles Matthias, Paul, and Barnabas were not made by our Saviour himself, but were elected by the Church, that is, by the assembly of Christians; namely, Matthias by the church of Jerusalem, and Paul and Barnabas by the church of Antioch; so were also the *presbyters* and *pastors* in other cities, elected by the churches of those cities. For proof whereof, let us consider, first, how St. Paul proceeded in the ordination of presbyters in the cities where he had converted men to the Christian faith, immediately after he and Barnabas had received their apostleship. We read that *they ordained elders in every church* (Acts 14:23); which at first [290] sight may be taken for an argument that they themselves chose and gave them their authority; but if we consider the original text, it will be manifest that they were authorized and chosen by the assembly of the Christians of each city. For the words there are *cheirotonesantes autois presbuterous kat' ekklesian*, that is, *when they had ordained them elders by the holding up of hands in every congregation.* Now it is well enough known that in all those cities the manner of choosing magistrates and officers was by plurality of suffrages; and, because the ordinary way of distinguishing the affirmative votes from the negatives was by holding up of hands, to ordain an officer in any of the cities was no more but to bring the people together to elect them by plurality of votes, whether it were by plurality of elevated hands, or by plurality of voices, or plurality of balls, or beans, or small stones, of which every man cast in one, into a vessel marked for the affirmative or negative; for divers cities had divers customs in that point. It was therefore the assembly that elected their own elders; the Apostles were only presidents of the assembly to call them together for such election, and to pronounce them elected, and to give them the benediction, which now is called consecration. And for this cause they that were presidents of the assemblies, as in the absence of the Apostles the elders were, were called *proestotes* and in Latin *antistites*; which words signify the principal person of the assembly, whose office was to number the votes, and to declare thereby who was chosen; and where the votes

were equal, to decide the matter in question by adding his own, which is the office of a president in council. And, because all the churches had their presbyters ordained in the same manner, where the word is *constitute*, (as Titus 1:5) *hina katasteses kata polin presbuterous, For this cause left I thee in Crete, that thou shouldest constitute elders in every city*, we are to understand the same thing; namely, that he should call the faithful together, and ordain them presbyters by plurality of suffrages. It had been a strange thing if in a town where men perhaps had never seen any magistrate otherwise chosen than by an assembly, those of the town, becoming Christians, should so much as have thought on any other way of election of their teachers and guides, that is to say, of their presbyters (otherwise called bishops), than this of plurality of suffrages, intimated by St. Paul in the word *cheirotonesantes* (Acts 14:23). Nor was there ever any choosing of bishops, before the emperors found it necessary to regulate them in order to the keeping of the peace amongst them, but by the assemblies of the Christians in every several town.

57. The same is also confirmed by the continual practice even to this day in the election of the bishops of Rome. For if the bishop of any place had the right of choosing another to the succession of the pastoral office, in any city, at such time as he went from thence to plant the same in another place, [then] much more had he had the right to appoint his successor in that place in which he
[291] last resided and died; and we find not that ever any bishop of Rome appointed his successor. For they were a long time chosen by the people, as we may see by the sedition raised about the election between Damasus and Ursinus; which Ammianus Marcellinus saith was so great that Juventius the Praefect, unable to keep the peace between them, was forced to go out of the city; and that there were above a hundred men found dead upon that occasion in the church itself. And though they afterwards were chosen, first, by the whole clergy of Rome, and afterwards by the cardinals; yet never any was appointed to the succession by his predecessor. If therefore they pretended no right to appoint their own successors, I think I may reasonably conclude they had no right to appoint the successors of other bishops without receiving some new power; which none could take from the Church to bestow on

them, but such as had a lawful authority, not only to teach, but to command the Church, which none could do but the civil sovereign.

58. The word *minister* in the original, *diakonos*, signifieth one that voluntarily doth the business of another man, and differeth from a servant only in this, that servants are obliged by their condition to what is commanded them; whereas ministers are obliged only by their undertaking, and bound therefore to no more than that they have undertaken; so that both they that teach the word of God and they that administer the secular affairs of the Church are both ministers, but they are ministers of different persons. For the pastors of the Church, called *the ministers of the word* (Acts 6:4) are ministers of Christ, whose word it is; but the ministry of a deacon, which is called *serving of tables* (Acts 6:2), is a service done to the church or congregation; so that neither any one man nor the whole Church could ever of their pastor say he was their minister; but of a deacon, whether the charge he undertook were to serve tables or distribute maintenance to the Christians when they lived in each city on a common stock or upon collections, as in the first times, or to take a care of the house of prayer, or of the revenue, or other worldly business of the Church, the whole congregation might properly call him their minister.

Ministers of the Church what.

59. For their employment as deacons was to serve the congregation, though upon occasion they omitted not to preach the Gospel, and maintain the doctrine of Christ, every one according to his gifts, as St. Stephen did; and both to preach and baptize, as Philip did; for that Philip, which preached the Gospel at Samaria (Acts 8:5), and baptized the eunuch (verse 38), was Philip the Deacon, not Philip the Apostle. For it is manifest that when Philip preached in Samaria (verse 1), the Apostles were at Jerusalem, and *when they heard that Samaria had received the word of God, sent Peter and John to them* (verse 14); by imposition of whose hands they that were baptized received (which before by the baptism of Philip they had not received) the Holy Ghost (verse 15). For it was necessary for the conferring of the Holy Ghost that their baptism [292] should be administered or confirmed by a minister of the word, not by a minister of the Church. And therefore to confirm the baptism of those that Philip the Deacon had baptized, the Apostles

sent out of their own number from Jerusalem to Samaria, Peter and John, who conferred on them that before were but baptized, those graces that were signs of the Holy Spirit, which at that time did accompany all true believers; which what they were may be understood by that which St. Mark (16:17) saith, *These signs follow them that believe in my name; they shall cast out devils; they shall speak with new tongues; they shall take up serpents; and if they drink any deadly thing, it shall not hurt them; they shall lay hands on the sick, and they shall recover.* This to do was it that Philip could not give, but the Apostles could and, as appears by this place, effectually did to every man that truly believed, and was by a minister of Christ himself baptized; which power either Christ's ministers in this age cannot confer, or else there are very few true believers, or Christ hath very few ministers.

And how chosen.

60. That the first deacons were chosen, not by the Apostles, but by a congregation of the disciples, that is, of Christian men of all sorts, is manifest out of Acts, 6, where we read that the Twelve, after the number of disciples was multiplied, called them together, and having told them that it was not fit that the Apostles should leave the word of God, and serve tables, said unto them (verse 3), *Brethren look you out among you seven men of honest report, full of the Holy Ghost, and of wisdom, whom we may appoint over this business.* Here it is manifest that though the Apostles declared them elected, yet the congregation chose them; which also is more expressly said where it is written that *the saying pleased the whole multitude, and they seven,* etc. (Acts 6:5).

Of ecclesiastical revenue under the law of Moses.

61. Under the Old Testament, the tribe of Levi were only capable of the priesthood and other inferior offices of the Church. The land was divided amongst the other tribes (Levi excepted) which by the subdivision of the tribe of Joseph into Ephraim and Manasseh were still twelve. To the tribe of Levi were assigned certain cities for their habitation, with the suburbs for their cattle; but for their portion they were to have the tenth of the fruits of the land of their brethren. Again, the priests for their maintenance had the tenth of that tenth, together with part of the oblations and sacrifices. For God had said to Aaron, *Thou shalt have no inheritance in their land, neither shalt thou have any part amongst them; I am thy part and thine inheritance amongst the children of Israel* (Num. 18:20). For

God being then King, and having constituted the tribe of Levi to be his public ministers, he allowed them for their maintenance the public revenue, that is to say, the part that God had reserved to himself; which were tithes and offerings; and that is it which is meant where God saith, I am thine inheritance. And therefore to the Levites might not unfitly be attributed the name of *clergy*, from [293] *kleros*, which signifieth lot or inheritance; not that they were heirs of the kingdom of God, more than other; but that God's inheritance was their maintenance. Now seeing in this time God himself was their King, and Moses, Aaron, and the succeeding high priests were his lieutenants; it is manifest that the right of tithes and offerings was constituted by the civil power.

62. After their rejection of God in the demanding of a king, they enjoyed still the same revenue; but the right thereof was derived from that, that the kings did never take it from them; for the public revenue was at the disposing of him that was the public person; and that, till the Captivity, was the king. And again, after the return from the Captivity, they paid their tithes as before to the priest. Hitherto therefore Church livings were determined by the civil sovereign.

In our Saviour's time, and after.

63. Of the maintenance of our Saviour and his Apostles, we read only they had a purse (which was carried by Judas Iscariot); and that of the Apostles such as were fishermen did sometimes use their trade; and that when our Saviour sent the twelve Apostles to preach, he forbade them *to carry gold, and silver, and brass in their purses, for that the workman is worthy of his hire*. By which it is probable their ordinary maintenance was not unsuitable to their employment; for their employment was *freely to give, because they had freely received* (verse 8); and their maintenance was the *free gift* of those that believed the good tiding they carried about of the coming of the Messiah their Saviour. To which we may add that which was contributed out of gratitude by such as our Saviour had healed of diseases; of which are mentioned *certain women which had been healed of evil spirits and infirmities; Mary Magdalen, out of whom went seven devils; and Joanna the wife of Chuza, Herod's steward; and Susanna, and many others, which ministered unto him of their substance* (Luke 8:2-3).

Matt. 10:9-10.

64. After our Saviour's ascension, the Christians of every city

Acts 4:34. lived in common upon the money which was made of the sale of their lands and possessions, and laid down at the feet of the Apostles, of good will, not of duty; for *whilst the land remained* saith St. Peter to Ananias, *was it not thine? And after it was sold, was it not in thy power?* (Acts 5:4). Which showeth he needed not have saved his land nor his money by lying, as not being bound to contribute anything at all unless he had pleased. And as in the time of the Apostles, so also all the time downward, till after Constantine the Great, we shall find that the maintenance of the bishops and pastors of the Christian Church was nothing but the voluntary contribution of them that had embraced their doctrine. There was yet no mention of tithes; but such was in the time of Constantine and his sons the affection of Christians to their pastors, as Ammianus Marcellinus saith, describing the sedition of Damasus and Ursinus about the bishopric, that it was worth their contention, in that the
[294] bishops of those times by the liberality of their flock, and especially of matrons, lived splendidly, were carried in coaches, and were sumptuous in their fare and apparel.

The ministers of the Gospel lived on the benevolence of their flocks.

1 Cor. 9:7.

65. But here may some ask whether the pastor were then bound to live upon voluntary contribution, as upon alms, *For who,* saith St. Paul, *goeth to war at his own charges? or who feedeth a flock, and eateth not of the milk of the flock?* And again, *Do ye not know that they which minister about holy things live of the things of the Temple; and they which wait at the altar partake with the altar* (verse 13); that is to say, have part of that which is offered at the altar for their maintenance? And then he concludeth, *Even so hath the Lord appointed that they which preach the gospel should live of the gospel.* From which place may be inferred, indeed, that the pastors of the Church ought to be maintained by their flocks; but not that the pastors were to determine either the quantity or the kind of their own allowance, and be, as it were, their own carvers. Their allowance must needs therefore be determined either by the gratitude and liberality of every particular man of their flock or by the whole congregation. By the whole congregation it could not be, because their acts were then no laws; therefore the maintenance of pastors before emperors and civil sovereigns had made laws to settle it was nothing but benevolence. They that served at the altar lived on what was offered. So may the pastors also take what is offered them by their

flock, but not exact what is not offered. In what court should they sue for it who had no tribunals? Or if they had arbitrators amongst themselves, who should execute their judgements when they had no power to arm their officers? It remaineth therefore that there could be no certain maintenance assigned to any pastors of the Church, but by the whole congregation; and then only when their decrees should have the force, not only of *canons*, but also of *laws*; which laws could not be made but by emperors, kings, or other civil sovereigns. The right of tithes in Moses' Law could not be applied to then ministers of the Gospel, because Moses and the high priests were the civil sovereigns of the people under God, whose kingdom amongst the Jews was present; whereas the kingdom of God by Christ is yet to come.

66. Hitherto hath been shown what the pastors of the Church are; what are the points of their commission, as that they were to preach, to teach, to baptize, to be presidents in their several congregations; what is ecclesiastical censure, viz., excommunication, that is to say, in those places where Christianity was forbidden by the civil laws, a putting of themselves out of the company of the excommunicate, and where Christianity was by the civil law commanded, a putting the excommunicate out of the congregations of Christians; who elected the pastors and of the Church, that it was the congregation; who consecrated and blessed them, that it was the pastor; what was their due revenue, that it was none but their own possessions, and their own labour, and the voluntary contributions of devout and grateful Christians. We are to consider now [295] what office in the Church those persons have who, being civil sovereigns, have embraced also the Christian faith.

That the civil sovereign being a Christian has the right of appointing pastors.

67. And first, we are to remember that the right of judging what doctrines are fit for peace, and to be taught the subjects, is in all commonwealths inseparably annexed (as hath been already proved, Chapter eighteen) to the sovereign power civil, whether it be in one man or in one assembly of men. For it is evident to the meanest capacity that men's actions are derived from the opinions they have of the good or evil which from those actions redound unto themselves; and consequently, men that are once possessed of an opinion that their obedience to the sovereign power will be more hurtful to them than their disobedience will disobey the

laws, and thereby overthrow the commonwealth, and introduce confusion and civil war; for the avoiding whereof, all civil government was ordained. And therefore in all commonwealths of the heathen, the sovereigns have had the name of pastors of the people, because there was no subject that could lawfully teach the people, but by their permission and authority.

68. This right of the heathen kings cannot be thought taken from them by their conversion to the faith of Christ, who never ordained that kings, for believing in him, should be deposed, that is, subjected to any but himself, or, which is all one, be deprived of the power necessary for the conservation of peace amongst their subjects and for their defence against foreign enemies. And therefore Christian kings are still the supreme pastors of their people, and have power to ordain what pastors they please, to teach the Church, that is, to teach the people committed to their charge.

69. Again, let the right of choosing them be, as before the conversion of kings, in the Church, for so it was in the time of the Apostles themselves (as hath been shown already in this chapter); even so also the right will be in the civil sovereign, Christian. For in that he is a Christian, he allows the teaching; and in that he is the sovereign (which is as much as to say, the Church by representation), the teachers he elects are elected by the Church. And when an assembly of Christians choose their pastor in a Christian commonwealth, it is the sovereign that electeth him, because it is done by his authority; in the same manner as when a town choose their mayor, it is the act of him that hath the sovereign power; for every act done is the act of him without whose consent it is invalid. And therefore whatsoever examples may be drawn out of history concerning the election of pastors by the people or by the clergy, they are no arguments against the right of any civil sovereign, because they that elected them did it by his authority.

70. Seeing then in every Christian commonwealth the civil sovereign is the supreme pastor,[1] to whose charge the whole flock
[296] of his subjects is committed, and consequently that it is by his authority that all other pastors are made, and have power to teach and perform all other pastoral offices, it followeth also that it is

1 See also 42.71, 42.72, 42.80, 42.92, and 43.6.

from the civil sovereign that all other pastors derive their right of teaching, preaching, and other functions pertaining to that office, and that they are but his ministers; in the same manner as magistrates of towns, judges in courts of justice, and commanders of armies are all but ministers of him that is the magistrate of the whole commonwealth, judge of all causes, and commander of the whole militia, which is always the civil sovereign. And the reason hereof is not because they that teach, but because they that are to learn, are his subjects. For let it be supposed that a Christian king commit the authority of ordaining pastors in his dominions to another king (as divers Christian kings allow that power to the Pope), he doth not thereby constitute a pastor over himself, nor a sovereign pastor over his people; for that were to deprive himself of the civil power; which, depending on the opinion men have of their duty to him, and the fear they have of punishment in another world, would depend also on the skill and loyalty of doctors who are no less subject, not only to ambition, but also to ignorance, than any other sort of men. So that where a stranger hath authority to appoint teachers, it is given him by the sovereign in whose dominions he teacheth. Christian doctors are our schoolmasters to Christianity; but kings are fathers of families, and may receive schoolmasters for their subjects from the recommendation of a stranger, but not from the command; especially when the ill teaching them shall redound to the great and manifest profit of him that recommends them; nor can they be obliged to retain them longer than it is for the public good, the care of which they stand so long charged withal as they retain any other essential right of the sovereignty.

The pastoral authority of sovereigns only is *de jure divino*, that of other pastors is *jure civili*.

71. If a man therefore should ask a pastor, in the execution of his office (as the chief priests and elders of the people asked our Saviour), *By what authority doest thou these things, and who gave thee this authority?* (Matt. 21:23), he can make no other just answer but that he doth it by the authority of the commonwealth, given him by the king or assembly that representeth it. All pastors, except the supreme, execute their charges in the right, that is, by the authority of the civil sovereign, that is, *jure civili*. But the king, and every other sovereign, executeth his office of supreme pastor by immedi-

ate authority from God, that is to say, in *God's right*, or *jure divino*.[1] And therefore none but kings can put into their titles, a mark of their submission to God only, *Dei gratia Rex*, etc. Bishops ought to say in the beginning of their mandates, *By the favour of the King's Majesty, Bishop of such a diocese*; or as civil ministers, *In his Majesty's name*. For in saying, *Divina providentia*, which is the same with *Dei gratia*, though disguised, they deny to have received their authority [297] from the civil state, and slyly slip off the collar of their civil subjection, contrary to the unity and defence of the commonwealth.

Christian kings have power to execute all manner of pastoral function.

72. But if every Christian sovereign be the supreme pastor of his own subjects, it seemeth that he hath also the authority, not only to preach, which perhaps no man will deny, but also to baptize, and to administer the sacrament of the Lord's Supper and to consecrate both temples and pastors to God's service;[2] which most men deny, partly because they use not to do it, and partly because the administration of sacraments, and consecration of persons and places to holy uses, requireth the imposition of such men's hands as by the like imposition successively from the time of the Apostles have been ordained to the like ministry. For proof therefore that Christian kings have power to baptize and to consecrate, I am to render a reason both why they use not to do it, and how, without the ordinary ceremony of imposition of hands, they are made capable of doing it when they will.

73. There is no doubt but any king, in case he were skilful in the sciences, might by the same right of his office read lectures of them himself by which he authorizeth others to read them in the universities. Nevertheless, because the care of the sum of the business of the commonwealth taketh up his whole time, it were not convenient for him to apply himself in person to that particular. A

1 See also 42.110 and 42.119. The issue of whether the episcopacy was *de jure divino* (by divine right) and how the episcopacy should be treated was hotly debated in 1640 and 1641. Some wanted the bishops excluded from the House of Lords and some wanted episcopacy abolished altogether. Lucius Cary, Lord Falkland, gave an anti-episcopal speech in the House of Commons in February, 1641. He said, "I doe not believe them to bee *Jure divino* … I neither consider them as necessary, nor as unlawful … but as convenient or inconvenient" (*Speech Made to the House of Commons Concerning Episcopacy*, p. 15). Although he did not want the episcopacy eliminated, he wanted it reformed and did not rule out its abolition if reform failed.

2 I know of no other major thinker who claimed that the monarch of England had the power to consecrate priests and bishops. See also 42.70.

king may also, if he please, sit in judgement to hear and determine all manner of causes, as well as give others authority to do it in his name; but that the charge that lieth upon him of command and government constrain him to be continually at the helm, and to commit the ministerial offices to others under him. In the like manner our Saviour (who surely had power to baptize) baptized none himself, but sent his Apostles and Disciples to baptize. So John 4:2.
also St. Paul, by the necessity of preaching in divers and far distant places, baptized few; amongst all the Corinthians he baptized only Crispus, Gaius, and Stephanas; and the reason was because his 1 Cor. 14:16.
principal charge was to preach. Whereby it is manifest that the 1 Cor. 1:17.
greater charge, such as is the government of the Church, is a dispensation for the less. The reason therefore why Christian kings use not to baptize is evident, and the same for which at this day there are few baptized by bishops, and by the Pope fewer.

74. And as concerning imposition of hands, whether it be needful for the authorizing of a king to baptize and consecrate, we may consider thus.

75. Imposition of hands was a most ancient public ceremony amongst the Jews, by which was designed, and made certain, the person or other thing intended in a man's prayer, blessing, sacrifice, consecration, condemnation, or other speech. So Jacob, in blessing the children of Joseph, *Laid his right hand on Ephraim the younger, and his left hand on Manasseh the firstborn* (Gen. 48:14); and this he [298]
did wittingly (though they were so presented to him by Joseph as he was forced in doing it to stretch out his arms across) to design to whom he whom he intended the greater blessing. So also in the sacrificing of the burnt offering, Aaron is commanded *to lay his hands on the head of the bullock* (Exod. 29:10); and *to lay his hand on the head of the ram* (verse 15). The same is also said again, Lev. 1:4, and 8:14. Likewise Moses when he ordained Joshua to be captain of the Israelites, that is, consecrated him to God's service, *laid his hands upon him, and gave him his charge* (Num. 27:23), designing and rendering certain who it was they were to obey in war. And in the consecration of the Levites God commanded that *the children of Israel should put their hands upon the Levites* (Num. 8:10). And in the condemnation of him that had blasphemed the Lord, God commanded that *all that heard him should lay their hands on his head, and*

*that all the congregation should stone him* (Lev. 24:14). And why should they only that heard him lay their hands upon him, and not rather a priest, Levite, or other minister of justice, but that none else were able to design and demonstrate to the eyes of the congregation who it was that had blasphemed and ought to die? And to design a man, or any other thing, by the hand to the eye is less subject to mistake than when it is done to the ear by a name.

76. And so much was this ceremony observed that in blessing the whole congregation at once, which cannot be done by laying on of hands, yet Aaron *did lift up his hand towards the people when he blessed them* (Lev. 9:22). And we read also of the like ceremony of consecration of temples amongst the heathen, as that the priest laid his hands on some post of the temple, all the while he was uttering the words of consecration. So natural it is to design any individual thing rather by the hand, to assure the eyes, than by words to inform the ear, in matters of God's public service.

77. This ceremony was not therefore new in our Saviour's time. For Jairus, whose daughter was sick, besought our Saviour not to heal her, but *to lay his hands upon her, that she might be healed* (Mark 5:23). And *they brought unto him little children, that he should put his hands on them, and pray* (Matt. 19:13).

78. According to this ancient rite, the Apostles and presbyters and the presbytery itself laid hands on them whom they ordained pastors, and withal prayed for them that they might receive the Holy Ghost; and that not only once, but sometimes oftener, when a new occasion was presented; but the end was still the same, namely a punctual and religious designation of the person ordained either to the pastoral charge in general or to a particular mission. So *The Apostles prayed, and laid their hands* (Acts 6:6) on the seven deacons; which was done, not to give them the Holy Ghost (for they were full of the Holy Ghost before they were cho-
[299] sen, as appeareth immediately before, verse 3), but to design them to that office. And after Philip the Deacon had converted certain persons in Samaria, Peter and John went down *and laid their hands on them, and they received the Holy Ghost* (Acts 8:17). And not only an Apostle, but a presbyter had this power; for St. Paul adviseth Timothy, *Lay hands suddenly on no man* (1 Tim. 5:22); that is, design no man rashly to the office of a pastor. The whole presbytery laid

their hands on Timothy, as we read, 1 Timothy 4:14, but this is to be understood as that some did it by the appointment of the presbytery, and most likely their *proestos*, or prolocutor, which it may be was St. Paul himself. For in his second Epistle to Timothy, chapter 1, verse 6, he saith to him, *Stir up the gift of God which is in thee, by the laying on of my hands* (where note, by the way, that by the Holy Ghost is not meant the third person in the Trinity, but the gifts necessary to the pastoral office). We read also that St. Paul had imposition of hands twice; once from Ananias at Damascus at the time of his baptism (Acts 9:17–18); and again at Antioch, when he was first sent out to preach (Acts 13:3). The use then of this ceremony considered in the ordination of pastors was to design the person to whom they gave such power. But if there had been then any Christian that had had the power of teaching before, the baptizing of him, that is, the making him a Christian, had given him no new power, but had only caused him to preach true doctrine, that is, to use his power aright; and therefore the imposition of hands had been unnecessary; baptism itself had been sufficient. But every sovereign, before Christianity, had the power of teaching and ordaining teachers; and therefore Christianity gave them no new right, but only directed them in the way of teaching truth; and consequently they needed no imposition of hands (besides that which is done in baptism) to authorize them to exercise any part of the pastoral function, as namely, to baptize and consecrate. And in the Old Testament, though the priest only had right to consecrate, during the time that the sovereignty was in the high priest, yet it was not so when the sovereignty was in the king; for we read that Solomon blessed the people, consecrated the Temple, and pronounced that public prayer (1 Kings 8), which is the pattern now for consecration of all Christian churches and chapels; whereby it appears he had not only the right of ecclesiastical government, but also of exercising ecclesiastical functions.

The civil sovereign if a Christian is head of the Church in his own dominions.

79. From this consolidation of the right politic and ecclesiastic in Christian sovereigns, it is evident they have all manner of power over their subjects that can be given to man for the government of men's external actions, both in policy and religion, and [they] may make such laws as themselves shall judge fittest, for the government of their own subjects, both as they are the commonwealth

and as they are the Church; for both State and Church are the same men.[1]

80. If they please, therefore, they may (as many Christian kings [300] now do) commit the government of their subjects in matters of religion to the Pope; but then the Pope is in that point subordinate to them and exerciseth that charge in another's dominion *jure civili*, in the right of the civil sovereign; not *jure divino*, in God's right (and may therefore be discharged of that office when the sovereign for the good of his subjects shall think it necessary). They may also, if they please, commit the care of religion to one supreme pastor (or to an assembly of pastors) and give them what power over the Church or one over another, they think most convenient; and what titles of honor, as of bishops, archbishops, priests, or presbyters, they will; and [they may] make such laws for their maintenance (either by tithes or otherwise) as they please, so [long as] they do it out of a sincere conscience, of which God only is the judge. It is the civil sovereign that is to appoint judges and interpreters of the canonical scriptures; for it is he that maketh them laws. It is he also that giveth strength to excommunications; which but for such laws and punishments as may humble obstinate libertines, and reduce them to union with the rest of the Church, would be contemned. In sum, he hath the supreme power in all causes, as well ecclesiastical as civil, as far as concerneth actions and words, for those only are known and may be accused; and of that which cannot be accused, there is no judge at all, but God, that knoweth the heart. And these rights are incident to all sovereigns, whether monarchs or assemblies; for they that are the representants of a Christian people are representants of the Church; for a Church and a commonwealth of Christian people are the same thing.

Cardinal Bellarmine's books *De Summo Pontifice* considered.

81. Though this that I have here said, and in other places of this book, seem clear enough for the asserting of the supreme ecclesiastical power to Christian sovereigns, yet because the Pope of Rome's challenge to that power universally hath been maintained chiefly, and I think as strongly as is possible, by Cardinal Bellarmine in his controversy *De Summo Pontifice*, I have thought it

1 See also 42.70–42.72, 42.80 and 42.86.

necessary, as briefly as I can, to examine the grounds and strength of his discourse.

82. Of five books he hath written of this subject, the first containeth three questions; one, which is simply the best government, *monarchy*, *aristocracy*, or *democracy*, and concludeth for neither, but for a government mixed of all three; another, which of these is the best government of the Church, and concludeth for the mixed, but which should most participate of monarchy; the third, whether in this mixed monarchy, St. Peter had the place of monarch. Concerning his first conclusion, I have already sufficiently proved (chapter 18) that all governments, which men are bound to obey, are simple and absolute. In monarchy there is but one man supreme, and all other men that have any kind of power in the state have it by his commission, during his pleasure, and execute it in his name; and in aristocracy and democracy, but one supreme assembly, with the same power that in monarchy belongeth to the monarch, which is not a mixed, but an absolute [301] sovereignty. And of the three sorts, which is the best is not to be disputed where any one of them is already established; but the present ought always to be preferred, maintained, and accounted best, because it is against both the law of nature and the divine positive law to do anything tending to the subversion thereof. Besides, it maketh nothing to the power of any pastor (unless he have the civil sovereignty) what kind of government is the best, because their calling is not to govern men by commandment, but to teach them and persuade them by arguments, and leave it to them to consider whether they shall embrace or reject the doctrine taught. For monarchy, aristocracy, and democracy do mark out unto us three sorts of sovereigns, not of pastors; or, as we may say, three sorts of masters of families, not three sorts of schoolmasters for their children.

The first book.

83. And therefore the second conclusion, concerning the best form of government of the Church, is nothing to the question of the Pope's power without his own dominions; for in all other commonwealths his power, if he have any at all, is that of the schoolmaster only, and not of the master of the family.

84. For the third conclusion, which is that St. Peter was monarch of the Church, he bringeth for his chief argument the

place of St. Matthew 16:18–19, *Thou art Peter, and upon this rock I will build my church*, etc. *And I will give thee the keys of heaven; whatsoever thou shalt bind on earth shall be bound in heaven, and whatsoever thou shalt loose on earth shall be loosed in heaven.* Which place, well considered, proveth no more but that the Church of Christ hath for foundation one only article; namely, that which Peter, in the name of all the Apostles professing, gave occasion to our Saviour to speak the words here cited. Which that we may clearly understand, we are to consider, that our Saviour preached by himself, by John Baptist, and by his Apostles, nothing but this article of faith, *that he was the Christ*; all other articles requiring faith no otherwise than as founded on that. John began first, preaching only this, *The kingdom of God is at hand* (Matt. 3:2). Then our Saviour himself preached the same (Matt. 4:17): and to his twelve Apostles, when he gave them their commission (Matt. 10:7), there is no mention of preaching any other article but that. This was the fundamental article, that is the foundation of the Church's faith. Afterwards the Apostles being returned to him, he asketh them all, not Peter only, *who men said he was* (Matt. 16:13); and they answered that *some said he was John the Baptist, some Elias, and others Jeremias, or one of the Prophets*; then he asked them all again (not Peter only), *Whom say ye that I am?* (verse 15). Therefore St. Peter answered (for them all), *Thou art Christ, the Son of the living God*; which I said is the foundation of the faith of the whole Church; from which our Saviour takes the occasion of saying, *upon this stone I will build my*
[302] *Church*; by which it is manifest that by the foundation-stone of the Church was meant the fundamental article of the Church's faith. But why then (will some object) doth our Saviour interpose these words, *Thou art Peter*? If the original of this text had been rigidly the reason would easily have appeared. We are therefore to consider that the Apostle Simon was surnamed *Stone* (which is the signification of the Syriac word *cephas*, and of the Greek word *petrus*). Our Saviour, therefore, after the confession of that fundamental article, alluding to his name, said (as if it were in English) thus, Thou art *Stone*, and upon this Stone I will build my Church; which is as much as to say, This article, that *I am the Christ*, is the foundation of all the faith I require in those that are to be members my Church. Neither is this allusion to a name an unusual

thing in common speech; but it had been a strange and obscure speech, if our Saviour, intending to build his Church on the person of St. Peter, had said, *Thou art a stone, and upon this stone I will build my Church*, when it was so obvious, without ambiguity, to have said, *I will build my Church on thee*; and yet there had been still the same allusion to his name.

85. And for the following words, *I will give thee the keys of heaven*, etc., it is no more than what our Saviour gave also to all the rest of his Disciples, *Whatsoever ye shall bind on earth shall be bound in heaven. And whatsoever ye shall loose on earth shall be loosed in heaven* (Matt. 8:18). But howsoever this be interpreted, there is no doubt but the power here granted belongs to all supreme pastors; such as are all Christian civil sovereigns in their own dominions. Insomuch as if St. Peter, or our Saviour himself, had converted any of them to believe him and to acknowledge his kingdom; yet because his kingdom is not of this world, he had left the supreme care of converting his subjects to none but him; or else he must have deprived him of the sovereignty to which the right of teaching is inseparably annexed. And thus much in refutation of his first book, wherein he would prove St. Peter to have been the monarch universal of the Church, that is to say, of all the Christians in the world.

The second book.

86. The second book hath two conclusions; one, that St. Peter was Bishop of Rome, and there died; the other, that the Popes of Rome are his successors; both which have been disputed by others. But supposing them true; yet if by Bishop of Rome be understood either the monarch of the Church, or the supreme pastor of it, not Silvester, but Constantine (who was the first Christian emperor) was that bishop; and as Constantine, so all other Christian emperors were of right supreme bishops of the Roman Empire. I say, of the Roman Empire, not of all Christendom, for other Christian sovereigns had the same right in their several territories, as to an office essentially adherent to their sovereignty; which shall serve for answer to his second book.

The third book.

87. In the third book he handleth the question whether the Pope be Antichrist. For my part, I see no argument that proves he [303] is so, in that sense the Scripture useth the name; nor will I take any argument from the quality of Antichrist to contradict the authori-

ty he exerciseth, or hath heretofore exercised, in the dominions of any other prince or state.[1]

88. It is evident that the prophets of the Old Testament foretold, and the Jews expected, a Messiah, that is, a Christ, that should re-establish amongst them the kingdom of God, which had been rejected by them in the time of Samuel when they required a king after the manner of other nations. This expectation of theirs made them obnoxious to the imposture of all such as had both the ambition to attempt the attaining of the kingdom, and the art to deceive the people by counterfeit miracles, by hypocritical life, or by orations and doctrine plausible. Our Saviour therefore, and his Apostles, forewarned men of false prophets and of false Christs. False Christs are such as pretend to be the *Christ*, but are not, and are called properly *Antichrists*, in such sense as when there happeneth a schism in the Church by the election of two Popes, the one calleth the other *Antipapa*, or the false Pope. And therefore Antichrist in the proper signification hath two essential marks; one, that he denieth Jesus to be Christ; and another that he professeth himself to be Christ. The first mark is set down by St. John in his first Epistle, 4.3, *Every spirit that confesseth not that Jesus Christ is come in the flesh is not of God; and this is the spirit of Antichrist.* The other mark is expressed in the words of our Saviour, *Many shall come in my name, saying, I am Christ* (Matt. 24:5); and again (verse 23), *If any man shall say unto you, Lo, here is Christ, there is Christ, believe it not.* And therefore Antichrist must be a false Christ; that is, some one of them that shall pretend themselves to be Christ. And out of these two marks, *to deny Jesus to be the Christ* and *to affirm himself to be the Christ*, it followeth that he must also be an *adversary of Jesus the true Christ*, which is another usual signification of the word Antichrist. But of these many Antichrists, there is one special one, *ho Antichristos, the Antichrist*, or *Antichrist* definitely, as one certain person; not indefinitely *an Antichrist.* Now seeing the Pope of Rome neither pretendeth himself, nor denieth Jesus to be the Christ, I perceive not how he can be called Antichrist; by which word is not meant one that falsely pretendeth to be *his* lieutenant, or vicar general, but to be *his*. There is also some mark of

---

1 Many Protestants in the seventeenth century thought that the pope was the antichrist. Hobbes's view is moderate.

the time of this special Antichrist, as when that abominable destroyer, spoken of by Daniel, shall stand in the holy place (Matt. 24:15), and such tribulation as was not since the beginning of the world, nor ever shall be again, insomuch as if it were to last long, *no flesh could be saved; but for the elect's sake those days shall be shortened* (Matt. 24:22), (made fewer). But that tribulation is not yet come; for it is to be followed immediately by a darkening of the sun and moon, a falling of the stars, a concussion of the heavens, and the glorious coming again of our Saviour in the clouds (Matt. 24:22). And therefore *the Antichrist* is not yet come; whereas many Popes are both come and gone. It is true, the Pope, in taking upon him [304] to give laws to all Christian kings and nations, usurpeth a kingdom in this world, which Christ took not on him; but he doth it not *as Christ*, but as *for Christ*, wherein there is nothing of *the Antichrist.*

Dan. 9:27

The fourth book.

89. In the fourth book, to prove the Pope to be the supreme judge in all questions of faith and manners, *which is as much as to be the absolute monarch of all Christians in the world*, he bringeth three propositions; the first, that his judgements are infallible; the second, that he can make very [real] laws, and punish those that observe them not; the third, that our Saviour conferred all jurisdiction ecclesiastical on the Pope of Rome.

Texts for the infallibility of the pope's judgement in points of faith.

90. For the infallibility of his judgements, he allegeth the Scriptures; the first, that of Luke 22:31, *Simon, Simon, Satan hath desired you that he may sift you as wheat; but I have prayed for thee, that thy faith fail not; and when thou art converted, strengthen thy brethren.* This, according to Bellarmine's exposition, is that Christ gave here to Simon Peter two privileges; one, that neither his faith should fail, nor the faith of any of his successors; the other, that neither he nor any of his successors should ever define any point concerning faith or manners erroneously, or contrary to the definition of a former Pope; which is a strange and very much strained interpretation. But he that with attention readeth that chapter shall find there is no place in the whole Scripture that maketh more against the Pope's authority than this very place. The priests and scribes, seeking to kill our Saviour at the Passover, and Judas possessed with a resolution to betray him, and the day of killing the Passover being come, our Saviour celebrated the same with his Apostles, which he said, till the kingdom of God was come he would do no more,

and withal told them that one of them was to betray him. Hereupon they questioned which of them it should be; and withal, seeing the next Passover their master would celebrate should be when he was king, entered into a contention who should then be the greatest man. Our Saviour therefore told them that the kings of the nations had dominion over their subjects, and are called by a name in Hebrew that signifies bountiful; but I cannot be so to you; you must endeavour to serve one another; I ordain you a kingdom, but it is such as my Father hath ordained me; a kingdom that I am now to purchase with my blood, and not to possess till my second coming; then ye shall eat and drink at my table, and sit on thrones, judging the twelve tribes of Israel. And then addressing himself to St. Peter, he saith, *Simon,* Simon, Satan seeks, by suggesting a present domination, to weaken your faith of the future; but I have prayed for thee, that thy faith shall not fail; thou therefore (note this) *being converted, and understanding my kingdom as of another world, confirm the same faith in thy brethren.* To which St. Peter answered (as one that no more expected any authority in this world), *Lord, I am ready to go with thee, not only to prison, but to*
[305] *death.* Whereby it is manifest, St. Peter had not only no jurisdiction given him in this world, but a charge to teach all the other Apostles that they also should have none. And for the infallibility of St. Peter's sentence definitive in matter of faith, there is no more to be attributed to it out of this text than that Peter should continue in the belief of this point, namely, that Christ should come again and possess the kingdom at the day of judgement; which was not given by this text to all his successors; for we see they claim it in the world that now is.

91. The second place is that of Matthew 16:18, *Thou art Peter, and upon this rock I will build my Church, and the gates of hell shall not prevail against it.* By which, as I have already shown in this chapter, is proved no more than that the gates of hell shall not prevail against the confession of Peter, which gave occasion to that speech; namely this, that *Jesus is Christ the Son of God.*

92. The third text is John 21:16–17, *Feed my sheep*; which contains no more but a commission of teaching.[1] And if we grant the rest of the Apostles to be contained in that name of *sheep*, then it is

---

1 See also 42.99 and 42.133.

the supreme power of teaching; but it was only for the time that there were no Christian sovereigns already possessed of that supremacy. But I have already proved that Christian sovereigns are in their own dominions the supreme pastors,[1] and instituted thereto by virtue of their being baptized, though without other imposition of hands. For such imposition, being a ceremony of designing the person, is needless when he is already designed to the power of teaching what doctrine he will, by his institution to an absolute power over his subjects. For as I have proved before, sovereigns are supreme teachers, in general, by their office, and therefore oblige themselves, by their baptism, to teach the doctrine of Christ; and when they suffer others to teach their people, they do it at the peril of their own souls; for it is at the hands of the heads of families that God will require the account of the instruction of his children and servants. It is of Abraham himself, not of a hireling, that God saith, *I know him that he will command his children, and his household after him, that they keep the way of the Lord, and do justice and judgement* (Gen. 18:19).

93. The fourth place is that of Exod. 28:30, *Thou shalt put in the breastplate of judgement, the Urim and the Thummim*; which he saith is interpreted by the Septuagint, *delosin kai aletheian* (that is, *evidence* and *truth*) and thence concludeth, God hath given evidence and truth (which is almost infallibility) to the high priest. But be it evidence and truth itself that was given, or be it but admonition to the priest to endeavour to inform himself clearly, and give judgement uprightly; yet in that it was given to the high priest, it was given to the civil sovereign; for such, next under God, was the high priest in the commonwealth of Israel, and is an argument for evidence and truth, that is, for the ecclesiastical supremacy of civil [306] sovereigns over their own subjects, against the pretended power of the Pope. These are all the texts he bringeth for the infallibility of the judgement of the Pope, in point of faith.

94. For the infallibility of his judgement concerning manners, he bringeth one text, which is that of John, 16:13 *When the Spirit of truth is come, he will lead you into all truth*; where, saith he, by *all truth* is meant, at least, *all truth necessary to salvation*. But with this mitigation, he attributeth no more infallibility to the Pope than to any

Texts for the same in point of manners.

1 See also 42.70–72, 42.80, 42.86, and 43.6.

man that professeth Christianity and is not to be damned; for if any man err in any point, wherein not to err is necessary to salvation, it is impossible he should be saved; for that only is necessary to salvation without which to be saved is impossible. What points these are I shall declare out of the Scripture in the chapter following. In this place I say no more but that though it were granted the Pope could not possibly teach any error at all, yet doth not this entitle him to any jurisdiction in the dominions of another prince, unless we shall also say a man is obliged in conscience to set on work upon all occasions the best workman, even then also when he hath formerly promised his work to another.

95. Besides the text, he argueth from reason, thus. If the Pope could err in necessaries, then Christ hath not sufficiently provided for the Church's salvation, because he hath commanded her to follow the Pope's directions. But this reason is invalid, unless he show when and where Christ commanded that, or took at all any notice of a Pope. Nay, granting whatsoever was given to St. Peter was given to the Pope, yet seeing there is in the Scripture no command to any man to obeyeth him when his commands are contrary to those of his lawful sovereign.

96. Lastly, it hath not been declared by the Church, nor by the Pope himself, that he is the civil sovereign of all the Christians in the world; and therefore all Christians are not bound to acknowledge his jurisdiction in point of manners. For the civil sovereignty and supreme judicature in controversies of manners are the same thing; and the makers of civil laws are not only declarers, but also makers of the justice and injustice of actions, there being nothing in men's manners that makes them righteous or unrighteous, but their conformity with the law of the sovereign. And therefore when the Pope challengeth supremacy in controversies of manners, he teacheth men to disobey the civil sovereign; which is an erroneous doctrine, contrary to the many precepts of our Saviour and his Apostles delivered to us in the Scripture.

97. To prove the Pope has power to make laws, he allegeth many places; as first, Deut. 17:12: *The man that will do presumptuously, and will not hearken unto the priest (that standeth to minister there before the Lord thy God, or unto the judge), even that man shall die, and*
[307] *thou shalt put away the evil from Israel.* For answer whereunto we are

to remember that the high priest, next and immediately under God, was the civil sovereign; and all judges were to be constituted by him. The words alleged sound therefore thus, *The man that will presume to disobey the civil sovereign for the time being, or any of his officers, in the execution of their places, that man shall die*, etc., which is clearly for the civil sovereignty, against the universal power of the Pope.

98. Secondly, he allegeth that of Matt. 16, *Whatsoever ye shall bind*, etc., and interpreteth it for such *binding* as is attributed to the Scribes and Pharisees, *They bind heavy burdens, and grievous to be borne, and lay them on men's shoulders* (Matt. 23:4); by which is meant, he says, making of laws, and concludes thence that the Pope can make laws. But this also maketh only for the legislative power of civil sovereigns; for the Scribes and Pharisees sat in Moses' chair, but Moses next under God was sovereign of the people of Israel; and therefore our Saviour commanded them to do all that they should say, but not all that they should do; that is, to obey their laws, but not follow their example.

99. The third place is John 21:16, *Feed my sheep*;[1] which is not a power to make laws, but a command to teach. Making laws belongs to the lord of the family, who by his own discretion chooseth his chaplain, as also a schoolmaster to teach his children.

100. The fourth place, John 20:21, is against him. The words are, *As my Father sent me, so send I you.* But our Saviour was sent to redeem (by his death) such as should believe, and by his own and his Apostles' preaching to prepare them for their entrance into his kingdom; which he himself saith is not of this world, and hath taught us to pray for the coming of it hereafter, though he refused to tell his Apostles when it should come (Acts 1:6-7); and in which, when it comes, the twelve Apostles shall sit on twelve thrones (every one perhaps as high as that of St. Peter), to judge the twelve tribes of Israel. Seeing then God the Father sent not our Saviour to make laws in this present world, we may conclude from the text that neither did our Saviour send St. Peter to make laws here, but to persuade men to expect his second coming with a steadfast faith; and in the meantime, if subjects, to obey their princes; and if princes, both to believe it themselves and to do

1 See also 42.92 and 42.133.

their best to make their subjects do the same, which is the office of a bishop. Therefore this place maketh most strongly for the joining of the ecclesiastical supremacy to the civil sovereignty, contrary to that which Cardinal Bellarmine allegeth it for.

101. The fifth is Acts 15:28, *It hath seemed good to the Holy Spirit, and to us, to lay upon you no greater burden than these necessary things, that ye abstain from meats offered to idols, and from blood, and from things strangled, and from fornication.* Here he notes the word *laying of burdens* for the legislative power. But who is there that, reading this [308] text, can say this style of the Apostles may not as properly be used in giving counsel as in making laws? The style of a law is, *we command*; but, *we think good*, is the ordinary style of them that but give advice; and they lay a burden that give advice, though it be conditional, that is, if they to whom they give it will attain their ends; and such is the burden of abstaining from things strangled, and from blood, not absolute, but in case they will not err. I have shown before (Chapter 25) that law is distinguished from counsel in this, that the reason of a law is taken from the design and benefit of him that prescribeth it;[1] but the reason of a counsel, from the design and benefit of him to whom the counsel is given. But here, the Apostles aim only at the benefit of the converted Gentiles, namely, their salvation; not at their own benefit; for having done their endeavour, they shall have their reward, whether they be obeyed or not. And therefore the acts of this council were not laws, but counsels.

102. The sixth place is that of Rom. 13, *Let every soul be subject to the higher powers, for there is no power but of God*; which is meant, he saith, not only of secular, but also of ecclesiastical princes. To which I answer, first, that there are no ecclesiastical princes but those that are also civil sovereigns and their principalities exceed not the compass of their civil sovereignty; without those bounds, though they may be received for doctors, they cannot be acknowledged for princes. For if the Apostle had meant we should be subject both to our own princes and also to the Pope, he had taught us a doctrine which Christ himself hath told us is impossible, namely, *to serve two masters*. And though the Apostle say in another place, *I write these things being absent, lest being present I should use*

1 See also 25.3.

*sharpness, according to the power which the Lord hath given me* (2 Cor. 13:10); it is not that he challenged a power either to put to death, imprison, banish, whip, or fine any of them, which are punishments, but only to excommunicate, which, without the civil power, is no more but a leaving of their company, and having no more to do with them than with a heathen man or a publican; which in many occasions might be a greater pain to the excommunicant than to the excommunicate.

103. The seventh place is 1 Cor. 4:21, *Shall I come unto you with a rod, or in love, and the spirit of lenity?* But here again, it is not the power of a magistrate to punish offenders, that is meant by a rod; but only the power of excommunication, which is not in its own nature a punishment, but only a denouncing of punishment, that Christ shall inflict, when he shall be in possession of his kingdom, at the day of judgement. Nor then also shall it be properly a punishment, as upon a subject that hath broken the law; but a revenge, as upon an enemy or revolter that denyeth the right of our saviour to the kingdom; and therefore this proveth not the legislative power of any bishop that has not also the civil power.

104. The eighth place is 1 Tim. 3:2, *A bishop must be the husband but of one wife, vigilant, sober,* etc., which he saith was a law. I [309]
thought that none could make a law in the Church but the monarch of the Church, St. Peter. But suppose this precept made by the authority of St. Peter; yet I see no reason why to call it a law, rather than an advice, seeing Timothy was not a subject, but a disciple of St. Paul; nor the flock under the charge of Timothy, his subjects in the kingdom, but his scholars in the school of Christ. If all the precepts he giveth Timothy be laws, why is not this also a law, *Drink no longer water, but use a little wine for health's sake*? And why are not also the precepts of good physicians so many laws, but that it is not the imperative manner of speaking, but an absolute subjection to a person, that maketh his precepts laws?

105. In like manner, the ninth place, 1 Timothy 5:19, *Against an elder receive not an accusation, but before two or three witnesses*, is a wise precept, but not a law.

106. The tenth place is Luke 10:16, *He that heareth you, heareth me; and he that despiseth you, despiseth me.* And there is no doubt but he that despiseth the counsel of those that are sent by Christ

despiseth the counsel of Christ himself. But who are those now that are sent by Christ but such as are ordained pastors by lawful authority? And who are lawfully ordained that are not ordained by the sovereign pastor? And who is ordained by the sovereign pastor in a Christian commonwealth that is not ordained by the authority of the sovereign thereof? Out of this place therefore it followeth that he which heareth his sovereign, being a Christian, heareth Christ; and he that despiseth the doctrine which his king, being a Christian, authorizeth despiseth the doctrine of Christ, which is not that which Bellarmine intendeth here to prove, but the contrary. But all this is nothing to a law. Nay more, a Christian king, a pastor and teacher of his subjects makes not thereby his doctrines laws. He cannot oblige men to believe, though as a civil sovereign he may make laws suitable to his doctrine, which may oblige men to certain actions, and sometimes to such as they would not otherwise do, and which he ought not to command; and yet when they are commanded, they are laws; and the external actions done in obedience to them, without the inward approbation, are the actions of the sovereign, and not of the subject, which is in that case but as an instrument, without any motion of his own at all, because God hath commanded to obey them.

107. The eleventh is every place where the Apostle, for counsel, putteth some word by which men use to signify command, or calleth the following of his counsel by the name of obedience. And therefore they are alleged out of 1 Cor. 11:2, *I commend you for keeping my precepts as I delivered them to you*. The Greek is, *I commend you for keeping those things I delivered to you, as I delivered them*. Which is far from signifying that they were laws, or anything else,
[310] but good counsel. And that of 1 Thess. 4:2, *You know what commandments we gave you*; where the Greek word is *paraggelias edokamen*, equivalent to *paredokamen, what we delivered to you*, as in the place next before alleged, which does not prove the traditions of the Apostles to be any more than counsels; though as is said in the eighth verse, *he that despiseth them, despiseth not man, but God*; for our Saviour himself came not to judge, that is, to be king in this world; but to sacrifice himself for sinners, and leave doctors in his Church, to lead, not to drive men to Christ, who never accepteth forced actions (which is all the law produceth), but the inward

conversion of the heart, which is not the work of laws, but of counsel and doctrine.

108. And that of 2 Thess. 3:14, *If any man obey not our word by this epistle, note that man, and have no company with him, that he may be ashamed*, where from the word *obey*, he would infer that this epistle was a law to the Thessalonians. The epistles of the emperors were indeed laws. If therefore the Epistle of St. Paul were also a law, they were to obey two masters. But the word *obey*, as it is in the Greek *hupakouei*, signifieth *hearkening to*, or *putting in practice*, not only that which is commanded by him that has right to punish, but also that which is delivered in a way of counsel for our good; and therefore St. Paul does not bid kill him that disobeys, nor beat, nor imprison, nor amerce [punish] him, which legislators may all do; but avoid his company, that he may be ashamed; whereby it is evident it was not the empire of an Apostle, but his reputation amongst the faithful, which the Christians stood in awe of.

109. The last place is that of Heb. 13:17, *Obey your leaders, and submit yourselves to them, for they watch for your souls, as they that must give account*; and here also is intended by obedience, a following of their counsel; for the reason of our obedience is not drawn from the will and command of our pastors, but from our own benefit, as being the salvation of our souls they watch for, and not for the exaltation of their own power and authority. If it were meant here that all they teach were laws, then not only the Pope, but every pastor in his parish should have legislative power. Again, they that are bound to obey their pastors have no power to examine their commands. What then shall we say to St. John, who bids us *not to believe every spirit, but to try the spirits whether they are of God, because many false prophets are gone out into the world?* (1 John 4:1). It is therefore manifest that we may dispute the doctrine of our pastors, but no man can dispute a law. The commands of civil sovereigns are on all sides granted to be laws; if any else can make a law besides himself, all commonwealth, and consequently all peace and justice, must cease; which is contrary to all laws, both divine and human. Nothing therefore can be drawn from these or any other places of Scripture to prove the decrees of the Pope, where he has not also the civil sovereignty, to be laws.

The question of superiority between the pope and other bishops.

110. The last point he would prove is this, *that our Saviour Christ*
[311] *has committed ecclesiastical jurisdiction immediately to none but the Pope.* Wherein he handleth not the question of supremacy between the Pope and Christian kings, but between the Pope and other bishops. And first, he says it is agreed that the jurisdiction of bishops is at least in the general *de jure divino*,[1] that is, in the right of God; for which he alleges St. Paul, Ephes. 4:11, where he says that Christ, after his ascension into heaven, *gave gifts to men, some Apostles, some prophets, and some evangelists, and some pastors, and some teachers*; and thence infers they have indeed their jurisdiction in God's right, but will not grant they have it immediately from God, but derived through the Pope. But if a man may be said to have his jurisdiction *de jure divino*, and yet not immediately; what lawful jurisdiction, though but civil, is there in a Christian commonwealth that is not also *de jure divino*? For Christian kings have their civil power from God immediately; and the magistrates under him exercise their several charges in virtue of his commission; wherein that which they do is no less *de jure divino mediato* than that which the bishops do in virtue of the Pope's ordination. All lawful power is of God, immediately in the supreme governor, and mediately in those that have authority under him; so that either he must grant every constable in the state to hold his office in the right of God or he must not hold that any bishop holds his so, besides the Pope himself.

111. But this whole dispute, whether Christ left the jurisdiction to the Pope only or to other bishops also, if considered out of those places where the Pope has the civil sovereignty, is a contention *de lana caprina* [about trifles]; for none of them, where they are not sovereigns, has any jurisdiction at all. For jurisdiction is the power of hearing and determining causes between man and man and can belong to none but him that hath the power to prescribe the rules of right and wrong; that is, to make laws; and with the sword of justice to compel men to obey his decisions, pronounced either by himself or by the judges he ordaineth thereunto, which none can lawfully do but the civil sovereign.

112. Therefore when he allegeth, out of the sixth chapter of Luke, that our Saviour called his disciples together and chose

---

1 See also 42.71.

twelve of them, which he named Apostles, he proveth that he elected them (all, except Matthias, Paul, and Barnabas), and gave them power and command to preach, but not to judge of causes between man and man; for that is a power which he refused to take upon himself, saying, *Who made me a judge, or a divider, amongst you?* and in another place, *My kingdom is not of this world.* But he that hath not the power to hear and determine causes between man and man cannot be said to have any jurisdiction at all. And yet this hinders not but that our Saviour gave them power to preach and baptize in all parts of the world, supposing they were not by their own lawful sovereign forbidden; for to our own sovereigns Christ himself and his Apostles have in sundry places expressly commanded us in all things to be obedient. [312]

113. The arguments by which he would prove that bishops receive their jurisdiction from the Pope (seeing the Pope in the dominions of other princes hath no jurisdiction himself) are all in vain. Yet because they prove, on the contrary, that all bishops receive jurisdiction, when they have it, from their civil sovereigns, I will not omit the recital of them.

114. The first is from Numbers 11, where Moses, not being able alone to undergo the whole burden of administering the affairs of the people of Israel, God commanded him to choose seventy elders, and [God] took part of the spirit of Moses, to put it upon those seventy elders; by which is understood, not that God weakened the spirit of Moses, for that had not eased him at all, but that they had all of them their authority from him; wherein he doth truly and ingenuously interpret that place. But seeing Moses had the entire sovereignty in the commonwealth of the Jews, it is manifest that it is thereby signified that they had their authority from the civil sovereign; and therefore that place proveth that bishops in every Christian commonwealth have their authority from the civil sovereign; and from the Pope in his own territories only, and not in the territories of any other state.

115. The second argument is from the nature of monarchy, wherein all authority is in one man and in others by derivation from him. But the government of the Church, he says, is monarchical. This also makes for Christian monarchs. For they are really monarchs of their own people, that is, of their own Church (for

the Church is the same thing with a Christian people); whereas the power of the Pope, though he were St. Peter, is neither monarchy, nor hath anything of *archical* nor *cratical*, but only of *didactical*; for God accepteth not a forced, but a willing obedience.

116. The third is from that the See of St. Peter[1] is called by St. Cyprian, the *head*, the *source*, the *root*, the *sun*, from whence the authority of bishops is derived. But by the law of nature, which is a better principle of right and wrong than the word of any doctor that is but a man, the civil sovereign in every commonwealth is the *head*, the *source*, the *root*, and the *sun*, from which all jurisdiction is derived. And therefore the jurisdiction of bishops is derived from the civil sovereign.

117. The fourth is taken from the inequality of their jurisdictions; for if God (saith he) had given it them immediately, he had given as well equality of jurisdiction, as of order; but we see some are bishops but of one town, some of a hundred towns, and some of many whole provinces; which differences were not determined by the command of God; their jurisdiction therefore is not of God, but of man; and one has a greater, another a less, as it pleaseth the Prince of the Church. Which argument, if he had proved before that the Pope had had a universal jurisdiction over all Christians, had been for his purpose. But seeing that hath not
[313] been proved, and that it is notoriously known the large jurisdiction of the Pope was given him by those that had it, that is, by the emperors of Rome (for the Patriarch of Constantinople, upon the same title, namely, of being bishop of the capital city of the Empire, and seat of the emperor, claimed to be equal to him), it followeth that all other bishops have their jurisdiction from the sovereigns of the place wherein they exercise the same; and as for that cause they have not their authority *de jure divino*; so neither hath the Pope his *de jure divino*, except only where he is also the civil sovereign.

118. His fifth argument is this; *If bishops have their jurisdiction immediately from God, the Pope could not take it from them, for he can do nothing contrary to God's ordination*; and this consequence is good and well proved. *But* (saith he) *the Pope can do this, and has done it.*

---

1 A 'see' is the territory within which a bishop has jurisdiction. The See of St. Peter is Rome, because Peter is said to be the first bishop of Rome.

This also is granted, so he do it in his own dominions or in the dominions of any other prince that hath given him that power, but not universally, in right of the popedom; for that power belongeth to every Christian sovereign within the bounds of his own empire and is inseparable from the sovereignty. Before the people of Israel had by the commandment of God to Samuel set over themselves a king after the manner of other nations the high priest had the civil government; and none but he could make nor depose an inferior priest. But that power was afterwards in the king, as may be proved by this same argument of Bellarmine; for if the priest, be he the high priest or any other, had his jurisdiction immediately from God, then the king could not take it from him (*for he could do nothing contrary to God's ordinance*). But it is certain that King Solomon deprived Abiathar the high priest of his office (1 Kings 2:26) and placed Zadok in his room (verse 35). Kings therefore may in the like manner ordain and deprive bishops, as they shall think fit, for the well governing of their subjects.

119. His sixth argument is this; if bishops have their jurisdiction *de jure divino* (that is, *immediately from God*) they that maintain it should bring some word of God to prove it; but they can bring none. The argument is good; I have therefore nothing to say against it. But it is an argument no less good to prove the Pope himself to have no jurisdiction in the dominion of any other prince.

120. Lastly, he bringeth for argument the testimony of two Popes, Innocent and Leo; and I doubt not but he might have alleged, with as good reason, the testimonies of all the Popes almost since St. Peter; for, considering the love of power naturally implanted in mankind, whosoever were made Pope, he would be tempted to uphold the same opinion. Nevertheless, they should therein but do as Innocent and Leo did, bear witness of themselves, and therefore their witness should not be good.

121. In the fifth book he hath four conclusions. The first is *that the Pope is not lord of all the world*; the second, *that the Pope is not lord of all the Christian world*; [314] the third, *that the Pope (without his own territory) has not any temporal jurisdiction* DIRECTLY. These three conclusions are easily granted. The fourth is *that the Pope has (in the dominions of other princes) the supreme temporal power* INDIRECTLY;

Of the Pope's temporal power.

which is denied; unless he mean by *indirectly* that he has gotten it by indirect means, then is that also granted. But I understand that when he saith he hath it *indirectly*, he means that such temporal jurisdiction belongeth to him of right, but that this right is but a consequence of his pastoral authority, the which he could not exercise, unless he have the other with it; and therefore to the pastoral power, which he calls spiritual, the supreme power civil is necessarily annexed; and that thereby he hath a right to change kingdoms, giving them to one, and taking them from another, when he shall think it conduces to the salvation of souls.

122. Before I come to consider the arguments by which he would prove this doctrine, it will not be amiss to lay open the consequences of it, that princes and states that have the civil sovereignty in their several commonwealths may bethink themselves whether it be convenient for them, and conducing to the good of their subjects (of whom they are to give an account at the day of judgement) to admit the same.

123. When it is said the Pope hath not (in the territories of other states) the supreme civil power *directly*, we are to understand he doth not challenge it, as other civil sovereigns do, from the original submission thereto of those that are to be governed. For it is evident, and has already been sufficiently in this treatise demonstrated, that the right of all sovereigns is derived originally from the consent of every one of those that are to be governed; whether they that choose him do it for their common defence against an enemy, as when they agree amongst themselves to appoint a man or an assembly of men to protect them, or whether they do it to save their lives, by submission to a conquering enemy. The Pope therefore, when he disclaimeth the supreme civil power over other states *directly*, denieth no more but that his right cometh to him by that way; he ceaseth not for all that to claim it another way; and that is, without the consent of them that are to be governed, by a right given him by God (which he calleth *indirectly*) in his assumption to the papacy. But by what way soever he pretend, the power is the same; and he may (if it be granted to be his right) depose princes and states, as often as it is for the salvation of souls, that is, as often as he will; for he claimeth also the sole power to judge whether it be to the salvation of men's souls, or not. And this is

the doctrine, not only that Bellarmine here, and many other doctors teach in their sermons and books, but also that some councils have decreed, and the Popes have accordingly, when the occasion hath served them, put in practice. For the fourth council of Lateran (held under Pope Innocent the Third in the third Chapter, *De Haereticis*), hath this canon: *If a king, at the Pope's admonition, do not purge his kingdom of heretics, and being excommunicate for the same, make not satisfaction within a year, his subjects are absolved of their obedience.* And the practice hereof hath been seen on divers occasions; as in the deposing of Childeric, King of France; in the translation of the Roman Empire to Charlemagne; in the oppression of John, King of England; in transferring the kingdom of Navarre; and of late years, in the league against Henry the Third of France, and in many more occurrences. I think there be few princes that consider not this as unjust and inconvenient; but I wish they would all resolve to be kings or subjects. Men cannot serve two masters. They ought therefore to ease them, either by holding the reins of government wholly in their own hands or by wholly delivering them into the hands of the Pope, that such men as are willing to be obedient may be protected in their obedience. For this distinction of temporal and spiritual power is but words. Power is as really divided, and as dangerously to all purposes, by sharing with another *indirect* power, as with a *direct* one. But to come now to his arguments. [315]

124. The first is this, *The civil power is subject to the spiritual; therefore he that hath the supreme power spiritual hath right to command temporal princes, and dispose of their temporals in order to the spiritual.* As for the distinction of temporal and spiritual, let us consider in what sense it may be said intelligibly that the temporal or civil power is subject to the spiritual. There be but two ways that those words can be made sense. For when we say one power is subject to another power, the meaning either is that he which hath the one is subject to him that hath the other, or that the one power is to the other as the means to the end. For we cannot understand that one power hath power over another power, or that one power can have right or command over another; for subjection, command, right, and power are accidents, not of powers, but of persons. One power may be subordinate to another, as the art of a

saddler to the art of a rider. If then it be granted that the civil government be ordained as a means to bring us to a spiritual felicity, yet it does not follow that if a king have the civil power and the Pope the spiritual, that therefore the king is bound to obey the Pope, more than every saddler is bound to obey every rider. Therefore as from subordination of an art cannot be inferred the subjection of the professor; so from the subordination of a government cannot be inferred the subjection of the governor. When therefore he saith the civil power is subject to the spiritual, his meaning is that the civil sovereign is subject to the spiritual sovereign. And the argument stands thus; *the civil sovereign is subject to the spiritual; therefore the spiritual prince may command temporal princes.* Where the conclusion is the same with the antecedent he should

[316] have proved. But to prove it, he allegeth first, this reason, *Kings and popes, clergy and laity, make but one commonwealth; that is to say, but one Church; and in all bodies the members depend one upon another; but things spiritual depend not of things temporal; therefore temporal depend on spiritual, and therefore are subject to them.* In which argumentation there be two gross errors; one is that all Christian kings, popes, clergy, and all other Christian men make but one commonwealth; for it is evident that France is one commonwealth, Spain another, and Venice a third, etc. And these consist of Christians, and therefore also are several bodies of Christians, that is to say, several churches;[1] and their several sovereigns represent them, whereby they are capable of commanding and obeying, of doing and suffering, as a natural man; which no general or universal Church is, till it have a representant, which it hath not on earth; for if it had, there is no doubt but that all Christendom were one commonwealth, whose sovereign were that representant, both in things spiritual and temporal; and the Pope, to make himself this representant, wanteth three things that our Saviour hath not given him, to *command*, and to *judge*, and to *punish*, otherwise than, by excommunication, to run from those that will not learn of him; for though the Pope were Christ's only vicar, yet he cannot exercise his government till our Saviour's second coming; and then also it is not the Pope, but St. Peter himself, with the other Apostles, that are to be judges of the world.

---

1 See also 39.5.

125. The other error in this his first argument is that he says the members of every commonwealth, as of a natural body, depend one of another. It is true they cohere together, but they depend only on the sovereign, which is the soul of the commonwealth; which failing, the commonwealth is dissolved into a civil war, no one man so much as cohering to another, for want of a common dependence on a known sovereign; just as the members of the natural body dissolve into earth for want of a soul to hold them together. Therefore there is nothing in this similitude from whence to infer a dependence of the laity on the clergy or of the temporal officers on the spiritual, but of both on the civil sovereign, which ought indeed to direct his civil commands to the salvation of souls; but is not therefore subject to any but God himself. And thus you see the laboured fallacy of the first argument, to deceive such men as distinguish not between the subordination of actions in the way to the end, and the subjection of persons one to another in the administration of the means. For to every end, the means are determined by nature or by God himself supernaturally; but the power to make men use the means is in every nation resigned (by the law of nature, which forbiddeth men to violate their faith given, to the civil sovereign).

126. His second argument is this: *Every commonwealth (because it is supposed to be perfect and sufficient in itself) may command any other* [317] *commonwealth not subject to it, and force it to change the administration of the government; nay depose the prince, and set another in his room, if it cannot otherwise defend itself against the injuries he goes about to do them; much more may a spiritual commonwealth command a temporal one to change the administration of their government, and may depose princes, and institute others, when they cannot otherwise defend the spiritual good.*

127. That a commonwealth, [in order] to defend itself against injuries, may lawfully do all that he hath here said is very true; and hath already in that which hath gone before been sufficiently demonstrated. And if it were also true that there is now in this world a spiritual commonwealth, distinct from a civil commonwealth, then might the prince thereof, upon injury done him or upon want of caution that injury be not done him in time to come, repair and secure himself by war; which is, in sum, deposing, killing, or subduing, or doing any act of hostility. But by the same

reason, it would be no less lawful for a civil sovereign, upon the like injuries done or feared, to make war upon the spiritual sovereign; which I believe is more than Cardinal Bellarmine would have inferred from his own proposition.

128. But spiritual commonwealth there is none in this world; for it is the same thing with the kingdom of Christ; which he himself saith is not of this world, but shall be in the next world, at the resurrection, when they that have lived justly, and believed that he was the Christ, shall, though they died *natural* bodies, rise *spiritual* bodies; and then it is that our Saviour shall judge the world, and conquer his adversaries, and make a spiritual commonwealth. In the meantime, seeing there are no men on earth whose bodies are spiritual, there can be no spiritual commonwealth amongst men that are yet in the flesh; unless we call preachers, that have commission to teach and prepare men for their reception into the kingdom of Christ at the resurrection, a commonwealth; which I have proved already to be none.

129. The third argument is this; *It is not lawful for Christians to tolerate an infidel or heretical king, in case he endeavour to draw them to his heresy, or infidelity. But to judge whether a king draw his subjects to heresy, or not, belongeth to the Pope. Therefore hath the Pope right to determine whether the prince be to be deposed, or not deposed.*

130. To this I answer that both these assertions false. For Christians or men of what religion soever, if they tolerate not their king, whatsoever law he maketh, though it be concerning religion, do violate their faith, contrary to the divine law, both natural and positive; nor is there any judge of heresy amongst subjects but their own civil sovereign. *For heresy is nothing else but a private opinion, obstinately maintained, contrary to the opinion which the public per-*
[318] *son* (that is to say, the representant of the commonwealth) *hath commanded to be taught.* By which it is manifest that an opinion publicly appointed to be taught cannot be heresy; nor the sovereign princes that authorize them, heretics. For heretics are none but private men that stubbornly defend some doctrine prohibited by their lawful sovereigns.

131. But to prove that Christians are not to tolerate infidel or heretical kings, he allegeth a place in Deuteronomy 17:15, where God forbiddeth the Jews, when they shall set a king over them-

selves, to choose a stranger: and from thence inferreth that it is unlawful for a Christian to choose a king that is not a Christian. And it is true that he that is a Christian, that is, he that hath already obliged himself to receive our Saviour, when he shall come, for his king, shall tempt God too much in choosing for king in this world one that he knoweth will endeavour, both by terror and persuasion, to make him violate his faith. But, it is (saith he) the same danger to choose one that is not a Christian for king, and not to depose him when he is chosen. To this I say, the question is not of the danger of not deposing; but of the justice of deposing him. To choose him may in some cases be unjust; but to depose him, when he is chosen, is in no case just. For it is always a violation of faith, and consequently against the law of nature, which is the eternal law of God. Nor do we read that any such doctrine was accounted Christian in the time of the Apostles; nor in the time of the Roman Emperors, till the popes had the civil sovereignty of Rome. But to this he hath replied that the Christians of old deposed not Nero, nor Dioclesian, nor Julian, nor Valens, an Arian, for this cause only, that they wanted temporal forces. Perhaps so. But did our Saviour, who for calling for might have had twelve legions of immortal, invulnerable angels to assist him, want forces to depose Caesar, or at least Pilate, that unjustly, without finding fault in him, delivered him to the Jews to be crucified? Or if the Apostles wanted temporal forces to depose Nero, was it therefore necessary for them in their epistles to the new made Christians to teach them (as they did) to obey the powers constituted over them (whereof Nero in that time was one), and that they ought to obey them, not for fear of their wrath, but for conscience sake? Shall we say they did not only obey, but also teach what they meant not, for want of strength? It is not therefore for want of strength, but for conscience sake, that Christians are to tolerate their heathen princes or princes (for I cannot call any one whose doctrine is the public doctrine, a heretic) that authorize the teaching of an error. And whereas for the temporal power of the Pope, he allegeth further that St. Paul appointed judges under the heathen princes of those times, such as were not ordained by those princes (1 Cor. 6) it is not true. For St. Paul does but advise them to take some of their brethren to compound their differences, as arbitrators, rather [319] than to go to law one with another before the heathen judges; which is a wholesome precept, and full of charity, fit to be practiced also in the best Christian commonwealths. And for the danger that may arise to religion, by the subjects tolerating of a heathen or an erring prince, it is a point of which a subject is no competent judge; or if he be, the Pope's temporal subjects may judge also of the Pope's doctrine. For every Christian prince, as I have formerly proved, is no less supreme pastor of his own subjects than the Pope of his.

132. The fourth argument is taken from the baptism of kings; wherein, that they may be made Christians, they submit their sceptres to Christ and promise to keep and defend the Christian faith. This is true; for Christian kings are no more but Christ's subjects; but they may, for all that, be the Pope's fellows; for they are supreme pastors of their own subjects; and the Pope is no more but king and pastor, even in Rome itself.

133. The fifth argument is drawn from the words spoken by our Saviour, *Feed my sheep*;[1] by which was given all power necessary for a pastor; as the power to chase away wolves, such as are heretics; the power to shut up rams, if they be mad, or push at the other sheep with their horns, such as are evil (though Christian) kings; and power to give the flock convenient food; from whence he inferreth that St. Peter had these three powers given him by Christ. To which I answer that the last of these powers is no more than the power, or rather command, to teach. For the first, which is to chase away wolves, that is, heretics, the place he quoteth is, *Beware of false prophets which come to you in sheep's clothing, but inwardly are ravening wolves* (Matt. 7:15). But neither are heretics false prophets, or at all prophets; nor (admitting heretics for the wolves there meant) were the Apostles commanded to kill them, or if they were kings, to depose them; but to beware of, fly, and avoid them. Nor was it to St. Peter, nor to any of the Apostles, but to the multitude of the Jews that followed him into the mountain, men for the most part not yet converted, that he gave this counsel, to beware of false prophets; which therefore, if it confer a power of chasing away kings, was given not only to private men, but to men that were not at all Christians. And as to the power of separating

---

1 See also 42.92 and 42.99.

and shutting up of furious rams (by which he meaneth Christian kings that refuse to submit themselves to the Roman pastor), our Saviour refused to take upon him that power in this world himself, but advised to let the corn and tares grow up together till the day of judgement; much less did he give it to St. Peter, or can St. Peter give it to the Popes. St. Peter, and all other pastors, are bidden to esteem those Christians that disobey the Church, that is, (that disobey the Christian sovereign) as heathen men and as publicans. Seeing then men challenge to the Pope no authority over heathen [320] princes, they ought to challenge none over those that are to be esteemed as heathen.

134. But from the power to teach only, he inferreth also a coercive power in the Pope over kings. The pastor (saith he) must give his flock convenient food; therefore food; therefore the pope may and ought to compel kings to do their duty. Out of which it followeth that the Pope, as pastor of Christian men, is king of kings; which all Christian kings ought indeed either to confess or else they ought to take upon themselves the supreme pastoral charge, every one in his own dominion.

135. His sixth and last argument is from examples. To which I answer, first, that examples prove nothing; secondly, that the examples he allegeth make not so much as a probability of right. The fact of Jehoiada in killing Athaliah (2 Kings 11) was either by the authority of King Joash, or it was a horrible crime in the high priest, which ever after the election of King Saul was a mere subject. The fact of St. Ambrose, in excommunicating Theodosius the Emperor (if it were true he did so), was a capital crime. And for the Popes, Gregory I, Gregory II, Zachary, and Leo III, their judgements are void, as given in their own cause; and the acts done by them conformably to this doctrine are the greatest crimes (especially that of Zachary) that are incident to human nature. And thus much of *power ecclesiastical*; wherein I had been more brief, forbearing to examine these arguments of Bellarmine, if they had been his as a private man, and not as the champion of the Papacy against all other Christian princes and states.

[321]

# CHAPTER XLIII

## OF WHAT IS NECESSARY FOR A MAN'S RECEPTION INTO THE KINGDOM OF HEAVEN

The difficulty of obeying God and man both at once,

1. The most frequent pretext of sedition and civil war in Christian commonwealths hath a long time proceeded from a difficulty, not yet sufficiently resolved, of obeying at once both God and man then when their commandments are one contrary to the other. It is manifest enough that when a man receiveth two contrary commands and knows that one of them is God's, he ought to obey that and not the other, though it be the command even of his lawful sovereign (whether a monarch or a sovereign assembly) or the command of his father. The difficulty therefore consisteth in this, that men, when they are commanded in the name of God, know not in divers cases whether the command be from God or whether he that commandeth do but abuse God's name for some private ends of his own.[1] For as there were in the Church of the Jews many false prophets that sought reputation with the people by feigned dreams and visions; so there have been in all times in the Church of Christ false teachers that seek reputation with the people by fantastical and false doctrines, and by such reputation, as is the nature of ambition, to govern them for their private benefit.

Is none to them that distinguish between what is and what is not necessary to salvation.

2. But this difficulty of obeying both God and the civil sovereign on earth, to those that can distinguish between what is necessary and what is not necessary for their reception into the kingdom of God, is of no moment. For if the command of the civil sovereign be such as that it may be obeyed without the forfeiture of life eternal, not to obey it is unjust; and the precept[2] of the apostle takes place, *Servants, obey your masters in all things*; and *Children, obey your parents in all things*; and the precept of our Saviour, *The Scribes and Pharisees sit in Moses' chair; all therefore they shall say,*

---

1 This is not as difficult a problem as Hobbes makes it seem here. Given his earlier stated view that the subject gives up his decision-making right to the sovereign, it is unlikely that a conflict can arise. See 43.22. Hobbes has given a philosophical justification for the defense, "I was just obeying orders."

2 Recall that there are two kinds of precepts: commands and counsels. The precepts of the Apostles were counsels, not commands. See also 43.5.

*that observe, and do.* But if the command be such as cannot be obeyed, without being damned to eternal death, then it were madness to obey it, and the counsel of our Saviour takes place, *Fear not those that kill the body, but cannot kill the soul* (Matt. 10:28).[1] All men therefore that would avoid both the punishments that are to be in this world inflicted for disobedience to their earthly sovereign and those that shall be inflicted in the world to come for disobedience to God have need be taught to distinguish well between what is, and what is not, necessary to eternal salvation.

[322]

All that is necessary to salvation is contained in faith and obedience.

3. All that is NECESSARY *to salvation* is contained in two virtues, *faith*[2] *in Christ*, and *obedience to laws*.[3] The latter of these, if it were perfect, were enough to us.[4] But because we are all guilty of disobedience to God's law, not only originally in Adam, but also actually by our own transgressions, there is required at our hands now, not only *obedience* for the rest of our time, but also a *remission* of sins for the time past; which remission is the reward of our faith in Christ. That nothing else is necessarily required to salvation is manifest from this, that the kingdom of heaven is shut to none but to sinners; that is to say, to the disobedient, or transgressors of the law; nor [is it shut] to them, in case they repent, and believe all the articles of Christian faith necessary to salvation.

What obedience is necessary.

4. The obedience required at our hands by God, that accepteth in all our actions the will for the deed, is a serious endeavour[5] to obey him; and is called also by all such names as signify that

1 Others worried about the same problem of knowing what to do when there appeared to be a conflict between God's commands and the sovereign's: "[Thomas] Scott believed in the divine backing given to royal authority ('God hath appointed Kings and Judges to bee life tenants and Deputies in his steade'); he believed, too, that decisions of the king-in-parliament were to be 'obeyed for conscience sake'; and that if the king, should command something contrary to God's wishes the subject must (of course) obey God rather than man, but should 'suffer what is injoyned by him [i.e. the king]' ..." (Glenn Burgess, *The Politics of the Ancient Constitution*, University Park, PA: Pennsylvania UP, 1992. p. 137).

2 Faith is "keeping of promise" (14.11).

3 See 43.19 for a summary.

4 If human beings were perfectly obedient, they would not have needed the redemption of Jesus. Notice Hobbes's emphasis on obedience.

5 Endeavoring to do something is trying to do it. Many Protestants, because of their uncompromising adherence to the belief that faith and grace, not works, are salvific, did not even require a person to try to be good. Goodness was a consequence of having faith.

endeavour. And therefore obedience is sometimes called by the names of *charity* and *love*, because they imply a will[1] to obey; and our Saviour himself maketh our love to God, and to one another, a fulfilling of the whole law; and sometimes by the name of *righteousness*, for righteousness is but the will to give to every one his own, that is to say, the will to obey the laws; and sometimes by the name of *repentance*, because to repent implieth a turning away from sin, which is the same with the return of the will to obedience. Whosoever therefore unfeignedly desireth to fulfil the commandments of God, or repenteth him truly of his transgressions, or that loveth God with all his heart and his neighbour as himself, hath all the obedience necessary to his reception into the kingdom of God; for if God should require perfect innocence, there could no flesh be saved.

And to what laws.

5. But what commandments are those that God hath given us? Are all those laws which were given to the Jews by the hand of Moses the commandments of God? If they be, why are not Christians taught to obey them? If they be not, what others are so, besides the law of nature? For our Christ hath not given us new laws, but counsel[2] to observe those we are subject to; that is to say, the laws of nature, and the laws of our several sovereigns; nor did he make any new law to the Jews in his Sermon on the Mount, but only expounded the laws of Moses, to which they were subject before. The laws of God therefore are none but the laws of nature, whereof the principal is that we should not violate our faith,[3] that is, a commandment to obey our civil sovereigns, which we constituted over us by mutual pact one with another. And this law of God, that commandeth obedience to the law civil, commandeth by consequence obedience to all the precepts[4] of the Bible; which, as I have proved in the precedent chapter, is there only law where the civil sovereign hath made it so; and in other places [it is nothing] but counsel, which a man at his own peril may without injustice refuse to obey.

---

1 A will is the last desire before acting (6.53).

2 See also 43.2.

3 The third law of nature is 'Keep your covenants'. "The failing of performance [of a covenant] is violation of faith" (14.11). Hobbes uses religious concepts such as faith and covenant in order to emphasize the seriousness of the matter. It is also the case that the civil state does what the Christian religion had promised for the 'next life'.

4 Notice the contrast in this sentence between precepts and laws.

6. Knowing now what is the obedience necessary to salvation and to whom it is due, we are to consider next, concerning faith, whom and why we believe, and what are the articles or points necessarily to be believed by them that shall be saved. And first, for the person whom we believe, because it is impossible to believe any person before we know what he saith, it is necessary he be one that we have heard speak.[1] The person therefore whom Abraham, Isaac, Jacob, Moses, and the prophets believed was God himself, that spake unto them supernaturally; and the person whom the Apostles and Disciples that conversed with Christ believed, was our Saviour himself. But of them to whom neither God the Father nor our Saviour ever spake, it cannot be said that the person whom they believed was God. They believed the Apostles and after them the pastors and doctors of the Church that recommended to their faith the history of the Old and New Testament; so that the faith of Christians ever since our Saviour's time hath had for foundation, first, the reputation of their pastors, and afterward, the authority of those that made the Old and New Testament to be received for the rule of faith; which none could do but Christian sovereigns, who are therefore the supreme pastors and the only persons whom Christians now hear speak from God; except such as God speaketh to in these days supernaturally. But because there be many false prophets *gone out into the world*, other men are to examine such spirits, as St. John adviseth us, *whether they be of God, or not* (1 John 4:1). And, therefore, seeing the examination of doctrines belongeth to the supreme pastor, the person which all they that have no special revelation are to believe is, in every commonwealth, the supreme pastor, that is to say, the civil sovereign.[2] [323]

In the faith of a Christian, who is the person believed.

7. The causes why men believe any Christian doctrine are various; for faith is the gift of God and he worketh it in each several man by such ways as it seemeth good unto himself. The most ordinary immediate cause of our belief, concerning any point of Christian faith, is that we believe the Bible to be the word of God.[3] But why we believe the Bible to be the word of God is

The causes of Christian faith.

---

1 See also 7.7.

2 See also 42.70–2, 42.80 and 42.86.

3 Philosophical theologians had long distinguished between faith and reason. Hobbes makes the faith part of that distinction do more work than his predecessors. The

much disputed, as all questions must needs be that are not well stated. For they make not the question to be, *Why we believe it*, but *How we know it*; as if *believing* and *knowing* were all one. And thence while one side ground their knowledge upon the infallibility of the Church and the other side on the testimony of the private spirit, neither side concludeth what it pretends. For how shall a man know the infallibility of the Church but by knowing first the infallibility of the Scripture? Or how shall a man know his own private spirit to be other than a belief grounded upon the authority and arguments of his teachers or upon a presumption of his own gifts? Besides, there is nothing in the Scripture from which can be inferred the infallibility of the Church; much less, of any particular Church; and least of all, the infallibility of any particular man.

[324] Faith comes by hearing. 8. It is manifest, therefore, that Christian men do not know, but only believe the Scripture to be the word of God, and that the means of making them believe, which God is pleased to afford men ordinarily, is according to the way of nature, that is to say, from their teachers. It is the doctrine of St. Paul concerning Christian faith in general, *Faith cometh by hearing*[1] (Rom. 10:7), that is, by hearing our lawful pastors. He saith also, *How shall they believe in him of whom they have not heard? And how shall they hear without a preacher? And how shall they preach, except they be sent?* (verses 14–15). Whereby it is evident that the ordinary cause of believing that the Scriptures are the word of God is the same with the cause of the believing of all other articles of our faith, namely, the hearing of those that are by the law allowed and appointed to teach us, as our parents in their houses, and our pastors in the churches; which also is made more manifest by experience. For what other cause can there be assigned why in Christian commonwealths all men either believe or at least profess the Scripture to be the word of

---

question, 'How do we know that the Bible is true?' is a confused question. Believing and knowing are not the same thing. People believe the Bible; they do not know that it is true, according to Hobbes (43.8). Most scholars think that because Hobbes is so rationalistic, he cannot be serious about believing the Bible. I think that because Hobbes's beliefs were so odd in nonreligious areas, e.g., his beliefs that points have extension and that sovereigns have absolute authority, oddity alone cannot be a good reason for thinking he did not sincerely hold a proposition.

1 See also 29.8.

God, and in other commonwealths scarce any, but that in Christian commonwealths they are taught it from their infancy, and in other places they are taught otherwise?

9. But if teaching be the cause of faith, why do not all believe? It is certain therefore that faith is the gift of God,[1] and he giveth it to whom he will. Nevertheless, because to them to whom he giveth it, he giveth it by the means of teachers, the immediate cause of faith is hearing. In a school, where many are taught and some profit, others profit not, the cause of learning in them that profit is the master; yet it cannot be thence inferred that learning is not the gift of God. All good things proceed from God; yet cannot all that have them say they are inspired; for that implies a gift supernatural and the immediate hand of God, which he that pretends to, pretends to be a prophet, and is subject to the examination of the Church.

10. But whether men know, or believe, or grant the Scriptures to be the word of God, if out of such places of them as are without obscurity I shall show what articles of faith are necessary, and only [articles] necessary for salvation, those men must needs know, believe, or grant the same.

The only necessary article of Christian faith.

11. The (*unum necessarium*), only article of faith, which the Scripture maketh simply necessary to salvation is this, that JESUS IS THE CHRIST.[2] By the name of *Christ* is understood the King which God had before promised by the prophets of the Old Testament to send into the world, to reign (over the Jews and over such of other nations as should believe in him) under himself eternally, and to give them that eternal life which was lost by the sin of Adam. Which, when I have proved out of Scripture, I will further show when, and in what sense, some other articles may be also called *necessary*.

[325]

Proved from the scope of the Evangelists.

12. For proof that the belief of this article, *Jesus is the Christ*, is all the faith required to salvation, my first argument shall be from the scope of the evangelists, which was, by the description of the life of our Saviour, to establish that one article, *Jesus is the Christ*. The sum of St. Matthew's Gospel is this, that Jesus was of the stock

1 Hobbes holds the orthodox view that faith is a gift, that is, a grace, from God. '*Gratia*' in Latin means gift, and the word 'grace' comes from it.

2 See also 42.13, 42.29, 42.34, and 43.18.

of David, born of a virgin, which are the marks of the true Christ; that the Magi came to worship him as King of the Jews; that Herod for the same cause sought to kill him; that John the Baptist proclaimed him; that he preached by himself and his Apostles that he was that King; that he taught the law, not as a scribe, but as a man of authority; that he cured diseases by his word only and did many other miracles, which were foretold the Christ should do; that he was saluted King when he entered into Jerusalem; that he forewarned them to beware of all others that should pretend to be Christ; that he was taken, accused, and put to death for saying he was King; that the cause of his condemnation, written on the cross, was JESUS OF NAZARETH, THE KING OF THE JEWS. All which tend to no other end than this, that men should believe that *Jesus is the Christ*. Such therefore was the scope of St. Matthew's Gospel. But the scope of all the evangelists, as may appear by reading them, was the same. Therefore the scope of the whole Gospel was the establishing of that only article. And St. John expressly makes it his conclusion, *These things are written, that you may know that Jesus is the Christ, the Son of the living God* (John 20:31).

From the sermons of the Apostles.

13. My second argument is taken from the subject of the sermons of the Apostles, both whilst our Saviour lived on earth, and after his ascension. The Apostles in our Saviour's time were sent *to preach the kingdom of God* (Luke 9:2); for neither there, nor Matt. 10:7, giveth he any commission to them other than this, *As ye go, preach, saying, the kingdom of heaven is at hand*; that is, that Jesus is the *Messiah*, the *Christ*, the *King*, which was to come. That their preaching also after his ascension was the same is manifest out of the Acts 17:6, *They drew*, saith St. Luke, *Jason and certain brethren unto the rulers of the city, crying, These that have turned the world upside down are come hither also, whom Jason hath received. And these all do contrary to the decrees of Caesar, saying that there is another king, one Jesus*. And out of the second and third verses of the same chapter, where it is said that St. Paul, *as his manner was, went in unto them; and three Sabbath days reasoned with them out of the Scriptures; opening and alleging that Christ must needs have suffered, and risen again from the dead, and that this Jesus is Christ.*

From the easiness of the doctrine.

14. The third argument is from those places of Scripture by which all the faith required to salvation is declared to be easy. For if an inward assent of the mind to all the doctrines concerning

Christian faith now taught (whereof the greatest part are disputed) were necessary to salvation, there would be nothing in the world so hard as to be a Christian. The thief upon the cross, though repenting, could not have been saved for saying, *Lord, remember me* [326]
*when thou comest into thy kingdom*, by which he testified no beliefs of any other article, but this, that *Jesus was the King*. Nor could it be said (as it is Matt. 11:30) that *Christ's yoke is easy, and his burden light*; nor that *little children believe in him*, as it is, Matt. 18:6. Nor could St. Paul have said (1 Cor. 1:21), *It pleased God by the foolishness of preaching, to save them that believe*; nor could St. Paul himself have been saved, much less have been so great a doctor of the Church so suddenly, that never perhaps thought of transubstantiation, nor purgatory,[1] nor many other articles now obtruded.

From formal and clear texts.

15. The fourth argument is taken from places express, and such as receive no controversy of interpretation; as first, John 5:39, *Search the Scriptures, for in them ye think ye have eternal life, and they are they that testify of me.* Our Saviour here speaketh of the Scriptures only of the Old Testament; for the Jews at that time could not search the Scriptures of the New Testament, which were not written. But the Old Testament hath nothing of Christ but the marks by which men might know him when he came, as that he should descend from David, be born at Bethlehem, and of a virgin, do great miracles, and the like. Therefore to believe that this Jesus was, he was sufficient to eternal life; but more than sufficient is not necessary; and consequently no other article is required. Again, *Whosoever liveth and believeth in me shall not die eternally* (John 11:26). Therefore to believe in Christ is faith sufficient to eternal life; and consequently no more faith than that is necessary. But to believe in Jesus, and to believe that Jesus is the Christ, is all one, as appeareth in the verses immediately following. For when our Saviour had said to Martha, *Believest thou this?* (verse 26) she answereth, *Yea, Lord, I believe that thou art the Christ, the Son of God, which should come into the world* (verse 27). Therefore this article alone is faith sufficient to life eternal, and more than sufficient is not necessary. Thirdly, John 20:31, *These things are written that ye might believe, that Jesus is the Christ, the Son of God, and that believing ye might have life through his name*. There, to believe that *Jesus is the*

1 See also 43.17, 44.16, 44.30–4, 44.37, 44.40, 46.21, 46.27, and 47.14.

*Christ* is faith sufficient to the obtaining of life; and therefore no other article is necessary. Fourthly, 1 John 4:2, *Every spirit that confesseth that Jesus Christ is come in the flesh is of God*. And 1 John 5:1, *Whosoever believeth that Jesus is the Christ is born of God*. And verse 5, *Who is he that overcometh the world, but he that believeth that Jesus is the Son of God?* Fifthly, Acts 8:36–37, *See*, saith the eunuch, *here is water, what doth hinder me to be baptized? And Philip said, If thou believest with all thy heart thou mayst. And he answered and said, I believe that Jesus Christ is the Son of God*. Therefore this article believed, *Jesus is the Christ*, is sufficient to baptism, that is to say, to our reception into the kingdom of God, and, by consequence, only necessary. And generally in all places where our Saviour saith [327] to any man, *Thy faith hath saved thee*, the cause he saith it is some confession which directly, or by consequence, implieth a belief that *Jesus is the Christ*.

From that it is the foundation of all other articles.

16. The last argument is from the places where this article is made the foundation of faith; for he that holdeth the foundation shall be saved. Which places are first, Matt. 24:23, *If any man shall say unto you, Lo, here is Christ, or there, believe it not, for there shall arise false Christs, and false prophets, and shall shew great signs, and wonders*, etc. Here, we see, this article, *Jesus is the Christ*, must be held, though he that shall teach the contrary should do great miracles. The second place is Gal. 1:8, *Though we, or an angel from heaven, preach any other gospel unto you than that we have preached unto you, let him be accursed*. But the gospel which Paul and the other Apostles preached was only this article, that *Jesus is the Christ*; therefore for the belief of this article, we are to reject the authority of an angel from heaven; much more of any mortal man, if he teach the contrary. This is therefore the fundamental article of Christian faith. A third place is 1 John 4:1, *Beloved, believe not every spirit. Hereby ye shall know the Spirit of God; every spirit that confesseth that is come in the flesh is of God*. By which it is evident that this article is the measure and rule by which to estimate and examine all other articles, and is therefore only fundamental. A fourth is Matt. 16:18, where, after St. Peter had professed this article, saying to our Saviour, *Thou art Christ the Son of the living God*, our Saviour answered, *Thou art Peter, and upon this rock I will build my Church*; from whence I infer that this article is that on which all other doc-

trines of the Church are built, as on their foundation. A fifth is (1 Cor. 3:11-12, etc.), *Other foundation can no man lay than that which is laid, Jesus is the Christ. Now if any man build upon this foundation, gold, silver, precious stones, wood, hay, stubble; every man's work shall be made manifest; for the day shall declare it, because it shall be revealed by fire, and the fire shall try every man's work, what sort it is. If any man's work abide which he hath built thereupon, he shall receive a reward. If any man's work shall be burnt, he shall suffer loss; but he himself shall be saved, yet so as by fire.* Which words, being partly plain and easy to understand and partly allegorical and difficult, out of that which is plain may be inferred that pastors that teach this foundation, that *Jesus is the Christ*, though they draw from it false consequences (which all men are sometimes subject to), they may nevertheless be saved; much more that they may be saved, who, being no pastors, but hearers, believe that which is by their lawful pastors taught them. Therefore the belief of this article is sufficient; and by consequence, there is no other article of faith necessarily required to salvation.

17. Now for the part which is allegorical, as that *the fire shall try every man's work*, and that they *shall be saved, but so as by fire*, or *through fire* (for the original is *dia puros*), it maketh nothing against this conclusion, which I have drawn from the other words that are plain. Nevertheless, because upon this place there hath been an argument taken to prove the fire of purgatory,[1] I will also here offer you my conjecture concerning the meaning of this trial of doctrines and saving of men as by fire. The Apostle here seemeth to allude to the words of the Prophet Zachary [Zechariah], who, speaking of the restoration of the kingdom of God, saith thus, *Two parts therein shall be cut off, and die, but the third shall be left therein; and I will bring the third part through the fire, and will refine them as silver is refined, and will try them as gold is tried; they shall call on the name of the Lord, and I will hear them* (Zech. 13:8-9). The day of judgement is the day of the restoration of the kingdom of God; and at that day it is that St. Peter tells us shall be the conflagration of the world, wherein the wicked shall perish; but the remnant which God will save shall pass through that fire unhurt, and be therein (as silver and gold are refined by the fire from their dross) tried, and

[328]

2 Peter 3:7, 10, 12.

1 See also 12.42, 43.14, 44.16, 44.30-4, 44.37, 44.40, 46.26, 46.27, and 47.14.

refined from their idolatry, and be made to call upon the name of the true God. Alluding whereto, St. Paul here saith that *the day* (that is, the day of judgement, the great day of our Saviour's coming to restore the kingdom of God in Israel) shall try every man's doctrine, by judging which are gold, silver, precious stones, wood, hay, stubble; and then they that have built false consequences on the true foundation shall see their doctrines condemned; nevertheless they themselves shall be saved, and pass unhurt through this universal fire, and live eternally, to call upon the name of the true and only God. In which sense there is nothing that accordeth not with the rest of Holy Scripture, or any glimpse of the fire of purgatory.

In what sense other articles may be called necessary.

18. But a man may here ask whether it be not as necessary to salvation to believe that God is Omnipotent Creator of the world, that Jesus Christ is risen, and that all men else shall rise again from the dead at the last day, as to believe that *Jesus is the Christ.* To which I answer, they are; and so are many more articles; but they are such as are contained in this one, and may be deduced from it, with more or less difficulty. For who is there that does not see that they who believe Jesus to be the Son of the God of Israel and that the Israelites had for God the Omnipotent Creator of all things, do therein also believe that God is the Omnipotent Creator of all things? Or how can a man believe that Jesus is the king that shall reign eternally, unless he believe him also risen again from the dead? For a dead man cannot exercise the office of a king. In sum, he that holdeth this foundation, *Jesus is the Christ*, holdeth expressly all that he seeth rightly deduced from it and implicitly all that is consequent thereunto, though he have not skill enough to discern
[329] the consequence. And therefore it holdeth still good that the belief of this one article is sufficient faith to obtain remission of sins to the penitent and consequently to bring them into the kingdom of heaven.

That faith and obedience are both of them necessary to salvation.

19. Now that I have shown that all the obedience required to salvation consisteth in the will to obey the law of God, that is to say, in repentance; and all the faith required to the same is comprehended in the belief of this article, *Jesus is the Christ*; I will further allege those places of the Gospel that prove that all that is necessary to salvation is contained in both these joined together. The

men to whom St. Peter preached on the day of Pentecost, next after the ascension of our Saviour, asked him, and the rest of the Apostles, saying, *Men and brethren, what shall we do?* (Acts 2:37). To whom St. Peter answered (in the next verse), *Repent and be baptized every one of you, for the remission of sins, and ye shall receive the gift of the Holy Ghost.* Therefore repentance and baptism, that is, believing that *Jesus is the Christ*, is all that is necessary to salvation. Again, our Saviour being asked by a certain ruler, *What shall I do to inherit eternal life?* (Luke 18:18) answered (verse 20), *Thou knowest the commandments, Do not commit adultery, Do not kill, Do not steal, Do not bear false witness, Honour thy father and thy mother*, which when he said he had observed, our Saviour added, *Sell all thou hast, give it to the poor, and come and follow me*; which was as much as to say, rely on me that am the king. Therefore to fulfil the law, and to believe that Jesus is the king, is all that is required to bring a man to eternal life. Thirdly, St. Paul saith, *The just shall live by faith* (Rom. 1:17), not every one, but the *just*; therefore *faith* and *justice* (that is, the *will to be just*, or *repentance*) are all that is necessary to life eternal. And our Saviour preached, saying, *The time is fulfilled, and the kingdom of God is at hand; repent and believe the Evangel* (Mark 1:15), that is, the good news that the Christ was come. Therefore to repent, and to believe that Jesus is the Christ, is all that is required to salvation.

What each of them contributes thereunto.

20. Seeing then it is necessary that faith and obedience (implied in the word repentance) do both concur to our salvation, the question by which of the two we are justified is impertinently disputed. Nevertheless, it will not be impertinent to make manifest in what manner each of them contributes thereunto, and in what sense it is said that we are to be justified by the one and by the other. And first, if by righteousness be understood the justice of the works themselves, there is no man that can be saved; for there is none that hath not transgressed the law of God. And therefore when we are said to be justified by works, it is to be understood of the will, which God doth always accept for the work itself, as well in good as in evil men. And in this sense only it is that a man is called *just* or *unjust*; and that his justice justifies him, that is, gives him the title, in God's acceptation of *just*, and renders him capable of *living by his faith*, which before he was not. So that justice justi-

[330] fies in that sense in which to *justify* is the same as that to *denominate a man just*; and not in the signification of discharging the law, whereby the punishment of his sins should be unjust.

21. But a man is then also said to be justified when his plea, though in itself insufficient, is accepted, as when we plead our will, our endeavour to fulfil the law, and repent us of our failings, and God accepteth it for the performance itself. And because God accepteth not the will for the deed, but only in the faithful, it is therefore, faith that makes good our plea; and in this sense it is that faith only justifies; so that *faith* and *obedience* are both necessary to salvation, yet in several senses each of them is said to justify.

Obedience to God and to the civil sovereign not inconsistent whether Christian,

22. Having thus shown what is necessary to salvation, it is not hard to reconcile our obedience to God with our obedience to the civil sovereign, who is either Christian or infidel. If he be a Christian, he alloweth the belief of this article, that *Jesus is the Christ*; and of all the articles that are contained in, or are by evident consequence deduced from it; which is all the faith necessary to salvation. And because he is a sovereign, he requireth obedience to all his own, that is, to all the civil laws; in which also are contained all the laws of nature, that is, all the laws of God; for besides the laws of nature and the laws of the Church, which are part of the civil law (for the Church that can make laws is the commonwealth), there be no other laws divine. Whosoever therefore obeyeth his Christian sovereign is not thereby hindered neither from believing nor from obeying God. But suppose that a Christian king should from this foundation, *Jesus is the Christ*, draw some false consequences, that is to say, make some superstructions of hay or stubble, and command the teaching of the same; yet seeing St. Paul says he shall be saved, much more shall he be saved that teacheth them by his command, and much more yet, he that teaches not, but only believes his lawful teacher. And in case a subject be forbidden by the civil sovereign to profess some of those his opinions, upon what just ground can he disobey? Christian kings may err in deducing a consequence, but who shall judge? Shall a private man judge when the question is of his own obedience? Or shall any man judge but he that is appointed thereto by the Church, that is, by the civil sovereign that representeth it? Or if the Pope or an Apostle judge, may he not err in deducing of a conse-

quence? Did not one of the two, St. Peter or St. Paul, err in a superstructure, when St. Paul withstood St. Peter to his face? There can therefore be no contradiction between the laws of God and the laws of a Christian commonwealth.

23. And when the civil sovereign is an infidel, every one of his own subjects that resisteth him sinneth against the laws of God (for such are the laws of nature), and rejecteth the counsel of the Apostles that admonisheth all Christians to obey their princes, and all children and servants to obey their parents and masters in all things. And for their *faith*, it is internal and invisible; they have the license that Naaman[1] had and need not put themselves into danger for it. But if they do, they ought to expect their reward in heaven and not complain of their lawful sovereign, much less make war upon him. For he that is not glad of any just occasion of martyrdom has not the faith he professeth, but pretends it only, to set some colour upon his own contumacy. But what infidel king is so unreasonable as, knowing he has a subject that waiteth for the second coming of Christ, after the present world shall be burnt, and intendeth then to obey him (which is the intent of believing that Jesus is the Christ), and in the meantime thinketh himself bound to obey the laws of that infidel king, which all Christians are obliged in conscience to do, to put to death or to persecute such a subject?[2]

Or infidel.

[331]

24. And thus much shall suffice, concerning the kingdom of God and policy ecclesiastical. Wherein I pretend not to advance any position of my own, but only to show what are the consequences that seem to me deducible from the principles of Christian politics (which are the Holy Scriptures), in confirmation of the power of civil sovereigns and the duty of their subjects. And in the allegation of Scripture, I have endeavoured to avoid such texts as are of obscure or controverted interpretation, and to allege none but in such sense as is most plain and agreeable to the harmony and scope of the whole Bible, which was written for the re-establishment of the kingdom of God in Christ. For it is not the bare words, but the scope of the writer, that giveth the true light by which any writing is to be interpreted; and they that insist upon

1 See 43.23.
2 Hobbes could be naïve.

single texts, without considering the main design, can derive no thing from them clearly; but rather, by casting atoms of Scripture as dust before men's eyes, make everything more obscure than it is, an ordinary artifice of those that seek not the truth, but their own advantage.

# PART IV

[333]

# OF THE KINGDOM OF DARKNESS

## CHAPTER XLIV

## OF SPIRITUAL DARKNESS FROM MISINTERPRETATION OF SCRIPTURE

The kingdom of darkness what.

Eph. 6:12
Matt. 12:26
Matt. 9:34
Eph. 2:2
John 16:11

1. Besides these sovereign powers, *divine* and *human*, of which I have hitherto discoursed, there is mention in Scripture of another power, namely, that of *the rulers of the darkness of this world, the kingdom of Satan,* and *the principality of Beelzebub over demons;* that is to say, over phantasms[1] that appear in the air. For which cause Satan[2] is also called *the prince of the power of the air,* and (because he ruleth in the darkness of this world) *the prince of this world.* And in consequence hereunto, they who are under his dominion, in opposition to the faithful (who are the *children of the light*), are called the *children of darkness.* For seeing Beelzebub is prince of phantasms, inhabitants of his dominion of air and darkness, the children of darkness and these demons, phantasms or spirits of illusion, signify allegorically the same thing. This considered, the kingdom of darkness, as it is set forth in these and other places of the Scripture, is nothing else but a *confederacy of deceivers that, to obtain dominion over men in this present world, endeavour, by dark and erroneous doctrines, to extinguish in them the light both of nature and of the gospel, and so to disprepare them for the kingdom of God to come.*[3]

---

1 See also 34.25, 36.2, 45.14, 44.13, 44.16, 44.21, 45.2, 45.4, 45.8, 45.10, and 45.14.

2 See also 38.12–13, 42.24, 44.2, 44.27, and 45.7.

3 The Pope is a member of the Kingdom of Darkness, but is not the Antichrist (42.87).

[334] The Church not yet fully freed of darkness.

2. As men that are utterly deprived from their nativity of the light of the bodily eye have no idea at all of any such light, and no man conceives in his imagination any greater light than he hath at some time or other perceived by his outward senses, so also is it of the light of the gospel and of the light of the understanding that no man can conceive there is any greater degree of it than that which he hath already attained unto. And from hence it comes to pass that men have no other means to acknowledge their own darkness but only by reasoning from the unforeseen mischances that befall them in their ways. The darkest part of the kingdom of Satan is that which is without the Church of God, that is to say, amongst them that believe not in Jesus Christ. But we cannot say that therefore the Church enjoyeth, as the land of Goshen, all the light which to the performance of the work enjoined us by God is necessary. Whence comes it that in Christendom there has been, almost from the time of the Apostles, such jostling of one another out of their places, both by foreign and civil war, such stumbling at every little asperity of their own fortune and every little eminence of that of other men, and such diversity of ways in running to the same mark, *felicity*, if it be not night amongst us or at least a mist? We are therefore yet in the dark.

Four causes of spiritual darkness.

3. The enemy has been here in the night of our natural ignorance and [has] sown the tares of spiritual errors; and [has done] that, first, by abusing and putting out the light of the Scriptures. For we err, not knowing the Scriptures. Secondly, by introducing the demonology[1] of the heathen poets,[2] that is to say, their fabulous doctrine concerning demons, which are but idols, or phantasms of the brain, without any real nature of their own, distinct from human fancy; such as are dead men's ghosts and fairies and other matter of old wives' tales. Thirdly, by mixing with the Scripture divers relics of the religion and much of the vain and erroneous philosophy of the Greeks, especially of Aristotle.[3] Fourthly, by mingling with both these, false or uncertain traditions, and feigned or uncertain history. And so we come to err *by giving heed to seducing spirits*, and the demonology of such *as speak lies in*

---

1 See also 40.14, 44.16, 45.2, and 47.15.

2 See also 12.6, 38.6, 45.33, and 45.38.

3 See also 46.11–14 and 47.16.

*hypocrisy* (or, as it is in the original, *of those that play the part of liars* (1 Tim. 4:1) *with a seared conscience*, that is, contrary to their own knowledge. Concerning the first of these, which is the seducing of men by abuse of Scripture, I intend to speak briefly in this chapter.

Errors from misinterpreting the Scriptures concerning the kingdom of God.

4. The greatest and main abuse of Scripture and to which almost all the rest are either consequent or subservient is the wresting of it to prove that the kingdom of God, mentioned so often in the Scripture, is the present Church or multitude of Christian men now living,[1] or that, being dead, are to rise again at the last day. Whereas the kingdom of God was first instituted by the ministry of Moses over the Jews only, who were therefore called his peculiar people, and ceased afterward, in the election of Saul, when they refused to be governed by God any more and demanded a king after the manner of the nations; which God [335] himself consented unto, as I have more at large proved before, in the 35 chapter. After that time, there was no other kingdom of God in the world, by any pact or otherwise, than he ever was, is, and shall be king of all men and of all creatures, as governing according to his will, by his infinite power. Nevertheless, he promised by his prophets to restore this his government to them again, when the time he hath in his secret counsel appointed for it shall be fully come, and when they shall turn unto him by repentance and amendment of life. And not only so, but he invited also the Gentiles to come in and enjoy the happiness of his reign on the same conditions of conversion and repentance. And he promised also to send his Son into the world, to expiate the sins of them all by his death and to prepare them by his doctrine to receive him at his second coming. Which second coming not yet being, the kingdom of God is not yet come, and we are not now under any other kings by pact but our civil sovereigns, saving only that Christian men are already in the kingdom of grace, inasmuch as they have already the promise of being received at his coming again.

As that the kingdom of God is the present Church.

5. Consequent to this error that the present Church is Christ's kingdom, there ought to be some one man or assembly by whose mouth our Saviour, now in heaven, speaketh and giveth law and which representeth his person to all Christians or divers men or

1 Cf. 35.7, 35.11, 35.13, 38.5, 41.3, and 41.4.

divers assemblies that do the same to divers parts of Christendom. This power regal under Christ being challenged universally by the Pope, and in particular commonwealths by assemblies of the pastors of the place (when the Scripture gives it to none but to civil sovereigns), comes to be so passionately disputed that it putteth out the light of nature and causeth so great a darkness in men's understanding that they see not who it is to whom they have engaged their obedience.

And that the pope is his vicar general.

6. Consequent to this claim of the Pope to be vicar general of Christ in the present Church (supposed to be that kingdom of his to which we are addressed in the gospel) is the doctrine that it is necessary for a Christian king to receive his crown by a bishop, as if it were from that ceremony that he derives the clause of *Dei gratia* in his title; and that then only is he made king by the favour of God when he is crowned by the authority of God's universal vicegerent on earth; and that every bishop, whosoever be his sovereign, taketh at his consecration an oath of absolute obedience to the Pope. Consequent to the same is the doctrine of the fourth Council of Lateran, held under Pope Innocent the Third (Chapter 3, *De Haereticis*), *that if a king, at the pope's admonition, do not purge his kingdom of heresies, and being excommunicate for the same, do not give satisfaction within a year, [then] his subjects are absolved of the bond of their obedience.* Where, by heresies are understood all opinions which the Church of Rome hath forbidden to be maintained.
[336] And by this means, as often as there is any repugnancy between the political designs of the Pope and other Christian princes, as there is very often, there ariseth such a mist amongst their subjects, that they know not a stranger that thrusteth himself into the throne of their lawful prince, from him whom they had themselves placed there; and, in this darkness of mind, [they] are made to fight one against another, without discerning their enemies from their friends, under the conduct of another man's ambition.

And that the pastors are the clergy.

7. From the same opinion, that the present Church is the kingdom of God, it proceeds that pastors, deacons, and all other ministers of the Church take the name to themselves of the *clergy*, giving to other Christians the name of *laity*, that is, simply *people*. For *clergy* signifies those whose maintenance is that revenue which God, having reserved to himself during his reign over the Israelites, assigned to the tribe of Levi (who were to be his public ministers

and had no portion of land set them out to live on, as their brethren) to be their inheritance. The Pope therefore (pretending the present Church to be, as the realms of Israel, the kingdom of God), challenging to himself and his subordinate ministers the like revenue as the inheritance of God, the name of *clergy* was suitable to that claim. And thence it is that tithes and other tributes paid to the Levites as God's right, amongst the Israelites, have a long time been demanded and taken of Christians by ecclesiastics, *jure divino*, that is, in God's right. By which means, the people everywhere were obliged to a double tribute: one to the state, another to the clergy; whereof that to the clergy, being the tenth of their revenue, is double to that which a king of Athens (and esteemed a tyrant) exacted of his subjects for the defraying of all public charges. For he demanded no more but the twentieth part, and yet abundantly maintained therewith the commonwealth. And in the kingdom of the Jews, during the sacerdotal reign of God, the tithes and offerings were the whole public revenue.

8. From the same mistaking of the present Church for the kingdom of God came in the distinction between the *civil* and the *canon* laws; the civil law being the acts of sovereigns in their own dominions, and the canon law being the acts of the Pope in the same dominions. Which canons, though they were but canons, that is, rules propounded, and but voluntarily received by Christian princes, till the translation of the Empire to Charlemagne; yet afterwards, as the power of the Pope increased, became rules commanded; and the emperors themselves (to avoid greater mischiefs, which the people blinded might be led into) were forced to let them pass for laws.

9. From hence it is that in all dominions where the Pope's ecclesiastical power is entirely received, Jews, Turks, and Gentiles are in the Roman Church tolerated in their religion as far forth as in the exercise and profession thereof they offend not against the civil power; whereas in a Christian, though a stranger, not to be of the Roman religion is capital, because the Pope pretendeth that all Christians are his subjects. For otherwise it were as much against [337]
the law of nations to persecute a Christian stranger for professing the religion of his own country, as an infidel, or rather more, inasmuch as they that are not against Christ are with him.

10. From the same it is that in every Christian state there are

certain men that are exempt, by ecclesiastical liberty, from the tributes and from the tribunals of the civil state; for so are the secular clergy, besides monks and friars, which in many places bear so great a proportion to the common people, as if need were, there might be raised out of them alone an army sufficient for any war the Church militant should employ them in against their own or other princes.

Error from mistaking consecration for conjuration.

11. A second general abuse of Scripture is the turning of consecration into conjuration or enchantment. To *consecrate* is in Scripture to offer, give, or dedicate in pious and decent language and gesture a man or any other thing to God, by separating of it from common use; that is to say, to sanctify or make it God's, and to be used only by those whom God hath appointed to be his public ministers (as I have already proved at large in the 35 chapter), and thereby to change, not the thing consecrated, but only the use of it, from being profane and common, to be holy and peculiar to God's service. But when by such words the nature or quality of the thing itself is pretended to be changed, it is not consecration, but either an extraordinary work of God or a vain and impious conjuration. But seeing (for the frequency of pretending the change of nature in their consecrations) it cannot be esteemed a work extraordinary, it is no other than a *conjuration* or *incantation*, whereby they would have men to believe an alteration of nature that is not, contrary to the testimony of man's sight and of all the rest of his senses. As for example, when the priest, instead of consecrating bread and wine to God's peculiar service in the sacrament of the Lord's Supper (which is but a separation of it from the common use to signify, that is, to put men in mind of, their redemption by the Passion of Christ, whose body was broken and blood shed upon the cross for our transgressions) pretends that by saying of the words of our Saviour, *This is my body* and *This is my blood*, the nature of bread is no more there, but his very body; notwithstanding there appeareth not to the sight or other sense of the receiver anything that appeared not before the consecration. The Egyptian conjurers that are said to have turned their rods to serpents and the water into blood are thought but to have deluded the senses of the spectators by a false show of things; yet [they] are esteemed enchanters. But what should we have thought of them if

there had appeared in their rods nothing like a serpent and in the water enchanted nothing like blood, nor like anything else but water, but that they had faced down the king, that they were serpents that looked like rods and that it was blood that seemed water? That had been both enchantment and lying. And yet in this daily act of the priest, they do the very same, by turning the [338] holy words into the manner of a charm, which produceth nothing new to the sense; but they face us down, that it hath turned the bread into a man, nay, more, into a God, and require men to worship it as if it were our Saviour himself present, God and Man, and thereby to commit most gross idolatry. For if it be enough to excuse it of idolatry to say it is no more bread, but God; why should not the same excuse serve the Egyptians, in case they had the faces to say the leeks and onions they worshipped were not very leeks and onions, but a divinity under their *species* or likeness? The words, *This is my body*, are equivalent to these, *This signifies or represents, my body*; and it is an ordinary figure of speech; but to take it literally is an abuse; nor, though so taken, can it extend any further than to the bread which Christ himself with his own hands consecrated. For he never said that of what bread soever any priest whatsoever should say, *This is my body* or *This is Christ's body*, the same should presently be transubstantiated.[1] Nor did the Church of Rome ever establish this transubstantiation till the time of Innocent the Third; which was not above five hundred years ago, when the power of Popes was at the highest and the darkness of the time grown so great, as men discerned not the bread that was given them to eat, especially when it was stamped with the figure of Christ upon the cross, as if they would have men believe it were transubstantiated, not only into the body of Christ, but also into the wood of his cross, and that they did eat both together in the sacrament.

Incantation in the ceremonies of baptism.

12. The like incantation, instead of consecration, is used also in the sacrament of baptism, where the abuse of God's name in each several person, and in the whole Trinity, with the sign of the cross at each name, maketh up the charm. As first, when they make the holy water, the priest saith, *I conjure thee, thou creature of water, in the*

1 See also 37.13.

*name of God the Father Almighty, and in the name of Jesus Christ his only Son our Lord, and in virtue of the Holy Ghost, that thou become conjured water, to drive away all the powers of the enemy, and to eradicate, and supplant the enemy*, etc. And the same in the benediction of the salt to be mingled with it, *that thou become conjured salt, that all phantasms and knavery of the Devil's fraud may fly and depart from the place wherein thou art sprinkled; and every unclean spirit be conjured by him that shall come to judge the quick and the dead.* The same in the benediction of the oil, *that all the power of the enemy, all the host of the Devil, all assaults and phantasms of Satan, may be driven away by this creature of oil.* And for the infant that is to be baptized, he is subject to many charms: first, at the church door the priest blows thrice in the child's face and says, *Go out of him, unclean spirit, and give place to the Holy Ghost the Comforter.* As if all children, till blown on by the priest, were demoniacs. Again, before his entrance into the church, he saith as before, *I conjure thee, etc., to go out, and depart from*
[339] *this servant of God*; and again the same exorcism is repeated once more before he be baptized. These and some other incantations are those that are used instead of benedictions and consecrations in administration of the sacraments of baptism and the Lord's Supper, wherein everything that serveth to those holy uses, except the unhallowed spittle of the priest, hath some set form of exorcism.

And in marriage, in visitation of the sick, and in consecration of places.

13. Nor are the other rites, as of marriage, of extreme unction, of visitation of the sick, of consecrating churches and churchyards, and the like, exempt from charms, inasmuch as there is in them the use of enchanted oil and water, with the abuse of the cross, and of the holy word of David, *asperges me Domine hyssopo*, as things of efficacy to drive away phantasms and imaginary spirits.

Errors from mistaking eternal life and everlasting death.

14. Another general error is from the misinterpretation of the words *eternal life*, *everlasting death*, and the *second death*.[1] For though we read plainly in Holy Scripture that God created Adam in an estate of living for ever, which was conditional, that is to say, if he disobeyed not his commandment, which was not essential to human nature, but consequent to the virtue of the tree of life, whereof he had liberty to eat, as long as he had not sinned; and that he was thrust out of Paradise after he had sinned, lest he should eat thereof and live for ever; and that Christ's Passion is a

1 See also 38.1–3.

discharge of sin to all that believe on him, and by consequence, a restitution of eternal life to all the faithful, and to them only; yet the doctrine is now and hath been a long time far otherwise, namely, that every man hath eternity of life by nature, inasmuch as his soul is immortal. So that the flaming sword at the entrance of Paradise, though it hinder a man from coming to the tree of life, hinders him not from the immortality which God took from him for his sin nor makes him to need the sacrificing of Christ for the recovering of the same; and consequently, not only the faithful and righteous, but also the wicked and the heathen, shall enjoy eternal life, without any death at all, much less a second and everlasting death. To salve this, it is said that by *second and everlasting death* is meant a second and everlasting life, but in torments, a figure never used but in this very case.

15. All which doctrine is founded only on some of the obscurer places of the New Testament; which nevertheless, the whole scope of the Scripture considered, are clear enough in a different sense, and unnecessary to the Christian faith. For supposing that when a man dies, there remaineth nothing of him but his carcass, cannot God, that raised inanimated dust and clay into a living creature by his word, as easily raise a dead carcass to life again, and continue him alive for ever or make him die again by another word? The *soul* in Scripture signifieth always either the life or the living creature, and the body and soul jointly, the *body alive*. In the [340]
fifth day of the Creation, God said, Let the waters produce *reptile animae viventis*, the creeping thing that hath in it a living soul; the English translate it, *that hath life*. And again, God created whales, *et omnem animam viventem*, which in the English is, *every living creature*. And likewise of man, God made him of the dust of the earth and breathed in his face the breath of life, *et factus est homo in animam viventem*, that is, *and man was made a living creature*. And after Noah came out of the ark, God saith, he will no more smite *omnem animam viventem*, that is, *every living creature*. And, *Eat not the blood, for the blood is the soul*; that is, *the life*. From which places, if by *soul* were meant a *substance incorporeal*, with an existence separated from the body, it might as well be inferred of any other living creature, as of man. But that the souls of the faithful are not of their own nature, but by God's special grace, to remain in their bodies from

the resurrection to all eternity, I have already, I think, sufficiently proved out of the Scriptures, in the 38 chapter. And for the places of the New Testament where it is said that any man shall be cast body and soul into hell fire, it is no more than body and life; that is to say, they shall be cast alive into the perpetual fire of Gehenna.

As the doctrine of purgatory and exorcisms, and invocation of saints.

16. This window it is that gives entrance to the dark doctrine, first, of eternal torments and afterwards of purgatory,[1] and consequently of the walking abroad, especially in places consecrated, solitary or dark, of the ghosts of men deceased, and thereby to the pretences of exorcism and conjuration of phantasms, as also of invocation of men dead; and to the doctrine of indulgences, that is to say, of exemption for a time or for ever, from the fire of purgatory, wherein these incorporeal substances are pretended by burning to be cleansed and made fit for heaven. For men being generally possessed, before the time of our Saviour, by contagion of the demonology[2] of the Greeks, of an opinion that the souls of men were substances distinct from their bodies, and therefore that when the body was dead, the soul of every man, whether godly or wicked, must subsist somewhere by virtue of its own nature, without acknowledging therein any supernatural gift of God's; the doctors of the Church doubted a long time what was the place which they were to abide in, till they should be reunited to their bodies in the resurrection, supposing for a while, they lay under the altars; but afterward the Church of Rome found it more profitable to build for them this place of purgatory, which by some other Churches, in this later age, has been demolished.

The texts alleged for the doctrines aforementioned have been answered before.

17. Let us now consider what texts of Scripture seem most to confirm these three general errors I have here touched. As for those which Cardinal Bellarmine hath alleged for the present kingdom of God administered by the Pope (than which there are none that make a better show of proof), I have already answered them,[3] and made it evident that the kingdom of God, instituted by Moses, ended in the election of Saul; after which time the priest of
[341] his own authority never deposed any king. That which the high priest did to Athaliah was not done in his own right, but in the

1 See also 12.32, 43.14, 43.17, 44.30–4, 44.37, 44.40, 46.21, and 47.14.

2 See also 40.14, 44.3, 45.2, and 47.15.

3 See 42.81ff.

right of the young King Joash, her son. But Solomon in his own right deposed the high priest Abiathar and set up another in his place. The most difficult place to answer, of all those that can be brought to prove the kingdom of God by Christ is already in this world, is alleged, not by Bellarmine, nor any other of the Church of Rome, but by Beza,[1] that will have it to begin from the resurrection of Christ. But whether he intend thereby to entitle the presbytery to the supreme power ecclesiastical in the commonwealth of Geneva (and consequently to every presbytery in every other commonwealth) or to princes and other civil sovereigns, I do not know. For the presbytery hath challenged the power to excommunicate their own kings, and to be the supreme moderators in religion, in the places where they have that form of church government, no less than the Pope challengeth it universally.

Answer to the text on which Beza inferreth that the kingdom of Christ began at the Resurrection.

18. The words are, *Verily I say unto you, that there be some of them that stand here, which shall not taste of death, till they have seen the kingdom of God come with power* (Mark 9:1). Which words, if taken grammatically, make it certain that either some of those men that stood by Christ at that time are yet alive or else that the kingdom of God must be now in this present world. And then there is another place more difficult; for when the Apostles after our Saviour's resurrection and immediately before his ascension, asked our Saviour, saying, *Wilt thou at this time restore again the kingdom to Israel?*, he answered them, *It is not for you to know the times and the seasons, which the Father hath put in his own power; but ye shall receive power by the coming of the Holy Ghost upon you, and ye shall be my witnesses both in Jerusalem, and in all Judea, and in Samaria, and unto the uttermost part of the earth* (Acts 1:6). Which is as much as to say, My kingdom is not yet come nor shall you foreknow when it shall come; for it shall come as a thief in the night; but I will send you the Holy Ghost, and by him you shall have power to bear witness to all the world (by your preaching) of my resurrection, and the works I have done and the doctrine I have taught, [in order] that they may believe in me and expect eternal life at my coming again. How does this agree with the coming of Christ's kingdom at the resurrection? And that which St. Paul says, *That they turned from idols, to serve the living and true God, and to wait for His Son from*

1 Theodore Beza (1519-1605) converted to Calvinism in 1549. See also 44.40.

*heaven* (1 Thes. 1:9-10), where to wait for his Son from heaven is to wait for his coming to be king in power; which were not necessary if his kingdom had been then present. Again, if the kingdom of God began (as *Beza* on that place (Mark 9:1) would have it) at the resurrection, what reason is there for Christians ever since the resurrection to say in their prayers, *Let thy kingdom come*? It is
[342] therefore manifest that the words of St. Mark are not so to be interpreted. There be some of them that stand here, saith our Saviour, that shall not taste of death till they have seen the kingdom of God come in power. If then this kingdom were to come at the resurrection of Christ, why is it said, *some of them*, rather than *all*? For they all lived till after Christ was risen.

Explication of the place in Mark 9:1.

19. But they that require an exact interpretation of this text, let them interpret first the like words of our Saviour to St. Peter concerning St. John, *If I will that he tarry till I come, what is that to thee?* (John 21:22), upon which was grounded a report that he should not die. Nevertheless the truth of that report was neither confirmed, as well grounded, nor refuted, as ill grounded on those words, but left as a saying not understood. The same difficulty is also in the place of St. Mark. And if it be lawful to conjecture at their meaning, by that which immediately follows, both here and in St. Luke, where the same is again repeated, it is not improbable to say they have relation to the Transfiguration, which is described in the verses immediately following, where it is said that *After six days Jesus taketh with him Peter, and James, and John* (not all, but some of his Disciples) *and leadeth them up into an high mountain apart by themselves, and was transfigured before them. And his raiment became shining, exceeding white as snow; so as no fuller on earth can white them. And there appeared unto them Elias with Moses, and they were talking with Jesus*, etc. So that they saw Christ in glory and majesty, as he is to come, insomuch as *they were sore afraid*. And thus the promise of our Saviour was accomplished by way of vision. For it was a vision, as may probably be inferred out of St. Luke, that reciteth the same story, and saith that Peter and they that were with him were heavy with sleep (Luke 9:28); but most certainly out of Matt. 17:9 where the same is again related; for our Saviour charged them, saying, *Tell no man the vision until the Son of Man be risen from the dead*. Howsoever it be, yet there can from thence be taken no

argument to prove that the kingdom of God taketh beginning till the day of judgement.

20. As for some other texts to prove the Pope's power over civil sovereigns (besides those of Bellarmine), as that the two swords that Christ and his Apostles had amongst them were the spiritual and the temporal sword, which they say St. Peter had given him by Christ, and that of the two luminaries, the greater signifies the Pope, and the lesser the king, one might as well infer out of the first verse of the Bible that by heaven is meant the Pope and by earth the king; which is not arguing from Scripture, but a wanton insulting over princes that came in fashion after the time the popes were grown so secure of their greatness as to contemn all Christian kings, and treading on the necks of emperors, to mock both them and the Scripture, in the words of the ninety-first Psalm, *Thou shalt tread upon the lion and the adder; the young lion and the dragon thou shalt trample under thy feet.*

Abuse of some other texts in defense of the power of the Pope.

21. As for the rites of consecration, though they depend for the most part upon the discretion and judgement of the governors of the Church and not upon the Scriptures; yet those governors are obliged to such direction as the nature of the action itself [343] requireth, as that the ceremonies, words, gestures be both decent and significant, or at least conformable to the action. When Moses consecrated the tabernacle, the altar, and the vessels belonging to them, he anointed them with the oil which God had commanded to be made for that purpose (Exod. 40); and they were holy. There was nothing exorcised, to drive away phantasms. The same Moses (the civil sovereign of Israel), when he consecrated Aaron (the high priest) and his sons, did wash them with water (not exorcised water), put their garments upon them, and anointed them with oil; and they were sanctified, to minister unto the Lord in the priest's office, which was a simple and decent cleansing and adorning them before he presented them to God, to be his servants. When King Solomon (the civil sovereign of Israel) consecrated the temple he had built (2 Kings 8), he stood before all the congregation of Israel; and having blessed them, he gave thanks to God for putting into the heart of his father to build it and for giving to himself the grace to accomplish the same; and then [he] prayed unto him, first, to accept that house, though it were not

The manner of consecrations in the Scripture was without exorcisms.

suitable to his infinite greatness; and to hear the prayers of his servants that should pray therein, or (if they were absent) towards it; and lastly, he offered a sacrifice of peace offering; and the house was dedicated. Here was no procession; the King stood still in his first place; no exorcized water; no *Asperges me*, nor other impertinent application of words spoken upon another occasion, but a decent and rational speech, and such as in making to God a present of his new-built house was most conformable to the occasion.

22. We read not that St. John did exorcize the water of Jordan, nor Philip the water of the river wherein he baptized the eunuch, nor that any pastor in the time of the Apostles did take his spittle and put it to the nose of the person to be baptized, and say, *in odorem suavitatis*, that is, *for a sweet savour unto the Lord*; wherein neither the ceremony of spittle, for the uncleanness, nor the application of that Scripture, for the levity, can by any authority of man be justified.

The immortality of man's soul, not proved by Scripture to be of nature but of grace.

23. To prove that the soul, separated from the body, liveth eternally, not only the souls of the elect, by especial grace and restoration of the eternal life which Adam lost by sin and our Saviour restored by the sacrifice of himself to the faithful, but also the souls of reprobates, as a property naturally consequent to the essence of mankind, without other grace of God but that which is universally given to all mankind, there are divers places which at the first sight seem sufficiently to serve the turn; but such as when I compare them with that which I have before (chapter 38)[1] alleged out of the fourteenth of *Job* seem to me much more subject to a diverse interpretation than the words of Job.

24. And first there are the words of Solomon, *Then shall the dust*
[344] *return to dust, as it was, and the spirit shall return to God that gave it* (Eccles. 12:7). Which may bear well enough (if there be no other text directly against it) this interpretation, that God only knows (but man not) what becomes of a man's spirit when he expireth; and the same Solomon, in the same book, delivereth the same sentence in the sense I have given it. His words are, *All go to the same place; all are of the dust, and all turn to dust again; who knoweth that the spirit of man goeth upward, and that the spirit of the beast goeth down-*

1 See 38.4.

*ward to the earth?* (Eccles. 3:20-21). That is, none knows but God; nor is it an unusual phrase to say of things we understand not, *God knows what* and *God knows where.* That of Genesis 5:24, *Enoch walked with God, and he was not; for God took him,* which is expounded, Hebrews, 11:5, *He was translated, that he should not die; and was not found, because God had translated him. For before his translation, he had this testimony, that he pleased God,* making as much for the immortality of the body as of the soul, proveth that this his translation was peculiar to them that please God, not common to them with the wicked, and depending on grace, not on nature. But on the contrary, what interpretation shall we give, besides the literal sense of the words of Solomon, *that which befalleth the sons of men befalleth beasts, even one thing befalleth them; as the one dieth, so doth the other; yea, they have all one breath* (one spirit)*; so that a man hath no pre-eminence above a beast, for all is vanity* (Eccles. 3:19). By the literal sense, here is no natural immortality of the soul,[1] nor yet any repugnancy with the life eternal, which the elect shall enjoy by grace. And, *Better is he that hath not yet been than both they* (Eccles. 4:3), that is, than they that live or have lived; which, if the soul of all them that have lived were immortal, were a hard saying; for then to have an immortal soul were worse than to have no soul at all. And again, *The living know they shall die, but the dead know not anything* (Eccles. 9:5), that is, naturally, and before the resurrection of the body.

25. Another place which seems to make for a natural immortality of the soul is that where our Saviour saith that Abraham, Isaac, and Jacob are living; but this is spoken of the promise of God and of their certitude to rise again, not of a life then actual; and in the same sense that God said to Adam that on the day he should eat of the forbidden fruit, he should certainly die; from that time forward he was a dead man by sentence, but not by execution, till almost a thousand years after. So Abraham, Isaac, and Jacob were alive by promise, then, when Christ spoke, but are not actually till the resurrection. And the history of Dives and Lazarus make nothing against this, if we take it (as it is) for a parable.

26. But there be other places of the New Testament where an immortality seemeth to be directly attributed to the wicked. For it

---

1 See also 38.4, 44.15, and 44.24.

is evident that they shall all rise to judgement. And it is said besides, in many places, that they shall go into *everlasting fire, ever-*
[345] *lasting torments, everlasting punishments; and that the worm of conscience never dieth*; and all this is comprehended in the word *everlasting death*, which is ordinarily interpreted *everlasting life in torments*. And yet I can find nowhere that any man shall live in torments everlastingly.[1] Also, it seemeth hard to say that God, who is the Father of mercies, that doth in heaven and earth all that he will, that hath the hearts of all men in his disposing, that worketh in men both to do and to will, and without whose free gift a man hath neither inclination to good nor repentance of evil, should punish men's transgressions without any end of time, and with all the extremity of torture that men can imagine, and more. We are therefore to consider what the meaning is of *everlasting fire*, and other the like phrases of Scripture.

27. I have showed already that the kingdom of God by Christ beginneth at the day of judgement; that in that day the faithful shall rise again with glorious and spiritual bodies and be his subjects in that his kingdom, which shall be eternal; that they shall neither marry, nor be given in marriage, nor eat and drink, as they did in their natural bodies, but live for ever in their individual persons, without the specifical eternity of generation; and that the reprobates also shall rise again to receive punishments for their sins, as also that those of the elect, which shall be alive in their earthly bodies at that day, shall have their bodies suddenly changed, and made spiritual and immortal. But that the bodies of the reprobate, who make the kingdom of Satan,[2] shall also be glorious or spiritual bodies, or that they shall be as the angels of God, neither eating nor drinking nor engendering, or that their life shall be eternal in their individual persons, as the life of every faithful man is or as the life of Adam had been if he had not sinned, there is no place of Scripture to prove it, save only these places concerning eternal torments, which may otherwise be interpreted.

28. From whence may be inferred that, as the elect after the resurrection shall be restored to the estate wherein Adam was before he had sinned, so the reprobate shall be in the estate that

---

1 See also 38.14–15.

2 See also 38.12–13, 42.24, 44.2, and 45.7.

Adam and his posterity were in after the sin committed, saving that God promised a redeemer to Adam, and such of his seed as should trust in him and repent, but not to them that should die in their sins, as do the reprobate.

29. These things considered, the texts that mention *eternal fire*, *eternal torments*, or *the worm that never dieth*, contradict not the doctrine of a second and everlasting death,[1] in the proper and natural sense of the word *death*. The fire or torments prepared for the wicked in Gehenna, Tophet, or in what place soever, may continue forever; and there may never want wicked men to be tormented in them, though not every nor any one eternally. For the wicked, being left in the estate they were in after Adam's sin, may at the resurrection live as they did, marry, and give in marriage, and have gross and corruptible bodies, as all mankind now have, and consequently may engender perpetually, after the resurrection, as they did before; for there is no place of Scripture to the contrary. For St. Paul, speaking of the resurrection (1 Cor. 15), understandeth it only of the resurrection to life eternal and not the resurrection to punishment. And of the first, he saith that the body is *sown in corruption, raised in incorruption; sown in dishonour, raised in honour; sown in weakness, raised in power; sown a natural body, raised a spiritual body*. There is no such thing can be said of the bodies of them that rise to punishment. So also our Saviour, when he speaketh of the nature of man after the resurrection, meaneth the resurrection to life eternal, not to punishment. The text is Luke, 20, verses 34–6, a fertile text: *The children of this world marry and are given in marriage; but they that shall be counted worthy to obtain that world and the resurrection from the dead, neither marry nor are given in marriage. Neither can they die any more; for they are equal to the angels, and are the children of God, being the children of the resurrection*. The children of this world that are in the estate which Adam left them in shall marry and be given in marriage, that is, corrupt, and generate successively, which is an immortality of the kind, but not of the persons of men; they are not worthy to be counted amongst them that shall obtain the next world, an absolute resurrection from the dead, but only a short time, as inmates of that world, and to the end only to receive condign punishment for their contumacy. The elect are the only

Eternal torments what.

[346]

1 See also 38.14.

children of the resurrection; that is to say, the sole heirs of eternal life; they only can die no more. It is they that are equal to the angels, and that are the children of God, and not the reprobate. To the reprobate there remaineth after the resurrection a *second* and *eternal* death, between which resurrection and their second and eternal death is but a time of punishment and torment, and to last by succession of sinners thereunto as long as the kind of man by propagation shall endure, which is eternally.

Answer of the texts alleged for purgatory.

30. Upon this doctrine of the natural eternity of separated souls is founded, as I said, the doctrine of purgatory.[1] For supposing eternal life by grace only, there is no life but the life of the body and no immortality till the resurrection. The texts for purgatory alleged by Bellarmine out of the canonical Scripture of the Old Testament are, first, the fasting of David for Saul and Jonathan, mentioned 2 Sam. 1:12, and again, 2 Sam. 3:35, for the death of Abner. This fasting of David, he saith, was for the obtaining of something for them at God's hands, after their death, because after he had fasted to procure the recovery of his own child, as soon as he knew it was dead, he called for meat. Seeing then the soul hath an existence separate from the body, and nothing can be obtained by men's fasting for the souls that are already either in heaven or hell; it followeth that there be some souls of dead men that are neither in heaven nor in hell; and therefore they must be in some third place, which must be purgatory. And thus with hard strain-
[347] ing, he has wrested those places to the proof of a purgatory, whereas it is manifest that the ceremonies of mourning and fasting, when they are used for the death of men whose life was not profitable to the mourners, they are used for honour's sake to their persons; and when it is done for the death of them by whose life the mourners had benefit, it proceeds from their particular damage; and so David honoured Saul and Abner with his fasting, and, in the death of his own child, recomforted himself by receiving his ordinary food.

31. In the other places which he allegeth out of the Old Testament, there is not so much as any show or colour of proof. He brings in every text wherein there is the word *anger* or *fire* or *burning* or *purging* or *cleansing*, in case any of the fathers have but in a

1 See also 12.32, 43.14, 43.17, 44.16, 44.31–4, 44.37, 44.40, 46.21, and 47.14.

sermon rhetorically applied it to the doctrine of purgatory, already believed. The first verse of Psalm 37, *O Lord, rebuke me not in thy wrath, nor chasten me in thy hot displeasure*, what were this to purgatory, if Augustine had not applied the *wrath* to the fire of hell and the *displeasure* to that of purgatory? And what is it to purgatory, that of Psalm 66.12. *We went through fire and water, and thou broughtest us to a moist place*, and other the like texts (with which the doctors of those times intended to adorn or extend their sermons or commentaries) haled to their purposes by force of wit?

Places of the New Testament for Purgatory answered.

32. But he allegeth other places of the New Testament that are not so easy to be answered. And first that of Matt. 12:32, *Whosoever speaketh a word against the Son of Man, it shall be forgiven him; but whosoever speaketh against the Holy Ghost, it shall not be forgiven him neither in this world, nor in the world to come*; where he will have purgatory to be the world to come, wherein some sins may be forgiven which in this world were not forgiven; notwithstanding that it is manifest there are but three worlds: one from the creation to the flood, which was destroyed by water and is called in Scripture *the old world*; another from the flood to the day of judgement, which is *the present world*, and shall be destroyed by fire; and the third, which shall be from the day of judgement forward, everlasting, which is called *the world to come*; and in which it agreed by all there shall be no purgatory; and therefore the world to come and purgatory are inconsistent. But what then can be the meaning of those our Saviour's words? I confess they are very hardly to be reconciled with all the doctrines now unanimously received; nor is it any shame to confess the profoundness of the Scripture to be too great to be sounded by the shortness of human understanding. Nevertheless, I may propound such things to the consideration of more learned divines, as the text itself suggesteth. And first, seeing to speak against the Holy Ghost, as being the third person of the Trinity, is to speak against the Church, in which the Holy Ghost resideth, it seemeth the comparison is made between the easiness of our Saviour in bearing with offences done to him while he himself taught the world, that is, when he was on earth, and the severity of the pastors after him, against those which should deny their authority, which was from the Holy Ghost. As if he should say, you that deny my power, nay, you that shall crucify me, shall be pardoned by me, [348]

as often as you turn unto me by repentance; but if you deny the power of them that teach you hereafter, by virtue of the Holy Ghost, they shall be inexorable, and shall not forgive you, but persecute you in this world, and leave you without absolution (though you turn to me, unless you turn also to them), to the punishments, as much as lies in them, of the world to come. And so the words may be taken as a prophecy or prediction concerning the times, as they have long been in the Christian Church; or if this be not the meaning (for I am not peremptory in such difficult places), perhaps there may be place left after the resurrection for the repentance of some sinners. And there is also another place that seemeth to agree therewith. For considering the words of St. Paul, *What shall they do which are baptized for the dead, if the dead rise not at all? Why also are they baptized for the dead?* (1 Cor. 15:29), a man may probably infer, as some have done, that in St. Paul's time there was a custom, by receiving baptism for the dead (as men that now believe are sureties and undertakers for the faith of infants that are not capable of believing) to undertake for the persons of their deceased friends, that they should be ready to obey and receive our Saviour for their king at his coming again; and then the forgiveness of sins in the world to come has no need of a purgatory. But in both these interpretations, there is so much of paradox that I trust not to them, but propound them to those that are thoroughly versed in the Scripture, to inquire if there be no clearer place that contradicts them. Only of thus much, I see evident Scripture to persuade me that there is neither the word nor the thing of purgatory, neither in this nor any other text; nor anything that can prove a necessity of a place for the soul without the body, neither for the soul of Lazarus during the four days he was dead, nor for the souls of them which the Roman Church pretend to be tormented now in purgatory. For God, that could give a life to a piece of clay, hath the same power to give life again to a dead man, and renew his inanimate and rotten carcass into a glorious, spiritual, and immortal body.

33. Another place is that of 1 Cor. 3, where it is said that they which build stubble, hay, etc., on the true foundation, their work shall perish; but *they themselves shall be saved; but as through fire*; this fire he will have to be the fire of purgatory. The words, as I have

said before, are an allusion to those of Zech. 13:9, where he saith, *I will bring the third part through the fire, and refine them as silver is refined, and will try them as gold is tried*, which is spoken of the coming of the Messiah in power and glory, that is, at the day of judgement and conflagration of the present world, wherein the elect shall not be consumed, but be refined, that is, depose their erroneous doctrines and traditions and have them, as it were, singed off, and shall afterwards call upon the name of the true God. In like manner, the Apostle saith of them that, holding this foundation, *Jesus is the Christ*, shall build thereon some other doctrines [349] that be erroneous, that they shall not be consumed in that fire which reneweth the world, but shall pass through it to salvation, but so as to see and relinquish their former errors. The builders are the *pastors*; the foundation, that *Jesus is the Christ*; the stubble and hay, *false consequences drawn from it through ignorance or frailty*; the gold, silver, and precious stones are their *true doctrines*; and their refining or purging, the *relinquishing of their errors*. In all which there is no colour at all for the burning of incorporeal, that is to say, impatible [incapable of suffering] souls.

Baptism for the dead, how understood.

34. A third place is that of 1 Cor. 15, before mentioned, concerning baptism for the dead, out of which he concludeth, first, that prayers for the dead are not unprofitable; and out of that, that there is a fire of purgatory; but neither of them rightly. For of many interpretations of the word baptism, he approveth this in the first place, that by baptism is meant (metaphorically) a baptism of penance; and that men are in this sense baptized when they fast and pray and give alms; and so baptism for the dead and prayer for the dead is the same thing. But this is a metaphor, of which there is no example, neither in the Scripture nor in any other use of language, and which is also discordant to the harmony and scope of the Scripture. The word *baptism* is used for being dipped in one's own blood, as Christ was upon the cross, and as most of the Apostles were, for giving testimony of him (Mark 10:38, Luke 12:50). But it is hard to say that prayer, fasting, and alms have any similitude with dipping. The same is used also, Matt. 3:11 (which seemeth to make somewhat for purgatory) for a purging with fire. But it is evident the fire and purging here mentioned is the same whereof the Prophet Zechariah (13:9) speaketh, *I will bring the third*

*part through the fire, will refine them,* etc. And St. Peter after him, *That the trial of your faith, which is much more precious than of gold that perisheth, though it be tried with fire, might be found unto praise, and honour, and glory at the appearing of Jesus Christ* (1 Peter 1:7); and St. Paul, *The fire shall try every man's work of what sort it is* (1 Cor. 3:13). But St. Peter and St. Paul speak of the fire that shall be at the second appearing of Christ; and the Prophet Zechariah, of the day of judgement. And therefore this place of St. Matthew may be interpreted of the same, and then there will be no necessity of the fire of purgatory.[1]

35. Another interpretation of baptism for the dead is that which I have before mentioned, which he preferreth to the second place of probability. And thence also he inferreth the utility of prayer for the dead. For if after the resurrection such as have not heard of Christ or not believed in him, may be received into Christ's kingdom, [then] it is not in vain, after their death, that their friends should pray for them till they should be risen. But granting that God at the prayers of the faithful may convert unto him some of those that have not heard Christ preached and consequently cannot have rejected Christ and that the charity of men in that point cannot be blamed; yet this concludeth nothing for purgatory,[2]
[350] because to rise from death to life is one thing, to rise from purgatory to life is another, as being a rising from life to life, from a life in torments to a life in joy.

36. A fourth place is that of Matt. 5:25: *Agree with thine adversary quickly, whilst thou art in the way with him, lest at any time the adversary deliver thee to the judge, and the judge deliver thee to the officer, and thou be cast into prison. Verily I say unto thee, Thou shalt by no means come out thence, till thou hast paid the uttermost farthing.* In which allegory, the offender is the sinner; both the adversary and the judge is God; the way is this life; the prison is the grave; the officer, death; from which the sinner shall not rise again to life eternal, but to a second death, till he have paid the utmost farthing or Christ pay it for him by his Passion, which is a full ransom for all manner of sin, as well lesser sins as greater crimes, both being made by the Passion of Christ equally venial.

1 See also 12.32, 43.14, 43.17, 44.16, 44.30–3, 44.37, 44.40, 46.21, and 47.14.

2 See also 12.32, 43.14, 43.17, 44.16, 44.30–4, 44.37, 44.40, 46.21, 46.27, and 47.14.

37. The fifth place is that of Matt. 5:22: *Whosoever is angry with his brother without a cause shall be guilty in judgement. And whosoever shall say to his brother,* RACHA, [*raca*] *shall be guilty in the council. But whosoever shall say, Thou fool, shall be guilty to hell fire.* From which words he inferreth three sorts of sins and three sorts of punishments, and that none of those sins, but the last, shall be punished with hell fire; and consequently, that after this life there is punishment of lesser sins in purgatory.[1] Of which inference there is no colour in any interpretation that hath yet been given of them. Shall there be a distinction after this life of courts of justice, as there was amongst the Jews in our Saviour's time, to hear and determine divers sorts of crimes, as the judges and the council? Shall not all judicature appertain to Christ and his Apostles? To understand therefore this text, we are not to consider it solitarily, but jointly with the words precedent and subsequent. Our Saviour in this chapter interpreteth the Law of Moses, which the Jews thought was then fulfilled when they had not transgressed the grammatical sense thereof, howsoever they had transgressed against the sentence or meaning of the legislator. Therefore, whereas they thought the sixth Commandment was not broken but by killing a man, nor the seventh, but when a man lay with a woman not his wife, our Saviour tells them, the inward anger of a man against his brother, if it be without just cause, is homicide. You have heard, saith he, the Law of Moses, *Thou shalt not kill*, and that *Whosoever shall kill shall be condemned before the judges*, or before the session of the Seventy; but I say unto you, to be angry with one's brother without cause or to say unto him *Racha*, or *Fool*, is homicide, and shall be punished, at the day of judgement and session of Christ and his Apostles, with hell fire. So that those words were not used to distinguish between divers crimes and divers courts of justice and divers punishments; but to tax the distinction between sin and sin, which the Jews drew not from the difference of the will in obeying God, but from the difference of their temporal courts of justice, and to show [351]
them that he that had the will to hurt his brother, though the effect appear but in reviling or not at all, shall be cast into hell fire by the judges and by the session, which shall be the same, not different, courts at the day of judgement. This considered, what can

1 See also 12.32, 43.14, 43.17, 44.16, 44.30–4, 44.40, 46.21, and 47.14.

be drawn from this text to maintain purgatory, I cannot imagine.

38. The sixth place is Luke 16:9: *Make ye friends of the unrighteous Mammon, that when ye fail, they may receive you into everlasting tabernacles.* This he alleges to prove invocation of saints departed. But the sense is plain, that we should make friends with our riches of the poor, and thereby obtain their prayers whilst they live. *He that giveth to the poor lendeth to the Lord.*

39. The seventh is Luke 23:42: *Lord, remember me when thou comest into thy kingdom.* Therefore, saith he, there is remission of sins after this life. But the consequence is not good. Our Saviour then forgave him and, at his coming again in glory, will remember to raise him again to life eternal.

40. The eighth is Acts 2:24, where St. Peter saith of Christ, *that God had raised him up, and loosed the pains of death, because it was not possible he should be holden of it.* Which he interprets to be a descent of Christ into purgatory, to loose some souls there from their torments, whereas it is manifest that it was Christ that was loosed. It was he that could not be holden of death or the grave, and not the souls in purgatory. But if that which Beza says in his notes on this place be well observed, there is none that will not see that instead of *pains*, it should be *bands*; and then there is no further cause to seek for purgatory in this text.

[352]

## CHAPTER XLV

## OF DEMONOLOGY AND OTHER RELICS OF THE RELIGION OF THE GENTILES

The original of demonology.

1. The impression made on the organs of sight by lucid bodies either in one direct line or in many lines, reflected from opaque or refracted in the passage through diaphanous bodies, produceth in living creatures, in whom God hath placed such organs, an imagination of the object from whence the impression proceedeth; which imagination is called *sight* and seemeth not to be a mere imagination, but the body itself without us, in the same manner as when a man violently presseth his eye, there appears to him a light without and before him, which no man perceiveth but himself,

because there is indeed no such thing without him, but only a motion in the interior organs, pressing by resistance outward, that makes him think so. And the motion made by this pressure, continuing after the object which caused it is removed, is that we call *imagination* and *memory*,[1] and, in sleep, and sometimes in great distemper of the organs by sickness or violence, a *dream*,[2] of which things I have already spoken briefly in the second and third chapters.

2. This nature of sight having never been discovered by the ancient pretenders to natural knowledge, much less by those that consider not things so remote (as that knowledge is) from their present use, it was hard for men to conceive of those images in the fancy and in the sense otherwise than of things really without us; which [images] some [people], because they vanish away, they know not whither nor how, will have to be absolutely incorporeal, that is to say, immaterial, or forms without matter (colour and figure, without any coloured or figured body), and that they can put on airy bodies, as a garment, to make them visible when they will to our bodily eyes; and others say [they] are bodies and living creatures, but made of air or other more subtle and ethereal matter, which is, then, when they will be seen, condensed. But both of them agree on one general appellation of them, DEMONS.[3] As if the dead of whom they dreamed were not inhabitants of their own brain, but of the air or of heaven or hell, not phantasms, but ghosts, with just as much reason as if one should say he saw his own ghost in a looking-glass or the ghosts of the stars in a river, or call the ordinary apparition of the sun of the quantity of about a foot, the demon or ghost of that great sun that enlighteneth the whole visible world; and by that means [they] have feared them, as things of an unknown, that is, of an unlimited power to do them good or harm; and consequently, [they have] given occasion to the [353]
governors of the heathen commonwealths to regulate this their fear by establishing that DEMONOLOGY[4] (in which the poets, as principal priests of the heathen religion, were specially employed or reverenced) to the public peace and to the obedience of sub-

1 See also 2.2–4.

2 See also 2.5–6.

3 See also 8.25, 12.16, 34.15, 34.18, and 36.2.

4 See also 40.14, 44.3, 44.16, and 47.15.

jects necessary thereunto, and to make some of them good *demons* and others evil; the one as a spur to the observance, the other as reins to withhold them from violation of the laws.

What were the demons of the ancients.

3. What kind of things they were to whom they attributed the name of *demons* appeareth partly in the genealogy of their gods, written by Hesiod, one of the most ancient poets of the Grecians, and partly in other histories, of which I have observed some few before, in the twelfth chapter of this discourse.

How that doctrine was spread.

4. The Grecians, by their colonies and conquests communicated their language and writings into Asia, Egypt, and Italy; and therein, by necessary consequence, their *demonology*, or, as St. Paul calls it, *their doctrines of devils.* And by that means the contagion was derived also to the Jews, both of Judaea and Alexandria, and other parts, whereinto they were dispersed, and the name of *demon* they did not, as the Grecians, attribute to spirits both good and evil, but to the evil only. And to the good *demons* they gave the name of the Spirit of God and esteemed those into whose bodies they entered to be prophets. In sum, all singularity, if good, they attributed to the Spirit of God, and if evil, to some *demon*, but a *kakodaimou,* an evil *demon*, that is, a *devil*. And therefore, they called *demoniacs*, that is, *possessed by the devil*, such as we call madmen or lunatics or such as had the falling-sickness, or that spoke anything which they, for want of understanding, thought absurd. As also of an unclean person in a notorious degree, they used to say he had an unclean spirit; of a dumb man, that he had a dumb devil; and of *John the Baptist* (Matt. 11:18), for the singularity of his fasting, that he had a devil; and of our Saviour, because he said, he that keepeth his sayings should not see death *in aeternum*, *Now we know thou hast a devil; Abraham is dead, and the prophets are dead.* And again, because he said *they went about to kill him*, the people answered, *Thou hast a devil: who goeth about to kill thee?* (John 7:20). Whereby it is manifest that the Jews had the same opinions concerning phantasms, namely, that they were not phantasms, that is, idols of the brain, but things real and independent on the fancy.

How far received by the Jews.

John 8:52.

Why our Savior controlled it not.

5. Which doctrine, if it be not true, why (may some say) did not our Saviour contradict it and teach the contrary? Nay, why does he use on divers occasions such forms of speech as seem to confirm it? To this I answer that, first, where Christ saith, *A spirit*

*hath not flesh and bone* [Luke 24:39], though he show that there be spirits; yet he denies not that they are bodies. And where St. Paul says, *We shall rise spiritual bodies* [1 Cor. 15:44], he acknowledgeth the nature of spirits, but that they are bodily spirits; which is not difficult to understand. For air and many other things are bodies, though not flesh and bone, or any other gross body to be dis- [354] cerned by the eye. But when our Saviour speaketh to the devil and commandeth him to go out of a man, if by the devil be meant a disease, as frenzy or lunacy or a corporeal spirit, is not the speech improper? Can diseases hear? Or can there be a corporeal spirit in a body of flesh and bone, full already of vital and animal spirits? Are there not therefore spirits, that neither have bodies, nor are mere imaginations? To the first I answer that the addressing of our Saviour's command to the madness or lunacy he cureth is no more improper than was his rebuking of the fever or of the wind and sea; for neither do these hear. Or [it is no more improper] than was the command of God to the light, to the firmament, to the sun, and stars, when he commanded them to be; for they could not hear before they had a being. But those speeches are not improper, because they signify the power of God's word; no more therefore is it improper to command madness or lunacy (under the appellation of devils by which they were then commonly understood) to depart out of a man's body. To the second, concerning their being incorporeal, I have not yet observed any place of Scripture from whence it can be gathered that any man was ever possessed with any other corporeal spirit but that of his own by which his body is naturally moved.

The Scriptures do not teach that spirits are incorporeal.

6. Our Saviour, immediately after the Holy Ghost descended upon him in the form of a dove, is said by St. Matthew 4:1 to have been *led up by the Spirit into the wilderness*; and the same is recited (Luke 4:1) in these words, *Jesus being full of the Holy Ghost, was led in the Spirit into the wilderness.* Whereby it is evident that by *Spirit* there is meant the Holy Ghost. This cannot be interpreted for a possession. For Christ and the Holy Ghost are but one and the same substance, which is no possession of one substance or body by another. And whereas in the verses following he is said *to have been taken up by the devil into the holy city, and set upon a pinnacle of the temple*, shall we conclude thence that he was possessed of the

devil, or carried thither by violence? And again, *carried thence by the devil into an exceeding high mountain, who showed him thence all the kingdoms of the world*, wherein we are not to believe he was either possessed or forced by the devil, nor that any mountain is high enough, according to the literal sense to show him one whole hemisphere. What then can be the meaning of this place, other than that he went of himself into the wilderness, and that this carrying of him up and down, from the wilderness to the city, and from thence into a mountain, was a vision? Conformable whereunto is also the phrase of St. Luke, that he was led into the wilderness, not *by*, but *in* the Spirit, whereas, concerning his being taken up into the mountain and unto the pinnacle of the temple, he speaketh as St. Matthew doth, which suiteth with the nature of a vision.

7. Again, where St. Luke says of Judas Iscariot that *Satan entered into him, and thereupon that he went and communed with the chief priests, and captains, how he might betray Christ unto them* [Luke 22:3-
[355] 4], it may be answered that by the entering of Satan (that is, the enemy)[1] into him is meant the hostile and traitorous intention of selling his Lord and Master. For as by the Holy Ghost is frequently in Scripture understood the graces and good inclinations given by the Holy Ghost; so by the entering of Satan may be understood the wicked cogitations and designs of the adversaries of Christ and his Disciples. For as it is hard to say that the devil was entered into Judas, before he had any such hostile design; so it is impertinent to say he was first Christ's enemy in his heart and that the devil entered into him afterwards. Therefore the entering of Satan and his wicked purpose was one and the same thing.

8. But if there be no immaterial spirit nor any possession of men's bodies by any spirit corporeal, it may again be asked why our Saviour his Apostles did not teach the people so and in such clear words as they might no more doubt thereof. But such questions as these are more curious than necessary for a Christian man's salvation. Men may as well ask why Christ, that could have given to all men faith, piety, and all manner of moral virtues, gave it to some only, and not to all, and why he left the search of natural causes and sciences to the natural reason and industry of men

1 See also 38.12–13, 42.24, 44.2, 44.27, and 45.7.

and did not reveal it to all or any man supernaturally, and many other such questions, of which nevertheless there may be alleged probable and pious reasons. For as God, when he brought the Israelites into the Land of Promise, did not secure them therein by subduing all the nations round about them, but left many of them, as thorns in their sides, to awaken from time to time their piety and industry, so our Saviour, in conducting us toward his heavenly kingdom, did not destroy all the difficulties of natural questions, but left them to exercise our industry and reason, the scope of his preaching being only to show us this plain and direct way to salvation, namely, the belief of this article, *that he was the Christ, the Son of the living God, sent into the world to sacrifice himself for our sins, and, at his coming again, gloriously to reign over his elect, and to save them from their enemies eternally*, to which the opinion of possession by spirits or phantasms is no impediment in the way, though it be to some an occasion of going out of the way and to follow their own inventions. If we require of the Scripture an account of all questions which may be raised to trouble us in the performance of God's commands, we may as well complain of Moses for not having set down the time of the creation of such spirits, as well as of the creation of the earth and sea, and of men and beasts. To conclude, I find in Scripture that there be angels[1] and spirits, good and evil, but not that they are incorporeal, as are the apparitions men see in the dark or in a dream or vision, which the Latins call *spectra* and took for *demons*. And I find that there are spirits corporeal, though subtle and invisible, but not that any man's body was possessed or inhabited by them, and that the bodies of the saints shall [356] be such, namely, spiritual bodies, as St. Paul calls them.

The power of casting out devils, not the same it was in the primitive Church.

9. Nevertheless, the contrary doctrine, namely, that there be incorporeal spirits, hath hitherto so prevailed in the Church that the use of exorcism (that is to say, of ejection of devils by conjuration) is thereupon built, and, though rarely and faintly practised, is not yet totally given over. That there were many demoniacs in the primitive Church and few madmen, and other such singular diseases, whereas in these times we hear of, and see many madmen, and few demoniacs, proceeds not from the change of nature, but of names. But how it comes to pass that whereas heretofore the

1 See also 34.23.

Apostles, and after them for a time the pastors of the Church, did cure those singular diseases, which now they are not seen to do, as likewise, why it is not in the power of every true believer now to do all that the faithful did then, that is to say, as we read *in Christ's name to cast out devils, to speak with new tongues, to take up serpents, to drink deadly poison without harm taking, and to cure the sick by the laying on of their hands* (Mark 16:17), and all this without other words but in the name of Jesus, is another question. And it is probable that those extraordinary gifts were given to the Church for no longer a time than men trusted wholly to Christ and looked for their felicity only in his kingdom to come; and consequently, that when they sought authority and riches and trusted to their own subtlety for a kingdom of this world, these supernatural gifts of God were again taken from them.

Another relic of gentilism, worshipping of images, left in the Church, not brought into it.

10. Another relic of Gentilism is the *worship of images*, neither instituted by Moses in the Old, nor by Christ in the New Testament, nor yet brought in from the Gentiles, but left amongst them, after they had given their names to Christ. Before our Saviour preached, it was the general religion of the Gentiles to worship for gods those appearances that remain in the brain from the impression of external bodies upon the organs of their senses, which are commonly called *ideas, idols, phantasms, conceits*, as being representations of those external bodies which cause them and have nothing in them of reality, no more than there is in the things that seem to stand before us in a dream. And this is the reason why St. Paul says, *We know that an idol is nothing* [1 Cor. 8:4], not that he thought that an image of metal, stone, or wood was nothing, but that the thing which they honored or feared in the image and held for a god was a mere figment, without place, habitation, motion, or existence, but in the motions of the brain. And the worship of these with divine honour is that which is in the Scripture called idolatry and rebellion against God. For God being King of the Jews and his lieutenant being first Moses and afterward the high priest, if the people had been permitted to worship and pray to images (which are representations of their own fancies), they had had no further dependence on the true God, of whom there can
[357] be no similitude, nor on his prime ministers, Moses and the high priests; but every man had governed himself according to his own

appetite to the utter eversion [overturning] of the Commonwealth, and their own destruction for want of union. And therefore the first law of God was: *they should not take for gods*, ALIENOS DEOS,[1] *that is, the gods of other nations, but that only true God, who vouchsafed to commune with Moses, and by him to give them laws and directions for their peace, and for their salvation from their enemies.* And the second was that *they should not make to themselves any image to worship, of their own invention.* For it is the same deposing of a king to submit to another king, whether he be set up by a neighbour nation or by ourselves.

Answer to certain seeming texts for images.

11. The places of Scripture pretended to countenance the setting up of images to worship them or to set them up at all in the places where God is worshipped, are, first, two examples: one of the cherubim over the Ark of God, the other of the brazen serpent; secondly, some texts whereby we are commanded to worship certain creatures for their relation to God, as to worship his footstool, and lastly, some other texts, by which is authorized a religious honouring of holy things. But before I examine the force of those places, to prove that which is pretended, I must first explain what is to be understood by *worshipping*, and what by *images* and *idols*.

What is worship.

12. I have already shown, in the twentieth chapter of this discourse, that to honour[2] is to value highly the power of any person and that such value is measured by our comparing him with others. But because there is nothing to be compared with God in power, we honour him not, but dishonour him, by any value less than infinite. And thus honour is properly of its own nature secret and internal in the heart. But the inward thoughts of men, which appear outwardly in their words and actions, are the signs of our honouring; and these go by the name of *worship*,[3] in Latin, *cultus*. Therefore, to pray to, to swear by, to obey, to be diligent and officious in serving, in sum, all words and actions that betoken fear to offend or desire to please is *worship*, whether those words and actions be sincere or feigned, and because they appear as signs of honouring are ordinarily also called *honour*.

1 See also 30.7 and 42.37.

2 See also 31.8ff.

3 See also 31.8ff.

Distinction between divine and civil worship.

13. The worship we exhibit to those we esteem to be but men, as to kings and men in authority, is *civil worship*; But the worship we exhibit to that which we think to be God, whatsoever the words, ceremonies, gestures, or other actions be, is *divine worship*. To fall prostrate before a king, in him that thinks him but a man, is but civil worship; And he that but putteth off his hat in the church, for this cause, that he thinketh it the house of God, worshippeth with divine worship. They that seek the distinction of divine and civil worship, not in the intention of the worshipper, but in the words *douleia* and *latreia*, deceive themselves. For whereas
[358] there be two sorts of servants: that sort which is of those that are absolutely in the power of their masters, as slaves taken in war, and their issue, whose bodies are not in their own power (their lives depending on the will of their masters, in such manner as to forfeit them upon the least disobedience), and that are bought and sold as beasts, were called *douloi*, that is properly, slaves, and their service, *douleia*; the other, which is of those that serve for hire, or in hope of benefit from their masters voluntarily, are called *thetes*, that is, domestic servants; to whose service the masters have no further right than is contained in the covenants made betwixt them. These two kinds of servants have thus much common to them both, that their labour is appointed them by another; and the word *latris* is the general name of both, signifying him that worketh for another, whether as a slave or a voluntary servant. So that *latria* signifieth generally all service; but *douleia* the service of bondmen only, and the condition of slavery; and both are used in Scripture, to signify our service of God, promiscuously. *Douleia*, because we are God's slaves, *latreia*, because we serve him; and in all kinds of service is contained, not only obedience, but also worship, that is, such actions, gestures, and words as signify *honour*.

An image what. Phantasms.

14. An *image* (in the most strict signification of the word) is the resemblance of something visible: in which sense the fantastical forms, apparitions, or seemings of visible bodies to the sight, are only *images*; such as are the show of a man or other thing in the water, by reflection or refraction; or of the sun or stars by direct vision in the air, which are nothing real in the things seen nor in the place where they seem to be; nor are their magnitudes and figures the same with that of the object, but changeable, by the

variation of the organs of sight or by glasses, and are present oftentimes in our imagination and in our dreams, when the object is absent; or changed into other colours, and shapes, as things that depend only upon the fancy. And these are the *images* which are originally and most properly called *ideas* and *idols*, and derived from the language of the Grecians, with whom the word *eido* signifieth *to see*. They are also called PHANTASMS,[1] which is in the same language, *apparitions*. And from these images it is that one of the faculties of man's nature is called the *imagination*. And from hence it is manifest that there neither is, nor can be, any image made of a thing invisible.

15. It is also evident that there can be no image of a thing infinite;[2] for all the images and phantasms that are made by the impression of things visible are figured. But figure is quantity every way determined; and therefore there can be no image of God, nor of the soul of man, nor of spirits, but only of bodies visible, that is, bodies that have light in themselves, or are by such enlightened.

Fictions.

16. And whereas a man can fancy shapes he never saw, making up a figure out of the parts of divers creatures, as the poets make their centaurs, chimeras, and other monsters never seen, so can he [359] also give matter to those shapes and make them in wood, clay, or metal. And these are also called images, not for the resemblance of any corporeal thing, but for the resemblance of some fantastical inhabitants of the brain of the maker. But in these idols, as they are originally in the brain, and as they are painted, carved, moulded or molten in matter, there is a similitude of the one to the other, for which the material body made by art may be said to be the image of the fantastical idol made by nature.

Material images.

17. But in a larger use of the word *image* is contained also any representation of one thing by another. So an earthly sovereign may be called the image of God, and an inferior magistrate the image of an earthly sovereign. And many times in the idolatry of the Gentiles there was little regard to the similitude of their material idol to the idol in their fancy, and yet it was called the image of it. For a stone unhewn has been set up for Neptune and divers

1 See also 34.25, 36.2, 44.1, 44.13, 44.16, 44.21, 45.2, 45.4, 45.8, 45.10, and 45.14.

2 See also 3.12, 12.6, 31.28, and 45.12.

other shapes far different from the shapes they conceived of their gods. And at this day we see many images of the Virgin Mary and other saints, unlike one another, and without correspondence to any one man's fancy, and yet serve well enough for the purpose they were erected for, which was no more but by the names only to represent the persons mentioned in the history; to which every man applieth a mental image of his own making, or none at all. And thus an image, in the largest sense, is either the resemblance or the representation of some thing visible, or both together, as it happeneth for the most part.

18. But the name of idol is extended yet further in Scripture, to signify also the sun or a star or any other creature, visible or invisible, when they are worshipped for gods.

Idolatry what. 19. Having shown what is *worship*, and what an *image*, I will now put them together, and examine what that IDOLATRY is which is forbidden in the second Commandment, and other places of the Scripture.

20. To worship an image is voluntarily to do those external acts which are signs of honouring either the matter of the image, which is wood, stone, metal, or some other visible creature, or the phantasm of the brain for the resemblance or representation whereof the matter was formed and figured, or both together as one animate body composed of the matter and the phantasm, as of a body and soul.

21. To be uncovered before a man of power and authority or before the throne of a prince or in such other places as he ordaineth to that purpose in his absence is to worship that man or prince with civil worship, as being a sign, not of honouring the stool or place, but the person and is not idolatry. But if he that doth it should suppose the soul of the prince to be in the stool or should present a petition to the stool, [then] it were divine worship, and idolatry.

[360] 22. To pray to a king for such things as he is able to do for us, though we prostrate ourselves before him, is but civil worship, because we acknowledge no other power in him but human. But voluntarily to pray unto him for fair weather or for anything which God only can do for us is divine worship and idolatry. On the other side, if a king compel a man to it by the terror of death

or other great corporal punishment, it is not idolatry. For the worship which the sovereign commandeth to be done unto himself by the terror of his laws is not a sign that he that obeyeth him does inwardly honour him as a god, but that he is desirous to save himself from death, or from a miserable life; and that which is not a sign of internal honour is no worship and therefore no idolatry. Neither can it be said that he that does it scandalizeth or layeth any stumbling block before his brother, because how wise or learned soever he be that worshippeth in that manner, another man cannot from thence argue that he approveth it, but that he doth it for fear; and that it is not his act, but the act of his sovereign.

23. To worship God in some peculiar place or turning a man's face towards an image or determinate place is not to worship or honour the place or image, but to acknowledge it holy, that is to say, to acknowledge the image or the place to be set apart from common use; for that is the meaning of the word *holy*; which implies no new quality in the place or image, but only a new relation by appropriation to God and therefore is not idolatry, no more than it was idolatry to worship God before the brazen serpent or for the Jews, when they were out of their own country, to turn their faces (when they prayed) toward the temple of Jerusalem, or for Moses to put off his shoes when he was before the flaming bush, the ground appertaining to Mount Sinai, which place God had chosen to appear in and to give his laws to the people of Israel, and was therefore holy ground, not by inherent sanctity, but by separation to God's use, or for Christians to worship in the churches which are once solemnly dedicated to God for that purpose by the authority of the king or other true representant of the Church. But to worship God as inanimating or inhabiting such image or place, that is to say, an infinite substance in a finite place, is idolatry; for such finite gods are but idols of the brain, nothing real, and are commonly called in the Scripture by the names of *vanity*, and *lies*, and *nothing*. Also to worship God, not as inanimating or present in the place or image, but to the end to be put in mind of him or of some works of his, in case the place or image be dedicated or set up by private authority and not by the authority of them that are our sovereign pastors, is idolatry. For

the Commandment is, *Thou shalt not make to thyself any graven image.* God commanded Moses to set up the brazen serpent; he did not make it to himself; it was not therefore against the Commandment. But the making of the golden calf by Aaron and the
[361] people, as being done without authority from God, was idolatry; not only because they held it for God, but also because they made it for a religious use, without warrant either from God their Sovereign, or from Moses that was his lieutenant.

24. The Gentiles worshipped for gods, Jupiter and others that, living, were men perhaps that had done great and glorious acts, and, for the children of God, divers men and women, supposing them gotten between an immortal deity and a mortal man. This was idolatry, because they made them so to themselves, having no authority from God, neither in his eternal law of reason nor in his positive and revealed will. But though our Saviour was a man, whom we also believe to be God immortal and the Son of God;[1] yet this is no idolatry, because we build not that belief upon our own fancy or judgement, but upon the word of God revealed in the Scriptures. And for the adoration of the Eucharist, if the words of Christ, *This is my body*, signify *that he himself, and the seeming bread in his hand, and not only so, but that all the seeming morsels of bread that have ever since been, and any time hereafter shall be, consecrated by priests, be so many Christ's bodies, and yet all of them but one body*, then is that no idolatry, because it is authorized by our Saviour; but if that text do not signify that (for there is no other that can be alleged for it), then, because it is a worship of human institution, it is idolatry. For it is not enough to say, God can transubstantiate the bread into Christ's body, for the Gentiles also held God to be omnipotent, and might upon that ground no less excuse their idolatry, by pretending, as well as others, a transubstantiation of their wood and stone into God Almighty.

25. Whereas there be [those] that pretend divine inspiration to be a supernatural entering of the Holy Ghost into a man and not an acquisition of God's graces by doctrine and study, I think they are in a very dangerous dilemma. For if they worship not the men whom they believe to be so inspired, they fall into impiety, as not adoring God's supernatural presence. And again, if they worship

1 See also 34.14.

them they commit idolatry; for the Apostles would never permit themselves to be so worshipped. Therefore the safest way is to believe that by the descending of the dove upon the Apostles and by Christ's breathing on them when he gave them the Holy Ghost and by the giving of it by imposition of hands, are understood the signs which God hath been pleased to use, or ordain to be used, of his promise to assist those persons in their study to preach his kingdom, and in their conversation, that it might not be scandalous, but edifying to others.

Scandalous worship of images.

26. Besides the idolatrous worship of images, there is also a scandalous worship of them, which is also a sin, but not idolatry. For idolatry is to worship by signs of an internal and real honour; but scandalous worship is but seeming worship, and may sometimes be joined with an inward and hearty detestation, both of the image and of the fantastical demon or idol to which it is dedicat- [362] ed; and proceed only from the fear of death or other grievous punishment; and is nevertheless a sin in them that so worship, in case they be men whose actions are looked at by others as lights to guide them by; because following their ways, they cannot but stumble and fall in the way of religion: whereas the example of those we regard not, works not on us at all, but leaves us to our own diligence and caution, and consequently are no causes of our falling.

27. If therefore a pastor lawfully called to teach and direct others, or any other, of whose knowledge there is a great opinion, do external honour to an idol for fear, unless he make his fear and unwillingness to it as evident as the worship, [then] he scandalizeth his brother by seeming to approve idolatry. For his brother arguing from the action of his teacher or of him whose knowledge he esteemeth great, concludes it to be lawful in itself. And this scandal is sin, and a scandal given. But if one being no pastor nor of eminent reputation for knowledge in Christian doctrine do the same and another follow him, this is no scandal given; for he had no cause to follow such example, but is a pretence of scandal, which he taketh of himself for an excuse before men. For an unlearned man that is in the power of an idolatrous king or state, if commanded on pain of death to worship before an idol, he detesteth the idol in his heart, he doth well; though if he had the

fortitude to suffer death, rather than worship it, he should do better. But if a pastor, who as Christ's messenger has undertaken to teach Christ's doctrine to all nations, should do the same, it were not only a sinful scandal, in respect of other Christian men's consciences, but a perfidious forsaking of his charge.

28. The sum of that which I have said hitherto, concerning the worship of images, is this, that he that worshippeth in an image or any creature, either the matter thereof or any fancy of his own which he thinketh to dwell in it or both together or believeth that such things hear his prayers or see his devotions, without ears or eyes, committeth idolatry. And he that counterfeiteth such worship for fear of punishment, if he be a man whose example hath power amongst his brethren, committeth a sin. But he that worshippeth the Creator of the world before such an image or in such a place as he hath not made or chosen of himself, but taken from the commandment of God's word, as the Jews did in worshipping God before the cherubim and before the brazen serpent for a time and in or towards the temple of Jerusalem, which was also but for a time, committeth not idolatry.

29. Now for the worship of saints and images and relics and other things at this day practised in the Church of Rome, I say they are not allowed by the word of God nor brought into the
[363] Church of Rome from the doctrine there taught, but partly left in it at the first conversion of the Gentiles and afterwards countenanced and confirmed and augmented by the bishops of Rome.

Answer to the argument from the cherubim, and brazen serpent.

30. As for the proofs alleged out of Scripture, namely, those examples of images appointed by God to be set up, they were not set up for the people or any man to worship, but that they should worship God himself before them, as before the cherubim over the Ark and the brazen serpent. For we read not that the priest or any other did worship the cherubim. But contrarily we read (2 Kings 18:4) that Hezekiah broke in pieces the brazen serpent which Moses had set up, because the people burnt incense to it. Besides, those examples are not put for our imitation, that we also should set up images, under pretence of worshipping God before them; because the words of the second Commandment, *Thou shalt not make to thyself any graven image*, etc., distinguish between the images that God commanded to be set up and those which we set

up to ourselves. And therefore from the cherubim or brazen serpent to the images of man's devising, and from the worship commanded by God to the will-worship of men, the argument is not good. This also is to be considered, that as Hezekiah broke in pieces the brazen serpent, because the Jews did worship it, to the end they should do so no more, so also Christian sovereigns ought to break down the images which their subjects have been accustomed to worship, that there be no more occasion of such idolatry. For at this day the ignorant people, where images are worshipped, do really believe there is a divine power in the images, and are told by their pastors that some of them have spoken and have bled, and that miracles have been done by them; which [miracles] they apprehend as done by the saint, which they think either is the image itself or in it. The Israelites, when they worshipped the calf, did think they worshipped the God that brought them out of Egypt, and yet it was idolatry, because they thought the calf either was that God or had him in his belly. And though some man may think it impossible for people to be so stupid as to think the image to be God or a saint or to worship it in that notion; yet it is manifest in Scripture to the contrary; where, when the golden calf was made, the people said, *These are thy gods, O Israel* and where the images of Laban are called his gods. And we see daily by experience in all sorts of people that such men as study nothing but their food and ease are content to believe any absurdity, rather than to trouble themselves to examine it, holding their faith as it were by entail unalienable, except by an express and new law.

Exod. 32:2.
Gen 31:30.

31. But they infer from some other places that it is lawful to paint angels and also God himself, as from God's walking in the garden, from Jacob's seeing God at the top of the ladder, and from other visions and dreams. But visions and dreams, whether natural or supernatural, are but phantasms; and he that painteth an image of any of them maketh not an image of God, but of his own phantasm, which is making of an idol. I say not that to draw a picture after a fancy is a sin, but when it is drawn, to hold it for a representation of God[1] is against the second Commandment and can be of no use but to worship. And the same may be said of the images of

Painting of fancies no idolatry, but abusing them to religious worship is.

[364]

1 See also 3.12.

angels and of men dead, unless as monuments of friends or of men worthy remembrance. For such use of an image is not worship of the image, but a civil honouring of the person, not that is, but that was; but when it is done to the image which we make of a saint, for no other reason but that we think he heareth our prayers and is pleased with the honour we do him, when dead and without sense, we attribute to him more than human power; and therefore it is idolatry.

32. Seeing therefore there is no authority, neither in the Law of Moses nor in the Gospel, for the religious worship of images or other representations of God which men set up to themselves or for the worship of the image of any creature in heaven or earth or under the earth; and whereas Christian kings, who are living representants of God, are not to be worshipped by their subjects by any act that signifieth a greater esteem of his power than the nature of mortal man is capable of, it cannot be imagined that the religious worship now in use was brought into the Church by misunderstanding of the Scripture. It resteth therefore that it was left in it by not destroying the images themselves in the conversion of the Gentiles that worshipped them.

How idolatry was left in the Church.

33. The cause whereof was the immoderate esteem and prices set upon the workmanship of them, which made the owners, though converted from worshipping them as they had done religiously for demons, to retain them still in their houses, upon pretence of doing it in the honor of Christ, of the Virgin Mary, and of the Apostles, and other the pastors of the primitive Church, as being easy, by giving them new names, to make that an image of the Virgin Mary and of her Son our Saviour, which before perhaps was called the image of Venus and Cupid, and so of a Jupiter to make a Barnabas, and of Mercury, a Paul, and the like.[1] And as worldly ambition, creeping by degrees into the pastors, drew them to an endeavour of pleasing the new-made Christians, and also to a liking of this kind of honour, which they also might hope for after their decease, as well as those that had already gained it, so the worshipping of the images of Christ and his Apostles grew more and more idolatrous, save that somewhat after the time of Constantine divers emperors and bishops and general councils

1 See also 12.6, 44.3, and 45.38.

observed and opposed the unlawfulness thereof, but too late or too weakly.

Canonizing of saints.

34. The canonizing of saints is another relic of Gentilism;[1] it is neither a misunderstanding of Scripture nor a new invention of the Roman Church, but a custom as ancient as the commonwealth of Rome itself. The first that ever was canonized at Rome was Romulus, and that upon the narration of Julius Proculus, that swore before the Senate, he spoke with him after his death and was assured by him he dwelt in heaven, and was there called Quirinus, [365] and would be propitious to the state of their new city; and thereupon the Senate gave public testimony of his sanctity.[2] Julius Caesar and other emperors after him had the like testimony, that is, were canonized for saints; for by such testimony is CANONIZATION now defined and is the same with the *apotheosis* of the heathen.

The name of Pontifex.

35. It is also from the Roman heathen that the popes have received the name and power of PONTIFEX MAXIMUS. This was the name of him that in the ancient commonwealth of Rome had the supreme authority under the Senate and people of regulating all ceremonies and doctrines concerning their religion; and when Augustus Caesar changed the state into a monarchy, he took to himself no more but this office and that of tribune of the people (that is to say, the supreme power both in state and religion); and the succeeding emperors enjoyed the same. But when the Emperor Constantine lived, who was the first that professed and authorized Christian religion, it was consonant to his profession to cause religion to be regulated (under his authority) by the bishop of Rome, though it do not appear they had so soon the name of Pontifex, but rather that the succeeding bishops took it of themselves, to countenance the power they exercised over the bishops of the Roman provinces. For it is not any privilege of St. Peter, but the privilege of the city of Rome, which the emperors were always willing to uphold, that gave them such authority over other bishops, as may be evidently seen by that, that the bishop of Constantinople, when the Emperor made that city the seat of the Empire, pretended to be equal to the bishop of Rome, though at

1 See also 47.12.

2 The story is in Livy, *History of Rome* Book I, chapter 16.

last, not without contention, the Pope carried it and became the *Pontifex Maximus*, but in right only of the Emperor and not without the bounds of the Empire nor anywhere after the Emperor had lost his power in Rome, though it were the Pope himself that took his power from him. From whence we may by the way observe that there is no place for the superiority of the Pope over other bishops, except in the territories whereof he is himself the civil sovereign, and where the emperor, having sovereign power civil, hath expressly chosen the Pope for the chief pastor under himself of his Christian subjects.

Procession of images.

36. The carrying about of images in procession is another relic of the religion of the Greeks and Romans; for they also carried their idols from place to place, in a kind of chariot, which was peculiarly dedicated to that use, which the Latins called *thensa* and *vehiculum Deorum*; and the image was placed in a frame or shrine, which they called *ferculum*. And that which they called *pompa* is the same that now is named *procession*; according whereunto, amongst the divine honours which were given to Julius Caesar by the Senate, this was one, that in the pomp or procession at the Circaean games, he should have *thensam et ferculum*, a sacred chariot and a shrine, which was as much as to be carried up and down as a god, just as at this day the popes are carried by Switzers[1] under a canopy.

[366]

Wax, candles, and torches lighted.

37. To these processions also belonged the bearing of burning torches and candles before the images of the gods, both amongst the Greeks and Romans. For afterwards the emperors of Rome received the same honor, as we read of Caligula, that at his reception to the Empire he was carried from Misenum to Rome in the midst of a throng of people, the ways beset with altars and beasts for sacrifice and burning *torches*, and of Caracalla, that was received into Alexandria with incense and with casting of flowers, and *dadouxias*, that is, with torches; for *Dadouxoi* were they that amongst the Greeks carried torches lighted in the processions of their gods. And in process of time the devout but ignorant people did many times honour their bishops with the like pomp of wax candles and the images of our Saviour and the saints, constantly, in

1 The Swiss Guard, the Pope's security force.

the church itself. And thus came in the use of wax candles and was also established by some of the ancient councils.

38. The heathens had also their *aqua lustralis*, that is to say, *holy water*. The Church of Rome imitates them also in their *holy days*. They had their *bacchanalia*, and we have our *wakes*, answering to them; they their *saturnalia*, and we our *carnivals* and Shrove Tuesday's liberty of servants; they their procession of *Priapus*, we our fetching in, erection, and dancing about Maypoles; and dancing is one kind of worship. They had their procession called *Ambarvalia*, and we our procession about the fields in the Rogation week.[1] Nor do I think that these are all the ceremonies that have been left in the Church from the first conversion of the Gentiles; but they are all that I can for the present call to mind. And if a man would well observe that which is delivered in the histories concerning the religious rites of the Greeks and Romans, I doubt not but he might find many more of these old empty bottles of Gentilism which the doctors of the Roman Church, either by negligence or ambition, have filled up again with the new wine of Christianity, that will not fail in time to break them.

## CHAPTER XLVI [367]

## OF DARKNESS FROM VAIN PHILOSOPHY, AND FABULOUS TRADITIONS

What philosophy is.

1. By Philosophy is understood *the knowledge acquired by reasoning, from the manner of the generation of anything, to the properties; or from the properties, to some possible way of generation of the same; to the end to be able to produce, as far as matter and human force permit, such effects as human life requireth.*[2] So the geometrician, from the con-

1 See also 12.16 and 45.33.

2 Hobbes gives a similar definition in *De Corpore* (1655), 1.2 in *English Works*, ed. Willam Molesworth, vol. 1: "Philosophy is the knowledge, acquired through correct reasoning, of effects or phenomena from the conception of their causes or generations, and also of generations which could exist from the knowledge of their effects" (my translation from the Latin version). Much of *De Corpore* was probably complete or in a good draft by 1650.

struction of figures,[1] findeth out many properties thereof, and from the properties, new ways of their construction by reasoning, to the end to be able to measure land and water, and for infinite other uses. So the astronomer, from the rising, setting, and moving of the sun and stars in divers parts of the heavens, findeth out the causes of day and night, and of the different seasons of the year, whereby he keepeth an account of time; and the like of other sciences.

Prudence no part of philosophy.

2. By which definition it is evident that we are not to account as any part thereof that original knowledge called experience, in which consisteth prudence, because it is not attained by reasoning, but found as well in brute beasts as in man;[2] and is but a memory of successions of events in times past, wherein the omission of every little circumstance altering the effect, frustrateth the expectation of the most prudent: whereas nothing is produced by reasoning aright, but general, eternal, and immutable truth.

No false doctrine is part of philosophy:

3. Nor are we therefore to give that name to any false conclusions; for he that reasoneth aright in words he understandeth can never conclude an error:

No more is revelation supernatural:

4. Nor to that which any man knows by supernatural revelation, because it is not acquired by reasoning:[3]

Nor learning taken upon credit of authors.

5. Nor that which is gotten by reasoning from the authority of books; because it is not by reasoning from the cause to the effect nor from the effect to the cause, and is not knowledge, but faith.

Of the beginnings and progress of philosophy.

6. The faculty of reasoning being consequent to the use of speech, it was not possible but that there should have been some general truths found out by reasoning, as ancient almost as language itself. The savages of America are not without some good moral sentences; also they have a little arithmetic, to add and divide in numbers not too great; but they are not therefore philosophers. For as there were plants of corn and wine in small [368] quantity dispersed in the fields and woods before men knew their

---

1 Making something is the paradigm of scientific knowledge because one is then certain of the cause of the effect. So knowledge of geometry is more certain than knowledge of physics. See also 46.11.

2 See also *De Corpore* 1.2

3 Hobbes draws a sharp line between faith and reason, belief and knowledge (7.5, 7.7).

virtue or made use of them for their nourishment or planted them apart in fields and vineyards, in which time they fed on acorns and drank water; so also there have been divers true, general, and profitable speculations from the beginning, as being the natural plants of human reason.[1] But they were at first but few in number; men lived upon gross experience; there was no method, that is to say, no sowing nor planting of knowledge by itself, apart from the weeds and common plants of error and conjecture. And the cause of it being the want of leisure from procuring the necessities of life and defending themselves against their neighbours, it was impossible, till the erecting of great commonwealths, it should be otherwise. *Leisure* is the mother of *philosophy*; and *commonwealth*, the mother of *peace* and *leisure*. Where first were great and flourishing cities, there was first the study of *philosophy*. The Gymnosophists of India, the Magi of Persia, and the Priests of Chaldaea and Egypt are counted the most ancient philosophers; and those countries were the most ancient of kingdoms. Philosophy was not risen to the Grecians and other people of the West, whose commonwealths, no greater perhaps than Lucca or Geneva, had never peace but when their fears of one another were equal; nor the leisure to observe anything but one another. At length, when war had united many of these Grecian lesser cities into fewer and greater, then began seven men, of several parts of Greece, to get the reputation of being wise, some of them for moral and politic sentences and others for the learning of the Chaldaeans and Egyptians, which was astronomy and geometry. But we hear not yet of any schools of philosophy.

Of the schools of philosophy amongst the Athenians.

7. After the Athenians, by the overthrow of the Persian armies, had gotten the dominion of the sea and thereby, of all the islands and maritime cities of the archipelago, as well of Asia as Europe, and were grown wealthy, they that had no employment, neither at home nor abroad, had little else to employ themselves in but either, as St. Luke says, *in telling and hearing news* (Acts 17:21), or in discoursing of philosophy publicly to the youth of the city. Every master took some place for that purpose: Plato, in certain public walks called Academia, from one Academus; Aristotle in the walk

1 Hobbes uses this same analogy in *De Corpore* 1.1.

of the temple of Pan, called Lycaeum; others in the Stoa or covered walk, wherein the merchants' goods were brought to land; others in other places, where they spent the time of their leisure in teaching or in disputing of their opinions; and some in any place where they could get the youth of the city together to hear them talk. And this was it which Carneades also did at Rome, when he was ambassador, which caused Cato to advise the Senate to dispatch him quickly, for fear of corrupting the manners of the young men that delighted to hear him speak, as they thought, fine things.

8. From this it was that the place where any of them taught and disputed was called *schola*, which in their tongue signifieth *leisure*,
[369] and their disputations, *diatribae*, that is to say, *passing of the time*. Also the philosophers themselves had the name of their sects, some of them, from these their schools; for they that followed Plato's doctrine were called *Academics*, the followers of Aristotle, *Peripatetics*, from the walk he taught in, and those that Zeno taught, *Stoics*, from the *Stoa*, as if we should denominate men from More-fields, from Paul's Church, and from the Exchange, because they meet there often to prate and loiter.

9. Nevertheless, men were so much taken with this custom, that in time it spread itself over all Europe and the best part of Africa, so as there were schools, publicly erected and maintained, for lectures and disputations, almost in every commonwealth.

Of the Schools of the Jews.

10. There were also schools anciently, both before and after the time of our Saviour, amongst the Jews; but they were schools of their law. For though they were called *synagogues*, that is to say, congregations of the people; yet, inasmuch as the law was every Sabbath day read, expounded, and disputed in them, they differed not in nature, but in name only, from public schools, and were not only in Jerusalem, but in every city of the Gentiles where the Jews inhabited. There was such a school at Damascus, whereinto Paul entered, to persecute. There were others at Antioch, Iconium and Thessalonica, whereinto he entered, to dispute. And such was the synagogue of the Libertines, Cyrenians, Alexandrians, Cilicians, and those of Asia; that is to say, the school of Libertines, and of Jews, that were strangers in Jerusalem: and of this school they were that disputed with St. Stephen (Acts 6:9).

11. But what has been the utility of those schools? What science is there at this day acquired by their readings and disputings? That we have of geometry, which is the mother of all natural science, we are not indebted for it to the schools. Plato, that was the best philosopher of the Greeks, forbade entrance into his school to all that were not already in some measure geometricians. There were many that studied that science to the great advantage of mankind; but there is no mention of their schools; nor was there any sect of geometricians; nor did they then pass under the name of philosophers. The natural philosophy of those schools was rather a dream than science and set forth in senseless and insignificant language, which cannot be avoided by those that will teach philosophy without having first attained great knowledge in geometry. For nature worketh by motion, the ways and degrees whereof cannot be known without the knowledge of the proportions and properties of lines and figures. Their moral philosophy is but a description of their own passions. For the rule of manners, without civil government, is the law of nature, and in it, the law civil, that determineth what is *honest* and *dishonest*, what is *just* and *unjust*, and generally what is *good* and *evil*. Whereas they make the rules of *good* and *bad* by their own *liking* and *disliking*, by which means, in so great diversity of taste, there is nothing generally [370] agreed on, but every one doth, as far as he dares, whatsoever seemeth good in his own eyes, to the subversion of commonwealth. Their logic, which should be the method of reasoning, is nothing else but captions of words and inventions how to puzzle such as should go about to pose them. To conclude, there is nothing so absurd that the old philosophers (as Cicero saith, who was one of them) have not some of them maintained. And I believe that scarce anything can be more absurdly said in natural philosophy than that which now is called Aristotle's *Metaphysics*, nor more repugnant to government than much of that he hath said in his *Politics*, nor more ignorantly, than a great part of his *Ethics*.[1]

The school of the Grecians unprofitable.

12. The school of the Jews was originally a school of the law of Moses, who commanded that at the end of every seventh year, at the Feast of the Tabernacles, it should be read to all the people,

The school of the Jews unprofitable.

1 See also 44.3.

that they might hear and learn it (Deut. 31:10). Therefore the reading of the law (which was in use after the Captivity) every Sabbath day ought to have had no other end but the acquainting of the people with the Commandments which they were to obey and to expound unto them the writings of the prophets. But it is manifest, by the many reprehensions of them by our Saviour, that they corrupted the text of the law with their false commentaries and vain traditions; and so little understood the prophets that they did neither acknowledge Christ nor the works he did, of which the prophets prophesied. So that by their lectures and disputations in their synagogues, they turned the doctrine of their law into a fantastical kind of philosophy, concerning the incomprehensible nature of God and of spirits, which they compounded of the vain philosophy and theology of the Grecians, mingled with their own fancies, drawn from the obscurer places of the Scripture, and which might most easily be wrested to their purpose; and from the fabulous traditions of their ancestors.

University what it is.

13. That which is now called a *university* is a joining together and an incorporation under one government, of many public schools in one and the same town or city, in which the principal schools were ordained for the three professions, that is to say, of the Roman religion, of the Roman law, and of the art of medicine. And for the study of philosophy it hath no otherwise place than as a handmaid to the Roman religion; and since the authority of Aristotle is only current there, that study is not properly philosophy (the nature whereof dependeth not on authors), but *Aristotelity*. And for geometry, till of very late times it had no place at all, as being subservient to nothing but rigid truth. And if any man by the ingenuity of his own nature had attained to any degree of perfection therein, he was commonly thought a magician, and his art diabolical.

Errors brought into religion from Aristotle's Metaphysics.

[371] 14. Now to descend to the particular tenets of vain philosophy, derived to the universities and thence into the Church, partly from Aristotle, partly from blindness of understanding, I shall first consider their principles. There is a certain *philosophia prima* on which all other philosophy ought to depend, and consisteth principally in right limiting of the significations of such appellations or names, as are of all others the most universal, which limitations serve to

avoid ambiguity and equivocation in reasoning and are commonly called definitions,[1] such as are the definitions of body, time, place, matter, form, essence, subject, substance, accident, power, act, finite, infinite, quantity, quality, motion, action, passion, and divers others, necessary to the explaining of a man's conceptions concerning the nature and generation of bodies. The explication (that is, the settling of the meaning) of which, and the like terms, is commonly in the Schools called *metaphysics*, as being a part of the philosophy of Aristotle, which hath that for title. But it is in another sense; for there it signifieth as much as *books written or placed after his natural philosophy*; but the Schools take them for *books of supernatural philosophy*; for the word *metaphysics* will bear both these senses. And indeed that which is there written is for the most part so far from the possibility of being understood and so repugnant to natural reason, that whosoever thinketh there is anything to be understood by it must needs think it supernatural.

Errors concerning abstract essences.

15. From these metaphysics, which are mingled with the Scripture to make School divinity, we are told there be in the world certain essences separated from bodies, which they call *abstract essence and substantial forms*, for the interpreting of which jargon, there is need of somewhat more than ordinary attention in this place. Also I ask pardon of those that are not used to this kind of discourse for applying myself to those that are. The world (I mean not the earth only, that denominates the lovers of it *worldly men*, but the *universe*, that is, the whole mass of all things that are) is corporeal, that is to say, body; and hath the dimensions of magnitude, namely, length, breadth, and depth, also every part of body is likewise body and hath the like dimensions, and consequently every part of the universe is body, and that which is not body is no part of the universe; and because the universe is all that which is no part of it is *nothing* and consequently *nowhere*. Nor does it follow from hence that spirits are *nothing*; for they have dimensions and are therefore really *bodies*, though that name in common speech be given to such bodies only as are visible or palpable, that is, that have some degree of opacity; but for spirits, they call them incorporeal, which is a name of more honour and may therefore with more piety be attributed to God himself, in whom we consider

1 See also 4.12-13.

not what attribute expresseth best his nature, which is incomprehensible, but what best expresseth our desire to honour him.

[372] 16. To know now upon what grounds they say there be essences abstract or substantial forms, we are to consider what those words do properly signify. The use of words is to register to ourselves and make manifest to others the thoughts and conceptions of our minds. Of which words, some are the names of the things conceived, as the names of all sorts of bodies that work upon the senses and leave an impression in the imagination; others are the names of the imaginations themselves, that is to say, of those ideas or mental images we have of all things we see or remember; and others again are names of names, or of different sorts of speech, as *universal,*[1] *plural, singular*, are the names of names; and *definition, affirmation, negation, true,*[2] *false, syllogism, interrogation, promise, covenant*, are the names of certain forms of speech. Others serve to show the consequence or repugnance of one name to another, as when one saith, *A man is a body*, he intendeth that the name of *body* is necessarily consequent to the name of *man*, as being but several names of the same thing, *man*; which consequence is signified by coupling them together with the word *is*. And as we use the verb *is*; so the Latins use their verb *est*, and the Greeks their *esti* through all its declinations.[3] Whether all other nations of the world have in their several languages a word that answereth to it or not, I cannot tell; but I am sure they have not need of it; for the placing of two names in order may serve to signify their consequence, if it were the custom (for custom is it that gives words their force), as well as the words *is*, or *be*, or *are*, and the like.

17. And if it were so, that there were a language without any verb answerable to *est* or *is* or *be*; yet the men that used it would be

---

1 According to Hobbes, the word 'universal' names or is a name of words such as 'tree', 'cat', and 'human', because 'tree', 'cat', and 'human' are names of many individual objects. The word 'plural' names such words as 'trees', 'cats', and 'humans' while the word 'singular' names such words as 'tree', 'cat', and 'human'.

2 The word 'true' names the sentence 'Snow is white' while the word 'false' names the sentence, 'Snow is not white'.

3 Something is needed to distinguish an arbitrary placement of one word next to other words and sentences (or other meaningful units of language) in which some connection obtains among the words. English uses the word 'is' in its various forms to show that 'Snow is white' is a sentence. A word is actually not essential to indicate that the string of words is a sentence; word order is sufficient, as Hobbes notes in 46.17.

not a jot the less capable of inferring, concluding, and of all kind of reasoning, than were the Greeks and Latins. But what then would become of these terms, of *entity*, *essence*, *essential*, *essentiality*,[1] that are derived from it, and of many more that depend on these, applied as most commonly they are? They are therefore no names of things, but signs, by which we make known that we conceive the consequence of one name or attribute to another, as when we say, *A man is a living body*, we mean not that the *man* is one thing, the *living body* another, and the *is* or *being*, a third, but that the *man* and the *living body* is the same thing, because the consequence, *If he be a man, he is a living body*, is a true consequence, signified by that word *is*. Therefore, *to be a body, to walk, to be speaking, to live, to see*, and the like infinitives; also corporeity, walking, speaking, life, sight, and the like, that signify just the same, are the names of *nothing*, as I have elsewhere more amply expressed.

18. But to what purpose (may some man say) is such subtlety in a work of this nature, where I pretend to nothing but what is necessary to the doctrine of government and obedience? It is to this purpose, that men may no longer suffer themselves to be abused by them that by this doctrine of *separated essences*, built on the vain [373]
philosophy of Aristotle, would fright them from obeying the laws of their country, with empty names, as men fright birds from the corn with an empty doublet, a hat, and a crooked stick.[2] For it is upon this ground that, when a man is dead and buried, they say his soul (that is his life) can walk separated from his body, and is seen by night amongst the graves. Upon the same ground, they say that the figure and colour and taste of a piece of bread has a being there, where they say there is no bread;[3] and upon the same ground they say that faith and wisdom and other virtues are sometimes *poured* into a man, sometimes *blown* into him, from heaven, as

1 Hobbes holds that 'redness' and 'swiftness' are meaningful because they are formed from words that name actual objects, 'red' and 'swift'. He thinks that words invented by scholastic philosophers, such as 'entity' and 'essence', can be seen to be meaningless, because the word that they are formed from, namely, the Latin word for 'is', is not essential to language.

2 Hobbes is talking about Aristotelian scholastic philosophy in a work on government because these philosophers use their (absurd) metaphysical views to frighten people into believing things that influence people's political beliefs and behavior. His rhetorical questions at the end of the paragraph are supposed to indicate the political use of the metaphysical doctrines.

3 See also 5.15, 8.27, 43.14, 44.11, and 45.24.

if the virtuous and their virtues could be asunder and a great many other things that serve to lessen the dependence of subjects on the sovereign power of their country. For who will endeavour to obey the laws, if he expect obedience to be poured or blown into him? Or who will not obey a priest, that can make God, rather than his sovereign; nay, than God himself? Or who that is in fear of ghosts will not bear great respect to those that can make the holy water that drives them from him? And this shall suffice for an example of the errors which are brought into the Church from the *entities* and *essences* of Aristotle, which it may be he knew to be false philosophy, but wrote it as a thing consonant to, and corroborative of, their religion, and fearing the fate of Socrates.

19. Being once fallen into this error of separated essences, they are thereby necessarily involved in many other absurdities that follow it. For seeing they will have these forms to be real, they are obliged to assign them some place. But because they hold them incorporeal, without all dimension of quantity, and all men know that place is dimension, and not to be filled but by that which is corporeal, they are driven to uphold their credit with a distinction, that they are not indeed anywhere *circumscriptive*, but *definitive*. Which terms being mere words, and in this occasion insignificant, pass only in Latin, that the vanity of them may be concealed. For the circumscription of a thing is nothing else but the determination or defining of its place; and so both the terms of the distinction are the same. And in particular, of the essence of a man, which (they say) is his soul, they affirm it to be all of it in his little finger, and all of it in every other part (how small soever) of his body; and yet no more soul in the whole body than in any one of those parts. Can any man think that God is served with such absurdities? And yet all this is necessary to believe, to those that will believe the existence of an incorporeal soul, separated from the body.

20. And when they come to give account [of] how an incorporeal substance can be capable of pain and be tormented in the fire of hell or purgatory, they have nothing at all to answer, but that it cannot be known how fire can burn souls.[1]

---

1 It is absurd for scholastic philosophers, who think that the soul is immaterial, to talk about the fire of purgatory or hell causing pain to a soul.

21. Again, whereas motion is change of place and incorporeal substances are not capable of place, they are troubled to make it seem possible how a soul can go hence,[1] without the body, to heaven, hell, or purgatory, and how the ghosts of men (and I may add of their clothes which they appear in) can walk by night in churches, churchyards, and other places of sepulture. To which I know not what they can answer, unless they will say, they walk *definitive*, not *circumscriptive*, or *spiritually*, not *temporally*, for such egregious distinctions are equally applicable to any difficulty whatsoever. [374]

*Nunc-stans.*

22. For the meaning of *eternity*, they will not have it to be an endless succession of time; for then they should not be able to render a reason how God's will and pre-ordaining of things to come should not be before his prescience of the same, as the efficient cause before the effect or agent before the action, nor of many other their bold opinions concerning the incomprehensible nature of God. But they will teach us that eternity is the standing still of the present time, a *nunc-stans* (as the Schools call it), which neither they nor any else understand, no more than they would a *hic-stans* for an infinite greatness of place.

One body in many places, and many bodies in one place at once.

23. And whereas men divide a body in their thought, by numbering parts of it, and in numbering those parts, number also the parts of the place it filled, it cannot be but in making many parts, we make also many places of those parts; whereby there cannot be conceived in the mind of any man more or fewer parts than there are places for; yet they will have us believe that by the almighty power of God, one body may be at one and the same time in many places;[2] and many bodies at one and the same time in one place, as if it were an acknowledgement of the Divine Power to say, that which is, is not; or that which has been, has not been. And these are but a small part of the incongruities they are forced to from their disputing philosophically, instead of admiring and adoring of the divine and incomprehensible nature, whose attributes

1 It is absurd for scholastic philosophers, who think that the soul is immaterial, to talk about the soul walking or going any place.

2 A body is the kind of thing that fills up a place and can only be in one place. But, according to the scholastic theory of transubstantiation, the body of Jesus in the Eucharist is in many places at the same time.

cannot signify what he is, but ought to signify our desire to honour him with the best appellations we can think on.[1] But they that venture to reason of his nature, from these attributes of honour, losing their understanding in the very first attempt, fall from one inconvenience into another, without end and without number; in the same manner, as when a man ignorant of the ceremonies of court, coming into the presence of a greater person than he is, used to speak to, and stumbling at his entrance, to save himself from falling, lets slip his cloak; to recover his cloak, lets fall his hat; and, with one disorder after another, discovers [exposes] his astonishment and rusticity.

Absurdities in natural philosophy, as gravity the cause of heaviness. [375]

24. Then for physics, that is, the knowledge of the subordinate and secondary causes of natural events, they render none at all but empty words. If you desire to know why some kind of bodies sink naturally downwards toward the earth and others go naturally from it, the Schools will tell you, out of Aristotle, that the bodies that sink downwards are heavy; and that this heaviness is it that causes them to descend. But if you ask what they mean by *heaviness*, they will define it to be an endeavour to go to the center of the earth, so that the cause why things sink downward is an endeavour to be below, which is as much as to say that bodies descend or ascend, because they do. Or they will tell you the center of the earth is the place of rest and conservation for heavy things, and therefore they endeavour to be there, as if stones and metals had a desire or could discern the place they would be at, as man does, or loved rest, as man does not, or that a piece of glass were less safe in the window than falling into the street.

Quantity put into body already made.

25. If we would know why the same body seems greater, without adding to it, one time than another; they say, when it seems less, it is *condensed*, when greater, *rarefied*. What is that *condensed* and *rarefied*? Condensed is when there is in the very same matter less quantity than before, and rarefied, when more. As if there could be matter that had not some determined quantity, when quantity is nothing else but the determination of matter; that is to say, of body, by which we say one body is greater or lesser than another by thus, or thus much. Or as if a body were made without any quantity at all and that afterwards more or less were

1 See also 31.8, 31.14, and 31.28.

put into it, according as it is intended the body should be more or less dense.

26. For the cause of the soul of man, they say, *creatur infundendo* and *creando infunditur*; that is, *It is created by pouring it in*, and *[It is] poured in by creation*.

Pouring in of souls.

27. For the cause of sense, an ubiquity of *species*, that is, of the *shows* or *apparitions* of objects, which when they be apparitions to the eye is *sight*; when to the ear, *hearing*; to the palate, *taste*; to the nostril, *smelling*; and to the rest of the body, *feeling*.

Ubiquity of apparition.

28. For cause of the will to do any particular action, which is called *volitio*, they assign the faculty, that is to say, the capacity in general, that men have to will sometimes one thing, sometimes another, which is called *voluntas*, making the power the cause of the act, as if one should assign for cause of the good or evil acts of men their ability to do them.[1]

Will, the cause of willing.

29. And in many occasions they put for cause of natural events their own ignorance, but disguised in other words, as when they say, fortune is the cause of things contingent, that is, of things whereof they know no cause, and as when they attribute many effects to occult qualities, that is, qualities not known to them, and therefore also (as they think) to no man else, and to *sympathy, antipathy, antiperistasis, specifical qualities*, and other like terms, which signify neither the agent that produceth them nor the operation by which they are produced.

Ignorance an occult cause.

30. If such *metaphysics* and *physics* as this be not *vain philosophy*, there was never any; nor needed St. Paul to give us warning to avoid it. [376]

31. And for their moral and civil philosophy, it hath the same or greater absurdities. If a man do an action of injustice, that is to say, an action contrary to the law, God, they say, is the prime cause of the law and also the prime cause of that and all other actions, but no cause at all of the injustice, which is the inconformity of the action to the law. This is vain philosophy. A man might as well say that one man maketh both a straight line and a crooked, and another maketh their incongruity. And such is the philosophy of

One makes the things incongruent, another the incongruity.

1 Scholastic philosophers, not realizing that a will is simply the last desire a person has before acting, invent a special faculty that causes acts of will. Actually, they just invent a word, '*voluntas*', because there is no such faculty of willing. A similar point is made in the next paragraph.

all men that resolve of their conclusions before they know their premises, pretending to comprehend that which is incomprehensible, and of attributes of honour to make attributes of nature, as this distinction was made to maintain the doctrine of free will, that is, of a will of man not subject to the will of God.

Private appetite [is] the rule of public good and evil.

32. Aristotle and other heathen philosophers define good and evil by the appetite of men, and well enough, as long as we consider them governed every one by his own law. For in the condition of men that have no other law but their own appetites, there can be no general rule of good and evil actions. But in a commonwealth this measure is false. Not the appetite of private men, but the law, which is the will and appetite of the state, is the measure. And yet is this doctrine still practiced, and men judge the goodness or wickedness of their own and of other men's actions, and of the actions of the commonwealth itself, by their own passions; and no man calleth good or evil but that which is so in his own eyes, without any regard at all to the public laws, except only monks and friars, that are bound by vow to that simple obedience to their superior to which every subject ought to think himself bound by the law of nature to the civil sovereign. And this private measure of good is a doctrine, not only vain, but also pernicious to the public state.

And that lawful marriage is unchastity.

33. It is also vain and false philosophy to say the work of marriage is repugnant to chastity or continence, and by consequence to make them moral vices, as they do that pretend chastity and continence for the ground of denying marriage to the clergy. For they confess it is no more but a constitution of the Church that requireth in those holy orders that continually attend the altar and administration of the Eucharist, a continual abstinence from women, under the name of continual chastity, continence, and purity. Therefore they call the lawful use of wives[1] want of chastity and continence, and so make marriage a sin, or at least a thing so impure and unclean as to render a man unfit for the altar. If the law were made because the use of wives is incontinence and contrary to chastity, then all marriage is vice. If because it is a thing too impure and unclean for a man consecrated to God, [then] much more should other natural, necessary, and daily works,

1 Hobbes's choice of words here betrays an unfortunate patriarchal point of view.

which all men do, render men unworthy to be priests, because they are more unclean. [377]

34. But the secret foundation of this prohibition of marriage of priests is not likely to have been laid so slightly as upon such errors in moral philosophy, nor yet upon the preference of single life to the estate of matrimony, which proceeded from the wisdom of St. Paul, who perceived how inconvenient a thing it was for those that in those times of persecution were preachers of the gospel and forced to fly from one country to another, to be clogged with the care of wife and children; but [this prohibition was laid] upon the design of the popes and priests of after times, to make themselves the clergy, that is to say, sole heirs of the kingdom of God in this world, to which it was necessary to take from them the use of marriage, because our Saviour saith that at the coming of his kingdom the children of God *shall neither marry, nor be given in marriage, but shall be as the angels in heaven*, that is to say, spiritual.[1] Seeing then they had taken on them the name of spiritual, to have allowed themselves (when there was no need) the propriety of wives, had been an incongruity.

And that all government but popular is tyranny:

35. From Aristotle's civil philosophy, they have learned to call all manner of commonwealths but the popular (such as was at that time the state of Athens) *tyranny*. All kings they called tyrants,[2] and the aristocracy of the thirty governors set up there by the Lacedaemonians that subdued them, the thirty tyrants, as also to call the condition of the people under the democracy, *liberty*. A *tyrant* originally signified no more, simply, but a *monarch*. But when afterwards in most parts of Greece that kind of government was abolished, the name began to signify, not only the thing it did before, but with it the hatred which the popular states bore towards it, as also the name of *king* became odious after the deposing of the kings in Rome, as being a thing natural to all men to conceive some great fault to be signified in any attribute that is given in despite [spite], and to a great enemy. And when the same men shall be displeased with those that have the administration of

---

1 The Roman Catholic popes do not allow priests to marry because they claim that they rule the kingdom of God, and Jesus said that "at the coming of his kingdom the children of God *shall neither marry, nor be given in marriage*."

2 See also 19.2 and "A Review and Conclusion" 9.

the democracy or aristocracy, they are not to seek for disgraceful names to express their anger in; but [they] call readily the one *anarchy* and the other *oligarchy* or the *tyranny of a few*. And that which offendeth the people is no other thing but that they are governed, not as every one of them would himself, but as the public representant, be it one man or an assembly of men, thinks fit, that is, by an arbitrary government; for which they give evil names to their superiors, never knowing (till perhaps a little after a civil war) that without such arbitrary government, such war must be perpetual, and that it is men and arms, not words and promises, that make the force and power of the laws.

That not men, but law governs.

36. And therefore this is another error of Aristotle's politics, that in a well-ordered commonwealth, not men should govern, but the laws. What man that has his natural senses, though he can
[378] neither write nor read, does not find himself governed by them he fears and believes can kill or hurt him when he obeyeth not? or that believes the law can hurt him, that is, words and paper, without hands and swords of men? And this is of the number of pernicious errors; for they induce men, as oft as they like not their governors, to adhere to those that call them *tyrants*, and to think it lawful to raise war against them; and yet they are many times cherished from the pulpit, by the clergy.

Laws over the conscience.

37. There is another error in their civil philosophy (which they never learned of Aristotle, nor Cicero, nor any other of the heathen), [namely] to extend the power of the law, which is the rule of actions only, to the very thoughts and consciences of men, by examination and *inquisition* of what they hold, notwithstanding the conformity of their speech and actions. By which, men are either punished for answering the truth of their thoughts or constrained to answer an untruth for fear of punishment. It is true that the civil magistrate, intending to employ a minister in the charge of teaching, may enquire of him if [whether] he be content to preach such and such doctrines, and, in case of refusal, may deny him the employment. But to force him to accuse himself of opinions, when his actions are not by law forbidden, is against the law of nature, and especially in them who teach that a man shall be damned to eternal and extreme torments, if he die in a false opinion concerning an article of the Christian faith. For who is there

that knowing there is so great danger in an error, whom the natural care of himself compelleth not to hazard his soul upon his own judgement, rather than that of any other man that is unconcerned in his damnation?

Private interpretation of law.

38. For a private man, without the authority of the commonwealth, that is to say, without permission from the representant thereof, to interpret the law by his own spirit, is another error in the politics, but not drawn from Aristotle nor from any other of the heathen philosophers. For none of them deny but that in the power of making laws is comprehended also the power of explaining them when there is need. And are not the Scriptures, in all places where they are law, made law by the authority of the commonwealth and, consequently, a part of the civil law?

39. Of the same kind it is also when any but the sovereign restraineth in any man that power which the commonwealth hath not restrained, as they do that impropriate the preaching of the gospel to one certain order of men, where the laws have left it free. If the state give me leave to preach or teach, that is, if it forbid me not, no man can forbid me. If I find myself amongst the idolaters of America, shall I that am a Christian, though not in orders, think it a sin to preach Jesus Christ, till I have received orders from Rome? Or when I have preached, shall not I answer their doubts and expound the Scriptures to them; that is, shall I not teach? But for this may some say, as also for administering to them the [379] sacraments, the necessity shall be esteemed for a sufficient mission; which is true. But this is true also: that for whatsoever a dispensation is due for the necessity, for the same there needs no dispensation when there is no law that forbids it. Therefore to deny these functions to those to whom the civil sovereign hath not denied them is a taking away of a lawful liberty, which is contrary to the doctrine of civil government.

Language of School-divines.

40. More examples of vain philosophy, brought into religion by the doctors of School Divinity,[1] might be produced; but other men may if they please observe them of themselves. I shall only add this, that the writings of School divines are nothing else, for the most part, but insignificant trains of strange and barbarous

1 'School Divinity' refers to the theology of scholastic philosophers, who were influenced by Aristotle's philosophy. See note on page 49.

words or words otherwise used than in the common use of the Latin tongue, such as would pose Cicero and Varro and all the grammarians of ancient Rome. Which, if any man would see proved, let him (as I have said once before) see whether he can translate any School-divine into any of the modern tongues, as French, English, or any other copious language; for that which cannot in most of these be made intelligible is not intelligible in the Latin. Which insignificancy of language, though I cannot note it for false philosophy; yet it hath a quality, not only to hide the truth, but also to make men think they have it, and desist from further search.

Errors from tradition.

41. Lastly, for the errors brought in from false or uncertain history, what is all the legend of fictitious miracles in the lives of the saints and all the histories of apparitions and ghosts alleged by the doctors of the Roman Church, to make good their doctrines of hell and purgatory, the power of exorcism, and other doctrines which have no warrant, neither in reason nor Scripture, as also all those traditions which they call the unwritten word of God, but old wives' fables? Whereof, though they find dispersed somewhat in the writings of the ancient Fathers; yet those Fathers were men that might too easily believe false reports. And the producing of their opinions for testimony of the truth of what they believed hath no other force with them that (according to the counsel of St. John (1 John 4:1)), examine spirits than in all things that concern the power of the Roman Church (the abuse whereof either they suspected not or had benefit by it) to discredit their testimony in respect of too rash belief of reports, which the most sincere men without great knowledge of natural causes (such as the Fathers were) are commonly the most subject to. For naturally, the best men are the least suspicious of fraudulent purposes. Gregory the Pope and St. Bernard have somewhat of apparitions of ghosts that said they were in purgatory, and so has our Bede; but nowhere, I believe, but by report from others. But if they, or any other, relate any such stories of their own knowledge, they shall not thereby confirm the more such vain reports, but discover their own infirmity or fraud.

[380]

Suppression of reason.

42. With the introduction of false [philosophy], we may join also the suppression of true philosophy by such men as neither by lawful authority nor sufficient study are competent judges of the

truth. Our own navigations make manifest, and all men learned in human sciences now acknowledge [that] there are antipodes; and every day it appeareth more and more that years and days are determined by motions of the earth. Nevertheless, men that have in their writings but supposed such doctrine,[1] as an occasion to lay open the reasons for and against it, have been punished for it by authority ecclesiastical. But what reason is there for it? Is it because such opinions are contrary to true religion? That cannot be, if they be true. Let therefore the truth be first examined by competent judges or confuted by them that pretend to know the contrary. Is it because they be contrary to the religion established? Let them be silenced by the laws of those to whom the teachers of them are subject, that is, by the laws civil; for disobedience may lawfully be punished in them that against the laws teach even true philosophy. Is it because they tend to disorder in government, as countenancing rebellion or sedition? Then let them be silenced and the teachers punished by virtue of his power to whom the care of the public quiet is committed; which is the authority civil. For whatsoever power ecclesiastics take upon themselves (in any place where they are subject to the state) in their own right, though they call it God's right, is but usurpation.

## CHAPTER XLVII [381]

## OF THE BENEFIT THAT PROCEEDETH FROM SUCH DARKNESS, AND TO WHOM IT ACCRUETH

*He that receiveth benefit by a fact is presumed to be the author.*

1. Cicero maketh honourable mention of one of the Cassii, a severe judge amongst the Romans, for a custom he had in criminal causes (when the testimony of the witnesses was not sufficient) to ask the accusers, *cui bono*,[2] that is to say, what profit, honour, or other contentment the accused obtained or expected by the fact. For amongst presumptions, there is none that so evidently declareth the author as doth the BENEFIT of the action. By the same

---

1 Hobbes is probably thinking at least of Copernicus and Galileo.

2 See also 47.4 and 47.17.

rule I intend in this place to examine who they may be that have possessed the people so long in this part of Christendom with these doctrines contrary to the peaceable societies of mankind.

That the Church militant is the kingdom of God was first taught by the Church of Rome.

2. And first, to this error *that the present Church, now militant on earth, is the kingdom of God* (that is, the kingdom of glory, or the land of promise, not the kingdom of grace, which is but a promise of the land) are annexed these worldly benefits; first, that the pastors and teachers of the Church are entitled thereby, as God's public ministers, to a right of governing the Church, and consequently, because the Church and commonwealth are the same persons, to be rectors and governors of the commonwealth. By this title it is that the Pope prevailed with the subjects of all Christian princes to believe that to disobey him was to disobey Christ himself, and in all differences between him and other princes (charmed with the word *power spiritual*) to abandon their lawful sovereigns, which is in effect a universal monarchy over all Christendom. For though they were first invested in the right of being supreme teachers of Christian doctrine, by and under Christian emperors within the limits of the Roman Empire (as is acknowledged by themselves) by the title of Pontifex Maximus, who was an officer subject to the civil state; yet after the Empire was divided and dissolved, it was not hard to obtrude upon the people already subject to them another title, namely, the right of St. Peter, not only to save entire their pretended power, but also to extend the same over the same Christian provinces, though no more united in the Empire of Rome. This benefit of a universal monarchy, considering the desire of men to bear rule, is a sufficient presumption that the Popes that pretended to it and for a long time enjoyed it, were the authors of the doctrine by which it was obtained, namely, that the Church now on earth is the kingdom of Christ. For that granted, it must be understood that Christ hath some lieutenant amongst us by whom we are to be told what are his commandments.

[382] 3. After that certain Churches had renounced this universal power of the Pope, one would expect, in reason, that the civil sovereigns in all those Churches should have recovered so much of it as (before they had unadvisedly let it go) was their own right and in their own hands. And in England it was so in effect, saving that they by whom the kings administered the government of religion,

by maintaining their employment to be in God's right, seemed to usurp, if not a supremacy, yet an independency on the civil power; and they but seemed to usurp it, inasmuch as they acknowledged a right in the king to deprive them of the exercise of their functions at his pleasure.

4. But in those places where the presbytery took that office, though many other doctrines of the Church of Rome were forbidden to be taught; yet this doctrine, that the kingdom of Christ is already come and that it began at the resurrection of our Saviour, was still retained. But *cui bono*? What profit did they expect from it? The same which the popes expected: to have a sovereign power over the people. For what is it for men to excommunicate their lawful king, but to keep him from all places of God's public service in his own kingdom; and with force to resist him when he with force endeavoureth to correct them? Or what is it, without authority from the civil sovereign, to excommunicate any person, but to take from him his lawful liberty, that is, to usurp an unlawful power over their brethren? The authors therefore of this darkness in religion are the Roman and the Presbyterian clergy.[1]

And maintained also by the presbytery.

5. To this head, I refer also all those doctrines that serve them to keep the possession of this spiritual sovereignty after it is gotten. As first, that the *Pope, in his public capacity, cannot err.* For who is there that, believing this to be true, will not readily obey him in whatsoever he commands?

Infallibility.

6. Secondly, that all other bishops, in what commonwealth soever, have not their right, neither immediately from God nor mediately from their civil sovereigns, but from the Pope, is a doctrine by which there comes to be in every Christian commonwealth many potent men (for so are bishops) that have their dependence on the Pope, owe obedience to him, though he be a foreign prince; by which means he is able (as he hath done many times) to raise a civil war against the state that submits not itself to be governed according to his pleasure and interest.

Subjection of bishops.

1 Hobbes was trying to steer a course between Roman Catholicism and Presbyterianism. Like the Roman Catholics, he wanted the head of the Church to have absolute authority, and like the Presbyterians, he thought the head should not be the Pope. Unlike the Roman Catholics and the Presbyterians, he thought that the head of the Church should be the same as one's secular sovereign.

Exemptions of the clergy.

7. Thirdly, the exemption of these and of all other priests, and of all monks and friars from the power of the civil laws. For by this means, there is a great part of every commonwealth that enjoy the benefit of the laws and are protected by the power of the civil state, which nevertheless pay no part of the public expense, nor are liable to the penalties, as other subjects, due to their crimes, and, consequently, stand not in fear of any man, but the Pope, and adhere to him only, to uphold his universal monarchy.

The names of *sacerdotes* and *sacrificers*.

8. Fourthly, the giving to their priests (which is no more in the New Testament but presbyters, that is, elders) the name of *sacerdotes*, that is, sacrificers, which was the title of the civil sovereign
[383] and his public ministers, amongst the Jews, whilst God was their king. Also, the making the Lord's Supper a sacrifice serveth to make the people believe the Pope hath the same power over all Christians that Moses and Aaron had over the Jews, that is to say, all power, both civil and ecclesiastical, as the high priest then had.

The sacramentation of marriage.

9. Fifthly, the teaching that matrimony is a sacrament giveth to the clergy the judging of the lawfulness of marriages, and thereby of what children are legitimate, and consequently, of the right of succession to hereditary kingdoms.

The single life of priests.

10. Sixthly, the denial of marriage to priests serveth to assure this power of the Pope over kings. For if a king be a priest, he cannot marry and transmit his kingdom to his posterity. If he be not a priest, then the Pope pretendeth this authority ecclesiastical over him, and over his people.

Auricular confession.

11. Seventhly, from auricular confession they obtain, for the assurance of their power, better intelligence of the designs of princes and great persons in the civil state than these can have of the designs of the state ecclesiastical.

Canonization of saints and declaring of martyrs.

12. Eighthly, by the canonization[1] of saints and declaring who are martyrs, they assure their power in that they induce simple men into an obstinacy against the laws and commands of their civil sovereigns, even to death, if by the Pope's excommunication they be declared heretics or enemies to the Church, that is (as they interpret it) to the Pope.

---

1 See also 45.34.

Transubstantiation, penance, absolution.

13. Ninthly, they assure the same, by the power they ascribe to every priest of making Christ; and by the power of ordaining penance, and of remitting and retaining of sins.

Purgatory, indulgences, external works.

14. Tenthly, by the doctrine of purgatory,[1] of justification by external works, and of indulgences, the clergy is enriched.

Demonology and exorcism.

15. Eleventhly, by their demonology[2] and the use of exorcism, and other things appertaining thereto, they keep (or think they keep) the people more in awe of their power.

School divinity.

16. Lastly, the metaphysics, ethics, and politics of Aristotle,[3] the frivolous distinctions, barbarous terms, and obscure language of the Schoolmen, taught in the universities (which have been all erected and regulated by the Pope's authority), serve them to keep these errors from being detected, and to make men mistake the *ignis fatuus* of vain philosophy for the light of the Gospel.

The authors of spiritual darkness, who they be.

17. To these, if they sufficed not, might be added other of their dark doctrines, the profit whereof redoundeth manifestly to the setting up of an unlawful power over the lawful sovereigns of Christian people, or for the sustaining of the same when it is set up, or to the worldly riches, honour, and authority of those that sustain it. And therefore by the aforesaid rule of *cui bono*, we may justly pronounce for the authors of all this spiritual darkness, the Pope and Roman clergy and all those besides that endeavour to settle in the minds of men this erroneous doctrine, that the Church now on earth is that kingdom of God mentioned in the Old and New Testament.

18. But the emperors and other Christian sovereigns, under [384]
whose government these errors and the like encroachments of ecclesiastics upon their office at first crept in, to the disturbance of their possessions and of the tranquillity of their subjects, though they suffered the same for want of foresight of the sequel and of insight into the designs of their teachers, may nevertheless be esteemed accessories to their own and the public damage. For without their authority there could at first no seditious doctrine have been publicly preached. I say they might have hindered the same in the beginning; but when the people were once possessed

---

1 See also 12.32, 43.17, 44.16, 44.30–40, and 46.20–1.

2 See also 40.14, 44.3, 44.16, and 45.2.

3 See also 44.3 and 46.11–14.

by those spiritual men, there was no human remedy to be applied that any man could invent. And for the remedies that God should provide, who never faileth in his good time to destroy all the machinations of men against the truth, we are to attend his good pleasure that suffereth many times the prosperity of his enemies, together with their ambition, to grow to such a height as the violence thereof openeth the eyes, which the wariness of their predecessors had before sealed up, and makes men by too much grasping let go all, as Peter's net was broken by the struggling of too great a multitude of fishes; whereas the impatience of those that strive to resist such encroachment, before their subjects' eyes were opened, did but increase the power they resisted. I do not therefore blame the Emperor Frederick for holding the stirrup to our countryman Pope Adrian;[1] for such was the disposition of his subjects then, as if he had not done it, he was not likely to have succeeded in the empire. But I blame those that, in the beginning, when their power was entire, by suffering such doctrines to be forged in the universities of their own dominions, have held the stirrup to all the succeeding popes, whilst they mounted into the thrones of all Christian sovereigns, to ride and tire both them and their people, at their pleasure.

19. But as the inventions of men are woven, so also are they raveled out;[2] the way is the same, but the order is inverted. The web begins at the first elements of power, which are wisdom, humility, sincerity, and other virtues of the Apostles, whom the people, converted, obeyed out of reverence, not by obligation.

---

1 In 1155, after refusing to hold the bridle of the horse of Pope Adrian IV as he dismounted, Emperor Frederick I (Barbarosa) (c. 1125-1190) relented when he was assured that Charlemagne had done the same. The pope later claimed that the emperor was the pope's vassal. Frederick denied it and at a diet in Besançon declared that he was emperor "by the election of the princes and from God alone."

2 This paragraph and the next are an application of Hobbes's theory of synthesis and analysis applied to historical phenomena. Synthesis begins with one or more simple concepts or propositions and shows how other concepts or propositions cause or are constructed from them. Applied to this example, Hobbes is claiming to show how from the elements of one historical situation (that of the Apostles), another historical situation arose (that of the presbyters), and that in turn to another (that of the bishops). Analysis begins with a proposition describing some effect and breaks this proposition down into supposedly simpler components to show its possible cause. See also 46.1.

Their consciences were free, and their words and actions subject to none but the civil power. Afterwards the presbyters (as the flocks of Christ increased), assembling to consider what they should teach and thereby obliging themselves to teach nothing against the decrees of their assemblies, made it to be thought the people were thereby obliged to follow their doctrine, and, when they refused, refused to keep them company (that was then called excommunication), not as being infidels, but as being disobedient. And this was the first knot upon their liberty. And the number of presbyters increasing, the presbyters of the chief city or province got themselves an authority over the parochial presbyters, and appropriated to themselves the names of bishops. And this was a second knot on Christian liberty. Lastly, the bishop of Rome, in regard of the [385]
Imperial City, took upon him an authority (partly by the wills of the emperors themselves, and by the title of Pontifex Maximus; and at last when the emperors were grown weak, by the privileges of St. Peter) over all other bishops of the Empire. Which was the third and last knot and the whole synthesis and construction of the pontifical power.

20. And therefore the *analysis* or *resolution* is by the same way, but beginneth with the knot that was last tied, as we may see in the dissolution of the preterpolitical Church government in England. First, the power of the popes was dissolved totally by Queen Elizabeth;[1] and the bishops, who before exercised their functions in right of the Pope, did afterwards exercise the same in right of the Queen and her successors; though by retaining the phrase of *jure divino*, they were thought to demand it by immediate right from God.[2] And so was untied the first knot. After this, the Presbyterians lately in England obtained the putting down of episcopacy.[3] And so was the second knot dissolved. And almost at the

---

1 Hobbes may be thinking of such acts as "An Act Against the Bringing in and Putting in Execution of Bulls and Other Instruments from the See of Rome" (1571) and "An Act to Retain the Queen's Majesty's Subjects in their Due Obedience" (1581).

2 The claim that the episcopacy existed *jure divino* was hotly contested in the late 1630s, as the result of Archbishop William Laud's policies. See "Laud's Apologia," in *The Stuart Constitution*, 2nd ed., ed. J. P. Kenyon, (Cambridge: Cambridge UP, 1986), 147–8.

3 Episcopacy was abolished in England by Act of Parliament in 1646.

same time, the power was taken also from the Presbyterians.[1] And so we are reduced to the independency of the primitive Christians to follow Paul or Cephas or Apollos, every man as he liketh best.[2] Which if it be without contention and without measuring the doctrine of Christ by our affection to the person of his minister (the fault which the Apostle reprehended in the Corinthians) is perhaps the best: first, because there ought to be no power over the consciences of men, but of the word itself, working faith in every one, not always according to the purpose of them that plant and water, but of God himself, that giveth the increase. And secondly, because it is unreasonable in them, who teach there is such danger in every little error, to require of a man endued with reason of his own to follow the reason of any other man or of the most voices of many other men, which is little better than to venture his salvation at cross and pile.[3] Nor ought those teachers to be displeased with this loss of their ancient authority. For there is none should know better than they that power is preserved by the same virtues by which it is acquired, that is to say, by wisdom, humility, clearness of doctrine, and sincerity of conversation, and not by suppression of the natural sciences and of the morality of natural reason, nor by obscure language, nor by arrogating to themselves more knowledge than they make appear, nor by pious frauds, nor by such other faults as in the pastors of God's Church

---

1 This may be dated from Pride's Purge, December, 1648, when Colonel Pride refused to allow supposed presbyterian MPs into Parliament. The greatly reduced parliament acquired the name 'The Rump Parliament'.

2 Hobbes may or may not intend his comment sarcastically. Although it was still not especially difficult to find worship services conducted according to the Book of Common Prayer in London, many people considered the episcopal Church of England near death or dead. The two archbishoprics were vacant in 1651. The Archbishop of Canterbury, William Laud, was executed on 10 January 1645, and the Archbishop of York, John Williams, died on 25 March 1650. Neither would be replaced until the Restoration in 1660. Some bishops were in exile and others were in England but inactive. There was no effective leadership of the episcopal chuch. According to one estimate, about sixty percent of the clergy conformed to the new, anti-episcopal regime (J. R. H. Moorman, *A History of the Church in England*, 3rd ed. [London: A. & C. Black, 1972], 244-5); see also Stephen Neill, *Anglicanism* (Oxford UP, 1976), 157. Although Hobbes attended services conducted according to the Book of Common Prayer, he may have been reconciling himself to a state of numerous independent congregations.

3 I think Hobbes means by the flip of a coin. 'Cross and pile' refer to the head and tail of a coin. A 'pile' was the lower piece of a stamping machine that made coins.

are not only faults, but also scandals, apt to make men stumble one time or other upon the suppression of their authority.

21. But after this doctrine, *that the Church now militant is the kingdom of God spoken of in the Old and New Testament*, was received in the world, the ambition and canvassing for the offices that belong thereunto and especially for that great office of being Christ's lieutenant and the pomp of them that obtained therein the principal public charges, became by degrees so evident that they lost the inward reverence due to the pastoral function, insomuch as the wisest men of them that had any power in the civil state needed nothing but the authority of their princes to deny them any further obedience. For, from the time that the Bishop of Rome had gotten to be acknowledged for bishop universal, by pretence of succession to St. Peter, their whole hierarchy or kingdom of darkness may be compared not unfitly to the kingdom of fairies, that is, to the old wives' fables in England concerning ghosts and spirits, and the feats they play in the night. And if a man consider the original of this great ecclesiastical dominion, he will easily perceive that the papacy is no other than the ghost of the deceased Roman Empire, sitting crowned upon the grave thereof. For so did the papacy start up on a sudden out of the ruins of that heathen power.

Comparison of the papacy with the kingdom of fairies.

[386]

22. The *language* also which they use, both in the churches and in their public acts, being Latin, which is not commonly used by any nation now in the world, what is it but the ghost of the old Roman language?

23. The *fairies* in what nation soever they converse have but one universal king, which some poets of ours call King Oberon; but the Scripture calls Beelzebub, prince of demons. The *ecclesiastics* likewise, in whose dominions soever they be found, acknowledge but one universal king, the Pope.

24. The ecclesiastics are *spiritual* men and *ghostly* fathers. The fairies are *spirits* and *ghosts*. *Fairies* and *ghosts* inhabit darkness, solitudes, and graves. The *ecclesiastics* walk in obscurity of doctrine, in monasteries, churches, and churchyards.

25. The *ecclesiastics* have their cathedral churches, which, in what town soever they be erected, by virtue of holy water, and certain charms called exorcisms, have the power to make those

towns, cities, that is to say, seats of empire. The *fairies* also have their enchanted castles and certain gigantic ghosts that domineer over the regions round about them.

26. The fairies are not to be seized on, and brought to answer for the hurt they do. So also the *ecclesiastics* vanish away from the tribunals of civil justice.

27. The *ecclesiastics* take from young men the use of reason, by certain charms compounded of metaphysics, and miracles, and traditions, and abused Scripture, whereby they are good for nothing else but to execute what they command them. The *fairies* likewise are said to take young children out of their cradles, and to change them into natural fools, which common people do therefore call elves, and are apt to mischief.

28. In what shop or operatory the fairies make their enchantment, the old wives have not determined. But the operatories of the *clergy* are well enough known to be the universities, that received their discipline from authority pontifical.

29. When the *fairies* are displeased with anybody, they are said
[387] to send their elves to pinch them. The *ecclesiastics*, when they are displeased with any civil state, make also their elves, that is, superstitious, enchanted subjects, to pinch their princes, by preaching sedition; or one prince, enchanted with promises, to pinch another.

30. The *fairies* marry not; but there be amongst them incubi that have copulation with flesh and blood. The *priests* also marry not.

31. The *ecclesiastics* take the cream of the land by donations of ignorant men that stand in awe of them, and by tithes. So also it is in the fable of *fairies*, that they enter into the dairies and feast upon the cream, which they skim from the milk.

32. What kind of money is current in the kingdom of fairies is not recorded in the story. But the *ecclesiastics* in their receipts accept of the same money that we do; though when they are to make any payment, it is in canonizations, indulgences, and masses.

33. To this and such like resemblances between the *papacy* and the kingdom of *fairies* may be added this, that as the *fairies* have no existence but in the fancies of ignorant people, rising from the traditions of old wives or old poets, so the spiritual power of the *Pope*

(without the bounds of his own civil dominion) consisteth only in the fear that seduced people stand in of their excommunications, upon hearing of false miracles, false traditions, and false interpretations of the Scripture.

34. It was not therefore a very difficult matter for Henry the Eighth by his exorcism, nor for Queen Elizabeth by hers, to cast them out. But who knows that this spirit of Rome, now gone out, and walking by missions through the dry places of China, Japan, and the Indies, that yield him little fruit, may not return, or rather, an assembly of spirits worse than he, enter and inhabit this clean-swept house and make the end thereof worse than the beginning? For it is not the Roman clergy only that pretends the kingdom of God to be of this world and thereby to have a power therein, distinct from that of the civil state. And this is all I had a design to say, concerning the doctrine of the POLITICS. Which, when I have reviewed, I shall willingly expose it to the censure of my country.

# A *REVIEW* AND *CONCLUSION*

[389]

1. From the contrariety of some of the Natural Faculties of the Mind, one to another, as also of one Passion to another, and from their reference to Conversation, there has been an argument taken, to inferre an impossibility that any one man should be sufficiently disposed to all sorts of Civill duty. The Severity of Judgment, they say, makes men Censorious and unapt to pardon the Errours and Infirmities of other men: and on the other side, Celerity of Fancy makes the thoughts lesse steddy than is necessary, to discern exactly between Right and Wrong. Again, in all Deliberations, and in all Pleadings, the faculty of solid Reasoning, is necessary: for without it, the Resolutions of men are rash, and their Sentences unjust: and yet if there be not powerful Eloquence, which procureth attention and Consent, the effect of Reason will be little. But these are contrary Faculties; the former being grounded upon principles of Truth; the other upon Opinions already received, true, or false; and upon the Passions and Interests of men, which are different, and mutable.

2. And amongst the Passions, *Courage*, (by which I mean the Contempt of Wounds, and violent Death) enclineth men to private Revenges, and sometimes to endeavour the unsettling of the Publique Peace: And *Timorousnesse*, many times disposeth to the desertion of the Publique Defence. Both these they say cannot stand together in the same person.

3. And to consider the contrariety of mens Opinions, and Manners in generall, It is they say, impossible to entertain a constant Civill Amity with all those, with whom the Businesse of the world constrains us to converse: Which Businesse, consisteth almost in nothing else but a perpetuall contention for Honor, Riches, and Authority.

4. To which I answer, that these are indeed great difficulties, but not Impossibilities: For by Education, and Discipline, they may bee, and are sometimes reconciled. Judgment, and Fancy may have place in the same man; but by turnes, as the end which he aimeth at requireth. As the Israelites in Egypt, were sometimes fastened to their labour of making Bricks, and other times were ranging abroad to gather Straw: So also may the Judgement sometimes be fixed upon one certain Consideration, and the Fancy at another time wandring about the world. So also Reason, and Eloquence, (though not perhaps in the Natural Sciences, yet in the Morall)
[390] may stand very well together. For wheresoever there is place for adorning and preferring of Errour, there is much more place for adorning and preferring of Truth, if they have it to adorn. Nor is there any repugnancy between fearing the Laws, and not fearing a publique Enemy; nor between abstaining from Injury, and pardoning it in others. There is therefore no such Inconsistence of Humane Nature, with Civill Duties, as some think. I have known cleernesse of Judgment, and largenesse of Fancy; strength of Reason, and gracefull Elocution; a Courage for the Warre, and a Fear for the Laws, and all eminently in one man; and that was my most noble and honoured friend, Mr. *Sidney Godolphin*; who hating no man, nor hated of any, was unfortunately slain in the beginning of the late Civill warre, in the Publique quarrell, by an undiscerned, and an undiscerning hand.

5. To the Laws of Nature, declared in the 15. Chapter, I would have this added, *That every man is bound by Nature, as much as in him lieth, to protect in Warre the Authority, by which he is himself protected in time of peace.* For he that pretendeth a Right of Nature to preserve his owne body, cannot pretend a Right of Nature to destroy him, by whose strength he is preserved: It is a manifest contradiction of himselfe. And though this Law may bee drawn by consequence, from some of those that are there already mentioned; yet the Times require to have it inculcated, and remembered.

6. And because I find by divers English Books lately printed, that the Civill warres have not yet sufficiently taught men, in what point of time it is, that a Subject becomes obliged to the Conquerour; nor what is Conquest; nor how it comes about, that it

obliges men to obey his Laws:[1] Therefore for farther satisfaction of men therein, I say, the point of time, wherein a man becomes subject to a Conqueror, is that point, wherein having liberty to submit to him, he consenteth, either by expresse words, or by other sufficient sign, to be his Subject. When it is that a man hath the liberty to submit, I have shewed before in the end of the 21. Chapter; namely, that for him that hath no obligation to his former sovereign but that of an ordinary Subject, it is then, when the means of his life is within the Guards and Garrisons of the Enemy; for it is then, that he hath no longer Protection from him, but is protected by the adverse party for his Contribution. Seeing therefore such contribution is every where, as a thing inevitable, (not withstanding it be an assistance to the Enemy,) esteemed lawfull; a totall Submission, which is but an assistance to the Enemy, cannot be esteemed unlawful. Besides, if a man consider that they who submit, assist the Enemy but with part of their estates, whereas they that refuse, assist him with the whole, there is no reason to call their Submission, or Composition an Assistance; but rather a Detriment to the Enemy. But if a man, besides the obligation of a Subject, hath taken upon him a new obligation of a Souldier, then he hath not the liberty to submit to a new Power, as long as the old one keeps the field, and giveth him means of subsistence, either in his Armies or Garrisons: for in this case, he cannot complain of want of Protection, and means to live as a Souldier: But [391]
when that also failes, a Souldier also may seek his Protection wheresoever he has most hope to have it; and may lawfully submit himself to his new Master. And so much for the time when he may do it lawfully, if hee will. If therefore he doe it, he is undoubtedly bound to be a true Subject: For a Contract lawfully made, cannot lawfully be broken.

7. By this also a man may understand, when it is, that men may be said to be Conquered; and in what the nature of Conquest, and the Right of a Conquerour consisteth: For this Submission is it that implyeth them all. Conquest, is not the Victory it self; but the

1 Hobbes is probably thinking of the *de facto* theorists, according to whom a person owes obligation to whoever holds power. For Hobbes, power must be combined with the consent of the subject 'Review and Conclusion' 7. See also 20.10 and 21.21.

Acquisition by Victory, of a Right, over the persons of men. He therefore that is slain, is overcome, but not Conquered: He that is taken, and put into prison, or chaines, is not Conquered, though Overcome; for he is still an Enemy, and may save himself if hee can: But he that upon promise of Obedience, hath his Life and Liberty allowed him, is then Conquered, and a Subject; and not before. The Romans used to say, that their Generall had *Pacified* such a *Province*, that is to say, in English, *Conquered* it; and that the Countrey was *Pacified* by Victory, when the people of it had promised *Imperata facere*, that is, *To doe what the Romane People commanded them*: This was to be Conquered. But this promise may be either expresse, or tacite: Expresse, by Promise: Tacite, by other signes. As, for example, a man that hath not been called to make such an expresse Promise, (because he is one whose power perhaps is not considerable;) yet if he live under their Protection openly, hee is understood to submit himselfe to the Government: But if he live there secretly, he is lyable to any thing that may bee done to a Spie, and Enemy of the State. I say not, hee does any Injustice, (for acts of open Hostility bear not that name); but that he may be justly put to death. Likewise, if a man, when his Country is conquered, be out of it, he is not Conquered, nor Subject: but if at his return he submit to the Government, he is bound to obey it. So that *Conquest* (to define it) is the Acquiring of the Right of Soveraignty by Victory. Which Right is acquired in the people's Submission, by which they contract with the Victor, promising Obedience, for Life and Liberty.

8. In the 29. Chapter I have set down for one of the causes of the Dissolutions of Common-wealths, their Imperfect Generation, consisting in the want of an Absolute and Arbitrary Legislative Power; for want whereof, the Civill Soveraign is fain to handle the Sword of Justice unconstantly, and as if it were too hot for him to hold: One reason whereof (which I have not there mentioned) is this, That they will all of them justifie the War, by which their Power was at first gotten, and whereon (as they think) their Right dependeth, and not on the Possession. As if, for example, the Right of the Kings of England did depend on the goodnesse of the cause of *William* the Conquerour, and upon their lineall, and directest Descent from him; by which means, there would perhaps

be no tie of the Subjects obedience to their Soveraign at this day in all the world: wherein whilest they needlessely think to justifie [392] themselves, they justifie all the successfull Rebellions that Ambition shall at any time raise against them and their Successors. Therefore I put down for one of the most effectuall seeds of the Death of any State, that the Conquerors require not onely a submission of mens actions to them for the future, but also an Approbation of all their actions past; when there is scarce a Commonwealth in the world, whose beginnings can in conscience be justified.

9. And because the name of Tyranny,[1] signifieth nothing more, nor lesse, than the name of Soveraignty, be it in one, or many men, saving that they that use the former word, are understood to bee angry with them they call Tyrants; I think the toleration of a professed hatred of Tyranny, is a Toleration of hatred to Commonwealth in generall, and another evill seed, not differing much from the former. For to the Justification of the Cause of a Conqueror, the Reproach of the Cause of the Conquered, is for the most part necessary: but neither of them necessary for the Obligation of the Conquered. And thus much I have thought fit to say upon the Review of the first and second part of this Discourse.

10. In the 35. Chapter,[2] I have sufficiently declared out of the Scripture, that in the Common-wealth of the Jewes, God himselfe was made the Soveraign, by Pact with the People; who were therefore called his *Peculiar People*, to distinguish them from the rest of the world, over whom God reigned not by their Consent, but by his own Power: And that in this Kingdome Moses was Gods Lieutenant on Earth; and that it was he that told them what Laws God appointed them to be ruled by. But I have omitted to set down who were the Officers appointed to doe Execution; especially in Capitall Punishments; not then thinking it a matter of so necessary consideration as I find it since. Wee know that generally in all Common-wealths, the Execution of Corporeall Punishments was either put upon the Guards, or other Souldiers of the Sovereign Power; or given to those, in whom want of means, contempt of honour, and hardnesse of heart concurred, to make them sue for

---

1 See also 19.2 and 46.35.

2 See 35.5.

such an Office. But amongst the Israelites it was a Positive Law of God their Soveraign, that he that was convicted of a capitall Crime, should be stoned to death by the People; and that the Witnesses should cast the first Stone, and after the Witnesses, then the rest of the People. This was a Law that designed who were to be the Executioners; but not that any one should throw a stone at him before Conviction and Sentence, where the Congregation was Judge. The Witnesses were neverthelesse to be heard before they proceeded to Execution, unlesse the Fact were committed in the presence of the Congregation it self, or in sight of the lawfull Judges; for then there needed no other Witnesses but the Judges themselves. Neverthelesse, this manner of proceeding, being not thoroughly understood, hath given occasion to a dangerous opinion, that any man may kill another, in some cases, by a Right of Zeal, as if the Executions done upon Offenders in the Kingdome
[393] of God in old time, proceeded not from the Soveraign Command, but from the Authority of Private Zeal: which, if we consider the texts that seem to favour it, is quite contrary.

11. First, where the Levites fell upon the People, that had made and worshipped the Golden Calfe, and slew three thousand of them; it was by the Commandement of Moses, from the mouth of God, as is manifest, *Exod.*, 32. 27. And when the Son of a woman of Israel had blasphemed God, they that heard it, did not kill him, but brought him before Moses, who put him under custody, till God should give Sentence against him; as appears, *Levit.* 25. 11, 12. Again, (*Numbers* 25. 6,7.) when Phinehas killed Zimri and Cosbi, it was not by Right of Private Zeale: Their Crime was committed in the sight of the Assembly; there needed no Witnesse; the Law was known, and he the heir apparent to the Soveraignty; and, which is the principall point, the Lawfulnesse of his Act depended wholly upon a subsequent Ratification by Moses, whereof he had no cause to doubt. And this Presumption of a future Ratification, is sometimes necessary to the safety [of] a Common-wealth; as in a sudden Rebellion, any man that can suppresse it by his own Power in the Countrey where it begins, without expresse Lawe or Commission, may lawfully doe it, and provide to have it Ratified, or Pardoned, whilst it is in doing, or after it is done. Also, *Numb. 35.30* it is expressly said, *Whosoever shall kill the Murtherer, shall kill him*

*upon the word of Witnesses*: but Witnesses suppose a formall Judicature, and consequently condemn that pretence of *Ius Zelotarum*. The Law of Moses concerning him that enticeth to Idolatry, (that is to say, in the Kingdome of God to a renouncing of his Allegiance (*Deut.* 13. 8.) forbids to conceal him, and commands the Accuser to cause him to be put to death, and to cast the first stone at him; but not to kill him before he be Condemned. And (*Deut.* 17. ver. 4, 5, 6) the Processe against Idolatry is exactly set down: For God there speaketh to the People, as Judge, and commandeth them, when a man is Accused of Idolatry, to Enquire diligently of the Fact, and finding it true, then to Stone him; but still the hand of the Witnesse throweth the first stone. This is not Private Zeale, but Publique Condemnation. In like manner when a Father hath a rebellious Son, the Law is (*Deut.* 21. 18.) that he shall bring him before the Judges of the Town, and all the people of the Town shall Stone him. Lastly, by pretence of these Laws it was, that St. Stephen was Stoned, and not by pretence of Private Zeal: for before hee was carried away to Execution, he had Pleaded his Cause before the High Priest. There is nothing in all this, nor in any other part of the Bible, to countenance Executions by Private Zeal; which being oftentimes but a conjunction of Ignorance and Passion, is against both the Justice and Peace of a Common-wealth.

12. In the 36. Chapter I have said, that it is not declared in what manner God spoke supernaturally to Moses: Not that he spake not to him sometimes by Dreams and Visions, and by a supernaturall Voice, as to other Prophets: For the manner how he spake unto him from the Mercy-Seat, is expressely set down *Numbers* 7.89. in these words, *From that time forward, when Moses entred into the Tabernacle of the Congregation to speak with God, he heard a Voice which spake unto him from over the Mercy-Seat, which is over the Arke of the Testimony; from between the Cherubims he spake unto him*. But it is not declared in what consisted the praeeminence of the manner of Gods speaking to Moses, above that of his speaking to other Prophets, as to Samuel, and to Abraham, to whom he also spake by a Voice, (that is, by Vision) Unlesse the difference consist in the clearnesse of the Vision. For *Face to Face*, and *Mouth to Mouth*, can- [394]

not be literally understood of the Infinitenesse, and Incomprehensibility of the Divine Nature.[1]

13. And as to the whole Doctrine, I see not yet, but the Principles of it are true and proper; and the Ratiocination solid. For I ground the Civill Right of Soveraigns, and both the Duty and Liberty of Subjects, upon the known naturall Inclinations of Mankind, and upon the Articles of the Law of Nature; of which no man, that pretends but reason enough to govern his private family, ought to be ignorant. And for the Power Ecclesiasticall of the same Soveraigns, I ground it on such Texts, as are both evident in themselves, and consonant to the Scope of the whole Scripture. And therefore am perswaded, that he that shall read it with a purpose onely to be informed, shall be informed by it. But for those that by Writing, or Publique Discourse, or by their eminent actions, have already engaged themselves to the maintaining of contrary opinions, they will not bee so easily satisfied. For in such cases, it is naturall for men, at one and the same time, both to proceed in reading, and to lose their attention, in the search of objections to that they had read before: Of which, in a time wherein the interests of men are changed (seeing much of that Doctrine, which serveth to the establishing of a new Government, must needs be contrary to that which conduced to the dissolution of the old,) there cannot choose but be very many.

14. In that part which treateth of a Christian Common-wealth, there are some new Doctrines, which, it may be, in a State where the contrary were already fully determined, were a fault for a Subject without leave to divulge, as being a usurpation of the place of a Teacher. But in this time, that men call not onely for Peace, but also for Truth, to offer such Doctrines as I think True, and that manifestly tend to Peace and Loyalty, to the consideration of those that are yet in deliberation, is no more, but to offer New Wine, to bee put into New Casks, that both may be preserved together. And I suppose, that then, when Novelty can breed no trouble, nor disorder in a State, men are not generally so much inclined to the reverence of Antiquity, as to preferre Ancient Errors, before New and well proved Truth.

15. There is nothing I distrust more than my Elocution; which

---

1 See also 36.13.

neverthelesse I am confident (excepting the Mischances of the Presse) is not obscure. That I have neglected the Ornament of quoting ancient Poets, Orators, and Philosophers, contrary to the custome of late time, (whether I have done well or ill in it,) proceedeth from my judgment, grounded on many reasons. [395] For first, all Truth of Doctrine dependeth either upon *Reason*, or upon *Scripture*; both which give credit to many, but never receive it from any Writer. Secondly, the matters in question are not of *Fact*, but of *Right*, wherein there is no place for *Witnesses*. There is scarce any of those old Writers, that contradicteth not sometimes both himself, and others; which makes their Testimonies insufficient. Fourthly, such Opinions as are taken onely upon Credit of Antiquity, are not intrinsecally the Judgment of those that cite them, but Words that passe (like gaping) from mouth to mouth. Fifthly, it is many times with a fraudulent Designe that men stick their corrupt Doctrine with the Cloves of other mens Wit. Sixtly, I find not that the Ancients they cite, took it for an Ornament, to doe the like with those that wrote before them. Seventhly, it is an argument of Indigestion, when Greek and Latine Sentences unchewed come up again, as they use to doe, unchanged. Lastly, though I reverence those men of Ancient time that either have written Truth perspicuously, or set us in a better way to find it out our selves; yet to the Antiquity it self I think nothing due: For if we will reverence the Age, the Present is the Oldest; if the Antiquity of the Writer, I am not sure that generally they to whom such honor is given, were more Ancient when they wrote, than I am that am Writing: But if it bee well considered, the praise of Ancient Authors, proceeds not from the reverence of the Dead, but from the competition, and mutuall envy of the Living.

16. To conclude, there is nothing in this whole Discourse, nor in that I writ before of the same subject in Latine,[1] as far as I can perceive, contrary either to the Word of God, or to good Manners; or to the disturbance of the Publique Tranquillity. Therefore I think it may be profitably printed, and more profitably taught in the Universities, in case they also think so, to whom the judgement of the same belongeth. For seeing the Universities are the

1 Hobbes is referring to *De Cive* (1642, 1647).

Fountains of Civill and Morall Doctrine, from whence the Preachers, and the Gentry, drawing such water as they find, use to sprinkle the same (both from the Pulpit, and in their Conversation) upon the People, there ought certainly to be great care taken, to have it pure, both from the Venime of Heathen Politicians, and from the Incantation of Deceiving Spirits. And by that means the most men, knowing their Duties, will be the less subject to serve the Ambition of a few discontented persons, in their purposes against the State; and be the lesse grieved with the Contributions necessary for their Peace, and Defence; and the Governours themselves have the lesse cause, to maintain at the Common charge any greater Army, than is necessary to make good the Publique Liberty, against the Invasions and Encroachments of forraign Enemies.

17. And thus I have brought to an end my Discourse of Civill and Ecclesiasticall Government, occasioned by the disorders of the present time, without partiality, without application, and without other designe, than to set before mens eyes the mutuall Relation
[396] between Protection and Obedience; of which the condition of Humane Nature, and the Laws Divine, (both Naturall and Positive), require an inviolable observation. And though in the revolution of States, there can be no very good Constellation for Truths of this nature to be born under, (as having an angry aspect from the dissolvers of an old Government, and seeing but the backs of them that erect a new); yet I cannot think it will be condemned at this time, either by the Publique Judge of Doctrine, or by any that desires the continuance of Publique Peace. And in this hope I return to my interrupted Speculation of Bodies Naturall; wherein, (if God give me health to finish it,) I hope the Novelty will as much please, as in the Doctrine of this Artificial Body it useth to offend. For such Truth, as opposeth no man's profit, nor pleasure, is to all men welcome.

---

FINIS

---

# *Appendix A: From Robert Filmer,* Observations Concerning the Original of Government, Upon Mr. Hobbes's, Leviathan, etc.

Robert Filmer (c. 1588-1653) was a gentleman who was educated at Trinity College, Cambridge. Little noted in his own day, he is now best known as the target of John Locke's criticisms in the first of the *Two Treatises of Government.* Like Hobbes, Filmer believed in absolute sovereignty, as indicated by the title of his book, *The Necessity of the Absolute Power of all Kings* (1648). Filmer published *Observations Concerning the Original of Government, Upon Mr Hobbes's 'Leviathan', Mr Milton against Salmasius, and H. Grotius 'De Jure Belli'* in 1652. His theory is patriarchal; that is, he believes that a ruler's right comes from a father's right to rule. To put this slightly differently, the basis for political authority is the same as that for the authority of a father over his family. Filmer also believes political authority is grounded upon divine right; sovereigns govern by the authority of God. Although Hobbes gives lip service to the divine right theory and thinks that fathers often gave rise to governments by extracting an implicit covenant from their family members, he does not subscribe to the divine right theory or to patriarchalism.

Filmer's page references to *Leviathan* are to the original edition; these page numbers are printed in the margins within brackets in the text of this edition of *Leviathan.*

## *Observations Concerning the Original of Government, Upon Mr Hobbes's 'Leviathan', Mr Milton Against Salmasius, H. Grotius 'De Jure Belli'*

Robert Filmer

### I

If God created only Adam, and of a piece of him made the woman; [and] if by generation from them two as parts of them all mankind be propagated; [and] if also God gave to Adam not only the dominion over the woman and the children that should issue from them, but also over the whole earth to subdue it and over all the creatures on it, so that as long as Adam lived no man could claim or enjoy anything but by donation, assignation, or permission from him; [then] I wonder how the right of nature can be imagined by Mr. Hobbes, which he says, page 64, is a liberty for each man to use his own power as he will himself for preservation of his own life; a condition of war of everyone against everyone; a right of every man to everything, even to one another's body, especially since himself affirms, page 178, that originally the father of every man [Adam] was also his Sovereign Lord with power over him of life and death.[1]

II

Mr. Hobbes confesses and believes it was never generally so, that there was such a *jus naturae [right of nature]*; and if not generally, then not at all; for one exception bars all if he mark it well; whereas he imagines such a right of nature may now be practiced in America, he confesses a government there of families, which government how small or brutish soever (as he calls it) is sufficient to destroy his *jus naturale [natural right]*.

III

I cannot understand how this right of nature can be conceived without imagining a company of men at the very first to have been all created together without any dependency one of another; or as mushrooms *(fungorum more)* [as if] they all on a sudden were sprung out of the earth without any obligation one to another, as Mr. Hobbes' words are in his book *De Cive*, chapter 8, section 3: the Scripture teaches us otherwise, that all men came by succession, and generation from one man. We must not deny the truth of the history of the creation.

1 Thus the state of nature is not a state of war.

## IV

It is not to be thought that God would create man in a condition worse than any beasts, as if he made men to no other end by nature but to destroy one another, a right for the father to destroy or eat his children; and for children to do the like by their parents, is worse than cannibals [*De Cive*, 1.10]. This horrid condition of pure nature when Mr. Hobbes was charged with, his refuge was to answer, that no son can be understood to be in this state of nature. Which [this] is all one with denying his own principle; for if men be not free-born, it is not possible for him to assign and prove any other time for them to claim a right of nature to liberty, if not at their birth.

## V

But if it be allowed (which is yet most false) that a company of men were at first without a common power to keep them in awe, [then] I do not see why such a condition must be called a state of war of all men against all men. Indeed if such a multitude of men should be created as the earth could not well nourish, there might be cause for men to destroy one another rather than perish for want of food; but God was no such niggard in the creation; and there being plenty of sustenance and room for all men, there is no cause or use of war till men be hindered in the preservation of life, so that there is no absolute necessity of war in the state of pure nature. It is the right of nature for every man to live in peace, that so he may tend the preservation of his life, which whilst he is in actual war he cannot do. War of itself, as it is war, preserves no man's life; it only helps us to preserve and obtain the means to live. If every man tend the right of preserving life, which may be done in peace, there is no cause of war.

## VI

But admit the state of nature were the state of war; [then] let us see what help Mr. Hobbes hath for it. It is a principle of his that 'the law of nature is a rule found out by reason' (I do think it is given by God), page 64, 'forbidding a man to do that which is destructive to his life, and [forbidding him] to omit that by which he thinks it may be best preserved'. If the right of nature be a liberty for a man to do anything he thinks fit to preserve his life, then in the first place nature must teach him that life is to be preserved, and so consequently forbids to do that which may destroy or take away the means of life, or to omit that by which it may be preserved. And thus the right of nature and the law of nature will be all one;[1] for I think Mr. Hobbes will not say [that] the right of nature is a liberty for a man to destroy his own life. The law of nature might be better have been said to consist in a command to preserve or not to omit the means of preserving life, than in a prohibition to destroy, or to omit it.

## VII

Another principle I meet with, page 65. 'If other men will not lay down their right as well as he, then there is no reason for any to divest himself of his'. Hence it follows that if all the men in the world do not agree, no commonwealth can be established. [But], it is a thing impossible for all men in the world, every man with every man, to covenant to lay down their right. Nay it is not possible to be done in the smallest kingdom, though all men should spend their whole lives in nothing else but in running up and down to covenant....

## IX

... To authorize and give up his right of governing himself, to confer all his power and strength, and to submit his will to another is to lay down his right of resisting; for if right of nature be a liberty to use power for preservation of life, [then] laying down of that power must be a relinquishing of power to preserve or defend life; otherwise a man relinquishes nothing.

To reduce all the wills of an assembly by plurality of voices to one will is not a proper speech; for it is not a plurality but a totali-

1 According to Filmer, it follows from the right of nature and the law of nature that they are identical.

ty of voices which makes an assembly be of one will; otherwise it is but the one will of a major part of the assembly; the negative voice of any one hinders the being of the one will of the assembly. There is nothing more destructive to the true nature of a lawful assembly, than to allow a major part to prevail when the whole only hath right. For a man to give up his right to one that never covenants to protect is a great folly, since it is neither 'in consideration of some right reciprocally transferred to himself, nor can he hope for any other good, by standing out of the way, that the other may enjoy his own original right without hindrance from him by reason of so much diminution of impediments', page 66.

## X

*The liberty*, saith Mr. Hobbes, *whereof there is so frequent and honorable mention in the histories and philosophy of the ancient Greeks and Romans, and in the writings and discourse of those that from them have received all their learning in the politics, is not the liberty of particular men, but the liberty of the commonwealth. Whether a commonwealth be monarchical or popular, the freedom is still the same* [page 110]. Here I find Mr. Hobbes is much mistaken. For the liberty of the Athenians and Romans was a liberty only to be found in popular estates [states], and not in monarchies. This is clear by Aristotle, who calls a city a community of freemen, meaning every particular citizen to be free. Not that every particular man had a liberty to resist his governor or do what he list [liked], but a liberty only for particular men, to govern and to be governed by turns, *archein* and *archesthai* are Aristotle's words. This was a liberty not to be found in hereditary monarchies. So Tacitus mentioning the several governments of Rome, joins the consulship and liberty to be brought in by Brutus, because by the annual election of Consuls, particular citizens came in their course to govern and to be governed. This may be confirmed by the complaint of our author, which follows: *It is an easy thing for men to be deceived by the specious name of liberty; and for want of judgment to … mistake that for their private inheritance or birthright which is the right of the public only; and when the same error is confirmed by the authority of men in reputation for their writings on this subject, it is no wonder if it produce sedition and change of government….* [page 110]

## XIII

I cannot but wonder [that] Master Hobbes should say, page 112, the consent of a subject to sovereign power is contained in these words, *I authorize and do take upon me all his actions*' [page 87], in which there is no restriction at all of his own former natural liberty. Surely here Master Hobbes forgot himself; for before he makes the resignation to go in these words also, *I give up my right of governing myself to this man* [page 87]. This is a restriction certainly of his own former natural liberty when he gives it away; and if a man allow his sovereign to kill him which Mr. Hobbes seems to confess, how can he reserve a right to defend himself?[1] And if a man have a power and right to kill himself, [then] he does not authorize and give up his right to his sovereign, if he do not obey him when he commands him to kill himself.

## XV

... He [Hobbes] says, page 66, *A man cannot lay down the right of resisting them that assault him by force to take away his life; the same be said of wounds, chains and imprisonment.* Page 69. *A covenant to defend myself from force by force is void.* Page 68. *Right of defending life and means of living can never be abandoned.*

These last doctrines are destructive to all government whatsoever, and even to the *Leviathan* itself. Hereby any rogue or villain may murder his sovereign, if the sovereign but offer by force to whip or lay him in the stocks, since whipping may be said to be wounding, and putting in the stocks an imprisonment; so likewise every man's goods being means of living, if a man cannot abandon them, no contract among men, be it never so just, can be observed. Thus we are at least in as miserable a condition of war as Mr. Hobbes at first by nature found us.

1 According to Filmer, Hobbes's theory is contradictory.

# *Appendix B: From George Lawson,* An Examination of the Political Part of Mr. Hobbs His Leviathan

George Lawson (1598-1678) was educated at Emmanuel College, Cambridge, a Puritan college. Nonetheless he was an Arminian; that is, he believed in free will. Although he was a protégé of the archbishop of Canterbury, William Laud, who had been executed in 1645, Lawson was able to live undisturbed in England during the Civil Wars, and took the Engagement, a sworn oath to support the Commonwealth, in 1650. He published *An Examination of the Political Part of Mr Hobbs His Leviathan* in 1657. His more important book is *Politica Sacra & Civilis: or A Model of Civil and Ecclesiastical Government* (1660). Unlike Hobbes, who believes that God's natural sovereignty over human beings comes from his absolute power, Lawson holds that God has supreme authority over the universe because he created it.

Lawson's page references to *Leviathan* are to the original edition; these page numbers are printed in the margins within brackets in the text of this edition of *Leviathan*.

## *An Examination of the Political Part of Mr. Hobbs His Leviathan*

George Lawson

### The Epistle to the Reader

To glorify God and benefit man, both by doing good and preventing and removing evil, should be the endeavor, as it's the duty, of every Christian in his station. Upon this account I have undertaken this examination of Mr. Hobbs: I was indeed at the first unwilling, though solicited, to do any such thing; because upon the perusal of the political part of his *Leviathan*, I conceived, that as little good was to be expected, so little harm was to be feared from that book. Yet after that I understood by diverse learned and judicious friends, that it took much with many gentlemen and young students in the universities, and though it was judged to be a rational piece, I wondered; for though I knew the distemper of the times to be great, yet by this I found it to be far greater than I formerly suspected. And upon which consideration I judged it profitable and convenient, if not necessary, to say something to the gentleman; and did so. After that I had communicated my pains unto divers worthy and learned friends, they pressed me to give way to the printing of them, which I did, if they after serious perusal should find them worthy of the press. They were at length approved, and again by some desired to enlarge. But this I refused to do, both because there is very little, if any thing material at all in Mr. Hobbs his civil and ecclesiastical politics, omitted by me and not examined; and also because I had formerly finished a Treatise of Civil and Ecclesiastical Government [*Politica Sacra & Civilis: or A Model of Civil and Ecclesiastical Government*], which if it had not been lost by some negligence, after an *Imprimatur* was put upon it, might have prevented and made void the political part of Mr. Hobbs: and though one copy be lost, yet there is another, which may become public hereafter. When thou has read this brief examination, thou mayest, if judicious and impartial, easily judge, whether there be any thing in Mr. Hobbs which is either excellent or extraordinary: and whether there be not many things inconsistent, not only with the sacred Scriptures, but with the rules of right reason. But not willing to prepossess thee, I commit thee to God, and remain,

*Thine in the Lord,*
*Geo. Lawson.*

## Cap. [Chapter] I.

### *Of Mr. Hobbs his Leviathan, concerning the Causes, Generation, and Definition of a Commonwealth.*

Civil government derives its being from heaven;[1] for it is a part of God's government over mankind, wherein he uses the ministry of angels and the service of men; yet so, as that he reserves the supreme and universal power in his own hands, with a liberty to dispose the rulers of the world at will and pleasure, and transfer the

1 According to Lawson, human rulers have their authority by divine right, that is, given by God.

government of one nation to another; to lay the foundation of great empires, and again to destroy them for their iniquity. To think that the sole or principal cause of the constitution of a civil state is the consent of men, or that it aims at no further end than peace and plenty, is too mean a conceit of so noble an effect. And in this particular I cannot excuse Mr. Hobbs, who in the modeling both of a civil, and also of an ecclesiastical commonwealth, proceeds upon principles not only weak, but also false and dangerous. And for this reason I undertake him. This should have been done by some well-skilled in political learning, and not by me who do not profess it, as being a Divine and of the meanest among many. And my intention is not to inform my betters, who know the vanity and absurdity of his discourse, but to undeceive the ignorant reader, who may too easily be surprised.

The … seventeenth of his book, does inform us,
First, *That the end of civil government is security.*
Secondly, *This security cannot be had in the state of nature, because it is the state of war; nor by a weak, nor a great multitude, except united by one perpetual judgement.*
Thirdly, *A great multitude are thus united, when they confer all their power and strength upon one man or assembly of men, that may reduce all their wills by plurality of voices to one will, etc. From whence arises a common-wealth.*
Fourthly, *This common-wealth is defined and distributed.*

Against all this, something may be excepted. For first, that the state of nature is the state of war, may be doubted, if not denied. For man is a rational creature; and if he act according to his nature, he must act rationally. And though he may seek to preserve himself, and [do] that sometimes with the damage or destruction of another, yet he cannot, [and] may not do this unjustly, but [only] according to the laws of nature; which are two:

The first, *Love thy neighbor as thy self.*
The second, *Do as thou would be done unto.*

These tend directly unto peace, not unto war, which is unnatural; and they may be kept by multitudes of men not united in a civil state, or under a form of government. And this is evident from divine and profane histories. For families ... and also states both by confederation and without any such thing have lived peaceably together. When the Apostle [Paul] says, *The gentiles which have not the law, by nature do the things contained in the Law*, he does not mean by *nature* a commonwealth or form of government civil. It's true, the Apostle brings in a bill of indictment against all mankind, and accuses them, *that their feet are swift to shed blood. Destruction and calamity or misery are in their ways. And the way of peace they have not known*, Rom. 3:15-17. Yet he understands this not of nature, but the corruption of nature;[1] and the parties here accused are not men only as in the state of nature, but also under a government, and that [government] not only civil but ecclesiastical too. For such the Jews here charged, were. So that all that can be either by him evidently proved, or by others granted, is that if *by nature*, he mean corruption of nature, and the same not only original and native, but also acquired by perpetual acts, so far as to quench the light of nature and suppress the vigor of those principles which God left as relics of his image, then his position may be true, [namely] that the state of nature is the state of war. Secondly, that by a well-constituted civil government, to which nature inclines man, the laws of nature and peace may be more easily and better observed. ...

T.H. [Thomas Hobbes]: *The sovereign's actions cannot be accused of injustice by the subject, because he hath made himself author of all his actions. And no man can do injustice to himself. The sovereign may do iniquity, but not injustice.*

G.L. [George Lawson] 1. The sovereign's actions are to punish the evil and protect the good. As a sovereign, he can do no other actions, and these cannot be justly accused. 2. Neither can the consent of the people, nor does a commission of God give him any power to act contrary to these. 3. When he acts unjustly (for so he may do, and all iniquity is injustice) neither God nor the

---

1 According to Lawson, the state of nature is not a state of war, because human beings are rational.

people are authors of such action; for he was set up by them to do justly, and no ways else. 4. Civil justice and injustice, as they consist in formalities, differ much from moral and essential justice and injustice. In this respect a prince may be civilly just and morally unjust. 5. To accuse may be judicial, or extra-judicial. Judicially, a prince as a prince cannot be accused by his subject as such. Yet the subject may represent unto his sovereign his faults, and by way of humble petition, desire them to be reformed. …

T.H. (page 93): *If there had not first been an opinion received of the greatest part of England, that these powers were divided between the king, and the Lords and the Commons, the people had never been divided and fallen into these civil wars.*

G.L.: The cause moral of these wars was our sins. The political cause was the mal-administration; yet so, that all sides have offended through want of wisdom, and many other ways. The ignorance of politics in general, and of our own constitution in particular, cannot be excused or excepted. What the ancient constitution was, we know not certainly, though some relics of the same continued till our times. But the whole frame was strangely altered and corrupted. Many different opinions there be concerning our government; yet three amongst the rest are most remarkable. [First,] for one party conceives the king to be an absolute monarch. A second determines the king, peers, and Commons to be three co-ordinate powers; yet so that some of them grant three negatives, some only two. A third party gives distinct rights unto these three; yet in this they are sub-divided, and they would be thought to be more rational, who give the legislative power unto the Lords and Commons in one house; the judicial, to the Lords in a distinct house; and the executive to the king, who was therefore trusted with the sword both of war and justice. None of these can give satisfaction. There is another opinion, which puts the supreme power radically in the 40 counties, to be exercised by king, peers and Commons, according to certain rules, which by antiquaries in law, together with some experienced statesmen of this nation, might be found out, but are not. The seeds of this division were sown and began to appear before the wars; and the opinion that all these were only in one man, that is the king absolutely, some say, was the greatest cause, not only of the last, but also of other civil wars in former times; and it hath been observed, that every man liked that opinion best, which was most suitable to his own interest. Our several opinions in religion have heightened our differences, and hindered our settlement; yet religion is but pretended [a pretence]; for every party aims at civil power, not spiritual liberty from sin. And the power to settle us, thus woefully distracted, is only in God; and if he ever will be thus merciful unto us, the way whereby he will effect it, will be by giving the greatest power to men of greatest wisdom and integrity, not by reducing us unto one opinion, that all the powers civil must be in one, as the author does fondly fancy. Let the form be the best in the world, yet without good governors it's in vain. …

This man [Hobbes] deserves to be a perpetual slave; his intention is to make men believe that the kings of England were absolute monarchs, their subjects slaves, without propriety of goods or liberty of person, the parliaments of England merely nothing but shadows, and the members thereof but so many carriers of letters and petitions between home and the court. What he means by subordinate representatives, I know not. I think his intention is to oppose those who affirmed king, peers, and Commons to be co-ordinate, not subordinate powers, and all of them jointly to make up one supreme. Subordinate representatives or powers he may safely and must grant in all states. The word *representative* he either does not understand, or if he does, he intolerably abuses his unwary and unlearned reader by that term. A representative in the civil law, called *topoteretes*, is one who by his presence supplies the place of another that is absent, for some certain end, as to act that which another should do, but in his own person does not, yet with the consent of the person represented, so far as that the thing is judged to be done by him. And in this sense, the person representing is judged to be one with the person represented by fiction of law. And one may represent another as a superior, who may represent another in any act, so far as that other is in his power; or as an inferior, by a power derived from his superior; or as an equal by consent, so far as the person represented is willing, and the person representing will undertake to act for him. In all these representations, the *representee* and the representer are judged one person. In a free-state, a parliament is a representative of the whole body of the people; this we call a general representative. The reason of this representation is, because the whole body of a people cannot well act personally. What kind of representative the parliament of England was, is hard to know, except we knew certainly the first institution, which, by tract of time and many abuses of that excellent Assembly, is now unknown. It was certainly trusted with the highest acts of legislation, judgement, [and] execution. The whole body consisted of several orders and ranks of men, as of kings, peers, commons, the clergy. Whether they might meddle with the constitution or no, is not so clear; it's conceived they could not alter it, though they might declare it what it was. Their power was great without all doubt, yet not so great, but that it was bounded, and a later parliament might alter and reform what a former had established, which argues, that the 40 counties, and the whole body of the people whence all parliaments have their original [origin] and being, as they are parliaments, were above them. In this great assembly, the knights and burgesses did represent the counties and the boroughs, the convocation [represented] the whole body of the clergy; the peers, by ancient tenure, [represented] their families, vassals and dependants. But whom the king should represent is hard to determine. If the law did consider him as an infant, and this according to the constitution, he could represent no other person or persons. And if this be so, then there is plain reason why he never should have the title of representative; yet evident reason there is, why the rest should be called a representative; and the people are not representers, as he fondly imagines, but the persons represented. …

T.H.: *That by the liberty of the subject, the sovereign's power of life and death is neither abolished nor limited.*

G.L.: It's certain that the sovereign's power and the subject's liberty are consistent. For the sovereign may take away the life of his subject; yet according to the evidence of judgement, agreeable to law; [and] no otherwise. Yet he presupposes, 1. That the king is supreme and [is] the primary subject, owner and possessor of the original power, which sometimes may be; yet with us it's far otherwise. 2. That the power of civil sovereigns is absolute. For with him, [the following is true:]

T.H.: *Nothing the sovereign representative can do to a subject on what pretence so ever, can properly be called injustice or injury, because every subject is author of every act the sovereign does, so that he never wants right to anything, otherwise than as he himself is the subject of God, and bound thereby to observe the laws of nature. When … Jephthah sacrificed his daughter, and David murdered Uriah, both innocent, yet, they [Jephthah and David] did them [the daughter and Uriah] no injustice, etc.*

G.L.: Here he seems to contradict himself. For he grants two things. 1. That the sovereign is subject to God. 2. That in that respect he is bound to observe the laws of nature; yet he says, he can do no injustice to the subject, and that he hath right to anything, so yet as he is limited by subjection to God and the laws of nature. … [But] if he be God's subject, as certainly he is, it follows that in that respect he is but trusted as a servant with the administration of the power civil; [and it follows] that he is fellow-subject with his subjects; [and it follows that] he may do injustice, as one fellow subject may wrong another.

Secondly, if he be bound to observe the laws of nature, which are the laws of God; then, 1. he is not absolute, or *solutus legibus* [*free of the laws*]. His power is limited and bounded by these laws. 2. Then he hath no power to murder, oppress, and destroy his innocent subjects, who are more God's than his, and only trusted by God in his hands for to be protected, righted in all just causes, and vindicated from all wrongs. 3. No prince or sovereign can assume, or any people give to any person or persons, any the least power above, or contrary unto the laws of nature. These laws are the moral precepts of eternal justice and equity, from which all civil laws have their rise, and are either conclusions drawn from them, or certain rules tending to the better observation of them. Which things well considered, do make it very evident how little the power of civil lords and princes must needs be. In some few indifferent things, they may be absolute, have arbitrary power, and be in some respect above those constitutive laws which they themselves enact.

His instance in Jephthah gives them power above, and contrary to the laws of God and nature. Yet who will grant him that Jephthah sacrificed his daughter? The text will not evince it; for it only says that whatsoever comes forth of my doors to meet me, &c. shall be the Lord's, or I will offer it up for a burnt-offering (Judges 11:31).[1] …

The example of David murdering Uriah can much less prove the absolute power of sovereigns to take away the lives of their innocent subjects.[2] For, David hath no such power: for, 1. He was no absolute prince, but limited both by the written laws of God, and also the natural. 2. Neither he nor any other can have any such power, because man cannot; God does not give any such power. 3. David did not only iniquity, but injustice to Uriah. … But … let me digress a little and search out the reason and cause of the power of life and death, as in the hands of civil sovereigns. To this end, observe that no man hath absolute power of his own life, as he hath of his goods. Man may have the use and possession, but not the propriety [property] and dominion of it. Therefore it's granted on all hands that though a man's life be said to be his own; yet he may not also be *felo de se*, and kill himself; he is not master of his life so far, as to have any power or liberty to do any such thing. It is true that God, who is Lord of life and death, gives liberty to man in some cases to hazard, [and] in some he commands to lay down his life. He may hazard it in a just war and defense of his own country, and also of himself, against an unjust invader. He must lay down his life; and God commands it for the testimony of Christ, in which case he that loses it shall find it. From all this it follows that no people can, by making a sovereign, give any absolute power of life and death unto him. For nothing can give that which it hath not; neither can they make themselves authors of the unjust acts of their sovereign, much less of his murders, and taking away the lives of their innocent subjects. *Id enim quisque potest quod jure potest.* [Anyone can do that which is done by right.] If thus it be, then they must have the power to take away life from God, who alone hath power of life; and this power he only gives in case the subject be guilty of such crimes as by his laws are capital. …

---

1 Lawson is wrong about what Jephthah swore to at Judges 11:31 and wrong to deny that Jephthah sacrificed his daughter. Judges 11:39 says, "her father … did with her according to the vow which he had vowed …"

2 See 21.7.

T. H. pages 111–13: *The liberty of the subject is in such things as are neither determined by his first submission to the sovereign power, nor by the laws.*

G. L.: This is the substance of three pages, and amounts to so much as may easily be comprised in a few words. For when a subject is not bound either by the laws of the constitution or administration, he is free according to Mr. Hobbs his judgement. Yet in proper sense in both these cases, he is no subject; but *dominus* [lord] and far more than *liber* [free]. The civilians [civil lawyers] do better determine the liberty of the subject to be *postestatem agendi sub publicae defensionis praesidio* [the power of acting under the protection of the public defense] though this be no perfect definition. As before, so now I say, that liberty here is not opposed to obligation, but servitude. For to be subject to a wise sovereign according to just laws is so much liberty as any reasonable man can desire; for in this respect he is rather subject to God than man; and to serve him is doubtless perfect freedom. As no sovereign should be denied so much power as to protect the least, if innocent, and to punish the greatest, if guilty; so no subject should be bound to do evil, which is servitude and bondage indeed, or restrained from doing that good which God commands him. Civil government was never ordained by God to be destructive either of moral or divine virtues, or of the noble condition of man as a rational creature. Therefore regular submission unto supreme power, will never stand with any obligation unto evil, or contract for protection except in innocency. Paul pleading before Festus says, *If I be an offender or have committed any thing worthy of death, I refuse not to die* (Acts 25:11). How can this stand with what this author says, when he affirms that it's lawful for a man guilty and condemned to save himself if he can, I leave to others for to examine. From the Apostle's words it's evident, he desires no protection, even of himself, as worthy of death, neither hath God given any power to man to save in such a case. …

*Of the Second Part, the Twenty-fourth of the Book; Of Nutrition and Procreation of a Commonwealth.*

Two things only in this Cap. I question: the 1. concerning the original of propriety [property]. The 2. concerning a standing revenue of the crown. …

For 1. we find propriety of goods and lands in several families, which are of no commonwealth. 2. The constitution of any commonwealth does presuppose this propriety, without which there can be no buying, selling, exchanging, stealing, restitution; otherwise the eighth commandment, *Thou shalt not steal,* could not be a law of nature, nor bind any man, except in a commonwealth; and so before a commonwealth be instituted in a community or people, there could be no sin in stealing. 3. All that may be granted in this point is that the sovereign may preserve and regulate propriety, both by laws and judgements. Yet the author makes all men brutes, nay wild and ravenous beasts, and birds of prey, until they have made themselves slaves unto some absolute sovereign, and such they must be, either beasts by the law of nature, or slaves by the law of the civil state. 4. As for his instance in the land of Canaan divided by lots to be chosen before Eleazer the high priest, and Joshua the general, it's impertinent and false [see *Leviathan* 24.6]. For, 1. Israel before it was molded into a commonwealth, had propriety in their goods. 2. The propriety of that land was at the first and continued in God; for they were but God's tenants in a special and peculiar manner, so as no people in the world was; therefore no man could alienate nor mortgage beyond the year of Jubilee, at which time God seemed to renew their leases … 3. When they had in common conquered, and taken possession of the land, it was theirs, so far as God had conveyed it, in common. 4. It was for peace and order, as also for to preserve the distinction of tribes divided; yet so as the sovereign dividing it was God, who ordered the lot. Eleazer and Joshua were but superintendents of the lot, and no sovereigns; neither had they any the least propriety more than others of the people. The text expressly says, that when they had made an end of dividing the land, they gave Joshua Timnath Serah in Mount Ephraim for his inheritance (Joshua 19:49–50), where it is to be observed, that the people gave it him. …

### *Of the Second Part. The 25th of the Book 'Of Counsel'*

… [G. L.]: That command should be for the benefit of the party commanding, and counsel for the good of the party counseled, is merely accidental in ways essential to them. And though sometimes both the intention and the event of both may be such as he determines, yet we know it is many times otherwise. For commands may sometimes, nay often, be beneficial to the party commanded, and intended to be so; as counsel may be intended, not only for the good of the party counseled, but also counseling; and also prove so to be.…

For one and the same sentence may be a command, a counsel and an exhortation too, yet in different respects; as it binds [it is] a command, as it directs a counsel, as it incites an exhortation.

T. H.: *The legislator in all commonwealths is the sovereign. Again, the commonwealth is the legislator by the representative.*[1]

G. L.: That *pars imperans* [the commanding part] is the legislator in every state must needs be granted; but that the commonwealth should be the legislator, either by or without *pars imperans*, the sovereign, I do not understand. For it consists of two parts, the sovereign and the subject; and if the whole commonwealth make laws, then the subject as well as the sovereign is legislator. In a republic or free-state, there is a difference between the sovereign and the subject, much more in other models and forms. Therefore he must needs speak either improperly or untruly, when he says the state is legislator.

T. H.: … *The sovereign is not subject to the civil laws, because he hath power to make and repeal them at pleasure.*[2]

G. L.: That the sovereign in divers respects and especially as a sovereign is not subject unto but [is] above the laws is a certain truth. For laws do bind the subject, not the sovereign, to obey or be punished; but the sovereign does command as superior, not obey as inferior; [and he] does punish [and] is not punished. The power to

1 See 26.5.
2 See 26.6.

make a law, when there is none, and to repeal after that it's made is sufficient evidence of his superiority, as also dispensations in judgements and pardons be. Yet this supreme will, legislative over men, is subject to the superior will of God, and must neither make, nor repeal laws, but according to wisdom and justice.

T. H.: ... *Custom is not law by long continuance of time, but by consent of the sovereign.*[1]

G. L.: ... For if the sovereign only be the legislator, then continuance of time and practice of the people, though universal, cannot make a law. The sovereign must give either an express or tacit consent; and this consent is then most evident when he makes the custom a rule in judgment and observes it. And the civilians [civil lawyers] well observe that besides continuance of time and the sovereign's consent, a third thing is required, and that is, that the beginning of it be reasonable, as the author here does note.

T. H.: ... *The law of nature and the civil law contain each other, and are of equal extent. For the laws of nature, which consist in equity, justice, gratitude and other moral virtues on these depending, in the condition of mere nature, are not properly laws, but qualities, that dispose men to peace and obedience; when a commonwealth is once actually settled, then are they laws, etc.*[2]

G. L.: 1. This is no conclusion from the definition, except he mean that the rule of right and wrong be the law of nature. 2. The laws of nature are the laws of God, and not of man; and not only subjects, but sovereigns are bound by them. 3. Therefore they bind not as commanded by the civil sovereign, but as written by the hand of heaven in the heart of man. Neither is that which afterwards he makes the difference between the law of nature and the law of civil governors, any difference at all, that the one is written, the other not. For both are written, one by the hand of man, though every civil law be not written, and the other by the hand of God: the one in the heart, the other upon some other material substance; and that which is written in the heart, may be written out of it. 4. Equity, justice, gratitude and other moral virtues, are not laws of nature, but either habitual or actual conformities unto

1 See 26.7. and 26.9. See also *Dialogue Between a Philosopher and a Student of the Common Laws*, etc. in *English Works*, ed. Molesworth, vol. 6, p. 61, and *De Cive* 14.15.

2 See 26.8.

the laws of nature. 5. How the laws of nature, and laws civil should be of equal extent, and yet contain one another, and be parts one of another, I do not understand. 6. A law of nature is only then a civil law, when it's declared to be so by the civil sovereign, yet it's a law before. 7. For the most part, learned men do understand by the laws of nature certain divine principles imprinted upon the heart of man; by the laws of nations, more immediate; by the laws civil, more remote conclusions of constitutive laws civil.

T. H.: *1. How can a man without supernatural revelation, be assured of the revelation received by the declarer of those laws?*[1]

*2. How can he be bound to obey them?*

*The answer to the first, by sanctity, miracle, wisdom, success, without particular revelation, it's impossible for a man to have assurance of a revelation made to another. Therefore no man can infallibly know by natural reason that another hath had a supernatural revelation of God's will, but only a belief.*

G. L.: This presupposes, 1. That there is a positive law of God. 2. This positive law is declared and witnessed to be the law of God. 3. That this testimony concerning this law is divine and infallible. 4. That it is such, because it's grounded on and agreeable to an immediate revelation from God of that law to him that does declare it, as to Moses, the Prophets or Apostles. For God formerly spoke unto the fathers by the prophets, in the latter times to their children by his Son first and after by his Apostles. The question here is not how we shall attain a demonstrative, clear or intuitive knowledge of the matter of the law, nor the manner of the revelation; but how we may be assured that the declaration or testimony of him to whom the revelation was made, is divine, that we may believe it as divine and from God. The means whereby the divinity of the testimony was made evident at the first were extraordinary as signs, wonders, and diverse miracles and gifts of the Holy Ghost, according to his own will (Heb. 2:4). But after that, upon these divine attestations, the Gospel was generally received in all nations, and the prophecies of the Old Testament in this particular fulfilled, these ceased; yet one thing always did, and ever will manifest the testimony and doctrine of the Gospel to be divine, and that is the Holy Ghost, who (by his powerful working

---

1 See 26.40.

upon the hearts of men, seriously attending to this truth, whereby a great change both inwardly in their hearts, and outwardly in their lives is wrought) does mightily confirm it. And those who find, and feel in themselves the effects of sanctification and heavenly comfort, can no ways doubt, but are assured that God was in the Prophets and Apostles, and did speak by them. Besides when we consider, 1. That the more we understand them, the more excellency of wisdom we find in them. 2. That these positives are agreeable and no ways contrary to pure morals. 3. That they conduce effectually to holiness and eternal life. 4. That they were approved, received by the best men in the world, and sealed with the blood of many martyrs, we must needs be fully satisfied that they are not false, feigned, fantastic conceits of deluded men, and not only so, but all these things may persuade any rational man to try upon practice, whether they be divine or no. And this never any did, but found the Apostles' doctrine to be of God. If we had nothing but the universal and perpetual agreement and tradition of the Church of all places and times, affirming the Scripture to be the Word of God, it were sufficient to produce in a rational man a greater measure of belief, than any book or history in the world can possibly require or deserve. For this universal testimony of the best in several parts of the world, at such a distance as that they in their time neither heard of, nor knew one another, makes it more credible than any humane history can be. But to return unto Mr. Hobbs, I say it's possible, and not impossible to know the divinity of the testimony or declaration immediately, but not of the revelation or matter revealed. Yet that such a revelation, and such a thing revealed there was, is known in some measure by consequence. And the divine authority of this testimony may be infallibly known, and that by natural reason, yet by it as elevated and more perfected by outward representation and inward sanctification. And the matter of the revelation to another, together with the manner, may be believed, though not known. For when we once know that God hath revealed it, we believe the thing revealed to be true, though by artificial and intrinsical arguments we cannot prove it to be so. For the testimony of God may be evident, though the thing testified be hidden and above our reason. The conclusion is that we may have an infallible knowledge of the positive laws of God, so far as to know that they are from him, and are his laws, and that without particular revelation, that they were revealed to another. …

T. H.: *That the subject in the first constitution laid aside his power of self-preservation by hurting, subduing, killing others in his own defense; and so did not give it, but left to the sovereign.*[1]

G. L.: This is ridiculous, absurd, and grounded upon his false principles. For, 1. The sovereign is the minister of God and is bound to do (so that he keep within the compass of his commission) that which God would do, and that is to punish evil. And as all his power of making laws, judgement, peace, war, etc. are from God, so is this amongst the rest. By whom he is made a sovereign, from him he hath the sword to punish. Men may give their consent that such a man or such a company of men shall reign, but the power is from God, not them. 2. In the constitution of a supreme governor, no man can covenant to be protected or defended in doing evil. Neither can any or all higher powers in the world justly promise to protect any in evil; neither hath any man any power unjustly to preserve himself. For that of the author, that in the state of nature every man hath right to every thing, is absolutely false and abominable. When a man subjects himself unto a sovereign ordained of God, not only to protect the good, but to punish the evil, he cannot except himself from his punitive power, if he do ill; because he subjects according to the just laws of God and cannot lawfully do any other ways. So that power to punish is given by God, not left by man unto higher powers civil. …

T. H.: *A second cause of weakening and dissolving a state are certain doctrines. The first, that every private man is judge of good and evil actions.*[2]

G. L.: Judgement is public or private; public no private man can pass; private he may; and that most of his own actions, and others too. The acts of others are private and public; of both these he may judge. Public acts of the governors are laws, judgements, [and] execution. Even of laws he may, he must within himself, so far as they are a rule and bind him, enquire, examine and determine, whether good or evil. Otherwise, he can perform but only a blind obedience to the best; and if he conform unto the unjust, he in

---

1 See 28.2.

2 See 29.6.

obeying man, disobeys God, which no good man will do. In other acts which are apparently just, we may judge of them truly as they are, and no otherwise. Yet this must not be done to palliate our disobedience to that which is just, or raise sedition, or rebel; but we may complain to God, and by our humble prayers seek redress. …

T. H.: *A fourth opinion repugnant to the nature of a commonwealth is this, that he that hath the sovereign power, is subject to the civil laws.*[1]

G. L.: There is no doubt but that this is destructive of government and contrary to the very nature and essence of a commonwealth; the essential parts whereof are, *imperans & subditus* [*commanding and being subdued*], the sovereign and the subject; take this difference away, [and] you confound all, and turn the commonwealth into a community; yet though sovereigns are above their own laws, (how otherwise could they dispense with them and repeal them?) wise men have given advice to princes for to observe their own laws, and that for example unto others; and good princes have followed this advice. Sovereigns are to govern by laws, not to be subject unto them. But what this man means by sovereign, in the hypothesis, is hard to know. For he presupposes all sovereigns absolute, and all kings of England such sovereigns; and so in general it may be granted, that all sovereigns are above the laws civil; yet the application of this rule to particular princes of limited power, may be false and no ways tolerable. …

T. H.: *A fifth doctrine which tends to the dissolution of a commonwealth is that every man hath an absolute propriety in his goods, such as excludes the right of the sovereign. Every man hath indeed a propriety that excludes the right of the subject which is derived from the sovereign, without whose protection every man should have equal right to the same.*[2]

G. L.: 1. If the subject have propriety, as the author grants, it must needs be absolute and must needs exclude not only the right of the fellow-subject, but of the sovereign too. For propriety in proper sense is an independent right of total alienation, without any license of a superior or any other. 2. This propriety is not derived from the sovereign, except he be despotical; and such indeed the author affirms all sovereigns to be; and in that respect

1 See 29.9.
2 See 29.10.

the subjects can neither have propriety nor liberty; therefore he contradicts himself, when he says in many places, that the sovereign is absolute, and here, that the subject hath propriety. 3. It's to be granted that even in a free-state the subjects' propriety cannot [be] free from the public charges; for as a member of the whole body, he is bound to contribute to the maintenance of the state, without the preservation whereof he cannot so well preserve his own private right. 4. Propriety is by the law of nature and nations at least agreeable unto both. And when men agree to constitute a commonwealth, they retain their proper right, which they had unto their goods before the constitution, which does not destroy, but preserve propriety, if well ordered. For men may advance a sovereign without any alienation of their estates. No man hath any propriety from God, but so as to be bound to give unto the poor, relieve the distressed, and maintain the sovereign in his just government; yet this does not take away, but prove propriety, because every one gives, even unto the commonwealth, that which is his own, not another man's, nor his sovereign's, who may justly in necessary cases, for the preservation of the state, impose a just rate upon the subject.

But if the reader seriously consider the author's discourse in other parts of his book, he may easily know whereat he aims. For, 1. he makes all sovereigns absolute. 2. The kings of England to be sovereigns. And 3. in that respect to have a power to raise subsidies and moneys without a parliament. And 4. hath made that a mortal disease of our state, which is a great preservative of our liberty. For the people always bear the purse and could not by the king be charged with the least, without their consent by their representative in the parliament. This did poise and limit the regal power, prevented much riot and excess in the court, made the prince frugal, and hindered unnecessary wars. Yet good princes and frugal, never wanted money, were freely supplied by their subjects, whilst they required in their need any thing extraordinary above the public revenue, in a right way by Parliament. ...

T. H.: *And as to rebellion in particular against monarchy, one of the most frequent causes is the reading of the books of policy and histories of the ancient Greeks and Romans, etc.*[1]

---

1 See 29.14.

G. L.: This has been formally examined. The reading of the books cannot do so much hurt, as this *Leviathan* may do. For it is far more dangerous and destructive of good government than any of their histories, which can do no hurt to any but such as are ignorant and ill-disposed. In those books they may read of kings and emperors, and of monarchies as well as free-states; and few are so void of understanding, but that they well know they are bound to their own form of government, and are not to covet every model they read of. Such men as he do shamefully debase free-state, as forms unlawful in themselves, and so flatter limited princes, as though they were absolute lords, and advance monarchy so high, as though it were the only form of government, so instituted by God and commanded; that all nations were bound unto it, and whosoever does not bow unto it, is a rebel against God. Yet he [God] never instituted immediately any commonwealth but one, and that was a free-state [Israel]; and when a king was desired, he was offended, and under a regal government it came to ruin. Whereas he thinks these books do teach regicide and killing of kings, he is much mistaken. For subjects to murder their lawful sovereigns, is an horrid crime, and so much the more to be detested, if done under the name of *tyrannicide*. To plead for tyrants really such as such, is to be abhorred. They pervert the very end of all government, abuse their power, act contrary to the laws of God and men, to the ruin of the state, are enemies of mankind, the chiefest agents for the devil. The question is, whether a people having power in their hands may not restrain or remove or put to death such men, as being guilty of many crimes, which the laws of God have made universally capital, so that no man in the world can plead exemption? Some think that they are to be left to God, and subjects must seek deliverance by prayers and tears; and the truth is, Christians as Christians, have no other remedy. Others conceive [that] they may be restrained, and that by force, and their own subjects do it. Others give this power only unto magistrates or to such as share with them in the supreme power: others are of a mind that seeing [since] they cease to be kings or sovereigns, they may be lawfully tried and put to death, as well as private men; and that without any ordinary jurisdiction. Others determine this to be lawful in such states as that of Lacedaemon in Greece and

Aragon in Spain. What the doctrine of the Church of Rome is cannot be unknown. For the Pope does arrogate an universal ecclesiastical jurisdiction, whereby he may excommunicate any Christian king that shall not obey his canons [laws] and edicts; and upon this sentence once given, he may depose him, free his subjects from their allegiance, and command them as Catholics to rise in rebellion against him; and some of them have taught, that it's a meritorious art to poison, stab, or any other way to murder kings for the promotion of the Catholic cause. This question, after the terms thereof clearly explicated, is of very great moment; and let men advise well how they do determine either in their own judgement privately, or before others. …

T. H.: *Some make the power of levying money depend upon a general assembly; of conduct and command upon one man; of making laws upon the accidental consent of three. Such government is no government, but a division of the commonwealth into three independent factions*, etc.[1]

G. L.: Here again he hath made the Parliament, which is the bulwark of, and best remedy for to preserve our liberty, a disease; and hath turned the king, peers, and Commons into three independent factions; and this government, he says, some call a mixed monarchy. Whether there can be a mixed state is a question in politics; yet if we understand what mixture is and could determine whether this mixture be in the supreme power as fixed in the constitution or exercised in the administration, we might more easily satisfy ourselves. But this hath not been exactly done. For it's probable that in the exercise of the supreme power, in the three acts of legislation, judgement, execution, there might be a mixture, and these brought to a just and regular temperament. But a mixed monarchy in proper sense there cannot be. Yet a limited and well-poised monarch there may be. To place the power legislative, which includes all the rest, in three co-ordinate parties, granting to every one of them severally a negative, to me seems irrational; for it may easily turn them who should be one, into three factions, as here it is affirmed. At least it will retard all businesses, which for dispatch, require secrecy and expedition. But to place the universal power originally in the general assembly without any negative; the judicial in the Lords, and the executive in the king, seems to be far

1 See 29.16.

more agreeable to the rules of reason. This some think was our ancient constitution, and the same excellent.

Difficulty of raising monies necessary for the defense and preservation of state, monopolies, [and] popularity in a subject are diseases which much weaken a state; there is no doubt of this. That one city should engross the wealth and strength of a nation, and be so rich and populous as to be able to set forth a potent army and maintain it, may be judged very dangerous to a commonwealth, as Mr. Hobbs informs us. By this city in particular, he means London, which, as some tell us, furnished the parliament with men and monies, whereby the king was vanquished and overthrown. Yet they seldom did assist the parliament but upon high terms and advantageous to themselves; in so much as their petitions were commands unto the parliament, which did depend more upon the city than the city upon them, by which means they might in time engross the whole power, and so rule the nation. Yet an army of their own did break their strength and reduce them upon their own terms; and it's clear [that] that city depends much upon the River [Thames], both for fuel, merchandize and provision, and by a wise provident counsel may be easily kept in order. And this might the more easily be done because the citizens have so many several interests, and the same inconsistent amongst themselves, as that they can hardly be united.

After all these diseases from within, which weaken and may dissolve a government, he informs of a destructive cause, and that is a foreign or intestine war, wherein the enemy obtains a final victory, so that the sovereign cannot protect his subjects in their loyalty. This indeed may cut off a line, change the governors, and alter the form of government. Yet in all this, the community may continue and never be like a subject matter without any form; but the government may be the same and the governors only altered; nay the constitution may stand firm, and the administration only varied; or if the form be changed, yet the privation of the former is an introduction of the latter. Here it's confessed that when the power of protection fails in the sovereign, obligation in the subject is taken away. But he starts a question, though with him no question, whether the right of a sovereign monarch can be extinguished by the act of another? He says it cannot. Yet experience tells us, it may. For a conquered monarch, fallen into the power of another, ceases to be a sovereign, and this is by the act of another. And again, if God by another take away his sword, though his person escape and be at liberty, he hath but the name and not the thing or real title. If his subjects, freed from obligation, because he can give no protection, do submit themselves unto another; yet he thinks, that if the power of an assembly be suppressed, their right is extinct. The assembly in an aristocracy or democracy, for such he means, may be extraordinary or ordinary; and the same [may be] the immediate subject of the supreme power or only trusted for a time with the administration and exercise thereof. And the power of an assembly may be suppressed for a time, and so only suspended, the assembly remaining still. Except he let us know what kind of assembly he understands, and what kind of suppression of power he means, he does nothing. An assembly whose power depends on a certain place, time, number, may lose their right, if once they be scattered or defective in that circumstance. …

Many of his rules [in chapter 20] I confess are good, but most of them are such as are very ordinary and commonly known. But in those points wherein he is singular, he can hardly be excused from error. His first and chiefest care after the good of the people is to preserve the absolute power of rulers, which he asserts to be their due; and lest they should lose any of them, he renews his catalogue of them again. These must be taught [to] the people, that they may know themselves to be absolute slaves. And princes must take heed of transferring any of sovereign rights unto another. But this was needless; for they have a desire of power before they do obtain it. And after they are once possessed of it, they not only keep that which is due, but also usurp far more than either God or man hath given them. Kings, who are but trusted with a limited power, endeavor to make themselves absolute lords; and despotical sovereigns must be petty deities. The best princes had always a greater care to exercise their power well than to enlarge it. And by their wisdom and justice have governed more happily than any of these absolute sovereigns, who desire rather to be great than good, and themselves more honorable than the people happy.

The errors of this author, vented in this part, as that sovereign power civil is absolute; a civil law against rebellion is no obligation; a good law is not a just law, because no law can be unjust. All his rules of government may be proved out of Scripture and other such like, I will not here examine, because some of them are ridiculous; some of them have been formerly answered: and his proof of these in his next part shall be discussed.

*Of … the 31st of the Book. Of the Kingdom of God by Nature.*

This chapter is the conclusion of the second part, the *Leviathan*, and makes way for the third following. The principal subject hereof is the laws of nature as distinct to laws supernatural. For he truly and wisely makes God the king and lawgiver both in the kingdom of God by nature and above nature. That God is the universal king by nature, he seems to prove out of the Scripture. …

[Cf. *Leviathan* 188] Obedience is due to God not merely as gratitude to a benefactor, but as a duty unto him as a lawgiver. For as a creator he may have a right to command, because by creation he hath an absolute propriety in his being, which is such as he is capable of a law. And creation is not considered as any kind of benefit, but such a benefit as his rational being was wholly derived from it, and also wholly and perpetually depends upon his preservation, and his eternal happiness upon his legislation and government. …

How far Mr. Hobbs is from the true understanding of worship in general and of the worship of God in particular may easily appear from this, that he makes worship to be nothing else but the outward signification by words and actions of internal honor; which with him is nothing else but the inward thought and opinion of the power and goodness of another. But neither is worship nor honor any such thing as he hath defined. And his discourse of worship with the distinctions will be found very poor upon examination, except we allow him a sovereign power over words to impose what signification upon them he pleaseth, and the same different from that wherein they are used in classical authors.

… If they [sovereigns] have no better directions, they may make use of his principles, as some have done to their ruin. Princes and ministers of state have no need to be taught them. For they know them too well and follow them too much.

# *Appendix C: From John Bramhall,* The Catching of Leviathan, or the Great Whale

John Bramhall (1594-1663), educated at Sidney Sussex College, Cambridge, made a good career in the Church of England. Having supported Thomas Wentworth's oppressive but efficient governance of Ireland in the early 1630s, he was made bishop of Derry in 1634. A Royalist, he fled England with William Cavendish, then marquis of Newcastle, after the battle of Marston Moor (1644). At the Restoration, Bramhall was made archbishop of Armagh, primate of Ireland. In Paris, a debate with Hobbes on free will, conducted in front of Newcastle, resulted in an exchange of treatises in the 1650s. Bramhall's *The Catching of Leviathan* was published (with the date 1658) as an appendix to *Castigations of Mr Hobbes His Last Animadversions, in the Case Concerning Liberty, and Universal Necessity* (1658). Hobbes replied in his *An Answer to a Book Published by Dr. Bramhall … called the 'Catching of the Leviathan'*, reprinted in volume 4 of William Molesworth's edition of Hobbes's *English Works*. His general estimate of Bramhall's criticisms applies equally well to his other critics:

> [Bramhall] hath put together divers sentences picked out of my *Leviathan*, which stand there plainly and firmly proved, and [he] sets them down without their proofs, and without the order of their dependence one upon another; and calls them atheism, blasphemy, impiety, subversion of religion, and by other names of that kind. My request unto you is that when he cites my words for erroneous, you will be pleased to turn to the place itself, and see whether they be well proved, and how to be understood ("To the Reader").

References that appear in the margin of the original edition of *The Catching of Leviathan* have been placed within the body of the text within parentheses. Page references to *Leviathan* are to the edition of 1651.

## *The Catching of Leviathan, or the Great Whale*

Demonstrating, out of Mr. Hobbs his own works, That no man who is thoroughly an Hobbist, can be a good Christian, or a good commonwealth's man or reconcile himself to himself. Because his principles are not only destructive to all religion, but to all societies; extinguishing the relation between prince and subject, parent and child, master and servant, husband and wife: and abound with palpable contradictions.

...

Our God is a perfect, pure, simple, indivisible, infinite essence; free from all composition of matter and form, of substance and accidents. All matter is finite, and he who acts by his infinite essence needs neither organs nor faculties nor accidents to render him more complete. But T. H. [Thomas Hobbes] his god is a divisible god, a compounded god, that hath matter and qualities or accidents. Hear himself. I [Hobbes] argue thus, *The divine substance is indivisible, but eternity is the divine substance. The major (premise) is evident because God is* Actus simplicissimus (the simplest act). *The minor (premise) is confessed by all men, that whatsoever is attributed to God, is God.* Now listen to his answer (Q p. 267): *The major is so far from being evident, that* Actus simplicissimus *signifies nothing. The minor is said by some men, thought by no man, whatsoever is thought is understood.* The major was this, *The divine substance is indivisible.* Is this far from being evident? Either it is indivisible or divisible. If it be not indivisible, then it is divisible, then it is materiate, then it is corporeal, then it hath parts, then it is finite by his own confession (*DC* 15.14) ... Thus he hath already destroyed the ubiquity, the eternity, and the simplicity of God. I wish he had considered better with himself, before he had desperately cast himself upon these rocks.

... My next charge is that he destroys the very being of God[1] and leaves nothing in his place but an empty name. For by taking away all incorporeal substances, he takes away God himself. The very name (saith he) of an incorporeal substance is a contradic-

1 According to Bramhall and many others, Hobbes's idea of God as material has atheistic consequences.

tion. And *to say that an Angel or Spirit is an incorporeal substance, is to say in effect that there is no Angel or Spirit at all* (*Lev.* p. 214). By the same reason to say that God is an incorporeal substance is to say there is no God at all. Either God is incorporeal, or he is finite and consists of parts and consequently is no God. This, that there is no incorporeal spirit, is the main root of atheism, from which so many lesser branches are daily sprouting up.

When they have taken away all incorporeal spirits, what do they leave God himself to be? He who is the fountain of all being must needs have a real being of his own. And what real being can God have among bodies and accidents? For they have left nothing else in the universe. Then T.H. may move the same question of God, which he did of devils. *I would gladly know in what classes of entities, the Bishop ranks God?* (Q p. 160) Infinite being and participated being are not of the same nature. Yet to speak according to human apprehension (apprehension and comprehension differ much; T.H. confesses that natural reason does dictate to us that God is infinite; yet natural reason cannot comprehend the infiniteness of God) I place him among incorporeal substances or spirits, because he hath been pleased to place himself in that rank, *God is a spirit* (John. 4:24). Of which place T.H. gives his opinion, that it is unintelligible, and all others of the same nature, *and fall not under human understanding* (*Lev.* p. 208).

They who deny all incorporeal substances can understand nothing by God, but either nature, not *naturam naturantem [nature naturing]*, that is, a real author of nature, but *naturam naturatam [nature natured]*, that is, the orderly concourse of natural causes (as T.H. seems to intimate), or a fiction of the brain without real being, cherished for advantage and politic ends, as a profitable error, howsoever dignified with the glorious title of *the eternal causes of all things*. …

*Every man therefore ought to consider who is the sovereign prophet, that is to say, who it is that is God's vicegerent upon earth, and hath next under God the authority of governing Christian men* … (*Lev.* p. 232). Upon his principles the case holds as well among Jews and Turks and heathens, as Christians. Then he that teaches transubstantiation in France, is a true prophet, he that teaches it in England, a false prophet. Then Samuel was a false prophet to contest with

Saul a sovereign prophet (1 Sam. 15). So was the man of God who submitted not to the more divine and prophetic spirit of Jeroboam (1 Kings 13). And Elijah for reproving Ahab (1 Kings 18). Then Micaiah had but his deserts to be clapped up in prison and fed with bread of affliction and water of affliction, for daring to contradict *God's Vicegerent upon earth* (2 Chron. 18). And Jeremiah was justly thrown into a dungeon, for prophesying against Zedekiah his liege lord (Jer. 38). If his principles were true, it were strange indeed, that none of all these princes, nor any other that ever was in the world, should understand their own privileges. And yet more strange, that God Almighty should take the part of such rebellious prophets, and justify their prophesies by the event, if it were true that *none but the sovereign in a Christian … commonwealth can take notice what is or what is not the word of God* (*Lev.* p. 250). …

And howsoever in words he deny all resistance to the sovereign, yet indeed he admits it. *No man is bound by his pacts whatsoever they be, not to resist him, who brings upon him death or wounds, or other bodily damage* (*DC* 2.18). (By this learning, the scholar, if he be able, may take the rod out of his master's hand and whip him.) It follows: *seeing therefore no man is bound to that which is impossible, they who are to suffer death or wounds or rather corporeal damage, and are not constant enough to endure them, are not obliged to suffer them.* And more fully: *In case a great many men together have already resisted the sovereign power unjustly, or committed some capital crime, for which every one of them expects death, whether have they not the liberty to join together, and assist and defend one another? Certainly they have, for they do but defend their lives, which the guilty man may as well do, as the innocent. There was indeed injustice in the first breach of their duty. Their bearing of arms subsequent to it, though it be to maintain what they have done, is no new unjust act* (*Lev.* p. 112). Why should we not change the name of *Leviathan* into the *Rebel's Catechism*? Observe the difference between the primitive spirit, and the Hobbian spirit. The Theban Legion of known valour in a good cause, when they were able to resist, did choose rather to be cut in pieces to a man, than defend themselves against their Emperor by arms, because they would rather die innocent, than live nocent [guilty]. But T.H. allows rebels and conspirators to make good their unlawful attempts by arms. Was there ever such a trumpeter of rebellion heard of before? Perhaps he may say that he allows them not to justify their unlawful acts, but to defend themselves. First this is contrary to himself, for he allows them *to maintain what they had unjustly done.* This is too much and too intolerable, but this is not all. Secondly, if they chance to win the field, [then] who must suffer for their faults? Or who dare thenceforward call their acts unlawful? …

His … [next] excess is a grievous one, that *before the institution of a commonwealth, every man had a right to do whatsoever he thought necessary to his own preservation, subduing, hurting, or killing any man, in order thereunto.* And *this is the foundation of that right of punishing which is exercised in every commonwealth* (*Lev.* p. 161). And his sentence in brief is this; that if the magistrate do examine and condemn the delinquent, then it is properly punishment; if not, it is an hostile act, but both are justifiable. Judge reader, whether thou wilt trust St. Paul or T.H. St. Paul tells us, that the magistrate is *the ordinance of God, the minister of God, the revenger of God* (Rom. 13:2, 13:4), the sword-bearer of God *to execute wrath upon him that does evil.*

No, says T.H.; punishment is not an act of the magistrate as he is a magistrate, or as he is an officer of God to do justice, or a revenger of evil deeds; but as he is the only private man who has not laid down his natural right to kill any man at his own discretion, if he do but suspect that he may prove noisome to him, or conceive it necessary for his own preservation. Who ever heard of such a right before, so repugnant to the laws of God and Nature? But observe reader what is the result of it, that the sovereign may lawfully kill any of his subjects, or as many of them as he pleases, without any fault of theirs, without any examination on his part, merely upon suspicion of the least crime, if he do but judge him to be hurtful or noisome, as freely as a man may pluck up a weed, because it hinders the nourishment of better plants. *Before the institution of a commonwealth every one may lawfully be spoiled or killed by every one, but in a commonwealth only by one* (*DC* 10.1), that is the sovereign. And *by the right of nature we destroy without being unjust, all that is noxious, both beasts and men.* He makes no difference between a Christian and a wolf. Would you know what is noxious with him, even *whatsoever he thinks can annoy him* (Q p. 116 and 140)? Who would not desire to live in his commonwealth, where the sovereign may lawfully kill a thousand innocents every morning to his breakfast? Surely this is a commonwealth of fishes, where the great ones eat the lesser.

It were strange if his subjects should be in a better condition for their fortunes than they are for their lives, no I warrant you; do but hear him. *Thy dominion and thy property is so great, and lasts so long, as the commonwealth* (that is, the sovereign) *will* (*DC* 12.7). Perhaps he means in some extraordinary cases? Tush, in all cases, and at all times. When thou did choose a sovereign, even in choosing him thou made him a deed of gift of all thou has. *Et tu ergo tuum jus civitate concessisti, and therefore thou has granted all thy right to the commonwealth.* (Ibid.) …

Another of his whimsies is: *that no law can be unjust; by a good law I mean, not just a law, for no law can be unjust, etc. It is in the laws of the commonwealth, as in the laws of gaming. Whatsoever the gamesters all agree on, is injustice to none of them* (*Lev.* p. 182). An opinion absurd in itself, and contradictory to his own ground. There may be laws tending to the contumely of God, to atheism, to denial of God's providence, to idolatry, all which he confesses to be crimes of high treason against God. There may be laws against the law of nature, which he acknowledges to be the *divine law, eternally, immutable, which God hath made known to all men, by his eternal word born in themselves, that is to say, natural reason* (*DC* 14.4) … The true ground of this and many other of his mistakes, is this, that he fancies no reality of any natural justice or honesty, nor any relation to the law of God or nature, but only to the laws of the commonwealth. So from one absurdity being admitted, many others are apt to follow.

His economics are no better than his politics. He teaches parents *that they cannot be injurious to their children, so long as they are in their power* (*DC* 9.7). Yes, too many ways, both by omission and commission. He teaches mothers *that they may cast away their infants, or expose them at their own discretion lawfully* (*DC* 9.2) …

What horrid doctrines are these? It may be he will tell us that he speaks only of the state of mere nature, but he does not; for he speaks expressly of commonwealths and parallels fathers with kings and lords, to whom he ascribes absolute dominion, who have no place in his state of mere nature; for therein, according to his grounds, the children have as much privilege to kill their parents, as the parents to kill their children, seeing he supposes it to be a state of war of all men against men.

And if he did speak of the state of mere nature, it were all one. For first his state of mere nature is a drowsy dream of his own feigning, which looks upon *men as if they were suddenly grown out of the ground like mushrooms* (*DC* 8.1). The primogenious and most natural state of mankind was in Adam before his fall, that is, the state of innocence. Or suppose we should give way to him to expound himself of the state of corrupted nature, that was in Adam and his family after his fall. But there was no such state of mere nature as he imagines. There was religion, there were laws, government, society; and if there ever were any such barbarous savage rabble of men, as he supposes, in the world, it is both untrue and dishonorable to the God of nature, to call it the state of mere nature, which is the state of degenerated nature. He might as well call an hydropical distemper, contracted by intemperance or any other disease of that nature, the natural state of men. But there never was any such degenerate rabble of men in the world, that were without all religion, all government, all laws, natural and civil, no, not amongst the most barbarous Americans (who except some few criminal habits, which those poor degenerate people, deceived by national custom, do hold for noble) have more principles of natural piety, and honesty, and morality, than are readily to be found in his writings. As for the times of civil war, they are so far from being without all pacts and governors, that they abound overmuch with pacts and governors making policy not only to seem, but to be double. …

How repugnant is this which he says of the mother's dominion over her children, to the law of nations? By the law of the twelve tables a father might sell his child twice, *bis vanum dicat*. The mother had no hand in it. Neither does the judicial laws of the Jews, dissent from this (Exod. 21. 7). *If a man sell his daughter to be a maid servant* (Num. 30. 4). So likewise a child's vow might be invalidated by the authority of a father, but not of a mother. …

My … harping-iron is aimed at the head of his Leviathan, or the rational part of his discourse, to show that his principles are contradictory one to another, and consequently destructive one of another. It is his own observation: *That which takes away the reputa-*

*tion of wisdom in him that formeth a religion or addeth to it when it is already formed is the enjoining of a belief of contradictories; for both parts of a contradiction cannot possibly be true. And therefore to enjoin the belief of them, is an argument of ignorance* (*Lev.* p. 58). How he will free himself from his own censure, I do not understand; let the reader judge.

He affirms that an hereditary kingdom is the best form of government: *We are made subjects to him upon the best condition, whose interest it is that we should be safe and sound. And this comes to pass when we are the sovereign's inheritance* (that is, in an hereditary kingdom), *for every one does of his own accord study to preserve his own inheritance* (*DC* 10.18). Now let us hear him retract all this: *There is no perfect form of government where the disposing of the succession is not in the present sovereign* (*Lev.* p. 99). And whether he *transfer it by testament, or give it, or sell it, it is rightly disposed* (*DC* 9.13; *Lev.* p. 193).

He affirms *that which is said in the Scripture, it is better to obey God than man, has place in the kingdom of God by pact, and not by nature.* [*Lev.* 193] One can scarcely meet with a more absurd senseless paradox, that in God's own kingdom of nature (where he supposes all men equal, and no governor but God) it should not be better to obey God than man, the Creator than the created, the sovereign rather than a fellow-subject. Of the two it had been the less absurdity to have said that it had place in the kingdom of God by nature, and not by pact, because in the kingdom of God by pact, sovereigns are as *mortal gods.*

Now let us see him Penelope-like, unweave in the night what he had woven in the day: *It is manifest enough, that when man receives two contrary commands, and knows that one of them is God's, he ought to obey that, and not the other, though it be the command even of his lawful sovereign* (*Lev.* p. 321). Take another place more express, speaking of the first kingdom of God by pact with Abraham, etc. He has these words: *Nor was there any contract which could add to, or strengthen the obligation, by which both they and all man else were bound naturally to obey God Almighty* (*Lev.* p. 249). And before any such kingdom of God by pact, *As the moral law they were already obliged, and needed not have been contracted withal.* (Ibid.) He fancies that God reigns by pact over Adam and Eve, but *this pact became presently void* (*DC* 6.2. and 6.1). And if it had stood firm, what kingdom of God by nature could have been before it? But he reckons his kingdom of God by pact from Abraham, *from him the kingdom of God by pact takes its beginning*. But in Abraham's time, and before his time, the world was full of kings; every city had a king; was it not better for their subjects to obey God than them? Yet that was the kingdom of God by nature, or no kingdom of God at all.

Sometimes he says the laws of nature are laws: *whose laws (such of them as oblige all mankind) and in respect of God, as he is the god of nature, are natural, in respect of the same God, as he is King of Kings, are laws* (*Lev.* p. 185); and *right reason is a law* (*DC* 2.1). And he defines the law of nature to be *the dictate of right reason*. Where by the way observe what he makes to be the end of the laws of nature: *the long conservation of our lives and members, so much as in our power*. By this the reader may see what he believes of honesty, or the life to come. At other times he says that they are no laws.[1] *Those which we call the laws of nature, being nothing else but certain conclusions understood by reason of things to be done; or to be left undone. And a law, if we speak properly and accurately, is the speech that commands something by right to others, to be done, or not to be done, speaking properly, they are not laws, as they proceed from nature* (*DC* 3.33).

It is true, he adds in the same place, that *as they are given by God in holy Scripture, they are most properly called laws, for the holy Scripture is the voice of God ruling all things for the greatest right*. But this will not solve the contradiction, for so the laws of nature shall be no laws to any but those who have read the Scripture, contrary to the sense of all the world. And even in this he contradicts himself also. *The Bible is a law? to whom? to all the world; he knows it is not: how came it then to be a law to us? Did God speak it* vive voce *to us? Have we any other warrant for it than the word of the prophets? Have we seen the miracles? Have we any other assurance of their certainty, than the authority of the Church?* (Q p. 136.) And so he concludes that the authority of the Church is the authority of the commonwealth, the authority of the commonwealth, the authority of the sovereign, and his authority was given him by us. And so *the Bible was made law by the assent of the subjects*. (Ibid.) And *the Bible is their only*

1 According to Bramhall, Hobbes contradicts himself by holding that the laws of nature are laws and that they are not laws.

*law, where the civil Sovereign has made it so* (*Lev.* p. 332). Thus in seeking to prove one contradiction we have met with two.

He teaches: *that the laws of nature are eternal and immutable, that which they forbid can never be lawful, that which they command never unlawful* (*DC* 3.29). At other times he teaches, that *in war, and especially in a war of all men against all men, the laws of nature are silent* (*DC* 5.2). And that they do not oblige as laws, before there be a commonwealth constituted. *When a commonwealth is once settled, then are they actually laws, and not before* (*Lev.* p. 138).

He says *true religion consists in obedience to Christ's lieutenants, and in giving God such honour, both in attributes and actions, as they in their several lieutenancies, shall ordain* (Q pp. 334, 341). Which lieutenant upon earth is the *supreme civil magistrate.* And yet contrary to this he excepts from the obedience due to sovereign princes, *all things that are contrary to the laws of God, who rules over rulers.* Adding that *we cannot rightly transfer the obedience due to him upon men* (*DC* 6.13). And more plainly, *If a sovereign shall command himself to be worshipped with divine attributes and actions, as such as imply an independence upon God, or immortality, or infinite power, to pray unto them being absent, or to ask those things of them which only God can give, to offer sacrifice, or the like. Although Kings command us we must abstain* (*DC* 15.18). He confesses *that the subjects of Abraham had sinned, if they had denied the existence or providence of God, or done anything that was expressly against the honour of God, in obedience to his commands* (*DC* 16.17). And *actions that are naturally signs of contumely cannot be made by human power a part of divine worship, cannot be parts of divine worship* (*Lev.* p. 192), and yet religion may consist in such a worship, is a contradiction.

He confesses *that if the commonwealth should command a subject to say or do something that is contumelious unto God, or should forbid him to worship God, he ought not to obey* (*DC* 15.18). And yet maintaineth *that a Christian holding firmly in the faith of Christ in his heart, if he be commanded by his lawful sovereign, may deny Christ with his tongue*, alleging, *that profession with the tongue is but an external thing.* And *that it is not he in that case, who denies Christ before men, but his governor, and the law of his country* (*Lev.* p. 271). Hath he so soon forgot himself? Is not the denial of Christ contumelious to God?

He affirms that *if a sovereign shall grant to a subject any liberty inconsistent with sovereign power, if the subject refuse to obey the sovereign's command, being contrary to the liberty granted, it is a sin, and contrary to his duty, for he ought to take notice of what is inconsistent with sovereignty, etc. And that such liberty was granted through ignorance of the evil consequence thereof* (*Lev.* p. 157). Then a subject may judge not only what is fit for his own preservation, but also what are the essential rights of sovereignty, which is contrary to his doctrine elsewhere. *It belongs to kings to discern what is good and evil; and private men, who take to themselves the knowledge of good and evil, do covet to be as kings, which consisteth not with the safety of the commonwealth* (*DC* 12.1); which he calls *a seditious doctrine*, and one of the *diseases of a commonwealth* (*Lev.* p. 168). Yet such is his forgetfulness that he himself licenses his own book *for the press*, and to *be taught in the universities*, as containing nothing contrary to the *word of God or good manners*, or to *the disturbance of public tranquility* (*Lev.* p. 395). Is not this to take to himself the knowledge of good and evil?

In one place he says that *the just power of sovereigns is absolute, and to be limited by the strength of the commonwealth, and nothing else* (*DC* 6.18). In other places he says his power is to be limited by the laws of God and nature. As *there is that in heaven, though not on earth, which he should stand in fear of, and whose laws he ought to obey* (*Lev.* p. 167). And *it is true, that sovereigns are all subject to the laws of nature, because such laws be divine, and cannot by any man or commonwealth be abrogated* (*Lev.* pp. 199, 169). In one place he maintains that *all men by nature are equal among themselves* (*DC* 1.3). In another place, that *the father of every man was originally his sovereign Lord, with power over him of life and death* (*Lev.* p. 178). …

I chanced to say, that if a child, before he have the use of reason, shall kill a man in his passion; yet because he had no malice to incite him to it nor reason to restrain him from it, he shall not die for it in the strict rules of particular justice, unless there be some mixture of public justice in the case, showing only what was the law, not what was my opinion. An innocent child for terror to others, in some cases may be deprived of those honours and inheritances, which were to have descended upon him from his father, but not of his life. Amazia slew the murderers of the king his father,[1] ... *All punishments of innocent subjects, be they great or little, are against the law of nature. For punishment is only for transgression of the law, and therefore can be no punishment of the innocent* (2 Chron. 25:4). Yet within a few lines after he changes his note. *In subjects who deliberately deny the authority of the commonwealth established, the vengeance is lawfully extended, not only to the fathers, but also to the third and fourth generation.* (Ibid.) His reason is because *this offence consists in renouncing of subjection: so they suffer not as subjects, but as enemies.* Well, but the children were born subjects as well as the father, and they never renounced their subjection, how come they to lose their birth-right, and their lives for their fathers' fault, if there can be no punishment of the innocent; so the contradiction stands still.

But all this is but a copy of his countenance, I have showed formerly expressly out of his principles, *that the foundation of the right of punishing, exercised in every commonwealth,* is not the right of the sovereign for crimes committed, but *that right which every man by nature had to kill every man.* Which right, he says, every subject has renounced, but the sovereign, by whose authority punishment is inflicted, hath not. So if he do examine the crime in justice, and condemn the delinquent, then is properly punishment. If he do not, then it is an hostile act, but both ways just and allowable. Reader, if thou please to see what a slippery memory he has, [then] for thine own satisfaction, read over the beginning of the eight and twentieth chapter of his *Leviathan.* Innocents cannot be justly punished, but justly killed upon his principles.

But this very man, who would seem so zealous sometimes for human justice, that there can be no just punishment, but for crimes committed, how stands he affected to divine justice? He regards it not at all, grounding everywhere God's right to afflict the creatures upon his omnipotence: and maintaining that God may as justly afflict with eternal torments without sin, as for sin. *Though God have power to afflict a man, and not for sin, without injustice, shall we think God so cruel, as to afflict a man, and not for sin, with extreme and endless torments? Is it not cruelty? No more than to do the*

1 Amazia [Amaziah] reigned as king of Judah from around 800 B.C. to about 783. He was the son of King Joash [Jehoash], not to be confused with King Jehoash of Israel.

*same for sin, when he that afflicts might without trouble have kept him from sinning* (Q p. 13). Whether God do afflict eternally, or punish eternally; whether the sovereign proceed judicially, or in a hostile way, so it be not for any crime committed; it is all one as to the justice of God and the sovereign, and all one as to the sufferings of the innocent. But *it may and doth often happen in commonwealths that a subject may be put to death by the command of the sovereign power, and yet neither do the other wrong* (*Lev.* p. 105); that is to say, both be innocent, for that is the whole scope of the place. It is against the law of nature to punish innocent subjects, says one place, but innocent subjects may lawfully be killed or put to death, says another.

Sometimes he makes the institution of sovereignty to be only the laying down the right of subjects, which they had by nature. *For he who renounces or passes away his right, gives not to any other man, a right which he had not before, because there is nothing to which every man had not right by nature, but only stands out of his way, that he may enjoy his own original right, without hindrance from another* (*Lev.* p. 65). And elsewhere, *The subjects did not give the sovereign that right, but only in laying down theirs, strengthened him to use his own, etc.* (*Lev.* p. 162). *So it was not given, but left to him, and to him only. And the translation of right doth consist only in not resisting* (*DC* 2.4). He might as well have said, and with as much sense: *the transferring of right doth consist in not transferring of right.*[1] At other times he makes it to be a surrender, *or giving up of the subjects right to govern himself to this man. A conferring of all their power and strength upon one man, that may reduce all their wills by plurality of voices to one will. An appointing of one man to bear their person, and acknowledge themselves to be the authors of whatsoever the sovereign shall act, or cause to be acted in those things which concern the common safety; a submission of their wills to his will, their judgements to his judgement* (*Lev.* p. 87). And *David did no injury to Uriah, because the right to do what he pleased, was given him by Uriah himself* (*Lev.* p. 109). Before we had a transferring without transferring; now we have a giving up without giving up, an appointing or constituting, without appointing or constituting, a subjection without subjection, an authorizing without authorizing. What is this?

---

1 According to Bramhall, Hobbes contradicts himself by holding that people give up their rights to govern themselves, and that they do not give up this right.

He says that *it cannot be said honourably of God, that he has parts or totality, which are the attributes of finite things* (*DC* 15.14). If it cannot be said honourably of God that he has parts or totality, then it cannot be said honourably of God that he is a body; for every body has parts and totality. Now hear what he says, *Every part of the universe is body; and that which is no body, is no part of the universe. And because the universe is all that which is no part of it, is nothing* (*Lev.* p. 371). Then if God have no parts and totality, God is nothing. Let him judge how honourable this is for God. …

He says, *Christ had not a kingly authority committed to him by his father in the world, but only consiliary and doctrinal* (*DC* 17.6). He says on the contrary *that the kingdom of Judea was his hereditary right from King David, etc. And when it pleased him to play the king, he required entire obedience* (Matt. 21.2), *Go into the village over against you, and straightaway ye shall find an ass tied, and a colt with her, loose them and bring them unto me. And if any man say ought unto you, ye shall say, the Lord hath need of them* (*DC* 11.6).

He says, *the institution of eternal punishment was before sin* (*DC* 4.9) and *if the command be such as cannot be obeyed without being damned to eternal death, then it were madness to obey it* (*Lev.* p. 321). And *what evil hath excommunication in it, but the consequent, eternal punishment?* (*DC* 17.25). At other times he says there is no eternal punishment. *It is evident that there shall be a second death of every one that shall be condemned at the day of Judgement, after which he shall die no more* (*Lev.* p. 245). He who knoweth no soul nor spirit, may well be ignorant of a spiritual death.

A principal cause of his errors is a fancying to himself a general state of nature, which is so far from being general, that there is not an instance to be found of it in the nature of things, where mankind was altogether without laws and without governors, guided only by self interest, without any sense of conscience, justice, honesty, or honour. He may search all the corners of America with a candle and lantern at noon day, and after his fruitless pains, return a *non est inventus [it has not been found]*.

Yet all plants and living creatures are subject to degenerate and grow wild by degrees. Suppose it should so happen that some remnant of men, either chased by war or persecution or forced out of the habitable world for some crimes by themselves committed or being cast by shipwreck upon some desert, by long conversing with savage beasts, lions, bears, wolves and tigers, should in time becomes more brutish (it is his own epithet) than the brutes themselves, would any man in his right wits make that to be the universal condition of mankind, which was only the condition of an odd handful of men or that to be the state of nature, which was not the state of nature, but an accidental degeneration?

He that will behold the state of the nature rightly, must look upon the family of Adam and his posterity in their successive generations from the creation to the deluge and from the deluge until Abraham's time, when the first kingdom of God by pact as supposed by T.H. to begin. All this while (which was a great part of that time the world has stood) from the creation lasted the kingdom of God by nature, as he phrases it. And yet in those days there were laws and government, and more kings in the world, than there are at this present. We find nine kings engaged in one war; and yet all their dominions but a narrow circuit of land (Gen. 14). And so it continued for diverse hundreds of years after, as we see by all those kings which Joshua discomfited in and of Canaan. Every city had its own king. The reason is evident; the original right of fathers of families was not then extinguished.

Indeed T.H. supposes that men did spring out of the earth like mushrooms or mandrakes: *That we may return again to the state of nature, and consider men as if they were even now suddenly sprouted and grown out of the earth, after the manner of mushrooms, without any obligation of one to another* (*DC* 8.1). But this supposition is both false and atheistical, howsoever it dropped from his pen. Mankind did not spring out of the earth, but was created by God, not many suddenly, but one to whom all his posterity were obliged as to their father and ruler.

A second ground of his errors is his gross mistake of the laws of nature, which he relates most imperfectly, and most untruly. A moral heathen would blush for shame to see such a catalogue of the laws of nature.

First he makes the laws of nature to be laws and no laws: just as *a man and no man, hit a bird and no bird, with a stone and no stone, on a tree and no tree*: not *laws* but *theorems*, laws which require not *performance* but *endeavors*, laws which were silent, and could not be put in execution in the state of nature. *Where nothing was another man's, and therefore a man could not steal; where all things were common, and therefore no adultery; where there was a state of war, and therefore it was lawful to kill; where all things were defined by a man's own judgement, and therefore what honors he pleased to give unto his father; and lastly, where there were no public judgements, and therefore no use of witnesses* (*DC* 14.9). As for the first table he does not trouble himself much with it, except it be to accommodate it unto kings. Every one of these grounds here alleged are most false, without any verisimilitude in them; and so his superstructure must needs fall flat to the ground.

Secondly he relates the laws of nature most imperfectly, smothering and concealing all those principal laws, which concern either piety, and our duty towards man.

Thirdly, sundry of those laws which he is pleased to take notice of are either misrelated or misinterpreted by him. He makes the only end of all the laws of nature to be *the long conservation of a man's life and members*, most untruly. He makes every man by nature *the only judge of the means of his own conservation*, most untruly. His father and sovereign in the weightiest cases is more judge than himself. He says that *by the law of nature every man has right to all things, and over all persons*, most untruly. He says the natural condition of mankind is *a war of all men against all men*, most untruly. And that *nature dictates to us to relinquish this* feigned *right of all men to all things*, most untruly. And that *nature dictates to a man to retain his right of preserving his life and limbs, though against a lawful magistrate*, lawfully proceeding, most untruly. I omit his uncouth doctrine about pacts made in the state of nature, and that he knoweth no gratitude, but where there is a trust, *fiducia*. These things are unsound, and the rest of his laws, for the most part, poor trivial things, in comparison of those weightier dictates of nature, which he has omitted.

All other writers of politics do derive commonwealths from the sociability of nature, which is in mankind, most truly. But he will have the beginning of all human society to be from mutual fear, as much contrary to reason as to authority. We see some kind of creatures delight altogether in solitude, rarely, or never in company. We see others (among which is mankind), delight altogether in company, rarely, or never in solitude. Let him tell me what mutual fear of danger did draw the silly bees into swarms; or the sheep and doves into flocks; and what protection they can hope for, one from another? and I shall conceive it possible, that the beginning of human society might be from fear also.

And thus having invented a fit foundation for his intended building, ycleped [called] *the state of mere nature*, which he himself first devised for that purpose, he hath been long modeling and framing to himself a new form of policy, to be built upon it. But the best is, it has only been in paper. All this while he has never had a finger in mortar. This is the new frame of *absolute sovereignty*, which T.H. knew right well would never stand; nor he should be ever permitted to rear it up in our European climes [territory] or in any other part of the habitable world, which had ever seen any other form of civil government. Therefore he has sought out for a fit place in America, among the savages, to try if perhaps they might be persuaded that the laws of God and nature, the names of good and evil, just and unjust, did signify nothing but at the pleasure of the sovereign prince.

And because there has been much clashing in these quarters about religion, through the distempered zeal of some, the seditious orations of other, and some pernicious principles, well meant at first, but ill understood, and worse pursued. To prevent all such garboiles [disturbances] in his commonwealth, he has taken an order to make his sovereign to be *Christ's lieutenant upon earth, in obedience to whose commands true religion doth consist.*[1] Thus making policy to be the building, and religion the hangings, which must be fashioned just according to the proportion of the policy; and (not as Mr. [Thomas] Cartwright[2] would have had it) making religion to be the building, and policy the hangings, which must be conformed to religion.

Well the law is costly, and I am for an accommodation, that T.H. should have the sole privilege of setting up his form of gov-

---

1 See 42.11.

2 Thomas Cartwright (c. 1535-1603), Calvinist theologian who had a famous debate (1574-7) with John Whitgift. Cartwright's views were presbyterian, and he held that church and state were independent while Whitgift upheld the official view of the Church of England.

ernment in America, as being calculated and fitted for that meridian. And if it prosper there, then to have the liberty to transplant it hither: who knows (if there could but be some means devised to make them understand his language) whether the Americans might not choose him to be their sovereign? But all the fear is that if he should put his principles in practice, as magisterially as he does dictate them, his supposed subjects might chance to tear their *mortal God* in pieces with their teeth, and entomb his sovereignty [in] their bowels.

# *Appendix D: From William Lucy,* Observations, Censures and Confutations of Notorious Errours in Mr. Hobbes His Leviathan

William Lucy (1594-1677) received his B.A. from Trinity College, Oxford, and then studied law at Lincoln's Inn. He never practiced because he took a position at Caius College, Cambridge. He became bishop of St. David's at the Restoration. His *Observations, Censures and Confutations of Notorious Errours in the 12, 13, and 14 Chapters of Mr Hobs*[1] *His Leviathan* appeared in 1657, under the pseudonym William Pyke, Christophilus [lover of Christ]. It was enlarged and republished with a simpler title — the chapter allusions were dropped — in 1663. Lucy was a conventional thinker of the mid-seventeenth century, an Arminian in theology and an Aristotelian scholastic in philosophy. Hobbes refers to Lucy, under the name "Pike," in *Considerations Upon the Reputation and Loyalty, Manners, and Religion of Thomas Hobbes* (ed. Molesworth, vol. 4, p. 435) and *Six Lessons to the Savilian Professors of the Mathematics* (ed. Molesworth, vol. 7, p. 354).

### *Observations, Censures and Confutations of Notorious Errours in Mr. Hobbes His Leviathan, and other his Bookes*

[Hobbes says] *every man hath so much experience, as to have seen the Sun, or other visible objects, by reflection in the water, and the glasses, and this alone is sufficient for this conclusion, that* color *and* image *may be there where the thing seen is not* [*Elements of Law, Natural and Politic,* Part 1, c. 2, sec. 5] ... He should have proved first that color and image are the same, which he knows is denied by all his adversaries; color is in the object of sight, but there is no need of the image, where the substance is, nor can the image of color be in the same subject with the color. ... I say then that color is in the object, but image is not. ...

But he [Hobbes] urgeth again that *diverse times men see the same*

1 Hobbes's name was spelled in various ways. I have retained the spelling that exists in the text.

*object double, as two candles for one, which may happen by distemper* [ibid.] … I answer to this that this double sight may be two ways, either by a distemper of the organ or by a false reflection in the medium. The first I have had and have been cured by physick. The second is easy, for there may be multiplying glasses, and many such instruments, which may deliver the species double, and then the color or object must appear such; but here is no reason to prove that the color is not in the object, because *Quicquid recipitur, recipitur ad modum recipientis [Whatever is received is received according to the mode of the thing receiving]*. If the eye be indisposed, it must needs follow that the species shall be qualified accordingly. And for the medium or middle place or mean, which transports the species to the eye, it must needs be that the liquor will taste of that tap out of which it runs; that every story is enlarged or lessened, multiplied or diminished, according to the disposition of the deliverer, and so the indisposition of the medium varying the species, it must needs be that the color must appear such, although it be other. … [T]he image or species … is not in the object, but the color is.

He [Hobbes] begins thus: *The fool hath said in his heart there is no such thing as justice; and sometimes also with his tongue seriously alleging that every man's conservation and contentment being committed to his care, there could be no reason why every man might not do what he thought conduced thereunto; and therefore also to make or not make, keep or not keep, covenants, was not against reason, when it conduced to one's benefit* [p. 72]. Thus he makes the fool to confirm his wicked conclusion; and for my part, I think the fool's argument is unanswerable, out of Mr Hobbes his principles. For if it be true, as he hath supposed, that every man hath a natural right to every thing, and every man's conservation and contentment is committed to his own charge, and that no man can renounce by any covenant his right to defend himself from death, wounds, imprisonment, which he delivered in his 66 page … then he can by no covenant be obliged to forsake any thing, but only such little things as are scarcely considerable in justice.

… If a man take from any act or habit those circumstances which make it evil, [then] it will be good; but I am persuaded that a fear of God is so rooted in the hearts of men, that although men may darken the light, and clear light out of it, with wicked reasoning; although men may hinder the vivacity in the opposition of it, by customary inhabiting, reigning sins; yet it cannot be so extirpated, but that it will appear and break out sometimes in action. And although a fool or wicked man may sometimes *say so*; yet other times he will not believe his own words, and must oft fear he is in the wrong. This kind of reasoning either Mr. Hobbes taught, or learned from him; for I am persuaded never man disputed so high conclusions out of such impossible supposals, as he hath; such is this, *if there were no fear of God*. Let us see the force of the fool's argument; it seems to affirm that injustice, *taking away the fear of God, will stand with that reason which dictateth to every man his own good*; I am persuaded it is good when injustice may be committed where is no commonwealth, when men commit injustice so secretly that no magistrate may take notice of it; for if no God, no heaven or hell … for good or ill actions; and then a man's considerations are chiefly about his own ease, pleasure, and contentment in his bodily and sensitive life; but yet I must add one restraint to the fool's proposition. Injustice may stand with that reason which prescribes his own good, that is, his pleasure or contentment; but not with right reason, for right reason prefers the public good before the private, which cannot subsist without justice. …

The question, according to his [Hobbes's] own framing is *whether it be profitable to deceive or not*; his answer is drawn from a declaration that that man [the fool] should make, [namely] *that he thinks it fit to deceive*, which no man but a verier [bigger] fool than he … did ever do.[1] There is no power to act any great wickedness; but under the show of piety, not by professing to deceive, but by professing not to deceive. Oaths, covenants, protestations, cursing of themselves, are the horrid masks of impiety, which wicked men use to deceive with. The devil can no way so efficaciously deceive, as by putting on the shape or likeness of an angel; … sometimes

1 Lucy is calling attention to an ambiguity in Hobbes's discussion of the problem of the fool. If the fool is clever, he will not tell people that he thinks it is right to deceive them. And against this fool, Hobbes has no good answer, according to Lucy. But in the passage that Lucy alludes to, "he which declares he thinks it reason to deceive those that help him can in reason expect no other means of safety" (15.5), the fool is foolish because he admits to being a deceiver. Although Hobbes is able to refute this foolish fool, he fails to refute the clever fool, a person all too well-known in the world.

urging the Scripture itself, as with our Savior. That child of the devil, who will prosper in this world, must not protest and declare that he will deceive, but protest against it. …

Now my conclusion is that all deceit is injustice, all injustice unprofitable, because against the most sacred lawmaker, who will avenge it here or hereafter, whether men take notice of it or no. Evil and injustice will hunt the wicked person; only honesty and justice will bring a man peace and prosperity at the last. …

*A person is he who doth or speaks any thing* [p. 80], and this is as full as his [Hobbes's definition]; for whosoever doth or speaks his words or deeds are considered either as his own or another's … *When they are considered as his own* (that is, those actions or words) *then is he called a* Natural Person; *and when they are considered as representing the words and actions of another then he is a* feigned *or* artificial person. Thus may a man be distinguished into a true and counterfeit[1] man; and no more than the picture or the image of a man is a true man, no more is *a feigned or artificial person,* a true *person*; and yet this *feigned or artificial person* does as fully agree to his definition, as the *true person*; which shows the definition to be to blame. The *metaphysicians* have an undoubted axiom, that *ens* and *verum convertuntur [being* and *truth are interchangeable]*; what is not truly such is not such. If then such a man, whom he names be but a *feigned person,* he is not a *person truly,* and then not *a person*; yet we shall find him endeavoring to set him out, as the only *true person,* presently afterward with his grammar rules. …

*So* (saith he) *that a* person *is the same that an* actor *is, both on the stage and in common conversation; and, to* personate, *is to* act *or* represent *himself or another*. This is it I foretold you of, that although a *feigned* thing cannot be a *true* thing, yet he makes the *feigned* only the true, and the *representer* only to be the true *person,* not to be who is *represented*; and although in his definition he said that *a person is he whose words or actions are considered as his own, etc.* and in his following division there was a *natural* and a *feigned* person; yet here he makes all persons *feigned,* and their words or actions to be others. If he answer that his words were *represent himself or another,*

1 Lucy is unfairly taking 'feigned' to mean 'counterfeit' and thus concluding that a feigned or artificial person is not really a person. By 'feigned' in 'feigned person' Hobbes simply means a person who is created by human beings.

then if he *act himself,* it is enough to constitute him a person. I reply that what it is to *act himself,* he has expressed in the words immediately preceding, *a person is the same that an actor is, both on the Stage and in common conversation.* Now no man can properly be said to *act himself* or *represent himself,* for the actor and the acted, the representer and the represented are two. He proceeds, *and he that acteth another is said to bear his person, or act in his name.* Very true, but if he bears *another's person,* the *other* is the *person,* not he that bears it. The constable bears [and] represents the person of a King, but is not his person; so doth a player; this makes all against himself, … [Hobbes] labors to show that the representer is the person, but his argument proves only the represented is the person; and this we shall find in the ancient tragedies and comedies put out. The critics, which puts them out, calls the *persons* those which were *represented,* not the *actors,* as is to be seen in *Seneca* and *Terence,* etc.; not that I deny this word has sometimes been used by writers, as Mr. *Hobbes* expresses it; but I deny that that is the universal acception of that word, or that Mr *Hobbes* his argument doth show, that it was ever so accepted. But rather clean contrary; the *person* is he who is represented, not the representer. …

A *person* then, taken in the most received conceit [concept] that *divines* and *philosophers* acknowledge is defined by Boethius, [in] *De duabus naturis,* to be *rationalis, naturae individua substantia: An individual substance of a rational nature*: This definition is most generally received, and I doubt not, but it will abide the test, when it is clearly explained, which I shall endeavor to do[1] …

First, a *person* is a *substance;* by that term it is opposed to all *accidents,* and things only *imaginary;* it is an *individual substance,* by that term it is opposed to those [that] are called *second substances,* … as a man or a lion. … The last term in this definition is that it is *rationalis,* of a *reasonable nature*: this word *reasonable* must be understood of any intellectual nature, whether by discourse or else, and so it comprehends all divine, angelical, or whatsoever. … Mr. *Hobbes* [should] have not suffered himself to be transported with the imagination of how this word is used upon the *stage* … [I]n words,

1 Lucy is simply unwilling to consider Hobbes's unconventional definitions of persons. Lucy is refusing to understand 'person' in any sense other than the conventional scholastic definition that originated with Boethius (c. 480–c. 586).

we are not always to consider their etymology, but how they are used. …

In the 82 page, … he saith that *the true God may be personated.* This phrase gave me an amazement, for I cannot call to mind any such expression made either in *Scripture* or orthodox *ecclesiastical* writers, and understanding *personating* in that sense that Mr Hobbes doth. … [T]o say that *the true God may be personated* by any thing which is not God was too great an exaltation of the *creature*, and diminution of his excellency; but yet thus he doth, as appears by his instance *as he was first by* Moses, *who governed the Israelites (that were not his, but God's people) not in his own name with* hoc dicit Moses [Moses says this], *but in God's name with* hoc dicit Dominus [the Lord says this] *first by Moses.* I am persuaded he can never show me that the true God was ever personated by Moses. …

# *Appendix E: From Thomas Tenison,* The Creed of Mr. Hobbes Examined in a Feigned Conference between Him and a Student in Divinity

Thomas Tenison (1636–1715) received his B.A. from Corpus Christi College, Cambridge, and was privately ordained a priest by the bishop of Salisbury about 1659 because the Commonwealth had outlawed the episcopal Church of England. During the Restoration, he was made a fellow of Corpus Christi College, but he also held Church offices that gave him a good living. He became bishop of Lincoln in 1692 and archbishop of Canterbury in 1695.

It was at Corpus Christi College that he became influenced by the Cambridge Platonists, especially Ralph Cudworth. He, like the Cambridge Platonists, abhorred Hobbes's materialism. Thus, in *The Creed of Mr. Hobbes Examined*, published in 1670, Tenison asserts that God is not a body and that Hobbes confuses an idea with an image. Humans can have an idea of God without having an image of him, because, being immaterial, God cannot be sensed.

## *The Creed of Mr. Hobbes Examined in a Feigned Conference between Him and a Student in Divinity*

### Thomas Tenison

I have sometimes heard the substance of them [Hobbes's views] comprised in twelve Articles, which sound harshly to men professing Christianity; and they were delivered under the Title of the *Hobbist's Creed*, in such phrase and order as followeth.

"I believe that God is Almighty matter; that in him there are three Persons, he having been thrice represented on earth; that it is to be decided by the Civil Power, whether he created all things else; that angels are not incorporeal substances (those words implying a contradiction), but preternatural impressions on the brain of man; that the soul of man is the temperament of his body;

that the liberty of will in that soul is physically necessary; that the prime Law of Nature in the soul of man is that of self-love; that the law of the civil sovereign is the obliging rule of good and evil, just and unjust; that the books of the Old and New Testaments are made canon and law by the civil powers; that whatsoever is written in these books, may lawfully be denied even upon oath (after the laudable doctrine and practice of the Gnostics) in times of persecution, when men shall be urged by the menaces of authority; that hell is a tolerable condition of life, for a few years upon earth, to begin at the general resurrection; and that heaven is a blessed estate of good men, like that of Adam before his fall beginning at the general resurrection, to be from thenceforth eternal upon earth in the Holy-Land."...

### [Concerning Ideas, Images, and God]

Student: If God be a body, seeing man may have an image of extension and of all the possible figures, which may be made by the varieties of extension in matter, what hindereth that we may not have, in your gross way, an image of God? But because he is an immaterial substance, we cannot indeed have any bodily remembrance of him; but there is in every man a power to have an idea of him.[1] For, although it hath been said that there have been found whole nations (as in the Western World in Brazil) who have lived without the least suspicion of an infinite being, yet there is no nation so very barbarous, wherein the inhabitants have no faculty at all of exciting in them this idea of God. And here I cannot but reprehend it, as a very shameful error, in a man who placeth truth in the right ordering of names, and pretendeth to begin the sci-

1 Tenison criticizes Hobbes for refusing to recognize a distinction between an image, which is closely connected with sensation, and an idea, which is conceptual. We cannot imagine things that are not material or could not be sensed, but that does not mean that they cannot be conceived of or understood by the human mind, according to Tenison. He thinks that humans have no image of God because God is not a body, but humans can have an idea of God. It is not clear whether Tenison has adequately explained what an idea is: "By [an] idea is understood, not merely a corporeal similitude, but any notion without imagery, and whatsoever occureth in any perception: the very form of cogitation, whereby I become conscious to my self that I have perceived, is an idea."

ences, by settling first the significations of their words, to confound the names of *image* and *idea*, as if they were terms of equal importance. It is also an argument of thickness of mind, of a soul not yet advanced above the power of fancy, to say that no man hath or can have any kind of conception without an image, as if nothing were authentically written upon the table of our minds, without a real and sensible impression affixed to it. … By [an] idea is understood, not merely a corporeal similitude, but any notion without imagery, and whatsoever occureth in any perception: the very form of cogitation, whereby I become conscious to my self that I have perceived, is an idea. … [There is a] difference betwixt the idea of God in a perspicuous mind, and the notion of a God taken through the pictures of imagination.

# *Appendix F: From Samuel Pufendorf,* Of the Law of Nature and Nations

Samuel Pufendorf (1632-1694), born in Saxony, was educated at Leipzig and then Jena. In Jena he read the works of both Hugo Grotius (1583-1645), a famous Dutch political philosopher, and Hobbes. He taught philosophy first at the university in Heidelberg and then at the University of Lund, Sweden. In addition to his university teaching Pufendorf at various times was a tutor and historiographer.

His first book, *Elementorum jurisprudentiae universalis* [*Elements of Universal Jurisprudence*], was published in 1660. His most important book was *De Jure Naturae et Gentium* [*Of the Law of Nature and Nations*], published in 1670. The translation used in this appendix is by Basil Kennett, from the third edition, which appeared in 1717. Pufendorf's goal in *Of the Law of Nature and Nations* was to build on but also to correct, by his lights, the natural law theories of Grotius and Hobbes. From Grotius, Pufendorf took the idea that man was sociable, if not naturally, then at least by necessity, and also the idea that natural law theory can achieve the same rigor as mathematics. On another matter Pufendorf parted with Grotius. Grotius was notorious in some circles for saying that the law of nature would "apply though we should even grant, what without the greatest wickedness cannot be granted, that there is no God, or that he has no care of [providence over] human affairs" ("Prolegomena," *De Iure Belli ac Pacis Libri Tres* [*Three Books on the Law of War and Peace*] 1625). Pufendorf refused to countenance the possibility that God might not exist. From Hobbes, Pufendorf took the idea that human desire for self-preservation was fundamental to natural law and also the idea that natural law theory should argue from *a priori* premises. In contrast to Hobbes, Pufendorf thought that humans were sociable by necessity, as mentioned above.

## *Of the Law of Nature and Nations*

### Samuel Pufendorf

... It may not be improper here to examine that assertion of Mr. Hobbs which he hath laid down in ... his *Leviathan* ... *Now seeing all men, by nature, had a right to all things, they had a right every one of them to reign over all the rest. But because this right could not be obtained by force, it concerned the safety of everyone laying aside that right, to set up men with sovereign authority by common consent to rule and defend them: Whereas if there had been any man of power irresistible, there had been no reason why he should not by that power have ruled and defended both himself and them according to his own discretion.* ... [*Lev.* 187] Now in this discourse there are several things that deserve to be censured. For, in the first place, it may be questioned whether or no those two expressions, *A right of sovereignty* (upon account of strength) *is granted by nature*, and *A right of, etc, is not taken away by nature*, hang very well together. Because in most cases, my not taking away a thing is by no means an argument that I therefore grant it.[1] And since *not to be taken away* and *to be granted* are different things, such a right may seem to be granted by some other principle than nature, though nature doth not *take it away*. Besides, that maxim, *All men by nature had a right to everything*, ought to be interpreted with great caution. By *right* he means liberty, which every man hath of using his natural faculties according to reason. Therefore his principle, in a sound sense, will amount to no more than this: By nature, that is, upon the removal of all law, every man may fairly use his natural strength against those whom his reason instructs him thus to deal with, for the sake of his preservation. But it does not hence follow that barely by natural strength an obligation, properly so called, may be laid on another. For to *compel* and to *oblige* are different matters; and though natural strength may be sufficient for the former, yet the latter cannot be performed by that superiority alone.[2] For even according to Mr. Hobbes's own

1 For example, it may be the case that Ava does not take Bill's apple from him, but she did not give it to him.

2 Obligation is a normative notion. It requires some moral or political force. Compelling something is not a normative notion. It involves only physical force. If a person has an obligation to someone, he does not have a right to resist that person.

notion, as one man hath a right of compelling others, so those others have a right of resisting him. But now obligation cannot stand with a right of resisting, because it presupposes such reasons as inwardly affecting men's consciences make them conclude, by the judgment of their own mind, that they cannot honestly and therefore rightly resist. And though it be irrational to contend violently against a superior strength and by that means to draw upon ourselves greater mischiefs; yet there remains in us a right of trying all ways either to drive off the force by the dexterous application of other force or to elude it by subterfuge and escape. But neither can this right consist with that obligation which is precisely so termed, and which Grotius commonly opposeth to extrinsical. So that, on the whole matter, by bare force, not the right of resistance, but only the exercise of it, is extinguished. ... Mr. Hobbes himself acknowledgeth that a captive of war, although capable of obligation, yet is under none whilst he is restrained only by natural bond and before the interposition of any faith or compact; and that therefore such an one may give his conqueror the slip or may assault him violently, as soon as he finds the opportunity. ...

When we pay those things which are due upon the pact of a society with a member or a member with a society, ... we are said to exercise distributive justice. For whenever a man is received into a society, a pact is either expressly or at least tacitly made between the society and the member now to be introduced, by which the society engageth to give him a just share and proportion of the goods which it enjoys as a common body; and the member promiseth that he will bear his proper and equal part of those burdens which conduce to the preservation of the society, considered as such. The exact determination of the proper share of goods to be assigned to the member is made according to the rule and value of the pains or charges employed by him towards preserving the common society in proportion to the pains or charges contributed by the other members. On the other hand, the determination of the proper share of burdens to be laid on the members is made according to the value of the benefits received by him from the society, considered in proportion to the advantages which the rest of the members enjoy. Hence, since it generally happens that one member contributes more towards the preservation of the society than another and that one likewise exceeds another in deriving advantage from it, the reason is very apparent why, upon the supposal of many persons, and of this inequality amongst them, we ought in the exercise of distributive justice, to observe a comparative equality. ... Thus, for instance, if six things of the same value are to be distributed amongst Caius, Seius, and Titius, upon supposition that Titius exceeds Caius in a triple proportion, and Seius in a double, Titius shall have three, Seius two, and Caius one. Nor is it requisite to this equality that the reward fully answer and come up to the merits of the person. ... And the same rule must be followed in distributing burdens. ...

As for what Mr. Hobbes allegeth to overthrow this *reflective equality*, that *I may of my own goods distribute least to him that deserves most, and most to him that deserves least, provided I pay but for what I bargain for*; and useth the authority of our Savior, in the 20th of St. Matt. ver. 13, etc. to confirm his opinion. All this, if rightly considered, makes nothing to the purpose. For in the place of Scripture cited above, it is shown indeed that he doth not offend against commutative justice (which governs the contracts about hire, etc.) who out of his liberality gives to some a larger reward than their service deserves; or who, to the wages due upon this commutative justice, adds something out of free bounty, which is comprehended under universal justice. ... Mr. Hobbes hath advanced one single notion of justice to comprehend every kind, making it nothing else but a keeping of faith and fulfilling of covenants, which opinion he borrowed from Epicurus. [See Diogenes Laertius, Book 10 near the end.] Commutative justice, he says, takes place in contracts, as in buying and selling, hiring and letting to hire, lending and borrowing, exchanging, bartering, and the like. Distributive justice (though improperly so called) is, he says, *the justice of an arbitrator, which being trusted by them who make him arbitrator, if he perform his trust, he is said to distribute to every man his own*. Nor will he allow any other equality to be observed but this, that since we are all equal by nature, one man ought not to arrogate to himself more right than he allows another, unless he hath obtained a greater right than ordinary, by the intervention of covenants. Farther, since according to his sentiments an injury or an unjust action or omission is nothing else but the violation of a covenant, he hence infers that we cannot offer an injury to a man unless we have before covenanted with him. This assertion is founded on his old maxim of *the right of every man to all things,* which he hath stretched far beyond its just limits; so that he imagines before any covenant is made … every man hath a right of doing to others what he pleaseth; and thus, only using his right, he cannot be said to commit an injury. But … nature allows a man to use all such means as reason shall judge conducible to his firm and lasting preservation, as indeed Mr. Hobbes himself in his definition of right inserts the use of reason. But now sound reason will never advise us, out of our own pleasure and humor, to put such affronts on another, as cannot but provoke him to war or to a reciprocal desire of hurting us. Besides it implies a manifest contradiction to say that upon the supposal of many men equal in rights, each of them hath a right to all things; since the right of one man to all things, if it hath any effect, must extinguish the rights of the rest; and if the right hath no effect upon the others, it is useless, absurd, and ridiculous. For in moral account, *not to be* and *not to be effectual* are much the same. And indeed, how can we call that a right which another may oppose with an equal right? Who would say, *I had the right of commanding a man*, if he, by the same right of commanding a man, might despise my order? Or that I had a right of beating another when he too had a right of returning my blows, and, if he pleased, with advantage and increase? 'Tis certain therefore that he that doth these things to another hath no right of doing them and consequently is injurious. On the contrary, the other party hath a right that such things should not be put upon him and is therefore injured. Thus we see that such right as being violated produceth an injury is not only acquired by covenant, but was given at first by nature without the intervention of any human act. …

Having arrived to know what justice is, we may easily settle our notions of injustice, and of its several species. An action, then, is unjust either when we apply it designedly to a person to whom we owed a different action, or when we deny another somewhat which was really his due. That is, we are equally guilty of a breach of justice by doing any evil to another which we had no right to do, and by taking from another or denying him any good which he had a fair title to require. …

But an unjust action, proceeding from intention, and trespassing on the perfect right of another, is in one word called *injury*. By the natural state of man in our present inquiry, we do not mean that condition which is ultimately designed [for] him by nature, as the most perfect and most agreeable; but such state as we may conceive man to be placed in by his bare nativity, abstracting from all the rules and institutions, whether of human invention or of the suggestion and revelation of heaven. …

We are ready to acknowledge it for a most certain truth that all mankind did never exist together in a mere natural state, inasmuch as upon the divine authority of Scriptures, we believe all human race [*sic.*]to have proceeded from one original pair. Now it's plain that Eve was subject to Adam, Gen. 3:16, and those who were born of these primitive parents, and so on, did immediately fall under paternal authority and under family government. But such a state might have befallen mankind if, as some of the heathens believed, they had in the beginning of their being, leapt out of the earth like frogs or had come up from seed, like Cadmus's human crop (Ovid, *Metamorphoses* Book 3, vv. 122-3), which fable is, methinks, a very exact representation of that state of nature and of that war of all men against all, which Hobbes would introduce. …

A state of nature then did never naturally exist unless qualified and, as it were, in part; namely, while some party of men joined with some more in a civil body or in some confederacy like that; but still retained a natural liberty against all others. …

As to Mr. Hobbes's reasons, they are easily answered. In the first place, those cannot immediately hurt one another who are divided by distance of place; for he who is absent cannot hurt me, except by some body else who is present, and my possessions cannot be destroyed unless by one upon the spot. Therefore, those who live separately or at a distance from one another can offer no mutual hurt so long as they continue thus distant, it doth not appear why such men should not rather be reckoned friends than enemies. [Hobbes] acknowledgeth no more than one covenant of each man to each man; frequently representing and declaring that there passeth no covenant between the prince or the senate and his subjects. Indeed, we may easily gather from the design of his books of policy, which is clearly discovered in his *Leviathan*, the reason that put him upon his assertion. His principal aim was to oppose those seditious and turbulent spirits who in his time labored to bring down the regal power to their own model and either utterly to extinguish or to render it inferior to the subjects. To cut off from these men their ordinary plea for rebellion which was that there is a reciprocal faith between the prince and the people, and that when the former departs from what he engaged by promise, the latter are released from their obedience, as also to hinder restless and factious persons from interpreting every action of their prince, which suited not with their own humor, as a breach of his faith; he resolves to deny that there is any such thing as a covenant between subjects and their sovereign. … [However] this consideration doth by no means make it necessary for us to deny what is as clear as the light and to acknowledge no covenant in a case where there is certainly a mutual promise for the performance of duties not before required. Whilst I voluntarily subject myself to a prince, I promise obedience and engage his protection; on the other hand, the prince when he receives me as a subject, promiseth his protection, and engageth my obedience. Before this reciprocal promise, neither was he bound to protect me, nor I to obey him, at least by any perfect obligation. And who will not pretend to say that an act of this kind doth not fall under the head of covenants? Nor is this covenant useless because they who by their own free choice appoint a king over themselves seem beforehand to have entered into an agreement for the advancing such a particular person to the throne. For as the bare election without the acceptance of the party elected confers on him no power over the rest, so 'tis plain enough from the nature of the business that they who freely put themselves under the power of another desire he should in the exercise of that power pursue the end for which it was given him; and that he received the power on this condition that those who conferred it on him should not, by his means, miss their aim. They who create a sovereign, therefore, as they at the same time promise whatever the nature of subjection requires; so, on the other part, engage him to endeavor the procuring of all those benefits for the sake of which civil governments are introduced. And what can we call this but the entering into covenant?

# *Appendix G: From Edward Hyde,* A Brief View and Survey of Mr Hobbes His Leviathan

Edward Hyde (1609-1674), like Hobbes, was born in Wiltshire and attended Magdalen Hall, Oxford, though Hyde was twenty years younger. He was a member of Lord Falkland's intellectual circle at Great Tew, where he may have met Hobbes. He was a moderate monarchist, opposing the doctrine of absolute sovereignty but stalwart in defending the monarchy. He thought that parliament was not an independent political entity but was part of "the king in parliament." Although he voted to impeach Strafford, he eventually sided with the king in the Civil War.

He came to know Hobbes well when they were both in exile in Paris. At the Restoration, Hyde was made earl of Clarendon and was one of Charles II's most important counselors until, being made scapegoat, he was again forced to flee to Paris. Bitter in exile, he might have fumed over the good fortune of Hobbes, a summer patriot, and not even a sunshine soldier, while he, faithful Hyde, was disgraced and in effect ostracized. He vented his spleen in a book, the full title of which is *A Brief View and Survey of the Dangerous and Pernicious Errors to Church and State, in Mr Hobbes His Book, entitled Leviathan*, published in 1676, two years after his death. While he had liked Hobbes's *De Cive* (1642, 1647), he hated *Leviathan*; and he surmises in various places that Hobbes had altered his theory in order to ingratiate himself with the "usurper" Oliver Cromwell.

If Hyde's many criticisms are reduced to three, they are that Hobbes is wrong in holding that all people are born equal, that Hobbes's political theory is inconsistent with English law, and that the lessons of biblical history show Hobbes's theory to be false.

Hyde's prose is maddeningly prolix and serpentine. Many of the deletions indicated in the text are cut from the middle of a sentence.

All internal page references are to the 1651 edition of *Leviathan*.

## *A Brief View and Survey of Mr Hobbes His Leviathan*

Edward Hyde, Earl of Clarendon

### The Introduction

... [T]here are many who, being delighted with some new notions and the pleasant and clear style throughout the book, have not taken notice of those down-right conclusions which overthrow or undermine all those principles of government, which have preserved the peace of this kingdom through so many ages, even from the time of its first institution; or restored it to peace, when it had at some times been interrupted; and [they have taken] much less [notice] of those odious insinuations and perverting [of] some texts of Scripture, which do dishonor and would destroy the very essence of the religion of Christ. And when I called to mind the good acquaintance that had been between us and what I had said to many who I knew had informed him of it, and which indeed I had sent to himself upon the first publishing of his *Leviathan*, I thought myself even bound to give him some satisfaction why I had entertained so evil an opinion of his Book. ...

### The Survey of Chapters 13, 14 , 15, 16

[These] chapters, will require a little more disquisition, since under the pretence of examining, ... what the natural condition of mankind is, he takes many things for granted which are not true, as that *nature has made all men equal in the faculties of body and mind* (page 60), and imputes that to the nature of man in general, which is but the infirmity of some particular men; and by a mist of words, under the notion of explaining common terms (the meaning whereof is understood by all men, and which his explanation leaves less intelligible than they were before), he dazzles men's eyes from discerning those fallacies upon which he raises his structure ... . And whosoever looks narrowly to his preparatory assertions shall find such contradictions as must destroy the foundation of all his new doctrine in government, of which some particulars shall be mentioned anon.[1] So that if his maxims of one kind were marshalled together, collected out of these four chapters, and applied to his other maxims which are to support his whole *Leviathan*, the one would be a sufficient answer to the other; and so many inconsistencies and absurdities would appear between them, that they could never be thought links of one chain … [How can] a man of Mr. Hobbes's sagacity … reproach the Schools for absurdity in saying that *heavy bodies fall downwards out of an appetite to rest, thereby ascribing knowledge to things inanimate* [page 4]; and himself [in] describing the nature of foul weather, say, *that it lieth not in a shower or two of rain, but in an inclination thereto of many days together* [page 62], as if foul weather were not as inanimate a thing as heavy bodies, and inclination did not imply as much of knowledge as appetite does. In truth, neither … signifies in the before-mentioned instances more than a natural tendency to motion and alteration.

When God vouchsafed [condescended] to make man after his own image and in his own likeness …, it cannot be imagined but that at the same time he endued him with reason and all the other noble faculties which were necessary for the administration of that empire and the preservation of the several species which were to succeed the creation. And therefore to uncreate him to such a baseness and villainy in his nature … is a power that God never gave to the devil; nor has any body assumed it, till Mr. Hobbes took it upon him. Nor can anything be said more contrary to the honor and dignity of God almighty than that he should leave his master workmanship, man, in a condition of war of every man against every man,[2] in such a condition of confusion *that every man has a right to every thing, even to one another's body* (page 64), inclined to all the malice, force and fraud that may promote his profit or his pleasure, and without any notions of, or instinct towards, justice, honor, or good nature, which only makes mankind superior to the beasts of the wilderness. Nor had Mr. Hobbes any other reason to degrade him to this degree of bestiality, but that he may be fit to wear those chains and fetters which he has provided for him. He

1 According to Clarendon, Hobbes often contradicts himself.

2 According to Clarendon, it is an insult to God to claim that the natural condition of human beings is a state of war.

deprives man of the greatest happiness and glory that can be attributed to him, … that gentleness and benevolence towards other men, by which he delights in the good fortune and tranquility that they enjoy. … Man only [according to Hobbes] … is obliged for his own benefit and for the defense of his own right to worry and destroy all of his own kind, until they all become yoked by a covenant and contract that Mr. Hobbes has provided for them, and which was never yet entered into by any one man, and is in nature impossible to be entered into.[1]

After such positive and magisterial assertions against the dignity and probity [honesty] of mankind … the instances and arguments given by him are very unweighty and trivial to conclude the nature of man to be so full of jealousy and malignity, as he would have it believed to be from that common practice of circumspection and providence which custom and discretion has introduced into human life. For men shut their chests in which their money is … as that it may be preserved from thieves; and they lock their doors [in order] that their houses may not be common; and [they] ride armed and in company, because they know that there are ill men, who may be inclined to do injuries if they find an opportunity.[2] Nor is a wariness to prevent the damage and injury that thieves and robbers may do to any man an argument that mankind is in that man's opinion inclined and disposed to commit those outrages. If it be known that there is one thief in a city, all men have reason to shut their doors and lock their chests; and if there be two or three drunkards in a town, all men have reason to go armed in the streets to control the violence or indignity they might receive from them. Princes are attended by their guards in progress and all their servants [are] armed when they hunt without any apprehension of being assaulted, custom having made it so necessary, that many men are not longer without their swords than they are without their doublets, who never were jealous that any man desired to hurt them. …

He is very much offended with Aristotle, for saying in the first

---

1 According to Clarendon, no one has ever entered into a covenant or contract in the state of nature, and it is impossible to do so.

2 According to Clarendon, people lock doors and chests to protect against the very few people who are criminals.

book of his *Politics*, that by nature some are fit to command, and others to serve; which he says is not only against reason, but also against experience, for *there are very few so foolish that had not rather govern themselves, than be governed by others* (page 77). Which proposition does not contradict anything said by Aristotle, the question being whether nature has made some men worthier, not whether it has made all others so modest as to confess it; and [his view] would have required a more serious disquisition, since it is no more than is imputed to horses and other beasts, whereof men find by experience that some by nature are fitter for nobler uses and others for vile and to be only beasts of burden. But, indeed, [this] he says is the law of nature: *that every man must acknowledge every other man for his equal by nature* (page 77); which may be true as to the essentials of human nature; and yet there may be inequality enough as to a capacity of government.[1] But whatever his opinion is, we have Solomon's judgement against him. *Insipiens erit servus sapientis [And the foolish one will be servant to the wise one]* (Proverbs 11:29). And many learned men are of opinion, that the Gibeonites, who by the help of an impudent lie found the means to save their lives, were a people by nature of low and abject spirits, fit only to do the low and mean services for which they were prepared. And some of the Fathers believe that when the Patriarch Jacob, in his dying prophesy of Issachar, declared *Issachar is a strong ass, couching down between two burdens. And he saw that rest was good, and the land that it was pleasant, and bowed his shoulder to bear, and became a servant unto tribute* (Gen. 49:14–15). And 'tis very true, that Aristotle did believe that Divine Providence does show and demonstrate who are fit and proper for low and vile offices, not only by very notable defects in their understandings, incapable of any cultivation, but by some eminent deformity of the body (though that does not always hold) which makes them unfit to bear rule. And without doubt, the observation of all ages since that time has contributed very much to that conclusion which Mr. Hobbes so much derides, of inequality by nature, and that nature itself has a bounty which she extends to some men in a much superior degree than she does to others. Which is not contradict-

---

1 According to Clarendon, it is a simple fact that some people by nature are more fit to govern than others.

ed by seeing many great defects and indigencies [deficiencies] of nature in some men, wonderfully corrected and repaired by industry, education, and above all, by conversation [social interaction]; nor by seeing some early blossoms in others, which raise a great expectation of rare perfection, that suddenly decay and insensibly wither away by not being cherished and improved by diligence, or rather by being blasted by vice or supine laziness. Those accidents may sometimes happen, do not very often, and are necessary to awaken men out of the lethargy of depending wholly upon the wealth of nature's store. … And every man's experience will afford him abundance of examples in the number of his own acquaintance, in which, of those who have always had equal advantages of education, conversation, industry, and, it may be [perhaps], of virtuous inclination, it is easy to observe very different parts and faculties. … [In contrast] others, born and bred with the same care, wariness, and attention, and with all the visible advantages and benefits which the other enjoyed, remain still of a heavier and a duller alloy, less discerning to contrive and foresee, less vigorous to execute, and in a word, of a very different classis [class] to all purposes; which can proceed from no other cause, but the distinction that nature herself made between them in the distribution of those faculties to the one with a more liberal hand than to the other. …

But where are those maxims to be found which Mr. Hobbes declares and publishes to be the laws of nature, in any other author before him?[1] That is only properly called the Law of Nature that is dictated to the whole species, as to defend a man's self from violence and to repel force by force. [Laws of Nature are] not all that results upon prudential motives unto the mind of such as have been cultivated by learning and education. … For under what other notion can that reasonable conclusion … be called the law of nature, which is his fifteenth law, *That all men that mediate peace be allowed safe conduct?* (page 78). And of this kind much of the body of his law of nature is compiled; which I should not dislike, the style being in some sense not improper, but that I observe that from some of these conclusions which he pronounces to be

1 According to Clarendon, Hobbes's supposed laws of nature are not genuinely such because he is the only one who affirms them; and genuine laws of nature need to be known by all people.

*immutable and eternal as the laws of nature* (page 79), he makes deductions and inferences to control opinions he dislikes and to obtain concessions which are not right, by amusing men with his method and confounding, rather then informing, their understandings by a chime of words in definitions and pleasant instances. ... And it is an unanswerable evidence of the irresistible force and strength of truth and reason that whilst men are making war against it with all their power and stratagems, somewhat does still start up out of the dictates and confessions of the adversary that determines the controversy and vindicates the truth from the malice that would oppress it. How should it else come to pass that Mr. Hobbes, while he is demolishing the whole frame of nature for want of order to support it and makes it unavoidably necessary for every man to cut his neighbor's throat, to kill him who is weaker than himself and to circumvent and by any fraud destroy him who is stronger [would] set down such a body of laws prescribed by nature itself, as are *immutable and eternal*?[1] ... If the law of the Gospel [be], *Whatsoever you require that others should do to you, that do ye to them*, [and] if it be the law of nature that every man strive to accommodate himself to the rest, as he says it is, and *that no man by deed, word, countenance or gestures, declare hatred or contempt for another* (page 76); [and] if all men are bound by the law of nature *that they that are at controversy, submit their right to the judgement of an arbitrator* (page 78), ... [then] how come they to fall into that condition of war, as to be every one against everyone, and to be without any other cardinal virtues, but of force and fraud? It is a wonderful thing that a man should be so sharp-sighted, as to discern mankind so well enclosed and fortified by the wisdom of nature and so blind as to think him in a more secure estate by his transferring of right to another man, which yet he confesses is impossible entirely to transfer.[2] ...

What greater contradiction can there be to the peace which he would establish upon those unreasonable conditions than this liberty, which he says can never be abandoned, and which yet may

1 According to Clarendon, it is not possible both for Hobbes's laws of nature to exist and for people in their natural condition to be in a state of war.

2 According to Clarendon, it is incredible that Hobbes should think that people are intelligent enough to deduce the laws of nature and yet so stupid as to transfer their rights to others.

dissolve the peace every day?[1] And yet he says, *This is granted to be true by* all *men, in that they lead criminals to execution and prison with armed men, notwithstanding such criminals have consented to the law by which they are condemned* (page 70). Which indeed is an argument that men had rather escape than be hanged; but no more an argument that they have a right to rescue themselves than the fashion of wearing swords is an argument that men are afraid of having their throats cut by the malice of their neighbors. …

Without doubt, no man is *dominus vitae suae [lord of his own life]*, and therefore cannot give that to another, which he has not in himself. God only has reserved that absolute dominion and power of life and death to himself, and by his putting the sword into hand of the supreme magistrate, has qualified and enabled him to execute that justice which is necessary for the peace and preservation of his people, which may seem in a manner to be provided for by Mr. Hobbes' law of nature, if what he says be true, *that right to the end contains right to the means* (page 68). And this sole proposition, that men cannot dispose of their own lives, has been always held as a manifest and undeniable argument, that sovereigns never had, nor can have their power from the people. …

## The Survey of Chapters 17, 18

Mr. Hobbes having taken upon himself to imitate God and [having] created man after his own likeness, given him all the passions and affections which he finds in himself, he prescribes him [man] to judge of all things and words, according to the definitions he sets down, with the authority of a Creator. … He comes at last to institute such a commonwealth as never was in nature or ever heard of from the beginning of the world till this structure of his, and … [he] gives the man he hath made the sovereign command and government of with such an extent of power and authority as the Great Turk hath not yet appeared to affect.

… He will not find one government in the world, of what kind soever, so instituted, as he dogmatically declares all government to be; nor was mankind in any nation since the creation upon such a

1 According to Clarendon, for Hobbes to hold that people retain the liberty of self-preservation contradicts his view about how peace is established.

level, as to institute their government by such an assembly and election, and covenant, and consent, as he very unwarrantedly more than supposes. And it was an undertaking of the more impertinence, since by his own rule, *where there is already erected a sovereign power* (page 95), which was then and still is in every kingdom and state in Europe, and for aught we know in the whole world, *there can be no other representative of the people, but only to certain particular ends limited by the sovereign* [page 95]. So that he could have no other design but to shake what was erected; and the government was not at that time in any suspense but in his own country, by the effect of an odious and detestable rebellion. …

It had been kindly done of Mr. Hobbes, if according to his laudable custom of illustrating his definitions by instances … he had to this his positive determination added one instance of a government so instituted. There is no doubt there are in all governments many things done by and with the consent of the people … but that any government was originally instituted by an assembly of men equally free and that they ever elected the person who should have the sovereign power over them is yet to be proved; and till it be proved, must not be supposed, to raise new doctrines, upon which shake all government.

… [I]f Mr. Hobbes did not affect to be of the humor of those unreasonable gamesters [whom he describes on page 19] … I say, if Mr. Hobbes were not possessed by this supercilious spirit which he condemns, [then] since this his institution of sovereignty is a mere imagination, he might with as much reason … because it would have carried with it more equality and consequently more security, have supposed a covenant to be on the sovereign's part. … [He] will not admit that they who are his subjects make any covenant with their sovereign to obey him; which if he did, he could as well covenant again with them to govern righteously[1] without making them the judges of his justice or himself liable to their control and jurisdiction. So that the sovereign hath no security for the obedience of his people, but the promise they have made to each other; and consequently if they rebel against him, he cannot complain of any injustice done to him, because they have

1 According to Clarendon, Hobbes should have had people make a covenant with their sovereign to govern righteously.

broke no promise they made to him. And truly, by his own logic, they may release to one another when they think it convenient.[1] Whereas if the promises be mutual, I do not say *conditional*, the sovereign must not be at the mercy of his subjects; but as they put themselves under his power, so tyrannically (which will be a proper and significant word against all his interpretation) by which they have as much obligation upon him to be just, as he hath upon them to be obedient, which is no other, than that they swerve from justice, if they withdraw their obedience from him. This had been a more natural and equitable institution, and more like to have lasted, having in it the true essential form of contracts, in which it will never be found that one party covenants and the other not; which is the reason Mr. Hobbes himself gives, why no covenant can be made with God, and that *the pretence of covenant with God, is so evident a lie, even in the pretenders' own consciences, that it is not only an act of an unjust, but also of a vile and unmanly disposition* (page 89), which assertion is destructive of our religion and against the express sense of Scripture.

The impossibility alleged [by Hobbes] for such a covenant, because it could not be done before he was sovereign, for that the subjects who submit to him were not yet one person, and after he is sovereign what he does is void, is but a fancy of words which have no solid signification. …

It is to no purpose to examine the prerogatives he [Hobbes] grants to his sovereign, because he founds them all upon a supposition of a contract and covenant that never was in nature nor ever can reasonably be supposed to be; yet he confesses it to be *the generation of the great Leviathan* (page 87), and which, falling to the ground, all his prerogatives must likewise fall too; and so much to the damage of the sovereign power (to which most of the prerogatives are due), that men will [be] apt to suppose that they proceed from a ground which is not true, and so be the more inclined to dispute them. Whereas those prerogatives are indeed vested in the sovereign by his being sovereign; but he does not become sovereign by virtue of such a contract and covenant, but are of the essence of his sovereignty. … And here he supposes again that

1 According to Clarendon, Hobbes's views make government unstable because subjects are free to release each other from their covenant.

whatsoever a sovereign is possessed of is of his sovereignty; and therefore he will by no means admit that he shall part with any of his power which he calls *essential and inseparable rights* [page 93], and that whatever grant he makes of such power, the same is void; and he does believe that this sovereign right was at the time when he published his book so well understood (that is, [Oliver] Cromwell liked his doctrine so well) that it would be generally acknowledged in England at the next return of peace. Yet he sees himself deceived. It hath pleased God to restore a blessed and a general peace, and neither king nor people believe his doctrine to be true or consistent with peace.

… And there is too much cause to fear that the unhappy publication of this doctrine against the liberty and propriety [property][1] of the subject (which others had the honor to declare before Mr. Hobbes, though they had not the good fortune to escape punishment as he hath done, I mean Dr. [Roger] Manwaring, and Dr. [Robert] Sibthorpe) contributed too much thereunto.

… [Hobbes's ignorance causes him to marvel that] he that had the sovereignty [in England] from a descent of six hundred years was alone called *sovereign*, had the title of *Majesty* from every one of his subjects, and was unquestionably taken by them for their king, was notwithstanding never considered as their representative, that name without contradiction, passing for the title of those men which at his command were sent up by the people to carry their petitions and give him, if he permitted it, their advice; which he says *may serve as an admonition for those that are the true and absolute representative of a people* (which he hath made his sovereign to be) *to take heed how they admit of any other general representative upon any occasion whatsoever* (page 95). … And if Mr. Hobbes did not make war against all modesty, he would rather have concluded that the title of the representative of the people was not to be affected by

---

1 "But one man's liberty can be another man's slavery. … For the Parliamentary electorate — gentry and merchants — the most important liberty to be defended was the sanctity of private property; and the institution on which they relied to safeguard property was Parliament, the representative body of the propertied class. For most of the population, owning no property or very little, the sanctity of private property was not a major issue" (Christopher Hill, *Liberty Against the Law*. London: Penguin, 1997, 19-20). Hyde was an MP in the 1640s but ultimately sided with the king.

the king than that, for want [lack] of understanding, his Majesty should neglect to assume it or that his faithful counsel and his learned judges, who cannot be supposed to be ignorant of the regalities of the crown, should fail to put him in mind of so advantageous a plea, when his fundamental rights were so foully assaulted and in danger.[1] But though the king knew too well the original [source] of his own power to be contented to be thought the representative of the people; yet if Mr. Hobbes were not strangely unconversant with the transactions of those times, he would have known … that the King frequently and upon all occasions reprehended [reprimanded] the two Houses, both for assuming the style and appellation of parliament, which they were not, but in and by his Majesty's conjunction with them, and for calling themselves the Representative of the People, which they neither were, or could be to any other purpose than to present their petitions and humbly to offer their advice, when and in what his Majesty required it; and this was as generally understood by men of all conditions in England, as it was that rebellion was treason. But they who were able by false pretences and under false protestations to raise an Army, found it no difficult matter to persuade that army and those who concurred with them, that they were not in rebellion. …

## The Survey of Chapter 20

… And in the first place we must deny … Mr. Hobbes this ground-work, *that war is founded in nature*, which gives the stronger a right to whatever the weaker is possessed of;[2] so that there can be no peace or security from oppression, till such covenants are made, as may appoint a sovereign to have all that power which is necessary to provide for that peace and security; and out of and by this institution, his magistrate grows up to the greatness and size of his Leviathan. But we say that peace is founded in nature and that when the God of nature gave his creature, man, the dominion over the rest of his creation, he gave him likewise natural strength and

1 According to Clarendon, the king of England is the sovereign of the people, not their representative.

2 According to Clarendon, peace is founded in nature; and God gave people the skills to govern the world.

power to govern the world with peace and order. And how much soever he lost by his own integrity by falling from his obedience to his creator and how severe a punishment soever he underwent by that his disobedience, it does not appear that his [Adam's] dominion over mankind was in any degree lessened or abated. So that we cannot but look upon him [Adam], during his life, as the sole monarch of the world; and that lasted so long, as we may reasonably compute, that a very considerable part of the world that was peopled before the Flood was peopled in his life, … so that his dominion was over a very numerous people. And during all that time, we have no reason to imagine that there was any such instrument of government by covenants and contracts. …

… After the Flood, we cannot but think that Noah remained the sole monarch of the world during his life. …

We are not obliged, nor indeed have any reason to believe, that God was offended with the Children of Israel for desiring a king,[1] which was a government [he] himself had instituted over them and to which they had been long accustomed, and [the Children of Israel] had undergone much misery and confusion whilst there was no king in Israel; but [God was offended] for their mutinous manner of asking it, and the reason they gave for it, [namely] that they might be like other nations, which God had taken all possible care that they should not be, and enjoined them to learn nothing of them. And the description, which Samuel made of the exorbitant power of kings, which indeed the kings of the nations did exercise, by whose example they desired to be governed, was rather to terrify them from pursuing their foolish demand, than to constitute such a prerogative as the king should use whom God would appoint to go in and out before them; which methinks is very manifest, in that the worst kings that ever reigned over them, never challenged or assumed those prerogatives. Nor did the people conceive themselves liable to those impositions, as appears by the application they made to Rehoboam upon the death of Solomon, that he would abate some of that rigor his father had exercised towards them. …

---

1 According to Clarendon, God was not offended that Israel wanted a king to rule them.

… And it is not Mr. Hobbes's authority that will make it believed that he who desires more liberty demands an exemption from all laws, by which all other men may be masters of their lives, and that every subject is author of every act the sovereign doth, upon the extravagant supposition of a consent that never was given; and if it were possible to have been given, must have been void at the instant it was given, by Mr. Hobbes's own rules, as shall be made out in its place. …

Mr. Hobbes is too much conversant in both those learned languages to wish that the Western world were deprived of the Greek and Latin tongues for any mischief they have done; and upon my conscience, whatever errors may have been brought into philosophy by the authority of Aristotle, no man ever grew a rebel by reading him. … And if Mr. Hobbes would take a view of the insurrections and the civil wars which have at any time been stirred up in the Western parts, he will not find that they have been contrived or fomented by men who had spent much time in the reading Greek or Latin authors. … And I believe had Mr. Hobbes been of this opinion when he taught Thucydides to speak English, which book contains more of the science of mutiny and sedition, and teaches more of the oratory that contributes thereunto, than all that Aristotle and Cicero have, he would not have communicated such materials to his countrymen. …

But [in order] that this supreme sovereign, whom he hath invested with the whole property and liberty of all his subjects and so invested him in it that he hath not power to part with any of it by promise or donation or release, may not be too much exalted with his own greatness, he [Hobbes] hath humbled him sufficiently by giving his subjects leave to withdraw their obedience from him when he hath most need of their assistance; for *the obligation of subjects to the sovereign is understood* (he says) *to last as long, and no longer, then the power lasts to protect them* (page 114). So that as soon as any town, city, or province of any prince's dominions is invaded by a foreign enemy or possessed by a rebellious subject that the prince for the present cannot suppress … the people may lawfully resort to those who are over them; and for their protection [the people may] perform all the offices and duties of good subjects to them. *For the right men have by nature to protect themselves when none else can protect them, can by no covenant be relinquished, and the end of obedience is protection, which wherever a man sees it either in his own or in another's sword, nature applies his obedience to it, and his endeavours to maintain it* (page 114). And truly it is no wonder if … subjects take the first opportunity to free themselves from such a sovereign as he hath given them, and choose a better for themselves. Whereas the duty of subjects is … another kind of duty and obedience to their sovereign than to withdraw their subjection because he is oppressed; and [true subjects] will prefer poverty and death itself before they will renounce their obedience to their natural prince or do any thing that may advance the service of his enemies. And since Mr. Hobbes gives so ill a testimony of his government *that it is in its own nature not only subject to violent death by foreign war, but also from the ignorance and passion of men that it hath in it from the very institution many seeds of natural mortality by internal discord* (page 114), worse than which he cannot say of any government, we may very reasonably prefer the government we have and under which we have enjoyed much happiness, before his which we do not know, nor any body hath had experience of. …

Whether the relation of subjects be extinguished in all those cases, which Mr. Hobbes takes upon him to prescribe, as [for example] imprisonment, banishment, and the like, I leave to those who can instruct him better in the Law of Nations, by which they must be judged, notwithstanding all his appeals to the Law of Nature; and I presume if a banished person *during which*, he says, *he is not the subject* (page 114), shall join in an action under a foreign power against his country, wherein he shall with others be taken prisoner, … he shall be judged as a traitor and rebel, which he could not be, if he were not a subject. … Surely this woeful desertion and defection in the cases above mentioned, which hath been always held criminal by all law that hath been current in any part of the world, received so much countenance and justification by Mr. Hobbes his book and more by his conversation that [Oliver] Cromwell found the submission to those principles produced a submission to him [Cromwell], and the imaginary relation between protection and allegiance, so positively proclaimed by him, prevailed for many years to extinguish all visible fidelity to the King, whilst he [Hobbes] persuaded many to take the Engagement as a thing lawful and to become subjects to the usurper [Cromwell], as to their legitimate sovereign. …

It appears at last why by his institution he would have the power and security of his sovereign wholly and only to depend upon the contracts and covenants which the people make one with another, to transfer all their rights to a third person (who shall be sovereign) without entering into any covenant with the sovereign himself, which would have divested them of that liberty to disobey him … [Th]en he says, *if a monarch shall relinquish the sovereignty both for himself, and his heirs, his subjects return to the absolute liberty of nature. Because though nature may declare who are his sons and who are the nearest of his kin, yet it dependeth on his own will who shall be his heir; and if he will have no heir, there is no sovereignty or subjection* [page 114]. This seems the hardest condition for the poor subject that he can be liable unto, that when he hath divested himself of all the right he had, only for his sovereign's protection, that he may be redeemed from the state of war and confusion that nature hath left him in and hath paid so dear for that protection, it is left still in his sovereign's power to withdraw that protection from him, to renounce his subjection, and without his consent to transfer the sovereignty to another, to whom he hath no mind to be subject. One might have imagined that this new trick of transferring and covenanting had been an universal remedy, that being once applied would forever prevent the ill condition and confusion that nature had left us in, and that such a right would have been constituted by it, that sovereignty would never have failed to the world's end. And that when the subject can never retract or avoid the bargain he hath made, how ill soever he likes it or improve it by acquiring any better conditions in it, it shall notwithstanding be in the sovereign's power … to leave him without any protection, without any security, and as a prey to all who are too strong for him. This indeed is the greatest prerogative that he hath conferred upon his sovereign, when he had given him all that belongs to his subjects, that when he is weary of governing, he can destroy them by leaving them to destroy one another.

… And whereas he hath in his eighteenth chapter pronounced

*the right of Judicatory of hearing and deciding all controversies which concern law, either civil or natural, or concerning fact* (page 91) to be inseparably annexed to the sovereignty, and incapable of being aliened and transferred by him; and afterwards [he] declares *that the judgements given by judges qualified and commissioned by him to that purpose are his own proper judgements and to be regarded as such*, which is a truth generally confessed; in this chapter, against all practice and all reason, he degrades him from at least half that power, and fancies a judge to be such a party that if the litigant be not pleased with the opinion of his judge in matter of law or matter of fact, he may therefore (*because they are both subjects to the sovereign* (page 125)) appeal from his judge, and ought to be tried before another: for those the sovereign may hear and determine the cause himself if he please; yet if he will appoint another to be judge, it must be such a one as they shall both agree upon.

... Notwithstanding that *the law is reason* and *not the letter, but that which is according to the intention of the legislator* (*that is of the sovereign*) *is the law* (page 139), yet when there is any difficulty in the understanding the law, the interpretation thereof may reasonably belong to learned judges, who by their education and the testimony of their known abilities before they are made judges, and by their oaths to judge according to right, are the most competent to explain those difficulties, which no sovereign as sovereign can be presumed to understand or comprehend. And the judgements and decisions those judges make are the judgements of the sovereigns who have qualified them to be judges and who are to pronounce their sentence according to the reason of the law, not the reason of the sovereign. And therefore Mr. Hobbes would make a very ignorant judge, when he would not have him versed in the study of the laws, but only a man of good natural reason and of a right understanding of the Law of Nature. ... For to what purpose is all the distinction and division of laws into human and divine, into natural and moral, into distributive and penal, when [a person is the] sovereign? [T]*he Law of Nature is a part of the civil law in all commonwealths in the world*, and that though *it be naturally reasonable, yet it is by the sovereign power that it is law*, and he says likewise, *that all laws written and unwritten, and the Law of Nature itself, have need of interpretation* (page 138). And then he makes his supreme sovereign the only legitimate interpreter. So that he hath the Law of Nature as much in his power as under his jurisdiction, as any other part of the civil law. And yet he confesses his subject is not bound to pay obedience to any thing that his sovereign enjoins against the Law of Nature. In such labyrinths men entangle themselves who obstinately engage in opinions relating to a science they do not understand. ... I believe every man who reads Mr. Hobbes observes that when he entangles himself in the Laws of England and affects to be more learned in them than the Chief Justice Cook [Edward Coke[1]], the natural sharpness and vigor of his reason is more flat and insipid than upon other arguments, and he makes deductions which have no coherence, and in a word loses himself in a mist of words that render him less intelligible than at other times ...

## The Survey of Chapter 28

... There cannot be a more pernicious doctrine and more destructive to peace and justice, than that all men who are not subjects are enemies, and that against enemies, whom the commonwealth judges capable to do them hurt, it is lawful by the original right of nature to make war; which would keep up a continual war between all princes, since they are few who are not capable to do hurt to their neighbors. Nor can this mischief be prevented by any treaty or league; for whilst they are capable of doing hurt, the lawfulness still remains, and being the original right of nature, cannot be extinguished. ... [And] because in *War the Sword judgeth not, nor doth the victor make distinction of nocent* [culpable] *and innocent, nor has other respect of mercy, than as it conduceth to the good of his own people* (page 165), he makes no scruple to tell Cromwell *that as to those who deliberately deny his authority ... the vengeance is lawfully extended, not only to the fathers, but also to the third and fourth generations not yet in being, and consequently innocent of the fact for which they are afflicted, because they that so offend suffer not as subjects but as enemies,* towards whom the victor may proceed as he thinks fit and best for himself. After the giving which advice, it was a marvelous confidence that introduced him into the king's

---

1 Edward Coke (1552–1634) was England's leading theorist of the common law. This sometimes put him into opposition to King James I and later Charles I. His commentaries on the *Tenures* of Sir Thomas Littleton (c. 1422–81), an English jurist, are among his most famous works.

presence and encouraged him still to expect that his doctrine should be allowed to be industriously taught and believed. …

## The Survey of Chapter 30

Mr. Hobbes having invested his sovereign with so absolute power and omnipotence, we have reason to expect that in this Chapter of his office, he will enjoin him to use all the authority he has given him … And least [less] he should forget the rights and power he hath bestowed upon him, he recollects them all in three or four lines, amongst which he puts him in mind that he hath power to levy money when, and as much as in his own conscience, he shall judge necessary. And then [Hobbes] tells him [the sovereign] that it is against his duty to let the people be ignorant or misinformed of the grounds and reasons of those his essential rights, that is, that he is obliged to make his Leviathan canonical scripture, there being no other book ever yet printed that can inform them of those rights, and the grounds and reason of them.

… In the meantime he must not take it ill that I observe his extreme malignity to the Nobility, by whose bread he hath been always sustained [and] who must not expect any part, at least any precedence in his institution [government]; that in this his deep meditation upon the ten commandments and in a conjuncture when the Levellers[1] were at highest and the reduction of all degrees to one and the same was resolved upon and begun and exercised towards the whole Nobility with all the instances of contempt and scorn he chose to publish his judgement, as if the safety of the people required an equality of persons, and that *the honour of great persons is to be valued for their beneficence, and the aids they give to men of inferior rank or not at all; and that the consequence of partiality towards the great, raised hatred, and an endeavour in the people to pull down all oppressing and contumelious greatness* (*Lev.* 180), language lent to or borrowed from the Agitators of that time.

---

1 The Levellers advocated such reforms as voting rights for all males, except servants. Their views, popular among the parliamentary army of the mid-1640s, were debated at the Putney Debates of 1647. Prominent Levellers include John Lilburne, Richard Overton, and William Walwyn.

## The Survey of Chapter 31

… It is one of the unhappy effects, which a too gracious and merciful indulgence ever produces in corrupt and proud natures, that they believe that whatsoever is tolerated in them is justified and commended; and because Mr. Hobbes hath not received any such brand which the authors of such doctrine have been usually marked with, nor hath seen his book burned by the hand of the hangman, as many more innocent books have been, he is exalted to a hope that the supreme magistrate will at some time so far exercise his sovereignty, as to protect the public teaching of his principles and convert the truth of his speculation into the utility of practice. But he might remember, and all those who are scandalized, that such monstrous and seditious discourses have so long escaped a judicial examination and punishment, must know that Mr. Hobbes his *Leviathan* was printed and published in the highest time of Cromwell's wicked usurpation; for the vindication and perpetuating whereof, it was contrived and designed, and when all legal power was suppressed; and upon his Majesty's blessed return, that merciful and wholesome Act of Oblivion,[1] which pardoned all treasons and murders, sacrilege, robbery, heresies and blasphemies, as well with reference to their writings as their persons, and other actions, did likewise wipe out the memory of the enormities of Mr. Hobbes and his *Leviathan* …

We shall conclude here our disquisition of his policy and government of his commonwealth with the recollecting and stating the excellent maxims and principles upon which his government is founded and supported, [in order] that when they appear naked and uninvolved in his magisterial discourses, men may judge of the liberty and security they should enjoy, if Mr. Hobbes' doctrine were inculcated into the minds of men …

1. *That the king's word is sufficient to take any thing from any subject [more] than there is need, and that the king is judge of that need.* Page 106, cap. 20. part. 2.

---

1 By the Act of Oblivion (1660), Charles II "pardoned, released, indemnified, discharged and put in utter oblivion … all manner of treasons, misprisions of treason, murders, felonies, offences, crimes, contempts and misdemeanours counselled, commanded, acted or done" that led to or were committed during the English Civil War and the Interregnum (*The Stuart Constitution*, 2nd ed., ed. J.P. Kenyon. (Cambridge: Cambridge UP, 1986), 340).

*2. The liberty of a subject lieth only in those things, which in regulating their actions, the sovereign hath pretermitted, such as is the liberty to buy and sell, and otherwise to contract with one another; to choose their own abode, their own diet, their own trade of life, and institute their children as they themselves think fit, and the like. Page 109, cap. 21. part. 2.*

*3. Nothing the sovereign can do to a subject, on what pretence soever, can properly be called injustice or injury. Page 109.*

*4. When a sovereign prince putteth to death an innocent subject, though the action be against the Law of Nature, as being contrary to equity, yet it is not an injury to the subject, but to God. Page 109.*

*5. No man hath liberty to resist the word of the sovereign; but in case a great many men together, have already resisted the sovereign power unjustly, or committed some capital crime, for which every one of them expecteth death, they have liberty to join together, and to assist and defend one another. Page 112.*

*6. If a sovereign demand, or take any thing by pretence of his power, there lieth in that case no action at law. Page 112.*

*7. If a subject be taken prisoner in war, or his person or his means of life be within the guards of the enemy, and hath his life and corporal liberty given him on condition to be subject to the victor, he hath liberty to accept the condition, and having accepted it, is the subject of him that took him. Page 114.*

*8. If the sovereign banish the subject, during the banishment he is no subject. Page 114.*

*9. The obligation of subjects to the sovereign, is as long, and no longer than the power lasteth, by which he is able to protect them. Page 124.*

*10. What ever promises or covenants the sovereign makes are void. Page 89.*

*11. He whose private interest is to be judged in an assembly, may make as many friends as he can; and though he hires such friends with money, yet it is not injustice. Page 122, cap. 22. part. 2.*

*12. The propriety which a subject hath in his lands, consisteth in a right to exclude all other subjects from the use of them, and not to exclude their sovereign. Page 128, cap. 24. part. 2.*

*13. When the sovereign commandeth a man to do that which is against law, the doing of it is totally excused; when the sovereign commandeth anything to be done against law, the command as to that particular fact is an abrogation of the law. Page 157, cap. 27. part. 2.*

*14. Though the right of a sovereign monarch cannot be extinguished by the act of another, yet the obligation of the members may; for he that wants protection, may seek it anywhere, and when he hath it, is obliged (without fraudulent pretence of having submitted himself out of fear) to protect his protector as long as he is able. Page 174 cap. 29. part. 2.*

If upon the short reflections we have made upon these several doctrines, as they lie scattered over his book and involved in other discourses, the view of the naked propositions by themselves, without any other clothing or disguise of words, may better serve to make them odious to king and people; and that the first will easily discern, to how high a pinnacle of power soever he would carry him, he leaves him upon such a precipice, from whence the least blast of invasion from a neighbor or from rebellion by his subjects may throw him headlong to irrecoverable ruin. And the other [the people] will as much abhor an allegiance of that temper that by any misfortune of their prince they may be absolved from, and cease to be subjects, when their sovereign hath most need of their obedience. And surely if these articles of Mr. Hobbes's creed be the product of right reason and the effects of Christian obligations, the Great Turk may be looked upon as the best philosopher and all his subjects as the best Christians.

# Index

**Note**: The page references for many entries is selective. A comprehensive index would be unusable because many terms occur repeatedly in the text.